MYSTIC MEG'S ASTROLIFE

Meg Markova has been the astrologer for the *News Of The World* for the last ten years. Her sun sign is Leo, and she shares a garden flat in London with her cats.

Your lovelife, emotions, sexual power, outer and inner personality, your relationships with partners and family ... To get the full picture, Mystic Meg starts with your sun sign then, with at-a-glance tables, reveals your rising sign, Venus sign and Mars sign. If you were born in early January, you know your sun sign is Capricorn, but you could have Aries as your rising sign, Scorpio as your Venus sign, and Cancer as your Mars sign. Yes, there could be four different zodiac signs at work on your personality – and you need to know them all. Now you can ... and that will help you be the successful, special person you were born to be.

AstroLife is not just for one year of your life – *AstroLife* is for all of your life!

ACKNOWLEDGMENTS

For input, friendship, and encouragement, I would like to give special thanks to Maggie Innes, and to Kate Andrew, Angela Wilkes, Ann Tucek, Hilary Scott and Millicent Taylor.

MYSTIC MEG'S ASTROLIFE

The complete astrological guide to love, life and relationships

WARNER BOOKS

A *Warner* Book

First published in Great Britain by Warner Books in 1992
Reprinted 1995 (twice)

A CIP catalogue record for this book
is available from the British Library.

ISBN 0 7515 0010 0

Printed in England by Clays Ltd, St Ives plc

Warner Books
A Division of
Little, Brown and Company (UK)
Brettenham House
Lancaster Place
London WC2E 7EN

Contents

Introduction

Astrology does not set your life and your character in cement, it tells you what you can be. The position of the sun and the planets when you were born gives you the ingredients for your life. The more you know about them, the better you can build the life you want, using your strengths, and knowing what parts of your character need to change and grow. Though simply living your life might eventually teach you some of these things, astrology makes sure you know them in time to be your best self.

There is more than one zodiac sign at work. The boss sign is your SUN SIGN, based on the position of the sun on the day of the year you were born. My tables will give you your RISING SIGN, based on the sun's position at the time of day you were born. The way your sun and rising signs match up is the key to your personality. There are 12 different ways of being an Aries, and 12 different ways of being each of the sun signs. If you don't know your time of birth, don't worry, you'll recognise yourself.

Then, from the yearly tables, you'll find your VENUS SIGN, based on the position of the planet Venus when you were born. This reveals more about your emotions. And your MARS SIGN, based on the position of Mars when you were born, tells you more about your sex drive and life drive.

If you were born in early April, for instance, you already know ARIES is your sun sign, but you could have VIRGO as your rising sign, PISCES as your Venus sign and SAGITTARIUS as your Mars sign.

As you read through this book, you'll discover your personal pack of zodiac signs, and how to use it, in life and in love, to be the wonderful person you were born to be. There are no good and bad zodiac signs – you just need to know how to use them.

PART ONE

AstroLove

Love secrets of your sun sign
and your 12 love matches

SUN SIGNS

ARIES
March 21 to April 20
Element: Fire
Planet: Mars

TAURUS
April 21 to May 21
Element: Earth
Planet: Venus

GEMINI
May 22 to June 21
Element: Air
Planet: Mercury

CANCER
June 22 to July 22
Element: Water
Ruler: Moon

LEO
July 23 to August 23
Element: Fire
Ruler: Sun

VIRGO
August 24 to September 22
Element: Earth
Planet: Mercury

LIBRA
September 23 to October 23
Element: Air
Planet: Venus

SCORPIO
October 24 to November 22
Element: Water
Planets: Pluto/Mars

SAGITTARIUS
November 23 to December 21
Element: Fire
Planet: Jupiter

CAPRICORN
December 22 to January 20
Element: Earth
Planet: Saturn

AQUARIUS
January 21 to February 18
Element: Air
Planets: Uranus/Saturn

PISCES
February 19 to March 20
Element: Water
Planets: Neptune/Jupiter

The sun changes signs at a slightly different time each year and can be in one sign in the morning, another by the afternoon. If you were born near the beginning or end of your sign, look up your year in the sun sign tables on page 829 to find your true sun sign.

Aries in Love

THE WONDERFUL YOU

You have the passion power and the fiery charm to polevault your way into romance. And there is a heartful of loyal love locked away for the perfect partner. But until you find that partner, you will be happy playing the passion field. Your boldness and enticing independence and that sex-light in your eyes, signalling that anything could happen, make you irresistible. Even people you have known for years often turn out to have secretly adored you.

Changes and challenges sharpen your love skills. You have clever charm, blended with a straightforward and almost childlike approach to life that charges right through the defences others may have hoisted around their hearts.

Romance with you need never tumble into a routine with your impulsive, exciting, and smart ideas to keep sex sizzling. Partners love the way you make them laugh and the raw dash and courage you show. Once you are really in love, you'll risk anything.

As an Aries you give generously, with both mind and body, and you have the openness to ask for what you want – and the power to get it.

Your enthusiasm and optimism add good flavouring to the love relationship. You do flourish on flirtation. And, though you leap into love without looking, you rarely waste emotional energy on regrets over bad landings.

Yet when you are truly and lastingly in love, you slip out of that swashbuckler's skin and unveil a touching tenderness and vulnerability.

Your heart may be easy to catch, but it is the lover who also wins your mind who will bask in the beautiful light of Aries total loving.

THE WICKED YOU

You can love the chase more than real relationships, and your interest may seep away once you have won someone's love. And the love rules that should put someone out of your reach (like being your best friend's partner) are rules you smash your way through.

Then, when you have ripped away all resistance, you rush away to look for your next love challenge, not even glancing back at the wreckage you are leaving behind.

When you stay in a relationship, though, you can be too much of a controller, bossing partners about – in and out of the bedroom. You may not even notice yourself doing it. In fact, you can be so wrapped up in your own feelings you are too well insulated against other people's different needs and desires.

Compromise is not one of the words you store in your personal dictionary. The 'Me, Me, Me' inner cry that masterminds Aries' everyday life makes compromise almost impossible. In love, and everything else, when your Aries dark power is unleashed, you demand your own way – and fast.

And what happens when every one of those demands doesn't fall your way? Aries is more likely to leave than stay and work through problems.

You have an obsession with being in charge and knot the reins of romance very tightly to your own fingers. Trouble is, this makes it difficult for you to open up and admit you have a weaker, more needing side. And it is especially difficult for you to admit this to yourself.

It seems natural to set your lover a series of tests to prove commitment and make sure your love is deserved. Yet you will be astonished if any proof of love is expected from you, or any questions asked. You think that your being there is reward enough for your partner.

You will never be happy with someone who you think is a loser, but sometimes you set standards which everyone (except you) can see are ridiculously high. This can cut people out of your heart.

Aries can be the most selfish, most insensitive sign of all, and sometimes living with you is like being strapped on to a man-sized cheese grater. But when you are your Aries best, being with you is wonderful.

BEING YOUR ARIES BEST

Aries can make good loving even better by following these passion pointers. Forget that mental alarm clock you set to measure out love-time. Instead of rush-romancing, take it slow and relax into the lovemaking. That will untangle inner tensions and help you open up to feelings and emotions.

Believe that you don't have to be the boss – well, not all of the time. Let your partner make some of the decisions and respect opinions even when you don't agree with them. And showing that you do have a needing side doesn't make you weak, and certainly makes you more lovable.

Although you have a strong personality, you can be a very weak judge of other people. You have an extra helping of honesty and straightforwardness. Please don't assume that other people have this, too. Falling for every sob story, every twisted excuse, can trap you into trouble. Adding just a pinch of suspicion will help. Then you won't do that Aries slip-slide straight into those rotten relationships, even marriages, that can litter your lovelife.

Your temper can be a relationship wrecker, too. Put a timelock on it, and on your tongue. Count to at least 30 before shouting – and you will see that minor irritations can be smiled through. And that's much smarter than picking a fight on purpose to make things happen, just because you are bored.

Even an Aries romance can tumble into a sludge of same-again situations, but please don't just cut and run. You can be so busy blaming your partner that you quite forget to slice up a portion of the blame for yourself.

Love is communication, and it can only work when it is a two-way channel so, instead of running away, let your feelings out and your loved-one in.

ARIES SEXY SECRETS

Aries' love potion is energy. And the best pre-love match preparation is to rev up your body for romance with energetic dancing, a game of squash, or a sprint around the block. In fact, you may not even want to wait until you get back home, as outdoor loving is one of your favourite fantasies, and you'll cherish the partner who helps you to make it true.

Your hotspot is your face, and a lover who wants to give you total pleasure will start with cool fingers stroking the letters of your name on your forehead, then letting the tongue replace fingers for gentle butterfly kisses on your eyelids, then the soft rasping of a tongue sliding along your cheekbone and travelling on to your lips. Your lover should spend time stroking your temples and letting fingers travel through your hair, massaging the tension away.

The cold smoothness of satin on your skin, followed by hot breath – contrasts of all kinds work for Aries. That's why you can go from the pure fun of tickling, teasing and silly forfeit games to the deep, desperate, driving love that makes you feel you are the most desirable person alive at that moment.

You can only get to this love-ecstasy land when you are brave enough to break free from that mental need you feel to be in control. Give yourself to the love moment and you will be richly rewarded – and so will your partner.

WOOING AND WINNING ARIES

Aries is so determined to get what Aries wants that you might think the way to hang on to an Aries heart is to willingly give in to every whim – in and out of bed. No, it's not that simple. The ideal partner is the one who can never be overpowered. A partner must be independent and have as many outside interests and friends as you do.

Getting your own way is no fun with a partner who hands it over; a yes from a yes-man isn't what Aries wants. Power-clashes are more your style, and you need a partner who is clever enough to let you get your own way (or, at least, seem to get your own way) three-quarters of the time, but convince you to give way on the rest.

You will be truly won by someone who has an overdose of energy and enthusiasm and loves to laugh at your boisterous jokes. You need someone who is a mental match for you, too; if you can't respect a partner's mind, the relationship will rot away as desire turns to despising.

Your lovers will need the confidence to adore you, without roping you to their side, and a slight mystery about themselves and what they do when you are flying free. Predictability puts out Aries love fires very fast. But, though a touch of jealousy may intrigue Aries, too much jealousy-stirring behaviour will smash the relationship.

Your feelings can't turn on to maximum love until you are sure you can totally trust a lover. You almost never ask for appreciation and support, yet you need someone who realises how much you need it, and gives it to you.

When you are truly in love, you are so strong, and so ready to risk all to protect your partner. Yet at the same time you are discovering and revealing the gentle loyalty and relaxed mind that helps you give and take love, and enjoy both.

LOVE MATCH

How Aries combines with each of the 12 sun signs

Aries with Aries

If you like your romance flavoured with red-hot rows and even hotter reconciliations – while those 'I am leaving you' suitcases are still packed – then same-sign loving is good for you. Besides, in the gaps between the fiery clashes, it can be the perfect matching of body and emotions.

You can both see what others miss as Aries strides boldly through life, and that's the heavily disguised need for praise, appreciation and reassurance. But it is more difficult to accept that a partner's need for freedom is just as great as your own.

This can be a brilliant lifetime match because you both bring to it honesty and optimism. So it is worth working at making the love last – by taking turns at being in charge, and diluting your bossiness. And you do need to try to be less demanding and less selfish. And, yes, that does mean both of you . . .

Aries with Taurus

Let's try something new, says Aries. No, let's persevere and get this right, says Taurus. Let's borrow money for a romantic holiday, says Aries. Let's put money into a savings account every week for our own home, says Taurus.

You and Taurus come into a relationship with opposite points of view. But Taurus does have a very high sex-rating and a deeply loyal love style, which just may make you stay true and put up with that Taurus jealousy and possessiveness.

This relationship easily rolls through a romance, and Aries has lessons to learn from the sign that is ahead of it in the zodiac. But for a lifetime together, there is a lot of adjusting to do. You need to slam the brakes on Aries' independence and accept the Taurus need for security – both in love commitment and in cash.

You will have to stretch your short supply of patience to squeeze in that Taurus stubbornness and you must never try to shove them into deals and decisions before they are ready. If you do all this, you will make a strong love match.

Aries with Gemini

Instant attraction guarantees you will make brilliant pals, as mind-to-mind contact really works. And that sets you up to be good lovers, too. Gemini's swift thinking and witty talking spell sex appeal to Aries. Conversations could go on all night – except that you need lots of time to communicate with body language. As lovers you are in competition to see who can be the most adventurous, who can give the most mutual pleasure. This can be a beautiful match if you can tame your Aries pride, which sees your Gemini partner's popularity as a sign that you will soon be rejected. That could make you take flight.

You will have to learn to let this partner chat and charm everyone in sight, and believe your Gemini will still come home to you. And dilute your bossy streak, too. Gemini needs to feel free, and if you don't give Gemini freedom, Gemini will take off. But if you appreciate each other, without trying to change each other, this can be a wonderfully happy match.

Aries with Cancer

At first, Cancer seems to do everything to please you and you love it. Then you get impatient and outrageously selfish, and your personalities crash into each other. You want immediate decisions, Cancer wants second opinions on everything. You are sure you make good decisions, Cancer wants insurance against bad decisions (they invented prenuptial agreements). Then there's jealousy. Both of you are chronic sufferers – Aries tends to run out, Cancer to simmer and sulk for years.

Yet it can be a good relationship. Cancer gives you the admiration, and the caring, that your confidence needs in large helpings, because Cancer is intuitive enough to see you need it, while most people think your confidence is steel-strong. Aries should put impatience on hold, give Cancer time and plenty of love reassurance. Then the relationship will be strong, and Cancer will reveal a wild and imaginative love style. There will still be rows, most of them over Aries' selfishness, but love will survive. And the long love afternoon making up could be sensational.

Aries with Leo

Choose Leo if you want to be part of a two-person fan club. Because when these two fire signs find each other, you have all the flattery and fun-loving warmth you need for love that lasts a lifetime. You are both strong enough to be soft with each other just enough of the time. Leo can see that behind your tough talk hides someone who does need looking after – well, some of the time – but can only really accept it from someone they admire. And Aries can see that behind the Leo sunny, confident, proud smiles is a heart that can be frighteningly tender and wonderfully true.

You do need to schedule time for some early battles, though, because deciding who leads can be tricky. And a clever Aries will give Leo the biggest share of leading roles, or at least make Leo think that is what's happening.

Because you both score high on energy, you can channel this into love communication through generous daily helpings of hugs that keep you warm for the love feasts. And they will be five-star.

This truly is a partnership to cherish, because you are able to be friends as well as lovers. And even your quarrels – and with such strong personalities there must be some – lead to reconciliations that make the loving sweeter. You can trust a Leo with your heart.

Aries with Virgo

This is a relationship that needs to be worked at. You may at first feel daunted when you see what looks like Virgo's chilly, controlled journey through life, while Virgo may look at your rushing, me-first approach and shudder at the chaos of it. But the gap between you can be bridged and it will help you find your gentler self, too.

Aries needs to show patience and resist the temptation to rush Virgo through the first steps of romance, and through life. Virgo must ration the criticisms and untie some of the worries that could distract from the loving. Because behind the cool Virgo gaze is one of the zodiac's best-kept secrets, and that's red-hot passion. And that is bliss for Aries. A relationship that could go the distance if you both accept that you won't always understand the workings of your partner's mind – but can go on loving when you don't.

Aries with Libra

You are opposite signs of the zodiac and you do much more than attract. As an Aries you ask for what you want, while Libra gets even more from you by charm. The lovemaking, as fire and air meet, is wonderful. And you both love and need freedom. That may sound perfect. But taking freedom for yourself is not the same as giving it. And it is Aries who suffers most and must guard against all the simmering resentment at the time Libra lavishes on outside friends and interests.

Temper and anger, whatever the reason, push Libras away, because they are always looking for balance and are afraid of their own temper that, if ever set free, can be awesome. That's why it's so well controlled.

If you can turn your temperature setting to cool, you will be rewarded with a hot line to Libra's heart and temptation-filled bedroom. And Libra can hold on to your love with witty love games, and cutting back just a bit on solo excursions with friends.

Aries with Scorpio

Approach with caution. This can be Fatal Attraction for Aries and powerfully erotic for both signs. Your bodies are beautifully in tune, but your minds are as different as fire and ice. The cool mystery that makes Scorpio irresistible to you at first later becomes a challenge, but if you push too much then that Scorpio mystery becomes a wall made of jagged glass and spikes of sarcasm that will deeply wound open, trusting Aries. Scorpio won't suffer and won't give up all those secrets.

You can race your way through an argument, and feel free to say whatever slips on to your tongue, then have it all over and forgotten. Not with Scorpio – every word will be stored and served up against you later. You need to develop a lot of control and, while that could even be good for you, it is so difficult.

This is a relationship only for the bravest Aries and you will have to accept that the total honesty you crave is never going to happen. Then it can be a rewarding relationship and Scorpio will be warmed by your Aries enthusiasm for life and energy for love.

Aries with Sagittarius

You start with all the pluses for marriage and long-term happiness. You are both adventurous, energetic, honest. What starts as a meeting of like minds and bodies can grow into true trust and love. The lovemaking starts as an adventure that never needs to stop. You can even disagree and still end up laughing at the rows and liking each other even more, because neither of you stores grudges, or stoops to sulking.

You are both fire signs, but Sagittarius is far more controlled. Because of this, Sagittarius, like no other sign, can understand Aries' fragile inner self, and protect you.

The only cloud is that Aries will expect loyalty, and Sagittarius is, at heart, the most easily tempted to stray. But it is worth working through that because this has all the other ingredients for caring, sharing superlove.

Aries with Capricorn

Capricorn can love you, but certainly won't feel the need to say so, or show so except when you are making love. As an Aries you are naturally demonstrative and this is a deep-rooted difference that can choke a love match. Then there is the cash. Aries loves to spend, and Capricorn loves to accumulate.

There is a strong seam of mutual fascination, though, and a powerful sex attraction that could be enough to start building a relationship that will need a good helping of compromises. You will have to cut back on spontaneity, especially when it comes to committing cash you share with Capricorn. And decide that Capricorn's ambitions will help mutual security instead of getting infuriated at the time Capricorn spends at work.

Most of all Aries must learn to live without too much proof of love. And Capricorn must learn to give Aries verbal love reassurance occasionally. With these rules, it can work as a long-term love especially as Capricorn loosens up with age, becoming just a touch more like Aries.

Aries with Aquarius

Sharing dreams, schemes and a view of the world that says everything is there to be explored, Aries and Aquarius can be marvellous soul mates and bedmates. You can create your own world, able to talk about anything and everything, with a hot line to each other's heart.

Yet there are differences. Aries will race into every new experience, Aquarius will work out the best way to taste and enjoy it. So you do need to be careful that Aquarius' detachment doesn't cool your Aries passion. You both need to accept that freedom and lack of possessiveness doesn't mean lack of love. And you both need to practise it, or jealousy might jinx this good relationship.

Aries with Pisces

Pisces' psychic-powered sex-sense can match Aries' aggression with perfect, soothing and sensual sex that makes the physical part of the relationship good. But the deep and sometimes dark depths of Pisces' emotions often don't get a look in as Aries speedboats along on the surface of the relationship. Yet it can work so well, if Aries adds gentle love words, and doesn't just take from this giver. And if Pisces isn't so intent on keeping Aries happy that false promises wind round the relationship – especially since Aries is so honest, you'll believe anything ... Aries must accept Pisces needs to keep secrets and not get frustrated by the mask of mystery that Pisces will sometimes wear. Then Pisces' gentle, skilful, cool caring will fascinate Aries into lifetime loving.

LIVING LOVE

Case history of an Aries woman and Cancer man, star-crossed lovers

Rosie thumped her foot on the brake pedal and the car screamed to a halt. 'Give me the map,' she yelled, grabbing the road atlas out of Ian's hands. 'If I leave it to you, we'll never get there . . . Do I have to do everything myself!'

This was the fifth time in five hours that Ian's nerves had been scraped by her sharp words, and he had felt her instant Aries anger. Each time his reaction was to sink into a silent, yet accusing Cancer mood.

'Don't just sit there and sulk.' Rosie spat the words out as she raced through the map book. 'Do something.' And he did. Still silent, he opened the car door, closed it with exaggerated care, and walked back to the centre of town and the railway station.

Yes, his face looked calm. But his thoughts steamed with resentment. 'That's the last time I go anywhere with her. I never wanted to go, I knew it would be awful. Why did I let her talk me into it – and why does she always have to drive? She must know that I hate navigating. I've had enough of being bossed around by her.'

Rosie ignored her tears, refused to even turn round to watch Ian walk away, and drove off. This had been another plan to put things right between them. Another plan gone wrong. 'I have to make all the decisions, organise everything. He never does – just blames me when things go wrong. And why do I have to drive . . .?'

In a star-crossed roller coaster of a relationship, this was far from the first time that Rosie and Ian had ended up feeling this way. Ever since they first met, in the canteen of the large company where they both worked, their life together had been punctuated by trouble, each pushing the other, testing their own love power, measuring the love they were getting.

Rosie was driving more slowly now, remembering how good their relationship had been at the beginning. Ian's devotion made her feel she was the most cherished woman in the world. He brought her flowers, wrote love notes, drew cartoons when work got too hectic. It was soothing for a go-getting Aries to be bathed with his gentle and caring kind of loving.

Then his moods showed up, uninvited, at the love feast. Disagreements plunged him into sulks, where a straightforward Aries would never go. She wanted a blazing 10-minute row, he would let feelings fester for weeks. Rosie would be amazed when he mentioned a sore point that she'd wiped out of her mind. He could be so secretive, too.

She knew that her naturally bossy nature had raced way out of control and was trampling the life out of the relationship – just because it was so easy to get him to cooperate with what she wanted. But she had underestimated the power of his jealousy – he coldly refused to even look at her for days after that harmless flirtation at the office party. If only he would say how he felt, instead of expecting her to guess. Even if she tried guessing, she knew she'd get it wrong.

Yet the anger was pushed right out of her mind as she remembered the way his face lit up when he saw her, the way he touched her, so slow, so tender. Yes, she'd go back to their home, sort everything out, a takeaway meal, an evening in bed . . .

But the house was empty. He had left her a note. It just said, 'Rosie – You will by now have decided exactly what we should do next. Well, sorry to disappoint you, but I have my own plan. I have gone away for a couple of days, then I'll contact you. Ian.'

Her auto-rage lasted only seconds this time, she respected

him for making his own plans, and she was intrigued. When he came back, they both wanted to start again. But he needed new rules, though he admitted the only way he could find of facing her was in a letter. 'You're always so sure, so impatient,' he said. 'It's easier to let you have your own way. But it makes me angry inside that I do.'

Rosie agreed when he said he wanted to go on writing whenever he needed to. She suggested they should make alternate decisions, each partner vowing not to criticise the other's efforts – but to give it their best shot. After all, they knew it would be their turn next.

Then they went shopping in a joke shop together and bought a hat with a pair of donkey's ears on it. It is kept on a hook in the hallway. Each time Ian sulked for longer than an hour, he had to wear it. Each time Rosie's temper tantrums started, she had to wear it. This did help – the eccentricity of it appeals to both the Aries and Cancer in them, and it does keep things in perspective.

After a year, Ian was able to stop writing letters and talk problems through with Rosie face to face. He still feels a sting of jealousy when he sees her laughing with another man. But he's secure enough to ignore it. Besides, now she knows how he feels, at parties she'll come to his side every now and then to whisper something naughty in his ear. After all, she knows how he loves secrets.

The hat still hangs in the hallway, just in case. But recently it started a slight disagreement – should they pack it in their honeymoon suitcase . . .?

Case history of an Aries man and Sagittarius woman, star-blessed lovers

Jack's fingers tapped out his impatience as the ringing tone reached 10. She wasn't in her office, she always answered by the second ring. But why would Elaine say she was working late when she wasn't?

Splinters of suspicion pierced his mind. He dialled the number again, very carefully. He looked at the photograph of her in the hallway, almost embarrassed to realise how much he missed her, even after four years together. 'But where are you?' he said as the relentless ringing tone told him she wasn't there.

Jack and Elaine had met, in fire sign style, at a fancy-dress party, after a sponsored assault course circuit. They had spent the day snaking through mud, swinging on ropes, battling over 10-foot walls. Their mind moves were very different, though. Elaine, as a Sagittarius, wanted to prove to herself that she could do it. Jack, as an Aries, wanted to prove it to everybody else.

At the party, the first thing Jack noticed about Elaine was the crowd of men around her. 'Just friends,' she said later. That was something of a chorus line throughout their relationship, because Elaine had just as many male friends as female.

That had challenged Jack at first with his full quota of Aries possessiveness. But he learned he could totally trust her and knew she would never lie to him. Now his mind was wavering. 'Maybe I've just never found out about her lies before . . .'

In the early days, finding out about each other, and how many mind patterns and opinions they shared, had been exhilarating. And the beautiful way their bodies matched in their days, and nights, of lovemaking was magic.

From music to food, holidays to cash ('If we've got it, we spend it'), they had agreed on almost everything. And, for both of them, that had fuelled the courage each needed to try the new experiences that made life good.

At the beginning, though, with the fiery intensity of their sun signs, all they had wanted was each other. They moved in together almost overnight, and didn't even quarrel over household chores, agreeing they should hire a cleaning lady.

They both had evenings off from the relationship to keep their separate circles of friends thriving, agreeing that freedom must be part of their relationship. Sometimes life was rushed, but it was fun.

Well, that was until month six, when Elaine casually mentioned that she was going to spend the weekend at the home of an old schoolfriend who was upset after a marriage breakup – and that his name was Graham. Jack's reaction stunned them both. His Aries insecurity, so cleverly hidden by his mask of boldness, suddenly broke free. 'Please don't go Elaine, I love you, I need you here with me.'

Those were the words Elaine had thought she'd never hear. Because, although they were so beautifully matched – and both knew it – neither she, nor Jack, had ever spoken about their feelings.

Both fiercely proud and determinedly independent, yet neither could risk showing their vulnerability first. Their bodies said it, not their brains.

'I love you back,' she said. 'I don't really want to spend the weekend without you, I was only going because I didn't think you'd miss me ... you're always so busy, so self-contained.'

That night was the first time they really talked, about feelings, about fears, about a future together. They knew that the casual way they had treated their love was their way of guarding against hurts. Now they felt truly free, yet truly together, because now they could show each other their weaknesses as well as strengths.

They made three decisions. First, that Elaine's friend should come and stay with both of them. Second, that they would keep one evening each week just for each other. No TV, no friends, no work, just talking heart to heart. Third, they decided to get married, now that commitment was no longer a dragon to fight and fear.

The marriage had been wonderful, full of sexy surprises, new ways to touch, taste, enjoy. Their honeymoon night had started with a midnight picnic on a private beach. The sand covered with the pure silk sheets she had secretly packed ...

That was why now, just one year later, he was ringing her office. He had arranged to arrive home a day early from a business trip, booked a table at a romantic restaurant. He had put the champagne on ice in the bedroom.

Of course, life together hadn't been all silk sheets and champagne. They had had some crockery-chucking rows . . . though now he couldn't remember why. But they had made up just as quickly. Both did flirt sometimes, but trust meant they could live with, even be proud of, their partner's popularity . . .

Until today . . . 'What about that new chap at work she said was so athletic. She's so gullible, she could fall for any chat-up lines. To think, we were talking about starting a family. Now this.'

Jealousy began to edge into his mind. Then Elaine walked in. As soon as he saw her smile, he wondered how he could ever have doubted her.

'I've been to see the doctor,' she said, and handed Jack a small slip of paper. 'Pregnancy test: Positive.' Jack reached for the champagne. 'Here's to the three of us.'

Taurus in Love

THE WONDERFUL YOU

Steadfast, sensual and sentimental – this is the Taurus love style, and the ingredients that can make you a magnet to the opposite sex. With your feet firmly on the ground, you're the picture of efficiency and organisation in everyday life, yet the lucky loved-one who unlocks the secret safe-box of physical delights behind that practical front is in for an unforgettable treat.

More than most other signs, Taurus understands, needs and believes in physical love and pleasure, but you also know exactly how to make a lover feel cherished and safe from life's dangers – because that's just how you like to feel yourself. Security is like oxygen to Taurus – when you are sure of a partner's love you let your inhibitions peel away one by one and invest in that relationship all the loyalty and romance for which you're famous.

You're choosy about long-term partners – and rightly so. Because once you've made your choice you'll stick by it, putting up with far more than other, less tolerant signs. You can be wrapped in old-fashioned romance, like bouquets of red roses, proposals on bended knees and white weddings with a team of tiny bridesmaids. Presents feature strongly in your love profile – you love giving them and, let's admit it, receiving them too.

You need plenty of storage space for a stash of past gifts, old love letters, photographs and even used tickets from shared outings – that's the sentimental side of Taurus that's so appealing.

Lovers, actual or would-be, also appreciate Taurus honesty, reliability and calmness in a crisis. But they soon realise you can only be pushed so far. Your natural, open approach to lovemaking is evidence of your deeply sensual self – but cuddles and friendly caresses are as vital to you as your own deep sex powers that last all night long, and the next day, too.

THE WICKED YOU

While your passion for physical satisfaction is one side of Taurus' earthy style, the other is a clashing near-obsession with order and control in your life. Trying to tighten a lover's strings too hard, both in bed and out of it, can lead that lover to cut and run, right away from you.

Too often, the stubborn side of you surfaces with a very blinkered view of life – it's how you want to see it, and that's that. But, unfortunately, love doesn't necessarily fit into such narrow definitions, it needs give and take, as well as freedom, to flourish.

A committed creature of habit, Taurus also tends to get trapped in petty routines and rituals, and so tangled up in day-to-day trivia you tumble out of touch with your true passion-packed self. And that's a five-star shame. So is your weakness for overwork, where you put all your energy into your job and have none left over for loving. Ironically, without the lashings of loving that are the Taurus lifeblood, you become less and less able to work well . . .

Change of any kind is something you stomp away from. Even if a relationship has long ago gone stale, Taurus will probably prefer to stick it out rather than either risk new ways to revive it or leave. The belief that love is for life goes bone-deep. You clamp yourself to the familiar, if unsatisfactory, partner you have, instead of risking your home and security on a chance of romance. What is yours is yours alone – you'll fight tooth and nail if an outsider threatens your cosy set-up, and it can be dangerous for anyone who jars that Taurus jealousy into life.

It is hard for you to accept that lovers need a life outside, yet such possessiveness can strangle passion. And beneath the calm face you present to the world, Taurus is often a seething stew of buried anger, fear and insecurity, which can seep out at quite the wrong moments. You're wonderfully fluent in body language, but have a lot to learn about other kinds of communication ...

BEING YOUR TAURUS BEST

Taurus can build permanent passion on that already firm foundation of physical pleasure by learning to let lovers lead their own lives. Give them room to breathe rather than hugging them so tight to your heart they feel trapped – love lesson number one for Taurus is to become less of a control freak. Try it – you may be surprised that the less you ask of a partner, the more that partner wants to give. Your sought-after security will be safer by leaving the door of the cell open than by slamming it shut.

Try to shake off your obsession with routine – it's the one thing that romance isn't made for. Change the things you do together, the places you go, even the food you eat. Learn to accept that a partner cannot stay the same forever, and neither can you. The worst mistake you can make is to refuse to recognise change as a natural part of life.

Although you savour sex most of all in the familiar surroundings of your own bed, every now and again you should open that bedroom door and find a different love location, starting in the house but eventually aiming further afield. Imagination won't be your strongest suit, until you let your sensual cells take over – then you'll be amazed.

Learning to ask for what you want is also important for Taurus. However shy you feel, expecting a lover to guess or just 'know' simply isn't fair and you must feel free to express anger or disappointment as soon as you feel them, not have them forced out of you months later.

Realising love grows stronger, not weaker, by being tested is a revelation to Taurus, as long as it doesn't come too late.

TAURUS SEXY SECRETS

The one object that has no place in a Taurus bedroom is a clock, for the one activity you won't, and can't, be hurried in is lovemaking. Not for you a quick nibble or the equivalent of sexy fast food – every session should be a feast of sensual pleasures setting you free to show your dazzling love skills.

The Taurus appetite for sex equals that for food, and you settle for nothing less than perfection in both. So the ideal evening might start with a candlelit table, lots of finger foods to slip between each other's lips, a glass of perfectly chilled champagne – you love the almost orgasmic bursting of the bubbles against the roof of the mouth.

Lovemaking for you is an all-over experience so, while burning incense or smelling a sultry fragrance turns on your sense of smell, you'll enjoy watching your lover undress slowly in front of you, then feeling the caress of a length of velvet gently pulled along the back of your supersensitive Taurus neck. Rich, opulent fabrics and slow, romantic music complete your perfect love set – anything, in fact, that appeals to your natural love of luxury.

Sex for Taurus is as natural as breathing but you need time to reach the real heights of passion. Once there, however, you can keep coming back for more all night long, stopping only to scoff a plateful of dark chocolate mousse or some other sinful dessert.

Although your physical side can tempt you to no-strings flings, sex and love are intermingled for Taurus – and the warmth and intimacy of the afterglow are just as important to you as the act itself. It's the one time you can let those defences down – to both speak and listen freely. And to keep you satisfied, touching must be an all-day thing – a loving cuddle, stroke of the cheek or suggestive squeeze while passing on the stairs keeps that passion pilot light inside you aflame night and day.

You like sex deep and real and aren't overkeen on toys or games – although dressing up often helps you let go even more. And, although you prefer passion in conventional places, getting in tune with the earthy element of your nature by making love outside on a bed of leaves, under the stars, could prove quite addictive.

WOOING AND WINNING TAURUS

Taurus twin loves are food and finances – so you're likely to meet a mate over a gourmet dinner, when your trays of food match in the canteen, even in a supermarket queue, or checking your balance at the bank. Your dream lover will match your hearty appetites for living, and especially loving, yet know how to weave a warm safety blanket of security around your heart, and the home you share. For while part of you is intrigued by daring romance, deep down you crave a happy-ever-after love affair that lasts for life.

A partner who betrays you, by even fleetingly flirting with someone else, will find that, though the Taurus temper is slow to spark, when it does it's an infernal inferno in seconds. Subtlety and hidden feeling are quite beyond you – with such a clear-cut, black-and-white view of the world, you need straight talking from a lover, someone who will, in turn, encourage you to speak out and say what you feel when you feel it. For you do have a tendency to store up minor hurts and hopes until they burst out at quite the wrong time.

Laughter leads to love for you, too – a lasting lover will be able to tease and ease you effortlessly out of those so-serious moods, and help you giggle away any inhibitions in bed by encouraging fun and frolics. You need someone who can cope with your need to be in control, yet guide you towards change so gradually you don't even notice – a lover who accepts that your extravagant ways are just part of your generous character, and who'll help you to be as tolerant of yourself as you are of others.

And, most of all, a heart twinned to Taurus must want eventually to share you with children. Although you may be in no hurry, a family of your own, one day, is the ultimate aim for tender Taurus, the final seal on a love founded on security and trust.

LOVE MATCH

How Taurus combines with each of the 12 sun signs

Taurus with Taurus

'I'm right' is the favourite phrase and deep belief for both of you. So you may spend too much of your time together either in sulky stand-offs over quite trivial things, or trapped in the endless routines and rituals that you both adore.

Sex can be richly rewarding, because you both know exactly what your partner needs. But out of the sheets this match can slip into stagnant, same-every-day ways. And that would be a shame, because there is so much that could go right, if you are both willing to work at it. A Taurus twosome must make conscious efforts to bring changes into their life together. And dare to laugh at each other, and themselves.

Never let shallow disagreements deepen into a canyon between you. Take turns to grit your teeth and make the first move. After all, you both know just how difficult it is for your think-alike, feel-alike partner to do it.

Taurus with Gemini

Firmly striding after practical satisfaction, well-earthed in reality, it's difficult for Taurus to cope with the Gemini world of imagination, and the quicksilver Gemini mind that skips from plan to plan with plenty of time allocated for fast flirting, too. Yet in bed all these differences can be fused together into a fantasy that's made into exciting fact.

Charming, and always exciting, the Gemini wealth of ideas and love of variety can leave Taurus feeling threatened. Gemini is a strayaway who could tug those Taurus heartstrings out of shape, time and again. Yet Taurus can learn so much. But you will have to learn to talk about how you feel, and Gemini will have to learn to listen. Taurus is a physical sign and Gemini's main drive is mental. Taurus needs to share ideas more, and Gemini must add extra helpings of hugs and kisses.

Taurus with Cancer

Cancer, the emotional challenger, finds a safe resting place in the calm Taurus heart. Both sides will grow into the relationship and develop an intuitive understanding of each other. Because Taurus' love style is naturally loyal and deep, you survive the Cancer mood swings and sulks.

There is a rich seam of agreement on everything from joint finances to joint views of the world, and of course how to put it to rights. The security of being loved by Taurus and, even better, feeling so needed, sets free those Cancer sexy flights of fantasy that turn bedtime into adventureland.

This relationship may start with lust at first sight, or grow from a friendship into a good marriage. Both can be racked by jealousy, yet both understand why loyalty matters. Just make sure that both partners' passion for the quiet life doesn't mean major issues get buried away, where they can fester. Remember that conflict can be constructive.

Taurus with Leo

Leo loves to give orders, Taurus hates to take them. Without a ton of compromise, these lovers can spend most of their time together stuck in a bog of stubborn stalemates, only emerging to have a mega-row that gives both heartache. But if Taurus is ready to take a back seat to Leo, or at least make it seem that way, and accept Leo's show-off style, both signs can grow in the dazzling light of shared loyalty and a passion for all things physical.

This turbulent twosome both need constant praise and affection – and jealous Taurus must try to turn a blind eye to Leo's basic need for freedom and flirtation. Domestic routine is death to the roaring, roaming lion, but spring a few sensual surprises and you'll have Leo Taurus-tamed forever . . .

Taurus with Virgo

Two solid-as-a-rock lovers who can move mountains together. Mind and body harmonise in a Taurus/Virgo twosome, as each gives the other what they need most – trust and true fidelity of the heart and tender comfort of the home.

Neither sign is prone to impulse or risky romance, yet, behind carefully closed bedroom doors, all caution falls away as kindness and caring lead to luscious lovemaking that's a sizzling shared secret. Each brings out the riches in the other in a love paradise. Taurus must keep communication lines open to counter Virgo's romantic reserve, and lead the way in loving touches – you'll get back far more than you give in this strong and trusting match that's made for marriage.

Taurus with Libra

Loving a Libra means living with a mind-changer who spends most of the time making, shaking and faking decisions – while sure-minded Taurus looks on in dismay. This match can make it, if you accept you'll never really know each other, and try to make plus rather than minus points out of deep differences. Taurus must also get a grip on jealousy that can burn this relationship. It's the one thing free-thinking and free-wheeling Libra won't stand for. But for exciting times in bed and out of it Libra is a sure winner, well worth pursuing even just for a short romance that will always have a precious place in your memory.

Taurus with Scorpio

The Scorpio appetite for bedroom feasts matches, and occasionally surpasses, Taurus, putting a sleek smile of sexual satisfaction on the Taurus face. Both signs share a strong streak of possessiveness, helping them wrap each other in a cocoon of intense, private love that's deep enough to last a lifetime.

But beware of secrets. With neither of you fond of frankness, keeping thoughts and feelings to yourselves could eat away at love's foundations. And Scorpio's sudden, deadly sarcasm can stifle your straightforward love. After all, you are on opposite sides of the zodiac wheel. But if you keep

Scorpio's heart full of peaceful harmony there will be no need for sarcasm to strike ...

Taurus with Sagittarius

Taurus tries to build a barrier of domestic bliss around freedom-loving Sagittarius – but to Sagittarius it can feel as comfortable as the cold bars of a cage. Madcap, messy and made for partygoing, Sagittarius intrigues and infuriates the quiet, organised Taurus. But it's a pairing that could work if Taurus can put togetherness before tidiness – and put up with the spell sparkling Sagittarius casts on the opposite sex! But this is the Fatal Attraction sign for Taurus.

Bedtime is bliss with fun and games galore, but the Sagittarius straight-to-the-point honesty can leave less resilient lovers reeling. Forget Taurus caution and tell the truth straight back to stop love stagnating. Provide a long enough leash and Sagittarius will wander right back to your organised home.

Taurus with Capricorn

Strong, steady meeting of like minds and bodies that can make the earth move ... and more. From money to menus these two agree, and share the same ultimate goals in love and life – a happy home and freedom from cash worries. Each understands the other's ambition and tendency towards stubbornness, and together they learn to take life less seriously.

Loving, loyal and faithful, a Taurus/Capricorn twosome gets more tender and trusting with passing time, so a match that starts out good ends up great. And, if both sides can learn to express their desires in and out of the bedroom, nothing will shake their rock-solid relationship.

Taurus with Aquarius

Body language bonds two opposites together – but learning to communicate out of bed takes a lot, lot longer! Passion can persevere, however, if you count to 10 when those eccentric ideas start to surface as Aquarius gets restless in established romance and you get suspicious.

Stubborn sulks are a setback on both sides, but that Taurus earthy physical nature combined with Aquarius' brilliant brain make for never a dull moment. Loving Aquarius means sharing this air sign with all the friends and groups who adore your Aquarius, too, and understanding that ideas will sometimes matter more than love to Aquarius – a trial for possessive Taurus that's worth taking time and trouble to overcome.

Taurus with Pisces

Firm friendship can form lasting love, given enough time and trouble. For Pisces' vague manner and reluctance to face facts can infuriate down-to-earth Taurus – not to mention the fishy distaste for all things financial. If Taurus can avoid falling out over money and Pisces' lack of interest in material things, and give Pisces the time alone needed to recharge the romance batteries, this twosome can build lifelong love on a base of sensual pleasure. Pisces will open up your mind with ideas to keep sex steamy, while you supply security. Pisces will always swim away from confrontations, so it's up to Taurus to get shared grievances out into the open, and keep them there.

Taurus with Aries

Strength with patience is one of your personal virtues, and you'll need all you can muster to put up with bossy Aries' sudden mood swings, instant schemes, and constant need to be in charge. Although sex between these two signs can be erotically electric and inhibition-free, it will take a lot of work for love to last.

Taurus must be prepared to indulge Aries' need for challenge and change without too much resistance, and give all the adoration and devotion Aries demands, and genuinely expects. In return you'll be guaranteed never a dull moment and lots of those surprise presents you so love. And, more precious still, someone who is truly proud of you and everything you achieve.

LIVING LOVE

Case history of a Taurus man and Leo woman, star-crossed lovers

With a hot chocolate drink in one hand and his Walkman playing his favourite classical music tape, Roger opened the scarlet envelope, and unfolded the sheets of paper inside. He knew what he was going to find – several pages covered in Rebecca's large, looped handwriting. 'Dear Rog,' he read, settling further into the armchair he'd had custom-built to give him maximum comfort.

'Imagine me writing a letter. I bet that's what you're thinking! Well, even a lazy Leo can make time for things when they really matter. The fact is, I've decided to take that posting to the Paris office. By the time you read this I'll be on the plane, heading for a new life.

'Please don't think too badly of me. I've tried so hard to get you to discuss this whole thing, but you always look at me as if I'm mad if I mention the words ambition or adventure – it must be that security-loving, home-loving Taurus in you. And I knew deep down you'd never uproot your whole life and move to a strange country just for me. Perhaps that's the main difference between us – you're so steady and practical, and I have to gamble on that better job. I would have explained it all to you, if only I'd thought you'd listen.

'Neither of us has been doing much listening lately, have we? All we seem to do is jog along in our friendly way, getting nowhere fast. Did you know, for instance, that I've been a bit upset lately because Janie, my best friend from school, lost her baby and can't have any more?' Roger shivered. He hadn't known that.

'Roger, darling,' he read on, 'Please don't think I'm

blaming you for the way things have been. I know I'm so demanding and childish at times and I need such a lot of loving. But if you don't tell me, and show me, you love me I find it hard to believe. And yes, I do need to go out with you, to show you off in public. I was withering away at home, but it always seems such a shame to drag you out when you're so contented.

'I can't go through any more of those icy silences that freeze my heart whenever I suggest anything new. The polite remarks at the breakfast table, two frosty backs turned in bed. If only things could be like they were when we first met . . . those fireside picnics on chocolates and champagne, the beautiful ring you bought me and hid in the plate of trifle, choosing our new bed together and trying out every one in the shop. You didn't care what other people thought back then, didn't mind sharing our love with the world. You made me feel like a star.

'Well, I guess it's just not meant to be. It's not enough for me to live in the shadows at home. I need other people around, excitement, company – being at the centre. So it's better to have a clean break like this, don't you think? When I mentioned this Paris job you didn't express an opinion, so I presume you don't care what I do. If only you knew how much I longed for you to say you'd come too. Perhaps I still do, but it's too late now. Be happy Roger. Rebecca.'

The autostop click from Roger's Walkman broke into his thoughts. Yes, it was time for him to leave for the airport. Getting that letter six months ago had shaken his whole secure world, and rereading it now brought back all the hurt bafflement he'd felt. He'd honestly thought they were both happy, with a calm, settled life – instead the cosy set-up had been choking the happiness out of Rebecca's life.

He'd resolved to do nothing, and managed it – for a while. He enjoyed the peace and quiet, no friends ringing up for Rebecca at midnight, no clothes all over the bedroom, no surprises on the credit card statement. But slowly he found himself longing to hear her key in the door, her laughter, feel her warm skin and smell the perfume she always wore. Finally, in an act so uncharacteristic it made him shake nervously, Roger charmed Rebecca's Paris address out of a workmate, bought a plane ticket and flew over to surprise her. He'd been amazed how good the rush of adrenalin made him feel, how much he enjoyed the attention on the aeroplane. It helped him understand a little why Rebecca needed excitement.

She seemed pleased to see him and they spent the weekend beginning again, sightseeing hand in hand, lingering over long French meals. When it was time for Roger to leave, both felt they still had a long way to go, and every two weeks after that they spent the weekend together alternately in Birmingham and Paris. Love had grown all over again, but Roger still felt Rebecca was holding something back. Today she was flying in to see him and if he'd been in any doubt about what he had to do, rereading that letter had convinced him . . .

Heads turned to stare at Roger as he reached the Arrivals Gate, but he didn't care. As he glimpsed Rebecca's blonde head approaching him through the crowd he watched her eyes widen in amazement as they took in the two huge bouquets of red roses, and the megaphone he held up to his mouth. 'Rebecca Harper,' Roger's voice boomed out across the concourse, 'I just want to tell the world I love you and I'm begging you to ma . . .' Enveloped in a warm hug, Roger never got to finish his speech.

Case history of a Taurus woman and Virgo man, star-blessed lovers

Sitting in the taxi as it sped towards the hospital, Fiona tried to concentrate on the blur of streets as they passed. The call had come just as she was putting the finishing touches to Bill's favourite pudding, the one with five different kinds of fruit in it (one she had to make a special trip into the next town to buy) that took about two hours to make. But she didn't mind at all – with all the determined devotion in her

Taurus soul, she loved to make special dishes for her husband, then bask in his enjoyment as he took his first bite . . .

'But Bill won't be home for dinner tonight,' Fiona thought, trying not to panic. Over the slightly crackly phone line, the nurse's voice had sounded quite calm – but was that just for Fiona's sake? 'Your husband's asked me to call you,' she said. 'He's here at Saint George's having a few tests after being taken ill at lunchtime – nothing to worry about. But could you bring some of his things in with you just in case he has to stay the night? Come to outpatients and ask for the Cardiac Unit.'

Those words 'Cardiac Unit' had echoed in Fiona's mind all the time she packed Bill's bag, but she couldn't help smiling fondly as she opened his cupboard and saw the shirts, suits and ties neatly hung in colour order, and all the shining shoes stacked neatly away. 'Typical Virgo,' she thought, remembering it was Bill's neatness that had first brought the two of them together. He'd helped her get the accounts in order at the film club where they were both members – then let her take all the credit for the immaculate columns of neat, precise figures.

From that first, cautious friendship, love had grown slowly in a magical summer of shared meals and outings to the seaside and the zoo. Like two sides of the same coin, Fiona and Bill discovered they shared many of the same views and aims in life – not for fame or fortune, but a home and family and securely invested income. Fiona loved Bill's stiletto-sharp mind and his lightning responses to situations that made her laugh and laugh – while he adored her sensuous lovemaking and the beautiful home she kept just as he liked it.

They both knew, from the earliest days of their relationship, that this was for keeps, yet Fiona was glad she and Bill hadn't rushed into things. She really appreciated the romance of his proposal, on one knee after dinner at their favourite restaurant. Nor had there been any question of them living together. For this conventional couple it was the white wedding, the works, surrounded by the family that meant so much to both – the only possible start to their life together.

As she recalled her marriage vows, a single tear ran down Fiona's pale cheek. 'We said we'd love each other till death us do part,' she thought sadly. 'Now it looks like that could be sooner than we suspected. Oh poor, poor, Bill . . .' She struggled to pull herself together, knowing, as so often in their marriage, she would have to be the strong one. It was a role Fiona relished, the chance to stick up for her man and support him through hard times.

They'd had their share of problems, when Bill was made redundant and retreated behind a shield of compulsive worrying. Fiona was so proud of him for fighting back and retraining in a completely different career. She'd spent that time boosting his confidence and offering steady reassurance and it gave her a warm glow inside to know how much he appreciated her help, even though he'd never say so. Unlike some couples they knew, communicating had never been a problem for Fiona and Bill – they seemed so much on the same wavelength there was no need for words. They'd built a comfortable home together, where each found the security essential to their survival.

Yes, there had been rows, or disagreements really – generally when Bill got exasperated with Fiona's lavish spending, or she took offence when he voiced one criticism too many. But they'd always been able to come to some compromise without too much trouble. 'Let's be reasonable' was their relationship's motto, Fiona thought with a grin. And it suited them both perfectly.

The only real problem had been the shallow rut they found themselves in after a couple of years, when domestic harmony left them so satisfied all they wanted was each other and their home. Life, and sex too, Fiona had to admit, became more than a touch predictable. Suddenly they realised they hadn't seen any of their friends, or gone out separately, for months. And they'd followed the same love-making routine time and time again.

The rut was simple to get out of, though. Bill brought home the evening-class prospectus and each chose a different class to attend. They held a party and invited all their friends, then agreed each should go out without the other at least once a month. It was like a breath of fresh air blowing through their marriage, Fiona remembered, leaving both so refreshed that sex improved on its own.

By now Fiona was outside the door marked Cardiac Unit, brushing the tears from her face and forcing a smile on her lips for Bill's sake. She opened the door and immediately saw him sitting there, his face pale and drawn. But when he saw her his grey eyes lit up and he smiled sheepishly. 'Indigestion,' he said with an embarrassed shrug. 'Oh Bill,' Fiona gasped, and gave him a gentle kiss. 'I love you. Now let's go home.'

Gemini in Love

THE WONDERFUL YOU

A fantasy master, or mistress, of mind as well as body, Gemini can send a shiver of excitement through every encounter, however ordinary. You have a way of suggesting what just might happen that has would-be lovers eating out of your hand, and a free-as-air independence that intrigues and attracts the most unlikely people! Your strongest love muscle is your brain – that's where you cultivate the witty charm and devastating chat-up lines you're famous for, as well as dreaming up the fabulous fantasies that make your established lovelife a refreshing spring of sexy surprises.

Talking, laughing and living very much for the moment, you're a born flirt who flits through life leaving a trail of broken hearts. You throw yourself heart-first into any new experience or affair that comes your way. You know the perfect partner for you is out there somewhere, so what's wrong with having a bit of fun while you look?

You're bright, dramatic and funny and certainly not one to bear a grudge or heave around a heartful of excess emotional baggage. What's done is done ... now what's next?

Endlessly inquisitive, you can find out all about a lover yet remain a mystery yourself – that's just the way you like it. Your rich imagination comes up with countless ways to tease and please a lover, and pens luscious love letters you'll probably prefer to deliver in person. You adore a passion challenge and must make the rules in love, weaving a web of gossamer charm around a lover but running a mile if they try to tie you down in turn. Having two or more lovers on the go at once is ideal for you – each meets the needs of part of your complex personality, yet your versatility and air of mystery mean you're more than enough for them.

THE WICKED YOU

Love can be just another game to Gemini, with you in the lead and losers left far, far behind. You so adore to dazzle you can be blinded by our own light and simply not notice the hurt and havoc your flirty ways leave in their wake. Too often you let your head rule your heart, mistaking witty words and empty promises for true feelings. However easily you think you can cut yourself off from intimacy, deep inside you're searching for security and long-lasting love, just like everybody else.

Needing to be the centre of attention, you enthral someone with tantalising talk and body language that promises limitless passion. Then, suddenly, you're off without a backward glance, since the intellectual satisfaction is all you're after.

Your sharp tongue can slice into a lover's heart, yet you're amazed and indignant should anyone criticise you.

Partners feel they can never pin you down or get to know the true you, and you have the same problem yourself. Forever moving on to something, or someone, new, you've no time for soul-searching or self-analysis. And the slightest suggestion of routine is sudden death to any Gemini romance. With a hazy picture in your head of Mr or Ms Perfect, you'll quickly write off anyone who doesn't measure up – and with your standards that's almost everyone!

Ever unpredictable, your affections are heart-stoppingly hot one minute, icy cold the next – lovers can get fed up waiting for a nice, no-demands warm patch in between. Although you long for total togetherness you're also scared of what it means in terms of gaining trust and losing (you think) lust. Surrounded by admirers and acquaintances, your fear of seeming less than perfect can make you the loneliest person inside.

BEING YOUR GEMINI BEST

Gemini excels in the early stages of love – tempting possible partners to your side and sticking them there with a love spell that combines irresistible charm and mysterious sex appeal. But what happens next? From shopping to sex, the day-to-day routine that tends to replace passion's first flush leaves Gemini cold – and looking around for a fresh conquest. So love lingers on a superficial level and never really reaches the hidden depths of caring and sharing your heart is capable of.

Quantity, instead of quality, in love will satisfy your thirst for variety but never fill the hidden lonely places. To do that, you must be prepared to meet boredom head-on instead of running away from it. Use your amazing imagination to winch your relationship out of the rut of routine. Accept responsibility, rather than simply sighing 'Enough!'

For all the talking Gemini does, often you actually say very little, and reveal even less of your innermost self. Thoughts and feelings, and that includes insecurities, must be shared – you prefer to keep your emotions private so you can stay in control, and indispensable. But how can a lover really know you that way?

Practise revealing a little secret every day, and build up to sharing your innermost love needs. It's true that too much togetherness can leave you feeling stifled – the answer is to avoid flinging yourself into a love affair body and soul and burning up too soon.

Keep up other interests and friendships, plus a circle of preferably solidly attached pals you can flirt with harmlessly any time you feel like it ... then you all go home to your respective partners. For it's the mental stimulation you crave; you can happily do without the physical follow-up. Save that for the one person who, as you slowly open up your heart, will learn to love the real you – and help you do the same.

GEMINI SEXY SECRETS

Arousal for Gemini starts with the ears – caressed with sexy whispers and promises of erotic treats ahead that send the wheels of your fantastic imagination whirring. A silent lover is as pointless as a punctured water bed to Gemini – your considerable sex drive will only be switched on to maximum by compliments. You want to be talked to throughout lovemaking and told afterwards, in no uncertain terms, how wonderful it was. Then you'll want to giggle and chat for hours, since keeping your brain entertained is just as important a part of the love act to you as stimulating your body.

Your natural curiosity and suppleness mean you're usually game to give most experiments a go. But you shy away from lovers who try to dominate or control you – there's only room for one boss in your bed, and that's you. You adore your body and like making love with the lights on and even some mirrors carefully positioned to show you at your best – or setting the timeswitch on the camera to star in your very own private centrefold.

Predictability is out, surprises are in, if love is to last past the first few dates for Gemini. You thrive on spur-of-the-moment loving, being rushed home from a party early because your partner can't wait to make love with you. Such powerful passions are just the proof you need that your irresistible charm is working.

Fantasies and games play a vital part in lasting love – like pretending your partner is a stranger. Your hands and arms are supersensual and a tongue trace on the palm of your hand or a slow and gentle hand massage is the ideal starter for a feast of mind and body thrills.

WOOING AND WINNING GEMINI

Patience and perseverance are the two most important qualities for anyone who wants to partner Gemini permanently, plus hot love reflexes and a generous helping of sex-imagination.

As well as constant variety and a steady stream of surprises, Gemini needs to be guided slowly and surely down from that castle in the clouds where nothing and no one else can really reach, and helped to grasp the reality of life and love.

But lovers have to be quick – look the other way and Gemini can be gone. Gemini's ideal mate is someone just as bright and versatile, able and willing to match the Gemini mental and physical agility, yet with a built-in resistance to the jealousy that's inevitable, paired with such a sparkling, attention-seeking star.

Gemini can't survive without freedom – as soon as ties become too obvious, an escape tunnel will be started. But Gemini can be gently coaxed to stay by being allowed to go out (and trusted to come home again) alone, and shown just enough love to keep a flame of intrigue alight. For as soon as Gemini knows a lover inside out (or thinks so), that's the time to start afresh. A lover can beat this need for challenge by always remaining partly a mystery to Gemini and never, ever, lapsing into predictability.

Prudish partners aren't for Gemini either, as wild ideas can easily shock. A huge effort is also needed to coax Gemini to reveal that true character, but it's worth it! Once inside, a deep, deep well of love and loyalty is on tap for life. Drink deeply from Gemini's refreshing spring every day and there will still be something new bubbling up to surprise you tomorrow.

LOVE MATCH

How Gemini combines with each of the 12 sun signs

Gemini with Gemini

Mirror images of each other's enthusiastic dreams and schemes, this same-sign pairing is high on ideas and fun, low on practical plans. No need to fear being too restricted here as each partner has such a wide range of outside friendships, and makes so few demands, you could end up wondering if there's a relationship at all.

Though both might try hard to avoid it, serious head-to-heart talking is needed, plus a two-sided effort to be honest about partnership problems, rather than rushing away from them. Brainstorming sessions and imaginative lovemaking, plus shared laughter, make this a twosome well worth working at, though it will never be a relaxing relationship.

Gemini with Cancer

Clingy Cancer ways frighten freedom-loving Gemini – and that's a shame. Because taking the time to trust the intensity and explore the depth of the warm Cancer heart can be the key to defrosting those Gemini loving feelings. These can be trapped in ice by that ultra-casual image and mind-over-body approach.

The Gemini need for bed games and role-playing can threaten Cancer security and fuel too many rows. But compromise is possible if Gemini is ready to put as much into the relationship as Gemini takes out. Then, instead of feeling locked in, you could just find that Cancer protective care helps you get even more from life.

Gemini with Leo

That Gemini gift of the gab finds an eager audience in flattery-loving Leo to form a mutual admiration club. Brilliant pals, this couple may delay taking things further, if only because there's so much to say and do along the way. Bedtime's a balmy mix of fun and fantasy, with both sides enjoying practical jokes as well as times of tender touching and strong passion. One shadow could be the loyal Leo lack of understanding of Gemini's flirting – it can batter that Leo pride. If Gemini can curb that need to seek the reassurance of constant conquests, Leo love could fill that vacant heart to overflowing.

Gemini with Virgo

Chaos versus order as Gemini's untidy life and swift-changing friendships make fastidious, sensible Virgo see several shades of red. Although you share sharpness of mind and talent for conversation, basic differences could easily drive you apart. Virgo saves, Gemini spends. Gemini breaks, Virgo mends. And that Gemini need for constant change and challenge simply infuriates strong, steady Virgo. This partnership can become permanent by each putting the other first for a change and talking through tensions before they pull so tight they snap the fragile thread of love. A relationship that repays hard work . . . if Gemini can wait that long!

Gemini with Libra

A meeting of minds and bodies that's made for love and marriage – as long as Libra sets the date. For calm, think-it-through Libra is just the link Gemini needs to connect with reality and make the most of those magical, and at times mysterious, mental powers.

The pair of you will enjoy thrashing out endless theories and plans together – Gemini germinates the idea while Libra lovingly tends it until it bears fruit. While between the sheets it's a race to see who can supply the sauciest suggestion! A quick-thinking, fast-talking twosome who take on the world together. Sexy, lit with laughter and genuinely funny – you even enjoy your occasional rows.

Gemini with Scorpio

On a purely physical level this love's a wonderful winner, as Scorpio's powerful passion partners Gemini's stop-at-nothing imagination. But when it's time to get out of bed, fireworks start. This pair could make Punch and Judy seem perfectly matched! Secretive, permanently plotting Scorpio is put on guard by Gemini's constant chatter and disregard for things that 'really matter'.

That day-trip-through-life Gemini charm jars Scorpio jealousy into life, leading to row after row. Scorpio emotions may run so deep that you feel you'd drown in them. Risky romance – it will repay constant effort with some sparkling times, but it will never be straightforward.

Gemini with Sagittarius

Immediate attraction between opposite signs means this relationship starts well. But it can falter as both battle over star billing – these two are tremendous talkers, but neither's too keen to do the listening a lasting love needs. Straightforward Sagittarius can find those Gemini sudden mind swings a total turn-off and you are neck and neck in the flirtation race. Marriage is more like a marathon, with Sagittarius often a reluctant starter.

Yet a marvellous match is possible if Gemini can just put a brake on that talk and communicate via feelings instead of words. It's easy to play with what the head says, but not the heart – actions will always convince cuddly Sagittarius. So forget that Gemini need to impress and let your true self show – it's a secret you can trust Sagittarius with for life.

Gemini with Capricorn

Clashes over cash, and rows over responsibility – or rather Gemini's lack of it – are the problem. Yet Capricorn's down-to-earth grasp of reality and stubborn insistence on being right can, on a good day, keep Gemini's airy ideas grounded in practicality and so see them through.

But on a bad day, that Capricorn cash-man caution and basic conventional work-ambitious nature can feel like a lead weight round fly-free Gemini's neck. If you can try to tame your Gemini extravagance, both with cash and charm, and coat Capricorn with enough compliments to prove love is safe, then permanent passion is possible. But both of you must accept you'll never speak quite the same love language.

Gemini with Aquarius

Tongues tangle first, in conversation that's so easy. Though this couple start with their lack of commitment in common, they build a rock-solid romance – that's part of the magic and mystery of this very special pairing.

Sharing a thirst for change and excitement means things never get dull between the sheets – neither knows what to expect next and that's what keeps both notorious away-players at home and happy! The only danger point is that Aquarius, with a tougher edge to the personality, may have too much power in the relationship. Guard against this and you can have a true meeting of minds and hearts.

Firing intimate questions, sparking quirky ideas off each other, Gemini and Aquarius are perfectly matched mentally too – each chasing their separate dreams, plus one joint one of a happy, ever-changing life together, forever.

Gemini with Pisces

So easily hurt and prone to periods of brooding depression, Pisces' darker side makes a difficult and challenging partner for keep-life-light Gemini. Yet there's a haunting charm and gentle innocence about Pisces that's irresistible, plus a natural willingness to adore that feeds Gemini's hunger for admiration. Pisces' intuitive love skills can also widen Gemini's lust horizons.

But jealous scenes and suspicion-stirred silences are inevitable as Pisces' need for total commitment clashes with run-around Gemini. You must try to coax out Pisces' deepest fears and defuse them. Then offer constant, patient proof of love for this relationship to last.

Gemini with Aries

The heat is on as Gemini's breath of fresh air fans the flames of Aries' enthusiasm, for each other and for every task they tackle together. And that should be quite a number, as this twosome's so full of fantastic ideas, the only problem is which to try first. You may never quite finish many of the things you start together, but there's always a new challenge to try – in between some luscious love-ins, that is, and your sexy togetherness can make rivals realise they'll never break you apart.

The only cloud trying to push into a crystal-clear horizon is Aries' bossy tendencies and the sometimes selfish brand of Aries loving. But if Gemini can grit those teeth into a grin and give way, now and then, to Aries' orders, the reward will be an inspiring passion that is never repetitive or routine.

Gemini with Taurus

While organised Taurus slow-marches through life and love, chaotic Gemini dances and prances all around, whispering seductive secrets in Taurus' ears and tempting with tantalising titbits of a shared future. Although a common fascination for all things sexual gets this partnership off on a firm footing, it takes determined effort, not something Gemini's known for, to get past a sensual fling.

There has to be a time-limit on how long even stay-at-home Taurus can wait for an absent Gemini. It could be suitcases on the pavement when you stay out late one too many times. But if you, as a Gemini, can clip your own wings enough to spend time at home, and slow down that racing brain power, this can work. And Taurus will enjoy persuading you that the pleasures of the body are a match for the pleasures of the mind. But beware of that Taurus possessive jealousy.

LIVING LOVE

Case history of a Gemini man and Pisces woman, star-crossed lovers

Sitting uncomfortably side by side, but with their shoulders sharply angled away from each other, in the waiting room signposted 'Marriage Guidance', John and Carol both wondered why they were there. A restless Gemini through and through, John fidgeted nervously in his seat, picking up magazines, doing a fast flick through them.

Pisces Carol, meanwhile, sat still and looked icily calm, while inside she was a simmering brew of emotions, regrets and guilt. 'Why on earth did I persuade John to come here?' she thought. 'After all, he's everything a wife could want – handsome, charming, full of ideas to give us a better life. What more could I ask for?'

As she shaped the question, however, Carol already knew the answer. She could ask for security, simplicity, understanding – just a little bit of John's packed schedule to sit and do nothing but be together. 'I want to be more than just another appointment in his crowded diary,' she thought. 'I want to be special.'

'You want what?' John asked. Carol had spoken her last thought aloud. Immediately she felt her Pisces reserve swim up and start to swallow her courage – but this time she fought back. After all, what did she have left to lose now? 'I want to be special,' Carol repeated, and felt a slight sense of relief at the obvious bafflement in John's eyes. 'But Carol, of course you're special, you're my wife, I don't know what I'd do without you . . .' But even as he said the words, John realised he was just serving up a stock response. As always he was relying on his easy Gemini charm to sweet-talk Carol into seeing things his way – and letting him get on with his life.

If he was forced to admit it, that passive admiration was one of the reasons he'd been so attracted to Carol when they met in the travel agency where he worked and she'd come for advice on a holiday with her mother.

Her calmness had been a soothing balm to John's restless spirit. She never questioned his right to do whatever he liked, but was always there waiting for him when he got home, with a long cool drink, a long hot bath and a long sensual night of lovemaking. Then next day when he was up early and packing for another business trip, she waved him off with that sweet, self-contained smile.

'Have I taken you for granted?' John asked suddenly, taking his wife's hand and looking, really looking at her, for the first time in months. He realised with a start how beautiful she was, with such pale skin, deep blue eyes and shining straight hair.

This time, no cleverly convincing excuses came to his lips, although Carol was expecting them. She had heard them so often. Sorry he couldn't make the concert, that business meeting had gone on too long ... Lovely dinner but he had to meet his accountant for a rush deal ... Tell baby Harry that Daddy was sorry but he'd read him a story tomorrow night. It had taken five years, but finally she couldn't bear for her and the children to be so low on his list of personal priorities. Yet looking at John now, the thought of leaving him made her shudder. She knew, under all the frustration and the hurt, her love for him was still there.

And what hurts there had been – that affair she found out about when John's mistress phoned the house one night, glossed over by John's seemingly genuine remorse and promises never to stray again. The teaching career she gave up for him in the early days of their marriage because he wanted her to be always at home for him. That's how their whole marriage seemed to have been – her giving and John taking. Driven on by her new courage, Carol told him so.

'But why did you never say anything?' John asked. 'I know I'm away often on business, but I'd love it if you asked to come along so I could show you off. But you never seemed keen to be away from home. Every time I start to talk about our marriage you somehow manage to switch the conversation to something completely different. You always seemed so happy to take a back seat ... and as for the children, I admit I've always felt an outsider in that relationship – you seem to have such a closeness with them you don't need anyone else.'

Suddenly, there in that bare waiting room, all the problems of Carol and John's five years together seemed so clear. Both agreed they had slotted into set roles early on in their marriage – John as the gregarious, go-getting husband, Carol the stay-at-home wife. But gradually these roles had taken them over, until they found it impossible to escape.

Holding hands, each promised to reveal, and change if possible, two things they were unhappy with ... just for starters. 'First, I think I'd like to get a job,' said Carol, smiling, 'so I have a life of my own away from home to talk to you about. Second, I want you to say what you really mean and not just give me the answer you think I want to hear ...'

John nodded slowly, 'My turn?' he said. 'I want you to disagree with me sometimes and make suggestions on how you would like our life to go, rather than just nodding and smiling. I know I have some wild ideas, but I rely on you to keep my feet on the ground, that's why I love you. And number two, I want us to book into that hotel by the river – yes, right now – for an afternoon of love and ...' Here he leaned over and whispered gently in Carol's ear, then gave her one of those smiles she could never resist.

When the marriage guidance counsellor came looking for them, all she found in the waiting room were two cups of cold coffee and two empty vinyl chairs.

Case history of a Gemini woman and Libra man, star-blessed lovers

Peter was surprised at how free and light he felt as he snapped the small box closed and slipped it in his jacket pocket. If he hurried, he could just catch Sharon as she left work at the town's major department store. What was it this week, kitchen utensils or luscious lingerie? Sharon was such a born saleswoman it wouldn't make any difference, she'd have disposed of all her stock, and have orders for more, long before the store's closing time. That Gemini chat and charm power again, thought Peter, remembering how the two of them had met ...

Dressed in his normal college lecturing outfit, of denim shirt and worn tweed jacket, he stood in front of the tie counter for 15 minutes weighing up, in classic Libra style, each design. Not because he was indecisive, but because he wanted to get the right answer. 'The green's quite smart, but is it too dull? I like the stripes, but what shirt would I wear with it ...?' Then Sharon had come back from her lunch-break and wham! Within two minutes she was parcelling up both ties for him.

That was how their whole relationship had been. Mesmerised by Sharon's sparkling chatter, sensational smile and open manner, he was still wrestling with his Libra caution to ask her out when she did it for him: 'A group of us are going dry-slope skiing tomorrow night – would you like to come along?'

From then on, life had been a laugh-a-minute stream of outings. Sharon seemed to know so many people, sometimes Peter despaired of remembering all their names. And in true Gemini fashion she was forever starting new and more exciting projects, only to stop them when something even more fascinating came along. Peter grinned as he remembered the skiing only lasted long enough for Sharon to fill her tiny flat with salopettes and great big hairy boots. Then came squash (rackets and designer sports kit), then learning Spanish (a hugely expensive set of language tapes), then fostering animals for an animal charity ...

As Sharon and Peter talked, while the food got cold on the plates, swopped books and planned the round-the-world trip both dreamed of, they realised they had fallen in love, and it was the most natural and easy thing in the world to make their mutual delight in each other physical ...

That was about a year ago now, the happiest and headiest 12 months Peter had ever known, thanks to Sharon. However well he felt he knew her, every day brought a new surprise. Up until a week ago, he always thought that was because, while deeply and lastingly in love, the two of them had always maintained their separate lives and kept their independence.

Weekends were always together times but, although each kept a selection of outfits at the other's flat, Sunday nights found them kissing goodbye and going their separate ways. Peter, like all Libras, was secretly set in his private, well-organised ways. He loved the peace and quiet of his book-lined living-room and the neat, orderly, very masculine bathroom. He couldn't see the logic of living together. Sharon liked listening to loud music at six in the morning, while doing her Callanetics (latest fad). They were perfectly happy as they were ... weren't they?

So he was amazed when, last Sunday, as he was packing up his dirty laundry to leave, tears started rolling down Sharon's face. 'What's the matter?' Peter asked, genuinely shocked. 'I don't want you to go, I want you to stay, so we can be like a real couple,' Sharon said, a noticeable shake in her normally happy-go-lucky voice.

Then it all came out. How she felt their love would never go any further unless they took the risk of being together all the time. How easy (but unsatisfying) it was to be happy when each could get up and leave any time they wanted. And how she had hinted for weeks she was ready to move in with him, but Peter had ignored her hints.

He had to admit that was true. His Libra logic argued against change, when they were both so happy. 'Anyway, I thought you wanted to be free,' he said. 'Yes, I do,' replied Sharon. 'But I also want to try moving our relationship on. Don't you think it's worth the risk?'

Risk was one word Peter always crossed out of his mental dictionary – it was poison to his let's-make-sure Libra nature. There could be someone even better out there for him.

Wasn't that typical of Sharon's Gemini wild irresponsibility – jump straight in and worry about the consequences later? What if things didn't work out between them? What if she got fed up with him when she saw him every day? Her sunny personality was like a magnet to other men, what if one of them suddenly seemed a better bet? Living together would make it much tougher for him to restart his life if things went wrong.

Genuinely astonished by Peter's doubts, Sharon did everything she could to reassure him. 'Peter, it's you I love, that's why I want to be with you all the time,' she said. 'We can be together permanently and still keep all our different interests, we won't suddenly find each other boring just because we share the same toothpaste in the morning. We have so much in common and love each other so much, surely more time together can only make things better?'

Now, after a week of arguing with himself, Peter realised that for both of them it was time to trust the message of the heart – not the head. Talking and analysing had always been a strength – now he realised it might also be the major weak spot in their love.

It might be logical to live apart, but it might be a true love-adventure to live together. At last Peter realised that if Sharon – beautiful, magical Sharon – was prepared to take the risk, he should be, too. 'Together we'll make it work,' he thought tenderly as he slipped the little box into her hand. Inside, sparkling on its bed of black velvet, was the key to his front door – and a solid gold heart made into a key-ring with her name on it.

Cancer in Love

THE WONDERFUL YOU

Mysterious Cancer lives, and loves, with deep, and sometimes dark, emotional intensity and thrives on old-fashioned courtesy and courtship. No impulsive headstrong and heart-long dives into passion for Cancer – you're cautious and peer into every little part of an admirer's personality before you slowly start to let your soft, sensual centre show.

The public face you present to the world is sometimes polished and hard, sometimes serene and caring, but underneath you're a wobbly mass of insecurities that only a tried and trusted lover can banish forever. Then Cancer, lastingly in love, can summon up almost magical stocks of sexy surprises and turn countless fabulous fantasies into thrilling fact. Not to mention the loving loyalty Cancer is famous for, and the way you adore to spoil and pamper your other half, enfolding them in a blanket of devotion that makes them long to stay by your side forever.

You're prepared to wait while that subtle Cancer magic weaves its secret spell around a lover's heart, and you have tuned into your partner's hopes and desires. You like your loving steady and secure and, before Cancer can truly let go, you need the permanent promise of a wedding ring. But that certainly won't stop first-time acquaintances falling for the sensual secret they can read in your shy, sidelong glances.

Like a still, dark pool you contain hidden depths – no matter how many times lovers dip into your cool, calm waters there are still more surprises to intrigue minds and capture hearts.

THE WICKED YOU

Moods, moods and more moods are the downfall of most moon-ruled Cancerians – more unpredictable than the weather, your mood can change from minute to minute, without your lover having the slightest inkling why. You expect others to be as subtle and sensitive as you are, then explode with exasperation when they fall, inevitably, short of your standards.

That inbuilt Cancer mothering instinct can too easily turn to smothering – suffocating with a passion so intense it can send a lover running for cover.

You can also be manipulative, using sly, subtle digs and, often, sarcasm, to get your own way rather than coming straight out and saying what you want. For that would involve confrontation and, perhaps, conflict – something Cancer would do almost anything to avoid.

Caught up in your own needs and insecurities, to the point of near-obsession, you can be cruel and relish revenge. You'll spend days flexing your powerful imagination to dream up fiendish ways of getting your own back on someone who's hurt you.

Forgive and forget doesn't figure in Cancer's life scheme; you rarely forgive and never forget. Lovers are frequently baffled as you dredge up old grudges and disagreements from the depths of your heart, sometimes months or even years afterwards. A bit of a pessimist, even when passion's going wonderfully well, you're gloomily dwelling on What Could Go Wrong. You avoid making decisions yourself and that forces a lover to make them. Then you bitterly blame that lover for messing things up.

BEING YOUR CANCER BEST

Nestling inside every Cancer is a vast reservoir of romantic, and raunchy, loving, just waiting to be tapped. But to reach it, any lover must fight a way through formidable protective fences. Many who might make you very happy never make it past the first barrier – a heart-freezing Cancer sulk, perhaps, or sudden temper tantrum.

You need to realise it takes two to make a relationship work, so try meeting a lover half-way rather than waiting in your ivory tower for that lover to arrive and rescue you. Some might decide it's not worth the bother!

Don't be scared to show your sensitive soul – a true Mr or Ms Right will be immediately captivated by it. And, hard though it may be, control those seesawing moods, or at least give a storm warning when one's brewing so everyone can take cover!

Practise spelling out what you want or what's bothering you – write it down, if you can't bring yourself to say it – rather than expecting a partner to pick up signals so subtle they're more or less invisible.

Take care you don't get stuck in the grudge sludge. It's such a waste of very special Cancer imagination and energy that you could put to far more satisfying use.

Put pessimism on ice by living for the present rather than fretting about the future. And, while partners appreciate your loyal devotion, do make sure passion doesn't become a prison through your near-neurotic possessiveness. Accept you can't control a loved one's every move and offer them more freedom. You may find they want less – because they can't get enough of the magical mystery tour of Cancer loving.

CANCER SEXY SECRETS

Water is the one element guaranteed to get Cancer going – the slower and more sensually, the better. A long, hot, scented bath to share with someone special, making love in the shower, on a water bed or even in the sea, as waves wash over you ... all appeal to Cancer's view of sex as a delicious shared secret. Emotional sensitivity is mirrored by supremely sensitive skin that thrills to slow touching as gentle fingers trace the cheekbone, outline the lips, find the pulse in the throat, and then as a tongue tracking the same pattern with an aching, exciting slowness – everywhere.

Candlelight and soft, caressing music, perhaps some juicy strawberries or grapes to feed each other during a long feast where love is the main course. Your sexy hotspots are the breasts or chest (being brushed here with a lover's warm breath or newly washed hair sends senses soaring).

Constant reassurance in the form of whispered compliments and nerve-shivering suggestions keeps Cancer anxieties at bay. Often you prefer to play the passive role in lovemaking, yet your endlessly erotic imagination will go along with a lover's wish to experiment. Then, because your fantasy is often much better than that of your partner, you end up in charge.

But you also adore straightforward sex; the only essential element you need is love. Affairs on a purely physical footing can't ever really work for you. Perfect lovemaking for Cancer starts with the security of feeling loved – then you are really able to let go and reach your core of pure passion.

WOOING AND WINNING CANCER

Casual and couldn't-care-less lovers need not apply for the post of Cancer's permanent partner. The one thing you must have is committed adoration, and a large portion of it. You need someone strong enough to survive all those maddening mood swings, sexy enough to bring out Cancer's secret sensual self. Someone self-confident enough to take a back seat sometimes so Cancer can shine. Your ideal lover must also be able to tune into whatever wavelength your thoughts and feelings are on at any one time, and think ahead to find ways round that Cancer dread of confrontation. You'll want to woo or be wooed with every romantic cliché in the book, from bouquets of red roses and bottles of champagne to a candlelit proposal.

Your partner will have to wait patiently until you've convinced yourself and cautiously made your decision.

You also need someone who can accept your Cancer need for secrets and tendency to be selfish. Someone to teach you that there is nothing to fear from sharing, who can help you to slowly loosen up and, eventually, let go that vice-like grip on the heartstrings.

Your partner must be firm but also prepared to let you control your life together, to a certain extent, without ever trying to boss you around, and not get claustrophobic as Cancer clings on so tight. Your partner will be richly rewarded, though, because once you do make a commitment to love, you offer total loyalty, the ability to make a lover feel the most looked-after person alive, and an irresistibly vulnerable centre that, once glimpsed, is impossible to forget.

LOVE MATCH

How Cancer combines with each of the 12 sun signs

Cancer with Cancer

Double helpings of insecurity mean this relationship is built on constantly shifting sand, as each partner tiptoes round the other's feelings and neither dares speak their mind, or their heart. Both are well supplied with love to give and caring that is sometimes so intense it becomes controlling. But, to truly succeed, a Cancer couple needs to learn to take, too, or what starts as a red-hot romance can soon freeze in the icy blast of boredom.

First lesson: these same-sign lovers must remember that real love can survive angry rows far more easily than moody sulks. Second lesson: don't jail yourselves away from the world with just possessive passion for company – you need input from less intense friends and family to help you both lighten up.

Cancer with Leo

There can be lots of laughs, at least to start with, as the wacky humour of Cancer and Leo collides – and Leo's warm passion style has you purring with sensual pleasure. But storm clouds soon appear on the horizon as Cancer's shower of pessimism dulls Leo's sunny outlook and your wily, sometimes sarcastic, ways wound that straightforward Leo soul.

A brilliant short-term romance, this love can last if Cancer can avoid jealousy and deflect Leo's bossy tendencies with a smile rather than a resentful sigh. Bossman Leo must learn it's dangerous to take you for granted. No nagging is another golden rule, plus an effort to leap before you look in lovemaking, just once in a while.

Cancer with Virgo

A natural friendship that merges into long-lasting love, as Virgo is so dependable – and that is a fair swop for Cancer's sensitive caring. Agreeing on everything from saving money to saving the whale, this compassionate couple make the world safe for each other and their love.

But it's all too easy for the safe and familiar to push passion out of bed, so both must make an effort to keep sex spontaneous and not too serious. If Cancer can conquer that compulsion to cling and doesn't infect Virgo with the gloom both can be susceptible to, this can be an equal, sharing passion that goes from good to better.

Cancer with Libra

Starts well with humour and high ideals, but soon cracks start to show as cool Libra won't ever really give up searching, always checking in case there's an even better partner out there, and that crushes Cancer. Libra may refuse to give Cancer much-needed commitment and security and Cancer's moon-ruled moods infuriate Libra.

It's a passion stalemate between two signs who both hate scenes, and are each so wrapped up in themselves they may find it impossible to see what's going wrong.

Sincere effort will be needed to make it work long term – constant straight talking and a two-sided promise to dive beneath the surface pretence to real deep feeling underneath. And it's worth the effort, because Libra needs the tender care of Cancer's special love recipe.

Cancer with Scorpio

Love and lust at first, and last, sight – this is a near-magical match of true soul mates. Normally both secretive and cautious, Cancer and Scorpio together find complete trust and understanding in each other, enough to share their most intimate secrets, hopes and fears.

Sex can be sensational, with Scorpio's legendary energy more than matched by Cancer's wicked imagination, and no holds barred approach, in bed and anywhere else that takes their fancy! Cemented together in a cocoon of warm and wonderful security, they'd happily wave the rest of the world goodbye forever. But Scorpio will have to remember kindness, and Cancer must make Scorpio feel in charge of the relationship – at least some of the time.

Cancer with Sagittarius

If these body buddies could stay in bed all the time they'd have a match made in heaven – it's light the touch paper and get between the covers! But as soon as they start trying to get on in everyday life it's an earth-shattering clash.

Your tender, caring heart can't help trying to calm Sagittarius' adventurous one, while the Sagittarius blunt and to-the-point comments can all too easily wound your ultra-sensitive soul.

It can work out if Cancer is willing, and able, to develop a tougher skin that's remark-resistant, and quell that deep-down desire to worship – Sagittarius will stick around far longer if shown indifference instead of adoration. And Sagittarius needs to realise how important family life is to Cancer and cooperate with all that in-law visiting.

Cancer with Capricorn

What starts as fiery passion can be all too quickly quenched as Capricorn's practical, and occasionally cold, approach to love slaps down Cancer's all-feeling love style. And Capricorn will always be a little in love with work. Yet these opposites do have quite a few things in common, from a shared love of saving rather than spending cash to a matching pair of carefully concealed soft centres – Capricorn inside a coat of moody sarcasm.

Kisses can turn to curses unless both concentrate on what they have in common, rather than dwelling on differences, and Cancer tries to see life, and love, in a rather less emotional way.

Cancer with Aquarius

There will be clashes over commitment, or lack of it, as Aquarius refuses to be handcuffed at home by Cancer's clinging love – and is constantly exasperated by the Cancer need for security and secrecy. Meanwhile, Cancer can't cope with that Aquarius absent-mindedness and generosity of heart that reaches out to everyone, not just Cancer. This is the Fatal Attraction match for Cancer – because the Aquarius ability to stay free is the irresistible challenge for locked-up-in-love Cancer.

This pairing can work if you accept you'll never own or completely understand Aquarius, and make a circle of outside friends and interests. Casual Aquarius must take time and trouble to reassure Cancer that love is always there, although it may never be obvious.

Cancer with Pisces

This telepathic twosome take love onto a higher plane, so perfect is their understanding of each other and their needs, both body and soul. Pisces is the sympathetic listener you long for, to whom you can pour out the hopes and fears you would never dare tell anyone else. And both halves of this couple are such dreamers they really do dwell together in their own special world. Add to this the element of erotic imagination each brings to lovemaking and the result is a chance-in-a-million romance that grows into giving, living love that's the envy of all you meet.

But Cancer may find the Pisces casual attitude to money a nerve-racker. And you could drift together into drinking and eating too much. Cancer will have to stay watchful, but it's more than worth it.

Cancer with Aries

Cancer's supersensitive subtleties are wasted on straightforward Aries, who's too busy rushing around and changing the world to take time to coax Cancer into a deep love relationship.

Yet, when fiery Aries wants to row and clear the air, more likely than not Cancer will retreat into a silent sulk – and the fog of misunderstanding thickens even more. All is forgotten between the sheets when Cancer mystery complements Aries imagination marvellously.

If you can accept that confrontation is a necessary part of passion, then love can last; but you'll need to believe that Aries restlessness is natural and does not mean you are failing to keep Aries interested.

Cancer with Taurus

A quiet, calm pairing that still sees the funny side of love – both are prone to get the giggles at the most erotic moments! While Cancer is happy to provide the loving devotion Taurus needs, the more even-tempered Taurus has the patience and inner strength to put up with Cancer's changeable moods, even though Taurus is often far from understanding them.

Both love their hearth and home, and adore a shared session of cooking followed by a further feast of loving. Add to this their mutual and careful respect for cash, and need for long-term commitment, to get a rock-solid romance that's made for loving, loyal marriage. But you need to make sure that familiar cosiness doesn't take the passion out of the relationship, and that Taurus doesn't have too much of a monopoly on decision-making.

Cancer with Gemini

A volatile mix of feeling and thinking. Emotional Cancer needs to be needed non-stop, while Gemini's ever-moving mental powers sprint from one love-challenge to the next, leaving Cancer much too often home – alone. This can make for an intriguing affair if both partners accept their differences, and resist impulses to change each other's characters.

But long term it can be tricky, unless you accept that Gemini's charm can't be kept just for you, and you can conquer resentful feelings. And Gemini must never scorn your serious love ways. When it works, it's brilliant, as both love to talk and can dazzle each other with daring suggestions in bed.

LIVING LOVE

Case history of a Cancer woman and Aquarius man, star-crossed lovers

Sally had started on her second box of tissues before she managed to finish packing her bag. But then, as she struggled to ram the clothes in and force the bag shut, the zip burst. She started weeping again. As she was calming down, she caught sight of the framed photograph on the bedside table of Colin and herself. It was taken on their last holiday together, arms around each other, big smiles, straw sunhats ...

In an action that jarred her caring Cancer soul, she snatched the photograph and hurled it to the floor. 'Two-timing slimy lying rat!' Sally yelled. As the picture, frame and all, bounced underneath the bed and she heard the crisp cracking of glass, Sally's heartbroken sobs changed to near-hysterical giggles. 'If I could just see myself, cool, calm, collected Sally, ranting and raving like some sort of lunatic. I'll just finish packing then I'm off – best thing I ever did.'

Yet, however hard she tried to convince herself, the words rang hollow in her heart. She knew, deep down, that the best thing she ever did was fall for the cool charm of Aquarius Colin. If she walked out on him now, she'd be turning her back on all the excitement and fun he brought, turning her life from light to dark.

'But at what price?' Regret deepened her voice to a rough whisper. 'I can't go on being hurt and deceived like this. He promised me he'd try to change – and now look what's happened.'

Yet, Colin had always been completely honest about his character. 'Don't try to tie me down, Sal,' he'd said when her loving Cancer mothering started to take over and organise his life, and timetable his days. 'I've got to be able to get up and go whenever I want to – that's the only way I'll stay! Try to shut me in a cage, however warm and wonderful it may be, and I'll do everything I can to escape. But leave the door open and I'll happily curl up with you in one corner forever.'

Completely against her inbuilt Cancer need for security, Sally had tried to give Colin the freedom he needed – but not asking where he'd been when he came home, and smiling when he made instant deep friendships with strangers at parties, had sometimes sliced too deep into her heart.

'Am I too sensitive?' she asked herself, repeating the words Colin often said. She knew there was some truth in this, but also that Colin was far from blameless. He knew his blond good looks and easy charm were like a magnet to other women, and sometimes he seemed almost to taunt Sally with it. 'But you know it's you I love, I always come home to you,' Colin would say. 'I just like mixing and talking with different people, that's all.'

When she was thinking straight she knew Colin wouldn't lie to her, yet still the daggers of doubt wounded her.

Their last bust-up six months ago had been their worst, when Colin had gone off for a weekend charity run, telling her only minutes before he left. Sally had fled to her sister's, then wondered if it was worth going on. Yet she couldn't get out of her mind the wonderful, laughter-rich times she and Colin had shared. The way he could tease her out of those Cancer dark moods. The way, while making love, he whispered compliments that made her feel the most wanted woman in the world. 'Can't live with him, can't live without him,' she'd thought, then looked up to find his worried face at the window.

'Don't leave me, Sally,' he'd said. 'I need you.' It didn't sound much, but that admission from normally no-commitments, no-promises Colin had been the turning point in their relationship – or so Sally had thought, until today.

Realising she truly did need commitment from him, Colin had told her every day how much he loved her, and usually made a point of telling her exactly where he was and who with. Better still, he sometimes took her with him, so now they shared things far more, rather than leading separate lives. On Sally's part, she'd stifled her natural Cancer desire to suffocate Colin with love, developed more interests of her own and didn't cross-examine him about mystery absences. She'd also promised to control those lightning mood changes that baffled and frustrated Colin. It had gone so well, until now!

Walking from her Spanish class, she happened to glance into an open pub doorway and saw Colin there, his blond head bent, deep in close and secretive conversation with Sally's own sister.

As Sally rushed home, all her new-found confidence fell away. Hating herself, for the first time in months she went through the pockets of Colin's jacket – and stared in stunned disbelief at the scrap of paper with the scribbled phone number of her best friend, Jackie.

'There's no going back this time, I've been betrayed,' Sally thought, as she threw the last of her clothes into the second case. But, almost to punish herself, she decided to take the photograph of herself and Colin. She knelt down to retrieve it from under the bed. In the dusty darkness, she caught sight of something. It was a square box with Barton's Birthday Bakery written on the side. As she pulled it out, Sally also saw a piece of paper taped to the top. There, in Colin's writing, was her sister's name, with 'organise drinks' written beside it. Underneath was 'Jackie – party tapes,' another of her friends paired up with 'cold buffet' and her own Mum's name with, written beside it, 'Take Sally out for the day so we can get the party ready.'

In her upset state, she'd completely forgotten her birthday next day – but Colin hadn't. 'He must have been planning this surprise for weeks. Maybe he's changed more than I realised. And so have I,' she thought, throwing clothes back into drawers and dabbing her red eyes with cold water. 'All I need now is my chance to prove it.'

Case history of a Cancer man and Scorpio woman, star-blessed lovers

Monday morning, and the hands of the office clock were barely on 8.30 a.m. when Mark sat down at his desk. He breathed a huge sigh of relief when, looking over at Rachel's corner of the open-plan office, he spotted an empty swivel chair. 'Thank goodness she isn't in yet,' he thought. 'I don't think I could have faced her this morning, knowing what I do.'

He knew even his Cancer fascination with secrets would have crumbled in the face of Rachel's X-ray Scorpio stare. But how difficult it had been to persuade her not to see him over the weekend. They had been going out together for nearly a year now and were almost inseparable, spending every spare moment in each other's flats and in each other's arms.

Right from the start, the breathtaking strength of the physical attraction between them had astonished Mark, who'd never felt anything like it for any woman before. It was partly Rachel's Scorpio energy, which radiated out of her even when she was doing something ordinary like washing-up, and partly her darker, more thoughtful side.

Linking paperclips together in a snaking chain to form her initials, Mark remembered how it was Rachel's pride that first brought them together. Although they'd worked in the same charity office for months, and Mark had longed to speak to beautiful, mysterious Rachel, it took the introduction of new technology to do the trick. For every time he passed Rachel's desk, with its new computer terminal, he saw her glaring at it. Something told him not to offer help. Instead, he tapped her on the shoulder and said, 'I'm having such trouble making sense of my computer manual. Can we run through it together?'

In the end, Rachel thought she understood it all far faster than Mark, but it didn't matter because he was so ecstatic to be spending time with her. When he was close to Rachel he felt so alive, her energy seemed to stream into him and help him see the world in a whole new way.

'Is this love?' he asked himself, but ever the cautious Cancer he made no moves towards her, so sure she'd reject him. Then one evening, when the two of them were the only ones left in the office, she took his face between her hands and kissed him. 'Mark, I love you,' she said, 'and I'm fed up waiting for you to do something!'

From that day on, things had gone from good to better between them. Although both were ambitious and driven at work, in their different ways, away from the office the tenderness and understanding between them took Mark's breath away.

With other relationships he'd found girls almost resented his need to worship and look after them. But Rachel took it for the compliment he meant it to be, and often said he was the first man to understand her – to free her from jealousy by making her feel she was the important one in the relationship.

Once moody and too often pessimistic, Mark realised after about six months with Rachel that he couldn't remember the last time he'd felt the moon's changeable pull wreck his mood. And he knew that, although her Scorpio temper had a real sarcastic sting in its tail for those silly enough to stir it up, that power had never been turned on him. And she laughed at his jokes, too – nothing made him feel better than seeing her smile after a rough week at work.

The only thing that grated on her nerves had been Mark's bone-deep need to keep secrets, from everyday things like the size of a restaurant bill to details of previous girlfriends. Rachel had tried to coax or trick them out of him, until

Mark explained how his secrets were like a security blanket. However stupid he knew he was being, he simply had to keep some things to himself. He'd really admired Rachel for the way she'd accepted that. The depth of her trust touched his heart.

'Mind you,' he thought now, 'this is one secret even I couldn't have kept from Rachel.' That's why he had asked her not to see him over the weekend, although he couldn't say why – and had seen her shiver of suspicion. There would be plenty of time to face her once she'd heard the news. 'Won't be long now,' he thought, as the hands of the clock slid towards 9 o'clock.

Working together had turned out better than he expected, partly because both of them had made a conscious effort to switch off from each other while in the office. They both loved their work, almost as much as they loved each other, so neither saw any need to leave. But it had been difficult, the last two weeks, knowing they were both in line for the top promotion – and there were no other candidates. Both tried not to show how much they wanted it, and failed miserably. And Mark couldn't help wondering and worrying what difference it would make to their relationship.

'Well, that's something we'll just have to work out ... together,' he thought now, remembering the letter he'd received in the internal post on Friday afternoon offering him the job. Rachel had been out at a conference, so he immediately went to discuss the situation with his boss. And when he came out, Mark realised Rachel would have to be told the news officially first, which was why he insisted they spend the weekend apart.

Here she was now, wearing that dark pink dress he bought for her, giving him her special smile. Still Mark was certain he'd made the right decision. 'Some things are more important than work,' he said to himself as Rachel was called, at once, into the boss's office to be told the promotion was hers. Mark's only condition had been she must never know he'd already turned it down. 'Good job I can keep a secret, really,' he smiled, as he waited to congratulate her.

Leo in Love

THE WONDERFUL YOU

Like a child in a sweet factory, previewing all the pleasures on offer, uncertain which to sample first – that's Leo newly in love. You are a genuine romantic who adores the fun, flirtatious stage of a relationship when, bit by bit, you allow your true loving soul to be eased and teased out of that often showy surface gloss.

But not before you have tied a lover to you forever with a dazzling display of your sunny, funny talents. You are unique both between the ears and between the sheets, and make any partner feel like the luckiest lover alive. When you're not splashing out on more-than-you-can-really-afford gifts for a loved-one, you are staging dramatic ways to show how much you care – spraying 'I adore you' in whipped cream on a partner's car, or sending an embarrassingly large bunch of roses to be delivered in a public place.

Tender and, once you give your trust, true forever, your loyalty is legendary, and anyone foolish enough to threaten your lover's security will fling open the door of that Leo blast furnace of a temper.

One of the most physical of signs, when you know you are loved, you're warm and loving and thrive on giving and receiving lots of hugs, kisses and touching. Without this life-cherishing contact, Leo's spark will flicker and die.

On the outside, you can seem super-self-sufficient, even bossy, but a major part of Leo's magic is your childlike capacity for joy and wonder at the world. This helps keep love fresh and fun, and can make any life you touch a lot more worth living. Add to this a double helping of pride, a dash of creativity and sex appeal that shimmers across the most crowded room, and it is easy to see why Leo loving is incomparable and unforgettable.

THE WICKED YOU

Turning life into a drama, with you as the star, can be your downfall. Once the first red-hot flush of passion cools, you find it difficult to settle for the day-to-day domesticity of love, and may even start creating scenes or shouting matches for the sheer pleasure and excitement of it. Because, with a rather pompous pride, you believe you deserve better.

You want love to be effortless and everlasting, and often, for the first few weeks at least, it is. But as soon as your idealised lover's character-cracks start to show, rather than help patch them up, you may run out, all the time refusing to believe you could possibly have any faults of your own.

Leo demands more adoration than the average megastar. A lover must be a personal fan club of one and worship your every move, or you'll lose interest. You love giving advice and loathe taking it.

Often you see passion as just another game, with you calling all the shots. And sometimes you manipulate partners to be the answer to your own problems, without the slightest thought for how they feel themselves.

Working at a relationship is about as attractive to you as working at the washing-up – you leave mundane activities like that to more ordinary, less high-and-mighty star signs. You can't bear to be neglected or ignored. If you are, that natural Leo flair for the dramatic can sour, turning your tongue vicious and vindictive and magnifying your already above-average Leo vanity into a mega-monstrous conceit that puts off both present and possible partners. You're also the easiest victim for the false flatterer.

BEING YOUR LEO BEST

First lesson for Leo is that true and lasting love won't just happen. After a flying start, it needs a little adjustment of the controls if it isn't to crash-land on the rocky slopes of your low boredom threshold.

The answer isn't looking for a new diversion, either, however challenging and attractive you may find the prospect. Try instead to channel that Leo laughter and gift for fun into the relationship you already have, and take things one day at a time.

Trust that a partner truly does love and adore you, and free that loved-one from the burden of having to spell it out every day. Yes, you may like all the attention, but do you really need it?

The hardest challenge of all will be to face up to your own faults – and, yes, even Leos have some – as well as a very carefully hidden, but real, layer of insecurity, which can sometimes make you seem cold and haughty. If you're going to hand out criticism so generously, you must be ready to receive some, too. Instead of just fuming about that criticism, listen, and try to change your supremely self-centred life views.

You find being in love the easiest thing in the world. It's everyday living with love you find difficult – a symptom of your fundamentally childish nature. Learning how to share, accepting life and love can't always be neatly analysed into right and wrong, nice and nasty, accepting a supporting role instead of always needing to be the star performer – all these are part of a growing-up process that will, to your surprise, leave Leo richer in love, and life. For that shadowy feeling you sometimes get of being alone in the world, on a different level from everyone else, isn't always a pleasant one. Yes, you are strong, but accepting you have weaknesses will make you stronger still.

LEO SEXY SECRETS

Your combination of flaming passion and shaming cheek

can add up to marvel-a-minute lovemaking. The more lavish the surroundings, the better Leo likes it, so soft lights, satin sheets and a bottle of champagne on ice set the scene perfectly for your love performance. And that's just what it is. Let your natural, dramatic tendencies take over and you can make each bedtime more unexpected, and exciting, than the last. You adore dressing up, sometimes disguising yourself, or your lover, as a nun of sensuality, hidden in wraps of black silk until the warmth of love makes that silk caress and outline your body. Uniforms, too, are a special treat, because you so like to be in charge. You relish meeting a lover in a bar and pretending to be strangers, or making an afternoon rendezvous at a hotel.

But you are less happy bringing others' fantasies to flesh – the only star of this show must be Leo! You'll undress slowly, as your lover, an audience of one, watches entranced, and will get extra turned on if there are mirrors all around the room, including one on the ceiling. A secret turn-on spot for you is the spine – you'll thrill to a slow, tongue-tip trace sliding down it, or a sliver of ice guided with the gentlest of hands. Plenty of foreplay is the key to Leo love happiness – you need lots of kissing, and the hard contrast of teeth, not biting but sliding along your flesh. The perfect accompaniment is endless flattery and compliments – and you will soon dump a lover who fails to deliver. You are good at showing a lover what you want, but should take time to ask questions and find out what your partner wants.

A born gambler, Leo will also suggest a game of 'Dare', with forfeits like posting a letter dressed in nothing but a raincoat, but you should resist pushing a lover too far with your dares. Keep it part of the fun that makes loving Leo as thrilling as a lifetime at the fair. But do beware of shutting off your mind as you enjoy the pleasures of the body. True love is a mixture of mental and physical – once Leo learns that, relationships will stop being performances and become truly satisfying.

WOOING AND WINNING LEO

Wanted – someone secure enough in themselves to offer round-the-clock reassurance and attention, yet not so confident they'll cadge the limelight from Leo. Strong enough to lead, yet preferring to follow . . . sounds a bit of a tall order? That could be why lasting love sometimes proves difficult for Leo. Difficult, but far from impossible.

The perfect life partner for you will also match you in two essential elements – sense of humour and physical strength. For who can really see a whining wimp sharing a positive Leo's life for keeps? One of the best places to seek out Mr or Ms Right is a sports event of some kind – preferably open air – or at a comedy show or film. You'll be laughing all the way to the lovebank.

Your ideal lover will appreciate Leo's childish verve for the gift it is, and not try to make you always live in the adult world, will be patient through your rare moods of roaring misery, and will see through that bold, brash surface to the sensitive centre underneath.

A partner must never let Leo feel neglected or second best. That's like stealing the sun from your world. Of course, you also need to be gently prodded if you're becoming too lazy and complacent, and steered towards being less self-centred. You should be encouraged to talk problems through rather than just wiping the slate clean and starting again with someone new. Since boredom is the biggest bugbear of Leo relationships – plus your bossiness – anyone who sticks at your side must be prepared to work hard to rout routine and smash smugness. But you'll make it a labour of love, rewarding your partner with lifelong loyalty and a tender, private version of Leo's sociable public face.

LOVE MATCH

How Leo combines with each of the 12 sun signs

Leo with Leo

This funning, stunning pair will score 10 out of 10 in

compatibility where it counts to them – each can understand only too well the other's need for admiration and constant variety. And between the sheets there's not a shy inhibition between you! Like a forest fire, hot love can flare up again at the most unexpected times, but might burn you up too when you play serious power games.

When both want to lead in life-planning, neither is going to follow, and plate-smashing clashes over who's in charge are only too likely. And there are problems linked to those lion-sized egos. If each roaring individual can shut up and listen from time to time, and if an attempt is made at sharing and taking turns at laying down the law, this warm and wonderful twosome can take love to unique new levels. Especially if one of you is the gentler, quietly persuasive, warmer-hearted Leo type.

Leo with Virgo

A tricky pairing, but when it works it can be wonderful, for calm Virgo can provide the perfect adoring audience Leo needs, while the Leo optimism and good nature helps cancel out the darker shadows of Virgo's personality. Too often, though, exasperated by Leo's happy-go-lucky, show-off ways, Virgo implodes into a never-never land of nag, nag, nag – and nothing's more guaranteed to chill Leo's warmth. Leo always needs the flattery that comes from flirting, and that will stretch Virgo's trust. With a generous helping of tolerance on both sides, and at least some effort to understand each other's obsessions and modify your own, this relationship can work.

Leo with Libra

Both signs score top marks for optimism and outgoing natures and you are a pair of pleasure-lovers. Libra falls for Leo's sexiness and Leo loves the flattery that spills so easily from Libra lips. But it's differences rather than similarities that make for lasting love in this match. For it's Libra's agile mental powers and ability to coax Leo into agreeing to things, and thinking it was a Leo idea anyway, that cuts out a lot of the power battles that tend to overshadow Leo relationships.

But problems could arise from Leo's basically do-it-now nature and Libra's thinking one. When Leo wants to act, Libra wants to talk it through again, and this combination of too much fire and air could flare out of control. But it's always fun cooling things down again.

Leo with Scorpio

As a Leo, of course, you won't admit it, but Scorpio is the one sign that could scare you. Scorpio can provide all the total loving Leo needs, but it certainly won't be without strong strings. First, that Leo must beat back that basically bossy nature. Second, that that roaring temper is tamed. And third, that Leo must economise on both dreams and debts. If it sounds like a tall order, it is, but worth it to keep the fuse lit on this relationship's explosive sex.

There could be quarrels over who gives the orders – Leo shouts while Scorpio schemes and wins. And this pairing that starts with a sex shock to both hearts could sour all too soon when Scorpio's sharp taste for revenge lashes Leo's vulnerable inner self one time too many. Yet Scorpio's deeper understanding of life can make Leo the loving, dependable partner you really want to be.

Leo with Sagittarius

Laughing all the way to the altar, if Leo can coax Sagittarius there, this is a meeting of like minds, like bodies and, most important, like funny bones. For it's a shared sense of humour that keeps this couple's love fresh, plus a healthy respect for each other's independence and a bottomless well of outrageous schemes to stop sex going stale.

Care is recommended, however, around two such towering tempers – like the iceberg, both signs show only a tiny fraction of the rage they're capable of, and say things in anger they regret when it's too late. Sagittarius can take the criticism, accepting that everyone has faults. Leo believes everyone has faults – except Leo. There can be too much competition, too, about who makes decisions, but this pair both enjoy the challenge.

Leo with Capricorn

While calculating Capricorn works and stores up money, impulsive spend-it Leo roars – and the already wide chasm between this couple can soon turn into the Grand Canyon. Not only do they live and love at different speeds, but in their separate ways both are hugely selfish and stubborn. It can be difficult to get any decisions made about the relationship's future.

Happiness can be had, however, if Leo can swallow at least some of that pride and let Capricorn rule some of the time, and tries not to suffocate the cool, cautious Capricorn with too much all-out adoration. And remember, this is romance, not a battleground.

Leo with Aquarius

With both sides inclined to drop a dreary relationship rather than work at repairing it, this could be short-lived once the thrill of stupendous sex fades and everyday routine rears its ugly head. Be ready for row upon row, with two lovers quick to bicker. You are both generous, but Leo concentrates warmth on a partner. Aquarius, at the opposite side of the zodiac wheel, likes to be generous to the world, and this can make a partner feel cheated of the number one spot.

Leo must try to accept Aquarius' unreliability and rather casual approach to a partner, then subtly chip away at changing the underlying attitude rather than charge at it head-on. Then this can be a pair of brilliant buddies who grow into a caring, daring couple and spend a lifetime together without getting bored.

Leo with Pisces

Pisces' heaving emotions, often cleverly concealed by a skin of steel, bewilder the open heart of Leo. And fire sign Leo sometimes has to work hard to stay alight, deluged by negative water sign Pisces. Yet straightforward Leo finds something irresistible about Pisces' mysterious looks, which promise the hidden erotic delights Leo loves, and make Pisces the Fatal Attraction sign for Leo. And there's a soft gentleness and natural adoration in Pisces that soon has Leo purring protectively.

If Leo uses more than natural tact, learns not to expect quick decisions and can stomach those Pisces moods, plus the times when Pisces is so desperately needing, this pair can make a lovers' compromise – Pisces coddling big kid Leo and Leo offering devoted protection in return. Don't ever expect it to be an easy option, but it can be rewarding.

Leo with Aries

Two larger-than-life personalities add up to larger-than-love passion – a made-in-heaven match that just gets better and better. When Aries and Leo can stop talking and admiring each other's talents long enough to get into bed, ecstasy is guaranteed, followed by a tender time of pillow talk where, bit by bit, each can let their brave mask slip to reveal the true, vulnerable self underneath.

Trust is the most vital element here – it means so much to these two fiery signs to know that their sensitive secrets are safe with each other. Aries may forget to give Leo enough flattery, and tussles over who takes the lead are inevitable. They can lead each other into trouble with a shared casual attitude to money, and Aries' restlessness is dangerously matched with Leo's love of gambling with emotions. But occasional spats could never wipe the loving smiles from these faces.

Leo with Taurus

Two luxury-loving signs who feel strongly attracted to each

other – but there'll be plenty of tears flowing, too. Leo's fast decisions feel too much like being controlled to Taurus. Home-happy Taurus will never tame Leo's wandering ways, and loving ties will soon come to feel like clanking chains of boredom and duty. Add to this a couple of iron wills and some nerves of steel, and it's just as well you both have hearts of gold to see you through.

Taurus may need gold in the bank, too, to satisfy Leo. But when the lights go out, all differences are soon forgotten in the shared physical joy that's as simple as breathing to Leo and Taurus, but a lot more fun. And it is more than worth making sure that stubborn squabbles don't wear your love away.

Leo with Gemini

Leo loves Gemini's athletic mind, leaping from scheme to scheme, and that ever-ready charm. Gemini adores the warmth and wonderful loyalty that make Leo the strongest, truest friend. This pair kick off as pals and will always find talking to each other rewarding, as both thrive on variety and are exceptionally sociable. The only possible rain on this picnic could pour from Leo's lack of understanding of Gemini's inborn need to flirt. You need to believe that it's not lack of loyalty. But if Leo can keep to the same relaxed rules of friendship, even when this relationship turns to romance, and trust Gemini to roam and always return, these two build an everlasting love on the firmest foundations.

Leo with Cancer

An electric affair that may lose all its buzz if it's taken long term – Leo loses patience as Cancer moods put a dampener on the relationship. To begin with, it's heaven, as these two share laughing and loving in steamy sessions that match Leo strength with Cancer fantasies. But, although Cancer's gentleness starts by intriguing, it could end by infuriating, as Leo struggles to rescue that inborn fire from a deluge of watery pessimism and gloom. Cancer's gentle, nagging criticism can cut deep into Leo's self-esteem. The relationship can work if you put your own needs to one side at least some of the time and let Cancer think he or she has won the argument. Then you will be rewarded by Cancer caring and a lifetime of warm, supportive love.

LIVING LOVE

Case history of a Leo man and Capricorn woman, star-crossed lovers

For Judith, the electronic putter was the final straw. She said nothing when Stuart spent their holiday fund on a state-of-the-art compact disc player, although they already had a perfectly good stereo system. She smiled stoically when he came home with not one but three jackets (with matching ties) from a designer shop that was closing down – then produced a gorgeous but offensively expensive silk blouse for her. But the day he proudly showed her a long, thin box, with a price tag she at first mistook for a serial number, was the day her quiet Capricorn resolve finally cracked.

'Look, Judy,' Stuart said with typical Leo enthusiasm, 'it's the most fantastic thing, an electronic putter that lets you know, with this digital display unit, exactly how hard you've hit the golf ball so you can learn what works and what doesn't, and look it's got –'

Judith's voice broke into his chatter. 'Stuart,' she said, her fury barely concealed under an icy surface calmness. 'Yes, darling?' he said, looking flushed and boyish, for all the world like a child with a new toy, which in fact was what he was. 'Stuart,' Judith repeated, 'you don't even play golf.'

He had the grace to look a little sheepish. 'Well, I thought I might learn. I am naturally sporty, after all. And just think of the advantage I'll have . . .'

By now Judith wasn't listening. With tears starting from her eyes, she moved into the next room and leant her forehead against the wall. Another month of wondering whether there would be enough in their joint account to pay the mortgage, and the electricity bill was due too. And the twins needed new school shoes . . .

'If only Stuart would grow up a bit and stop being so extravagant,' Judith thought to herself. 'I'm so fed up with playing the heavy in this relationship, always criticising, counting the pennies. But one of us has to do it.'

Yet the wildly generous and ever-childish streak in Stuart was one of the main things that had drawn her to him when they first met. That had been at the local funfair, when both were just teenagers. She was lingering by the big wheel, wondering if she dared have a go on it, when she felt an arm go round her shoulders and deep but so friendly voice say, 'Don't be scared, I'll look after you.'

With Stuart by her side she almost enjoyed the thrills of the big wheel. Then, insisting on paying, he whisked her from dodgems to waltzers, helter-skelter to ghost train, pausing only to buy her a candy-floss on the way. Judith had seen Stuart at school and never dreamed she'd ever meet him – he was handsome and popular, why would he ever look at her with her serious face and boring, old-fashioned clothes?

Yet he not only looked at her, he loved her. No matter what happened, she knew that was true. She realised her quiet strength and capable nature balanced his recklessness, made him feel secure. And little by little, with tender trust and patient lovemaking, he had thawed out the layer of ice life had laid down around her body and soul.

It all seemed a long time ago. Now all Judith could remember of their seven-year marriage was worrying about Stuart's lack of concern for money and his general unwillingness to settle down. Their house was filled with electronic gadgets, her wardrobe with exotic clothes he had bought for her, and the twins' room with dozens of cuddly toys, including the two three-feet high rabbits he had struggled into the hospital with the day they were born.

True, Stuart earned a good salary at the advertising

agency, but who knew what hard times lay ahead? 'We've nothing saved up for a rainy day,' thought Judith, and it was like a knife through her cautious Capricorn heart.

'Maybe,' she thought, 'it's time to call it a day. I might be better off on my own with just two kids – instead of three, if you count Stuart. I'd have to get a job, but I could probably manage . . .' She felt Stuart's hand on her shoulder. 'Don't be scared love – I'll always look after you,' he said.

'No, you won't, you'll send me half mad with worry, you'll buy me sexy clothes that make me look ridiculous – do you call that looking after me? The only person you know how to look after is yourself!' As soon as Judith spoke, she regretted her words. Stuart looked so hurt. Why hadn't she just kept quiet?

'We're never going to agree on money, are we?' said Stuart softly. 'Why don't you open an account on your own? I'll pay all my salary into it and you can allocate me spending money. That way you'll be in control and can spend or save what you like, and I can have my hobbies and mini spending sprees with a clear conscience. There, look, you're smiling. Don't you think that's a good idea?'

Actually Judith was smiling at the thought of Stuart having any kind of conscience about money. Still, she was willing to give his idea a go – she knew how empty and dull her life would be without him.

In return, she would try to put the brakes on the black looks and bleak silences that shrouded their home. She knew it scraped the shine off Stuart's sunny nature, yet couldn't seem to stop herself criticising and carping. Sometimes she thought he went and spent more just because he knew she didn't want him to.

'We've had our problems, but you're still the best husband I know,' Judith said, and saw Stuart's chin lift. 'I'm going to take the electronic putter back to the shop,' he said. 'It's pretty boring . . .' ('Success!' Judith thought.) '. . . and anyway there's a computerised Esperanto dictionary I could swop it for.' 'Oh well, one day at a time,' sighed Judith. Two years on, that's still her motto. But she and Stuart, the boys – and the toys – are still together.

Case history of a Leo woman and Aries man, star-blessed lovers

As she rode her bike through the squash club gates, Lisa smiled as she looked out for David's car. Not that she could miss his Ariesmobile, as she called it – bright red, two-seater and very, very fast, it stood out rather among the dull-coloured saloons and estates in the car park. Yes, there it was, parked at an angle, as though he'd rushed in and jumped out, which, in fact, she was sure he had.

'Always in a hurry – and usually late!' she thought to herself, marvelling yet again at how tolerant she was of David's minor, and even major, faults. Every other lover who hadn't lived up to her rather lofty Leo ideals had got very short shrift indeed. And after all, she'd always had another admirer waiting in the wings to take their place.

'So what is it about David?' she thought to herself as she hooked her sports bag out of the front basket and headed for the swing doors. She'd found herself asking that question many times during the 18 months she'd been living with him.

'Certainly not his looks,' Lisa grinned, picturing David's rather battered face with its mischievous eyes and grin hovering never far from the mouth. It was his energy, joy at being alive, that matched her own, and his optimism. He had his own life and certainly didn't shower her with slavish devotion the way some other lovers had – surprisingly, Lisa found even her Leo love of adoration preferred things that way. She didn't feel she had anything to live up to. 'I suppose he just treats me like a real person, not some sort of goddess,' she thought.

It had been easy to let David see the sensitive self she had, in the past, felt almost ashamed of. She had confided her deepest Leo dreams to him – how she had always wanted to go to drama school and had only done a secretarial course because she wanted to work to help out at home. She confessed, almost guiltily, that she often felt unhappy with her life because she secretly felt she deserved better.

Other men would smile and say, 'But you're wonderful the way you are.' Not David. 'You do deserve better,' he'd said in his decisive Aries way, and next day had called in to the drama school and got some application forms for her. The thrill when she'd been accepted was unbelievable. That night she and David had celebrated in bed with a bottle of champagne, the way their bodies knew best.

Now Lisa was nearing the end of her first year at drama school, and it had been just as wonderful as she'd hoped. She had even had a five-second role in a TV commercial. Yet David had never made her feel she had him to thank for it – he knew she had her fiery Leo pride. In the same way he supported her, without being asked, simply by paying a cheque into her account every month. He knew she could never ask him for money. She could still go to her evening classes, the foreign films she liked, and see her own friends. She and David could keep up the separate interests that were vital for keeping that fire sign enemy, boredom, away.

To others on the outside, Lisa knew their relationship looked unconventional, but it suited them wonderfully well. In fact, the only hiccup in their blissful time together had happened when they'd made an effort to conform and live like 'other people'. Lisa had rushed home from college to cook a meal for David instead of sending out for a takeaway, they'd both gone to the supermarket on Saturday morning rather than running round to the late-night shop just as it closed, and they'd stopped going out separately.

Then one week when Lisa had got engrossed in her book and burnt supper again, and they'd found themselves bickering in a supermarket aisle over what brand of butter to buy, they decided enough was enough. 'I'd far rather have a happy you than a perfect shepherd's pie,' David had said. 'Forget the shopping – get out there and go to the disco with your pals.'

They both realised that separate interests were what kept the relationship alive. Enjoying time spent apart didn't mean they couldn't stay together, whatever other people might think. Since then each had gone off alone on days, weekends, even holidays, and it had been worth it just for the glorious reunions when they'd got back.

'So what is it about David?' thought Lisa again as she looked down onto the squash court and saw him warming up, a picture of concentration, as ever. 'He lets me be me, he lets me be free – because that's what he wants for himself. I respect him, I trust him, I guess I just love him. In fact I know I must love him,' she thought. 'Why else would a competitive Leo like me let him win at squash . . . every second time?'

Meanwhile, down on the squash court, as David rhythmically thumped the little rubber ball against the wall, he was thinking along the same lines. 'I'm so lucky. Lisa's funny, she's brave, independent and sexy. She doesn't put pressure on me to make life all right for her – she prefers to do that for herself. Remember when she went to college and got that old bike to get about on, rather than taking lifts from me?

'She's honest and loyal, ready to chase her dreams, not sit down and simply complain about how high up and far away they are. She knows love means living our own lives, not trying to live each other's, and not caring a bit what other people say. Do I love her? I reckon I must, otherwise why would a must-crush-the-competition Aries like me let her beat me at squash . . . every second time?'

Virgo in Love

THE WONDERFUL YOU

Your passion fires are the zodiac's best kept secret, as they secretly smoulder beneath a cool surface that can mislead some people into thinking you are cold-hearted. But the right partner will know different, and lovingly win your trust, to be rewarded with the warmth of your wild and wonderful passion.

No false heart affairs for Virgo. You would rather stay permanently pals than risk frittering away your carefully hoarded reserves of romance on someone unworthy. And this caution pays off, because, once you find the total love commitment you seek, you and your lucky lover will be transported to levels of ecstasy few ever find. And you'll be kept there by your natural enthusiasm and deep curiosity about physical pleasure.

Although Virgo can seem reserved, even prim, given the right encouragement, you'll not only try anything once, but file away the results for future reference, so you can improve on your performance next time.

Fed on the right amount of security and trust, your faithful heart will light up your whole being. A generous and giving partner, you love to look after others, and make yourself unforgettable with thoughtful surprise presents and caring acts – like taking all the kids out for the day because you know your partner is really tired.

You have a natural urge to protect, and adore to winkle out every little detail about a loved-one's personality – no matter how trivial. But although you can be wonderfully kind and helpful, Virgo's no doormat, and no-one makes the mistake of thinking this more than once. In fact, this strength makes you even more attractive to a partner, so don't be afraid to use it.

You have definite, and rather high, standards of right and wrong, acceptable and not, as any partner who dares to cross that line soon finds out – sometimes painfully. But with your witty ways and cool charm, they'll forgive you anything, and keep coming back for more. Unselfish and forever true, with the sort of uncensored sex that makes brains buzz and toes tingle, unleashed Virgo loving is superb.

THE WICKED YOU

The trouble with being born a perfectionist is that mad, messy life, and especially love, doesn't often, if ever, match up to Virgo expectations. So you can turn bitter and disappointed, finding fault with potential partners and driving away those you do feel attracted to with your constant criticism and sarcasm.

Yes, you know it's mostly a security smoke-screen to keep your deep-down self-doubts and shaky confidence secret, but it can work rather too well and become a silver knife you sharpen to cut out your own heart. One icicle-forming glare from those frosty eyes has would-be romancers running right out of your life. You tend to take duty to its limits, too, breaking your Virgo back to help others out when you should be thinking of yourself. Then you wonder why a rosy glow of romance has been completely doused by a deluge of resentment.

You can also be distant and undemonstrative, avoiding too-close personal touching even with a lover and unable to handle a spur-of-the-moment hug.

The two other main sensual spoilers for Virgo are worry and work.

Yes, you want to be anything and everything to a lover, and will make enormous efforts to tease and please in bed.

But you're supposed to enjoy yourself too! And constant fretting about where a relationship is going is one sure way to send it nowhere. For, while your partner's sure to savour the loving treats you supply, he or she would like you to try living for yourself now and then, rather than always giving.

Work is the other burden weighing on your conscientious Virgo heart. Whether it's a high-flying career in accountancy or the pile of ironing that's waiting to be done, your sense of duty tends to let work walk all over your life, and love.

You are forever doing favours for others, staying late to help out at the office, spending all evening cleaning so the kitchen floor sparkles. Lush, relaxing loving can be so easily forgotten in this frenzy of activity. Please try to live a little more for today. Tomorrow your list of 'must-do's' will still be there, but your mate might be gone. Remember your potential to be one of the best lovers in the zodiac – and you can live up to it.

BEING YOUR VIRGO BEST

Love isn't an exam, with a list of questions to be scored off as you answer them. That's the first lesson Virgo needs to learn. Try to see passion less as an all-or-nothing test, more as a natural part of life, and you'll have taken the first step towards relaxing in romance and learning to love yourself first, the first step to loving others.

Yes, you do deserve to be loved. Shocking though it may seem to you, a lover isn't going to leave just because you turn out to be less than perfect. In fact, they'll probably prefer you that way, but you must play your part by dropping all those impossibly high standards that even superman, or woman, would have trouble matching.

Give a little, live a little more. Positive steps towards a relaxation technique could stop Virgo worry and insecurity taking over your lovelife. Take up a sport instead, or get rid of pent-up tension and frustration by punching a feather pillow. Next time you find yourself faced with an endless list of 'essential' jobs, tear it up and take a child to the fair instead.

You've got so much love, so much laughter buried under that controlled Virgo surface, please do learn to let it out. All it takes is a slight adjustment of priorities. When you feel sexy, make the first move, even if the odd socks are waiting to be sorted. Partners will be thrilled, as they know how Virgo loathes to feel vulnerable and how you hate to leave a task undone.

Try to treat yourself as lovingly as you do others – buy feel-good underwear, exercise your body, set aside an hour or more every day to do something you want to do. Boosting your self-esteem will spice up sex and help silence the sarcastic criticism that sometimes slithers out before you can stop it. Most of all, accept that love can never be perfect – pretty good is enough for most people, so why not for Virgo, too?

VIRGO SEXY SECRETS

Starting slowly and then sensuously steaming towards the ultimate in satisfaction, successful sex for Virgo starts with one very important organ – the brain. For until a lover has been positively vetted by your brain, there's no way that lover will be allowed near your body. Seduction of Virgo's mind starts with an intellectual activity like visiting an exhibition, then, once interest is aroused, you'll want to share an intimate meal with a potential partner, and fire questions about everything from what side of the bed they sleep on to how many foreign languages they speak.

Even in established relationships, Virgo is addicted to asking questions and analysing a partner's motives over and over again. But a lover must not pry into Virgo's sacred secrets in return. Still, the suspense is worth it for the lucky ones who make it to Virgo's bed.

You plan and serve an exquisite menu of mouthwatering love treats that changes every night. The mood starts with slow music to help ease off those inborn Virgo inhibitions, smoochy dancing with lots of neck nibbling and the occasional lingering kiss, bodies slithering down the length of each other, plus unlimited whispers stressing how sexy you are, how desirable your body – a sure way to prise away the shell of practicality that blunts Virgo response. Music also helps keep your brain at bay, to give your body a chance for once.

Your secret sex-spot is the stomach, so the lightest of fingertips, circling there, can make your body flare with fierce desire. The longer foreplay lasts the better – letting go completely, so your mind totally yields to your body, is your secret of sexcess.

You must avoid scheduling sex into your routine. Make love when you happen to wake up in the middle of the night, or minutes before guests arrive for lunch.

Putting feelings into words can be Virgo's worst nightmare, but silence can sometimes strangle good sex. Whispering your pleasure, and eventually shouting it, will please your partner and help your inner tension unwind.

Start by sharing body language, in a scented bath together, or feeding each other mouthfuls of lemon mousse, without using a spoon. Watch an erotic film, then write down your secret fantasies and read them aloud – all help to unlock Virgo's passion potential.

As a change from adapting to others' wishes, try taking charge in love sometimes, dominating a passive partner into a frenzy with skilful caresses and silk scarves. Then change places so, just for once, you can forget everyone else and concentrate on your own pleasure. Turn that famous Virgo devotion on yourself and see why it leads to once-in-a-lifetime loving.

WOOING AND WINNING VIRGO

Even on your wedding day you're likely to be worrying about the future and whether love will last. So any permanent partner needs to be willing and able to put up with this, along with your basically practical and rather impersonal approach to life.

You could meet your match in a bookshop or DIY store,

and you will spend a long time analysing the relationship before you decide to commit your brain, or your body, to it.

Fleeting flings aren't Virgo's style at all – it's an every-night stand you seek, so potential life partners are advised not to rush things.

You demand perfection and could drive lesser people crazy with constant criticism and questions. So your star-matched mate will be someone with a far more secure self-image than yours, who takes life a lot less seriously and can adore you despite being told they're in the wrong.

You need a person who's comfortable in their own body and can gently coax Virgo towards being more physically demonstrative in everyday life, as well as providing a sensuously slow build-up to lovemaking – someone who can take the lead in bed but is prepared to share that leading role once Virgo's true sexy self surfaces. A partner must be generous enough to help you discover the delights of putting yourself first for a change. You need someone strong, yet someone who can tactfully point out when you work and worry too much. Someone who makes sure your lovelife isn't swamped by the details of daily life.

In return, Virgo will pamper a partner endlessly – from breakfast in bed to saving up secretly for a much-longed-for concert ticket. Virgo protects fiercely and offers a lifetime of loving devotion, as long as you're not taken for granted. But those who really know you won't risk doing that and losing your special loving.

LOVE MATCH

How Virgo combines with each of the 12 sun signs

Virgo with Virgo

What chance romance in a swift-to-find-fault twosome who both demand perfection, easily become obsessed with work and need lots of time alone? It could become a super-loyal love match of two people who really understand each other, if both sides can drop the intolerance, realise that no-one can be perfect – and stop suggesting their partner isn't.

You need to revamp priorities, too, so that work and duty move down your list, at least some of the time, to let love go to the top. That way you will be able to really make love the way you both need to. Together you can escape that sensuous shyness and slowly emerge into the lovelight, although this is a relationship that will always need true commitment and cooperation from both sides.

Virgo with Libra

What starts as a meeting of smart minds can all too soon become a relationship of grudge and drudge, as sociable, casual Libra lives life to the full, leaving the nuts and bolts of their relationship to Virgo. At first, Virgo could enjoy all the responsibility, but after a while it turns into rotting resentment, so Virgo needs to speak out before being taken for granted. You should also make an effort to join Libra's social scene rather than lurking alone, and put a brake on sarcastic barbs that puncture Libra's confidence. Then you'll find the mutual respect to add to the romantic ideals you already share. And that makes your relationship work.

Virgo with Scorpio

Physically a dream match, as Scorpio's secrets-reading sensuality sparks Virgo's own sex power and gives the confidence, and the leadership, Virgo loving needs. But things go well for this couple out of bed, too, as Scorpio's brave strength and protective nature ease away Virgo's worrying and sulking.

Virgo can see through that sometimes sarcastic Scorpio manner and is not scared away, but fascinated, by Scorpio's dark mystery. But you must control nagging and Scorpio must control jealousy – in case some cruel words escape from either, or both, that can't be forgiven or forgotten. And that must be avoided because very few relationships go so deep.

Virgo with Sagittarius

An industrious, sensible loner takes on a lazy, still-childish party animal – Virgo and Sagittarius could hardly have less in common if they tried. It starts with the fascination of something you can't understand, and Sagittarius' zest for life and love could help cautious Virgo shrug off some of those prize hang-ups, especially that habit of worrying what other people think. But soon Sagittarius' blunt remarks are hammering at Virgo's fragile confidence, and the chasm between the two lifestyles gets dangerously wide.

It will need constant work, with you prepared to give free-roaming Sagittarius a long love leash if passion isn't going to bolt away. But when it's good, it's very good because, despite deep differences, you can communicate, especially in the bedroom.

Virgo with Capricorn

Magically matched in a caring nature and caution, this twosome shares a reverence for money. Yet there is a seething cauldron of love fantasy under the rather straight surface. Virgo and Capricorn can fuse into a secure, strong-heart attachment. Each is eager not to rush things, which allows romance to grow from strength to strength and each partner to trust the other enough to share worries they normally would be embarrassed to let others even glimpse.

Loyal and dependable, neither would dream of letting a loved-one down, and Capricorn's mirror-image sense of duty frees you from the inner anger that stems from other star signs taking Virgo for granted. Virgo may still need to be led in bed in the early stages of the relationship, or sex could be suffocated by a plastic coating of respectability.

Virgo with Aquarius

Aquarius is the one sign that can make Virgo almost recklessly romantic. For Aquarius' brilliant brain and rather detached ways are almost addictive to even the most reserved Virgo, and Aquarius can truly need all the caring and life-organising Virgo does. But too soon, however, the curtains threaten to close on this relationship.

There is a danger that Aquarius stops fascinating and starts infuriating Virgo with all those love-the-world, impractical ways. The terror of being tied down could make Aquarius dash for the door out of domesticity before Virgo slams it shut. Yet it can work if Virgo settles for semi-detached loving, and both are really committed. It can give Aquarius the secure base they need and give Virgo a lifelong love mission.

Virgo with Pisces

The dreamer meets the schemer – and at first Pisces' sensitive, feel-a-way-through-life personality is enchanted by Virgo's ability to summon order out of chaos, calculate and plan a life-route and still stay caring and gentle. But before long trouble could be brewing, as Virgo tries to balance the relationship and the books, an impossible task with impulsive, creative Pisces around. After all, you are from opposite sides of the zodiac circle.

If Virgo can live a slightly less organised life, take the odd chance or make a spontaneous change of plan, impulsive Pisces will stick around longer than just a few heart-bursting years. And please, no nagging. Starting along that road with Pisces might mean never stopping – until you reach the divorce court. And that would mean losing a relationship that can provide, as opposites do, a lifetime of love learning.

Virgo with Aries

As matches go, it can be rather one-sided – and Aries is the Fatal Attraction sign for Virgo. Action-master Aries makes all the running while cool Virgo waits and watches, almost afraid to take the final step into commitment, yet secretly fascinated by that fiery personality and love power.

Hidden feelings are as much use as a chocolate teapot to upfront Aries, who needs love spelt out, and fast, or interest disintegrates. But if Virgo can force feelings into words and actions, and call a halt to cold criticism, what starts as mutual curiosity can grow into everlasting admiration and trust. Spontaneous Aries can be the perfect partner to annihilate deep-seated Virgo inhibitions. But Aries will have to be kind.

Virgo with Taurus

High-security love that willingly lasts into a life sentence, this can be a rock-solid romance between two signs who both appreciate the comforts of home and of each other. Virgo loves to nursemaid a partner and Taurus enjoys being on the receiving end of all that care. These two practical pals will slowly and surely build on a firm foundation of shared beliefs and earthy love power, with the warmth of Taurus balancing the cool skills of Virgo.

Taurus, with a more confident, calmer life view, helps round off the corners of Virgo's fussy worrying. The loving encouragement and praise Virgo provides can help Taurus make ambitions real. Both of you enjoy seizing and using opportunities, and understand why work matters. Together you'll both taste greater success in life and love, secure in total trust.

Virgo with Gemini

Virgo's reliance on routine and love of order, plus guilt binges, threaten this relationship, although it can start brilliantly with shared mental interests and easy conversation. But trying to tie Gemini down, even with the finest threads of passion, just makes Gemini fight even more furiously to be free.

As Virgo dreams of evenings together in a neat home, Gemini is on the outside – in a world filled with fun and people to charm. Too soon the Virgo calm and sweetness that first attracted Gemini can seem a crashing bore. It can work if you tolerate Gemini's constant need for change and chatting-up, and are lavish with your praise. But you must accept that no one person will ever meet all Gemini's needs.

It's never an easy option, though you can spend a happy lifetime trying to make it work.

Virgo with Cancer

A never-ending supply of sympathy and concern for each other keep this pair happily together, and they also share a superpractical approach to cash. Both are gentle and can, at first, be physically shy. Gradually discovering the delights of each other's body can make sex a constant source of happiness, provided this double helping of inner doubt doesn't mean first moves are never made.

If controlling Virgo can learn to cope with Cancer's dramatic mood swings without deploying that sharp sarcasm, and both make sure that lovemaking never becomes yawn-making, this couple can build a safe house of their love that shelters them both forever.

Virgo with Leo

As tricky as filling a lion's teeth without anaesthetic, this relationship is never simple. But alongside its ever-changing moods, it is sometimes sheer heaven. Virgo's inborn adoration is like nectar to the attention-loving Leo. And Virgo's listening skills are perfect for listen-to-me Leo. But if Leo's show-off bullying revs up too much, independent Virgo will only stand so much before striking back. And nothing can puncture the inflated balloon of Leo pride more permanently than a stiletto-sharp Virgo criticism.

If these two can learn tolerance, constantly remind themselves that neither is as self-contained as they seem, and concentrate on good points rather than bad, brilliant bedtimes can be the base for a good, learning-from-each-other relationship. But not one that can ever be taken for granted.

LIVING LOVE

Case history of a Virgo man and Gemini woman, star-crossed lovers

Steve was puzzled as he got off the bus and looked down the road. For he was sure he could see some red and yellow balloons hanging from his front door. 'What now? Does this mean we'll be subjected to another evening of Paula's hangers-on?' The questions grated in his mind.

Paula's 'hangers-on' was what he had christened the crowd of students from the college where she taught, who always seemed to be around, drinking tea and sometimes carelessly breaking his carefully chosen china, in their small kitchen or arguing in the hall. In fact, they were Paula's study group and she only had them round once a week, normally on the night Steve went to his chess club, so he didn't need to see them at all.

'It might do you good if you did,' Paula once said to him. 'They're full of optimism and fresh ideas. They might get you out of that rut.' A sociable, flexible Gemini, she simply couldn't understand that Steve's set ideas about life were what kept him sane – as a typical Virgo, he clung to what, and who, he knew and was secretly scared of too much change.

Still, since that row they had had last night, he had decided he must make an effort to be more adaptable. Even now, he couldn't believe that, after five years of marriage and two children, he and Paula could have argued over something so trivial. She was trying on a new dress, a perfect shade of blue that brought out the striking colour of her eyes. He was about to say how lovely she looked, when he saw the price tag and blurted out, 'Could a dress really cost that much?'

The smile froze on Paula's face. 'I bought it with my own money,' she said icily. 'I suppose you'd rather I went shopping at a jumble sale.' She ran into the bathroom and slammed the door. 'But Paula, I never thought . . .' he called through the door, jumping back as she came charging out in her underwear.

'No, I don't suppose you did,' she said angrily. 'But I can tell you now, Steve, I have had enough of your criticism and coldness. It seems I can't do anything right where you're concerned. If I go out, I should have been at home with you. If I do stay in, you fasten your eyes on a book or that model ship you're building and it's obvious you think I'm just in the way.

'If I cook a meal it's never quite right, there's always too much salt in this, too little sauce in that. If I have friends round, you slink off upstairs. If I buy a dress it's too expensive, but if I don't buy something new you say I look a mess. Is it a wife you want, or a robot programmed by you?'

Her words shocked Steve. He always thought his slight criticism kept Paula's feet on the ground. As an impulsive Gemini, she would chase all sorts of impossible rainbows if he wasn't there to keep an eye on her. Besides, she was always so charming and self-contained, with a host of admirers falling at her feet. If he was to be brutally honest, criticising her made Steve feel more secure because it gave him power over her.

He tried to explain this to Paula who sat on the bed and twisted her wedding ring, too tense for tears. She looked so young and so vulnerable. Steve wondered how he could ever have thought his criticisms wouldn't hurt her. It had been the safety net he had spun gradually since they first met at a wedding, where Paula's easy conversation, lit with her vivid imagination and excitement at life, had captivated the quieter, slower Steve.

At first he adored becoming part of her huge circle of friends, partly because he knew all the men envied him his place at Paula's side, and in her bed. Her optimism lifted him and he was able to ignore the instant friends-with-anyone approach and extravagance that were such a basic part of her character.

When did it all start to go sour? It had been a very gradual process of him retreating back within himself, closing doors behind him so Paula couldn't reach him or disturb his feelings. Had he really thought she wouldn't mind? Last night he had heard her sobs as she explained how much he had hurt her, how she had tried to get through to him and failed. She had decided their marriage must be over.

Steve was shocked into action. He took a deep breath and told Paula everything, unlocked his secret insecurities, and the self-protective instinct that made his tongue lash out with a criticism when really his heart was crying out to her.

She didn't scoff, but held him tight and at last was able to cry. Together, they drew up a new set of rules for their relationship. Rule number one, do more things together. Rule number two, make time to talk. Rule number three, Steve to criticise less. Rule number four, Paula to tell Steve when he's cutting himself off ... and so it went on. Steve wrote out the rules in his neat writing, and they stuck the paper above their bed – then lay side by side just touching, and talking more than they'd done for months.

Steve came to with a start, realising he was just outside his front door. He grinned, thinking, 'So what if she does have her hangers-on, sorry, students, round? Some of them can be quite good company. But what are these balloons for?'

He opened the door and saw Paula, quite alone, breathtaking in the new blue dress, with a bottle of champagne in her hands. 'Happy Anniversary,' she said. 'Here's to us and the new start we're making, together.' Steve frowned slightly, 'But ...' he began, stopping when he saw Paula's smile waver. No criticisms, he reminded himself and took her in his arms instead. Thank goodness for the Virgo organisation that had made him buy that perfect blue-stoned eternity ring today when he was passing the jeweller's shop. Later, but in a far from critical way, he would have to remind Paula their anniversary wasn't actually until next week. But meanwhile, they had some celebrating to do ...

Case history of a Virgo woman and Taurus man, star-blessed lovers

Wendy analysed the ceiling and made a mental note to fill those hairline cracks and repair it, as soon as she was up and about again. And those net curtains – how could she have missed such a disaster? Once sparkling white, they were now more a shade of cream, another job for next week. Hopefully before Ken noticed.

Sometimes it was a trial being a Virgo, she smiled, unable to let life simply slip by without at least attempting to make it perfect. Kept in bed by a heavy cold that was doing the rounds at work, she found it almost impossible to relax. She tried reading a book, then found herself making a list of people to write to, jobs to do.

More than anything else, she loathed being idle. Even three years with her patient, luxury-loving Taurus Ken hadn't cured her of that. She could hear him moving about downstairs in the kitchen, making her some lunch. Now he was coming up the stairs. 'Room service,' he said. And just seeing him made Wendy feel better already.

He plumped up her pillows and helped her sit up, then put a tray on her knees. On it, as a complete change to the spartan grilled food and healthy salad she normally ate, was a steaming plateful of egg and chips. 'Now, I want you to eat it all up,' Ken said, handing Wendy a fork. Almost against her better nature – just think of all those calories – she started eating. And found, to her astonishment, that it was absolutely delicious. 'I wonder why I don't let Ken do the cooking more often,' she thought. But she already knew the answer. She liked to be in control in the kitchen as in all other areas of their life together.

They had met at the local sports centre when both went to a badminton course – Wendy pristine in her perfectly creased shorts and brilliant white trainers, Ken looking much more comfortable in well-worn khaki shorts and a sports shirt he'd accidentally dyed pink via a mishap at the launderette. For all the 10 weeks of the course they had smiled and nodded to each other, both wanting to get to know each other better, both reluctant to make the first move. Then, on the last night, Ken had asked for Wendy's phone number, 'to arrange a match.'

It had turned out to be a love match, as slowly they discovered how much they complemented each other. Ken was the physical, touching type. Wendy wasn't – well, not at first – until she found her Virgo reserve fading whenever she was around him. Her attention to detail intrigued Ken, and soon he was asking her advice on everything from his cherished cash investments to which car to buy. And her 'mothering' nature was perfect.

It was far from one-sided, however. In return for his physical comforts, Ken gave Wendy the mental security she craved. She knew she could trust him absolutely and that he would always be there for her, vital if she was to let down her guard and give herself to him body and soul.

Wendy smiled now as she remembered all the 'firsts' Ken had introduced her to. Her first shared bath, all sensual warmth and soapy kisses. Her first massage, really helping her find the relaxation that came so hard to her Virgo self. It was wonderful to be with someone and not have to pretend, to really be herself.

'But am I?' she thought. 'Do I still try too hard to be the perfect wife and housekeeper, to always have everything in its place, not a speck of dust anywhere? Is that the real me, or just how I think I should be?' She had to admit it caused slight friction. Several times lately, for example, Ken had swept her in his arms and whispered, 'Come to bed, darling,' and she'd replied, 'In a minute, Ken. I'm writing up my work plan for the office' or 'Can't you wait until I've finished cleaning the cooker?'

Ken had shrugged and turned on the TV instead, and the moment was gone forever. Wendy knew he wouldn't care how shiny-clean the cooker was, so why was it so important to her?

'Maybe it's not so important now,' she laughed to herself.

It had taken being in bed for a week to show her what mattered in life. At first, she was almost annoyed to realise Ken was managing to look after himself, and her, perfectly well. But now it came as quite a relief not to feel the responsibility for the whole house rested on her shoulders. Ken wasn't the helpless, clueless individual she'd made him out to be in her head. After all, he had looked after himself perfectly well for years before they met.

Wendy suddenly felt much better. Next time Ken wanted to help, she decided, she'd let him – so what if the result wasn't as perfect as if she'd done it herself. She couldn't believe she'd let a stupid thing like housework come between them. She slid out of bed and went downstairs. Wendy peeked round the kitchen door and stifled a giggle as she saw Ken, in her plastic apron and rubber gloves, scrubbing at the top of the cooker with a worried look on his face. 'Leave that,' Wendy said. 'I've got something much more important I'd like you to do for me, in the bedroom.' 'And it's not washing the net curtains,' she smiled to herself.

Libra in Love

THE WONDERFUL YOU

Like a rainbow surprising a gloomy sky, Libra love is unforgettable. A blend of sexuality and confidence-winning charm, sexy-voiced Libra has the lines, and the moves, to make your target feel like the world's most wanted person. But once you have made the conquest, this willing would-be partner may have to wait in line, because Libra is in demand.

With inner attractiveness balanced by an outer sense of style, Libra is charming, disarming and far more content being a couple than living alone. You seek harmony in love as well as life, and will work hard to steam-iron away any creases in a relationship.

You are sensitive and yet so committed to seeing both sides of a situation that you will rarely lapse into rage or a sudden jealous tantrum. Shouting scenes are not your style.

The tiny details of togetherness that less thoughtful lovers let slip are Libra's loveblood. You will remember not just a birthday but what your partner was wearing when you first met, favourite names, places, foods – even down to the preferred flavour of fruit gums. This makes you sensational between the sheets, as each bedtime with Libra is a luxurious trip to past delights and even more thrilling present experiments. You feel life isn't complete without passion and adore being part of a permanent team of two against the world.

Marriage or similar commitment is your goal, but that doesn't mean you can't enjoy yourself on the way. You are sociable, fun and flirtatious, a fan of all things bright and beautiful, with such persuasive chat you could talk a Trappist monk into telling you a joke. When you turn all that star-power on one person, is it any wonder Libra loving is legendary?

THE WICKED YOU

How often do you stop and rethink when you should be doing something? For a major barrier stands between Libra and the lasting, uncomplicated love you long for – and that is your very own brain. You never stop considering, plotting and planning in a relationship, not because you are indecisive, but because you want to get the right, and the best, deal for yourself.

Incredibly vain, yet secretly insecure, you flourish on flattery and like nothing better than being hoisted on to a pedestal. But once up there, you find it hard to get down – and it can be lonely.

You are rarely happy with partners the way they are. Instead, you draw up an action plan to change your partner and will happily spend a lifetime working on it. You prefer the mental to the physical, thoughts to emotions, and shrink back from becoming too involved, even when you know a lover's crazy about you. So you could end up talking about love instead of showing it. The answer isn't moving on to someone who might be the perfect partner of your imagination, but being honest in the relationship you have. For although Libra goes to any lengths to reroute a discussion that's approaching a showdown, this anything-for-a-quietly-perfect-life policy just papers over the splits in love. Sooner or later they'll show through again, only bigger.

You know partners are putty in your hands, and yet you're so afraid of seeming vulnerable or imperfect that you hide insecurities rather than give a partner any advantage over you. But love can't live that lie forever.

Libra can also be manipulative, using charm and, sometimes, smarm to talk others into doing your dirty work. You might even get a go-between to tell a partner you want out. And when it comes to making decisions, forget it. You spend so long searching for perfect right answers, even if it's just deciding what to eat tonight, you can drive lovers mad. Smothering under layer upon layer of wheedling and wangling, you lose track of your true feelings, and lash out in a confused lather of complaints. Too often Libra forgets it takes two to make a relationship, and they can't both be you.

BEING YOUR LIBRA BEST

Lowering your super-high standards, putting those passion-choking thought-waves on hold and tuning, instead, into feelings and emotions is the way for Libra to locate happiness in real, rather than ideal, love. Try to forget your all-important image some of the time, and say or do something that exposes your secret vulnerable self, even if it's just giving a lover a spontaneous hug or confessing you'd rather they didn't go off on a separate holiday because you'll miss them. The hardest word to say is the first – but you owe it to yourself to at least try. Love built on honesty will last, but what hope is there for a relationship constructed on a rickety foundation of pretence and pride?

It is a revelation to Libra to realise passion doesn't evaporate just because you turn out not to be perfect. Yes, by involving soul, as well as body, you risk being hurt, the one thing cool Libra dreads. But you also risk being truly happy, the one thing brainbound Libra, a slave to logic and reason, longs for. Life, and love, can be uncomplicated – if you let them.

Practise being more direct, asking a lover straight out for what you want, rather than disguising it in a mask of false compliments and slippery suggestions. And stop delaying decisions while you wallow in both sides of a situation. Spend much longer sitting on the fence and you'll never be able to get off it.

Love is about two people's choices, so not even cool, charming Libra can have it all your way. The love maze can be a dangerous place for Libra because you're the world's best flirt and can have a total stranger in your power in seconds. But too often that stranger's good looks disguise a bad heart, and all the admiration and flattery a stranger can supply will never fill the empty space in you that's reserved for genuine, growing-through-life romance. So why risk everything, for nothing? Let a little more of your lovelight shine through every day and the real, satisfying love of one partner should see you through a lifetime.

LIBRA SEXY SECRETS

You adore a long, slow build-up to bedtime that involves tons of talking and preferably a touch (or more) of luxury. A rich French meal with lots of fingers to lick, a fresh fig, opening up like yielding female love flesh, followed by some slow dancing in a scented, candlelit room, with a lover's mouth, and eyes, telling you time and time again how attractive you look – that's the sort of evening that's sure to leave Libra in the mood for love.

Your mind is just as vital to Libra satisfaction as your body, so you also enjoy sharing fantasies and watching sexy film scenes with a lover, or reading erotic poems aloud to each other. A long, slow massage with warmed aromatic oils appeals to your supersensitive sense of smell, and finishing up with the lightest of circling movements, warm breaths and lip brushes on your lower back and buttocks – Libra's sex-spots – leaves every nerve ending in a state of exhilarating excitement. You like erotic jewellery worn in secret love places, hard gold against satin softnesses.

You love to be pursued and wooed, flattered and teased by a partner, as that feeds your need to feel both attractive and in control. Sexy notes slipped into your pocket as you leave for work, suggestive phone calls at lunchtime are perfect for Libra. And your all-star combination of quick wits and even quicker daring means you know how to keep things exciting.

Dressing up is another favourite love game – you adore looking your absolute best and can't relax if you feel your hair is a mess or you need a wash. This obsession with image can come between Libra and complete satisfaction as, terrified of letting go too much and looking silly, you're reluctant to give yourself completely. Try to believe you can only be loved more, not less, by giving up control now and then to a partner. Total trust is the only way for Libra to find the ultimate sexual pleasure.

WOOING AND WINNING A LIBRA

Libra's passion for putting on the ritz means you're likely to meet your star soul mate somewhere smart, like a swish dinner and dance or wedding reception. You'll be struck first by an attractive face and a well-dressed body, but if there's no brain to go with it, forget it. Love starts for Libra with fascinating conversation.

Your perfect partner also appreciates the good things in life and will pamper you endlessly with surprise presents plus a never-ending stream of compliments to boost your ever-fragile self-confidence. You need someone who can put up with your fascination with flirting, who can take a back seat at any social occasion while you work the room, yet always be there to back you up when you need it. Then keep the love spark well and truly lit with secret hand signals across everyone else's heads or a saucy coded language the two of you have concocted together . . . in bed, of course.

The ideal partner for you will be loyal and loving, patient, and strong enough to withstand, and ignore, your double-mindedness and realise that under that calm surface is a seething mass of fears and frustrations.

Your fate mate will work out fail-safe ways to help you cut out the clever chitchat and get straight to what counts. Without this a relationship with Libra might never get past the superficial. Your life and love mate will, of course, worship and adore you, but not let you get away with so much that you lose respect for them. Passionate in the bedroom, the best of pals out of it, any relationship that's 50 per cent Libra promises 100 per cent excitement.

LOVE MATCH

How Libra combines with each of the 12 sun signs

Libra with Libra

Two luxury lovers who make a warm oasis of comfort out of their love, a safe place to escape the trials of life. And because both of you have a fascinating blend of male and female in your personality mix, you understand each other better than any other combination of signs can. This couple only stops talking and complimenting each other when you find something even more interesting to do with your mouths. You share a desire to make the world perfect – and have fun doing it. But a double dose of Libra can also lead to frustration, as neither side wants to be the first to commit. A time limit on decisions and a determined effort to make feelings as important as thoughts can work wonders.

Libra with Scorpio

You can be a sexy twosome with seemingly endless appetites for love, from nibbles to five-course feasts. But so intense, so sure Scorpio can be infuriated by sunny Libra's mind-changes, while open Libra finds Scorpio's deep need for secrecy a frustrating mystery. And that equally deep Scorpio conviction that Scorpio is always right bewilders Libra.

Libra's flirting can light the touch paper on fiery Scorpio jealousy all too easily. Storms can be diverted if both sides vow to talk straight and keep no secrets, and if Libra uses all that easy charm to help Scorpio loosen up then it will be a partnership path well worth exploring.

Libra with Sagittarius

Fun on the run for this terrific twosome, who both talk a good love match and adore loving it up at parties. Sharing a basic honesty and warmth, Libra and Sagittarius start with a firm foundation of friendship and build up a long-lasting passion, brick by brick. But the whole thing can start to shake if Libra's need for commitment meets Sagittarius' need for anything but, or if Libra's faultless logic leaves fiery, all-action Sagittarius lost.

If Libra can remember romance is a two-person show, and let some of Sagittarius' snappy decision-making rub off, joint optimism and touching trust make this one of the zodiac's greatest love hits.

Libra with Capricorn

Serious Capricorn walks through life one considered step at a time, while Libra pushes ahead, turns back, and shoots off up dead ends, all the time cheerfully chatting. Capricorn realism versus Libra optimism, dark versus light – these two are so different they're completely charmed by each other at the start, and Capricorn loves Libra's lavish gifts and attention. Soon doubts can creep in as the gap between what they have in common becomes a passion gulf. Happiness may disappear when Libra starts to see the cautious other half as less partner, more parent. Yet it can work out if your love for Capricorn helps you treat life just a shade more solemnly. And if Capricorn confidence lets Libra chase dreams.

Libra with Aquarius

A gift of romance that mixes pleasure and mutual understanding and leaves both sides breathless with its sheer force of physical attraction. To outsiders, you may both seem like dreamers, yet when you two put your thoughtful heads together, your doubly dazzling brain-power leaves less electric twosomes lagging far behind. Squabbles over who's in charge may be the only cloud and, because Aquarius is stubborn, Libra will need to give way on most of the unimportant things and let Aquarius loose on those doing-good-for-the-world plans.

Yet this perfect pairing should still be teasing each other into laughter and bouncing ideas off each other when you cut the cake on your golden wedding anniversary.

Libra with Pisces

Mysterious Pisces starts as an irresistible challenge to conquest-keen Libra, but initial attraction soon wears thin as Pisces' clingy ways cover free spirit Libra in everlasting ivy, rooting you to the spot. And being constantly admired and adored can get too much, even for you.

Permanent partnership is possible if Libra can accept Pisces' need for security and curb solo socialising – because when Libra stays out late, Pisces may move out. Libra must try to feel, more than think, when it comes to love. Otherwise all-emotions Pisces could be turned off by Libra's too balanced, somewhat contrived approach. But it's well worth it just for the romance.

Libra with Aries

Two fiercely independent personalities, from opposite sides of the zodiac wheel, make for an eventful match, full of explosive sex and with both only too glad to go into extra time. But though it's a winning team, a double leadership challenge is likely. And when Libra's faultless logic slams up against Aries' impatient temper one time too many, the temptation is just to turn and walk away.

Yet it can be made to work as well out of bed as in it by using Libra charm to keep Aries calm, ignoring tantrums, and helping Aries see both sides of a situation rather than rushing straight in. Libra is so good at supplying the praise Aries thrives on, and feeding Aries pride. Aries can teach Libra though – the sort of night classes you'll be thrilled to attend!

Libra with Taurus

Long, lazy days and nights slowly discovering each other's bodies and enjoying a feast of exotic foods may well be how fellow luxury fans Libra and Taurus kick off their affair – unfortunately, you have to get up sooner or later. And Taurus is the Fatal Attraction sign for Libra, because of the Taurus rich, earthy sensuality.

But Libra mind swings are pure aggravation to the made-up mind of Taurus. Fair-thinking Libra finds Taurus stubbornness too much to take. And jealousy jinxes the precious loving. To make it long term, Libra must stay loyal – and act loyal. But a shared sense of humour and sheer delight between the sheets can make it worth working at.

Libra with Gemini

A merging of like-thinking stars gives each the chance to do the thing they love – communicate. But you do keep quiet long enough to enjoy breathtaking sex sessions. Both adore beauty, and Libra's calm is the perfect complement to Gemini's energetic get up and go, although Libra fairness can grate against Gemini optimism. Arguing, analysing, discussing – starting as perfect pals, this love match will always maintain a core of solid friendship that sees it through life's trials – even outside affairs, which are a danger. As for reaching the altar, it's a marriage made to measure. But it can be difficult for both of you to decide to go for commitment at the same time, and trust will need to be earned.

Libra with Cancer

Both love to laugh and adore making up their many rows in bed, yet this pair need very different things from the relationship. Cancer wants emotional security, instinctive understanding, total commitment to family. Libra wants to be admired, not just by a partner, but by the rest of the world, too. When sensitive Cancer clings, logical Libra feels bewildered, then trapped.

Cancer is a slave to emotions and Libra to thought, so true and lasting understanding may at times seem like an impossible dream. But a showdown is unlikely since both fight shy of rows. If Libra can freeze extravagance and impatience and spend endless energy coaxing Cancer out of moods, lifetime loving can happen, but this will never be a pairing either of you can take for granted.

Libra with Leo

A pair of talented talkers, co-stars of a warm relationship, both refuse to settle for second best, and won't have to in this romance. Libra's easy-going nature soothes the lion's roller coaster of a personality, while Leo's courage and refusal to regret can spur normally play-safe Libra into taking rewarding life risks.

The price to pay is letting Leo lead – or seem to – because as a quick-thinking Libra you know many wily ways to get what you really want! Be prepared for Leo tantrums, however, or being suddenly hit by that tornado of a temper could devastate Libra. You will need to limit the flirting you do when Leo is watching, because Leo needs the limelight and can't bear to feel the target of a joke. When the lights go out this couple communicate in the same body language.

Libra with Virgo

Virgo appreciates Libra's loving thoughtfulness, and the fact that no little favour goes unnoticed, while the sometimes scatty Libra finds Virgo-style organising the perfect antidote to chronic indecision. Both have calm surfaces that conceal a deep, deep well of sensual potential that make this a so-satisfying relationship, at least in the beginning.

There is a danger, though, that Virgo's criticism breaks loose and punctures Libra's personal pride one time too many. Libra may find Virgo's darker moods and highly strung scenes too much to understand or take, and there could be major rows over Virgo thrift and Libra lavish luxury spending. But it can work, when Virgo takes on more of Libra's optimism.

LIVING LOVE

Case history of a Libra woman and Taurus man, star-crossed lovers

Watching Rick putting the new bathroom cabinet together made Sarah shiver. Each slow, deliberate movement, the faithful way he read the instructions thoroughly then followed them to the letter. 'He's so dull,' she thought. 'Am I really stuck with him for the rest of my life? We're obviously unsuited, why did I ever marry a Taurus?'

She looked at her watch, nearly 4 p.m. and she knew exactly what was coming next. 'Any minute now,' she thought, 'he'll say, "Well Sarah, must be time for a cup of tea."' Two minutes later, Rick looked up and said just that – and was astonished to see just an empty space where his Libra wife of three years had been standing ready with the power drill. 'Typical of Sarah,' he thought to himself, 'so unpredictable.'

Rick and Sarah had known when they got married that their life views were worlds apart. Rick liked the solid, the respectable, the familiar, while Sarah craved change, variety and luxury. Yet the physical passion had been so intense, and they were so sure of their love, that they married just three months after they met. Sarah wondered if they had done the right thing. Yes, Rick was deeply respectable at heart and had wanted to 'make it legal', but was sexual perfection enough to base a life partnership on? Sex between Sarah and Rick was still so rich, so good. There were no problems there, unlike a lot of their friends. But more and more Sarah found herself asking whether that was enough to maintain a marriage.

She tried to talk to Rick, and always hit a wall of stubbornness. 'Let's not spoil what we have,' he always said. 'Everything will turn out all right, I know it will.' Sarah knew he saw himself as the strong, silent type, so this complacent 'pat on the head' for her as the little woman left her seething. Sometimes she felt she was invisible to her own husband – she couldn't even earn compliments when she dressed up for him any more.

Sarah started seeing her old pals for nights on the town, leaving Rick at home watching a video or rebuilding, bit by bit, the motorbike he'd been working on for years. Sometimes Sarah thought he loved that bike more than her.

Meanwhile, he was determined she would never know how jealous and fearful her nights out made him.

One night in a bar, when Sarah was being chatted up by a dark, beautifully dressed stranger, who soothed her with rich compliments and gave her all the attention missing at home, she thought to herself, 'Would Rick even care if I went to bed with another man?' So when the man asked her back to his house, she agreed. He lived not far from her, in a converted warehouse. It was elegantly furnished in black and white, and had cost a lot of money.

'If only I could get Rick interested in things like this,' Sarah thought wistfully. Then suddenly the man was pulling her down on to the black leather sofa, kissing her with exciting, unfamiliar lips tasting of the wine they had drunk. Then, on a low glass table by the sofa, she caught sight of a photograph of a smiling woman with a small boy on either side. 'Oh don't worry about them,' said the man. 'They're out of town for a week. And what they don't know won't hurt them, will it?'

His casually spoken words froze her. His attitude towards marriage was so like her own had become. Yet hearing it from someone else brought home just how cold and calculated it seemed. 'No, no,' she mumbled, pushing him off, then snatched up her coat and just ran.

Thankfully, Rick was still up when she got in, almost sobbing with a mixture of anger at herself and relief she'd not taken that step into infidelity. She saw his dear, worried face, and wondered how she could ever have questioned his caring for her? 'Oh Rick,' she said quietly, 'whatever are we going to do?'

After that night, both Sarah and Rick realised their marriage needed work to survive, that it wouldn't just come right on its own. Sarah confessed she had set impossible standards for Rick, so it was not surprising he failed when he was judged a loser by his own wife.

Rick gradually accepted marriage must be a partnership, and he must try not to plan every move for them, but adapt to what life may bring. 'You have to go with the flow sometimes,' explained Sarah, 'rather than try to dam up the river.'

'Am I really so boring, Sarah?' Rick asked as they lay together in bed one Sunday afternoon in the contented after-sex glow. Sarah thought back to the wonderful lovemaking they had just shared, the security she felt whenever Rick was close, the panic she had experienced when her idle idea of infidelity had almost become reality.

If she had learned one thing, it was that love couldn't be separated into head and heart, thinking and feeling. In the past she had done too much thinking, considering and condemning. Now she resolved to let her feelings and emotions do the talking instead.

'Boring, Rick?' she smiled, lightly stroking his chest. 'Ask me again in half an hour – we've got better things to do than talk right now.' That uncharacteristic impulsive action was the first of many in Sarah and Rick's new-style marriage. But perhaps the most important because it led to the conception of their adored daughter, who they both agreed was to be called Hope.

Case history of a Libra man and Aquarius woman, star-blessed lovers

Dean could hardly believe his eyes as he pushed open the slightly ajar front door, put his suitcase down in the hall and looked around. Just two days ago, when he left for his training course, the hall of their flat had been painted a neutral shade of magnolia. But now, from ceiling to floor, the hall walls were coated in sheet after sheet of tin foil, with huge yellow and red flowers stuck on and, here and there, a splodge of blue that he took to be a butterfly. The whole thing looked like a bad dream, or a reject set from Doctor Who.

'Debbie,' he called out. Then thought, 'Being a creative and original Aquarius is all very well, but she's really gone too far this time. And she's obviously been so carried away in her decorating she forgot to shut the front door – anyone could have walked in here.'

Already, however, Dean's inbuilt Libra sense of fairness was making him see the other side of things. 'Debbie's obviously spent ages doing this to surprise me. And on the whole, I suppose it's not so bad. It's the thought that counts, and it's certainly been thought about. It is partly my fault, too. After all, we have been talking about redecorating the hall for months now, but I could never make up my mind which style I preferred. Debbie must have just decided to go for it.'

Now Dean could just imagine Debbie's determined smile as she had the idea to decorate in tin foil – perhaps sparked by one of those trendy magazines she was always reading. Of course, the moment she had the idea, she would start. Even if it was one o'clock in the morning. That restless and rather eccentric centre in Debbie was one of the things that had attracted Dean to her.

They'd been 'just good friends' for ages before becoming involved, and both still valued the easy, affectionate friendship that was the base of their love. They really could tell each other anything and, in matching air-sign style, still spend hours arguing and analysing the world before slipping into bed to continue in the body language they both loved best.

Working as a counsellor, Dean sometimes grew weary of people's complicated problems, and Debbie's straightforward honesty was like a breath of fresh air, while she told him often enough she loved his calm acceptance of her rather more offbeat ideas.

There had been plenty of those, from setting up a helpline for depressed cats to ditching her job as an art teacher to travel round the world, drawing as she went. She got as far as Italy, then turned and came home, 'Because I missed you too much,' she told Dean. That same night they decided to move in together and somehow rustled up a mortgage for their small flat. 'Thank goodness something pushed us into doing it,' thought Dean now. 'Otherwise we would still be trying to make up our minds.'

Their joint indecisiveness had been one of the only problems in their relationship. Libra Dean found it hard to make up his mind because he was always worried he might choose the wrong way, while Aquarius Debbie always had something more interesting to do than make decisions about mundane things like what make of washing machine to buy. 'Ask me tomorrow, I'm meditating,' she'd say, or, 'Sorry, got to go out collecting for that new charity.'

They solved that one by setting a time limit on decisions, normally a week, and taking turns to make them more fun by presenting them like a mock advertising campaign. Dean could still remember how Debbie looked dressed up as a French chef, extolling the virtues of different non-stick pans. But somehow the hall colour had still remained undecided. Until now.

Life with Debbie was such fun. Yet the longer they lived together the more difficult it became to make the change from pals in the living-room to lovers in the bedroom. Sex became less frequent and less exciting. But one night they sat down and talked about it, and Debbie came up with a plan. 'Every week we must make love somewhere different, and never the same place twice,' she suggested. And after they'd exhausted the flat's possibilities they'd tried hotels, the garden shed, the back seat of the car, a secluded telephone box. The thrill of perhaps being caught appealed to their minds, the thrill of being together was enough for their bodies.

'With a woman like that, who cares about a few bits of tin foil,' thought Dean now. 'In fact, I think it's beginning to grow on me.' But as he pushed open the living-room door, he gasped in dismay. All the furniture he and Debbie had bought together was gone. Even the carpet was different. 'This is really too much.' Just then he heard a footstep in the hall. It was Debbie.

Before he could say a word, she asked, 'Dean, what are you doing here? You're lucky I didn't lock you in. I fed Harriet's cat and it was only when I got back upstairs to our flat that I realised I'd left her front door open. What do you think of her hall decoration? Pretty way out, eh? Dean?' The sound of Dean's laughter drowned her out. Absent-minded as ever, he realised he'd walked into the wrong flat . . . this was Harriet's downstairs, an exact copy of their own, except, of course, for the hall.

He looked at Debbie's pale skin and vulnerable eyes and took her in his arms. 'I think we should have ours done exactly the same,' he murmured into her hair. 'But meanwhile, does Harriet's hallway count as somewhere different . . .?'

Scorpio in Love

THE WONDERFUL YOU

Scorpio is the sexiest sign of all, with a delight in sensual pleasure and an X-ray, X-rated mind that sees exactly how to woo and win any potential partner. Passion is much more than a physical thing for Scorpio. When you are truly in love you are fiercely loyal, with feelings that are almost dangerously deep.

Love is a case of all or nothing and, while a lover is lazily basking in the tropical waters of Scorpio passion, it feels like heaven. Intuition is your private love strength, psychic ability to see straight into other people's minds and make their secret dreams, and their most daring fantasies, come true. Yet you always have a certain air of secrecy that makes you even more irresistible and keeps your lover under a spell. However well people think they know you, there's always another Scorpio surprise in there somewhere.

You are driven, determined and as single-minded as a guided missile when you're in pursuit of something, or someone, you want. As a Scorpio you set high standards for everyone, including yourself. You live and breathe passion and adore sex, the wilder the better. But that doesn't mean you're forever on the lookout for fresh bedmates. In fact, Scorpio prefers a lifetime of loving with a single partner, as long as it's one who will keep your appetites, and your thirst for change, satisfied.

For despite a longing for secure loving, somewhere inside Scorpio is an unshakeable drive to gamble, to test the limits of love, thinking 'Wonder what would happen if . . .'

You live, comfortably, on a knife-edge. Your strong belief in yourself and sheer bravado stop you falling off – well, most of the time. And, of course, when a gamble does pay off, the excitement is like pure oxygen to the flame of your lovelife.

THE WICKED YOU

The strongest sun has its shadow, and so does Scorpio loving. For under the surface layer of powerful, loyal passion is a domineering, cruel streak of jealousy that can too easily get out of control and rampage through the most secure of romances.

You can be painfully possessive, while still expecting partners to put up with your own love curiosity which may take you into other beds.

Superstrong yourself, you despise weakness and indecisiveness and will always strike first if you have the smallest suspicion that your own position is threatened. However much in love you may be, Scorpio self always tops your list of priorities. That makes you intolerant and quick to judge, condemn and as good as execute others before they can say a word in defence of their true innocence.

You need constant variety and excitement in love and may well be cruel when life is rolling along too tamely for your rather wilder tastes.

You want to trust, yet self-protection pulls you back into the darker places of distrust that inhabit your mind. You can be insensitive to other, more trusting hearts, almost arrogant, and sometimes seem coolly detached from everyday feelings and fears.

You see the secret side of people and this has its disadvantages, as well as potential pleasures, for you won't hesitate to use a lover's weaknesses in a fight if it suits you – all the while keeping your own insecurities a secret so your partner can't figure out your failings.

Scorpio's most frightening character flaw is sheer lust for power and willingness to use sex to get it. You're only too aware of the fascination others feel for you, but using it to manipulate them is far from fair – bad for them, and for you.

Experiencing such strong emotions and passions can have its minus points – without a close, caring relationship where you can let off steam without being scared of seeming stupid, emotion can build up inside Scorpio to such a pressure point that it threatens physical and mental health.

BEING YOUR SCORPIO BEST

All the essential factors are there for a lifetime of luscious loving: soaring sex drive, inbuilt loyalty and deep desire for one-to-one commitment. But Scorpio's secretive, manipulative side is the potent drop of acid that can poison future love happiness. The antidote is to loosen, and lighten, up. Learn to respect others for being different, instead of trying to mould them, whether they are willing or not, into your mirror image. Love and let love, and keep sex for the sharing pleasure it is, rather than a selfish tactic to keep you in control.

Love and sex often seem like completely separate things to Scorpio, but for others they must merge into one to make sense of life. You need to love with your mind as well as your body to try for the total trust that could transport Scorpio to sky-high levels of bliss. It won't always be easy, but it's not impossible.

As, one by one, you let your carefully concealed secret worries slip out of your heart, and realise the world doesn't end because you've shown a bit more of your vulnerable self, you'll find the Scorpio darkest green jealousy gets less and less able to damage you and your partner.

Learning to really relax is another essential element of Scorpio love success – deep breathing or even just a brisk walk followed by a long, warm bath when you feel tension revving up for a row will remove the stress from sex and help you savour it as a long, slow feast rather than frantic fast food.

As a Scorpio you need to use that steel-built determination to bulldozer away some of your detachment. You have so much intuition into how others feel, yet hold back from becoming too involved. Doesn't it get lonely up there on a level of your own? Come down to earth sometimes, open up to the uncertainties and the mistakes that are a natural part of being alive. You'll be happier, and so will your partner.

SCORPIO SEXY SECRETS

A slave to your senses, nothing turns Scorpio on more than an assault on all of them – simultaneously. Silky floor cushions, music with a loud, sexy beat, scented candles burning, spicy food to feed each other, followed by an icy mouthful of champagne drunk from places warmed by sexual heat. The list of Scorpio love treats has no end and, because of your thirst for constant variety, you're happy to try all of them, several times. That's even before you get as far as the bed where, like all other areas of your life, Scorpio demands to be in charge.

You adore watching a partner's pleasure as loving starts teasingly slowly with gossamer-fine caresses, both half dressed, black suspenders biting into soft flesh, desire taking you to the edge, excitement like hot liquid running through your veins. But then you cool it slightly to keep a lover lingering on the edge of ecstasy in an agony of passion.

But staying in control constantly can get wearying. Do try, however difficult it may be at first, to let a lover set the pace sometimes. Yes, your partner may lack your intuitive love skill to start with, but together you can work out ways to take turns at giving and receiving maximum pleasure – like the feel of silk gloves on the inside of your thighs, then the gentle slap-massage of leather gloves, or dressing up to give change-hungry Scorpio a different lover every night, and all sorts of love toys.

But while Scorpio loves to experiment, you will not follow a sex manual. Appeals to your rich imagination are more effective than any amount of gymnastic positions. Ringing you up at work to whisper erotic poetry down the phone. Suddenly stopping in the middle of a meal to rush upstairs. A list of sex instructions masquerading as a shopping list. There are a thousand and more different ways of subtly turning someone on and Scorpio is more than willing to try them all.

But once that desire switch is flicked, look out – there's no going back, and the intensity of Scorpio lovemaking can be a little scary until a lover gets used to it. The bedroom's the stage where star performer Scorpio feels most at home – but the act need never be the same twice.

WOOING AND WINNING SCORPIO

No wimps, worriers or time-wasters is the number one demand in Scorpio's choice of permanent partner. And a close second comes a skin thicker than rhino hide, because anyone looking to linger around Scorpio must be prepared to weather this sign's seesawing moods, sometimes unreasonable demands, constant need for change, and tendency to lash out with poisonous perfection when feeling threatened.

Your magic match must also stand up to you while still adoring you, make you the centre of their world yet still have a life of their own, and offer limitless support without expecting any kind of comforting in return. Sounds too tall an order to be possible? Well, there is certainly no shortage of would-be Scorpio partners to be found at the horror films, racetracks and football matches that keep Scorpio adrenalin at sky-high levels. And that's because you set equally high standards for your Scorpio self, including a lifelong loyalty and an appetite and enthusiasm for physical loving that can't be matched.

You have a deep respect for permanent commitment and long to meet that someone special, yet, even when you do, it's difficult for Scorpio to sink gratefully into the comfortable depths of a long-time love. Instead, you're forever testing the limits of your love, pushing things that little bit too far.

And, when the sailing's been a bit too plain for too long, you'll whip up a storm from somewhere to engineer the kind of relationship crisis Scorpio thrives on. So your partner needs to be always one step ahead of you, while letting you think you still have the upper hand.

Scorpio needs help to balance the many separate sides of your nature, so a partner must be confidently secure and full of clever tricks to help you relax and release the inner tension that can cause moods. Also essential are a lack of inhibitions, a good collection of cookery books, a strong sense of humour and a complete lack of jealousy, even if you are flirting madly with a complete stranger. When it comes to Scorpio loving, only the best will do and you are the zodiac sign most able to find it.

LOVE MATCH

How Scorpio combines with each of the 12 sun signs

Scorpio with Scorpio

Despite large helpings of mutual desire and a lovelife that makes the fattest sex manual seems short on ideas, this romance can soon become a race for number one position. The twin Scorpio curse is a double dose of competitiveness and a tendency to take the smallest slight too seriously.

Revenge takes the reins and suddenly what was a blazing love is a steaming ruin doused by a bucketful of bitchy back-biting. It needs effort on both sides sometimes to let things slide, and to curb a natural competition that can cancel out affection. But world-beating bedtimes and perfect understanding can be the reward when both concede just a little of your personal pride and escape the possessiveness.

Scorpio with Sagittarius

Freedom-loving Sagittarius clears away the dark cobwebs of Scorpio's hidden insecurity with positive optimism. It's an instant attraction that soon translates to bedtime capers with lots of laughter and intense, exciting loving.

But when Scorpio wants to talk future, Sagittarius wants to talk fun, and that basically different love view drives a wedge between you that's hard to shift. And when Sagittarius wants to go out alone, Scorpio may stay at home and brood over reprisals. It can work if Scorpio eases up on the intensity to give outgoing Sagittarius enough rope to enjoy that essential independence – and tries not to hug secret hurts to the heart where they grow into a bitter bile that sours any chance of long-term happiness. And Scorpio does have life lessons to learn from Sagittarius – especially the take-life-easier tricks.

Scorpio with Capricorn

Starting as faithful friendship and growing steadier and stronger as it's carefully fed with love, this relationship gains its staying power from a firm rooting in reality, with calm, strong Capricorn providing the perfect antidote to Scorpio's often unreasonable jealousy and suspicion.

But it can get so good both stop trying and you roll slowly into a rut that is difficult to escape. Capricorn could tire of Scorpio's dark moods and show the Capricorn talent for sarcasm that only makes Scorpio plan and plot even more.

If Scorpio can fight against taking this peace-loving partner for granted, it's love for life. And Capricorn discovers a sexual pleasure with in-love Scorpio that matches the wildest dreams, as Capricorn's own imagination is set free by intuitive Scorpio.

Scorpio with Aquarius

Extrovert, extravagant and exciting, that's how Aquarius first looks to a newly smitten Scorpio. Yet these same qualities put the first spanner in the love works. For though no-holds-barred fun between the sheets keeps a love spark flickering between these two, it needs constant cherishing and care to stop it dying out.

If Scorpio can stomach Aquarius' straight-talking, party-stalking ways without resorting to jealous outbursts or deep sulks, and turn an unseeing eye to that Aquarius lack of cash sense, then a future together is possible, especially if you convert stubborn quarrels to healing lovemaking sessions. And both need to accept that each of you will always keep a part of the heart a private place.

Scorpio with Pisces

Pisces' gently persistent passion chips away, little by clever little, at Scorpio's lifetime shell of mistrust, to get to the loving centre underneath. And once you realise your Scorpio pride or position has nothing to fear from the Pisces adoration, letting go of so much suspicion can prove a tremendous relief. Tough Pisces will never know all of your Scorpio secrets, and should accept this.

Protected by the almost mystical power of their love, these two deep, thoughtful signs communicate on a level all your own, and form a rock-solid relationship able to take on anything fate flings your way. A marvellous love match that matures to devoted marriage, which can cancel out all the dark doubts that attack these two signs.

Scorpio with Aries

Both are fiercely competitive and aiming for only one level in life – the top. And when Scorpio's magnetic mystery meets Aries' passionate fire the sexual relationship can be an instant success. But two such independent and competitive heads are in danger of smashing into each other, sooner rather than later, with Aries' temper fuse lit by Scorpio's smouldering suspicions, and Scorpio exasperated by Aries' flat refusal to be forcibly moulded into the perfect partner.

More respect for each other's opinions, and a flexible rather than fixed approach to future loving, could pull it through. But this passion, though powerful, will never prove a pushover and you could happily reach your silver wedding day still trying to figure each other out.

Scorpio with Taurus

The part of the Taurus mind that is firmly rooted in reality will help cancel out Scorpio's too-deep worries. The sexy surprises, and occasional outright shocks, that Scorpio keeps supplying intrigue the passionate Taurus and make bedtime never the same, just better.

A matching set of stubborn wills, though, could make for trouble, and there are over-generous portions of jealousy on both sides. Scorpio could try to at least sometimes accept the Taurus point of view, without always trying to impose a personal opinion, and open up enough to give the security-conscious Taurus the safe future the earth sign craves. Then this multi-million merger of signs, from the opposite sides of the zodiac wheel, could break the lovebank.

Scorpio with Gemini

A couple of cool customers – Scorpio is so sure of hurts ahead that a love-proof shield may always stay hoisted around the heart, and maybe wisely because Gemini can be the Fatal Attraction sign for Scorpio. Gemini may be so busy spreading love and affection that there isn't the time to simply sit and discover what makes a partner, like deep Scorpio, tick. Gemini approaches love like a sprinter, Scorpio is marathon-minded.

Despite a sex life full of outrageous ideas and physical success, this relationship will find it difficult to struggle down to the deeper level that is essential to lasting love. And the more Scorpio tries to chain up Gemini's cheeky flirting, the worse it gets, leading to bitter bust-ups and seemingly never-ending sulks. It needs much effort from both sides if a future together is to be more than a fabulous dream. But it is worth it, because Gemini knows how to stop you brooding and brings you into the light.

Scorpio with Cancer

Innocence and insight, sweetness and strength together, Scorpio and Cancer find good qualities you never knew you had, and help each other make the most of them and your life together. Both secretly tender – Scorpio can be outwardly tough and Cancer a strict conformist – these signs breathe a big sigh of relief to find someone you can trust absolutely with your deepest hopes and fears.

With all barriers down, it's full steam ahead to a sex life that's built on a base of mutual respect – and massive desire. And with two such inventive signs putting your minds and bodies together, the bedroom temperature never stops rising. Although this is a wonderfully star-blessed relationship, you must make sure that you remember the kindness Cancer needs. And you both need to ration the moods that affect your partner as much as they do you.

Scorpio with Leo

In the beginning, two big hearts join forces to come up with a spectacular love match. But all too soon these single-minded signs' pride is locked in combat. Both want the upper hand and neither is prepared to let the other's faults go unnoticed. Bitter bitching leads to constant criticism and to regular rows – and when Leo has felt the Scorpio sting one time too many, even the loving lion will stop sticking patches on rapidly deflating love.

Taking turns at decision-making, and thinking hard before blurting out hurts, could help this sex-powered pair build a good relationship. As a Scorpio you may not always believe Leo deserves praise, but you should give it anyway because Leo can't love, or live, happily without it.

Scorpio with Virgo

Take two tender souls, add a generous measure of trust, a dash of protectiveness and you have a twosome that could go the distance. Together, Scorpio and Virgo cook up a feast of fulfilling, faithful love from a constantly changing and challenging menu. Sensitive Virgo blossoms under the safe shelter of Scorpio's protection. The sometimes sharp-edged Scorpio puts jealousy on hold since Virgo unselfishness mostly makes it unnecessary.

Your powerful intuition sees the sexy secrets of Virgo loving, and that strong, caring heart other signs miss. And if you can really work on learning to let love flow instead of forcing it, and Virgo can curb that critical tongue, new levels of trust and lust make this love a winner.

Scorpio with Libra

Kicking off with a blistering Libra shot straight into Scorpio's vulnerable heart, this will never be a boring love game. But without a careful game strategy this could turn into a damaging defeat. Libra's casual ways clash painfully with Scorpio's intense ideas, and air and water elements, already so far apart, grow dangerously distant.

The harder Scorpio pushes for commitment, the more Libra resists. Tactful rethinking of expectations is essential if this is to last, yet both have much to gain. Libra finds more ambition and success with Scorpio in support, and Scorpio learns the difference between loving someone and controlling them.

LIVING LOVE

Case history of a Scorpio woman and Sagittarius man, star-crossed lovers

When the clock chimed the half-hour, Fran finally admitted that Alex wasn't coming. It was half-past seven, so the baseball exhibition match had already started. He should have arrived to pick the kids up at least half-an-hour ago. She looked at them sitting there in half-sized baseball hats and numbered T-shirts – Danny at 10 trying to look nonchalant but six-year-old Tim quite unable to hide his disappointment.

At that moment, with all the Scorpio intensity she was capable of, Fran felt almost murderous. If she could have got her hands on Alex Harrison at that moment – but who knew where he was. Instead, she decided on damage limitation. 'Come on, you two,' she said, to stop the disappointment hitting the boys too hard. 'Let's go ice-skating.'

An hour later, as she rested by the rink and watched Tim and Danny try to master staying upright, Fran's hot temper had cooled to iron determination. Whatever her feelings for Alex – and he was the best thing that had happened to her since her divorce – she simply couldn't let him mess up her kids like this, promising to take them places then either forgetting completely or turning up so late it wasn't worth going. A typical live-for-this-moment Sagittarius, it wasn't that Alex meant to let them down, he just couldn't seem to get himself organised enough to be at a set place at a set time. But for Tim and Danny, and for herself, Fran needed someone who was totally reliable. If Alex couldn't even get himself to the house when he said he would, how could she even think about accepting his proposal of marriage?

When Alex had held her close in bed and whispered, 'Be my wife, Fran, I love you so much,' part of her had wanted to say a fast yes. But her practical, family-centred Scorpio side had slapped down her passionate side and made her say, 'Well, I'll have to think about it. I have the boys to consider.'

She tried to explain to Alex how the very things she loved about him – his spontaneity, his happy-go-lucky attitude to life, his love of partying and meeting new people – were also the ones that made her doubt they had a future together as a married couple. 'While we're together like this, I can take it, but if we got married everything would change. You would have to share responsibility for the boys and the house, and really I don't know if you're ready, or willing, to do that,' she told Alex.

Yet even as she spoke, looking into Alex's deep, kind eyes brought home to Fran how much she loved him. Loved the way he refused to take her dark moods seriously and talked her out of them. Loved his laugh, his baffled look when he was trying to figure out a DIY problem, the way he always seemed to wear odd socks or shirts wrongly buttoned up.

His easy-going optimism was such an antidote to her own, often gloomy, pessimism. He even helped her come to terms with her possessive nature by showing her that, although he might chat and joke with other women all night, it was always Fran he came home to. Of course, jealous sparks had flown over the months they were together. Two such strong personalities had their share of raucous rows. Yet, whatever troubles they had, there was always a thread of deep mutual respect that, although stretched, never broke.

Fran didn't believe in happy ever after – her disastrous first marriage had burst that bubble. She knew, if they stayed together, that Alex would often exasperate and frustrate her, that often it would be like having three kids instead of just two. Was it worth the risk? Not if he doesn't compromise, she thought firmly to herself as she drove home, the car filled with the smell of the cheeseburgers and chips she bought Tim and Danny to try and help them forget Alex's non-show.

'Things are going to change around here,' she decided. 'It's time for Alex to face the fact that if he wants to marry me I come with all the trimmings, including these two boys. I'm fed up skirting round the issue, terrified to ask him to make a commitment to them in case I scare him off. So what if I do scare him off? He's not worth having in that case. But he's just got to realise that if he makes a promise to me or my boys, then he has to keep it. My family matters more than anything to me, and it will have to mean that much to him, too.'

The light on the answerphone was flashing when Fran let them into the darkened house. 'Well, if that's Alex, I am going to leave him to suffer,' Fran thought to herself, and took her time putting the boys to bed and making a leisurely cup of tea before sitting down to play the message. Anger and jealousy scorched into her mind as she heard a woman's voice.

'This is a message for Fran Cole. If you're wondering where Alex Harrison has got to –' 'Don't tell me,' shouted

Fran, 'He's been spending the evening with you.' '–he's been trapped in a lift at Bayswater station since 6.30. As policewoman on duty I was called to the scene and he insisted I get this message to you. He said you'd understand. The message is, "Tell my future wife and sons I'm ready for them now . . ."'

The station was just round the corner from her house, so Alex had been in plenty of time, and he was prepared to make the effort for the boys and herself. She felt excited, but ashamed, too, to have judged him so harshly. 'Alex isn't the only one with compromises to make,' she thought, and she picked up the phone to tell him just that.

Case history of a Scorpio man and Capricorn woman, star-blessed lovers

'To my best friend,' said the large anniversary card on the mantlepiece. Underneath, a message in Karen's neat, precise Capricorn writing started, 'Hey, happy anniversary, *olé*.' Joe smiled as he read it, remembering the incident on their Spanish honeymoon – two years ago now.

On a secluded sandy beach they swam and sunbathed nude, then made love, without, of course, applying the factor 20 sun cream to some vital parts. The result was a sunburn that made it impossible for him to sit down during the rest of the holiday. But it hadn't mattered a bit, since they were so aroused and fascinated by each other's bodies that they spent most of the fortnight trying out quite different positions.

That was just one of the funny stories that could still make Joe smile. He knew this made their love strong. They were the best of pals who could laugh together.

In fact, their relationship had started as friendship, when they met through Karen's brother and discovered a mutual interest in hang-gliding that led to many blustery afternoons soaring together over the coastline. It was nearly a year before they turned friendship into romance, and finally let the flicker of lust that had been glowing beneath the surface burst into a furnace of desire.

Karen confessed later she was wary of Joe because of his womanising reputation, and certainly before he met her he had had a long list of lovers. He always told himself it was just his natural superstrong Scorpio sex drive. But once he got together with Karen, felt the steady, faithful power of her love and knew, whatever happened, she would never let him down, the deeper, more romantic side of his Scorpio self took over. He hardly looked at another woman. They were married within months.

Of course, like any marriage, it had its problems, notably over Joe's near obsession with work now he had become a self-employed electrician, and his dark moods. At first Karen had resented being left alone at all hours of the day and night when Joe was called out on emergency jobs. Now she realised it was only temporary until he got established – and both appreciated more the time they did get to spend together.

She gradually learned to almost ignore Joe's moods, and at least not take them personally – accepting them as simply as much a part of him as the dagger-shaped mole on his right thigh.

Joe, in turn, helped Karen to become less single-minded about her work in childcare, and take life in general less seriously. Like many Capricorns, she seemed to feel the worries of the world were her responsibility, and spent hours on the phone advising friends and family, or dropping everything to rush off and help one of what he called the 'lame ducks' that seemed to litter her life. But she learned to make time for Joe, too, and through it all there had been the shared jokes, the friendly competition, the knowledge they were each other's best friends.

'But maybe too much friends, not enough lovers,' thought Joe. It was partly his fault, partly Karen's, but lately they seemed to have been operating on only the friendly level, forgetting the deep, powerful lovers' passion they once shared. They knew each other so well, had so few secrets, it was almost too easy to get by on just an odd peck on the cheek and lovemaking so familiar it was relaxing rather than exciting.

'That's going to change, starting tonight,' thought Joe, as he went through his plan again. First, meet Karen – who, right now was looking after a friend's child – in a new Italian restaurant. Then, as they were getting ready to leave the restaurant, call a taxi and whisk her off to the airport – and a surprise weekend in Venice. 'That will revive all the romance,' thought Joe, checking again that the tickets were in his inside pocket. He was already relishing taking Karen to a mystery destination – the atmosphere of the city of love would bring back all the old times.

When he arrived at the restaurant, however, and handed the two overnight bags to the waiter for safekeeping, Karen still hadn't arrived. Joe settled to a glass of red wine and waited. After 20 minutes he was beginning to get seriously worried. Had Karen had an accident?

A waiter tapped him on the shoulder and gestured towards the counter – there was a telephone call for him. Karen's voice was breathless. 'Oh Joe, I'm at the hospital. When I was on my way to the restaurant, I saw a woman at the bus stop in obvious pain, so I stopped to ask her what was wrong. She was in labour but didn't have the money for a cab to the hospital.

'I got one for her and tried to give her the money for the fare but she begged me to come with her. What could I do? She's got no-one. I'm so sorry Joe, our evening is ruined. But we'll have plenty more. Look, why don't you come here? The baby's almost born and we can have a double celebration.'

Which is how, despite his romantic ideas, Joe and Karen ended up spending their second wedding anniversary in a hospital waiting room – and a very surprised new mum was given the cash value of that Venice holiday to buy baby clothes. Joe suddenly realised romance between him and his wonderful, kind Karen had never died, in fact it was even better between friends. 'Who needs old times?' he whispered.

Sagittarius in Love

THE WONDERFUL YOU

You have a high-energy brand of loving that is unforgettable. With a childishly idealistic heart sheltering behind a confident, charming front, Sagittarius offers friendship that barely covers an elemental desire for coupling, which has even the newest acquaintance going weak at the knees, and the heart. Sagittarius is also a wonderful joker, with a huge stock of stories and opinions you really must share.

You are the most impulsive of all the sun signs, so partners could suddenly find themselves travelling on the Orient Express, when they were expecting cocoa in front of the telly. Enthusiasm, surprises and variety are central to your lovelife, which has to be a constantly changing kaleidoscope of colourful actions and words to keep your interest for long.

Energetic and easily bored, you're always on the go and shrug off petty love problems like possessiveness and jealousy. Freedom is as essential to Sagittarius as breathing, so you never dream of slapping the passion-cuffs on anyone else – and never let anyone restrict you.

Although you like to be in charge, you don't mind taking a back seat now and then, and you always stay on good terms with ex-partners, refusing to bow to the bitchy back-biting that can leave a bitter taste once a relationship crumbles away.

Sagittarius is a sexy show-off with an irresistible smile, honest to the core, and incapable of lying to a lover. Yes, sometimes the truth can hurt, but this certainly isn't the sun sign to wrap an unpleasant fact in comforting language – something partners soon come to appreciate.

The Sagittarius combination of lively brain and an often strong body makes sex an adventure – you savour every single moment of the sensual journey as well as the thrilling arrival at total ecstasy. But you are an unselfish lover who takes time to coax fantasies and secret fears out of partners, then spends endless effort and imagination either making them come true or banishing them forever. Life with super-sociable Sagittarius can be one long surprise party, with your lucky partner as the guest of honour.

THE WICKED YOU

Commitment smacks of rules and restrictions to roam-alone Sagittarius, who can't stand feeling the walls of cosy, comfy loving closing in. Allergic to routine and always aware of the other, perhaps better, options that might be waiting outside, your reluctance to make real decisions and commit yourself completely often exasperates partners who want to make what seems like a perfect love permanent.

You always want to keep checking that grass on the other side of the fence, just in case it's greener, and you certainly don't want to do away with your only chance of ever tasting it.

So, although Sagittarius can be deeply and lastingly loyal, you're far from naturally faithful and gallop away from responsibility. Growing up may, finally, be forced upon you, but you'll give it the slip for as long as you can. Sagittarius can also be slightly selfish, chasing after your own dreams and making plans for your future that don't include your lover.

You can become so obsessed with the large-scale problems of the world, you can't even see when a partner isn't happy, or claims to be happy when the opposite is true. When crossed, your sunny nature can suddenly turn cloudy, lashing unsuspecting loved ones with a shivery downpour of sarcasm and angry shouting.

You offer direct love, often matched with blunt remarks, which means that intense, emotional romance is not for you. You prefer to stay pals and keep love on a lighter note – partly because, under that casual front, you don't know how to handle closeness and are scared it might change you or your life.

You often prefer to walk away from a stale situation, or one that's getting serious. And you may commit your heart to someone who can never be totally free to love you, because that's one way to keep your own freedom.

In love, as in life, Sagittarius tends to start lots of things, finish much fewer. You're so active and energetic, there's no time to sit down quietly and take stock of your life. But if you truly want the settled, stable life you often dream of, you must make time. Chasing rainbows is wonderful fun, but one day you'll want to catch one, and you won't know how.

BEING YOUR SAGITTARIUS BEST

Can free-loving, free-living Sagittarius learn to love commitment? Yes, but only when that's what you really want. Start by looking at your relationship through your lover's eyes. You may only feel comfortable with the door marked Exit left ajar, but most other people would prefer to keep it slammed shut, and padlocked just in case.

True love can never take root in your freedom-based relationships until you can trust yourself not to stray, and be satisfied with what you have rather than what might just come along sometime in the future. Take too long doing this and your partner will be worn down by your casual ways and exhausted by chasing after you every time you go racing away from responsibility.

Yes, Sagittarius shouldn't be caged – but, deep down in that secretly sensitive heart, don't you long for the security that a lifetime of one-to-one loving could bring? A cage can be made of warm, loving bonds as well as cold steel.

You must learn not to make instant promises you can't,

or won't, keep. Your tongue is too good at sending all sorts of ideas and sensational suggestions spinning into lovers' ears. Then you're astonished when there are scenes later because you forget, or fail, to deliver. However transported you are by passion, do say only what you mean.

Try to tackle others' emotions with a little more tact – not everyone has your thick skin, so put the brakes on your Sagittarius bluntness. With practice, you'll be able to pick up pointers to a partner's mood, rather than being amazed when that love mate suddenly changes and starts accusing you of not caring.

Please accept that even you could do with leaning on others sometimes. Reach out when you feel low or confused, rather than just burying yourself in all-action work or play. You will learn that independence is not exterminated by admitting you need someone else. It could even grow stronger.

SAGITTARIUS SEXY SECRETS

You so adore lovemaking you want to tell the world, so secrets are something you are almost too keen to reveal to an audience of friends, or even workmates. From your direct stare that does strange, but wonderful, things to the opposite sex, to the firm, fit body that's built to make and break all the love rules, Sagittarius can often be a walking, talking sex symbol.

The ideal build-up to passion for this fire sign is an action-packed day outdoors – perhaps walking in the hills or horse-riding, or just working on the allotment or rowing on the local boating pond. Follow this with a loud party where you can show off your talking talent by keeping a crowd in stitches, while sending, and receiving, secret love messages over their heads from your lover. Then it's home for a lingering aromatherapy massage with a warmed erotic oil like ylang-ylang, concentrating on Sagittarius hotspots, the hips and thighs.

Loads of love talk, the more explicit the better, turns on

your brain while alternating tender and tough touch turns on your body. Soon that body, for once, seems to lose all its independent power as a heavy sex ache turns to blissful shivers that touch every nerve.

Sex is as natural as smiling to Sagittarius, and you do plenty of both. Most at home out of doors, you'll leap at the chance to swim naked, walk along a deserted beach and make love under the stars. Impulsive and imaginative, you thrive on change and danger, and can inspire even the shyest partner to make outrageous suggestions. Hang-ups have no place in Sagittarius' bedroom, nor do you like seductions that seem to last forever. Once you've made up your mind to make love you want to get on and do it – so you can start all over again.

Your lack of jealousy and inhibitions makes you keen to experiment with all sorts of lotions and potions, passion and positions. Remember others' feelings as well as your own, and there need be no end to the ecstasy.

WOOING AND WINNING SAGITTARIUS

If a wedding ring is a lover's goal, then that lover needs to think again when Sagittarius is the target. Sagittarius may have to be roped to the roof-rack of the car to get you to the wedding ceremony on time – or any time. Yet that doesn't mean you can't be loving and loyal for a lifetime – it just has to be on your terms. So you need a lover who is as independent and non-possessive as you are, who won't ask too many questions when you've been out late, and will turn a blind eye to the many fun flirtations that are all part of being you.

To stay the course with Sagittarius, a partner must value honesty above all else, be open and direct, and never try to manipulate you with sly schemes or play silly games to get you to prove your love. A partner must be strong enough to accept your need for freedom, yet soppy enough to celebrate the anniversary of the day you bought your first saucepan together. Your ideal mate must also be sensitive enough to realise when you need to stop achieving, slow down and get in touch with your secret self. And be mischievous enough to never stop surprising you, in bed and out. Your perfect partner needs the patience of a saint and the between-the-sheets skills of an accomplished sinner. 'Love me, love my crowd', could be your Sagittarius motto. Your partner also has to put up with the noisy social set that has you at its centre, not to mention the half-finished projects scattered all over the house, and the boring chores that somehow always get pushed to the bottom of the list as more exciting offers come along.

Hectic, humorous, and full of loving so hot it explodes thermometers, life with Sagittarius means being perfect pals and perfect lovers. You may resist being tied down legally, but when the right person comes along you'll give yourself body and soul, and no piece of paper could make that any more binding.

LOVE MATCH

How Sagittarius combines with each of the 12 sun signs

Sagittarius with Sagittarius

A matching set of calendars is essential for this go-anywhere partnership, so you can compare dates and make sure you are both around long enough to carry on a relationship. Otherwise you may only meet on the stairs. Perfect bed pals who find each other's energy and honesty fuels your own ideas, if you two can make time to sit down and really get inside your heads and hearts, this could be a gold-plated pairing. Though cash, as both are bound to be free-spenders, could spark a crisis.

Too often, frantic action takes the place of feelings and, with both too busy to notice, this affair can fizzle out. It's easier to be a roaming-free lover yourself than allow your partner to be one. But sensational loving makes it worth the freedom compromising that both need to do.

Sagittarius with Capricorn

Wanderlusting, optimistic Sagittarius wants a life full of change, while sometimes solemn Capricorn wants to stay at home. Impulsive Sagittarius leaps before looking into all sorts of scrapes, cleverly cautious Capricorn thinks twice before even daring to look. Wide apart though they seem, this couple's joint fascination with all things physical makes for a love match that's scorching short term, a bit shaky long term.

Lasting happiness is possible if Sagittarius can give suspicious Capricorn the promise of the faithful future Capricorn needs, and Capricorn rations the criticisms to the things that really do matter. Then Sagittarius is stabilised by Capricorn, and Capricorn catches optimism from Sagittarius.

Sagittarius with Aquarius

Two creative, charm-powered fun seekers, who are pals first, passion partners second. You rarely lose mutual respect for each other's freedom and that prevents the relationship becoming a prison. Yet it does forge a special love chain that keeps you together. Surprises and laughter light this meeting of minds and bodies – you two spend as much time sparking ideas off each other as making sparks fly between the sheets.

Danger alarms sound if either or both become so determined to stay free you ignore the other's hopes or dreams. And Aquarius could try to control and can show a cool side that damages Sagittarius.

Sagittarius with Pisces

Sagittarius may start off being delighted by the sheer adoration of a Pisces lover, but all too soon that dependent, occasionally desperate, attention has become a bit of a drag. For while Pisces thinks mainly of others, Sagittarius often thinks of self, and Pisces' dreams of evenings cuddling together in front of the TV are like a living nightmare to sociable Sagittarius.

Too different to ever enjoy effortless happiness, these two can make a go of it if Sagittarius remembers Pisces' super-sensitive side and need of loving protection and bites back blunt comments or criticism. But it will never be easy unless Pisces can unlearn that inborn jealousy and possessiveness and replace it with a dash of confidence borrowed from Sagittarius.

Sagittarius with Aries

Certainly not without its rocky spots, this is still a brilliant relationship – even the arguments are fun. Both fire signs are a bit bossy, and can be selfish. But when you get together the real affection and respect you feel for each other turns you into starry-eyed lovers, linked together forever yet still tasting the independence both treasure.

Solid-gold sex, five-star fun and togetherness so natural neither feels trapped make this passionate pairing a perfect bet for a lifetime together, with or without a wedding. But both must beware of tumbling into jealousy. By expecting the best out of each other, these blissfully compatible signs will get it.

Sagittarius with Taurus

Taurus thinks Sagittarius is a dream lover – so generous and the perfect passion match in bed. And when this couple pool a joint love of luxury living and eating, it makes a great feast. Until Taurus gets out a calculator to find out just how much of a free-spender Sagittarius is. Then differences start to dig in as possessive Taurus wants Sagittarius to account for every moment spent apart. And Taurus may try to tighten up Sagittarius' spontaneous approach to life.

Suddenly Sagittarius feels stifled, and starts to struggle. Compromise can come if Taurus attempts tolerance and worries a bit less about security. Sagittarius will need to modify that 'do-as-I-please' life slogan. But it will always be a relationship that needs commitment to make it work – and both could have much to gain.

Sagittarius with Gemini

One big question – is there room in the limelight for both these would-be stars to shine? Competition is the catch word for the Sagittarius and Gemini couple, as both are publicity seekers who are proud to be the centre of attention – and secretly expect to be. If you can work out some way to take turns on stage, and concentrate on sharing feelings as well as sex and that non-stop stream of ideas, this relationship can progress from no-strings pals to passionate lovers. But it needs serious effort from both sides to overlook small hurts and wounding words. You are on opposite sides of the zodiac wheel, which gives you the clearest view of each other's faults and vulnerable spots, and you will always need to balance that with compassion.

Sagittarius with Cancer

All the doting admiration and bedroom antics Sagittarius could ask for come pouring forth from passion's willing slave, Cancer, who is eager, and skilfully able, to please. At first, attention-loving Sagittarius thinks this must be heaven, and this is the Fatal Attraction sign for Sagittarius.

But before long a slow slide can start, as Cancer's caring becomes clinging, and the dense, warm stickiness of their love stifles the Sagittarius need to feel personal freedom. Soon tender feelings may be trampled under foot in the Sagittarius stampede to escape, unless Cancer can keep passion at simmering rather than boiling point, and you are ready to set limits on your Sagittarius freedom and flirtations. Then the harmony you feel at lights-out time can last all day.

Sagittarius with Leo

With the same warmth, the same generosity and sense of humour, this match is so seamless even aisle-shy Sagittarius won't complain about making it officially permanent. Two attention-grabbing go-getters, the fiery duo's most cherished jewel is the priceless trust they co-own, plus an ability to cheer each other up no matter what.

Leo's inborn romance brings out a soppy side Sagittarius never knew was there, while Sagittarius' 'so what' attitude helps Leo fret less about material things. But Sagittarius must stop short of making fun of Leo, and not spend too many evenings out alone and damage Leo's massive self-esteem. And, because you can both believe, so sincerely, that your needs matter most, you will both have to learn to give way – just a little. In return you will be gaining such a lot.

Sagittarius with Virgo

Once Virgo has straightened out Sagittarius' mess, made the meals Sagittarius eats on the run, and tried to get some sort of organisation into your life, there may not be enough time left for loving.

At the second sign of sharp Virgo criticism, Sagittarius may want to speed away. Unless you really take time to learn about each other's mind, you may not even be able to agree when to have a row. If Virgo praises more and criticises less and gives Sagittarius freedom, warm love is possible. And Sagittarius will then find Virgo's sex power and caring are worth staying for.

Sagittarius with Libra

Twice the charm and twice the sex drive equals half the predictability. This pair are made to share their hearts and hopes, but neither will truly know where they stand, not with a partner who matches them surprise for surprise. This relationship works best if it stays in the friendship zone for a while, and slowly pans out into passion. That way the securely built base of liking and communicating will be solid enough to withstand any number of shocks.

Each respects the other's need for independence, is full of outrageous romantic ruses, and loves to get out on the town. But occasionally Libra can find Sagittarius' naturally seductive ways too much to take, and Sagittarius must at least pretend to admire – even though you'll never really share – Libra's artistic efforts to make a stylish home.

Sagittarius with Scorpio

Scorpio's intensity starts off flattering but can get frightening, as powerful emotions, so soon on show, scare Sagittarius, who may feel a cage door is closing and take instant flight. Sex is show stopping, with both sides happy to take turns as scene-setter and stealer.

But Scorpio wants a lover body and soul, and the scraps Sagittarius is able to scatter instead just can't satisfy this all-or-nothing sign. A real effort to understand will have to be made by both of you to open up the communication lines. If each learns from the other, Scorpio how to take love more lightly, Sagittarius how to take love more seriously, then this relationship could last. But it will never be a tie to be taken for granted.

LIVING LOVE

Case history of a Sagittarius man and Pisces woman, star-crossed lovers

Phil let the phone ring his usual three times, then picked it up. 'Samaritans, how can I help you?' he said. At first there was, as so often, silence at the other end of the line. Finally a woman's voice came, so hesitant and sad it touched him to the depths of his generous Sagittarius soul.

'I'm at my wits' end, I just don't know what to do. I'm sorry, I know you have lots of more urgent calls to take, but I just had to ring. It's my husband, you see, I just can't get through to him any more and I'm sure he's seeing someone else.'

Phil's voice came out in a strangled croak, but his stock response didn't fail him. 'What makes you think that?' he asked. Again there was silence and then the sound of tears being wiped away. 'He stays out late and doesn't tell me where he is. He makes secret phone calls. He shuts me out from everything but the most mundane family activities. He's like a stranger. I just feel I can't go on like this, but what can I do? I love him so, I don't want to lose him, but there seems to be no way to get through to tell him.'

Phil knew the next question he must ask. 'Why can't you tell him?' he asked, consciously lowering his voice.

'Because I'm not the one who does the talking, or the doing, in our relationship.' The sound of bitterness was unmistakable, and shocked Phil. 'I'm the Pisces sponge, soaking up everyone else's hopes, fears and complaints, but with no-one to listen to mine. Because, even when I do talk, he doesn't seem to hear me. He is so used to walking all over me, not telling me anything he's doing, like I don't even matter. But every time I see him getting changed to go out, I know he's going to see someone else and my heart just splits in two.' Now over the crackly line came the sound of full-blown, heart-rending sobs.

While the caller composed herself, Phil's mind raced. What was he going to do, how should he respond to this outpouring of sheer despair? All his training hadn't prepared him for this. But he needn't have worried.

When the voice came again, it was with the new note of determination. 'Well, now I've got that off my chest, I feel better. I'm sorry to have taken up your time like this, but it really is the only way I could think of. I've made up my mind to leave. I'll take the children, of course, and start over on my own. Being alone is the last thing I want, but it'll be better than the loneliness of being with someone who doesn't love me or want me any more. That's all I have to say. Goodbye Phil.'

'Linda, wait . . .' Phil shouted down the phone. She listened, but then hung up. He looked wildly at his watch – his shift was over for the night. If he was quick, he could still catch her. He grabbed his coat and ran.

As Phil sped towards home, he was overcome with shame, and anger at himself, too. His own wife felt so cut off from him that the only way to be sure he would listen was to phone him on his Samaritans shift, pretending to be a stranger. 'I'm understanding and patient with complete strangers, but not with my Linda. How could things have got so bad between us?' he thought desperately.

There was no way to pinpoint a change in attitude. It had been such a gradual thing. When they were first together he basked in Linda's love, her eagerness to please and efforts not to place any restrictions on him, however hard it was for her basically possessive Pisces self.

They were so happy together, but, before long, he took her understanding for granted. It even grated a bit on him, and the more he could get away with, the more he did misbehave. Even down to having an affair. Of course, in her clear-sighted, quiet Pisces way, Linda was quite right. He had been seeing someone from work, nothing serious, of course, no strings, just the way he liked it.

But was that the way he liked it? Now, with the prospect of losing Linda forever, Phil realised for the first time how much he needed and appreciated the warm, loving home Linda had created for him and the children. It was his haven from the outside world where, he now saw, freedom was just another word for selfishness. 'Something I know plenty about,' he thought grimly.

'I've got a lot of growing up to do. Facing up to responsibility needn't mean giving up my whole self to someone else, just sharing myself,' he thought. 'And sharing the other person, too, which means listening to Linda and really trying to meet her halfway. She's done enough giving to last me a lifetime.'

By the time he raced up their garden path, Phil's Sagittarius conscience was as black as the darkness that surrounded him. But the commitment to change was giving him courage. He would be less selfish, more responsible, talk less, listen more. He would love Linda the way she deserved, with all his heart, not just the mean portion he felt he could spare. But would he get the chance?

The house was in darkness as he let himself in. 'Oh, no,' he moaned, flinging himself down on the sofa as though the life had suddenly gone out of him. Then he felt the gentlest of touches on his shoulder, 'Phil, I couldn't just leave like that. Do you think we could try again?' And he was hugging his sweet, loving wife close and vowing never to let her slip so far away from him again.

That was three years ago now, and he never has.

Case history of a Sagittarius woman and Leo man, star-blessed lovers

When Ann opened the front door and saw the whole gang standing there, she was amazed but, in true Sagittarius style, was not, of course, at a loss for words. 'Come on in,' she said. 'But why are you all here? Have I forgotten my own birthday? Or, worse still, have I forgotten Ray's?' She felt Ray come up behind her and put his hands around her waist, feeling the thrill she still experienced when he touched her, even after five years together. Ann thought how easily they had shrugged off the harsh words of a few moments before.

None of their friends would even guess that, just as the doorbell rang, they had been blazing their way through an argument, fighting over something that seemed important at the time, but now seemed irrelevant. At least she had time to put down the bag of washing she was about to hurl at Ray's arrogant Leo head!

Now, as usual, they were their normal warm, affectionate selves. Ann sometimes wondered whether their many fire-sign fights were the price they had to play for the pleasures of their love. Both big-hearted and, yes, big-headed, they did both like to be boss. Since their first meeting – on a day trip to France, of all places – they had constantly stretched their love to its absolute limits with tests set for each other, and explosive arguments when either of them failed to play the complex love game.

At first, Ann had revelled in Ray's constant demands for proof of her love, his exaggerated jealousy whenever she so much as went near another man. 'You can't love me any more,' he'd say in that dramatic Leo way of his. And, though the pure Sagittarius in her made her long to just walk away, Ann would find herself reassuring him over and over again. Until finally she had just had enough, blew her top, and then for a while it was bliss again. Until the next time. And lately, she realised uneasily, the rows were getting closer together.

Mind you, she was just as bad – chipping away at Ray's fierce Leo pride, showing him up in public by picking holes in stories he was telling. Making him wait for her praise when he achieved something, until his frustration and secret insecurity came pouring out in a stream of shouting. Yet neither could even begin to imagine life without the other. 'What are we playing at?' said Ann to herself, suddenly realising she was still standing in the way of the dozen or so members of their gang of friends on the doorstep. 'Er, come in then you lot. What is this, a delegation?'

'Well, yes, it is,' said Richard, a mutual friend who had organised the day trip where Ann and Ray met. Once everyone had settled down in the living-room – mostly on the floor because Ann and Ray were so seldom at home they didn't bother with much furniture – Richard took out a neatly folded sheet of paper, carefully unfolded it, and began reading from it.

'In the pub tonight we, the undersigned, hereafter referred to as the Friends of Ray and Ann, decided we can no longer allow the state of affairs to continue . . .' 'You can tell he's an accountant,' thought Ann, her mind already wandering. 'Is this another charity appeal or something?' '. . . in that the aforementioned Ray and Ann are in the process of tearing each other apart with petty power struggles and one-upmanship. The best relationship we have ever seen is going down the drain, and we don't intend to sit back and let this happen. We all hereby swear to use any, and all, means at our disposal to deal with these circumstances, should they arise:

1. Ann makes Ray look small in front of us (or vice versa).
2. Ray bosses Ann about or makes unreasonable demands on her loyalty (or vice versa).

3. Either of them purposely engineers a scene in public for whatever reason.
4. ....'

As he read on, Ann glanced over at Ray. He wasn't angry or even upset – she could see by the way he was, for once, lost for words that, like her, he realised the truth of what their friends were saying. He caught her eye and broke into a broad grin, making her heart do the flip somersault it always did when she realised how much he loved her.

That night, as they lay sleepily satisfied in rumpled sheets, Ann whispered to Ray, 'Have we really been so blind we need our friends to point out the way we're risking our relationship? Why couldn't we see it for ourselves? Or maybe we did, but in true fire-sign style we hoped it would just go away. Anyway, now things are going to be different,' she said decisively, as Ray nodded. 'But I wonder what they meant by "any means at our disposal" ...'

They soon found out. For over the next few weeks, although they tried so hard, Ann and Ray still occasionally found themselves slipping back into their old habits. One night in the pub, when Ray was very flamboyantly sulking because Ann was talking to another man, Richard got up and poured a pint of bitter over his head.

When Ray told a story about work and Ann kept chipping in with sarcastic comments, everyone got up and went to sit at the opposite end of the bar. The threat of being humiliated in public just made them think that little bit harder before they leapt in. Soon they couldn't even remember the last time they'd tried to test the limits of their love, and the funniest thing of all was that the less 'proof' they had, the less they needed. Their relationship went from strength to strength and became a true partnership of equals – with a little help from their friends.

Capricorn in Love

THE WONDERFUL YOU

Solid as a rock with 'softie' stamped through the centre, fiercely independent yet longing to delegate love and life decisions, a sexy tiger disguised as an ice-king polar bear, no sign is more full of contradictions than maddening, yet marvellous Capricorn. And that makes you a memorable lover.

Your core of precious, lifelong passion may be buried so deep under layers of fear, distrust and insecurity that it takes a lot of loving digging to reach it. But a partner who puts in the time and effort will be rewarded with priceless loyalty and sensational sex that just gets steamier and steamier.

Strong and self-sufficient, Capricorn is the calm, safe haven for lovers from life's storms. You're always there with an encouraging word and affectionate hug and an unshakeable faith in yourself that spreads to loved-ones too, making them feel so tenderly protected they can tackle the world's problems.

Slow to trust, and this can sometimes be mistaken for toughness, or even hostility, you intrigue by revealing, just a little at a time, the tremendous loving you're capable of. Soon would-be lovers are willing to promise anything to feel more of your earth-moving sex power. But you play it straight, rarely making any promises you can't keep, or leading people on. Love, like life, is mostly a very serious business to you, you don't fool around with other people's feelings, and certainly expect the same courtesy in return.

Practical through and through, you can put your eye for

detail into perfect play in a relationship. You remember your partner's favourite food or music, send cards that perfectly mirror a partner's taste, spend months tracking down a special book or antique. Combined with this thoughtfulness is a simmering sex drive that starts warm and just gets hotter and wilder when you totally trust your partner. You not only get better-looking with age, but sexier, too, so there's certainly no rush where Capricorn romance is concerned.

THE WICKED YOU

Cool and confident on the outside, inside Capricorn can be so gripped by fear and caution that you dig a wide moat around your heart that even the keenest lover can't cross. Then you wonder why you're feeling so lonely and left out. You find it hard to ask for what you want or show any signs of weakness, in bed and out of it. Yet if a partner misreads your mind, you slip into the darkest of moods.

It's a short step from protectiveness to possessiveness and one too easy for secretly vulnerable Capricorn to make once you let down your love guard. With often impossibly high standards, for yourself as well as others, you see life as divided very clearly into right and wrong, black and white, and may only realise very late on that love doesn't always fit into such rigid categories.

Lack of flexibility leads you to let love go rather than compromising your principles – then, when you want it back, it's already too late. As secure as a fly in a spider's web, Capricorn finds it difficult to relax and really trust a partner. Instead you're constantly questioning their motives, analysing every little movement or conversation for hidden meaning and, the moment you feel threatened, retreating behind a glacier of icy sarcasm.

You can be much too interested in status and the health of a partner's bank balance – a dual snobbishness that rules out too many potential partners if you let these ambitions run riot in your lovelife. Your personal ambitions may be so strong that they don't leave enough time and energy for love.

While one half of you fantasises about true romance with Mr or Ms Right, the other half is so fearful of the deep, dark power of passion that you cower away from commitment and keep your emotions firmly under lock and key. Sometimes you share your lovelife with more than one person – so you're not truly dependent on any one of them.

And yet you can suddenly fall for a smooth-talking, conning charmer. Strangely, Capricorn can get hopelessly emotionally entangled with quite the wrong person, after turning down much more dependable offers. And that happens when your secret sexy centre overrules that cooler, more capable head. Brief bliss is usually followed by boredom or soul-deep disappointment. But, being a Capricorn, you won't budge. Sex may be a chore, sharing non-existent, but you are too stubborn to be the one to admit love defeat.

Learning when to let go of a failed affair and free your heart for higher passion is one of Capricorn's life goals. You could spend more time than any other sun sign sulking and suffering in the acid atmosphere of love gone sour. Such a shame when you have so much to give, and so much to receive, too.

BEING YOUR CAPRICORN BEST

Get ready to plunge straight into the uncharted depths of desire even you may not realise you're capable of. First step is to follow feelings and shut down thoughts, at least some of the time. A partner may be madly in love with you, and your perfect match, but when the strongest sound is the buzzing of that Capricorn brain – 'How long can this happiness last?' – a perfect lover may move out looking for more trust. Logic is a cold bedfellow.

Love is not like a set of saucepans, guaranteed for so many years and able to be swopped if you decide you don't like it. It's unpredictable and uncontrollable, which is what most people find exciting about it – and so does Capricorn if you could only let yourself go enough to admit it.

It's easier to trust people than you think. Try a step-by-step approach, trust a little, then some more, until you feel ready – and you will – to confide in a partner completely. There's no rush. A safety catch on those Capricorn moods would also be a passion plus point. Few lovers really enjoy being subjected to an emotional helter-skelter time after time. Expect love to be good and your natural drive and enthusiasm can shine through. Think negative and all too soon you'll be struggling through thick black clouds of your own making.

Do try to drop the strong, capable mask sometimes so partners can actually see that vulnerable centre rather than vaguely sensing its presence. Let others be in charge sometimes, making decisions and steering lovemaking. Being constantly in control is exhausting, as you'll soon discover if you can give it up and wallow in sheer relaxation. Meditation, massage, regular exercise, and sharing your fears as well as your confidence, will all help take the stress out of sex and love and open up your Capricorn soul to its true passion potential.

CAPRICORN SEXY SECRETS

Slow and steady is the secret route to Capricorn pleasure. You need to start with whispered words and pleasure promises, perhaps in a public place. A generous helping of foreplay is essential to gradually thaw that cool front and leave mind and body deliciously aching for more. Slow, deep kisses and lots of help to slip out of your clothes should be followed by light lip traces and tongue tracking on your personal hotspot, the back of the knees. The gentlest of fingertips circling your thighs, fingernails lightly scoring silk flesh.

But things should go no further until you're ready – feeling rushed or pressured into going too far, too soon, will only send that Capricorn safety door slamming shut and put ultimate pleasure out of reach. Your practical, rather materialistic side means the setting must be right for sex –

clean sheets, soft classical music, and luxury food like smoked salmon or rum truffles to share. But your partner must not drop any crumbs in the bed, that's a real turn-off for you.

Although you may find sudden, uncontrollable lust irresistible, you usually prefer to stick to the bedroom and comfortable, rather than extreme, acrobatic positions. You don't need sex toys and fancy underwear – to straightforward Capricorn they just get in the way of the tight heat of sex itself, the true heartbeat of pure passion, where both are master and both are slave.

Clean skin, being able to set your own passion pace, and feeling secure enough to surrender totally to physical sensations add up to your fantasy lovemaking – then you are among the world's most satisfying, and satisfied, bedmates.

But you should try aromatic oils for massage, incense burning and candlelight to help you turn off your busy, ambitious mind. As trust grows between you, you'll find you never get bored as long as you're given all the time and attention you need. Reading erotic literature aloud to each other, slipping together into a scented bath, sharing a certain look that signals desire ... Capricorn may not be comfortable putting feelings into words, but with a special love language like this, who needs them?

WOOING AND WINNING CAPRICORN

Capricorn is likely to meet the perfect mate in a work setting (perhaps on a course together), or you may even opt for the cautious choice of a dating agency – ideal for finding out all about a would-be lover before you make a commitment. Slow to mature in many ways, you could play the field quite happily and settle down relatively late, but when you do take the plunge, as far as you're concerned, it's for keeps.

The ideal match for Capricorn is patient enough to put in hours of wooing and wheedling to help you drop those defence barriers, easy-going enough to weather some dark moods and physically strong enough to match your stamina between the sheets.

You need someone who believes in old-fashioned courtship, complete with promises and presents, who won't force you into a physical relationship before you're ready or try to tame your natural independence. Work and success are as necessary to Capricorn as breathing, and a lover must appreciate your ambitions.

Your best partner will encourage you to share your deepest fears and blackest despairs and bit by bit expose your secret sensitive centre, only to wrap it in a warm blanket of unconditional love. Aware of your general lack of trust, this partner will never break a promise or make you look small in public, share secrets you've confided or laugh at your funny little ways. You will get the respect you deserve, spiced up with the romance you desire, and in return you'll be the love of their life. Especially when that partner adds the fuel of total belief in your ambitions and talents. You secretly know your natural place is the top and will adore the partner who helps you to get there.

LOVE MATCH

How Capricorn combines with each of the 12 sun signs

Capricorn with Capricorn

In public this seems the perfect pairing – two practical, ambitious, penny-wise, cool customers who complement each other so well it's hard to see where one begins and the other ends. Twin Capricorns can understand, like no other sign, the insecurity behind that superconfident smile, the deep-seated dread of looking foolish by giving, and losing, a tender heart. It's good to have a partner who knows how important it is to be reliable.

But neither Capricorn wants to be the first to give ground, and what could be a deeply rewarding relationship may never get past a superficial stage, soured by squabbles over anything from sex to sport. And ambitions can sometimes become more important than love. But, because both of you work hard at relationships, you'll win through.

Capricorn with Aquarius

Like a wandering moth drawn back, time after time, to the steady beam of a reliable light bulb, star eccentric Aquarius can't resist Capricorn's calm, steady, loving glow – it provides the stability so often lacking in an Aquarius life. But, as the happiness of the honeymoon period wears off, Capricorn's caring arms can easily become chains, and that once-adored refusal to change seems nothing but dull stubbornness.

It will need effort on both sides to succeed – with Capricorn determined to loosen up, forget routine for once and respond with smiles instead of scolding when another Aquarius project collapses in an untidy heap. With both of you interested in the outside world – Capricorn to profit from it, Aquarius to explore and help it – you may need to work at finding enough time for your sexual relationship, which can be brilliant.

Capricorn with Pisces

Heads and hearts unite in a show-stopping twosome that adds Capricorn caution to Pisces tenderness yet comes up with a double act tough enough to take anything the world throws at it. Both halves of this equation feel safe and protected enough to let down their love guards – knowing the other will always be there with an understanding hug and caring word in this so genuine relationship. There's even a chance to laugh at each other, and at life.

Rows can be room-shakers, but they soon blow over, and the basic friendship that's this couple's foundation is built to last, as long as both beware of boredom in the bedroom and, as a practical Capricorn, you resist deluging Pisces' dream schemes with a too hefty helping of reality.

Capricorn with Aries

Athletic bedtime romps and powerful passion that seems unstoppable start this off on a high note, but soon the key changes to the clashing sound of rows. Upfront, aggressive Aries tries to ride roughshod over Capricorn's natural caution and can demand commitment long before the time is right, while Capricorn's sensible economy with feeling, and finances, is shocked by Aries' careless ways. And Aries is equally aggravated by your horribly harsh criticisms.

When resentment and frustration spread their freezing fingers around the relationship, it's time to review romance and put extra effort into communication. And it is worth it. As a Capricorn, you do sometimes have a self-damaging gloomy view of the world and non-stop Aries enthusiasm reaches right in and rescues you.

Capricorn with Taurus

Together these two can do the impossible, and have their feet on the ground, their heads in the clouds and their hearts in seventh heaven, with a mutual passion that perfectly meets each sign's need for simultaneous security and excitement. Both love luxury and making a cosy, comfy home to share, and neither can get enough of the warm, wonderful physical expression of your love that just gets more and more satisfying.

Total trust and lifelong loyalty are the final elements that help add up to ecstatic happiness even a double dose of stubbornness can't cloud – at least, not for very long. The only real danger is that love comes so easily to you that you can both slump into a rather self-satisfied dullness. So both need to add surprises, from time to time, both in and out of the bedroom.

Capricorn with Gemini

A perfect pairing, this, at least between the covers. But as the mist of mutual physical passion fades and careful Capricorn sees just what power to hurt gadabout Gemini has, coldness can freeze Capricorn's heart. Flirtatious and charming, Gemini tortures Capricorn's loyal, faithful soul without even realising, and all Capricorn's loving possessiveness looks like dreaded jealousy to committed freedom-fan Gemini. Capricorn's steady, relentless ambition and drive can confuse unimpressed Gemini.

Laughter and luscious sex can build a bridge over the love chasm between you two, but cash and control quarrels can knock it down brick by brick unless both tread carefully. And there are rewards when you do – as Gemini benefits from a slice of Capricorn seriousness and Capricorn from the lighter-look-at-life attitudes of Gemini.

Capricorn with Cancer

Cancer's gentle touch can fashion a tender new side from tough-nut Capricorn – and flick a switch marked 'sensual' that turns on electrifyingly sexy experiences. But happiness on the surface can be undermined by deep, dark differences that may seem destined to drive these two apart, unless there is a deal of effort on both sides – and you do come from opposite sides of the zodiac circle.

Supersensitive soul Cancer may never recover from exposure to Capricorn's practical, almost brutal approach to life, while you are amazed and appalled by Cancer's clinging, swinging moods. A vow of no secrets, no sulks from these two signs, who too easily descend into depression, helps smooth this rocky love path. Then you will successfully negotiate a lifetime together with a protective, planned-for-comfort-and-security homelife.

Capricorn with Leo

With lashings of loyalty and devotion, matching ambition and independence and a shared fascination for physical pleasure, this could be a world-beating combination – provided Leo and Capricorn have a live-in referee to blow the whistle on their many, many rows. And you, as a Capricorn, should remember that Leo is your Fatal Attraction sign, so guard against possessive, obsessional jealousy.

Two such strong wills, who both insist on being in charge, may make clashes inevitable. And it does need sacrifice, on both sides, and a sterling effort to take life and love a little less seriously to work long term. Capricorn must be prepared to give as well as demand, to indulge Leo's 'show you love me' demands and accept that glib Leo flashiness. This partnership is often dicey but never dull.

Capricorn with Virgo

Neither of you two would dream of proclaiming your passion from the rooftops, or even hinting. But what this love lacks in public displays, it more than makes up for in private warmth and tenderness. With a rich and real insight into how each other's mind and body work, Capricorn and Virgo can cut right through the barriers round both signs that baffle less thoughtful lovers.

Serious yet sexy, cool on the surface and a boiling pot of passion underneath – this luscious love is a delicious secret only you share, that starts brilliant and can get even better with every marvellous moment that passes. The only danger spots are that both you work too hard, and so may run out of the energy you need to fuel your sex life. And Virgo's nagging doubts occasionally infuriate the more sure-souled Capricorn.

Capricorn with Libra

Libra's charm and sexy tricks can change Capricorn from stubborn goat to frisky kid – and these two start the relationship with the lavish presents and luxury outings that Libra enjoys and teaches Capricorn to appreciate.

But, sooner or later, Capricorn gets serious – and can have all sorts of trouble coaxing a commitment from take-love-easy Libra who may want to stay free longer to see if a better lover comes along. Suddenly Capricorn changes from partner to parent, criticising the once-loved Libra antics and making romance rules that Libra is almost bound to break.

Yet it really is worth a rethink to make it last, and as a Capricorn you must learn flexibility and not view love as a winner-takes-all grudge match. And Libra will have to take finances more seriously and do that artful flirting only when safely out of range of Capricorn's baleful stare.

Capricorn with Scorpio

Made to be best mates and an even better marriage match, Scorpio and Capricorn share an almost daunting drive to succeed – to be number one in love, and in life. When each supports the other, you're unstoppable. But problems could start when this couple switch to being in competition and jealousy rips apart romance.

If you, as a Capricorn, school yourself to take a back seat occasionally, see Scorpio's possessive ways, which always threaten to topple over into jealousy, as a compliment rather than a threat and respond to scenes with smiles rather than sulks, this firecracker of a relationship can keep sparking sexily away forever. Though Scorpio will have to see that your occasional Capricorn coldness and emotional control don't mean that Scorpio sex magic isn't working.

Capricorn with Sagittarius

It often starts as a fabulous fling, with both sides addicted to sex and each other. But the fairytale starts to falter when Capricorn looks to live happily ever after, and Sagittarius is still keeping options open. As a home-loving Capricorn you may never get footloose fire sign Sagittarius shopping for saucepans while there's a party somewhere to go to, and this anti-commitment stance could stir up all sorts of storms unless Capricorn can let Sagittarius set the 'settling down' pace, however slow. And Sagittarius will have to give up some of that freedom, yet still help Capricorn to stop seeing life in such serious and sombre shades. Then you'll both see the loving and sexy sense of staying together.

LIVING LOVE

Case history of a Capricorn woman and Aries man, star-crossed lovers

It was after 5.30 p.m. on Friday before Nicola noticed the message in her diary, scribbled in Gary's fast scrawl: 'Please ring me so we can make an appointment to meet over the weekend.' Reading it, Nicola felt dismay, irritation and, finally, guilt. What were things coming to when her own husband had to make an appointment to see her?

Worst of all, she didn't know when she could fit him in – the representatives from that French firm were due in any moment and she'd promised her boss she'd spend the weekend showing them around the city and generally keeping them happy. 'I told Gary that, I must have,' she thought, doubting that her usually razor-sharp Capricorn organisation could have let her down. 'Gary must have forgotten,' she thought, 'typical Aries.' But her hand and heart were heavy as she picked up the phone.

When Gary answered, she could hear from his harassed tone and baby Fiona's whining in the background that things were not going well. 'Well, hello Nicola, so nice of you to call,' he said sarcastically. Nicola braced herself for yet another row. 'I'm sorry, Gary,' she said, trying to keep her voice calm. 'Things have been so hectic here.' She knew how lame that same excuse sounded, but it was true. Her job, as public relations director of a fast-forward fashion firm, had been such a break for her, after starting just two years before as a secretary. She had worked as hard as she could to make a success of it in the beginning.

The trouble was her boss had come to expect her commitment as a right. He didn't make any allowances for the fact she had a husband and young daughter at home. 'And, let's face it, nor have I recently,' thought Nicola, and wondered how she should tell Gary he'd be alone for the weekend . . . again.

As a naturally sociable, independent Aries, Gary found it

hard to be at home so much with only baby Fiona for company. Their role reversal had started when she was offered this, the job of her dreams, and Gary volunteered to give up his teaching post and look after the baby so she could accept it.

'I've always said I want to write that novel, now's my chance to try,' he told her. But caring for Fiona and the house was almost a full-time job. When he had a bit of spare time, he couldn't make himself sit at his typewriter. He didn't seem to have the mental energy for it. Yet they'd been so full of hope and confidence for the future just months ago when this arrangement had begun. When had it all started to go wrong?

Nicola realised the Capricorn ambition and drive to succeed had always been inside her, and she also knew it was one of the things that drew equally go-ahead, determined Gary to her in the first place. Always challenging and exciting sexually, their relationship had been stormy in many other areas too, especially the tussle over who should be boss, which was why she'd been amazed when Gary offered to take a back seat to let her career blossom. 'You'll do the same for me one day,' he'd said. 'After all, that's what a partnership is all about.'

Nicola snatched her wandering thoughts back to today and realised Gary was talking to her, his voice strained and tired through the telephone receiver. 'Well, will you or won't you be here tomorrow afternoon when I've promised Fiona we'll all go to the zoo?' snapped Gary. 'Yes, of course,' said Nicola, her mind racing as she wondered how the French delegation would take to a trip round the local zoo with her family.

'See you later, then,' said Gary, and hung up. In a painful flashback, Nicola suddenly remembered how once he would never hang up without telling her he loved her. 'Well, you never know what might happen, and I just want to make sure you know,' he would say with such a warm tenderness in his voice. Now it was hard to see how he would care if anything did happen, they'd drifted so far apart.

Yes, she sometimes felt Gary put too much pressure on her, but now Nicola could see immersing herself so much in work had been a partly self-inflicted burden, a means of escape from a marriage going wrong. With the total dedication only Capricorns could manage, she had cut herself off from everything else. Now she was forced to face the truth, she could see the marriage problems hadn't gone away, they'd just got worse. 'Life doesn't need to be all or nothing, for either of us,' she thought, picking up her briefcase and heading for her boss's door.

It was only seven o'clock when Gary heard Nicola's key in the lock, and he looked up from bathing Fiona in alarm. 'Something wrong?' he asked, a hint of that old love and concern momentarily crossing his face. 'No, but you had better get used to me being home at this time, because that's how it's going to be from now on,' said Nicola with a smile, picking up the bath sponge and tickling a delighted Fiona. 'Now, Gary, I believe your typewriter's through there somewhere . . . I'll call you when the dinner's ready.'

As she watched his strained features soften into a smile, Nicola felt something of the old heart-jolt. Maybe it's not too late, she thought. She kept the best bit of news for bedtime. Then she'd tell Gary she was going to work only four days a week for more pay.

'You work so very hard you fit five days into four anyway . . . and how about a payrise?' her boss had said. But as an ever-cautious Capricorn, Nicola decided she would keep that information to herself just for now, and let Gary believe she had fought for the time off. 'We need all the help we can get,' she thought. 'But we'll make it.' And they did.

Case history of a Capricorn man and Virgo woman, star-blessed lovers

Graham scowled at his reflection in the steamy bathroom mirror, and wondered if he'd ever get his hair to sit right. Its unruly curliness had always offended his practical, organised Capricorn soul. 'Oh well,' he sighed, 'Sandy likes it and that's the main thing.' His reflection smiled back at him the grin of pure delight that always came when he thought of Sandy, his girlfriend of two years and soon, he hoped, his fiancée.

'But is it too soon to ask her to marry me?' he wondered, going over and over the subject as he had for months – almost, in fact, since he and Sandy had met, at a mutual friend's 21st birthday party. From the moment their eyes met over a plate of garlic bread, Graham had felt there was something special about Sandra, or Sandy as she preferred to be called.

Born a Virgo, her practical nature matched his own so well. She never mocked his check-the-facts approach to life, but seemed to appreciate the loyalty and true devotion he offered – matched with his hard-work ambitions. Both were reserved, quiet in company, but liked nothing more than a good laugh. It was great to discover gradually that they shared the same taste in films and comedy. And even more wonderful months later, once both had realised this love was for keeps, to unhurriedly discover the hidden secrets and delights of each other's bodies.

'Mind you, it was no thanks to me we even got that far,' thought Graham now, almost blushing as he remembered how difficult he'd found it to push Capricorn caution aside long enough to simply ask Sandy out. Despite being given all the encouragement a girl could decently manage, at the end of that party Graham's head had still been debating asking her for a date. Then he looked round and found she was gone.

Travelling home alone on the bus, Graham was kicking himself for missing his chance. Then he found a folded piece of paper in his pocket, and he pulled it out. In very neat handwriting it read: 'Play-safe Virgos don't normally do things like this, but I reckon this time it's worth the risk. If you'd like to see me sometime, here's my phone number . . . Sandy.'

Just realising what it must have cost her to put her heart on the line like that touched something deep inside Graham. As soon as he got home, he dialled Sandy's number, and the relationship that was to become the best thing in his life began.

'The best thing in my life – so why am I so scared to make it permanent?' Graham asked himself. Not like the friends of Sandy's whose wedding he was now dressing up to go to. This wedding had really been a spur-of-the-moment thing, with the invitation arriving at Sandy's flat just a week before the big day. 'Oh, they're like that, impulsive ... you know, romantic,' Sandy had said when she told him about it. 'That's why you've never met them, they went off travelling abroad when we all left school, and they've only just arrived back in Britain.'

In her precise, caring Virgo way, Sandy had told him exactly what he was to wear to the register office ceremony. 'Wear your dark-blue suit, white shirt and that lovely silvery tie,' she said. 'I'll take care of the flowers for your button-hole when I get mine. And Graham, do go easy on the Brylcreem, your curls really are nice.'

Graham tried to avert his eyes from those dreaded curls now as he gave his finished look the once-over in the mirror. As ever, ready a good 15 minutes before he needed to be, he sat down to read the paper. But his mind was buzzing.

'Would we ever get married on the spur of the moment like this couple?' he thought idly. 'No chance! Sandy's loving, caring, sexy and the most wonderful woman I've ever met, but impulsive she certainly isn't. No – our wedding, if, I mean when, it happens, will probably involve months of meticulous planning.' He realised with a start that he was feeling quite wistful. 'We're not surprise sort of people really, I suppose. Could that be the one thing missing in our relationship?'

By the time the taxi driver rang the doorbell, Graham had made up his mind. Yes, he would ask Sandy to marry him – not tomorrow, or 'maybe next week', but tonight.

Where better than at someone else's wedding reception?

What if everybody stared at him? As long as his beloved Sandy said yes, for once he wouldn't care how silly he looked. Maybe we can have some surprises in our lives after all, Graham thought.

As the taxi pulled up outside the register office, Graham realised he was longing to see Sandy's face. They'd travelled separately because the register office was just round the corner from her flat. He scanned the crowd waiting outside, but there was no sign of her.

As Graham looked, however, he was surprised. 'Steve – I didn't know you knew this couple too!' he said, slapping his brother on the back, 'Oh, quite well, really,' said Steve with a grin. 'And so do Mum and Dad,' he went on. Graham was surprised again at the sight of his parents, looking so dressed up.

'But have you seen the bride? She's really something special.' Steve steered Graham towards a slight figure in a white dress, her hair a mass of tiny flowers. As she turned, looked deep into his eyes and smiled hesitantly, Graham thought he had never seen Sandy look so beautiful.

So much for no surprises in our lives, he thought, trying in vain to maintain his Capricorn calm as the pieces of the puzzle fell into place. 'Sandy has organised this surprise wedding for me, because she really does want to marry me – I don't even have to ask,' he thought. 'But I'm going to!'

'Sandy, will you marry me?' Graham whispered. 'Yes,' she replied, 'as long as it's in the next five minutes. I'm not giving you a chance to change your mind.' Hand in hand, they walked into their wedding.

Aquarius in Love

THE WONDERFUL YOU

Freedom is the key feature in Aquarius love relationships. Naturally independent and never clingy, you give lovers all the room they need to grow and develop, and expect the same privileges, and respect, in return. The most routine day can be turned into an adventure, with your constantly new ideas, your unconventional, occasionally bizarre, view of life. Aquarius loving is like a current of cool, fresh air that leaves even the most jaded nerve endings tingling.

You're rarely jealous or possessive and seek a true relationship of equals, with both sides of a couple making decisions and sharing home responsibilities. It may be a dream that doesn't often come true, but that does nothing to dampen your star-sent enthusiasm.

You're honest, almost to a fault, and have the sort of imagination that makes you whisk a partner off to the coast in the middle of the night (by motorbike) or plan a cosy supper for the two of you on a roundabout in the middle of a town bypass. If Aquarius is feeling romantic, anything, anywhere and any time goes. Although your own feelings are often discreetly concealed, you have a natural knack for wheedling others' intimate secrets out of them, and so make a superb listener – what lover can resist that?

You're quick to compliment and slow to judge, an unselfish daydream believer who wants to save the world and believes passionately in countless good causes. Aquarius goes to the limit, and sometimes an interesting bit further, to be fair and broad-minded in any situation, and your unshockable nature puts all sorts of saucy experiments on the love menu.

Although you're anything but vain, and rarely deliberately set out to attract the opposite sex, there's a magical mystery about you that's irresistible on first meeting, and just gets more addictive. In classic air sign style, mental attraction is just as vital to you as physical – sensational sex starts in your brain, not your body.

THE WICKED YOU

Too much thinking, too much restlessness, and too little doing, touching and feeling – that is the Aquarius love weakness. Brain can boss body to such an extent that emotional reactions are out of the question. You often find it much easier, and safer, to give your loving care to a charity rather than to a love-hungry partner. True intimacy and commitment in a one-to-one relationship are tricky when you take such pride in making sure no-one ever knows your secret self. You sometimes even keep your vulnerable feelings secret from yourself. Control is your catchword, and it may take Aquarius years to realise it's one that is an ill-fitting match for the heart.

The casual detachment from life that keeps others at arm's length can also put true love out of your reach, unless you're prepared to take a deep breath and dive right in. You must accept that you can't always stand aside calmly pulling everyone else's strings like an all-powerful puppet master.

Almost obsessive self-sufficiency means that even when Aquarius wants to share problems or fears with someone else, you simply don't know how – and both partners and pals tend to drift away because they're convinced you don't need them.

All too often, Aquarius spends life dreaming of perfect passion, then stopping short, paralysed by fear, whenever that fantasy love becomes even a vague reality. This also makes you prone to sudden infatuations with sexy strangers, trampling underfoot long-term relationships that suddenly seem deadly dull.

The need for change and new challenges is central to every Aquarius character. Swopping new love for old every time you feel like it may be the 'free' and 'equal' thing to do. But if you never let love get beyond the superficial level, never allow a lover to see the needing, trusting, worrying soul so carefully concealed under that casual, carefree surface – then your love dreams may turn into a nightmare of wasted opportunities.

BEING YOUR AQUARIUS BEST

To start a true two-way love communication, Aquarius must stretch that star-given imagination even further and try to put yourself in a lover's place – to see how your inborn independence could look like indifference, and your need for control like life manipulation. Yes, these are part of what makes you unique, but perhaps you could settle for feeling just a little more ordinary, and a little less lonely.

If logic has ousted lust in your lovelife, it's time to do first, and deliberate later. When your brain starts sending out those 'getting too close', 'getting too dependent' alarm signals, use manual override by giving your partner a huge hug. Yes, the depth of feelings and emotions you miss are all there, you've just mislaid the combination for unlocking them. Plenty of one-to-one talking, really revealing your feelings rather than skating around them, and admitting your weaknesses as well as your strengths, are all different shots that lead to the same goal, your long-term security and happiness.

Too much intimacy leaves you feeling decidedly uncomfortable, so you shy away from it – then yearn for what you're missing. At times you do want to show your secret, vulnerable side to a lover, to get some real support. But you fear that, if you do, the prison door will slam shut behind you and you'll never be able to escape. The answer, again, is not to think about it – just do it. And your flexible Aquarius brain will find ways to cope.

If love is to last, it's vital to recognise your weak spots as well as your strengths, so that a sudden stab of lust for an attractive stranger won't lead to love destruction. Since your best affairs are dreamt up in your head, anyway, why not keep this person as a fantasy lover and enjoy a mental fling with them – and let your partner reap the benefits of the outrageous sex adventures it sparks. So body and brain can work together, instead of against each other all the time.

As an Aquarius you also need to learn to let others help you, as well as helping them. You really can't solve every problem on your own. Avoid channelling too much energy into overwork, picking arguments just to demonstrate your superior brain power, and separating sex from love, and you will achieve the true equality that's your ideal. And you deserve it.

AQUARIUS SEXY SECRETS

Boundless mental and physical energy plus a wacky, off-beat way of looking at the world make Aquarius one of the most adventurous of lovers – countless surprises between the sheets put bedmates devotedly under your spell forever. A fantasy night for you would be filled with both mystery and challenges – beginning with food you've never tried before, perhaps fed to you blindfold so you can guess what it is, followed by a trip to a planetarium to tune into the wider powers of the universe. Or even just a romantic walk in the open air to gaze at the stars together.

To turn on your mind, as well as body, you adore bedtime stories full of sexy promises. Or try a game of Truth or Dare to help you flick off that switch marked 'Control' – taking it in turns to reveal secrets, thoughts and feelings, with delicious forfeits.

A deep bath spiked with musk oil helps the senses sharpen, and switches off the mind. Slipperiness of soap in places that feel so good. Soft strokes with a nail brush then more harshly so skin tingles. A shower spray reaching everywhere, soft towels, total warm excitement. The main love feast starts with delicate tongue flicks, at first barely touching, and the most teasing of kisses along the back of your calves send electric passion signals to your brain.

It is important for you to switch to a passive role sometimes and take a share of pleasure rather than always trying to be in the driving seat. Truly sensational sex involves taking, as well as giving, letting yourself take centre stage rather than simply directing or spectating.

With few inhibitions and a fascination for all things new, Aquarius can be an extra-experimental lover keen to take on any challenge.

Yet, however sensational the sex, unless it can be combined with love you'll never feel truly satisfied. Take time in your life for warm hugs, kissing and hair-stroking sessions that don't lead to sex but encourage trust and intimacy to grow. Make a deal with a partner that one night you'll stop yourself making moves and be on the receiving end instead. Soon you'll see that all the adventure and variety Aquarius craves can come from the same relationship that gives you security and love. Relax and you can have it all.

WOOING AND WINNING AQUARIUS

Where will you, as an Aquarius, meet your match? First choice is somewhere exotic, as you are a skilful holiday romancer, or you might land a lover at a foreign film or ethnic music concert. Super-sociable Aquarius could also run into romance at a fancy-dress party or even on TV's 'Blind Date'. Swept away by your natural charm and zany style, lovers won't know what's hit them – but if jealousy or possessiveness seeps from a partner, then you'll be off.

The perfect lover for Aquarius has a difficult job, giving you both the devotion and attention you demand, plus unlimited freedom. You need someone secure enough to give you all the personal space you need, which could include living apart, or sleeping apart when you need privacy and time to think. Your lover should be physically open, warm and loving enough to conquer your Aquarius tendency towards emotional detachment.

You must have a partner who is a true believer in equality. There are no set male-female roles in an Aquarius household. Honest, unselfish and energetic, with a willingness to drop everything and chase rainbows with you, your partner should balance your often wild ways with a pair of feet planted firmly on the ground.

He, or she, must take time to coax confessions and secret vulnerability out of you and give you the confidence to invest in a one-to-one relationship instead of constantly looking around for new conquests. You need to be lovingly cocooned in passion layers that are elastic enough to stretch with, not against, you. Given freedom, fantasy lovemaking and help to find your own soft centre, Aquarius can be the most stimulating and satisfying of partners – with a built-in anti-boredom alarm.

LOVE MATCH

How Aquarius combines with each of the 12 sun signs

Aquarius with Aquarius

It's no-holds-barred bedtime romps with this pair of variety-loving pals who never run out of outrageous ideas and passion challenges. At first, you share a natural lack of jealousy and love of freedom that means angry scenes are rare. But what starts as a plus often becomes a minus and both may be too detached to bother whether love lasts or not, too unrealistic to believe relationships involve effort. And it may become more difficult to give a partner the freedom you take for yourself.

But this relationship could be a world-beater if only both sides concentrate on less talking, more touching, less mental, more physical, and really let each other into both lives and hearts. New places and new people will attract you both – try visiting them together.

Aquarius with Pisces

Toughness meets tenderness, zingy meets clingy. At first you, as an Aquarius, may bask in the glow of Pisces' absolute devotion and those clever please-you ways, and adore the romantic dreams you conjure up together. All too soon the more vulnerable Pisces demands start grating. Pisces wants constant togetherness, Aquarius needs time alone. Pisces always wants love to rule, but Aquarius often puts friendship in first place. And trusting Pisces' heart is an open book that careless Aquarius often rips up page by page. Then Pisces may tire of the tempest of such a changeable life.

Yet this could be such a good relationship if Aquarius tries to see life, and love, from a partner's point of view some of the time, and puts independence on hold. Try a little tenderness – you'll like it.

Aquarius with Aries

A double dose of independence, vitality and excitement makes for constant thrills and occasional spills. Both free-thinking, and perhaps too free-spending, Aries and Aquarius only fight over who's in line for the latest challenge, and who should be in charge – you both naturally assume this right. And when this competition spills over into the bedroom, nerve tingling times are guaranteed.

Yet though starred for success, this pairing can run into problems when so physical Aries wishes Aquarius could be more demonstrative, perhaps more sincere. But honest one-to-one talking can cure it as Aquarius dares to let emotions out of the secure box you lock them in, and Aries takes off those bossy boots. Just don't let complacency snuggle down between you in bed.

Aquarius with Taurus

Unstoppable force meets immoveable object when Aquarius' energy and drive for change clang up against Taurus' stubborn love of personal, dependable home comforts. Sex can be a passion feast of bodies – but reaching the brain is trickier.

For a while Aquarius will be charmed by steadfast and sensual Taurus' down-to-earth loving. But once the Taurus love of people-ownership shows itself and the love scissors come out to clip Aquarius' wings and optimistic cash habits, this relationship can prove dangerously unstable. Yet it can work with a real effort from Aquarius to stump up the security Taurus needs to thrive, although you can find this difficult because you will have to cut away all the pretence that safety-nets your own emotions. In return Taurus will take your side forever.

Aquarius with Gemini

Perfect passion partners who both treasure freedom and the fantasy lovemaking you share. This is a livewire love affair constantly crackling with new ideas and adventures – sex between you is never the same twice. Thinking so alike, you find the way through the maze of each other's personalities that can leave other signs baffled. Aquarius and Gemini form an exclusive club of soul mates against the rest of the world, while less lucky lovers can only look on in envy.

Complete trust makes faithful forever, stay together promises unnecessary. Both are irresistible to others but have sparkling eyes only for each other. An intriguing and inspiring match, your only problems come if friendship and shared work ambitions push passion out of the relationship, and if Aquarius edges too far ahead in making the decisions.

Aquarius with Cancer

Starts with smiles all round as Cancer's caring ways soothe Aquarius' restless spirit and start to build a cosy love nest for a shared future. Lovemaking is tender and true, sweetened by Cancer's at-first unconditional admiration. But one day Aquarius wakes up and realises that casually given promises have become shackles, and that Cancer's blanket of adoring love is starting to suffocate. Jealous scenes flare and once-flaming passion gets drowned in a deluge of bitter tears.

Yet this love can be a winner if there is compromise and commitment on both sides. There will have to be real Aquarius effort to conquer your own hidden doubts about your ability to truly love, and matching worries about rejection. Cancer will need to ration emotional moodswings that can turn Aquarius to ice. The reward is a partnership that never stops surprising both of you.

Aquarius with Leo

Surrounded by people, parties and passion, this union of two socially skilled sun signs can be dazzling in public – even more so in private. From opposite signs of the zodiac circle, Leo and Aquarius find each other an irresistible challenge, so different yet in some, not always good ways, so alike. Seeing your own selfishness mirrored in a partner is extra aggravating. But it's a fine line between spirited disagreements, interesting challenges and damaging rows, and it's a line this sizzling relationship soon crosses.

A few fights are inevitable in a partnership where both sides, with double-strength willpower, want to keep their finger on the power switch, and playing a supporting role simply isn't an option. Take turns at leading to keep love alive, lose a little of your self-importance, and you will be rewarded with a relationship that goes the distance and never gets dull.

Aquarius with Virgo

Virgo's cool charm and secret sex power intrigue Aquarius, and uninhibited bedtimes boost the total love score. And both of you think your way through life. But one big minus is Virgo's constant criticism and efforts to cage and rewire Aquarius' free-thinking mind. Then out comes Aquarius' tough, almost brutal honesty to crush Virgo's already eggshell-thin trust. True understanding and happiness can only come from more consideration on both sides.

If you, as Aquarius, can accept that criticism is sometimes deserved, and tread neatly around Virgo's so-sensitive feelings, and Virgo resists the temptation to inform you about all your flaws in fine detail, this romance can grow into a real understanding.

Aquarius with Libra

Laughter and loving bubble together in a heady brew that just gets stronger as time passes and makes both of you feel good, inside and out. With a shared view of life, Aquarius and Libra appreciate each other's strengths, are blissfully able to ignore each other's weaknesses, and uncover hidden layers of caring, commitment and fun. Built on a base of honesty and true friendship, this romance binds its two hearts together forever, yet lets each soar free towards new personal goals.

Both passionately believe in equality and keeping love fresh – the stuff from which happy-ever-after fairytales could be made. There is a shadow, though, over your sex life. Too much understanding can take the fire out of passion, but if you key this fact into your Aquarius imagination, then it shouldn't.

Aquarius with Scorpio

What draws light-loving Aquarius towards the mysterious dark depths of Scorpio? The excitement of exploring the unknown, the fascination of someone so very different, the powerful passion spell that Scorpio, sexiest of all signs, puts on inquisitive Aquarius. Meanwhile, Scorpio is able to tune into the depth of your feelings more easily than you can – with your Aquarius preference for staying on the surface.

But time can erase all this magic, and all that's left is Scorpio's intense moods, murky jealousy and driven determination to lock Aquarius' love away from the rest of the world. Rows are inevitable unless Aquarius can agree to some of Scorpio's 'act serious' rules, and really believe it's better to make up than break up. And for lifetime love

Scorpio will have to ration those skilful emotional games and replace jealousy with trust.

Aquarius with Sagittarius

It's fun on the run for this adventure-loving duo, and never a dull moment. Neither is known for tact, though, so this will never be too comfortable a pairing, and rollicking rows followed by making up and making love is the likely passion pattern. So it's lucky both thrive on it. 'Free and easy does it' is the love motto for Aquarius and Sagittarius, and each finds in the other the perfect travelling companion for a life-long voyage of discovery.

The only problems come if either tries to tame the other's independence, while, of course, hanging on to your own. And too many outside interests might gradually pull you apart. Avoid this and you'll be set for a lifetime of truly compatible love.

Aquarius with Capricorn

Supersteady Capricorn provides secretly sought-after stability and a reliable base in Aquarius' rather footloose life. And in return Aquarius lights up cobwebby corners of Capricorn's heart and shows how much fun falling in love can be. If only romance could stay that simple.

As early excitement starts to cool, Capricorn may carp on about commitment while Aquarius plots an easy escape route. The whole shaky structure could collapse. Yet it can work with understanding on both sides and a permanent promise from Aquarius to try to see things – some of the time – through Capricorn's more serious eyes and heart. In return Capricorn mustn't complain too much about Aquarius' more frequent time away from home. A bit of an odd couple who can triumph.

LIVING LOVE

Case history of an Aquarius man and Scorpio woman, star-crossed lovers

Neil woke at dawn. His eyes slowly opened and focused on the empty space on the pillow where Ginny's dark head should have been. He felt as if a tub of ice water had been poured over his head. Where was she?

As he struggled into his dressing gown, Ginny's words of the night before echoed in Neil's ears. 'You're so self-contained, so above it all,' she yelled, half-sobbing. 'You don't need me, you don't need anyone. I don't think you care if I live or die.'

'Ginny – no!' Neil had shouted, almost tripping as he followed her down the narrow stairs three at a time. She wouldn't have done anything stupid, would she? They'd been having so many violent rows recently, and although last night they'd 'made up' as usual by making frenzied love, the faraway look in her normally intense Scorpio eyes should have set alarm bells ringing in his head.

'But what did I do? I turned over and went to sleep. A perfect example of Aquarius indifference,' Neil thought angrily.

The extremes of emotions he felt came as a revelation to Neil. It helped him realise just how out of touch he was with his own feelings – and Ginny's, of course.

He was forced to admit that, time after time, she tried to bring up the subject of their two-year-old marriage, only to have him brush it aside like a troublesome buzzing fly. 'Not now, darling, I must finish this Open University essay,' he'd say. Or 'Why do you have to go on about feelings all the time? We're electric in bed, aren't we, so how can there be anything wrong?'

Perhaps that was just the problem – sex between him and Ginny had always been effortlessly ecstatic. And that hadn't changed even when rows were relentlessly ripping apart the rest of their shared life. So he fooled himself everything was okay, but not Ginny. She knew bodies couldn't do the sort of talking they needed – and she couldn't do it on her own, either.

Starved of communication and of the total commitment her loyal Scorpio soul needed (Neil had never let her feel too secure, 'just to keep her on her toes'), his once vibrant wife had shrivelled away before his eyes. And now, what had she done, had she hurt herself – or worse?

Sitting in the tiny kitchen, Neil thought of Ginny's fierce way of defending him if anyone spoke against him. Just five feet tall, she really would take on the world to save him. She loved – or at least had loved – him with an intensity his Aquarius self found quite frightening. She gave herself to him, body and soul, while he always held something back, a kind of marriage insurance policy. To start with, he was sure, Ginny hadn't noticed, but gradually, as the months went by, the jealousy and angry scenes had started.

The more she accused him of being too detached and uncaring, the more he withdrew and turned that bland smile on her which he knew infuriated her. Then the tears would come, and then the lovemaking.

'Did I really believe it made everything all right?' Neil wondered, slumping at the kitchen table. Ginny wasn't in the house, and hadn't left a note. Now worry gnawed away at his brain. What had happened to her? Suddenly the door swung open and there was Ginny – or was it?

Neil had to look twice before he recognised his wife. Her long dark hair was gone – in its place a bleached white crop cut that really suited her. She was wearing colours, dark red and orange, that Neil had never seen on her before. And she looked stunning.

'Right Neil,' Ginny said. 'Let's get down to business.' Her brisk, matter-of-fact tone was something he hadn't experienced before either. But, still reeling from the shock, it was her next words that really took Neil's breath away. 'Neil,' Ginny said, 'we've just been divorced. Our marriage wasn't working, never had, never would. So I hereby grant us a temporary divorce . . .'

Neil felt the room spin, this was all going far too fast. He didn't want a divorce, or did he? Suddenly he made sense of the rest of Ginny's speech, which was obviously well rehearsed.

'We can call it a day, or we can start from scratch and actually deal with all the problems we know we'll come up against, rather than running away from them (in your case) or getting in a state about them (in mine). Then if we feel we really do have a future together, well, we can undo our theoretical divorce and get married again. What do you say?'

Neil felt his head nod weakly. 'Oh and Neil, just one more thing . . .' added Ginny. 'No sex. At least not until we see whether we can make a go of things without it.' From that day on, Neil and Ginny began really getting to know and understand each other and making some of the compromises necessary to end the deadlock between them.

Neil was less detached and showed his feelings more to Ginny. She put her possessiveness on hold and tried her very best to control her deep, dark moods. Doing without sex was difficult, to begin with, but without that physical means of communication they had no choice but to talk. It was a real old-fashioned courtship with, underneath, the promise of heady delights ahead.

One evening, after a walk in the woods and shared sensual massage before a roaring log fire, they made love again, tenderly and with true love. 'Does that mean we're married again?' Neil asked eagerly afterwards, forgetting his Aquarius cool. 'Maybe,' smiled Ginny. 'We'll see.'

Case history of an Aquarius woman and Gemini man, star-blessed lovers

Joan collapsed giggling into the rickety canvas chair and exchanged a huge wink with her best friend Maggie – behind the back of the handsome man who'd just escorted her off the dance floor. 'Not bad looking,' Maggie mouthed at her, and Joan smiled back. 'Thanks so much,' she said breathlessly to the man, who she seemed to remember had told her his name was Jim. It was so difficult to hear anything with the music so loud.

'Jim' certainly wasn't bad looking. 'Once upon a time I'd have eaten him alive!' thought Joan in typical frank, Aquarius style as he walked off. 'But that was B.A. – Before Al. Now I've got him, what more could a girl ask for or need?' She scanned the crowded dance floor looking for that familiar tall figure. There! Al was standing diagonally across the room, deep in conversation with a woman sporting a startlingly revealing cleavage.

'Give a flirty Gemini an inch . . .' thought Joan to herself, smiling. Without a jealous bone in her body, in fact she was proud so many other women obviously found her Al charming and attractive – and she knew he felt the same way about her. Every week they came to the dance together, spent a couple of hours flirting and dancing with other people, then linked arms and went home together. It was just one aspect of their rather off-beat life together that astounded and even horrified some of their rather more conservative friends.

For a start, there was their stubborn refusal to live together. Both were so fiercely protective of their privacy and independence that they kept their separate homes and interests, and really couldn't imagine living any other way. 'Aren't you worried what Al gets up to when you're not around?' Maggie had asked Joan, who simply smiled serenely and said, 'If he wanted to get up to anything, wouldn't he do it whether I was there or not?'

Joan had no time for all the petty squabbles that seemed to haunt her friends' relationships – she and Al had been through that once already, thank you, in their first marriages, and once was enough.

Compared to her ex-husband, Al was a dream – none of that demanding to know where she'd been and who with, trying to tie her down to a drudge of domestic chores and damp down the independence she cherished. 'Can't imagine my ex waving me off alone on a walking holiday in Wales,'

Joan thought, 'or buying me a parachute jump for my birthday.'

She could still remember how thrilled she'd been by that gift, especially since she knew Al didn't have that much money to manage on. For his last birthday, thinking of that inborn Gemini vanity, she'd saved up to get Al a facial, massage and makeover at a local beauty salon. Always keen to try something new, he'd loved the experience. 'My ex would have had a seizure,' Joan giggled.

Joan and Al hadn't met in the most glamorous of circumstances. She was at the bus stop struggling with one supermarket carrier-bag too many, when he'd pulled up on his motorbike and offered her a lift. Needless to say, Joan jumped at the chance. When they got home Al came in for a cup of hot water (Joan did keep meaning to buy some more teabags, but kept forgetting) and they had seen each other almost every day since.

Joan wondered what she liked best about their relationship. 'It's easy,' she thought. 'We both like to try new things, to meet new people. We don't want to be tied down too much, but just enough. We never know what's going to happen next. We make each other laugh.'

Sometimes she really couldn't believe her luck. Mind you, it hadn't been roses all the way in the five years she and Al had been together. First of all they had to sort out the fact that they really were together. Although it was obvious, neither wanted to be first to admit it in the early days. Then there was the disastrous attempt at living together permanently that left both of them feeling awkward and resentful.

'I suppose we'd become too set in our ways. Maybe it would have worked if we'd given it more time,' Joan thought now. 'But thank goodness I didn't give up my own flat at the time. Love may be blind, but not that blind.' And anyway, she thought to herself with a grin, it was quite an adventure to take a change of clothes with her in her luckily huge handbag, just in case she landed up spending the night at Al's.

That was the thing that had scandalised her family – that she openly spent the night at Al's flat. Honestly, in this day and age, how could people be so old-fashioned? It was only now, after all these years, that they'd really come to terms with the relationship and more or less accepted it. Joan knew her family called them 'The Odd Couple' in secret – how Al had laughed when she told him about it.

Coming to with a start, she realised the music had stopped and fellow dancers were milling around in search of handbags and coats. Joan looked across the room and saw Al taking his leave of Miss Substantial Cleavage – kissing her hand, the cheeky thing. Then suddenly he was beside her, helping her into her coat.

'My place or yours?' Al whispered in her ear, and Joan felt her heart sing with happiness. She looked straight into his sparkling eyes, not noticing the wrinkles and grey hair that framed them. 'Yours,' she said decisively and, tenderly linking arms, they strolled off together – a 75-year-old 'Odd Couple' whose star-sent love would keep them forever young.

Pisces in Love

THE WONDERFUL YOU

Like a dark lake whose depths are carved too deep to reach, natural romantic Pisces has all the mystery, and more, a lover could desire. The way you can read a partner's every passion thought or feeling is further proof of your endless love potential, when you find the right, tender, sensitive partner.

Pisces is in love with love, and it shows. You adore the intrigue and excitement of that first meeting, the will-we, won't-we time when two hearts hang deliciously in the balance. You may even try to spin out this stage to make it last as long as possible, but few lovers subjected to your irresistible brand of temptation will complain.

Slowly, surely, you spin a web of devotion so gossamer-fine no lover can feel it, yet it can keep a lover by your side forever because you are one of the cleverest of secret manipulators. Pisces needs to be needed, and likes nothing better than dreaming up countless tiny ways to show that someone special your love is real, and irreplaceable.

You're the most generous of partners, much preferring to give rather than take, and you'd follow your chosen one anywhere, whether to a research station at the South Pole, or plunging into all sorts of outrageous bedtime adventures.

You're intense and serious, infatuated with all the dreams and drama of love affairs – and there is no shortage of willing contenders lining up. You'll suffer any amount of worries and woes in secret rather than see a loved-one hurt or scared. And you do thrive on looking after, and protecting, other people. You are supersensitive enough to coax out feelings others never knew they had. A specialist in romance – red roses, love poems, soft lights are just the beginning – Pisces passion is fantasy made flesh as only you know how.

THE WICKED YOU

So bound up, body and soul, in your idealised view of love, Pisces can catapult straight into disastrous infatuations and only get out with a heart badly bruised. You hoist a would-be partner on to a pedestal even when it's far from what that partner wants. You see your chosen one as the sexiest, most sincere lover who ever loved – but who could live up to that?

You forgive every fault, excuse every excess, until you almost force a partner to trample all over you, treating you like the doormat you've transformed yourself into. Then, one day, your rose-coloured specs come sliding off and all you can do is wail.

An easy target for a sexy yet insincere smile, you fall for disastrously unsuitable mates. Often love is less an attraction, more an addiction that makes you so good at deceiving yourself. And you can easily keep several of your hopeless passions running at the same time. Deep down you can be desperate for emotional support and reassurance, but too scared to ask for what you want. Your love tactics of winning by giving can be such a blinding obsession you forget how to take. What starts as a supportive love can run riot and become a suffocating clinging vine that tempts panicky lovers to cut free – and fast.

Broody and moody, so-intense Pisces can lack a sense of humour and the essential ability to, sometimes, laugh at life and love. It can't be Hollywood-style heavy breathing and bodice-ripping 24 hours a day. You can run a mile from a true partnership of equals, preferring instead to be a victim or a saviour on a hopeless mission to turn a bad relationship good. Yet even when you manage that, your darker side will be constantly chucking negative thoughts into your conscience. You are too good at reading 'hidden meanings' into an innocent remark and throwing jealous jabs. Your love suspicions may create a state of anxiety and misery.

BEING YOUR PISCES BEST

Forcing yourself to apply the passion brakes and not go revving wildly into every romance chance will help prevent that susceptible Pisces heart being left scarred and scared. Removing those rose-coloured glasses before, rather than after, an affair starts is highly recommended.

Try to let lovers be human, faults and all, rather than the cross between gods and Gone With The Wind characters your fantasy-mad mind fluffs up – and then just as suddenly deflates.

You really can't love others until you love yourself enough to stop secretly expecting things to go wrong. Tell yourself that you deserve good loving and you'll find the love confidence you so long for. Give yourself credit for your own ideas and achievements, make decisions for yourself. You may let people boss you around because you think that somehow it will make you more lovable. But if you get in touch with your natural Pisces strength and courage, which is a real part of your fascinating multiple personality, a lover will be even more intrigued.

Next step is to stop making love, and your lover, the be-all and end-all of your life. Find other projects to lavish your caring devotion on, and see how much easier it is to get love into focus when you're no longer hooked on it.

Yes, you can ask for what you want, both in and out of bed, but that doesn't guarantee you'll get it. For Pisces' next lesson to learn is that nothing in love is ever certain – and no amount of fretting and clever scheming could make it so.

Commitment can often leave Pisces confused. You give unconditional love, or at least you believe that you do, but can't quite seem to crack the happy-ever-after code. That's because a relationship requires both give and take – let it be too lop-sided and it'll flip right over. Put yourself on your partner's throne and you'll see how being worshipped can be a genuine burden, because it means that you have to be strong and perfect all the time.

You do have so much magical inner love energy, yet it can only be truly released when you take life less seriously. Stop brooding long enough to let your heart lift, and those lifelong love barriers will go down too, letting in the true love you need, for yourself and others.

PISCES SEXY SECRETS

The wonder ingredient in any Pisces passion potion is water, because its fluid, mysterious depths remind you of your inner self and it immediately washes away most of your inhibitions. Making love by, or in, the sea as warm waves lap lazily over your body is a Pisces love dream. Or, in cooler climates, a weekend in a seaside hotel, while the breakers crash against the rocks outside. Back home, you can always play a recording of the sea. A water bed or shared jacuzzi are also prime ingredients in your pleasure plans.

Sharing a shower with your lover, enjoying all the soft slipperiness of the soap, the fierce pressure of the water at full flow as it hits the skin, sets up pulses of pleasure. Then spend time on Pisces' sex centre – the feet – with fingers making firm circles on the sole, while the thumb gently presses the bones on top. Soon darts of exquisite pleasure will be shooting all over your completely relaxed body. Relaxation is the key to total Pisces ecstasy, and something that can never be achieved unless you give yourself the right to take pleasure as well as give it – without being gunned down by feelings of guilt.

As desire grows, fingers skim the whole body, the curve of the ankle, the soft skin of inner thighs, the opulence of body flesh, supersensitive inner arms, tongue-printing tiny circles everywhere. Kisses that start gently then turn greedy . . .

You also like erotic pictures and films, especially if you sit at opposite ends of the room and slap a ban on any kissing or touching until it's over – then you can't wait to get hold of each other.

Intrigue and mystery also turn Pisces on. You adore a sexy 'treasure hunt', with little clues left all around the house telling you to take off certain items of clothing or collect certain sex toys.

But while Pisces is pleased to experiment and rarely says no to any new games, do please beware of saying yes when you really want to say no. Fragile Pisces pride is easily humiliated, and if things don't work out as you want, or hope, you'll heap all the guilt on your own heart and let it hinder your passion progress. Take sex, like life, one step at a time, and look on the lighter side when you get the chance. More than other signs, you need to sleep in the same bed as your partner – the unconscious entwining of bodies is all part of your personal security system.

WOOING AND WINNING PISCES

A Pisces not surrounded by love is a fish out of water, so you need a partner who is prepared, like you, to make passion a priority – and, unlike you, to keep it in perspective. Your partner should be strong and sure, not likely to run a mile the more you need to lean, and able to accept your devoted love without trying to get too much control over you. Your Mr or Ms Right needs to be secure enough inside to help you establish your own store of self-esteem, and resist jealous outbursts when your often wandering eye strays towards a sexy outsider.

You'll meet at the cinema, the theatre, on or near a dance floor, or at the swimming pool. For Pisces love to last, partners must make sure you see them as they really are, not through eyes clouded by a haze of desire. So honesty, and self-knowledge, are added to the list of Pisces must-haves. Other partner plus points are a sense of humour, to help you lighten up, a flair for unusual surprises – the more romantic the better – and the maturity to refuse to rush things, however hard Pisces pushes.

Lack of bedtime inhibitions and a willingness to take the lead when the lights go out are also essential – passionate

Pisces will follow eagerly anywhere, anyhow, but it's perhaps expecting too much of your shy self to ask you to lead the way, until, of course, you've got your confidence.

You need someone who can show you the difference between infatuation and commitment, that reality, though at first tricky for you to see, can often be better and longer lasting than fantasy, someone who can show how much you're needed and nix those negative emotions that can make life seem so lacklustre. Then, as a Pisces, you will be able to live up to your potential as a lover who offers intense passion and healing compassion.

LOVE MATCH

How Pisces combines with each of the 12 sun signs

Pisces with Pisces

A merging of two romantic souls can be one of deep sensuality as you read each other's desires and have the surest touch in making those desires body-real. But you have a helping of emotions that is enough for at least six, and can generate such a thick steam of jealousy that you lose sight of each other.

You are good at reading each other's minds, not always such a good thing when one of you has the doubts that come into any relationship. And, because you both idealise each other and your relationship, the standards you set can be far too high. Yet this can be a terrific partnership if you both decide, having got over your mutual indecisiveness, to take life and love just a shade more lightly and make sure to keep up outside interests to stop your involvement with each other getting too intense and addictive.

Pisces with Aries

A match that can work well, although outsiders may wonder why. Pisces' apparently undemanding devotion is just the brand of loving Aries longs for, and the perfect boost for that big Aries ego. In return, Pisces is allowed to lean on sturdy Aries to your heart's content – and revels in handing over total responsibility for life and love. But for Aries, control may feel like it's too easily won, and it's a short step for Pisces from devotion to doormat. As Aries becomes more domineering and tender Pisces is too easily wounded, Aries could start to look for a more challenging romance. But it can be rescued if Pisces learns independence, self-sufficiency, and refuses to put up with hurtful actions. Then your Pisces mystery can keep Aries happily wondering if you will ever stop slipping just out of reach.

Pisces with Taurus

Taurus offers home-loving security, and calm certainty, like a strong, safe rock in the, at times, stormy ocean that is Pisces' life. This warmly understanding couple share true trust and the tender promise that neither will ever inflict hurt on purpose. Bedtimes are a blur of slow, sensual movement, and lovemaking can stay a strong part of the relationship forever. Pisces' imagination finds the Taurus appetite for physical pleasure blissfully rewarding and takes delight in dreaming up even more daring love thrills. One dark spot is that Taurus may find changeable Pisces' moods hard to handle. Taurus likes to take a firm grip on life and Pisces' slippery mood changes, and sometimes even character changes, too, make this tricky. But, because both of you are ready to sacrifice much for your generous-hearted loving, this is one of the best of all love matches.

Pisces with Gemini

For this twosome, it can be love at first sight for a couple who instantly intrigue each other. Pisces because of the hint of sensuous hidden depths that Gemini can't resist, Gemini because of a certain sunny charm that flicks a switch in Pisces' dark heart and floods it with light and hope.

But the light could start to fade, as Pisces puts a padlock on Gemini's freedom and could push Gemini into a fast-footed getaway. Pisces could swamp the keep-it-cool Gemini with an ocean of emotion, and Gemini just doesn't like being too heavily leaned on. If Gemini practises patience, and you, Pisces, develop self-reliance and cut down on possessiveness, this can work well and teach Gemini how to share feelings.

Pisces with Cancer

A double dose of dreaming keeps this couple's feet comfortably and neatly floating off the ground. It's one of the zodiac's best love matches and can stretch from first sight to last. Pisces and Cancer combine two deep-feeling, deep-caring hearts who can't believe their luck, as Cancer wants to protect, almost like a parent would, and Pisces has someone to lean on. Sex is a shared delight as each unselfishly strives, body and soul, to give the other ultimate pleasure. You both have the same problem, though, and that's moodiness. But provided it doesn't strike you simultaneously too often, you'll be fine. For both of you understand moods, and how important it is not to cause jealousy.

Pisces with Leo

Magically drawn by Pisces' mystery and gentle but so seductive ways, Leo will give you protection and take away your fears. While you, as a Pisces, are swiftly infatuated with Leo's strength and super-sociable ways, and put Leo on a pedestal to lavish with a devotion that can hide your powerful capacity for manipulation.

Soon, though, problems can start to creep in. Pisces pines for a commitment Leo may not feel ready to make. Leo gets impatient with Pisces' moods and shows a tough-talking and unpredictable temper that may send Pisces rushing away. Five-star sex acts as cement if bricks of trust, patience and two-way tolerance are there. And it is worth it because Leo does have a tender heart – and you need that.

Pisces with Virgo

Emotion-ruled Pisces is a tonic for too-practical Virgo and helps the serious, nursemaidy sign get in touch with that hidden sexy centre, while Virgo can persuade Pisces to add a dose of reality to that dreamworld and balance your often irrational mood swings. But where tidy Virgo orders organisation, Pisces creates chaos, and soon non-stop nagging and a minefield of misunderstanding take the place of once-tender togetherness. You can feed each other's worries, too, as Pisces' moods and Virgo's nerves meet head on. And you do come from opposite sides of the zodiac circle.

Passion-packed bedtimes are the key to success here and both must try to achieve the same honest communication out of the bedroom as in it. And it's more than worth it.

Pisces with Libra

Candlelit dinners, moonlight walks, presents and promises of love forever – the brew fermented by this twosome can be so heady and intoxicating it leaves both sides high on love and wanting nothing more than each other. But you should remember that, as a Pisces, Libra can be your Fatal Attraction.

Libra is likely to get the love chills first, as Pisces' loving embrace gets uncomfortably tight and cramps that famous flirting style. Then down falls Pisces, subjected to one logical Libra remark too often, and one Libra social outing alone too many.

If you both agree to accept, and not try to change, each other this relationship can work, especially if you share the decision-making you both find difficult, but Pisces must realise that Libra's most unlikely to volunteer to play life-support machine.

Pisces with Scorpio

Strength, support and an everlasting supply of sexy ideas, Scorpio brings all these, and much more, to this magic match, and in return is treated to the unique brand of super-sensitive caring only Pisces is capable of. Scorpio feels in charge, and that's just the way both partners like it, even though Pisces knows it's really equal billing. That darker, possessive streak in Scorpio never needs to surface because Pisces' passion is so plain to see and feel. Pisces' moods are mellowed by strong Scorpio as you both are inspired by the other into a change for the better.

Matching heart-for-heart in intensity, faithfulness and sexual compatibility, this couple are one of the matches best starred to spend a lifetime safe in each other's arms. There may be just a ripple of discontent, though, when Scorpio retreats into an occasional want-to-be-alone mood.

Pisces with Sagittarius

Mutual attraction of bodies is immediate but it may never be matched by a meeting of minds. For all-emotions, just-us-two Pisces and popular, partygoing Sagittarius are further apart than the North and South Poles, and could, without care, end up just as frosty.

If Sagittarius can try not to trample on all Pisces' tender hopes and dreams and plans for the perfect wedding (at least until past the first date), a compromise can be reached. And it often helps if you take the tension sparked by this relationship and turn it into energy to work together for a charity. That should make you relaxed enough to accept and even enjoy your differences.

Pisces with Capricorn

Heart is where the home is for these two security-loving signs, and they have a natural compatibility that sets up everlasting friendship and the strongest chances of fidelity. At first, as a Pisces, you will be drawn to Capricorn's calm, steady air, and adore the way Capricorn takes charge of the practicalities of life. While outwardly cool Capricorn can't help being captivated, and wonderfully warmed, by Pisces' all-or-nothing passion and even finds those maddening moods strangely fascinating, rather than aggravating.

If sex stays fresh this is a life sentence of love. There is just an occasional cloud when Capricorn's lack of sentimentality, and love of work, makes Pisces feel temporarily neglected.

Pisces with Aquarius

Aquarius breezes in and sends Pisces' heart spinning with lazy, crazy loving. But as a Pisces you feel insecure because Aquarius emotions will never be as deep as yours. When you try to secure Aquarius with your love chains, or at least cajole some sort of commitment, your love demands may make Aquarius run a mile. Suddenly the kindness of Aquarius affections turns to cruelty, and love is in danger of becoming a memory of what might have been.

Yet, when you work at this relationship, there are benefits for both of you. If Aquarius can try to give more, and Pisces to give less, and both partners really listen to each other, this pairing has potential. Though Aquarius will still have to be persuaded that staying home isn't just a failure to find something better to do.

LIVING LOVE

Case history of a Pisces woman and Libra man, star-crossed lovers

Afterwards, Melissa couldn't think why she and husband Andy had agreed to play the stupid game. She was usually so good at sensing when trouble was setting a trap. But super-sociable Libra Andy, with all eyes at the party on him, couldn't resist, of course. 'It's only a game,' he said.

The game, much favoured by Andy's business pals, was called Tell The Truth. Each person, in turn, was asked a deeply personal question and had to reply truthfully, however embarrassing the answer. Quite what the point of the game was, short of sparking off hoots of laughter,

Melissa couldn't grasp. But she knew Andy would refuse to be left out.

She dug her nails into her palms and fought back the tears as the raucous questions started. Quiet little James, from the accounts department, was asked, 'Where did you make love for the first time – if you ever have, of course?' and as he struggled to answer, Melissa shared his wounding embarrassment. Soon it would be her turn and then Andy's.

'Right, Melissa, here's your question. Is there anything you would die for?' She sighed with relief. The answer immediately leapt into her mind. She shot a glance at Andy, her husband for five far from tranquil years, and knew he was still the most important thing in her life. 'Yes,' she answered simply, 'my husband.'

Silence. She instinctively reached out to grasp Andy's hand but her fingers folded round thin air, and Melissa realised with a chill shiver that he had somehow shrunk away from her. Yes, she knew how much his logical air sign brain hated public displays of dependence, but surely this was an exception? She was simply telling the truth. Or was all this just another symptom of the downhill track their relationship seemed to be taking? The gap between them, he the cool thinker and she the warm feeler, had always been wide, but she believed they could always bridge it. Now she wasn't so sure.

The game moved on and it was Andy's turn to Tell The Truth. 'Now Andy,' she heard the host begin, 'you get the chance of a one-night stand with the woman of your dreams and your wife need never know. Do you take it?' Melissa breathed a sigh of relief again. She knew the answer to that one. Or did she? For Andy hesitated, smirked round the room, then answered, 'Well, maybe . . .' Melissa could not bear to hear another word and fled for home. She was soul-shocked that Andy would make a joke out of their marriage and contemplate being unfaithful to her.

She reached the small house they shared in the next street, and made herself a forget-it mug of whisky and hot water – lately, drinking seemed to take the sting out of her pain. She was sipping it in bed when Andy arrived. He came into the bedroom, 'Look, Missy, it was only a bit of fun – why must you always overreact so? You must know I'd never really be unfaithful to you, it wouldn't make sense.'

'Make sense, make sense,' screamed Melissa, 'that's all you logical Libras care about, isn't it? Well sometimes love just doesn't make sense. I "overreact", as you put it, because I love you and I care how you feel. Pity the feeling isn't mutual. I can't believe you humiliated me like that, in front of all those people.'

Andy's voice was even, measured – but his words were like spikes in Melissa's heart. 'Are you forgetting how you humiliated me? All that puppy dog devotion stuff is all right in private, but I don't really want it paraded in front of all our friends, thank you.'

Melissa felt panic rise like bitter bile. Deep inside, she knew, had always known, Andy found her clinging dependence suffocating, but he'd always kept their marriage on an even keel. His typical Libra charm, his jokes and the way he could lighten up the heaviest situation with a few logical words kept her intensity in check. Melissa knew her own generosity and unselfishness had contributed to their happiness. And they had been happy . . . but could they ever be again? They decided to try.

Melissa tried to cool her emotions. She knew she was addicted to letting her feelings spill over. She spent many anguished moments psyching herself up to make the moves away from the security she craved. She went on a weekend pottery course alone, and didn't check where Andy was every minute of every day.

But it was no good – before, she felt miserable sometimes, loved others. Now she just felt miserable. For however much Andy reassured her he did love her and wanted their marriage to last, Melissa couldn't get the memory of that night at the party out of her mind.

Looking for a go-between Melissa and Andy finally tried

counselling and found it was like Tell The Truth all over again, with often hurtful comments as they expressed hopes and fears. But the fact that Andy came to sessions at all was an indication to Melissa of how much he did care. And slowly, gradually, she came to see passion couldn't always be perfection, but it could be the best they could manage, together.

Her heart eased its stranglehold on Andy's and she discovered that the less she tried to bind him to her, the more attached he became. A year later, when they renewed their marriage vows, they knew each other far better than first time around – well enough never to play that party game again.

Case history of a Pisces man and Cancer woman, star-blessed lovers

Sean glanced up at the town hall clock as he drove past and saw that he still had plenty of time to reach the swimming baths and pick Diane up. He smiled as his mind flashed back to the day they first met, under that very clock. He'd been so nervous, especially since getting in touch with the dating agency was such a calculated thing for an emotion-led Pisces like him to do.

'I always had this idea true love would just happen,' he laughed to himself. 'It would be so romantic with roses, champagne, soft music, and me whispering in this mystery woman's ear, "Will you marry me?" Don't know how I thought this fantasy was ever going to come true when I hardly ever went anywhere except the supermarket, and worked from home.'

Eventually, flipping through the local paper one day, in his lunch hour, Sean had seen the headline on a quarter-page advertisement reading 'Why Not Give Love A Helping Hand?' At first, his automatic reaction was 'No way'. It was only a preview of himself in 40 years' time, picking up his pension and still hoping to meet that perfect woman, on the way to the post office, that spurred him on.

After a few false starts, he dialled the dating agency's number and got himself put on their books.

He had a couple of other dates before Diane and, for someone so shy, they were a frightening experience. One had been an excitable Sagittarius who talked non-stop and dragged him off to a funfair, the other another Pisces who'd just sat there fiddling with her buttons and hardly said a word. He'd been on the point of giving up when, that day under the clock, he met Diane. And yes, it really was love at first sight.

Born under the sign of Cancer, Diane was as easily hurt and gentle as himself. But she had such a wonderful sense of humour and infectious laugh that Sean felt, from that first moment, marvellously relaxed in her company.

What did they do on that first date? He couldn't really remember anything except being captivated by Diane's warm, expressive face and way she really seemed to listen to what he was saying. Sean even told her about his dream of a perfect love, and couldn't believe his ears when she answered, 'I have the same dream – but maybe it's not so impossible after all.'

From that day on, Sean and Diane were always together. Diane wasn't working then so they didn't have much money, but they liked nothing better than a picnic in the park, listening to music together, going swimming or sitting in Diane's little car looking at the stars and planning their future.

Yes, almost from the moment they first held hands both knew they had 'a future'. Sean wanted nothing more than to care for Diane, spoil and pamper her and shower her with presents and promises of eternal love. The depth of his feelings for her almost frightened him, sometimes. He felt his whole life, happiness, health even, depended on her.

That intensity had frightened Diane, too, he later found out. For although she had the same strength of feeling for him, she was able to love him without making her whole life revolve around him. She had interests, hobbies – she trained hard at swimming and won a place on a team, which thrilled her, but meant spending long hours in the pool away from him.

When Diane broke the news, her face clouded over at his angry expression. 'Sean, love, you've got to accept the fact that you don't own me. You're not responsible for me, I am,' Diane said gently. 'We've got such a good thing going here, I don't want to spoil it, but please try to let me go a little. I adore the way you care so much about me,' she went on, stroking his hand, 'but I'd like you to care about some other things as well.'

At the time, Sean had, with difficulty, bitten back the hurt, angry outburst that was his first reaction. Later, when he cooled down, he was able to see the wisdom of Diane's words. His saw that his intensity might make their love burn out before its time. 'We've got our whole lives ahead to love each other,' Diane whispered. 'So why try to crowd all the loving in now? Let's pace ourselves.'

It had been the one, not really black, more grey spot in their otherwise blissful relationship. Sean had looked in the local paper again, found an animal charity that was looking for volunteers and got caught up in helping out there, from fund-raising to nightshifts nursing sick animals. His almost obsessive passion faded to a far more lasting love founded in true friendship. Two years after they met, he and Diane were married.

Turning into the swimming pool car park now, Sean thought again how lucky he was. Diane really did seem to know him better than he knew himself, and their already perfect partnership had grown even stronger with time.

From the viewing gallery he saw her at the pool edge and hurried down to help her out of the water. It was one of the few times Diane made any concession to her disability. Mostly her strong arms could more than compensate for her paralysed legs, but the poolside was difficult for her to manage alone.

Her smile as she saw Sean approaching with the

wheelchair made him feel warm inside, and lucky to have such a beautiful, thoughtful, yet independent wife. He wondered when he had first realised that a wheelchair didn't mean Diane was dependent on him. He couldn't remember – but he knew it was just one of the lessons he had learned from his star match.

PART TWO

Your Rising Sign

Your sun sign personality,
chart of rising signs, and how your two
zodiac signs work together to shape
your personality

There is more than one zodiac sign in your AstroLife. You know your sun sign from the time of year you were born. If you were born on March 30, you know you are an Aries. If you were born on December 30, you know you are a Capricorn. Every year the sun moves through the 12 zodiac signs to give you your sun sign. But each day, as the sun rises and sets, it also moves through the 12 zodiac signs.

So the time of day you were born gives you a second zodiac sign, called your rising sign – because it is the zodiac sign rising over the eastern horizon at the time of your birth. So you can be an Aries sun sign, with a Libra rising sign, or a Capricorn sun sign with a Leo rising sign. There are 12 different ways of being an Aries – 12 different ways of being each of the 12 zodiac signs.

Your sun sign and rising sign combine to rule your AstroLife. When you know your rising sign, you will understand your own feelings and behaviour even better. The sun sign is the senior partner, but you need both to make the most of your AstroLife. Only those who know you really well will ever see and understand the side of you controlled by your rising sign.

IF YOU DON'T KNOW THE TIME YOU WERE BORN read the 12 match-ups under your sun sign, and you will recognise yourself.

IF YOU KNOW YOUR TIME OF BIRTH consult the chart that appears with your sun sign profile on the following pages, then read how your rising sign works with your sun sign.*

*The charts are calculated on Greenwich Mean Time (GMT) so, if you were born when the clocks are put forward for summer time, please deduct the time indicated on pages 846–48 before consulting the chart.

Once you know your rising sign, you may like to read that sign too in the AstroLove section of this book. And it's a good idea to check your weekly horoscope for both sun sign and rising sign.

Please don't feel disappointed if your sun sign and rising sign are the same – this makes you a very intense and fascinating version of your sign.

Sun Sign Aries

You're the sun sign that leaves the others standing. With an endless supply of energy, you can't understand why others might find you exhausting. Life's a load of fun and physical challenges for Aries – as an OAP you'll still be out running marathons. You're brave, too. If you see an old lady being mugged, a child or animal in danger, you'll rush in there – fists flying if need be. Unfairness or cruelty of any kind brings out the protective side of you and you'd risk anything for those you love.

Quick-witted, open and warm-hearted, you're great to be around, and have a knack of making things happen. Your fascinating personality seems never to be quite the same twice, but it's always extremely honest, positive and impulsive. Yes, you can be snappy and aggressive sometimes, and a slave to your strong sex drive. Your reckless nature makes you very risk- and accident-prone and you can't stand even a split second of boredom. As soon as work, play or partners start to seem dreary, your eyes can start to roam.

No job, however hard, is beyond you – according to yourself! But in fact, because you approach everything with buckets of self-confidence and the simple optimism of a child, you do achieve more than others even dream possible. Do try to let that impatient achiever's mask slip sometimes, however, or no-one will know what a tender, soppy centre is squirrelled away underneath.

You're a natural leader, and like being up in front. You owe your fiery temper to your ruler Mars, the planet of action and aggression. Luckily, your rage is snuffed out as quickly as a capped oilwell blaze. One minute you're shouting, the next smiling, and you're always first to wipe the slate clean, never stooping to silent sulks or grinding grudges.

You have to be where the action is, which makes you a fast-lane, thrilling lover – and a loyal, lifelong friend. You're always enthusiastic and can turn your natural competitive ways to your partner's advantage, producing greater and greater thrills for them.

Impulsive and generous, loved-ones are loaded down with gifts you've bought them, and you'll always put yourself out to help others. You can be forgetful and vague, and have a dread of any sort of details, especially financial. Yet your inborn seam of solid gold luck brings cash and career chances your way anyway.

You like to travel light and live for the moment, and you win friends easily. Any lover who's going to stay the Aries course needs to be a sparky sparring partner – game for anything in and out of bed and able to put up with your need to be free yet feel securely loved simultaneously.

Work off that excess energy and aggro through a sport or time-taking good cause, to give passion partners and friends a few well-earned breaks. And try to tame that rampant independence to let someone get really close.

The real you, Aries, will be revealed even more when you find the co-ruler of your life, your RISING SIGN, and see how it combines with your Aries sun sign.

You know what your SUN SIGN is – the day you were born makes you an Aries. Now, having checked the time of day you were born on the chart opposite, you know your RISING SIGN, too. If you don't know the exact time you were born, you'll soon spot yourself from the descriptions of each of the SUN SIGN/RISING SIGN combinations.

YOUR SUN SIGN IS **ARIES** – THIS CHART REVEALS YOUR RISING SIGN

If your date of birth is	If you were born between these times											
21–31 March	6:30 am to 7:44 am	7:45 am to 9:29 am	9:30 am to 11:59 am	12 noon to 2:44 pm	2:45 pm to 5:29 pm	5:30 pm to 8:14 pm	8:15 pm to 10:59 pm	11 pm to 1:29 am	1:30 am to 3:14 am	3:15 am to 4:29 am	4:30 am to 5:29 am	5:30 am to 6:29 am
1–10 April	6 am to 7:14 am	7:15 am to 8:59 am	9 am to 11:29 am	11:30 am to 2:14 pm	2:15 pm to 4:59 pm	5 pm to 7:44 pm	7:45 pm to 10:29 pm	10:30 pm to 12:59 am	1 am to 2:44 am	2:45 am to 3:59 am	4 am to 4:59 am	5 am to 5:59 am
11–20 April	5:15 am to 6:29 am	6:30 am to 8:14 am	8:15 am to 10:44 am	10:45 am to 1:29 pm	1:30 pm to 4.14 pm	4:15 pm to 6:59 pm	7 pm to 9:44 pm	9:45 pm to 12:14 am	12:15 am to 1:59 am	2 am to 3:14 am	3:15 am to 4:14 am	4:15 am to 5:14 am
YOUR RISING SIGN IS	TAURUS	GEMINI	CANCER	LEO	VIRGO	LIBRA	SCORPIO	SAGITTARIUS	CAPRICORN	AQUARIUS	PISCES	ARIES

Sun sign Aries/rising sign Taurus

You're torn two ways, your shimmering Aries flames often muffled by a damp shovelful of Taurus down-to-earthiness. One half of you wants to leap into life without a backward glance, the other demands time for a cautious, deliberate double-take. But this mixture of brilliant ideas and get-it-done determination does make sure you finish everything you do start!

Yours is a very powerful combination. It gives more staying power than the average flighty Aries, extra inner strength to help you shove your way straight to the top. And in the bedroom, Taurus' relaxed, supersensual side adds an extra element of excitement to Aries' enthusiasm, leaving lovers breathless and begging for more.

With a careful application of self-control, your Aries anger fuse fizzles slower. But when you do explode, everyone had better run for cover. It can take forever to cool that frightening fury. You love food, but as long as you listen to naturally sporty Aries as well as laid-back Taurus, you shouldn't find fitness too much of a problem.

Though you're extremely ambitious and often stubborn, childlike qualities like enthusiasm and innocence keep you forever young. Just be careful that home comforts, money in the bank and safe jobs don't push you to play safe instead of tackling your life's biggest challenges.

Sun sign Aries/rising sign Gemini

Fizzling with enough energy to light up countless lives, you also have the skill to juggle several jobs at once. If anyone can write a bestseller in between bringing up a family and holding down a full-time job, it's you!

A brainbox, brilliant storyteller and unusually skilled with your hands, do beware of using your tremendous talents to the wrong ends. Your persuasive patter could sell deep freezes to Eskimos, but that Aries conscience will always catch up with you, if your inborn corner-cutting and carelessness don't put a spanner in the works first!

Ideas fly from your never-still mind, but you'd do well to get them down on paper before the next brainwave comes along. Otherwise you can spend all your time dreaming, and none of it actually doing. Routines and offices bring out the caged beast in you, but remember you can easily inspire others to do work that bores you – so nicely they won't notice!

Fast food was invented for you, and you'll probably always burn up calories too fast to get fat. But you should sometimes make time to sit down and eat, as it may be your only chance to concentrate on family and friends.

Love will change your life, over and over again. It comes almost too easily – and you often talk yourself out of tight spots. Other people's partners spellbind you and you can't resist a challenge, like chasing someone who doesn't really care. But your heart's more tender than you realise.

Sun sign Aries/rising sign Cancer

Although you like to get your own way, you prefer manipulation by roundabout routes to head-on attack. Your rising sign dilutes your inborn drive and dynamism with just the right amount of gentleness and discretion. Even so, that quick Aries temper sometimes tears through your usually calm outer shell and no one thinks you're a soft touch for long, despite your caring ways. But you're not usually yelling for yourself – you always stick up for others hard done by.

Your fire and water mix often builds up such a high-pressure head of steam that you just have to let it off – and the dance floor is your favourite escape. You have Aries bravery, but it's more mental than physical – you'll fight for an idea but never raise your fists. And although your constant daydreaming conjures up highly original ideas, you also have a special flair for adapting other people's stale schemes to seem like new.

You were born to bounce between two paths – footloose freedom and a love of home sweet home. Should you take that exciting trip abroad or stay in and tile the toilet? Constant conflict means you may kick yourself for making the wrong choice, then turn it into a triumph anyway.

You make friends easily and are a born comedian, but please don't have too many laughs at other people's expense! When you believe in a cause you will move mountains, and apply the same unstoppable energy to love conquests.

Sun sign Aries/rising sign Leo

Fire meets fire from both your sun and rising signs for an inner inferno that makes you almost too hot to handle. Born leader or bossy, selfish dictator – you could easily be either, or both. Certainly power and success matter to you. You long to rub shoulders with the rich and powerful, but are held back by a lazy streak that prefers putting your feet up to putting your back into any project.

You're frank and open – what others see is generally what they get – and though you've a sudden, short-lived temper, you're never mean-minded or petty. You're first to make up and are always willing to ignore minor mistakes and faults in others, as long as they do the same for you.

Arrogance and pride can filter to the surface, but with that beaming smile never far away most people see straight through your swagger. A born scene-stealer and attention-grabber, it's just as well you're so naturally entertaining – no one minds letting you leap into the limelight or commandeer the karaoke machine.

You need a safety valve to stop you taking work problems out on your family – how about sport or amateur dramatics? Flattery can easily lead you astray and you're a sucker for expensive status symbols, but with your natural financial flair the money always seems to come from somewhere. And it's the same with love. Playful yet powerfully passionate, you guarantee a laughter and love-filled future.

Sun sign Aries/rising sign Virgo

Who dares wins, sometimes! For while the Aries side of you

can't wait to get stuck into danger and excitement, your Virgo inner core clamours to hold you back. Aries leaps first but Virgo must take a good look, with binoculars. You're never restrained long, but often that vital delay saves your skin.

Virgo brings a grain of common sense you'd otherwise lack. You're very capable and practical, with a good eye for detail and more sticking power than the average Aries. These second thoughts help cut back your share of accidents and mistakes and put the brakes on those risks you take.

Others open their hearts to you – you'd be an ideal Samaritan or counsellor – but although relationships do matter to you, you thoroughly enjoy your own company, too. With a new project never far from your mind, you like to sit down and work out whys and wherefores. Lovewise, you're exciting yet soothing too, because you're both fun-loving and lifelong faithful. You take vows oh so seriously. And because you are so honest, lovers always know you'll tell the truth, even if it isn't quite what they want to hear!

Your hatred of crowds comes out in occasional hermit-like urges to holiday alone miles from anywhere and anyone. You have a fascination with health, both your own and other people's, but do call a halt if it looks like turning into an obsession.

Sun sign Aries/rising sign Libra

Ever wondered why, in the middle of a slanging match, you have the sudden desire to quit quarrelling and start negotiating? Or halfway through some heavy-duty physical task, you break off because you've suddenly noticed how dirty it's making your hands? Well, your fastidious and style-conscious Libra side enjoys an argument just as much as your Aries one. But preferably it should be a mentally stimulating set-to, not a physical punch-up. And weaving all the broken bits together again afterwards is just as much fun for your secret peacemaking self.

With double your quota of charm – but absolutely no

smarm – others flock round you like moths to a bright light. Libra layers Aries bluntness with a light touch of tact, which stops you leaping straight into all sorts of misunderstandings. Your brain bubbles with bright ideas, and seems to operate on a different level to everyone else – studying comes easy at any age. Generally easy-going, you maintain a good balance and normally can handle any inner conflict. Dampening down either of your opposing halves, however, can make you ill, so you must try to express both.

You aren't as independent as you would like to be, preferring the support of a close pal to exploring life alone. And with that Aries act now, think later spirit watered down by Libra caution, you do tend to dither over life decisions, until a friend or lover gives you a much-needed shove.

Sun sign Aries/rising sign Scorpio

Your frantic me-first Aries drive gets a handy ally in deep and mysterious Scorpio – a poker face that hides your ambition long enough for you to get ahead of the game. Once you've programmed yourself with steel-jawed determination and unshakeable concentration, you're as hard to stop as a ticking timebomb. Your main challenge is to resist temptation to use your subtle power and superhuman energy for your own ends or without looking to the wider future.

Better watch your temper, too, for it can be truly terrible, and that twin-sign tongue has such a sarcastic edge! Yet you're never knowingly nasty and melt completely inside just seeing a cute picture or hearing a sentimental song from the past. One shadow to watch, though, is Scorpio-sparked jealousy which could cast a chill over Aries' sunny, non-possessive nature.

Emotionally, you're deep, dark and almost too passionate for most lovers! There's something irresistibly mysterious about you that keeps others coming back for more, and although they never get to know the complete you, the intense, smouldering bit you do reveal is more than enough!

You won't settle for second best, and if you can't find the

perfect mate, you prefer to go it alone. But you'd probably prove happiest linking hearts in a long-distance love match, with plenty of independence and the excitement of romantic meetings to fan the flames of desire.

Sun sign Aries/rising sign Sagittarius

Fiery and adventurous, you live for the moment, and your great sense of fun and sociability makes people feel good in your company. Your open friendliness and puppy-like devotion to those you love can evaporate, though, if someone tries too hard to tie you down!

Travel really turns you on. You can hardly wait to unpack your snowboots and skis before grabbing swimsuit and sunglasses and setting off in search of adventure again. And you're a dead cert for a steamy holiday romance.

You're totally blunt and tactless, which might lose you friends if they weren't so sure that you don't really mean what you just said.

Try not to spread yourself too thin or take on too much and end up letting everyone else, and yourself, down. You can easily whip up confidence and enthusiasm in others, so they'll do your dirty work, leaving you free to dream up those off-beat, brilliant ideas.

Fear's not something you know the meaning of, and you'll always launch in if you spot anything you reckon is unfair treatment of others. Your Sagittarius side lends you a natural luck, too, that keeps you out of mischief, often only just!

You work and play hard – too hard for some – and are a refreshing delight to be with, most of the time. Don't let your fear of being tied down stop you tuning in to love, though.

Sun sign Aries/rising sign Capricorn

Why does your natural cheery optimism give way to bouts of sadness and self-doubt? Could it be that murky Capricorn rising sign skulking behind the scenes? Most times, your secret practical side helps channel your energies into serious ambitions and good solid hard work. Together with your inspired, off-the-wall brainwaves, that gets you noticed. But it can also mean you need time off to sort your mind and heart out every so often.

Physically tough as old boots and with an ability to flourish under hardships that would floor most people, you can be reined back by a too-rigid respect for routine and tradition. Loosen up and listen more to your heart, not your head.

You thrive in big organisations, but do try not to trample on too many less ambitious workers on your way to the top. You're not as easily fooled by flattery as other Aries signs, and you really can get the last drop of work out of others – like those Egyptian pharaohs who got the pyramids built without lifting a finger themselves!

Anyone who chips beneath your crust will be surprised at the warmth of the sentimental heart you take great pains to hide. You're a most loyal lover and can make amazing sacrifices for your friends. You'll be most at peace with yourself if you listen to your optimistic side and don't set too much store by possessions.

Sun sign Aries/rising sign Aquarius

You're a bright-eyed adventurer with your sights set on the future. And magical Aquarius gives you such uncanny insight into life you're often thought to be a wacky eccentric. Don't be ashamed to be a one-off, always out of step with the crowd. As long as you aren't sidetracked into shocking others just for the sake of it, you will shoot all petty restrictions out of your path and soon zoom into a supersonic success zone all of your own.

Your ability to always see the whole picture means you are completely without prejudices. You take everyone just as you find them, and you certainly do seem to collect people – both friends and lovers. But hidden away beneath your sociable surface is a need to have everything on your own terms.

That means dumping pals or even partners when you feel like it, then taking them down from the shelf to be dusted off again when the mood takes you.

You also tend to go for quantity, not quality. You've a strong temper, though you lack malice, and your major secret shortcoming is thinking that if you can't be leader of the game then you won't play at all!

Freedom- and learning-loving, you never try to tie people down, or to force them to follow your lead. You care far more for people than things, yet may still have trouble expressing your feelings sometimes. Let actions speak louder than words, for no-one communicates better in body language.

Sun sign Aries/rising sign Pisces

Sensitive, dreamy Pisces makes you a slow-burner. You don't get angry at the first insult, but once your temper's torched you can be pretty hard to placate. And your misty mix of water and fire makes you charming, slightly lazy, head-in-the-clouds – all too easily losing yourself sometimes in the fog.

Pisces' influence sticks a spoiler on your potentially practical, get-on-with-it self. At worst, you can be lazy and hazy. But it can also bring out the free-thinker in you, making you impossible to bully into conforming. And there's a natural creative ability that your Aries drive could help convert to cash. But beware of Pisces' tendency to pig out on food and drink, for Aries has to do everything to excess!

Ward off twinges of self-pity when things go wrong and push yourself to the head of the queue at work – or you'll end up a frustrated follower, not king of the castle where you belong. Love is very important to you, but your heart bruises easily. Try to take time to think a new relationship through before you leap right in. What's your hurry!

You've a strong will, like all Aries types, but it can be very changeable, and your colourful imagination can come up with all manner of unrealistic fears. But no one is so tuned into others' feelings, yet independent, so thoughtful and kind without being any sort of walkover! When Pisces' misty moods loom on the horizon, Aries' optimism clears them pretty quick – you're not down for long, and never out!

Sun sign Aries/rising sign Aries

Twice the spice, or simply double trouble? Are you the bravest, cheeriest, strongest sign of all, or too much of a good thing?

When fire meets fire in both your sun and rising signs, you'll have to watch you don't blaze up in a splendidly showy burst ... only to fizzle out quickly once all the oxygen's used up, like a spectacular, short-lived firework.

Everything about you is larger than life, and louder! You've an explosive version of Aries' quick temper. And others find it so secretly funny that they'll light the touch paper and sit back to enjoy the show.

Impulsive and competitive, a challenge is like a red rag to a bull for you. You'd probably even try to race yourself if there was no one else around! But that doesn't mean you're a bad loser, far from it. Your inbuilt generosity makes you just as pleased about others' success.

You're a brilliant, headstrong self-starter, but a hopeless finisher – the original flashy hare beaten by a slow and steady tortoise. Other people are either totally for or against you – in your book there's no middle ground. You've got to let loose all that energy or you'll run round in circles forever.

You've unbreakable stamina but can be so selfish, without even realising. Try to share your heart, feelings, even fears, with loved ones a little more – you'll find it makes your everlasting fire burn even brighter.

Sun Sign Taurus

Sexy, sensitive beauty-lover, or grumpy glutton – you can be both, because you take such a delight in all things physical. So when your surroundings (preferably a pretty countryside scene) suit you, you feel satisfied and contented. And when other people are fitting in with your carefully worked out lifeplan, no one could be nicer. But when something's not right on the outside, your inner calm is the first to suffer...

The worst thing that can be said about you on a good day is you can be a bit dull, dependable and affectionate in a direct, cuddly way. But if someone presumes to prod you in a direction you don't want to take, or tries to change the ground rules of a relationship, then you see red. Your bad side's more pig-headed than bullish. You sulk, mumble and may drown your miseries in boozy binges or face-stuffing sessions that make a plague of locusts seem restrained. Eventually, you erupt into a blind rage that can be truly frightening to watch – and feel.

The good thing about your emotions is that they are very straightforward. What you see is what you get. You like to touch and be touched and are a sensual, rather than passionate, lover. Your love, once gained, is deep, simple and long-lasting. You like having a few close friends and spend much time and effort making the place you live in comfortable and easy on the eye. You are usually green-fingered, an excellent cook, and make things for your home that are both lovely to look at and completely practical.

You know exactly what you want in life, and work steadily until you get it. But your tendency is to tumble into a rut, and it's a real trial tempting you to try something new. Do lighten up that ultra-conservative outlook before you slump into a too-early old age. And be honest, now, are you really a generous gourmet, or just one more greedy slob? The truth is you do keep in touch with your body, no matter how many pounds you pile on, and even the most anti-exercise Taurus moves surprisingly well on the dance floor.

Money and material things do matter to you – too much, in fact. But your soulful side comes out in your strong feelings for animals and nature. You feel particularly happy when you can see big, spreading trees like oaks around you. You're more sensitive than your strong, silent image would suggest – after all, your ruling planet is all-caring Venus – and trying to bury your feelings could put a strain on even your chunky constitution, making you ill. So don't waste your time on sex-only affairs, or slumping in front of the telly with a takeaway when you should be out there sussing out new challenges. Shut out change and you might as well shut up shop altogether – you'll become too inflexible even for old friends to bear. Open up your ears, and your heart, long enough to really listen to what others are saying.

And now, Taurus, even more of the real you is revealed by discovering the co-ruler of your life – your RISING SIGN – and how it combines with your Taurus sun sign.

You know what your SUN SIGN is – the day of your birth makes you a Taurus. And once you've checked the time of day you were born against the chart opposite, you know your RISING SIGN too. If you don't know the exact time of your birth, don't worry – you'll soon spot yourself from the descriptions of each of the SUN SIGN/RISING SIGN combinations.

Sun sign Taurus/rising sign Gemini

Thank your lucky stars for a quirky touch of quicksilver from your chatty, charming rising sign. Gemini can fluff up your sometimes stodgy seriousness into a fresh-tasting soufflé. Still basically sensible, loyal and capable, you also

YOUR SUN SIGN IS **TAURUS** – THIS CHART REVEALS YOUR RISING SIGN

If your date of birth is	If you were born between these times											
21–30 April	5:45 am to 7:29 am	7:30 am to 9:59 am	10 am to 12:44 pm	12:45 pm to 3:29 pm	3:30 pm to 6:14 pm	6:15 pm to 8:59 pm	9 pm to 11:29 pm	11:30 pm to 1:14 am	1:15 am to 2:29 am	2:30 am to 3:29 am	3:30 am to 4:29 am	4:30 am to 5:44 am
1–10 May	5:15 am to 6:59 am	7 am to 9:29 am	9:30 am to 12:14 pm	12:15 pm to 2:59 pm	3 pm to 5:44 pm	5:45 pm to 8:29 pm	8:30 pm to 10:59 pm	11 pm to 12:44 am	12:45 am to 1:59 am	2 am to 2:59 am	3 am to 3:59 am	4 am to 5:14 am
11–21 May	4:45 am to 6:29 am	6:30 am to 8:59 am	9 am to 11:44 am	11:45 am to 2:29 pm	2:30 pm to 5:14 pm	5:15 pm to 7:59 pm	8 pm to 10:29 pm	10:30 pm to 12:14 am	12:15 am to 1:29 am	1:30 am to 2:29 am	2:30 am to 3:29 am	3:30 am to 4:44 am
YOUR RISING SIGN IS	GEMINI	CANCER	LEO	VIRGO	LIBRA	SCORPIO	SAGITTARIUS	CAPRICORN	AQUARIUS	PISCES	ARIES	TAURUS

show an endearing streak of scattiness now and then.

At work, Taurus persistence plus Gemini persuasiveness makes for an unbeatable mix. Among the most flexible types in a sign not famous for open-mindedness, you've a good eye for a business opportunity and a fast-talking tongue. But beware of relying too much on glib patter which can make you seem smarter and better informed than you really are. Make your inquiring mind work instead of making a beeline for superficial, get-rich-quick schemes.

Easily worried and prone to let life nibble at your nerves, inner anger inclines you to blow a fuse more often than you should. But, luckily, you don't stay furious for long and are able to keep friends for years. Your rising sign makes you more original and less ploddy than other Taurus types. You're likely to have hands fond of a fidget, and a slightly accelerated body clock, which means you can burn up calories fast and escape overweight.

You look younger than you are – a definite plus. But weighed against that is your sense of humour, which is very childish. You suppress worry and that can lead to nervous ailments and allergies, while your roving eye may produce repeated love problems. You need a patient partner!

Sun sign Taurus/rising sign Cancer

Home is definitely where your heart is – your emotional security is all tied up in bricks and mortar and you aim to own your own little castle as soon as possible. Ideally, you'd like to use it as a work base, too, perhaps making something useful and decorative.

You've a superstrong shot of money-awareness, thanks to your Cancer link, and your idea of heaven is umpteen rainy-day savings accounts. But don't let over-eagerness to earn, earn, earn make you a cash-hoarding bore. Ironically, you're quite easily parted from your savings – a real sucker for a sob story or money-making scheme.

On one level, you're supremely sensitive, charming and warm – the kind of person everyone would like to have stroking their brow on a sickbed. But when tender feelings are trampled by real or imagined cruelty you're prone to pig out on food and drink. Sex, however, you like to savour slowly, with gentle cuddles, not raunchy clinches.

You've a charming mask that conceals deep-seated ambition and a dreary tendency to sulk and live in the past when thwarted. And you'll probably never get right to the top of the tree because you're a closet copycat who would rather duplicate others' ideas than find your own.

Without someone to love you, you feel lost. But you can easily end up with the wrong mate because you're so change-every-day. Face up to what, and who, you want if you don't want to live a lie at home.

Sun sign Taurus/rising sign Leo

When it comes to grabbing golden opportunities, no-one could call you quick. You move about as fast as a sleepy snail, and can't change course without a massive reprogramming session. But when you do target some pet project or red-hot ambition, no-one can beat your dogged determination to hang on in there.

You're like a bulldozer with teeth, but too often your workaholic ways make others see you as a selfish, overbearing bully. You want the good life, stability, comfort and admiration – and you don't care how much that costs. Trouble is, you tend to use up other people's sweat as well. Many actually don't mind slaving away on your behalf because they're bewitched by your powerful personality. Generous when your life is ticking over smoothly, you like to entertain lavishly. You're good at turning a blind eye to others' problems if you've some of your own, though, and aren't as open-hearted as you'd like to believe...

No-one could call you petty and you have a volcanic temper that cools as quickly as it erupts. But you're easily hurt and, unlike a typical Taurus, you don't tend to forgive completely. As for love, remember that flamboyant gifts can't make up for hurt feelings. Think before you talk, and try not to take outside problems home. You're hot stuff in bed, but your insensitivity could mean you often wake up alone.

Sun sign Taurus/rising sign Virgo

Cautious, critical and practical to a fault, you only trust what you can see, feel, taste or hear. And even then, with the world's biggest bargain or most lasting love in your grasp, you're not going to rush it until you've taken legal advice! If a lover wanted to whisk you to a paradise island, you'd check the weather forecast and comb your hair first.

Still, your caution usually pays off and your criticism – although it can be spread too thick – is usually constructive. And you never trumpet 'Told you so!' to less thoughtful sun signs. All of which adds up to a pleasant person, certainly not the gossiping, griping nit-picker your critics sometimes make you out to be.

You're completely dependable, sincere in all you say, and helpful. Rarely a highflier yourself, you soon spot talent and achievement in others and make sure they get rewarded.

Virgo modesty tempers your Taurus temptation to muscle in, and although you're a hard taskmaster, you cast the same critical eye over your own faults. You loathe to throw anything away, and stored old newspapers and recycled jam jars long before Green hit the scene. But then you were just called mean! A double helping of earth signs makes you very materialistic – do let your sensual inner self stretch out sometimes.

Sun sign Taurus/rising sign Libra

Double Venus power makes you essentially sweet and gentle, mentally flexible and physically sensual. You must have beauty and plush, lush comfort around to survive, and your considerable charm really clicks in when the atmosphere's pleasant and relaxed.

But you do tend to drift through life, roping in new pals and hoping that they'll make all your major decisions for you. Your stay-at-home Taurus roots mix with Libra's occasional idleness to make you look lazier than you really are. Keep your mind, and your diary, open to activity if you don't want to get frozen like a fossil.

Of all Taurus types, you're the least likely to win the battle of the bulge without effort. For the only way you'll ever refuse a creamy cake is if your jaws are wired! Libra's scales will swing your moods violently at times, but you can always see both sides of an argument and calm down quite fast. Usually no-one wants to tangle with you, though, as you argue on long after your opponent's nodded off.

Willpower isn't a problem for you, if you can remind yourself you have Taurus endurance buried in there somewhere and try to aim in one direction at a time. You can work hard, in fits and starts, but money is a constant worry and you and your bank manager aren't likely to see eye to eye. Too often lust posing as love lets you down. But how often have you bolted when romance got routine?

Sun sign Taurus/rising sign Scorpio

Sensational – that's how your fans see you. But those who have suffered from your easy come, easy go attitude, uncertain temper and too-intense emotions reckon you're as dangerous as a runaway train and get out of your way, fast! There are no grey areas in your personality, and the pull of your rising sign makes you just too intense for some people to handle. You can also be maddeningly contrary – Taurus stubbornness is even more exaggerated – but in any conflict you grit your teeth and keep going to the bitter end.

This strength does also mean you barricade yourself away from anything you don't want to know about – you're supersensitive about your own needs, but can be blinkered and hard as nails about others'.

You've a small, tight-knit circle of friends, none of whom would dare let you down, and an equally small band of devoted loved-ones. Luckily, you mellow a bit as you get older and may even abandon one or two deeply held prejudices. You're happiest with a love partner who allows you to take them over – reworking both lives and wardrobe – but jealousy and over-possessiveness can cast a shadow over your closest relationships.

You never forget a hurt, and do have secret enemies. A passionate, curious and fascinating lover, you tend to use sex as a release for pent-up feelings, and for emotional reassurance. Try it sometimes, just for fun . . .

Sun sign Taurus/rising sign Sagittarius

Your star ingredients sit well together, as Taurus persistence gets a twist of flair. You're practical and philosophical, actually welcoming new ideas and following them through with never-say-die determination. You can be sensitive and tongue-tied, then do something bold and reckless. You beam out a brilliant ray of hope and youthfulness, but can spoil the image with shadows of sulkiness and irritability.

Unlike other Sagittarius rising signs, you have great patience with details. Coupled with your ability to shoulder an enormous workload, this should make sure you're never really short of cash. But, though you're money-conscious, you do have a tendency to blow cash on crazy schemes. Any windfall that comes your way will probably be as a result of lucky inheritance, rather than hard graft.

You have a typically Taurus love of the country, and your rising sign means you probably enjoy an outdoor sport or hobby, too. You're frank, honest and generous but often dive in to help when others don't want your assistance.

Life would be barren if you couldn't bask in mutual affection, and you are capable of loving very deeply indeed. Your heart will always be ruled by your head, however. Claustrophobia is your secret fear, and the one thing that can weaken your strong body is being trapped in the wrong job or relationship. You need plenty of time alone.

Sun sign Taurus/rising sign Capricorn

You'd make a marvellous murder detective – you're so

methodical, have such a clear sense of purpose, never rush, and plan everything extremely carefully. But your incredible ambition is usually channelled into more conventional jobs and you're likely to end up heading a bank or big business organisation. Power, one way or another, is what you're after.

Yours is a very capable combination, with a strong sense of purpose and determined set of life aims that make you very hard to discourage. Your rising sign helps lift your speed to a skip instead of the usual Taurus plod. And although you need physical comforting as much as the next Taurus, you can hide your amorous nature behind a seemingly severe front.

You do take emotional setbacks extremely hard, however, and your temper is unforgettably forceful and long-lasting. Your tendency to nurse heart-scars for years may make you postpone the marriage or full-time commitment you really need. Although you may be quite quiet with people you don't really know, you unbend with friends and need them to tide you over your bouts of moodiness.

You worry quite needlessly about your health, and if love hurts you can hide in brooding isolation. You work, and play, hard, and because you find it impossible to understand others' laziness or lack of cash sense, it's a waste of time anyone begging you for a hand-out.

Sun sign Taurus/rising sign Aquarius

You're the Taurus with the refreshing streak of unconventionality. You still stick close to home and appreciate your comforts, but that home could easily be a windmill or a houseboat. And you're more open-minded than some earth signs, prepared to listen and adapt. However, unlike a true Aquarius, your life revolves around routine and can career into chaos if your timetable's changed.

You also need the security of a family on your side before you can achieve anything. But you can run your home life like an army operation, making friends dread dropping in out of the blue, and guaranteeing a dull, drab social life.

Your inner tug of war is that you can look less straight than you feel and are constantly trying to choose between comforting, safe habits and thrilling, unknown challenges. You might even resolve this by leading a secret, double life. But more likely you'll get hitched early and stay together into old age. You can make necessary life changes without too much trouble, but your vision is never less than practical.

You're logical and lacking in prejudice – which makes you a rare Taurus indeed – but one weakness is your deep desire not to look a fool. If pushed into hasty decisions, you can make yourself sick, literally, and sulk angrily for days on end.

Sun sign Taurus/rising sign Pisces

You've a misty look in your eye and a vivid imagination, although 90 per cent of the time you tend to use it in mundane tasks, like home-decorating or cooking up special dishes. You are creative, but have enough Taurus practicality and determination to turn ideas into reality. With a rather rigid sun sign, you can stabilise your secret flyaway side. And you're objective enough to realise just when you're being over-sentimental.

Your warm, giving nature – and your good looks – can spell plenty of trouble in your lovelife. But many and varied affairs do have the advantage of teaching you a lot. Once your emotions are aroused, they can be dizzyingly difficult to dampen, unless you can stick to Taurus' 'Everything in moderation' motto.

In love with love, that's you. And you can wallow in muddy self-pity if your feelings aren't bounced back straightaway. Deep down, you need regular routine and emotional stability, but you're never going to get these organised unless you keep a tight rein on the drinking binges than could be your downfall.

Guard against fantasising about all the if-onlys in your

past, and keep your Taurus feet firmly on the ground by listening carefully to a close partner's advice. You come across as a kind person but, alas, some of your actions are sparked by a need to seem noble and good-hearted. In small, secret ways, you can be a real Scrooge.

Sun sign Taurus/rising sign Aries

When success is on offer, you're heading the queue. That Aries rising sign means you always lead with your hard, headstrong side, making you much more extrovert than you would be otherwise. You may also be superselfish – a trait you must stifle if partners are to stick around. Most of the time, you are sensible and practical, then all of a sudden you'll shoot off on some zany impulse, quite unlike Taurus. But this unpredictable quality could leapfrog you into a work position way above your natural abilities, so don't knock it!

You have a fiery temper that's quickly over and a blissful ignorance of when you're stamping on others with your two left feet. Money is your major motivator and you like it so much you will probably try to marry it. You can also make some rather cash-conscious friendships.

You're an ardent lover, though you watch the pennies however much you're smitten, and probably have at least one major love mistake hidden in your past. You work best putting someone else's brainwave into brilliant action, and think more quickly on your feet than other Taurus people. Energetic, pushy and ambitious, you must beware of exhausting yourself by too-sudden bursts of activity. You're the type who feels guilty for lounging around indoors all winter, then collapses on the squash court because you can't do anything by halves. You're likely to be one of life's late starters in education.

Sun sign Taurus/rising sign Taurus

Strength lies in your patient endurance, but you must gain control of your giant appetites if your double sign blend is to get you places. Built to last, you've a generously proportioned, muscular and shapely body – you risk wrecking your health with alternate binge blow-outs and crash diets. And because you won't deny yourself anything of life's physical joys, you may fritter away hard work and energy.

Long-suffering, a faithful friend, loyal lover and helpful, decisive workmate, you would benefit from more spontaneity in life. Lighten up, and don't keep insisting that you know best!

In fact, though you're proud of your opinions, you are mentally stuck in your mid-teens. You can't value what you can't see, so deeper emotions pass you by. Prone to hurry love, when you do win a partner – despite your lack of romantic subtlety – you tend to treat them as a prized possession rather than a person. Extra-strong Taurus influence makes you desperately drive to create beautiful things – and because you avoid the normal Taurus laziness trap, you could turn this into a money-spinning business.

Overwork could overstrain you, and health obsessions sap your mental strength. But you have it in you to become a millionaire – banking, the building trade and garden-linked jobs could bring later-life wealth.

Sun Sign Gemini

Freedom is your favourite name, and your motto should be 'I think . . .' If only you could stick to just one opinion on any subject! With mind-sharpening Mercury as your ruling planet, it's no wonder you've got a gadabout mind – you live inside your head and are so bright that, regardless of education or training, you're always at least two steps ahead of everyone else.

Your desire to be always up and active can be pretty unrelaxing, for other people. They may see you as a restless fidget, because as soon as you sit down one foot will begin to tap, your hand will reach for a magazine or TV remote control and your eyes dart round the room. Seconds later, you're making a cup of tea, then letting it go cold while you dial 'just one more' quick phone call.

Diaries and bulletin boards were invented for you and are often the only way to help you keep track of your feverish private life. Although your planetary personality can mean you'll two-time lovers and put friends on hold from time to time, you're usually so easy to talk to, pleasant, sympathetic and quick-witted, that you can charm your way out of the tightest corners and rearrange meetings before anyone has even realised how unreliable you are!

New faces, places and ideas constantly intrigue you and keep you young. But although you love learning new skills – and are so adaptable that you could probably make a go of most jobs – you favour short cuts and hate any drawn-out, hard-slog learning process. At your worst (and overtiredness brings out your terrible, twitchy side) you skim over life's surface, winging it with slippery patter and winning smiles when you should be getting down to work. You are a born salesperson but are even more smooth when it comes to escaping responsibility. You're simply never around to explain why your scheme's gone wrong!

In love, you're a famous flirt and a professional charmer, but you do need a strong, dependable partner to lean on for emotional support. You can be a fickle, selfish lover and any relationship will only stay the course if minds as well as bodies are well matched. But you're an ever-surprising friend who can bring sunshine into others' lives with just a phone call.

At work, you love handling more than one job at once, but could also waste your talents because you won't stick at things. Quick, inventive and able to adapt, you always want to try new places and new people, and this could sour personal happiness in the long run.

Stop joking your way out of situations you fear might take you out of your depth, and choose real love rather than chasing a fantasy. But use those brilliant storytelling skills to skate round life's real obstacles.

Stand by to discover even more about the real you, Gemini. Find the co-ruler of your life, your RISING SIGN, and see the difference it makes to your Gemini sun sign.

You know from the day you were born that your SUN SIGN is Gemini. Now, from checking the chart opposite for the time of day you were born you can find your RISING SIGN too, and discover its influence on your personality. If you don't know the exact time of your birth, you'll soon spot yourself by reading each description of the SUN SIGN/RISING SIGN combinations.

Sun sign Gemini/rising sign Cancer

Itchy feet lead you away from the nest early in life, but you may spend years trying to re-establish a safe, stable home for yourself. Unlike other Geminis, you often look for respon-

YOUR SUN SIGN IS **GEMINI** – THIS CHART REVEALS YOUR RISING SIGN

If your date of birth is	If you were born between these times											
22–31 May	6 am to 8:29 am	8:30 am to 11:14 am	11:15 am to 1:59 pm	2 pm to 4:44 pm	4:45 pm to 7:29 pm	7:30 pm to 9:59 pm	10 pm to 11:44 pm	11:45 pm to 12:59 am	1 am to 1:59 am	2 am to 2:59 am	3 am to 4:14 am	4:15 am to 5:59 am
1–10 June	5:30 am to 7:59 am	8 am to 10:44 am	10:45 am to 1:29 pm	1:30 pm to 4:14 pm	4:15 pm to 6:59 pm	7 pm to 9:29 pm	9:30 pm to 11:14 pm	11:15 pm to 12:29 am	12:30 am to 1:29 am	1:30 am to 2:29 am	2:30 am to 3:44 am	3:45 am to 5:29 am
11–21 June	4:45 am to 7:14 am	7:15 am to 9:59 am	10 am to 12:44 pm	12:45 pm to 3:29 pm	3:30 pm to 6:14 pm	6:15 pm to 8:44 pm	8:45 pm to 10:29 pm	10:30 pm to 11:44 pm	11:45 pm to 12:44 am	12:45 am to 1:44 am	1:45 am to 2:59 am	3 am to 4:44 am
YOUR RISING SIGN IS	CANCER	LEO	VIRGO	LIBRA	SCORPIO	SAGITTARIUS	CAPRICORN	AQUARIUS	PISCES	ARIES	TAURUS	GEMINI

sibility, and you're great at keeping in touch with those you love, no matter how far away. Cancer as a rising sign gives you a secret craving for security which almost, but not quite, cancels out your carefree nature.

You could easily solve this inner conflict by moving home often throughout your life, or putting down roots in several places at once. This combination also puts emotions on a knife-edge, and makes you easy prey to intense, sudden mood switches. Often miserly with money for yourself, you can also be a sucker for a pal's hard-luck story and get put upon time after time. You have a soft heart, but when relationships go sour – perhaps because real lovers can never match your fantasy ideal – you take it hard and hide away for a long time. You can drown in self-pity and surly sulks, but also have a hidden, self-destructive desire to suffer in love.

Forbidden fruit and the impossible-to-get fuel your appetite for intrigue, and not until quite late in life will you learn to stop chasing no-hope mates, and stop suffering those nervous skin and stomach problems. In a happy pairing, though, you're flexible, hard-working and sympathetic – the most supportive partner anyone could wish for.

Sun sign Gemini/rising sign Leo

Friendly, entertaining and witty, you're the most popular party guest around because you always manage to break the ice. You could even turn your sociable nature towards a profit, by selling, teaching, hosting a chat show or even telling jokes for a living. Chances are you'll enjoy flaunting your word power and larger-than-life personality as a sideline, especially between the sheets . . .

Basic Gemini charm and chatty versatility get a booster shot of Leo warmth and leadership, making you an ideal host or hostess too. But don't let your drive to entertain at all costs lead you into big-headed boasting or even lies! Turn the power of the spotlight down occasionally or you risk coming across as a shallow social butterfly who's more than a bit bossy.

Usually, though, you've a marvellous knack of getting your views across pleasantly and others love listening to you speak. Highly strung you may be, too, but though you fly off the handle fast, you forgive just as quickly. And the word 'grudge' isn't part of your vocabulary. But beware of flinging friends aside and then wondering why they're reluctant when you feel like making up.

Physically a knock-out yourself, you are drawn to strength and beauty in others, and may ignore potential dream lovers by going ga-ga over good looks. You gamble in love, but please don't take risks with sex if you value your health. Once in love, you're sincere and passionate.

Sun sign Gemini/rising sign Virgo

A double dose of big-thinker Mercury makes you agile, restless, very clever and keenly observant. You see life in brilliant bursts of light, but unless you can get control of your unpredictable energy early on, you fritter it away on empty chatter and dead-end schemes.

Working, and working fast, with words will be a winner for you, and despite jamming too many things into one day, you are one of the few Geminis who's never late! You have many friends, but few you really feel close to, perhaps because you tend to use people – never on purpose, of course!

You're far too fussy to find a love mate without a lot of effort, and even when you do, your bouts of super-criticism could drive them away again. But your cool eye for detail, common sense and tidiness can wrestle order out of any amount of chaos. If only your self-confidence was in such a well-controlled condition.

When you're in love, you often worry where your heart could lead that usually so-sensible head. So you end up making sarcastic, off-putting remarks, and will only tie down that romantic, butterfly heart when you stop trying to pull powerful, successful partners.

With a penetrating business mind, you're excellent at

balancing the books. And although you work methodically, your approach is never dull because of those dazzling flashes of inspiration. Use them wisely.

Sun sign Gemini/rising sign Libra

You are one of life's great companions, light of heart, a good mixer and born persuader. You can chat to anyone about anything and feel at home in any social event from the local bring-and-buy to Royal Ascot. At the same time you are restless – thanks to Gemini – and, as both your airy signs keep blowing your moods in umpteen directions at once, mighty changeable.

You'll always keep others on their toes, wondering which way you'll jump! Blessed with good intuition, you make a marvellous counsellor – Libra helps you listen, as well as offer sound and sympathetic advice. You can think fast and on your feet and would be suited to a career in politics, especially since you can always stay one step back from a controversial subject.

For one who loves a peaceful life and doesn't enjoy anger, you have a surprisingly quick temper – probably from trying too hard to sit on the fence. That inborn Libra balance pushes you to please all sides at once.

Movement and mental stimulation are must-haves in your life, but in love this can make you easily bored. You can be a daydream believer, too, putting more energy into imaginary affairs with pop stars and Hollywood heart-throbs than real-life responsibility. Generally, you can match-make and manage others' lovelives better than your own, but with the right tolerant partner, you're a cuddly, communicative and challenging lover.

Sun sign Gemini/rising sign Scorpio

While others flap around and panic in emergencies, yours is the one head that stays cool. You're used to fighting back your basic impulses, making you seem extremely proud, strong-willed, reserved and tough. But while these are qualities to count on in a crisis, in everyday life they can make you hard to get close to. And bottling up those powerful feelings can lead to almighty explosions, even stress-related illness, every now and then.

With its Scorpio shadow, your Gemini tongue gets a poisonous barb and your words can sometimes hurt far more than you know. But you still have a strange magnetism that draws many admirers, although only a few will meet your ever-exacting standards. Because you adore a murky secret, this can make you a cold, calculating lover. You want your partner to expose their vulnerable heart while you clutch all your love cards ever closer to your chest.

You have a reputation for over-the-top (and almost every other position) sex – yet if any sign is likely to hang on inside a hopelessly unhappy relationship, it's you. Scorpio pride and lasting loyalty make losing love an admission of defeat.

You have enormous reserves of physical and mental strength and your combination of Gemini curiosity and Scorpio dedication produce a razor-sharp mind that's made for in-depth insight and analysis. Always interested, and interesting, you make the world a lighter, brighter place.

Sun sign Gemini/rising sign Sagittarius

Constant activity of both brain and body is your trademark. You are always learning new things, but although you work hard and have a winning, friendly manner, you can't take being tied down. So success will only surface for you at work away from desk jobs. And because you tend to short-cut personal effort in favour of delegating the dirty work, you'll need to learn self-discipline to reach most life targets.

You are a lifelong student, but a natural teacher too. You think big, adore travel and are constantly heading for new horizons. In some respects you're everybody's pal, though you do reserve the right to up and off whenever the mood grabs you, even though this can look like abandoning old friends on a whim. Remember that most people don't find it so easy to switch relationships on and off as you do.

Your blunt, friendly manner can combine with keen observation to make you seem abrupt, sometimes positively tactless. But when you do point out someone's weaknesses or faults, it's with the best of intentions!

Inner enthusiasm can carry you away so much that you can't see that many of your plans don't stand a chance of success. And because your heart lives in the present, you can be a selfish, purely physical lover. Mind you, with your fit, sporty body, not many will complain. But do learn to listen if you'd like a gentler, more caring love.

Sun sign Gemini/rising sign Capricorn

You work doggedly, never ask for favours and can cope easily with problems that would floor others. Capricorn lends organisational ability to your lightning Gemini mind, a dash of reason to your intuition. So your decisions are very sound. You have an eagle eye for vital detail and are so persistent and ambitious that, if you don't get to the top of your chosen tree, it will only be because you choose to stop climbing.

Capricorn's nose-to-the-grindstone character counteracts your Gemini urge to spread yourself too thin, a magic combination. You're especially gifted with notes, both money and music, and although you crave recognition, you're as happy behind the scenes as in the spotlight. But do beware of laying down the law at home as well as work – less organised people will resent your house rules and obsession with checking every little fact and figure. And though you may make present sacrifices for a future goal, don't force others to follow suit against their will.

Your cool, almost calculating shell covers a sensual inner self, but you can spoil loving relationships with bouts of doom and gloom, and your suspicious, forceful temper. Try to forget, and forgive, minor faults if you want your lovelife to change from caterpillar to beautiful butterfly. And let your well-hidden physical warmth lead the way.

Sun sign Gemini/rising sign Aquarius

The cobwebs of tradition stand no chance against your unique blend of impatient, restless enthusiasm for change. You're a true thinker – open-minded, always able to hear every side of a story and free of the chains of prejudice and pride. You'd make a great judge! If only the training wasn't so long ... for the main drawback of your dancing mind is that you find it hard to stick to things and prefer chasing after a new challenge to completing a course.

Everything fast-moving appeals to you, from hair-raising fairground rides to jet travel. You're always on the scent of adventure, and parties, and this live-for-the-moment attitude affects most of your private life. So you can lose interest in lovers in record time, and relate better to large groups than individual friends. Those closest to you may feel they get a raw deal because, however happy-go-lucky you seem, deep down are strong likes and dislikes and a steel rod of self-sufficiency.

You've probably had more than your share of casual affairs that aroused your body but not your heart. Your strong temper and off-the-wall views aren't good love insurance either. But when you do fall in love it's head over heels, with any lasting love link brain-led, not bed-led.

You are always original, at home with both words and figures, and happiest in work that benefits other people. Tame that wild roaming mind, avoid unusual for unusual's sake – and don't let overwork undermine home life.

Sun sign Gemini/rising sign Pisces

This sympathetic, kind and affectionate combination would make you an ideal agony aunt or kindly uncle. Pisces gives you an almost psychic insight into others' feelings, while Gemini lets you detach your mind enough to offer sensible advice, without getting your own heart in too deep. You like people, and understand them, which makes you able to stand up for everyone else's rights except your own. But your fertile imagination and understanding of what makes people tick will always put you at the heart of life.

Your watery rising sign does unsettle your emotions to a significant extent, so when it comes to your own heart you find it hard to be objective. Blowing hot and cold in both friendship and romance, you need a strong home base to keep you on the straight and narrow. Your main problem will always be separating fantasy from fact.

Deep-rooted doubt about your own talents stops you pushing yourself forward, which could put the brakes on career progress – a great loss to the world. And sexually, you can be your own worst enemy, with an unhealthy hankering to be dominated by a partner who puts you down in public.

You also crave the impossible, then crash into a cocoon of comfort drinking or eating. That touch of Pisces can make you a pain to live with and you need a partner who's rock-solid emotionally strong. But unlike other Geminis, you always finish what you've started.

Sun sign Gemini/rising sign Aries

Your loud, unusual voice tells everyone you're on your way to join the party – and the action's about to hot up! Yours is a nervous energy, Aries flames fanned into far-flung sparks by Gemini's hyperactive air. The result is extreme restlessness – you've gone before some people have even realised you've arrived. But your readiness to leap right into the unknown, your drive to find out every fact on a given topic, and do it yesterday, make you very exciting company.

Adventure is food and drink to you, but sometimes you're just too quick off the mark. And this can cut short many a hopeful close encounter. You get bored so easily and at times have concentration levels less than zero. So it's a wonder any partner ever manages to hang on to you! But you do need loads of loving, ideally via a super-romantic set-up like a childhood sweetheart or exotic holiday affair.

You've selling power to beat all other signs, but whatever your work – and it must never be routine – you have to be in the front line. Ambition and enterprise are shadowed slightly by a headstrong streak and tendency to be put off too easily by slight setbacks. Your blazing temper doesn't last, thank goodness, and wise friends don't argue with your intense opinions. They just wait for them to change! Work on concentration and self-discipline, and pals will appreciate your many good points even more!

Sun sign Gemini/rising sign Taurus

You live to talk – usually out of turn! – and are a genuinely funny jokester who can also slaughter others with pointed sarcasm, only if they deserve it, of course! You don't make many enemies, but when someone has crossed you, you won't rest until they're flat on their back for you to wipe your feet on – a tactic that's a touch over the top for squabbles in supermarket car parks or with train-ticket inspectors!

Although not noted for ambition, you can get on despite yourself. For, once hooked on a job or subject, you won't let up until you've sucked every last drop of knowledge out of it. You're very good at spouting what you know, too – bosses notice you first because of your runaway mouth. But luckily your earthy rising sign anchors those gadabout Gemini roots and keeps your mind on your work until it's done.

Your touch of Taurus means you love your home, and your tummy. But Gemini can jinx all that – you spend ages on DIY, only to up and move to the other end of the country because you saw a tempting TV programme on it! Lovewise, you really would like to settle down ... only not just yet. A definitely domesticated, mature and understanding lover, probably a bit older than you, is your best bet. Because sex is essential to you, if that fizzles out so will love.

Your stubbornness may frustrate friends and family, but you also profit from the patience Gemini usually lacks.

Sun sign Gemini/rising sign Gemini

Congratulations, it's quads! And that means four different directions for your finely tuned, high-powered mind to fire off into at once. You can do it, of course, because of the unmatchable energy in your airy, imaginative personality.

To outsiders, you can seem as overcharged and over-the-top as a brilliant mad professor. You probably talk nineteen to the dozen, so quickly you need an interpreter, and send countless crazy ideas bouncing out of your never-still brain. When the mood to work takes you, though, you really are as well informed as you seem – as long as you resist impulses to rush and skimp.

If you can calm your stormy, flyaway nature and never give the clever conman in you a chance to rule, you could rise to great heights. In any job, a double dose of Gemini good luck and the ability to coolly come up with the goods even in panicky circumstances stand you in good stead.

But beware! Your charm (times four!), sympathetic ear and ability to smooth-talk your way out of anything may tumble you into terrible love tangles, and triangles! You can't remember what you've told, and to whom, and your affairs are littered with broken promises, stand-up dates and double bookings! Yet switch on one of those dazzling Gemini grins, say you're sorry, and lovers will forgive you anything. You'd make a starring professional actor, but even off stage you're great entertainment value!

Sun Sign Cancer

Although you're buffeted by powerfully strong feelings that crash over you like giant, foaming waves, on the outside you seem cool and controlled. It's just that, being so shy and sensitive, you need to keep your inner life a closed book where strangers are concerned. A sentimental nature doesn't make you wishy-washy, however. You're decisive – once you know what you want, you go all out to get it, only choosing a roundabout route rather than a direct hit and run.

While you hug your hidden self tight, you can't stand any other sort of secret – you'll create a scene if others pry into your private life, but it's okay for you to dig and delve into theirs. Normally, though, you're so perceptive, almost psychic, that you're first to sense what's going on, and going wrong, in other people's worlds.

Security is essential for you. Child or grown-up, your family holds centre stage in your thoughts and your heart, and you have a deep-seated desire to look after those you love. Naturally domesticated, you adore to cook and decorate, but do beware your protective instincts don't become smothering fussiness.

Traditional to the core, you place key importance on events and things connected to the past. You're so cautious that crucial chances and challenges often pass you by. But your skill at steering others to do what you want can help you catch up.

Easily impressed and reflecting others' emotions like a magic mirror, it doesn't follow that you're easily conned, for your sixth sense helps you pick out a trick a mile off.

Criticism, real or imagined, brings out the worst in you, by making you pull back inside your shell and stay there for a very long time. You're not keen on jokes at your own expense, either, and can sometimes be a self-pitying wet blanket. Your mood swings can be linked to the moon's cycle, but gardening or being near water can both help put the smile back on your face.

You can adapt to living alone, as long as there are plenty of sparkling sociable breaks to get together with family and friends. You go to great lengths to re-route rows, but when you're forced to defend yourself or loved-ones, you certainly don't pull any punches.

You're likely to be a late starter in the romance stakes, and are easily put off by coarseness or lack of mystery. It takes a long time for you to trust another with your heart. More sentimental than passionate, you are totally faithful and make an undemanding, understanding partner.

Duty and hard work drive you and you can get so caught up in a job or cause that you lose track of the outside world. But behind those shy defences is a dramatic, mysteriously powerful person who draws others, and keeps them, easily. The real you, Cancer, will be revealed even more when you find the co-ruler of your life, your RISING SIGN, because it combines with your Cancer sun sign in a way that's unique to you.

You know what your SUN SIGN is – the day you were born makes you a Cancer. Now, having checked the chart opposite for the time of day you were born, you know what your RISING SIGN is. If you don't know the exact time you were born, don't worry. You'll soon spot yourself from the descriptions of each of the SUN SIGN/RISING SIGN combinations.

Sun sign Cancer/rising sign Leo

Leo as a rising sign makes your home an open house. You adore entertaining on a small, and grand, scale – so once inside, visitors get all the caring attention they could want.

YOUR SUN SIGN IS **CANCER** – THIS CHART REVEALS YOUR RISING SIGN

If your date of birth is	If you were born between these times											
22–30 June	6:30 am to 9:14 am	9:15 am to 11:59 am	12 noon to 2:44 pm	2:45 pm to 5:29 pm	5:30 pm to 7:59 pm	8 pm to 9:44 pm	9:45 pm to 10:59 pm	11 pm to 11:59 pm	12 midnight to 12:59 am	1 am to 2:14 am	2:15 am to 3:59 am	4 am to 6:29 am
1–11 July	6 am to 8:44 am	8:45 am to 11:29 am	11:30 am to 2:14 pm	2:15 pm to 4:59 pm	5 pm to 7:29 pm	7:30 pm to 9:14 pm	9:15 pm to 10:29 pm	10:30 pm to 11:29 pm	11:30 pm to 12:29 am	12:30 am to 1:44 am	1:45 am to 3:29 am	3:30 am to 5:59 am
12–22 July	5:30 am to 8:14 am	8:15 am to 10:59 am	11 am to 1:44 pm	1:45 pm to 4:29 pm	4:30 pm to 6:59 pm	7 pm to 8:44 pm	8:45 pm to 9:59 pm	10 pm to 10:59 pm	11 pm to 11:59 pm	12 midnight to 1:14 am	1:15 am to 2:59 am	3 am to 5:29 am
YOUR RISING SIGN IS	LEO	VIRGO	LIBRA	SCORPIO	SAGITTARIUS	CAPRICORN	AQUARIUS	PISCES	ARIES	TAURUS	GEMINI	CANCER

Leo also lands you with a more open, drama-loving side than most Cancers, and lavishes lovers with a warm, obvious show of affection.

You'd make a good and adaptable actor, since your sun sign gives such insight into what makes others tick, and your rising sign lets you put it on public display. But this talent translates well to teaching, nursing and police work as well.

Yes, you do adore to own things and can get too keen on accumulating cash, but you turn this talent towards saving cash for others, too – and after all, you need a fair amount to keep up the lavish lifestyle you love!

You're no loner and wouldn't last long on a desert island without regular, warm loving. Your urge to create a drama out of nothing can ruin romance, and while you tease a partner with only a tiny part of the truth, you then explode because they can't read your mind!

Pettiness drives you away because you have a proud, kind and generous heart. Other people tend to put a lot of trust in you, and rightly so, because you'd do anything rather than let friend, family or workmate down. But when duty weighs you down too much, do get right away and take time for your own needs – no-one deserves it more.

Sun sign Cancer/rising sign Virgo

Those tender emotions are tucked away under an overlay of tough armour, thanks to your rising sign's shyness and need for secrecy. But blast down the barriers of your basic timidity and you make a wonderfully loyal friend and protective lover. For some reason, you shake off shyness best in group situations, so you tend to seek those out rather than spending spare time on a one-to-one basis.

Virgo brings a brilliant photographic memory while Cancer has a passion for the past. Combine the two, and the dream career for you could be linked to museums, antiques, or even writing historical novels.

In relationships, trivial detail tends to sidetrack you, but get a grip on that and you're thoughtful, helpful and deeply concerned for others' welfare. You've a skill for nursing, whether professionally or in a home crisis.

Your rising sign helps keep your runaway emotions under control, but once your sympathy's sparked, you are a steadfast friend to anyone down on their luck. But bite back that impulse to lecture them on 'what you should have done . . .' Slow to anger, you also forgive at snail's pace, and forgetting takes even longer! And your passion for neatness and tidiness borders on an obsession.

It's hard for you to lose yourself in love, and you're picking and poking at relationships constantly. Sex-based affairs are not your scene, and you may suffer many disappointments before finding warm love for life.

Sun sign Cancer/rising sign Libra

Home-hugging Cancer is at odds with Libra's impulse to reach out and socialise, but let yourself be lured out of your hideyhole shell to make friends and life can seem a lot less threatening. Your love of music should break the ice! You're a skilful people-watcher, very good at working out what the public want. So a career in marketing, public relations, or even running your own shop, could send you towards success. Luckily, you have a knack of rising to the top of most careers without too much effort.

With a sympathetic manner, good listening skills and a greatly-respected ability to make fair judgments, you're a born go-between. You'll do anything to beat injustice, and have enough tact to step in without starting a riot. But sometimes the decision timescale needs to be speeded up slightly – or you'll still be weighing up both sides when the argument's long gone.

Your rising sign's scales swing your already seesawing moods even more violently, and sadness can sweep over you suddenly. Anger can be extreme and violent too, but your major fault is becoming obsessed with work at the cost of everything, and everyone, else.

A happy-ever-after marriage is your aim, but if one love

doesn't make it, you tend to crash land and straight into the next. You feel insecure without a partner's approval, and can't buy a new coat or new kind of soap powder without a second opinion! Try to trust your own instincts.

Sun sign Cancer/rising sign Scorpio

Explosive as a box of fireworks, thankfully your touch paper doesn't get lit very often. For although your Scorpio side slips intense and powerful emotions into the cocktail, it also makes you less easily influenced than most other Cancer types. So you usually manage to master your mixed-up thoughts and feelings.

A stripe of Scorpio intuition on top of your basic coat of perception produces a powerfully psychic person who's magnetically attractive. Subtle, cunning and ambitious, you're the perfect plotter – with a strong streak of self-interest plus the ability to conceal it. As you get older, though, you become more genuinely caring towards others and may even have magical healing powers. Develop this deeper side of your nature to find fulfilment.

You see life as black and white, love and hate, and in romance you're far more of a game-player than head-over-heels victim. Secretly, you long for total power over a partner and may be too moody and complex for more straightforward lovers. You can also exploit your charm ruthlessly, while keeping at least one door in your own heart firmly locked . . . so frustrating!

When your rage, usually stoked by jealousy, boils over, others run for cover, leaving you alone and lolling in a deep, dark depression. By storing up sour feelings, you make yourself a target for future problems. Romance may be a rocky road for you, but ask for support to survive.

Sun sign Cancer/rising sign Sagittarius

No-one was ever less like their image – for though you come across as a fun-loving party animal, inside you're a shy and cautious soul who seldom sticks their nose far outside their own front door! Extra-strong family influence works to keep you close to home, but your sociable rising sign has made you more talkative than other Cancer types, even if you never reveal your real feelings. You're still touchy and supersensitive, though, and should let Sagittarius slowly wind down those steel shutters round your vulnerable self.

Love is something you've learned from stories and films rather than personal experience – and you'll always steer towards the sweetly sentimental rather than a passion-packed affair. But you are probably overprotective of your heart, and deep-seated pride plus an exaggerated sense of your own worth don't help you open up.

An amazingly loyal friend, you allow yourself to be put off possible love mates by trivial flaws. And you rarely let someone have your trust again once they've let you down. Perseverance isn't your strong point, because your rising sign lends you a restless streak. But on the plus side, this pushes you to be more adaptable to new surroundings, so you should aim for more than armchair travel. A big business job that takes you abroad, but also allows you to hide for long spells in home sweet home, would be your ideal. But any career must be routine-free.

Sun sign Cancer/rising sign Capricorn

Insight plus a generous jab of ambition combine to put your finger on the pulse and your name on that important door. You've a double, deep-seated desire for security and cash-backed power, and thrive when you're given your head and the chance to lead large groups.

The road you select to success will rarely be a straight one, but, thanks to your rising sign, you've all the self-discipline and drive you need to get there just the same. You'd never be taken for a true Capricorn, though – you're far too tolerant, and prefer to give in gracefully in arguments just to keep the peace.

Society's rules are for keeping, not chucking, as far as you're concerned. You're conventional, cautious and have a knack of stretching your cash and finding new ways of bringing more in. You may forgive, but you never forget a hurt. On the plus side, that long memory means many of your firmest friendships go way, way back.

Your main fault is getting too tangled up in others' problems. Please give up trying to sort them out single-handed, because it takes too heavy a toll on your delicate emotions. And if you do let yourself get down, dark depression can drag on for weeks.

A touch too keen on keeping up appearances, you can come across as cold and detached, even between the sheets – and sex takes a back seat to work. But any lover who lightens your heart can be sure of total devotion.

Sun sign Cancer/rising sign Aquarius

Still conventional at your very core, your adventurous rising sign helps widen your horizons and open up a whole new world of change and challenges. It also sharpens your already caring soul and spreads concern outside your immediate circle.

Ideally, you'd love a free-living, free-loving lifestyle, full of friends who are wacky one-offs. But with your watery side putting a slight damper on that, you hover in the safe shadows of a familiar setting, making the odd bold, brave dash into a dangerous love affair, unusual job or outrageous friendship.

Always open to fresh ideas, you are observant, inventive and drawn to all sorts of research, even secret. You're no snob, yet you still tend to inch up the social ladder, perhaps because your mixture of friendly caring and mysterious depths makes you irresistible.

Normally the sweetest-tempered of people, you will lash out in sudden anger if necessary, and others have learned to respect this. Basically buoyant, you're less affected by surroundings than other Cancer types and have considerable inner strength. But at work you're your own worst enemy if you let your thoughts linger gloomily on past hiccups and failures. Your sense of self-worth is as fragile as the finest crystal, and it's cost you even more, so protect it well by thinking positive. If lovers can accept your wide circle, you'll be loyal for life.

Sun sign Cancer/rising sign Pisces

Still waters run to unbelievable depths in your double water sign duo – you're so tuned in to others' thoughts and feelings it's a wonder you've time for your own. You're naturally self-protective, and know exactly how to avoid events and individuals that are likely to hurt you. But you also see straight to the centre of others' troubles and are especially good at advising them. Even strangers tend to open up to you because you seem so kind and sympathetic and have such an excellent bedside manner.

Romance is your rightful setting. Moody, but never mean, you're a magnificently imaginative lover, only too pleased to be swept off your feet by a wave of lust and emotion. Unfortunately, the down side of this is a fantasy addiction – you love being in love so much that any would-be long-term partner has to indulge your imagination in ever more outrageous ways, or risk your eyes, and heart, straying elsewhere.

You may often end up the 'other' man or woman and must guard against a selfish attitude in affairs. Watch out, too, that you don't drown your sorrows or find relief in bitter words when things aren't going your way, or become a slave to non-existent illnesses.

Gambling and fly-by-night financial schemes can be pitfalls for you, and you have an unhealthy tendency to live in the past. Your colourful imagination and emotions overwhelm you without some creative letting off steam.

Sun sign Cancer/rising sign Aries

Aries bravado boosts boldness – you're outspoken and your words always carry weight. Kind, sensitive and warm, you really do care about others very much. But you will always have to fight temptation to put yourself first, first, first. Your other unique qualities are a positive delight in chatting to strangers and a bottomless fund of unflagging energy. Even when you do retreat for a rest, or just some time alone, you make sure no-one catches you napping.

Now for the minus points. You seem to have been short-changed in that famous Cancer tact. Instead you're blunt and ruthless, ready to cut rudely across any talk that doesn't interest – or star – you. You're full of opinions and complaints, but not as good a judge of human nature as you think. You see only what you want to in close relationships, and you're tugged two ways as your conflicting signs tussle over their individual passions for home and freedom.

Love links may collapse when you dump a partner in favour of a tempting new offer. But you're never alone for long! Your pursuit of anyone, or anything, that takes your fancy is single-minded and single-handed. Rushing romance can rocket you into legal wrangles, but you don't mind falling sometimes if you're moving forward. Fire turns quiet Cancer courage flamboyant, you're always looking for ways to test yourself. Travel and sport are lucky for you.

Sun sign Cancer/rising sign Taurus

The kitchen or a comfy armchair is the centre of your world – no-one enjoys their home comforts, and home cooking, more! You could even have a ballooning body to prove it. But although you won't stray far from home and family, you love entertaining, too, and are great at it.

Unpretentious, friendly and tactful, you'll go out of your way to avoid making waves, or to calm them back down once they've started crashing. You just want a quiet life to enjoy your peace, although when stirred, you'll certainly leap to your own defence.

Your rising sign injects a touch of realism into dreamy Cancer, but that undiluted Taurus obsession with owning and controlling things is, thankfully, well watered down in you. You have a fine imagination, although you don't always give it free rein, which is a pity. Open up that fantasy factory more often, and make your talents work for you!

Singing and art attract you – you've a good voice and an eye for both the beautiful and the useful. But too often your passion for food and eating can replace romance, especially if you're feeling too tongue-tied to ask for what you really want in a relationship. Often passion is pushed back by pally companionship and, while that may be fine for you, partners probably want more.

Stable, patient, practical and cautious – they may sound dull, but yours are qualities in a million. Enjoy!

Sun sign Cancer/rising sign Gemini

Childlike, that's you – but it's an asset, not a fault! You're on younger people's wavelength and know just what makes them tick. But the influence of ever-so-caring Cancer means you genuinely like children. Even if you don't work in child-care, you'll be the most popular person among your own friends and family.

Even just a jot of Gemini airiness can make you seem superficial, a witty chatterbox whose patience runs out as quickly as sand through a sieve. But those deep-down, complicated Cancer emotions mean what you see is definitely not what you get. In fact you're ruled by your heart, not your head.

Your rising sign does set up an escape route from Cancer's routine rut, however, helping your head leap lightly towards new ideas. Considerate, caring and thoughtful, your slightly nervous energy may take its toll on your health – but makes you such fun to be around!

Yes, you do want security, but that could be supplied by two homes or two lovers. And you're more bored by your own company than most Cancers. Your quest for entertainment shoves social life into top gear, but also leads to broken promises, appointments and work deadlines.

Quickly and easily hooked on new romance, your so-short attention span can leave you open to better offers! You may lose out on love luck by trying to gain two goals. Lucky you're one of the most persuasive people around!

Sun sign Cancer/rising sign Cancer

Don't be shocked when, sometimes, a great tidal wave of emotion wells up and almost overwhelms you. It's just the moon making its double-strength pull on your feelings. Often dominated by self-obsessed thoughts, these bouts come from nowhere and leave you knocked out for weeks. And family and friends will just have to realise the only way out for you is quiet time alone to recover.

When this flood flows inwards, you may wonder why you were born with one protective skin too few. Few people are burdened, or blessed, with your supreme sensitivity. You live in a separate layer of life all your own and are often highly talented in music or art. And you can comfort yourself with the knowledge that whatever your life may be, it will never be dull or dreary.

Nothing's too good for those you love – but you do confine your calling for caring to too narrow a circle. And this can make you blind to real faults. It's hard, but you must accept that loved-ones are less than perfect, and so are you! You cling to the past and old, valuable objects, and your knowledge and delicate touch would make you an ideal museum worker. Counselling is another strength – your shoulder's often soggy from friends crying on it! And that warm, sexy voice is very pleasing and you often use it to nip would-be squabbles in the bud. Although you'll have your share of romantic disappointments, once in love you're a devoted and protective dream lover.

Sun Sign Leo

King of the stars, you're masterful and mighty, with a generous heart and a broad mind. But your down side is bossy, extravagant and outspoken – and you can be a bit lazy, vain and fall hard for flattery! One thing's for sure, you are impossible to ignore. Luckily for others, you've an inborn talent for leadership, and are incapable of taking any other position than up front. You excel at organising others and matching people to jobs. And whatever your physical size, you come across as larger and more lovable than life.

A bit of a show-off at times, you never bear a grudge and like to share any good fortune that comes your way. You can't bear being nagged but are happy to work hard, in your own time and following your own timetable. You'd never admit it, but you worry about looking good, and spend a huge amount of time doing your hair. And although you like to clown around when you're in a playful mood, being laughed at rather than with really hurts your pride.

Home is as lavish as you can manage – though usually anything but tidy – and you're happiest in open spaces. You like to fill it with people and animals, but there's a silent understanding that your word is law. You need lots of room, enough to fit in a doting audience wherever you are. And when it comes to love partners, you tend to hang on in there and try to make it work because of your old-fashioned values. And your pride. Let's not forget pride, because it's both your major strength and major weakness.

That gold-plated sense of self-worth hoists you to the top at work and privately guarantees your winnings in the love lottery. But it also makes it almost impossible for you to admit your mistakes. Pride pushes you to be stubborn and, unless you're careful, sets your opinions rock-solid. When your already dazzling confidence gets stoked up to scorching point, you become a tyrant who can't take criticism or listen to reasonable argument.

Generally the sun, your ruler, puts your emotions up front and keeps you frank, lively and flamboyantly cheerful. But when that glow gets clouded, you may suffer severe slabs of depression. You'll hide then from all but those closest to you.

It's essential that you let out anger and aggression or you may suffer from feverish illnesses or become accident-prone. Your courage helps you tackle tasks that others would find too terrifying. You always finish what you start and stand by friends through thick and thin, intriguing those close to you by being totally wrapped up in yourself yet so thoughtful towards others.

Gambling will always attract you, especially when hearts are at stake. You would give up everything for love. Your most delightful quality is a childlike enthusiasm for life which sweeps others along with you.

The real you, Leo, will be uncovered even more by finding your RISING SIGN, the co-ruler of your personality, and seeing just how it combines with your Leo sun sign.

You know what your SUN SIGN is – the day you were born makes you a Leo. Now that you've checked the time of day of your birth against the chart opposite, you know your RISING SIGN too. Even if you don't know the exact time you were born, you'll soon spot yourself from the rundown of each SUN SIGN/RISING SIGN combination.

Sun sign Leo/rising sign Virgo

Too much modesty from your rising sign can swamp your natural self-confidence, and make others wonder sometimes if you're really a Leo at all. But they sense there's a strong-

YOUR SUN SIGN IS **LEO** – THIS CHART REVEALS YOUR RISING SIGN

If your date of birth is	If you were born between these times											
23–21 July	7 am to 9:44 am	9:45 am to 12:29 pm	12:30 pm to 3:14 pm	3:15 pm to 5:44 pm	5:45 pm to 7:29 pm	7:30 pm to 8:44 pm	8:45 pm to 9:44 pm	9:45 pm to 10:44 pm	10:45 pm to 11:59 pm	12 midnight to 1:44 am	1:45 am to 4:14 am	4:15 am to 6:59 am
1–11 August	6:30 am to 9:14 am	9:15 am to 11:59 am	12 noon to 2:44 pm	2:45 pm to 5:14 pm	5:15 pm to 6:59 pm	7 pm to 8:14 pm	8:15 pm to 9:14 pm	9:15 pm to 10:14 pm	10:15 pm to 11:29 pm	11:30 pm to 1:14 am	1:15 am to 3:44 am	3:45 am to 6:29 am
12–23 August	5:45 am to 8:29 am	8:30 am to 11:14 am	11:15 am to 1:59 pm	2 pm to 4:29 pm	4:30 pm to 6:14 pm	6:15 pm to 7:29 pm	7:30 pm to 8:29 pm	8:30 pm to 9:29 pm	9:30 pm to 10:44 pm	10:45 pm to 12:29 am	12:30 am to 2:59 am	3 am to 5:44 am
YOUR RISING SIGN IS	VIRGO	LIBRA	SCORPIO	SAGITTARIUS	CAPRICORN	AQUARIUS	PISCES	ARIES	TAURUS	GEMINI	CANCER	LEO

willed, self-centred lion's heart beating behind your humble front, and that you're too sociable and tolerant of other people's views to be a true Virgo.

All the same, you're not as obviously a born leader as others of your sign and might choose to work behind the scenes rather than parading out in front. Strong feelings of right and wrong guide you and you're highly creative with an added edge of practicality. So you always finish what you start – and can often sell it, too!

Getting distracted by dragging details and being unable to sort out what really matters is the down side of that Virgo influence. But you can also spot key points that others might brush aside. Not for you the normal Leo habit of turning every emotion into an over-the-top production. But although your nature's more retiring than razzmatazz, you must guard against being too hard to get close to. The usually warm Leo sun can get clouded by doom and gloom.

In love, you want things perfect – or not at all! Too many pre-set conditions could frighten away would-be wooers, and your circle of friends, too, may suffer several cracks as someone fails to meet your sky-high standards. Workwise, your memory's your hottest property, but don't take too many risks – you lack pure Leo's gambling luck!

Sun sign Leo/rising sign Libra

You've a happy Leo knack for telling others what to do and still staying liked, because of your rising sign's diplomatic skills. Dramatic and magnetic, you can charm the socks off Royalty and skinheads alike, with a manner that manages to be both regal and chummy at the same time.

You're ultra-romantic, hot-loving and sincere, but slip all too easily into the role of generous jailor in love. You try to run all your close relationships on your own terms . . . and although you are an excellent and fair judge, you can't resist the temptation to lay down the law for your nearest and dearest as well!

You aim high at work and take a natural Leo pride in

whatever you achieve, but a double dose of laid-back laziness from both your signs can, sometimes, make you as hard to shift as an oil slick. Your friends find you delightful company – you're top of every party list – and you have a stronger feeling for teamwork, for sharing and giving, than most Leos. But your rising sign's swinging scales can make mood changes very abrupt.

Easy to enrage but simple to soothe, you normally give unpleasant scenes a miss, and when there's a decision to be made, you hesitate in far-from-fire-sign style. Your heart can't survive without a soul mate, but overdemanding partners soon get dumped and your spending habits can provoke rows. But you're one of the best and most skilful lovers, once matched to someone you respect.

Sun sign Leo/rising sign Scorpio

Your rising sign hurls a handful of gunpowder into your already fiery Leo personality, making you unpredictable, forceful and magnetic. There's frightening energy in this pairing, but bossiness can go overboard, making you constantly battle to dominate others.

Your determination to get to the top in any job, and stay there, is unstoppable, and your intuition and broad vision get added force from your love of hard work and supreme self-confidence. You're best off doing your own thing, of course. Even then, excess energy may need diverting sometimes into physically demanding sport if those you live with are to survive! You tend to hide your iron fist beneath Leo's soft kid gloves and only resort to a double sign show of strength when all else fails, and leave your opponents wondering just what hit them.

You can be an over-intense, over-extreme overworker – and play too hard, too. And your revenge on anyone foolish enough to cross you can be frightening! Anger often simmers in secret before erupting into cruel sarcasm, and being basically a show-off Leo, any tongue-lashings you deliver will be highly public.

For you, there's not much middle ground between love and hate, which means you can love more passionately than any other sign. You're attracted to strong types like yourself and, of course, celebrities. You could easily find fame yourself, with such limelight-loving ambition.

Sun sign Leo/rising sign Sagittarius

Two fire signs mixed make for a well-balanced nature and you're a particularly friendly, open and spontaneous Leo – loving, loyal and able to take most things in your stride. You're probably the most self-assured person there is, but something in your 'I'm all right, Jack' smugness can spark nastiness from others, and it isn't surprising. You try to throw a cloak of modesty over your amazing self-confidence every now and then, but it's so transparent that it doesn't fool anyone!

You take it for granted that others will look up to you – and, luckily, most of the time they do. A lifelong romantic, because you take your own freedom so much for granted you may not feel ready to pull your weight in a partnership until later life.

You're seldom held back by man-made obstacles and much prefer to look forward, not back. But although you are usually youthful and optimistic in outlook, you do have odd bursts of negative thinking. Playful and eager to learn, you'll probably spend some of your life far from your birthplace, and may even live in another, hotter, country. But wherever you're based will have a feel of Never Never Land because you hate getting to grips with growing up and dull old reality.

If fate flings bad things your way, you're tempted to up and leave, and start a new life somewhere else. But sometimes sticking it out can be very rewarding.

Sun sign Leo/rising sign Capricorn

Your rising sign makes you more stay-at-home than the average Leo, although you're still naturally sociable . . . and when it comes to the ambition bug, you're seriously infected! This star mix points to someone who rises to the top against all the odds. There's not much you wouldn't do to get ahead, though you never forget where you came from. But once your target, big or small, is in your sights, you don't take your eyes off it for a second.

Because you have a taste for the good things in life, you're prepared to work very hard indeed to get them. Your generosity tends to be personal in that it's limited to people you actually know. And although you're tolerant – too much so – with those you love, you can be overcritical and cruel to people outside that charmed circle.

Capricorn caution also controls your spending – most of the time! For while Leo's pockets are constantly open to offers of a party, your more cautious rising sign carefully takes credit cards and any big notes out of your wallet before you leave home, just in case! True, you can celebrate with the best, but you prefer to put your amazing energy to more sensible use.

In love, your warm heart hides behind a cool, calm mask, but anyone who manages to peek past it gets a completely genuine, faithful partner. Pride makes you endure heart pains in silence, so take extra long to choose a partner who really cares, and can keep up!

Sun sign Leo/rising sign Aquarius

You're not as me-mad as many Leos – your rising sign gives you a dreamy, anything-goes approach to life. You can have personal aims that don't become obsessions, and look to the far future in an objective way. It also gives you an extra-warm personality, going out of your way to help others. Though wanting to hug the whole world does of course fit in with your Leo drive to turn everything into a drama!

There can be an occasional clash between your Leo love of stardom and an Aquarius insistence on equal rights for all, Leo's urge to cling to fixed beliefs and your rising sign's fresh, ever-changing outlook. These tension knots can be most easily untangled when you're helping others on a large scale, and you should always work with people.

You certainly have the energy to keep two, even three, affairs on the boil and, not surprisingly, your lovelife will turn calmer when you leave your youth behind. You may lose your heart, more often than is good for you, but you never lose your head, making you ideal to have around in an emergency. And you have a far-from-usual Leo gift for working in partnership with others, though you do have to fight the impulse to take over!

Socially, you're quite modest and hate big, dressy do's, But you do have a mighty, though not malicious, temper. Your linked signs double stubbornness, but put you ahead of the game in observing human nature.

Sun sign Leo/rising sign Pisces

No wonder you long to be liked! Your dotty, dreaming drifter of a rising sign searches for love security, while your basic Leo personality is constantly on the lookout for affection, too. But in your lifelong search for good friends and lovers, you're also capable of short-lived, no-strings affairs, making you a bit of a mystery. You also appear innocent and easily led, as Pisces pushes you to experience anything new that comes your way. But there's still a natural authority hiding beneath your air of little boy, or little girl, lost.

Your big Leo heart is especially tender – you'd find it hard to harm a fly – and there's a superstrong ebb and flow to your emotions, thanks to Pisces. But your fire sign side makes sure you always keep the upper hand with feelings so they don't run, or ruin, your life. Whatever tears you may shed in private, your Leo pride will put a brave face on it in public. You know yourself far too well to let those doubts or that vulnerability hang out.

You may appear eccentric, and sometimes need lots of encouragement to reach life goals. But you probably will get to the top, even though you do it by the most roundabout route. Your anger simmers like a slow cooker, but once sparked, it's as hard to put out as a forest fire. And you can't cope with sudden upsets – except by panicking. In the long term, though, thoughtful caring wins you so many friends.

Sun sign Leo/rising sign Aries

Boss cat, that's you. A real trailblazer, an aggressive leader, outgoing and ever-optimistic, you never, but never, give up. Even on a shipwrecked raft, as the water lapped around your ears, you'd be sure a miracle rescue must be on its way. Your radiant charm wraps up your amazing ambition and takes the edge off a steely determination to achieve everything entirely on your own – which can catapult you into some catastrophic disasters!

Just as you rush heart-first into romance, 100 per cent convinced you'll live happily ever after, this time . . . so too you tackle work head-on and without even a moment's thoughtful hesitation. Your pride will never let you turn back, either, so it's just as well you're so adaptable! Steer your reckless aggro into sport or business instead, and resist the temptation to lord it over your family.

You're very competitive and would race your own shadow for want of something better – and your over-demanding ways could sabotage love affairs when they've hardly started. If anyone is daft enough to play victim, you can easily step into the bully's shoes. So chances are your over-impulsive, sexy nature will lead to early marriage.

At work, you can't take orders – but when given your own show to run, you're a creative change-maker. You do like to leave fiddly details to others, though. Patience is one virtue you lack. You want attention, food, love, sex and booze. And you want them now!

Sun sign Leo/rising sign Taurus

Strangers often take you for someone famous. You have a certain proud way of holding your head, you're probably good-looking and you move well, too. But the chances of you being really well known aren't too high, because your laid-back combination adds up to a lazy lion, full of star-making ideas but never quite getting round to action.

You certainly like your comforts and are born to be a leader as long as you learn from your mistakes. You'd be the kind of cowboy who rides straight into an Apache ambush, even though the warning signs are all there, just because you've decided to go that way and that's that.

There may be a clash between your rising sign's urge for security and an easy life and your sun sign's search for thrills and gambles. Taurus adds a footnote of financial caution, too, to your extravagance. Yours is a dynamic, dependable character and once you've committed your heart, you are usually faithful. Absolutely no-one and nothing can tire you out, either!

You've a strong home-loving side, and are probably still closely tied to your parents. You really need a safe haven to retreat to when life gets too difficult. Although you're perfectly capable of handling several crises at once, your approach can be rather heavy-handed. You'd save time and energy by not trying to smash your way through problems with a sledgehammer. A calm, cuddlesome lover, your relationships are the warmest, cosiest around.

Sun sign Leo/rising sign Gemini

You carry sunshine with you and have loads of friends, because you want to give them (and yourself, of course) the very best life can offer. No wonder plenty of people want to join your team. You're a Leo who's clearly going places, spurred on by your sun sign's determination and Gemini's way with words. You travel far by force of personality alone.

You enjoy working hard on behalf of those you adore and like nothing better than splashing out on fabulous presents for your family. Your rising sign gives you a taste for travel and makes you even more theatrical than most Leos. You're a witty, entertaining host and a laughter-making guest who can get any gathering off the ground.

That warm-as-toast Leo heart is teamed with a brilliant

brain, so you can get others eating out of your hand at work, leaving you free to dream up the big ideas. You never quite grow up or lose interest in learning, even when you're popping out to pick up your pension. You express yourself easily and with great drama, but you're quickly bored and prone to nervous exhaustion.

A passion for fresh faces and places can make life hard for your love, so the jealous type is not for you. Your temper has a low flashpoint but is easily soothed and you're always first to say sorry. Your heart may be a bit immature, but it's always in the right place.

Sun sign Leo/rising sign Cancer

Sentimental but never sickly, romantic with a realistic streak, always honest and sincere . . . you are one of the most sensitive of the Leo set. Yes, you can brood, sulk and generally mope around when you sense the spotlight isn't shining enough on you. And your rising sign has given you a rather thin skin and a gift for overreacting. Cancer makes you an emotional sponge, soaking up others' moods, good and bad. But Leo helps wring it all out again, through the creative outlet of drama.

Your opposing planetary influences are usually well balanced, but when a Leo gloom descends you may be sent tumbling towards paralysing self-pity and loneliness. Your inborn love of gold, both for its colour and what it can buy, is boosted by a cash-conscious rising sign, so no wonder your eyes light up and your heart leaps when you know you've got cash stashed away.

Family ties figure very large in your life and you like nothing better than cooking up a feast for loved-ones. In fact, you like showing off your skills so much you'd make an ideal TV chef, provided you can control your own foodie impulses enough not to get hugely fat!

Being cooped up drives you crackers and your changeable heart careers you through countless affairs. You hate anything low key or ordinary and can exaggerate just so you don't sound dull. But life around you is a colourful adventure and you've a knack of making others feel needed.

Sun sign Leo/rising sign Leo

Double your dose of pure Leo arrogance and what do you get? A pride of lions – a drama addict who's hooked on the spotlight and has a flair for showing the world only their best side. You're easy-going, incredibly generous, friendly and naturally commanding. You draw others towards your magnetic personality but need to be in charge or you'll move on to a new group. Writing, politics and acting all suit, but unless you tune into other people's feelings more, you could come a cropper in romance.

You do have one huge flaw, however ... megapride! It goes hand in hand with a vanity that makes you easy prey for sponging hangers-on and sweet-talking flatterers. You're bound to often feel let down by love, too, because you make no allowance for faults at the beginning. Honest and straightforward, you're one of the most upfront, open-book signs and expect everyone to be as trustworthy as you are. True love may take second place to your runaway ambition, too. Or you may try to turn partners into put-upon doormats, then impatiently kick them aside because they're not enough of a challenge.

At your worst, you're hot-headedly stubborn with a quick-flaring temper and refusal to listen to reason. Your lust rating is sky-high and could make love loyalty hard to hang on to. You can't take no for an answer once you fancy someone. But with such powerful creative energy, you're a lover in a million and won't face much rejection.

Sun Sign Virgo

If you meet a stranger on a narrow pavement and both hang back, quietly murmuring 'After you,' 'No – after you,' chances are you're both gentle, polite Virgos – especially if you find yourselves criticising each other's dress sense and dithering ways at the same time.

Sensible, solitary, but with a heart of solid gold, Virgo excels at work but appreciates enjoyable play, too – although you're usually too health-conscious to really let your hair down and get stuck into a social life.

You prefer to punch most of your considerable energies into practical work problems, and since you're a much-admired expert at sorting them out, why not enjoy it, too?

Because you've made something of a career out of criticism, you can give the impression you're a fault-finding fusspot who's too tightly wrapped in red tape and pointless detail. But really you're just pushed by your planet ruler, the thought-master Mercury, to be a perfection-seeker who lives through their mind rather than their body. So you're bound to live, eat and breathe work because your brain rarely switches off, even during sleep. But it has its up side . . .

You've a clear head and a cool heart that warms when you're doing what Virgo loves best – taking care of other people, often professionally. Your heart may not be stitched to your sleeve like the more demonstrative signs, but wherever you hide it, it's in the right place.

Nothing but the best is good enough for Virgo's mind and body. So you're very health-aware and protect your natural vitality by vetting carefully what food and drink goes down your throat. You may be a fan of food fads and diets, however, over-impressed by the word 'health' on the label.

You're very thorough, down to earth and well organised, and a bit of a loner deep down. You'd survive quite happily marooned on a desert island, so you demand a partner who's very much on the same wavelength. Your careful selection process means love mistakes are rare.

Not for you the trembling thrill of lust at first sight or instant friendships – you must weigh people up from a distance before committing yourself. You're hard to get to know, too, with your reserved ways and tendency never to use four words when one will do. But it's worth the effort, for Virgo loving is strong, lifelong and full of sexy surprises. In fact, you have a very powerful secret sex drive and, without sufficient lovemaking can become nervy and irritable.

Friends often call on you as a go-between to sort out their emotional problems and really value your advice. Any disadvantage in your arm's length, guarded manner is more than made up for by a nice, gentle sense of humour, genuine lifelong curiosity about people and a desire to please.

Are you ready to find out even more about the real you, Virgo? All will be revealed when you discover the co-ruler of your life, your RISING SIGN, and the way it combines with your Virgo sun sign.

You know what your SUN SIGN is from the the day you were born, which makes you a Virgo. Now, having checked the time of day you were born against the chart opposite, you know your RISING SIGN too. If you don't know the exact time you were born, you'll soon spot yourself from the descriptions of each of the SUN SIGN/RISING SIGN combinations.

Sun sign Virgo/rising sign Libra

Warm, loving Libra loosens your sun sign's inhibitions and make you less of a prisoner of sensible, but sometimes dull, routine. You may be fanatically neat and nit-picking, a rule-maker not breaker. But no one need ever know, since your

YOUR SUN SIGN IS **VIRGO** – THIS CHART REVEALS YOUR RISING SIGN

If your date of birth is	If you were born between these times											
24–31 August	7:30 am to 10:14 am	10:15 am to 12:59 pm	1 pm to 3:29 pm	3:30 pm to 5:14 pm	5:15 pm to 6:29 pm	6:30 pm to 7:29 pm	7:30 pm to 8:29 pm	8:30 pm to 9:44 pm	9:45 pm to 11:29 pm	11:30 pm to 1:59 am	2 am to 4:44 am	4:45 am to 7:29 am
1–11 September	7 am to 9:44 am	9:45 am to 12:29 pm	12:30 pm to 2:59 pm	3 pm to 4:44 pm	4:45 pm to 5:59 pm	6 pm to 6:59 pm	7 pm to 7:59 pm	8 pm to 9:14 pm	9:15 pm to 10:59 pm	11 pm to 1:29 am	1:30 am to 4:14 am	4:15 am to 6:59 am
12–22 September	6:15 am to 8:59 am	9 am to 11:44 am	11:45 am to 2:14 pm	2:15 pm to 3:59 pm	4 pm to 5:14 pm	5:15 pm to 6:14 pm	6:15 pm to 7:14 pm	7:15 pm to 8:29 pm	8:30 pm to 10:14 pm	10:15 pm to 12:44 am	12:45 am to 3:29 am	3:30 am to 6:14 am
YOUR RISING SIGN IS	LIBRA	SCORPIO	SAGITTARIUS	CAPRICORN	AQUARIUS	PISCES	ARIES	TAURUS	GEMINI	CANCER	LEO	VIRGO

Libra sunny smiles slide a pleasant mask onto that Virgo straight face.

You long to be accepted by friends and lovers but are often too shy to reach out for love. Your rising sign gives you an artistic touch and this can combine with your basically practical sun sign to bring a flair for decorating or graphic design.

Both signs in this set value order, neatness and a methodical approach to life – but do call 'Stop!' if you find yourself lining up all your shoes in rows or trying to select identical apples in the supermarket.

You'd make an excellent, thorough researcher, someone's priceless right hand. Venus-ruled Libra's warmth will help you to slap down sarcasm and lack of self-confidence and inspire you to shine up love links. But lasting romance is still likely to spark for you from the neighbouring computer terminal or production line – you can never totally separate business and pleasure!

Each of your two sides can get sidetracked by trivia, so you won't sprint up the success ladder. But you'll get further than you think. You must have a loving partner, but don't take troubles out on them again and again.

Sun sign Virgo/rising sign Scorpio

With eagle eyes always poised to pinpoint problems, you don't think twice about plunging straight in where angels fear to tread. If you can help, you will, which makes you an intensely loyal, caring friend – even when you're not getting your full 50 per cent of the deal.

You can also be a sharp-tongued, sharp-witted and argumentative enemy. Doing good is what makes you happiest, and you combine your Virgo taste for detail with a direct Scorpio approach and organisational skill. You are usually outspoken – especially for a deserving cause – but you do know when it's better to bite back that stinging tongue. Trouble is, you don't always apply your rules of perfection to yourself!

Your questioning mind puts you first in the queue for

nursing, teaching and medicine – jobs that rely on painstaking care as well as clever brains. But in your personal life, you are prone to extremes and only exercise can relax you. It takes you a long time – years perhaps – to trust someone enough to allow them to become a close friend or lover. And you can be cruelly cold.

Your talent for hiding feelings gives you the emotional edge, so make sure you pick a partner who can look after themselves. Jealousy brings out the beast in you, and if lovers let you down, you spend hours plotting vicious revenge. But your pool of deep, hidden passion means fascinating relationships will pepper your whole life.

Sun sign Virgo/rising sign Sagittarius

Friendship means so much to you. Unlike some other Virgos, you can even overlook major flaws in those you're close to, though you're still forever trying to fix and fiddle with their private lives! Yes, you're nosey and interfering, but your advice is usually welcome because friends realise you only want what's best for them.

Your patient and painstaking sun sign puts the brakes on any potential huffing, puffing and unrealistic plans provoked by your big-talking rising sign. But Sagittarius does lend a flourish to your sometimes obsessive fussiness and gives you a broader outlook on life. And though you're as organised and neat as any other Virgo, your rising sign makes you more open and approachable. It also shows you the plus points of pushing your below-the-surface nervous energy into sports or travel.

This is a very look-ahead sign, so you may neglect your own life while trying to sort out others' troubles. You need to be selfish sometimes, though, unless you want to be left on the shelf. You can seem cool, but you're never actually cruel.

Your free-falling, adaptable rising sign and your Virgo self-sufficiency do, however, let you find your way fast out of any love affair that starts fraying round the edges. Study and research are your first loves, but you'll probably still marry twice and form two major attachments, one with somebody socially high up, even famous.

Sun sign Virgo/rising sign Capricorn

A cucumber-cool customer, you don't waste precious time dawdling and daydreaming, but play everything straight down the line, by the rule book. Cautious, thorough, and extremely hard-working, you have to fight off a tendency to be an all-work-and-no-play type who tries to drive workmates equally hard.

Naturally reserved, you must try to let those barriers down a bit if you're to draw the emotional and sexual satisfaction you need. And remember, to stay fresh your lovelife needs changes, no matter how much you wish things could always stay the same.

Capricorn gives you a taste for life's luxuries, while Virgo doesn't mind going without, and this adaptable mixture drums you up the business talent to achieve fame and fortune. Although you're frightened of getting your fingers burned in love, you've a fantasy physical attractiveness which flings would-be loves at your feet.

Your talents lie in renovating and rescuing, anything from old cars to failing companies. Even sad, worn-out people! With Virgo's flair for organising and Capricorn's stop-at-nothing stamina, you'd make a good office manager, editor or market researcher. Any rescue operation where there's no room for mistakes or time for breaks would also suit your skills! Learning to relax would defuse fretting and let you take more pride in what you do achieve.

Sun sign Virgo/rising sign Aquarius

Deep-thinking and detail-conscious, your rising sign raises your eyes towards the future. But while Virgo is practical through and through, Aquarius' angle is more abstract – you can handle both the 'hows' and the 'what ifs' at the same time. You want to be of smiling service to others, and so are best suited to health care or a similar job where you're helping people get better against the odds. You'd give your last drop of blood for causes you believe in, but get more worked up about worldwide problems like saving whales or the ozone layer than personal needs or ambitions.

Lovers don't get quite the same level of tolerance and devotion as overseas orphans! In fact you are hard to please and are easily put off possible love matches by minor points such as unironed clothes or bad haircuts! You probably delay deep commitment until late in life – your rising sign sparks an extra taste for independence and you back away from displays of strong emotion.

You're not quite as practical as a Virgo should be – keener on thinking than doing. But there are some very original and far-sighted ideas brewing away in your brain. Despite all your caution, surprises are in store. A deeply fascinating love affair will fly out at you from somewhere completely unexpected. And you may well be the parent of twins! When you allow your fine mind to fly free, you're a gifted genius who others always take notice of.

Sun sign Virgo/rising sign Pisces

Deep-sea Pisces plunges your neat, orderly Virgo imagination into waters wider than those found inside the heated fish-tank! It makes you much more creative and boosts common sense with a touch of intuition, too. You're number one at helping anyone in desperate need, and though you'd never break the law yourself, you offer others who have a helping hand in a simple, kind way. But that doesn't mean you can't spot scroungers a mile off!

Your single-minded dedication to whatever work you're doing means you don't notice the dull, routine bits that might drive other sun signs demented. But, too often, you use work as a distraction to detour the uncomfortable lure of lust. While Virgo makes you fussy, passionate Pisces tries to push you into compromising positions with every glance, till your heart's in a spin. You may resort to drooling over someone out of reach like a film star!

Unlike many other Virgos, you're better off with a partner. Although you may think your heart's soft and tender, it's really steely enough to stand plenty of false starts until you finally find love. When weepy moods wash over you or you feel daydreamy, blame your rising sign for fine-tuning your feelings. Because you've helped countless friends sort themselves out, you're never short of sympathy. But you do tend to hang on to heartbreak, even when you're obviously being taken for a ride. Writing and work linked to food and drink will bring you success.

Sun sign Virgo/rising sign Aries

This is a duo that gets things done! Aries fans fire in your heart, while Virgo stays down to earth and practical, preventing that daft fire sign dash head-first into disaster. But you can find yourself torn two ways sometimes, between a desire to tread carefully and a who-cares fascination for challenges. Which can be exhausting for you and those who share your life.

You adore new ideas, yes, but being a basic Virgo you need to know how and why they work by taking them apart, piece by piece. With your endless energy and organised approach, no wonder you get on so well at work! You tend to turn your gifts towards serving others, but also have enough talent – plus patience to practise – to make music your future.

Although blocked nervous energy can end up as stomach or head pains, you're always interested in staying fit, particularly through special diet. You rush about more than other Virgos and can't stop problems picking away at you, so you'd rather be in charge and be confident of your own high standards than kowtow to someone less capable.

Often, though, you're not an obvious leader, more a backroom ideas person. You aren't as self-confident as Aries' brash tongue and sporty body seem, so you need a lover who makes you feel good and look good to the world. You're best with challenges that push you to your limits.

Sun sign Virgo/rising sign Taurus

This is a near-perfect pairing – your two signs fit together like hand and glove. Result – the most practical person around. You're modest and never make waves. You might seem stodgy to start with, but those close to you have come to appreciate what's underneath – a very tolerant, sympathetic person.

You will always put yourself out to help friends and family, even if it means turning out to collect them from an airport in the early hours, or lending a helping hand on a heavy-duty shopping trip when your favourite programme's on TV.

Affection matters more to you than to most Virgos, and your ideal is a pleasant job among nice people, preferably in leafy surroundings. You also hanker after a cosy home where you and those you love can unwind, and eat, to your heart's content. Laziness can fatten you up a treat, though, unless you jolt yourself into action at the gym or swimming pool.

You always see things through, but aren't particularly ambitious. Lovers find you totally trustworthy, loyal as they come. You prefer a partner who won't make too many demands, especially moneywise, but you secretly fret about losing your lover's interest, and so you go along with changes, just to please. But you'll go far because you never lose your sense of proportion or passion for homelife. Always have something to hug, even a furry pet!

Sun sign Virgo/rising sign Gemini

Your mega-dose of Mercury makes you rather restless and you need to find ways to rein in your free-range energies. You often find yourself polishing your desk, tidying cabinets, cleaning out cupboards and rejigging the garage, instead of getting on with a major job like earning your living!

You're even harder to satisfy than other Virgos, but your quick, questioning mind and outwardly sociable shine help you pass quickly on to fresh interests, or meet new lovers when old flames fail to measure up! In public, you would make a good professional critic, teacher or inspector, from buses to taxes. But in your private life you tend to give up on new relationships too readily due to the Gemini boredom factor, and may over-analyse too much.

You really enjoy being of help to others – yours is service with a smile and you're much more chatty than other Virgos. But though you have a deep sense of duty to someone once you've hitched your wagon to their heart, your taste for mind-games can make you too cool and detached at times.

Poor performance of any kind brings you out in a rash of criticism, but you still feel surprised when some of your love targets disappear! You're clever enough to win others round with words when you choose, though. Once you've learned to limit your workload, your great originality can shine through.

Sun sign Virgo/rising sign Cancer

You shine as a sympathetic saviour whenever a friend's in trouble because Cancer gives you a need to care. But remember you can risk your own health by taking on too many of other people's problems. Sometimes you need a bit of tender looking-after yourself, even if you have too much Cancer stubbornness to admit it!

Food preparation interests you a lot and you are likely to follow specific diets. You are prey to strange but unstoppable mood swings now and then because of your rising sign. And although Virgo usually keeps your view of life detached and sensible, you can submit to illogical sulks.

Your heart is easily hurt. Usually, you hug your wounds too close for others to see, but you should try to shift your double shot of self-sacrifice to let helping hands get closer. You enjoy changes of scene and can be an emotional mirror, reflecting other people's moods when you're with them.

Expect to reach a powerful position, but don't be surprised if your route's marred by a measure of scandal! At times you may lose your sense of proportion, and then loving is your best medicine. It gives you vitality, soothes your worries and boosts your confidence. You're happiest when you know someone really needs you. Money may be hard to come by to begin with as you lack natural cash luck, but when it does arrive it should last you a lifetime.

Sun sign Virgo/rising sign Leo

Hot stuff Leo links fiery enthusiasm and inspiration into your personality, but you always retain your practical, down-to-earth roots and never get carried away by the sound of your own voice. There's an extra tinge of warmth and generosity to your cool Virgo self, and you show your feelings far more readily. But there's enough Leo drama in you to help you hide your emotions when you want to, too!

Light touch, charm and friendliness make you popular and less of a shrinking violet. Your kind of Virgo certainly isn't always content to take a back seat.

That critical streak takes on a powerful but positive shade and your opinions are highly valued. But there are some minus points, too. Fire sign bigheadedness can reinforce your already set ideas, making you an unbearable know-all with opinions cast in concrete. And because you've such a high opinion of yourself, flattery can sweet-talk you into many stupid choices, especially between the sheets!

Love, plus Leo's desire for drama, can dominate your every waking moment. You retain basic Virgo fussiness and refusal to even consider second best, but then go on to combine it with a Leo wish to be seen in public only with a lover who makes you look good. Give yourself a break! You like collecting valuable things and must fight a tendency to see relationships in the same way. But once safely yours, nothing's too good for your love treasure.

Sun sign Virgo/rising sign Virgo

No other sign has your keen eye for all the tiny details of life – you're a walking microscope! You're so naturally observant that you could be a forensic scientist, store detective or psychologist. And, like a good mechanic, you've a special talent for finding and probing weak spots. You approach any problem, examine it from every angle, think for a few seconds, then deliver a spot-on breakdown.

But you're no nasty nit-picker who loves knocking holes in other people's ideas and dreams. You're just so practical that you can't rest until you've found out why things go wrong and then set about putting them right.

A slight meddler you may be, but one with a mission to make, do and mend! No-one resents you doing this, provided you don't turn your magnifying glass directly on them. Only your family and lovers know that you can turn into a bossy tyrant on the home-front, a perfectionist forever snatching tools, saucepans and dusters out of people's hands to show them how the job should be done!

Try to be more laid-back, or romance could cross the road rather than stay on your side. And you've so much to give the lucky person you choose as your lifetime love – a devotion to knowing every detail of a partner's likes and dislikes, and making their every fantasy into thrilling fact in the bedroom. Rock-solid romance that will always be a warm, safe refuge from the storms of everyday life.

Sun Sign Libra

Most Libras are very likeable, usually late and too often lazy-bones. You have the gift of good looks, often with the sort of perfect face that stops the traffic. And it's precisely because Libra looks so good (and you have people falling hopelessly for your charm from childhood onwards) that you're never punctual, and allow others to do your dirty work and take the blame for your mistakes. It's easy to act adorable when everyone's on your side from the start, isn't it?

In fact, Libra's main faults and advantages all arise because other people keep letting you off the hook. If anyone ever ticked you off when you showed up hours overdue, you'd soon kick those embedded bad habits of a lifetime. But that natural lack of worry means Libra will never turn into one of life's sloggers or plodders. You were born lucky, and with the trick of being able to think fast and on your feet. You can always say just the right thing with perfect timing, so to a large extent you lead a charmed, as well as charming, life.

Libra's like a delicate hothouse plant – place you in grotty, grubby surroundings or among crude, rude people who wear clashing colours and smell nasty and you'll shrivel away. You'll never lose that deep-down delicacy and desire for harmony and beauty.

Your greatest plus point lies in the way you handle people. You're kind, fair-minded and an excellent judge provided you don't swamp yourself with too many possibilities and can steel yourself to come down on just one side of the fence.

You hate hurting feelings and have a magical way of making bad news sound almost good. Not surprisingly, you put your diplomacy and charm to good use when it comes to Number One, and you know how to get your own way, subtly, if a bit selfishly. But you're thoughtful to others, too.

Love's vital for you, with passion planet Venus as your ruler, but, because you're a mind, not a body, person, you can think yourself in and out of love over and over again. And you rule sex right out if the setting's not right!

Emotionally, you can be shallow and more cool-hearted than you seem. And now and then, your machine-like mind blows a fuse and you'll plunge off the rails and into a deep depression. Your tactful, soothing manner goes out the window, too, when you see someone you love being mistreated, and switches to spectacular rage. Normally, you hate a row or anything that ruffles your elegant looks and perfectly groomed style. But you make an exception for injustice.

You can work hard – in fits and starts – but you must have civilised surroundings. If dumped in a jungle clearing, your camp would soon be fitted with a bath, shower and fridge-freezer run off the generator. Original and resourceful, you have a style all your own.

The real you, Libra, will be revealed even more when you find the co-ruler of your life, your RISING SIGN, and see how it combines with your Libra sun sign.

You know that the day you were born makes your SUN SIGN Libra. Now, by checking the time of day you were born on the chart opposite, you can find your RISING SIGN too. If you don't know the time of day you were born, you'll soon spot yourself from the descriptions of each of the SUN SIGN/RISING SIGN combinations.

Sun sign Libra/rising sign Scorpio

You're a born wrangler who can't resist an argument. Not a row, of course, merely a complicated, drawn-out and dramatic battle of wills. Deals and intrigues are such second nature that you have to force yourself not to start haggling over cereal packets in the supermarket.

YOUR SUN SIGN IS **LIBRA** – THIS CHART REVEALS YOUR RISING SIGN

If your date of birth is	If you were born between these times											
23–30 September	8:15 am to 10:59 am	11 am to 1:29 pm	1:30 pm to 3:14 pm	3:15 pm to 4:29 pm	4:30 pm to 5:29 pm	5:30 pm to 6:29 pm	6:30 pm to 7:44 pm	7:45 pm to 9:29 pm	9:30 pm to 11:59 pm	12 midnight to 2:44 am	2:45 am to 5:29 am	5:30 am to 8:14 am
1–11 October	7:45 am to 10:29 am	10:30 am to 12:59 pm	1 pm to 2:44 pm	2:45 pm to 3:59 pm	4 pm to 4:59 pm	5 pm to 5:59 pm	6 pm to 7:14 pm	7:15 pm to 8:59 pm	9 pm to 11:29 pm	11:30 pm to 2:14 am	2:15 am to 4:59 am	5 am to 7:44 am
12–23 October	7 am to 9:44 am	9:45 am to 12:14 pm	12:15 pm to 1:59 pm	2 pm to 3:14 pm	3:15 pm to 4:14 pm	4:15 pm to 5:14 pm	5:15 pm to 6:29 pm	6:30 pm to 8:14 pm	8:15 pm to 10:44 pm	10:45 pm to 1:29 am	1:30 am to 4:14 am	4:15 am to 6:59 am
YOUR RISING SIGN IS	SCORPIO	SAGITTARIUS	CAPRICORN	AQUARIUS	PISCES	ARIES	TAURUS	GEMINI	CANCER	LEO	VIRGO	LIBRA

Your Libra tact couples with Scorpio's sting to make you a very effective critic. You can deliver some quite near-the-knuckle comments, and all your victims can say is 'Thank you!' You're usually able to face up to reality better than most Libras, too. Your rising sign helps you clasp your courage in both hands and not delay sorting out personal dilemmas. That famous sun sign charisma isn't always upfront, though. Many with your sign mix are afraid of appearing soft-hearted, so you mask your true nature behind a rather severe, suspicious expression.

Your Scorpio side helps focus you, makes you more hard-edged and decisive than other can't-decide Libras. But you'll also have to guard against pigging out on food, drink and sex, because you're doubly sensual. You go in for great passions, and although many may not last, they're always intense. You may even marry several times. Your rising sign makes you prone to extremes and excess, sending Libra scales swinging crazily askew. But you've a knack of sorting out Libra money worries by energetic Scorpio moonlighting. You're not exactly a calm person, but like the eye of a storm, everything revolves round you.

Sun sign Libra/rising sign Sagittarius

Join Libra's airy charm to your rising sign's easy-come, easy-go joviality and they add up to one fun-filled, giant-size balloon. You cheer people up as you float by, never sticking around for long, and leave them so charmed they never realise you're all hot air and little else!

You're one of the best hosts around. Libra's tact and refinement mixes beautifully with Sagittarius' back-slapping humour to make you more cheerful than a Butlin's Redcoat – eager to make sure everyone's having a good time and not scared of looking silly yourself.

You very much want to be accepted. You excel in any job dealing with people, especially if it's linked to an after-hours social life. You've got to keep on the move, and won't be there when there's muck to clear up, but you always inspire others with your bright outlook and smile. Perhaps you sit and dream too much to get promoted fast, but few people notice how little you pull your weight!

Playful and charming, you have plenty of close encounters and a roving eye, but reason actually rules your heart. You can, unlike some Libras, get stir-crazy in relationships and need time to flit off alone occasionally. Your circle of friends stretches across the globe and you could take your time settling down.

You quite like gentle exercise – not just between the sheets – though you'll never be a true sporty Sagittarius. You thrive as part of a close-knit team.

Sun sign Libra/rising sign Capricorn

Increased mental sharpness and a liking for logic are the marks of this combination. Your Capricorn rising sign makes you more ambitious, too. It gets you up in the morning, and shoves you into the success race – though your peace-loving Libra nature softens the edges of that sharp-elbowed Capricorn action.

You're always polite and gracious, even when you're pushing past everyone else. You probably like work more than all other Libra types – but when times are slack or others don't expect much of you, you can slump into a stodgy sludge of idleness. True, your rising sign makes you slightly less self-indulgent, scoring six or seven out of 10 on the Libra spoil-yourself scale. But it won't actually stop you blowing a fortune on meals and clothes, it will just make you feel naughtier for doing it!

You hate making mistakes, and Capricorn can put you off trying in case you fail again. It also deepens your moods of depression when they come along. You're fair and particularly detached, but Capricorn plain-speaking sabotages your Libra diplomacy. You do have your sun sign's tact, but your timing's all wrong!

Endurance and determination have been mixed in your melting pot and that touch of Capricorn toughens up your character a treat. You're skilled at mixing pleasure with business, and like to get it on with lovers who can help you get on. They find you so fascinating they won't mind.

Sun sign Libra/rising sign Aquarius

Despite your scatty image, which you prefer to call interestingly eccentric, you're actually more practical and clued up than the average Libra and your thought processes are even more logical! You adore knowledge in all shapes and forms and have set your sights on the future. But because you think and dream on such a grand and hard-to-grasp scale, you're often misunderstood by more down-to-earth minds.

You're certainly a unique individual. As a youngster, your family probably despaired of your laziness and lack of achievement. Yet you're very creative and artistic and usually find enough inner strength to educate yourself and get on, better late than never. So no-one should ever write you off, Unlike most Libras, you're not desperately bothered what the world thinks of you. Aquarius opens up horizons and may even lead you to settle abroad for a nice slice of your life. Your Libra tendency to waver is largely wiped out by Aquarius, too, and when you do make up your mind, you may even tip into obsession. But soon it's all change all over again!

You're an excellent friend, loyal and defensive, and you can tolerate untidiness in your friends and surroundings better than most Libras. Emotional ups and downs, usually linked to your search for real love, can test your physical health. But you never lose interest, or faith, in people and places, so you never grow old.

Sun sign Libra/rising sign Pisces

You're just a sign combination who can't say no! You've such a sweet, gentle manner and you're so genuinely kind that, unless you get yourself a tough-nut partner or pal who'll slam doors and write nasty letters on your behalf, you could be put upon something rotten. And because you hate to break up any relationship and hurt feelings, you can stick around in a dead-end affair forever.

Your element of Pisces makes you extra naive, emotionally delicate and tender-hearted – but it also increases your artistic and musical flair. You're too shy to go out looking for fame, but probably so multi-talented you can't avoid it finding you anyway!

Your greatest flaw (apart from a tendency to turn to comfort drinking or eating) is your inability to make up your mind. As Libras go, you're way up among the star ditherers, as easily swayed as a cobweb in a breeze. Others often have to step in to make your decisions before the clock runs out. Your smart thinking-patterns, however, save you from being a sucker.

You do want to please – sometimes desperately – and can put your own needs on ice for ages while you fuss around other people. Sensual and in love with love, you'll have more than one serious relationship and are likely to be dominated in one of them. But your Pisces humour overlaying that stylish Libra sociability means you're never without friends or shoulders to cry on.

Sun sign Libra/rising sign Aries

Arguing makes you feel alive, opponents often feel like giving in before they start, because they know what a lengthy, polished and persistent performance is in store. Even when there's only one person around to spar with, you'll change sides or adopt a new, third opinion just to keep the chat lively and entertaining. Fire sign Aries mixes with your basic air sign for an easy way with words and a taste for manipulation. At times, you can gate-crash other people's conversations, but you usually speak with such charm and persuasion they don't mind.

Fiery Aries boosts energy levels, but makes you more rash than other Libras, so you are likely to spark off in several directions at once. You may also appear to be pushier than you are inside. And when, like any Libra, you fight for an underdog, you really pack quite a punch.

Falling in love is easy for you and you are likely to leap into an early marriage, and enjoy domestic dramas. But you do find it difficult to face up to emotional hitches, and would rather cut and run that confess to the world that you have made a mistake.

Love and sex bring you out in an acne of conflict. While Libra twitches for togetherness, Aries itches for a footloose loner's life. This means you can move between both moods in the same relationship – causing pain and confusion. But when you do finally commit to being part of a pair, your Aries dash of daring and survivor's instinct blends well with Libra's way with people to make good partnership.

Sun sign Libra/rising sign Taurus

Romance rules your whole life. It's bound to, with a double dollop of sensual, beauty-loving, creative planet Venus lined up in your birth chart. You have a special charm and such a talent for pleasing others through your tactful ways that you could almost make a career out of it. But you all too easily dribble away your energy and talents on bodice-ripping type romances that never get much further than your own imagination.

You can cancel out your disappointments with some physical and creative work like gardening, or making beautiful pictures, sounds and objects. With tubby, tolerant Taurus telling you to give in to pleasure, and love-specialist Libra at work, you never give up on your search for perfect passion. But it would be a good idea to channel your ambitions in some other directions, too.

Affable, and difficult to provoke – though explosive when pushed that notch too far – you get on with everyone and are a very huggy type. Music, friends, animals, nature, food and love are what you want. Loneliness, lack of home comforts are what you hate. You'd be lost without someone or something to love.

Beware your so-lazy streak which makes even climbing

into bed hard work. And do fight your stay-at-home nature to try a few of those changes and improvements you think about so much, but rarely follow through. You aren't too clever with money, but your warmth is priceless.

Sun sign Libra/rising sign Gemini

With two air signs doubling your thought and word power, you're as head-led as can be, and sail through life chiefly on personal charisma and sheer good luck. Your charm quota's so over the top it verges on smarm at times, and when it comes to actual work you're only too ready to let others take the strain. You'd be no use on the back of a tandem, with your feet up and your nose in a book while your partner turned puce with solo pedalling!

You've a great talent for speaking on cue, and this makes you appear even brainier than you are. You're soothing as a cup of hot chocolate and, unless the person you're dealing with is naturally negative, you can't put a foot wrong in personal relationships. Acting or design could be rewarding for you, but ever-active Gemini makes you extra prone to tackling too many jobs at once, and only quarter-finishing any of them. Gemini makes your mind fluttery while Libra's basically a languid looker-on, so you'll have to guard against being a shallow stick-at-nothing.

Get more businesslike if you want to make your mark on life, and get more rest for your mind's sake. Fun's what you're after from love, and any affair that can no longer provide that is heading for the scrapheap. Your laugh-a-minute manner attracts both friends and lovers, but you like forbidden fruit and are often tempted to use your quick wits to pinch someone else's partner. Resist it!

Sun sign Libra/rising sign Cancer

More domesticated than most Libras – who like a pretty, clean place only as long as they don't have to keep it that way themselves – your home's a showpiece, your cooking a triumph. While Cancer is privacy-loving, Libra likes the public, so you're forever inviting friends to drop by in droves. You certainly know an awful lot of people. Some of them are truly ghastly, some are real gems, but you give each equal weight and time.

With Libra's soothing ways and Cancer's listening skills, others pour their hearts' secrets out to you. Fair, balanced and keyed into emotions to a greater extent because of your watery rising sign, you tend to take careless remarks too much at face value.

Learn to be more choosy in love, too. That moon makes you a more intensely romantic lover than the average Libra, though you're still acting like a teenager well into middle age! Members of your family play leading roles in your life and you like to show how much you love them, often spending a fortune and endless time doing up your house for entertaining. Once you regard someone as yours, you can be clingy and aren't above emotional blackmail to keep their attention on the boil! You must loosen up more if you really want to keep a hearthold on someone special, and stop confusing love with ownership.

You must have security, including financial back-up. But you get more daring and individual as you get older.

Sun sign Libra/rising sign Leo

Peaceful, pally and pleasant-natured, your favourite position is stretched out on a sofa with friends and the hum of music and conversation around you. You're too much of a smiling drift-along to bother much with Libra-style debate, though that Leo fire can flip you into action when someone you like needs defending. Waves or rows generally, however, are what you want to avoid, so you shove under the carpet any upsetting flaws in those you know.

Libra makes you put everything off until next week, and added Leo leaves you even more unwilling to face unpleasant facts. You're good at delegating because it gives you more time to sit and daydream, and you're warm and charming enough to persuade everyone else it's a treat to do your washing-up or pick up your week's shopping. You could put on a pile of weight with Libra's sweet tooth and Leo's tendency never to walk when you can ride in comfort.

Thank goodness you're more alert mentally than you are physically! As a lover, you don't lean on your partner as much as other Libras, though your bossy rising sign means you've probably got to run the show on your terms all the time. And because you're extra money-conscious – making as well as spending cash easily – you could compromise your romantic Libra aims for a purely financial match! You're also too proud to sidestep heartbreak in good time, for fear of ridicule. Still, you thrive centrestage, so politics and showbiz are perfect careers.

Sun sign Libra/rising sign Virgo

Libra tends to put things off until tomorrow, but with Virgo as your rising sign, you might as well delay until the next decade! Your blend of critical perfection-seeker and fair-minded judge could make you the perfect referee, judge or umpire. But in your personal life, you're often cornered into doing precisely nothing because of all the ifs and buts you place in your own path. When you think about repainting your sitting-room, you realise the walls will have to be prepared first, so there's no point starting at all until you've chosen the best materials . . .

So it's not surprising that so much you do costs a packet and takes ages. And you only notice the tiny mistakes at the end of a job! Constantly getting ready to act, you never take off your gloves and get on with life.

Virgo could also leave you, unique among Libras, on your own! But it'll be through choice – if you can't find a lover you can show off, you'll pass on the wedding bells. You're a secret social climber but you're still capable of flashes of the most caring, sincere warmth – though you'd drop a pal double-quick who fell foul of the law.

Like all Libras, you're a party-lover. But Virgo stops you dancing on any tables when you get there – you mind your manners far too much for that! You're not easy to get to know and may nurse a sore heart from way back. Your biggest asset is your practical streak – you can hang on to money and are heaven-sent in any personal or public crisis.

Sun sign Libra/rising sign Libra

Comparing and analysing are like addictive drugs for you – you just can't stop weighing up everything, and everyone. But you can examine life until you lose what energy or motive you once had to act! You do come across as most agreeable – a yes-man or woman perhaps, but no-one was ever disliked for that! And sooner or later you find someone who wants to help pull your strings for life – the only way you'll ever use your considerable gifts for art, acting and music.

Peace is all you want and romance is more important to you than any dreary job you do just to earn a living. But you prefer love to be hassle-free and family life's fine as long as someone else acts as your fixer and DIY expert. You give new meaning to the phrase sleeping partner!

Charming, impossible, always late, and lovely to look at, you insist on the best of everything. You've such a sharpened sense of beauty that ugliness actually makes you ill. You are naturally incapable of working steadily – you either hibernate or work in a flat-out frenzy. You're a cash-keeping disaster but get bailed out by those who find you fun. You've a knack of lighting up any gathering and making everyone you meet feel wanted.

You're likely to be living with someone. You couldn't bear a moment on your own at home, an empty bed or just one place at table. Your hottest asset of all is your speed-learning skill, which can take you very far.

Sun Sign Scorpio

Scratching a Scorpio's surface quickly uncovers your two strongest driving forces – sex and secrets. Scorpios can't help but fascinate, and you usually get more offers of love than you can handle, even with such superhuman energy levels.

It doesn't matter a bit whether the secret's yours or has been haltingly confided by a friend. In both cases, you'd never spill the beans whatever the temptation. You really revel in your store of forbidden knowledge, despite the fact that you very rarely intend to cash in on it. But they do feed your other pressing and lifelong lust – for power. You have a seething, red-hot inferno of passions just waiting to erupt as soon as your strong self-control wavers. And though you make a good, loyal and hardworking servant, you're a power-crazy, even vicious, master!

In spite of a poker-faced cover-up and an ability to make do with just a few, dead-on-target words, you are so much at the mercy of your feelings. Anyone who gazes deeply into your burning, hypnotic eyes will get a clue as to how intense and passionate you really are. But by then, it's already too late for them to turn back.

Your extreme single-mindedness, which can slide into obsession, is what ensures your success. You work and play hard – at times too hard for your health – and see everything through to the bitter end. You can hypnotise those you fancy into a slave-like devotion, though you won't return the compliment until you feel total trust.

But the bad news is that, misdirected, your powerful personality is capable of violent, even criminal actions and intense cruelty. Those who disappoint or cheat you will feel the slicing edge of your tongue.

You have an excellent working-out mind but do best when you act on intuition. You can easily be lured by luxury and sensuality, especially towards out-of-bounds targets. Yet you are also capable of extreme levels of self-denial, great loyalty and faithfulness and, once you've got that jealousy under control, can have enduring long-term relationships that survive any emotional or financial upheaval.

Sex is a lifelong hobby, along with the mysteries of birth, death and the supernatural. You're hard to live with because you despise any show of weakness, and can turn in on yourself whenever your motives are questioned or someone seems to be moving away from your control. You're demanding, do nothing in half measures and hold rigidly fixed opinions, making you even more fascinating.

Try to stop living on those taut nerves if you're to avoid tension, insomnia and sudden, dramatic illnesses. Because you're such a very strong person, you will only be happy with an equally tough, though more flexible, mate. You expect a lot of others, even more of yourself.

Find out even more about the real you, Scorpio, by discovering the co-ruler of your life, your RISING SIGN, and the effect it has on your personality.

You know, from the date of your birth, that your SUN SIGN is Scorpio. Now, having checked the time of day of your birth against the chart opposite, you know your RISING SIGN too. Don't know the exact time you were born? Don't worry, you'll soon spot yourself from the rundown of each SUN SIGN/RISING SIGN combination.

Sun sign Scorpio/rising sign Sagittarius

Sagittarius gives you a matey manner and a flippancy that temporarily disguises your very deep-natured true self. You've loads of names and numbers in your address book but very few close friends, and never give your heart without cast-iron proof that your partner is trustworthy.

YOUR SUN SIGN IS **SCORPIO** – THIS CHART REVEALS YOUR RISING SIGN

If your date of birth is	If you were born between these times											
24–31 October	9 am to 11:29 am	11:30 am to 1:14 pm	1:15 pm to 2:29 pm	2:30 pm to 3:29 pm	3:30 pm to 4:29 pm	4:30 pm to 5:44 pm	5:45 pm to 7:29 pm	7:30 pm to 9:59 pm	10 pm to 12:44 am	12:45 am to 3:29 am	3:30 am to 6:14 am	6:15 am to 8:59 am
1–11 November	8:15 am to 10:44 am	10:45 am to 12:29 pm	12:30 pm to 1:44 pm	1:45 pm to 2:44 pm	2:45 pm to 3:44 pm	3:45 pm to 4:59 pm	5 pm to 6:44 pm	6:45 pm to 9:14 pm	9:15 pm to 11:59 pm	12 midnight to 2:44 am	2:45 am to 5:29 am	5:30 am to 8:14 am
12–22 November	7:45 am to 10:14 am	10:15 am to 11:59 am	12 noon to 1:14 pm	1:15 pm to 2:14 pm	2:15 pm to 3:14 pm	3:15 pm to 4:29 pm	4:30 pm to 6:14 pm	6:15 pm to 8:44 pm	8:45 pm to 11:29 pm	11:30 pm to 2:14 am	2:15 am to 4:59 am	5 am to 7:44 am
YOUR RISING SIGN IS	SAGITTARIUS	CAPRICORN	AQUARIUS	PISCES	ARIES	TAURUS	GEMINI	CANCER	LEO	VIRGO	LIBRA	SCORPIO

Your rising sign also brings out the athlete in you and tones down the hide-away streak. Its assertiveness combines with your Scorpio iron will to make you a ruthless defender of those you love and a powerful force to be reckoned with at work.

You seem far more tolerant and easy going than you really are and, strangely for a Scorpio, you can be easily taken in. You can usually see straight through a con at 40 paces, but Sagittarius generosity makes you susceptible to a well-rehearsed hard-luck story.

Clumsiness and outspokenness are among your other added extras, meaning you can lash out your sting-laden tail at the wrong people at the worst-picked times! You hurt lovers, too, by letting them know that, realistically, this is unlikely to be the 'Love That Lasts'.

Outgoing, affable and apparently open-minded, few people realise how rigid and unforgiving you can be – or that, despite your many lovers, emotionally you're very choosy. You just like having fun while waiting for the right one. But with a sexy imagination and superfit body like yours, no-one's complaining too loudly . . .

Sun sign Scorpio/rising sign Capricorn

Tough enough to obliterate opposition and capable of being completely ruthless, that's how the world sees you, thanks to your cool-headed rising sign blocking up your volcanic inner self under a hard crust of restraint and self-discipline. But every so often your passion erupts into view to prove you are a highly emotional Scorpio after all.

Most of the time, you bottle up that passion, and this control makes you a truly terrifying opponent and a sharp-edged, ultra-ambitious workmate. Friends and lovers get the best deal and find you an entirely honest, hotly emotional and deeply loyal partner who would leap between them and any oncoming train. Relationships matter very much to you, but you're also capable, in a work setting, of trampling on other people, as you trampoline your way to the top.

You score highly with those you are attracted to, but find it hard to relax in their company once you've got them alone. You can be over-serious and too intense for some tastes, but are as responsible as it's possible to be. Left alone too long, you may lapse into sulks and shadowy gloom. You are best in a team and need a partner with natural warmth, who is more spontaneous, to bring out the best in you.

Subtle, extremely smart, and a skilful administrator and negotiator, you are prepared to go to the limit for what, and who, you want. It's no wonder you usually get both.

Sun sign Scorpio/rising sign Aquarius

Maybe you don't set out to pull the wool over anyone's eyes, but your sign combination makes all appearances highly deceptive! Aloof, cool and head-led is how you come across, thanks to your Aquarius influence. But that boiling torrent of sexually charged feelings is just behind, waiting to burst through . . .

You're positive, hate having your views put down, and have a powerful Scorpio temper. But you are also more understanding than many who share your sun sign and have an extra helping of Aquarius look-forward to lighten any basic downbeat feelings. Your sun sign is firmly fixed but Aquarius puts a jot of Gipsy in your soul. This doesn't just spell itchy feet, but also boosts your uncanny insight into what makes others tick. With your blend of Scorpio's no-excuses realism and Aquarius' scientific curiosity, there aren't many motives you can't read.

Your moods are intense, but even those that wrench your heart aren't drawn out. You've a rare ability to square your chin and bounce back again with great emotional strength. You're more sympathetic than many a Scorpio, and despite analysis and diagnosis being your strongest skills, you are drawn towards the spiritual and occult. Some lovers may believe you're cold and too critical, but you have a genuine desire to help. Vigorous, intense and often inspiring, you'll always stand out in a crowd and can't fail to leave an unforgettable impression.

Sun sign Scorpio/rising sign Pisces

You seem kind, gentle, easily led – but nothing could be further from the truth. You've far more of a mind of your own than your swimming emotions and surface charm would suggest – you're so strong-willed, in fact, that some would find you obsessive. You simply can't take second best, or compromise.

Intuition is your prime asset, and you can peer beneath any mask, however murky. Highly imaginative, full of affection, and creative, you can achieve a lot. At times, however, your deep-flowing passions pull you this way and that and you can't stay in one place for long. Both your signs are water-based, so your emotions lead you by the nose and, when they do, little work gets done!

You can torment yourself, too, with wild ideas and fantasies. You like the good things in life, but won't harm others if you can help it. You've a pessimistic streak, though, and can court disaster and disappointment in relationships because your lovers are often so badly chosen. You can be unrealistic and over-ambitious, too, where work is concerned. And when things go wrong, beware of diving deep into drink or drugs!

You need a partner who'll give you a steady, secure background and a lot of dreamily romantic loving. Jobs linked to travel and foreign parts are lucky for you, as is creative writing. But remember that not everyone is as good at reading minds, and hearts, as you are.

Sun sign Scorpio/rising sign Aries

'What are you looking at?' is likely to be one of your favourite phrases, for double Mars trouble makes this a rather aggressive combination. Luckily, this explosive mixture is lightened by your being very warm-hearted and impulsive, too, thanks to Aries' influence.

Your great energy means you achieve so much. Loving and generous to those you adore, you are not so warm to those outside this charmed inner circle. Not many would dare to stand up to you in a row! But you reckon rows liven up life and rather enjoy exploding like a pressure cooker letting off steam. Aries shortens your fuse, yes, but it also leaves you less resentful, and quicker to forgive.

You can shove aside others' feelings because you must get your own way, and be tough on your family, too, even though you love them. Your feelings, deep as any Scorpio's, often land you in hot water and you may find the opposite sex a constant source of complications.

Your combination of quick decisions and the determination to see them through will help take you to the top, whatever your work. The other side of your unique coin is a ruthless, forceful streak that can overflow into mental cruelty. You want others to follow your advice to the letter and get very impatient when they don't.

Learn to be more spontaneous, so your pent-up passions can seep instead of burst out. The bigger the challenge, the more you dare. And of course, who dares wins.

Sun sign Scorpio/rising sign Taurus

Sex and money really matter to you, and often they are linked in your life. But the successful approach you use to earn your living doesn't work at all when it comes to lovemaking! You want to take over, totally dominate. And when you can't get what you want you turn as destructive as a toddler in a tantrum.

Yet although your personality pushes you towards life as a loner, you must realise you'll get nowhere without a partner. You find wooing's the easy bit, helped by all the little luxuries you've worked hard to pay for. But lovers try to break away once you build bars of your own suspicions round them. You know that you can love long and loyally, but always wonder if your partner is capable of similar devotion. Give them more leeway if you want to see your love light up.

Taurus makes your rage very hard to rouse, but it's impossible to turn it off once your red rag is out! You're very careful with money and possessions and more ambitious than most give you credit for. Faced with a new idea, your go-ahead

Scorpio brain can be held back by your cautious rising sign digging its heels in.

When life treats you badly, beware of the usual Taurus refuge, over-eating. Learn moderation and guard your kidneys' health with loads of pure water. You're at your best fighting from a corner and drive others as hard as yourself at work. You can achieve every dream.

Sun sign Scorpio/rising sign Gemini

Yours is an uneasy combination, since your two signs have little in common and must learn to rub along together. You swing between a Scorpio self-contained, intense personality and Gemini's desire to flit out there and get stuck into communicating left, right and centre. You're not as flexible and open-book as you seem, and although you can quickly become deeply fascinated with someone or something, you can drop the whole thing in double-quick time if a more appealing proposition pops up.

Your energy, like your loving, is erratic as well as erotic. You'd be taken more seriously if others could only keep up with your rapid U-turns. You can be a hurtful lover, promising the big romance but often delivering a pale, watered-down version. Even when your Scorpio passions are truly roused, you're capable of suddenly moving on. Your lovelife is actually more ruled by your mind than your heart and so you need to find partners who offer a challenge. Your most lasting love affairs are likely to be unusual, or outside the partnership you're supposed to be part of!

You're prone to fritter away your fantastic energies by taking on too many opposing tasks. But your probing Scorpio mind and curious Gemini flair make for a clever, subtle and experimental mix. You may have supernatural healing powers and will succeed in your sphere provided you carve a well-planned path and stick to it.

Sun sign Scorpio/rising sign Cancer

No-one feels more intensely than you. This is a highly charged mixture of water signs, so it's not surprising that you sometimes get hooked on your own emotional highs and lows! Your top priorities are romance, kids, poetry, animals and going out. Your home-loving rising sign means you like having people round to your place and you always seem to sense who needs entertaining and cheering up!

You love having a good time, and aren't as irresponsible as some other Scorpios. You prefer to keep your lines free in case of other offers and have a naughty tendency to run off with younger, better-looking partners! When these affairs don't work, you drown your miseries in drink or chocolate, and your sun sign's tendency to over-dramatise is heightened by Cancer's weepiness and self-pity.

You are capable of showing your deepest affections to someone, but often your family will get a better, more consistent brand of loving from you than a sex partner would. You are subtle, and though you appear open enough, you never give away more than suits your ends. You may plead poverty, but always have secret funds stashed away.

Problems arise when you try to mix work and love. Your mixture of signs may make you try to live in other people's pockets – possessiveness and jealousy put together with Cancer smothering can spell claustrophobia. You're the most far-sighted of all Scorpios, and despite a seething heart you seem ever calm.

Sun sign Scorpio/rising sign Leo

This is the most steadfast and dependable combination. You'll see things through, no matter how hard this might be, with the occasional Leo temptation to take the easiest way out blotting your record now and then. You are ambitious, but work aims often take a back seat to all the dramas in your private life!

Your rising sign sharpens your sense of self-worth and makes you extra proud, so that when you're hurt you never give up your chance of revenge . . . one day. This makes you a fearsome enemy, but an intensely loyal, loving and defensive friend.

You're sociable, but although you're a good mixer your ideas close-up are fixed and sometimes prejudiced. So no matter how wide your circle, opinions tend to be limited. You crave praise and approval more than most Scorpios, and like to throw your weight around, even if it's just to lord it over your neighbour in a parking-place squabble.

You've an insatiable appetite for sex! You give your all to each new affair and are a prime target to be flattered into bed. Emotional setbacks literally lay you low, though, and you need peace, love and harmony if a close partnership is to thrive.

You've many talents and may be drawn to selling, the theatre, medicine or the media. Dynamic, hot-tempered, active and exciting, power's your buzzword, so you need to take control. But not too much!

Sun sign Scorpio/rising sign Virgo

Sixth sense helps you always know exactly what must be done next. You've a great eye for detail, too, a gift from your rising sign. And this not-to-be-scorned skill can turn many a corner from failure to success.

Your worst fault is a lack of proportion. You can give too much weight to insignificant things and you tend to invent problems, fretting yourself into a host of imaginary illnesses. You confide in a few trusted friends but keep your cards clutched very close to your chest with the world at large.

In love, you find it very hard to express your deep feelings in words – only kisses and cuddles will do. You want to serve others, to please a partner in and out of bed, and are more caring than most Scorpios. You're very prickly about receiving favours, however, and will go to ridiculous lengths to avoid being in anyone's debt.

Persevering, determined and objective, you are extremely competent and capable of intense, white-hot concentration.

You long to control your own life, as well as other people's, and may be so self-sufficient you feel you don't need anyone to share your private life. Often, your identity is tied unhealthily to a job.

Virgo keeps your stormy emotions firmly under lock and key most of the time, bar the occasional stress-induced allergy or minor stomach problem. In times of trouble, others look to you for a cool head and leadership.

Sun sign Scorpio/rising sign Libra

An easy-going, friendly outer coat masks that glittering Scorpio eye that's forever plunging to the heart of other people's intentions. Your rising sign's witty tongue, which can sweeten your sour sarcasm, also serves to disguise what a shrewd cookie you really are!

You've a way with people, and that could combine with your sun sign's stick-at-it drive to succeed in making you an excellent public relations person. But you're such a speedy learner that many fields tempt you, including teaching and temping.

Your rising sign rockets already intense emotions to extremes, from outrageous optimism one moment down to blackest pessimism the next. You're magnetically attractive, but can be sexy but heartless, with lust not love sparking many of your affairs. You dabble in danger by chasing good looks and ignoring rings or any other commitment clues! Rows and separations could dog any marriage you make and there is bound to be more than one financially tangled love link. You only have to raise your eyebrows, however, to send out a sexy message others are desperate to reply to.

You are mysterious and magnetic, and even harder to get close to than other Scorpios. You're often not quite decided how you feel yourself – until you're sure you can read a partner like a book and they'll stick to your love terms!

Sun sign Scorpio/rising sign Scorpio

Extremely love-hungry, ever so intense and completely compelling, you've the pulling power of a giant magnet – and can be just as cold and metallic close up. Yet those who get past your stern outside discover a kindly heart, great honesty and devotion.

You want to dominate – your double-strength sign makes this a dead cert. And many of your romantic relationships fail, purely because you want to rule the roost. You must give partners more time to share your vision, not try to dictate to them. You go to extremes, both at work and at play, and have an unquenchable need to know . . . everything.

You have a huge physical capacity for lovemaking, but only reveal your true self to a select few. Romantic, sensual and passionate, you'd be the most exciting lover in the world if only you could keep that green-eyed monster under control! And you can't resist the dangerous appeal of an attractive stranger. SuperScorpio comes on too strong for many would-be lovers and you may not find the right blend of hot-blooded yet understanding partner until past your youth, and theirs. But it's such fun looking . . .

A self-controlled survivor, with your awesome drive and determination you've no time for flaggers or fakers, who probably fear you more than anything. An iron fist tucked inside a velvet glove, whatever your goal there's no stopping you once you've made up your mind to go for it!

Sun Sign Sagittarius

You take life at a gallop, you're outspoken, outdoors-loving and, more often than not, outrageous! You play for the fun of it and, though you like to win, the buzz of just taking part is enough. When outside challenges are thin on the ground, then you like to compete against your own past personal best.

You're honest to a fault, broad-minded, good-natured, dependable and generous. And also a bit of an escapist, with an ever-packed suitcase and one-way ticket tucked away somewhere safe in case you need to get away. But you can let your good intentions slump into selfishness, turning rude, rebellious and reckless when your major bugbear, boredom, looms.

Your strength lies in your trust and resilience, but your worst weak spot is communication breakdown. You're just not sensitive enough ever to fix this fault totally. Even your jokey manner tends towards the rather rough humour of slapstick, which makes more tender souls shrink away from you. But a sense of fun, even a rough and ready one, is better than none. And most people find your laugh-a-minute energy infectious.

Sociable, and soppy as a spaniel puppy, it's only when you drop one of your classic clangers that your lack of tact and delicacy really lets you down. Luckily, your basically kind nature usually filters through in time for forgiveness.

Energy and enthusiasm spring from you being a flexible fire sign, and for the most part you take a relaxed and optimistic view of life. Your self-confidence is hard to shake and you carry the flame of childhood innocence into your old age. You make a great parent, valuing others' freedom as much as your own.

Trouble is, this is a role you may not get to play. You're a red-blooded fire sign and enjoy a scorching sex life, but you may duck out of closer commitments and have been known to bolt from the altar. 'Don't fence me in' is your motto, and if work or love pins you in a corner, you soon become stressed.

At work, you're never short of inspiration but find details too dull to bother with. You may have been born under the generous, lucky planet Jupiter, but, if you don't check the nuts and bolts now and then, you'll find your wagon's only rolling on three wheels.

You can spread yourself too thin and end up letting people down. You must have fresh challenges, the more demanding the better. And if it's sporting or linked to dogs and horses, that's best of all. You need a job, and partner, to stimulate your mind. Happiest when fully stretched, you'll never stop learning new things, and thrive surrounded by people and noise. Clever, creative and inspiring, you can be childish, but keep childlike qualities like optimism and fresh-faced enthusiasm all your life.

Sagittarius, the true you will be revealed even more by finding the co-ruler of your life, your RISING SIGN, and how it combines with your Sagittarius sun sign.

You know what your SUN SIGN is – the day you were born makes you a Sagittarius. But if you check the time of day you were born against the chart opposite, you'll find your RISING SIGN too. If you don't know the exact time of your birth, you'll soon spot yourself from the descriptions of each SUN SIGN/RISING SIGN combination.

Sun sign Sagittarius/rising sign Capricorn

No, you may not laugh as readily as most Sagittarians, because your strict rising sign gives you a dignified, sometimes starchy, bearing, but you have a very well-balanced

YOUR SUN SIGN IS **SAGITTARIUS** – THIS CHART REVEALS YOUR RISING SIGN

If your date of birth is	If you were born between these times											
23–30 November	9:30 am to 11:14 am	11:15 am to 12:29 pm	12:30 pm to 1:29 pm	1:30 pm to 2:29 pm	2:30 pm to 3:44 pm	3:45 pm to 5:29 pm	5:30 pm to 7:59 pm	8 pm to 10:44 pm	10:45 pm to 1:29 am	1:30 am to 4:14 am	4:15 am to 6:59 am	7 am to 9:29 am
1–11 December	8:45 am to 10:29 am	10:30 am to 11:44 am	11:45 am to 12:44 pm	12:45 pm to 1:44 pm	1:45 pm to 2:59 pm	3 pm to 4:44 pm	4:45 pm to 7:14 pm	7:15 pm to 9:59 pm	10 pm to 12:44 am	12:45 am to 3:29 am	3:30 am to 6:14 am	6:15 am to 8:44 am
12–21 December	8:15 am to 9:59 am	10 am to 11:14 am	11:15 am to 12:14 pm	12:15 pm to 1:14 pm	1:15 pm to 2:29 pm	2:30 pm to 4:14 pm	4:15 pm to 6:44 pm	6:45 pm to 9:29 pm	9:30 pm to 12:14 am	12:15 am to 2:59 am	3 am to 5:44 am	5:45 am to 8:14 am
YOUR RISING SIGN IS	CAPRICORN	AQUARIUS	PISCES	ARIES	TAURUS	GEMINI	CANCER	LEO	VIRGO	LIBRA	SCORPIO	SAGITTARIUS

personality. Your basically humorous and humane outlook is given depth by Capricorn – and your breathless enthusiasm gets some sensible caution!

This is the sign mix of someone who's making their own luck and can come from nowhere to a high-powered position. Independent, talented and, thanks to Capricorn, practical in everyday and business matters, you can work hard behind the scenes to make yourself a tidy cash pile, though you're unlikely to be rich when you're young. Unless you're careful, work can push personal relationships aside. You make a faithful mate – more responsible than many of your sign – provided that you pick a tolerant, unpossessive partner, because you need several universes' worth of breathing space and, thanks to that touch of Capricorn, even more elbow room. A good mental match is doubly vital.

You do nothing without a purpose and your rising sign gives staying power to boost your keenness and curiosity. Thankfully, your crazy, caring core is never suffocated by Capricorn coolness, but you may become highly strung, moody and prone to health obsessions. Shyness may shake up your lovelife, but as in everything, once you have a clear goal to aim for, it's all systems go, go, go!

Sun sign Sagittarius/rising sign Aquarius

A fun-lover – and such fun as a lover, too – that's you! Your rising sign, the water-bearer, means you put your whole self into whatever you do. Coupled with that youthful Sagittarius spirit, you're the archer who hits any target you aim at.

Friendly and open, you have pals from every walk of life, and you're a great one for causes that will improve the whole world. But despite your generous, impulsive, forcefully outgoing nature, you usually hold back part of your heart until you're absolutely certain that you've found that special someone. Plenty of others are shown a good time, but don't realise they've never touched or known the real you . . .

Numerous short-lived affairs mixed with lengthy periods

of living alone seem to be your pattern, although once you do take the plunge, you're loyal and never play around. You must have space, though, and need to escape at regular intervals, ideally into a sporting or nature-linked hobby that stretches both mind and body.

You mean well but can be a touch cool, and oh so tactless! Your blunt words have plenty of people reaching for paper hankies. But you'd never give up on a chosen cause, even if membership was down to just you and your dog. Now and then your overconfident sun sign and dreamer Aquarius combine to bite you off more than you can chew, but usually others can't do enough to help you succeed.

Sun sign Sagittarius/rising sign Pisces

Your supersensitive watery rising sign makes you seem innocent, impractical and a bit of a daydreamer. It puts the brakes on your get-up-and-go and makes you want to swim with the flow rather than kick-start your own adventures. And it combines with your sun sign to make you twice as twitchy about responsibility and restrictions, though romance is a very powerful lure!

You're more moody and highly strung than most Sagittarians and far harder to get to know well. You're every bit as active, restless and ambitious as others of your sign, however, the major difference being that you dither, thanks to Pisces, and find it difficult to accept that your intense need for success brings responsibility, too.

This team also increases an existing tendency to exaggerate and sensationalise. But this is balanced by a boost in courtesy and caring for others. Your creative, restless mind will take you to the heights of any job, but you'll be at your best heading a large enterprise that serves people.

Extravagant and often carried away with love and money, you'll need a stable income and a feet-on-the-ground loving partner to keep your nervous tension under control. Your heart tends to get swept away, you make up magic personalities for your lovers, then wonder why they don't live up to them. Polish up common sense and your make-it-happen drive will move mountains.

Sun sign Sagittarius/rising sign Aries

Fire rules both your signs, and produces a combination that's really warm-blooded and warm-hearted! Hot-headed too, at times, with fuel-injected Aries aggression boosting your already larger-than-life sun sign!

But even though you can prickle unnecessarily at well-meant criticism, you're full of kindness, energy, optimism and self-confidence. People don't mind you bossing them about – they recognise that you're a natural trailblazer and are content to wing along in your wake. To keep good health, you need to channel your fizzing energy force into physical hard work and sport, or you'll get grumpy. Travel and sex are your tonics!

You've more than your share of hot loving needs but, although likely to get hitched early in life, and without the usual Sagittarius cold-feet caution, you're equally prone to up and off, leaving lovers in the lurch while you're hot on the scent of a new adventure. Daring, resourceful and ambitious, you must learn to persevere. You're direct, outspoken and don't know the meaning of tact. The truth may hurt, but you can't say anything else.

You're an open-handed friend who never skimps on cash, hospitality or help. As a lover you ooze sexiness and combine an athletic body with all-night-long energy. You're a jet-powered self-starter, though not much of a finisher. But does that really matter when you're living life so much to the full?

Sun sign Sagittarius/rising sign Taurus

You're a whirlwind whose wandering nature sends you all around the world. But you've a lucky pairing, so the end result of idealistic Sagittarius and steadfast Taurus is usually a charmed life. No wonder you get things done. Doubly capable, you can make even huge-scale plans look practical and inspire others to achieve them for you. You have a life-long urge to learn, and do so slowly and thoroughly, thanks to Taurus. But it's Sagittarius that raises your sights so high in the first place.

You do tend to close your ears once you've made up your mind, and even close friends hesitate to argue with you – not only do you have an explosive temper, but reason gets them nowhere! You've many friends from all walks of life and are a sensuous, if slightly self-centred lover. And you can be as possessive about your lover as you would be about a new car, since your rising sign makes you mad on owning and collecting things and people.

You also grab freedom yourself but grow grouchy when loved-ones try to stretch their wings – even you must admit that's unfair. You can push yourself when you have to, and you're not scared of responsibility. Less physically fit than the average Sagittarius, you do tend to over-eat. But you still like lots of fresh air and have a flair for gardening. Your warmth always wins you a helping hand and you're a dreamer, but a practical one. While your eyes scan the stars your feet stay firmly on solid ground.

Sun sign Sagittarius/rising sign Gemini

Your two signs combine to give you a double dose of itchy feet, so you can't tolerate even the mildest boredom for more than five minutes. Complicated, brainy and curious, you're a chatterbox, too. You crave company and actually make a fine friend – you're especially skilful at sorting out pals' problems. But you can break promises, just like a true Gemini, sometimes without realising. Your runaway mouth makes so many plans that sound fine and fun, but you don't give your mind time to catch up!

Romance is a jokey game to you. You can't resist a new face, and really relish a drawn-out, difficult courtship. It gives you a chance to flex your Gemini wits and suits your Sagittarius fear of too-close commitment. In fact, you prefer a stimulating chat to run-of-the-mill sex.

Flirting's your forte and you make lovely romantic phone calls. But while you can keep several loves simmering at once, they may well be all-verbal by-play and no naughty action! You excel in working partnerships and are brilliant at handling others' careers. Your blend of multi-talented, agile mind and all-over eagerness make you inventive with the odd flash of original genius. And though you get moody if ignored, you don't need great encouragement because of supreme Sagittarius self-confidence. Bending facts and a quick temper are your major faults, but you're so funny and popular most people forgive you anything!

Sun sign Sagittarius/rising sign Cancer

You're a bundle of contradictions as a result of the two-way tug of sign-led loyalties. Cancer makes you seem so sensitive when it comes to feelings – especially your own! – while Sagittarius sometimes turns you into a brutally tactless trampler of other people's confidence.

You're a love puzzle too – an up-and-off Sagittarian who still seems to need a nice little nest. So while one half is purring in pleasure at a newly decorated room, the other is leafing through travel brochures and booking a six-month safari!

Even when your rising sign helps you find true, close loving, your sun sign's busy sliding out of those warm embraces, ready to book a one-way ticket. Problem is, you want both commitment and freedom, blowing hot and cold and turning moody and self-pitying when others don't read you right. Your sun sign fears being trapped, your rising sign dreads rejection. No-one will win unless you take more chances.

Luckily, people persevere, partly because you're so nice-looking. Your hint of Cancer's crab makes you seem shyer than you really are, but also gives you extra staying power. You aim far higher than a true Cancer would, though, and are outgoing enough to wangle your way into any company. You've also got great intuition when it comes to second-guessing. Willing to try most things once, you'd go anywhere on earth to widen your horizons.

Sun sign Sagittarius/rising sign Leo

Fire! Fire! This hyperactive twosome blazes away to produce a sociable, sporty Sagittarius with natural leadership qualities, a royal manner – and pride that's as sensitive as sunburned skin. On the plus side, your sense of fun's so well developed that you could be a professional comic. You've a diploma in partying and all sorts of people are drawn to your warm, entertaining personality. Close up, your splash of Leo pride can put the skids on some friendships, though – and lovers need to learn a good line in massaging flattery if they're to keep you sweet!

Your smooth charm persuades others to turn a blind eye to your faults, such as your allergy to criticism. You're no fan of the grindstone, but you can shine effortlessly in some jobs, especially any linked to showbiz, sport, animals or youngsters. You're not sugary sentimental about children, but they instinctively like you. You treat life as one big joke, so are naturally on their level! You may bring colour into their lives without having any kids of your own.

Extremely effective – once you've overcome Leo's laid-back laziness – you nevertheless irritate stuffy bosses and serious workmates. Needless to say, you thrive best as your own boss! Your good looks and easy manner can be gold-getters, but you could gamble away gains. Full of fizz, fun and yourself, you were born to star.

Sun sign Sagittarius/rising sign Virgo

Ouch! You can be as prickly as a cactus, one that leaps right out of its pot to attack passers-by. Sagittarius' lack of tact plus Virgo's excess of criticism can hit home, hard. Yet you do care about other people's feelings. You just value honest opinions above kind white lies.

You can be just as tough on yourself. Your sun sign makes you want to be the best, naturally, and half of you believes you are! Until that Virgo half highlights every concealed crack and flaw. Result: a unique Sagittarius inferiority complex. Still, Virgo makes you a better settler-down than most others who share your sun sign. Your heart often gets the miseries because of lurking mistrust, though. Luck sends you a good selection of possible life mates, but fear of putting a foot wrong makes you miss some golden opportunities. You can also get sidetracked by silly details and tend to slap down friends' ideas. When love goes wrong you usually retreat to your family for a good moan, which is better than bottling it up and getting stomach trouble and rashes from stress.

You take life a touch too seriously, but you are inventive and have a flair for writing. Although your sign combination feels uncomfortable at times, you'll achieve more by selling yourself. Fake that self-confidence if necessary! Unlike a true Virgo, you're usually surrounded by people. Loyal with a sweet, kind heart, you never forget friends or duty.

Sun sign Sagittarius/rising sign Libra

Both your sides are people-linked, so you shine brightest whenever there's a gathering and music playing. You've a crammed diary and vast circle of acquaintances. Sweet-natured, ultra-friendly, adaptable and charming, Libra leaves you easily influenced by surroundings. It affects your emotional balance, too, so your heart runs on less of an even keel than a typical, sunny Sagittarius.

You're more of a sports spectator than player and you can be distinctly lazy when it comes to geeing yourself up for work. Romance rules your thoughts, and your imagination! You can pump up the merest show of politeness from someone you fancy into proof they're hot for you. Your sex drive is very high and you soon switch the glint in your eye to a new target if one proves a letdown. But you seek emotional and practical safety, and may chase the most unlikely partner because they offer secure comfort. Often in love with love, you rush fences and try to seize your happiness before its ripe.

Your creative talents include a Libra-linked flair for

making and decorating, but although you work hard and can turn your communication skills to good use, your income is never secure. Feast or famine's how your accounts work. Versatile and thoughtful, you're a happy blend of sense and sensitivity. You're the Sagittarius who most easily wins friends and, softly, secretly, influences people.

Sun sign Sagittarius/rising sign Scorpio

'Look out, slippery customer at work' could be posted on your door, especially where your job's concerned. Your rising sign makes you far more devious than any Sagittarius ought to be! More passionate and far more intense, too. You know exactly what you want, and Scorpio makes this extend to plenty of material possessions – and a total dread of owing money! You also know what you're good at and, with the booster rocket of Sagittarius self-confidence behind you, once you've rolled up your sleeves and attacked a project, it's not long before you've reached your goal.

Very strong-willed, sulky and hot-tempered when crossed, you can be so criticial. Scorpio gives you an extra-sharp tongue, reserved for your worst enemies, and a far more black-and-white view of the world than other fire signs. Sagittarius tolerance is well buried . . .

You were also born with a secret weapon. You're pretty hard to read yourself, but have a star-sent talent for telling others' thoughts. Power's what you seek and you value it particularly in love. You'll never refuse a challenge but in your case it's win or bust. You're afraid of really letting your feelings free, with some reason. Jealousy can turn your world upside down. Sex helps you relax best, but is also the source of your greatest worries. But outgoing Sagittarius links with Scorpio intensity to give you stupendous energy!

Sun sign Sagittarius/rising sign Sagittarius

You've a talent for making things happen and an impulse for adventure. You're very much an open book, independent, freedom-loving and generous. You love parties, adore being outdoors and have piles of pals who value your fail-safe flair for fun, sense of justice and endless energy. You can lose your cool, but normally reserve your aggression for when you think someone's had a raw deal, or you feel trapped!

In many ways you're a better friend than lover. Because you prefer partners who make limited demands on your heart, you can veer towards those already in a relationship. Sex is very important, too. You must both speak the same body language as well as sharing a brain wavelength, but you'll still bolt for freedom whenever doors look like slamming shut! Totally unpossessive yourself, you find it almost impossible to make allowances for possessiveness in others. You fling yourself into many passionate relationships, often long-distance, but seldom lose control all together.

Work or work-outs are your natural way of letting off steam. You're versatile in your job but have to go your own way, a self-starter who does best self-employed. You put in lots of mental effort and bubbling energy, and a constant quest for fresh fields takes you far if you pick an active job. Over-optimistic, you only stumble when things go wrong. You were born to organise and inspire.

Sun Sign Capricorn

Self-reliance, self-control and self-interested hard work are all part of you. You're stable, dependable, practical and very patient. But you can also be cool and care more for things than people. Actions, not words, are your tools and you wait and plan terribly carefully. Gradually and inevitably, like a guided missile, you work your way through any organisation and up the success ladder to the top. Once you've made your game plan, nothing can stop your progress.

If this sounds rather frightening, it can be, for those who aren't on your side. Your allies, though, know there's no-one they can trust or rely on more than you. You take life seriously and success is your aim. Saturn, your ruling planet, gives you endless powers of discipline and endurance. You're so self-contained that you could survive in the most desolate conditions if you had to. Yet you do care so deeply for others, too, and welcome and revel in responsibilities.

You're certainly not a laughterless workaholic – you have an irresistible, dry sense of humour and can leap through life in risk-ridden bounds, not just cautious plodding, when circumstances command. And part of your compulsion to work 24 hours a day comes from a natural need to feel secure financially. No matter how healthy your income, you've a deep-down fear that you will end up penniless, and less realistic signs' easy-going attitudes towards cash leaves you completely baffled.

You need to test and push yourself, just to see what the human mind and body is capable of – like a test pilot or marathon runner, forever stretching limits. You also need to know you can provide well for loved-ones. You make a faithful lover and an excellent parent – children know you will always be there for them.

One way you could get even closer to people is by learning to reveal your own thoughts and fears, opening up your heart more, learning to trust and taking emotions out of the freezer. Traditional to the core, you crave a conventional loving home set-up, and stable relationships. Yet you can make it difficult for yourself. For starters, you never want anything that comes too easy. You could compromise more and make allowances for minor faults.

You demand as much of yourself as of partners and friends, so do try to let your heart off the hook sometimes. Under that rock-solid surface is a true diamond – loyal, loving, pulse-stoppingly sexy and a partner who can be trusted to take care of any crisis. You always keep your word and promises and have an inner code of conduct you'd never break. Just knowing you are there brightens the day for so many people. A sure-footed high climber, your strength can win you the stars.

Now, Capricorn, it's time to discover even more about the real you, by finding your RISING SIGN, the co-ruler of your life which combines with your sun sign in a unique way.

You know what your SUN SIGN is – the date of your birth makes you a Capricorn. Now, having checked the chart opposite, you know your RISING SUN from the time of day you were born. Read on to find out what it reveals about you. If you don't know the exact time of your birth, don't worry. You'll soon spot yourself in one of the descriptions of SUN SIGN/RISING SIGN combinations.

Sun sign Capricorn/rising sign Aquarius

More objective, spontaneous and idealistic than most Capricorns, that's you. You're not as outgoing as a true Aquarius, of course, but yours is a go-for-it blend that mixes outrageous aims with your sun sign's practicality and ambition. So you

YOUR SUN SIGN IS **CAPRICORN** – THIS CHART REVEALS YOUR RISING SIGN

If your date of birth is	If you were born between these times											
22–31 December	9 am to 10:14 am	10:15 am to 11:14 am	11:15 am to 12:14 pm	12:15 pm to 1:29 pm	1:30 pm to 3:14 pm	3:15 pm to 5:44 pm	5:45 pm to 8:29 pm	8:30 pm to 11:14 pm	11:15 pm to 1:59 am	2 am to 4:44 am	4:45 am to 7:14 am	7:15 am to 8:59 am
1–11 January	8:30 am to 9:44 am	9:45 am to 10:44 am	10:45 am to 11:44 am	11:45 am to 12:59 pm	1 pm to 2:44 pm	2:45 pm to 5:14 pm	5:15 pm to 7:59 pm	8 pm to 10:44 pm	10:45 pm to 1:29 am	1:30 am to 4:14 am	4:15 am to 6:44 am	6:45 am to 8:29 am
12–20 January	8 am to 9:14 am	9:15 am to 10:14 am	10:15 am to 11:14 am	11:15 am to 12:29 pm	12:30 pm to 2:14 pm	2:15 pm to 4:44 pm	4:45 pm to 7:29 pm	7:30 pm to 10:14 pm	10:15 pm to 12:59 am	1 am to 3:44 am	3:45 am to 6:14 am	6:15 am to 7:59 am
YOUR RISING SIGN IS	AQUARIUS	PISCES	ARIES	TAURUS	GEMINI	CANCER	LEO	VIRGO	LIBRA	SCORPIO	SAGITTARIUS	CAPRICORN

probably get more done than many an Aquarius, despite their good intentions!

Yes, you can break rules at times. But that dyed-in-the-wool Capricorn caution does run very deep. Every now and then you surprise lovers, though, by fielding up-and-down feelings. You feel more loving and giving towards people as a whole (Aquarius influence again) than to any single person, until that rare lover comes along who can warm your heart fully. But you won't hesitate to help a friend or partner in distress, especially if you can see a logical solution.

You can be a rather aloof lover who likes secrecy and solitude, so your life partner will need to be an understanding type. But they'll be repaid with no-holds-barred bedtimes and a passion that starts strong and just gets better and better as years go by.

Workwise, you do best in big organisations and chances are you'll have to travel to earn your bread. Sensible and modest, you've a clear idea of what you want and where you're heading. People can take you for granted and offload extra responsibilities onto you, because they know you'll never let them, or yourself, down.

Sun sign Capricorn/rising sign Pisces

Pisces softens your heart and sends you seeking affection – you really do long to be liked. But Capricorn crops up in the strict standards you set yourself, especially in your lovelife, though you're much more easy going where others are concerned. You will always respond to a plea for help and you never sit in judgment on people.

You come across as a sympathetic soul, kind and hard-working – though you have an inner touch of sharp teeth behind that understanding smile. Generally, yours is a balanced blend of Capricorn clear-thinking and Pisces sensitivity. Your forceful, ever-present ambition is given a slightly softer edge, too. It's steered in the direction of others' welfare and you're particularly good with older people. Friends matter so much to you and you quickly dive to their defence.

Dreamy Pisces makes you appear to avoid decision-making, but really you just like to weigh everything up one more time, and never choke on major choices. You're a great team member at work. You tend to worry too much about money and need to escape both job and home occasionally – travel and music help you relax.

You probably prefer daydreaming to real flesh-and-blood romance for a long time. But the reality is that you need a stable base and lots of loving. Nagging's the one thing that will drive you away. Otherwise, as the most romantic Capricorn, you'll have cast-iron love commitments.

Sun sign Capricorn/rising sign Aries

You hold the best Capricorn cards for all-star success! You're sure-footed and determined enough to scrabble your way right up from the bottom of the heap to the heady heights. Usually with breathtaking speed, too!

Aries aggression makes you very sure of yourself and what you know you can do. Unlike other super-ambitious signs, though, you've a real head for heights and can hang indefinitely at the top once you've arrived. Challenge turns you on and, although Aries is something of a soft touch for flattering words, Capricorn keeps your eyes and mind on the job in hand. Remember it can get lonely up there, though – you might never admit it, but happy-ever-after loving and a houseful of kids to help with their homework is your secret dream.

Yet not only are you probably working too hard and too long hours to be in the running for happy families, but you can be cold, cynical and too hard on others to make finding a mate in the first place particularly easy! Give yourself a break and let that inner spring of sexy intrigue and infectious humour bubble to the surface! Burn off excess vitality in regular exercise and delegate more, at home and work. Unless you make a conscious effort to relax, love will bring out the worrier in you.

Your rising sign makes you hot-headed and hot-hearted, so

your eyes are sure to stray, but you'll soon see how to fit delicious risk factors into long-term romance . . .

Sun sign Capricorn/rising sign Taurus

Security is what you want – but you wouldn't say no to fame and fortune either. Your pair of signs are earthily practical and work well together. This is a positive, strong and very determined duo. A hint of Taurus idleness surfaces in you now and then, but you've too much Capricorn self-discipline to let it get the upper hand.

Careful planning and a gift for foreseeing the future accurately further fuel your success drive. Your ambitions are partly a Taurus desire to live well and partly a burning Capricorn need to be publicly patted on the back. You always get the job done. You're a razor-sharp manager, an effective executive and tackle everything you do with head-on honesty.

You've no time at all for fools or slackers, and you hate silly behaviour. Dependable and confident, you are usually able to make your base anywhere. Which is lucky, because your sign mix suggests that you'll be uprooted more than once, although each time one step nearer success. Your rising sign does make you a fraction fixed on one thoughtwave, and gives you a snappy, hard-to-soothe temper. You're not exactly Scrooge, but you know the value of money, and like lovers to spoil and pamper you. You prefer to show your own rock-solid emotions by thoughts and deeds rather than expensive presents.

Work linked to plants, land and education suits you best, and it takes a lot to stop your life progress.

Sun sign Capricorn/rising sign Gemini

Shrewd, logical and matter-of-fact, you work far too hard to be a real Gemini – but this glint of Mercury certainly brightens up your cautious Capricorn soul. Your two signs seem to be as different as chalk and cheese, yet they work well together, making you so mentally flexible that no-one can ever get one over on you! You say what you think, too, but with such

Gemini diplomacy your victims don't even notice you've insulted them!

There's a wickedly witty turn of phrase beneath your normally severe self. This earth-and-air mixture cuts both ways – it ties down your rising sign's fly-by-night talents and makes them deliver. And it whisks up those solid Capricorn abilities into projects others can get enthusiastic about. You're dependable, honorable, fair-minded and serious – but your rising sign also gives you a rather restless, inquisitive mind and increases your liking for people. It also makes you more of a flirt, which mixes up your lovelife no end because you're every bit as timid about commitment as the next Capricorn. It's likely you'll try to manage more than one relationship at once, but not being a true heart-free Gemini this could cause all sorts of complications.

You have a lower boredom threshold than other Capricorns, and need more sleep. Big business and crime-fighting are areas you could shine in and, provided you don't aim too high, you can run two careers at once.

Sun sign Capricorn/rising sign Cancer

Get out and get on, cries Capricorn, shoving you out into the world to achieve your ambitions. But it's much nicer staying here at home, murmurs the seductive little Cancer voice inside you. You do work as hard as anyone else born under your tough-minded sign, but you're also more home-orientated because of your Cancer influence. It means you handle people well – add that to your businesslike Capricorn drive for unlimited potential.

There's more warmth in you than many Capricorns – and marriage is positively good for you. You've an abrupt, abrasive manner and a razor-sharp tongue when hurt, and this can put would-be lovers right off! But those who stick around find you do need to closely share your emotions and have a tenderness that softens your no-nonsense inner self.

Traditional and highly protective, you never give up, even when all the odds are against you. When you do fall in love, you can throw aside your usual common sense, too, and become misty-eyed and supersensitive. Your biggest problem is treading the line between your often opposing signs. And watch out for your family smothering your lovelife by ringing you in the middle of a breathless bedroom bout! You can be driven from one relationship to the next one in a rather un-Capricorn way by your need to belong. But your most stable and satisfying love relationship will probably come your way in mid-life.

Sun sign Capricorn/rising sign Leo

More heart, more heat – that's what you get when Leo adds a flash of dash to your basically serious and capable Capricorn self. You also get generous leadership qualities which offset that go-it-alone tendency, and you do know how to back them up with drive and hard work.

You've a wonderful, but responsible, sense of humour – you're a joker who knows when to call a halt. But until you reach the top level in any job – where you're giving, not taking, orders – your working life won't be easy. You're not the slightest bit submissive or humble, so you hate being told what to do. But you will climb high through your combination of showman's flair and dogged determination.

You're actually less spontaneous and more cautious and negative than you appear, but as first impressions are the ones that count, Leo's done you a favour. Although you still appreciate time alone, it's an extra not an essential – and you're popular, hospitable and kind. But beware! Usually, your rising sign lends you optimism to burst through your pitch-black glooms, but when the Leo in you suffers wounded pride you can be doubly downcast.

You're not afraid of hard work, as long as it's not dirty. But you crumble too easily under criticism and work best for yourself or as a boss. More highly sexed, sensual and vain than just about every other Capricorn, you put your whole self into loving with flair and dare.

Sun sign Capricorn/rising sign Virgo

Practical, solemn, you seem to lead a sheltered life – but what inner harmony you have! Few personal problems hamper your hard-working and straight-dealing route to success. Your world's an earnest place but the lucky few get to feel and see the inner, earthy warmth that glows within you and can light up countless lives.

You're probably the most straightforward person in the world, as solid as Mount Everest and one of the best friends around. It's as a lover that you sometimes founder because your aloof manner can keep others at arm's length. No good for romance at all. What you class as dignified self-respect makes lovers feel completely unwanted. Secret affairs may prove a failing because you naturally take on others' problems and one thing leads to another . . . so be warned!

Virgo may make you imagine health problems, but your failure to relax probably lies behind most of your minor aches and pains. You need success and measure your worth by your work – an area of your life that needs untangling. You love the outdoors, especially gardening, and work best in anything linked to farming, food or land cultivation. Your miss-nothing approach also points to a banking career. Whatever you do, remember that scattering your interests leads to failure, as will short cuts and corner cutting. Your inner wisdom is your main strength, and what all your friends count on in a crisis.

Sun sign Capricorn/rising sign Libra

Polish, diplomacy and refinement are the gift of your rising sign. You certainly have sound business sense and are great boss material, but your Capricorn duty and ambition gets a charming cover-up from Libra. That means you're not all jabbing knees and elbows on your upward scramble to super-success!

You're humorous and warm-hearted, which shows in your stack of invitations. Yes, that Libra touch improves your image no end! You're also sentimental and romantically loving because of your Venus-ruled rising sign, but these qualities aren't too close to the surface. Close friends and loved-ones will have to scratch quite deep to find them – if you give them the chance.

You're so keen on pursuing possible lovers that you've got rather a wandering eye. Any partner of yours will have to be attractive, witty, understanding – and self-confident enough not to take your flirting seriously. It's pretty harmless in fact, because you're usually too busy working to follow through and, anyway, deep down you prefer loyalty to love.

Your rising sign can rock the boat in other ways, like blowing your finances in a spending binge and tipping moods into seesaw extremes. When you're down you can suffer Capricorn bleakness plus Libra 'Why bother?' But you're still the only Capricorn who can truly switch off, lie back and take life oh-so-easy.

Sun sign Capricorn/rising sign Scorpio

Super-ambitious, you don't just want to be totally successful yourself, you want all your family, friends and acquaintances to do well too! For that reason, you're forever shoving them forward. You've more than enough energy to spare to look after your interests, and theirs, at the same time!

Hopefully your loved ones won't mind you taking over. You do everything well, and to excess. You work extraordinarily hard and take great pride in your achievements. You buy the best because you know it will last and are thrifty in the extreme. Your active brain thrives on communication, so you're always on the phone, posting letters and recording messages for people. And your stamina extends to your off-duty times, as well, making you play as hard as you work.

Loyal and faithful, your rising sign gives you an added streak of possessiveness. You've a Scorpio-style temper and stinging tongue, too, and can be cruel to those who disappoint you. Your too-powerful emotions can drive lovers away, unless you're careful. These outbursts come as a surprise to those taken in by your cool appearance.

Your love links are liable to sudden take-offs, and abrupt endings! You've a steely core, though, and anyone who wants your heart must appeal first to your logical mind. Capable Capricorn plus shrewd Scorpio equals a quiet but deadly born leader who's irresistibly sexy.

Sun sign Capricorn/rising sign Sagittarius

Efficient, clever, ambitious . . . so what else is new about your kind of Capricorn? Sympathy for others, for a start. That's just one of the nice bonuses brought to you by friendly Sagittarius. It makes you more popular, less ruthless, and also broadens your mind. You want to follow lots of leads, and that endless curiosity helps keep you youthful, too. But your basically plodding self still needs to master each new course thoroughly before moving on to the next.

Compared to other Capricorns, you're more sociable and adventurous, even more fiercely independent and few could match your competitive spirit. You're extra keen on testing your endurance and make a rotten loser. The truth is, many of your pals tend to work in areas where they could do you some good. And your heart likes to bond to well-placed lovers, too, preferably rich ones! You're money-loving to the core and hoard fanatically, no matter how much you have already.

Hard to pin down, let alone partner in love, you need to make all the first moves and want a lover with a wide-awake mind. You can't help looking around for the Exit sign and could take years to settle down. One of your great skills is predicting popular trends – your down-to-earth side tunes you into public opinion, while your more way-out side helps you look ahead. Versatile and energetic, you shine where cash changes hands.

Sun sign Capricorn/rising sign Capricorn

You're the business, a head-down hard-grafter who can't be distracted until you've reached the bitter end of your chosen task. In fact, some might say you're all work and no play, but your satisfied lovers know better. Soaring ambition is well settled in you and marches hand in hand with your hunger to be in charge and in control. Saturn's influence makes you thorough as can be and so realistic. Impatient yet rule-mad, you won't make waves and are a hard taskmaster, particularly to yourself.

Your need to be constantly in control can hold back your lovelife a lot! And trying to make sure your heart never gets short-changed isn't a short cut to that once-and-forever great passion. Unless you put more time into your private life, it will remain shambolic, and mixing business with pleasure won't grab you a second date with anyone.

You're capable of great love but need so much reassurance before you'll lower your drawbridge that many lovers give up laying seige to your heart altogether. You, more than any other sign, need a partner and friends who'll help you laugh and let your hair down.

You worry quite a lot – tummy troubles and grey moods bring you down – but yours is still a tough and long-lived combination. You're heading high whatever happens, so do try to slow down a bit and make the trip more fun.

Sun Sign Aquarius

You're free as air, yet solidly fixed – that sounds like a contradiction, but shows what an unpredictable spirit you are. Being an air sign, you're a fast talker who needs to feel free. But you can cling fast to your opinions and don't like changing them. You're independent and must do your own thing, and even if that means stepping out from the crowd and looking rather odd, you don't care. In fact, you'd fight for everybody's right to do and say what they like.

At first handshake, you come across as very friendly. But although you care about people and the world in general, you're hard to get to know and reluctant to let a friend or lover come too close. Like a magical mirage, you disappear when reality closes in. Even though you can be a real revolutionary, it's your thoughts, not actions, that pack an outrageous punch and inspire all you meet.

Deep-down cautious, despite your mental daring, you thrive in clubs and organisations and often work for nothing to help those in need. And though you're an intelligent, inventive free-thinker, you also have a desire to dominate and force your views on others. So you're not half as tolerant as you seem!

Often, your ideas are ahead of their time, or even just plain crazy. With Uranus, the rebel planet, as your ruler, giving you inbuilt independence, nothing can stop your flow. Occasionally, you hit genius level!

Actually, you do need a love partner, because you find it hard to get along without constant reassurance. You can be loyal and faithful once your heart's made the right match. But, equally, you can't tolerate being held back in any way and find it so hard to express your feelings. So only cool, clever and understanding people need apply!

Good and lasting looks go with your sun sign, and your vitality and talk-to-me manner ensure that you're never short of admirers. You never judge lovers on their appearance, so it's likely that when you do settle down you'll pick an unlikely but blissfully happy match.

Although you need plenty of elbow room to pursue outside interests, these don't often include forbidden affairs. About the only thing that will make you flee your love nest is BO or bad teeth in a partner.

Fired up and full of ideas, you've sympathy in your eyes, a spring in your step and an ear for just about everyone. But, sadly, you can find it hard to give others the kind of reassurance you seek for yourself. You're often far more tense inside than your relaxed attitudes suggest. Work rarely gets you down, but feeling a situation is slipping out of your control can worry you sick. Just remember you're a match for anything life throws your way.

Now it's time to discover even more about the real you, by finding the joint ruler of your life, your RISING SIGN, and discovering the unique way it combines with your Aquarius sun sign.

You already know what your SUN SIGN is – the day you were born makes you an Aquarius. And once you've checked the time of day you were born against the chart opposite you'll know your RISING SIGN, too. Don't worry if you don't know the time of your birth exactly. You'll soon spot yourself in one of the SUN SIGN/RISING SIGN combinations.

Sun sign Aquarius/rising sign Pisces

With all-seeing eyes and almost magical intuition you bore through any false front to the real person underneath. Plus Pisces damps down your love of pure logic and gives you a more romantic window on the world.

Bored with routine, though you stick to it if it means freeing yourself for better things, you are frustrated without

YOUR SUN SIGN IS **AQUARIUS** – THIS CHART REVEALS YOUR RISING SIGN

If your date of birth is	If you were born between these times											
21–31 January	8:30 am to 9:29 am	9:30 am to 10:29 am	10:30 am to 11:44 am	11:45 am to 1:29 pm	1:30 pm to 3:59 pm	4 pm to 6:44 pm	6:45 pm to 9:29 pm	9:30 pm to 12:14 am	12:15 am to 2:59 am	3 am to 5:29 am	5:30 am to 7:14 am	7:15 am to 8:29 am
1–10 February	8 am to 8:59 am	9 am to 9:59 am	10 am to 11:14 am	11:15 am to 12:59 pm	1 pm to 3:29 pm	3:30 pm to 6:14 pm	6:15 pm to 8:59 pm	9 pm to 11:44 pm	11:45 pm to 2:29 am	2:30 am to 4:59 am	5 am to 6:44 am	6:45 am to 7:59 am
11–18 February	7:15 am to 8:14 am	8:15 am to 9:14 am	9:15 am to 10:29 am	10:30 am to 12:14 pm	12:15 pm to 2:44 pm	2:45 pm to 5:29 pm	5:30 pm to 8:14 pm	8:15 pm to 10:59 pm	11 pm to 1:44 am	1:45 am to 4:14 am	4:15 am to 5:59 am	6 am to 7:14 am
YOUR RISING SIGN IS	PISCES	ARIES	TAURUS	GEMINI	CANCER	LEO	VIRGO	LIBRA	SCORPIO	SAGITTARIUS	CAPRICORN	AQUARIUS

some way to let off artistic steam. You can accept reality because of your sun sign's practical grasp on life, but your rising sign sparks almost clairvoyant powers that go beyond the here and now. You can seem dithery at times but only because Pisces needs to make exactly the right choice. You're not putting off decisions, merely playing for time.

Because you hate upsetting people, you tend to say yes to everything, then quietly go off and do something different. Spontaneous and friendly, you are drawn to others and very well liked. You work best behind the scenes and put much effort into helping others.

Travel and love will always be linked in your life. Your emotions are often fired up, and you crave the high of a new love, then feel let down when things inevitably run down into routine. You can also torture yourself by dwelling on imaginary insults and might-have-been conversations! When life gets dreary, you whizz off to cloud-cuckoo-land, forgetting all the unpaid bills!.

Sun sign Aquarius/rising sign Aries

Physically and mentally adventurous, you adore new people and places, and fresh challenges. You don't mind stepping aside from the crowd and announcing outrageous opinions. Your rising sign brings daring and sunshine into your world and, in turn, you lighten up other people's lives.

This is a generous, warm and optimistic combination, full of sparks. You're not much of a sticker and can slither out when the going gets too tough, but that's because you like to live in the present and lack much of that famous Aquarius ability to see the future.

The Aries effect shortens your temper but lengthens your quota of kindness – you can be conned out of cash by a hard-luck story. Your ideas are so original, but can be too widely scattered to be any use. You should try to build up your attention span! Aries makes you more impatient, even when it comes to sex. You get bored so easily, and though you're a very keen bedmate and electrifying lover, you can cool off all too soon! You don't learn from past heartbreaks and tend to rush straight into new romance. You're quite likely to dash off with a string of identically wrong partners!

Practically tireless, you pour much of your amazing energy into two searches – for a grand passion and for a perfect, all-absorbing job. Yours is a mentally magnificent mix – you enjoy learning all your life, and go out of your way to stretch your brain cells.

Sun sign Aquarius/rising sign Taurus

Determined, strong and ambitious, you're a tough nut! Go-ahead Aquarius meets stay-at-home Taurus in an interesting mix which, against all odds, is also a comfortable match. You're pretty well balanced – you care about people and are far more generous than a true Taurus, although you wouldn't sacrifice an ounce of personal freedom to help someone, let's be honest.

A highly original thinker, your personal habits are still more or less fixed. Your rising sign makes you very stubborn and resistant to change – like a fragile houseplant shifted from one end of the windowsill to the other, you can go droopy and dried-up if circumstances are even slightly altered.

You're bound to end up in a good job – Taurus won't let you stay off the success track. But you often work so much that lovers feel neglected. Hyperpossessive, once a long-lusted-after love is yours you may lose interest and start working overtime again. So be warned!

Aquarius' self-control sticks around most of the time but extra pressure may make you blast off like a bouncing bomb. Others give that Taurus-triggered temper a wide berth. Still, your rising sign brings a down-to-earth sensuality that improves your heart's chances.

Your rising sign also makes you more worldlywise and businesslike than you seem, with practical groundwork that turns Aquarius flights of fancy into dreams come true.

Sun sign Aquarius/rising sign Gemini

You're like a gorgeous hummingbird, never still and ready to fly off in any direction you fancy. Your pair of ruling planets, Uranus and Mercury, join forces to make you extremely changeable, and your Gemini element leaves you constantly on the lookout for new challenges.

Brimful of ideas, some hare-brained, some brilliant, you place great importance on education and communication. Gemini makes you a great traveller, too, with a keen sense of adventure. And although you're easily irritated and wound-up, you also calm down quickly. You have an uncanny knack of being able to fit in almost anywhere and with all sorts of strange customs.

You enjoy change and variety in your lovelife. And Gemini joins a flirtatious frill to your basic Aquarius allergy to commitment. The result can be a sticky mess, peppered with broken promises. How often have you had to take the phone off the hook or run away just to escape?

You want a mate for playful fun rather than passionate affairs, and positively enjoy secrets and complications like juggling two romances at the same time. You're almost obsessively interested in other people's lives, but find it hard to turn curiosity into concern. You're generous, all right, and clever, but can scatter your talents and good intentions too widely to have any real effect. Focus more closely on real love, and the rest will follow.

Sun sign Aquarius/rising sign Cancer

Sensitive, vulnerable and ever-so-softly romantic, that's the way you seem, thanks to the influence of such a deep-feeling rising sign. But underneath, you're still detached, a typical Aquarius life looker-on. Now and then, though, dreamy Cancer gets down to work on your head-led sun sign and the result's an imagination so fertile it can take you far, far outside the real world.

Forever seeking life's deepest meaning, you reach out into the realm of sixth sense. You have a strong need to nurture, but are still more interested in people as a group than as individuals.

You're more of a thinking romantic than a doing one, too, though vulnerable Cancer's influence does make you keener than almost every other Aquarius on linking up permanently with a partner. You need a lover who makes you feel completely secure. Not for you a no-strings set-up or marriage of convenience. You want a deep, close relationship with your other half, upfront and honest.

Not terribly energetic, you love your home comforts and are one of the few Aquarius combinations who needs a prod to make them travel. Holding on to long-gone love can pull you back, and you like playing the martyr. But your so-what approach to life is your best safety valve. More logical than true Cancer, warmer than typical Aquarius, get set for long-term life and relationship success!

Sun sign Aquarius/rising sign Leo

Truly people-friendly, outgoing and optimistic, that's your sign blend – always ready to lend others a helping hand. You never bother to check if they want one, by the way, which may mean you need people more than they need you! Never mind, it's the thought that counts and, in your case, you're always thinking far ahead and on a very grand scale.

You can spotlight people's faults but usually like them anyway, because you're warmer than the average Aquarius. And, besides, where would you be without the adoring audience that dramatic showman Leo demands?

Partnerships – working ones rather than sexual ones – are your special talent. You thrive best when you've someone to bounce your highly original ideas off. In love, you've a deep need to define yourself through another person, but your Leo half can all too easily make you try your hand at emotional bullying. Any partner who stands for such nonsense, however, won't last long – needless to say, you've no time for people who let you boss them!

Firm, masterful and fair in working life, you prove a fine

leader, though workmates may occasionally complain about your long and loud lectures. There's one people-linked contradiction you can never quite work out. Do you care what others think, like Leo? Or does airy Aquarius tell world opinion to take a walk? Whatever happens, your winning mix makes an exciting, entertaining trendsetter.

Sun sign Aquarius/rising sign Virgo

Wise Virgo stitches your basic flyaway self to practicality. While your sun sign dreams the impossible dream, your rising sign sketches out cash-flow diagrams and tots up some vital statistics. Virgo also adds an ability to criticise both yourself and others – something most Aquarius people sadly lack. When Aquarius unselfishness adds in to Virgo's inborn need to do good, the result is a so-caring combination. Supportive as steel scaffolding, you give endless time, money and effort to help those in need.

You've an extra-cool head and strong sense of justice, but can lose your sense of proportion at times, bogged down in an obsession with trivial details. You may also be prone to habits that are too fixed, health obsessions and eating problems, and have a tendency to worry.

Lovewise, you can appear pretty cold and may have strained family relations in your past. Try oiling the wheels of loving with more laughter. You're drawn towards forbidden affairs and exciting secret meetings, but don't dabble more than your crystal-clear conscience can stand.

You tend to put love relationships under the microscope and can seem more restrained and old-fashioned than you really are. But you'll bloom like a desert flower given the right love and trust. You probably have a very striking appearance which attracts, and keeps, many. You're a realistic change-maker working for a wonderful world.

Sun sign Aquarius/rising sign Libra

Lucky you! Charming, witty and with an even-handed flair for both the artistic and scientific sides of life! You actually like studying, even if your restless rising sign only lets you concentrate in short bursts, so you're bound to end up working on something you enjoy and find fulfilling.

Love, your social life, children and animals are your priorities and you want a world that's pleasant and problem-free. Libra makes you so sensitive to your surroundings but can also bury your head in the sand to bypass confrontation. Your moods lurch from one extreme to another, and you're prone to spells of unbelievable sluggishness! Watch your main weaknesses – greed, laziness and sexual excess – and concentrate on the bonuses brought by your rising sign.

You're far more adaptable and easy-going than almost every other Aquarius, and far more hotly drawn to loving. In fact, it can become an obsession! You tend to prefer relationships that are well within their sell-by date and find it hard to stick with partners who've cosied down into comfy familiarity. Why not use that ever-active imagination to help keep romance alive?

Normally peace-loving, if someone pushes their luck with your good nature, you fizz with pent-up fury. Creative and competitive, you're a better thinker than doer but always such fun to have around.

Sun sign Aquarius/rising sign Scorpio

Already strong-willed, with Scorpio as your rising sign you can come on too forcefully! It makes you more intense, passion-filled and jealous so, unlike normally detached Aquarius, you rush into rows and rackets. You're quite critical and rather enjoy ripping other people's plans to shreds. You also love secrets and your sun sign interest in other people swells into an almost obsessive need to know what makes them tick.

What certainly isn't secret are your likes and dislikes, and your belief you always know best. You want to take over the world, for its own good, of course. There can be quite an inner clash between upright Aquarius' need for freedom and Scorpio's possessiveness. And when the chips are down in love affairs, you could find that green-eyed jailor Scorpio getting the upper hand.

Your lovelife is likely to have a very early start and carry on well into old age, with some secret affairs on the way. Self-centred, and well hidden even from yourself, you can be hard to get close to. Your eyes are ever alert for trouble, love chances and other people's soft spots, and when you set your heart against someone, you can make a terrifying enemy. For you can hate with cold Aquarius cleverness and cruel Scorpio heart!

Intensely loyal to family and a real hard worker, you're forever aiming to live life on a higher level. Your combined signs bring out the Gipsy in you.

Sun sign Aquarius/rising sign Sagittarius

Footloose funster Sagittarius teams up with your freedom-fan sun sign to make you the most self-sufficient soul around. A lifelong victim of wanderlust, you're so restless you just can't resist the chance of a trip, however short.

Generous, honest and able to think every problem through, you adore a good debate, especially when you can stick up for someone less strong. But you can also spout sermons when loving arms are needed or talk about sex and relationships when you should be listening to emotions.

Adventurous, go-ahead and with a horror of being tied down domestically, you need a soul mate who's as fun-loving and open-minded as you to make a strong, dynamic relationship. Chances are you'll spin through a wide mix of partners, though, because you get galloping panic at any sign of possessiveness, however slight. Even when you do settle, you still like to escape sometimes, and you must run your home life on your terms.

You've a fine sense of proportion and would rather have happiness and health than wealth. Work achievement can only be reached in a job that gets you out and about and gives plenty of thinking space. You feel the worries of the world deeply and have true helping instincts, so you may work with sick or needy people in your spare time. You can act the fool at times but you're no sucker – just a saint who brings out the very best in people.

Sun sign Aquarius/rising sign Capricorn

Unusually for an Aquarius, you seek security. Money worries keep you awake at night more than anything else and you're always straining your brain, wondering how you can boost your income. It's all because of one-step-at-a-time Capricorn.

Your mixture is also one of violent mood swings, from bright, mountain-top optimism to deep, dark gloom. But the good news is that, once you've made up your mind, you can work astonishingly hard and achieve an enormous amount.

Capricorn may make you a solitude-lover and reserved among strangers, but it also means that you're excellent in a crisis – the tougher, the better. It gives you authority and turns laid-back Aquarius into a well-organised whizz who flattens all obstacles.

You need a loving partner to boost your self-confidence – though you'd rather die than admit it! But marriage and other full-time commitments are hard for you and it's likely you'll be fixed up early in life, or not at all.

Unlike a true Capricorn, however, your heart can bleed for others. The idealistic edge is taken off but your essential caring warmth remains. Though your agile mind comes up with as many outrageous ideas as the next Aquarius, you're doubly cautious and need to feel accepted to feel good. So it's lucky that everyone you meet takes to you lovingly – and so lastingly.

Sun sign Aquarius/rising sign Aquarius

New ideas, new people, new projects, that's what you're all about. A true Aquarian, you manage both to stand back from life and fling yourself into the thick of others' troubles. You hold emotions under firm control yet are free with your flow of original ideas. Your circle of friends is very wide, and you need fresh stimulation all the time – in romance, too!

Logical, yet kind-hearted and helpful, you never lie and can sometimes come over as a bit strange. Seeming cold and emotionally switched-off, you're too self-conscious to surrender your heart easily, but are well capable of falling in love. It's just that, as with everything else, you insist on working to your own timetable. And being such a free spirit, you have to make sure you're sitting right beside the exit!

You prefer fresh intelligent chat to stale romantic moves any day, and once you've found a strong partner, your affection is everlasting. Technically minded, you need to be your own master at work. You've a knack for getting others to help and respect you.

You're not easy to live with, marching to your own music and always trying to match up to an impossible ideal. And though on the surface you seem simple and friendly, your interest can be very impersonal. Work to generate genuine warmth, guard against being different for different's sake and you'll be as nice as you wish to be!

Sun Sign Pisces

Feeling, rather than thinking, is your way. You're as adaptable and free-flowing as water – your element – and as hard to catch as the two fish, bound together but forever struggling to swim in opposite directions, that symbolise your sun sign.

Neptune, planet of imagination, is your ruler, which makes you hard to pin down, but also gives you amazing intuition. Highly emotional, you are strongly influenced by two things – other people and what's going on in your deepest secret mind. This doesn't make you weak and easily led, far from it. But it can mean you're very changeable and that you sometimes move in such mysterious ways that friends and family find you impossible to figure out.

You aim to be happy and optimistic, so when trouble rears, you often make your excuses and glide away. Unfortunately, most of your greatest headaches cannot be sidestepped, because they spring from within your feverish imagination and sometimes troubled emotions. And although you hate upsets, your inner feelers are so sensitive they can pick up the first tremors of trouble far in advance of anyone else. You're like the only person on board an ocean liner who knows a dangerous iceberg is looming.

No wonder you often try to escape from worldly troubles by daydreaming or looking for comfort in food, booze, or worse. You'd spend your whole life dreaming if you could.

You must try to find work that gives your intense, far-flung imagination some scope – jobs connected to film, TV or photography are ideal, or a travel agency.

You're lost without love in your life. Gentle, kind and easily moved by hard-luck stories, you're never short of friends, but you can too easily imagine that some of them are in love with you. Self-deception is one of your major failings and in friendships and affairs it can have disastrous consequences.

Being alone and abandoned is your worst nightmare, which may be why you try to force passion and commitment from the most unlikely people. When you do actually click with a partner, you're an excellent lover, caring and truly romantic. Your affair must always have an element of make-believe if it's to survive, however.

You're rather indecisive and often need others to bale you out of life's problem areas. This is because you're as good-natured and lacking in self-discipline as a young puppy, and far better at advising others than helping yourself! Discreetly generous, you've a well-hidden explosive temper and can get tetchy under pressure. But you're gentle at heart – a tender, tantalising lover and one of the kindest friends anyone could wish for.

The real you, Pisces, will be revealed even more when you find the co-ruler of your life, your RISING SIGN, and see how it combines with your Pisces sun sign.

You know what your SUN SIGN is – the day you were born makes you a Pisces. But now you can look more closely at yourself by checking the chart opposite for your RISING SIGN, from the time of day of your birth. And even if you don't know the exact time you were born, you'll soon spot yourself from the different descriptions of each SUN SIGN/RISING SIGN combination.

Sun sign Pisces/rising sign Aries

Pushy Aries adds extra thrust to your deep-water journey. You're a jet-propelled flying fish instead of an idly circling minnow. This flicker of rising sign fire makes you much more ambitious than the average Pisces, far readier to make up your mind and speak it!

YOUR SUN SIGN IS **PISCES** – THIS CHART REVEALS YOUR RISING SIGN

If your date of birth is	If you were born between these times											
19 Feb – 1 March	7:30 am to 8:29 am	8:30 am to 9:44 am	9:45 am to 11:29 am	11:30 am to 1:59 pm	2 pm to 4:44 pm	4:45 pm to 7:29 pm	7:30 pm to 10:14 pm	10:15 pm to 12:59 am	1 am to 3:29 am	3:30 am to 5:14 am	5:15 am to 6:29 am	6:30 am to 7:29 am
2–10 March	7:15 am to 8:14 am	8:15 am to 9:29 am	9:30 am to 11:14 am	11:15 am to 1:44 pm	1:45 pm to 4:29 pm	4:30 pm to 7:14 pm	7:15 pm to 9:59 pm	10 pm to 12:44 am	12:45 am to 3:14 am	3:15 am to 4:59 am	5 am to 6:14 am	6:15 am to 7:14 am
11–20 March	6:30 am to 7:29 am	7:30 am to 8:44 am	8:45 am to 10:29 am	10:30 am to 12:59 pm	1 pm to 3:44 pm	3:45 pm to 6:29 pm	6:30 pm to 9:14 pm	9:15 pm to 11:59 pm	12 midnight to 2:29 am	2:30 am to 4:14 am	4:15 am to 5:29 am	5:30 am to 6:29 am
YOUR RISING SIGN IS	ARIES	TAURUS	GEMINI	CANCER	LEO	VIRGO	LIBRA	SCORPIO	SAGITTARIUS	CAPRICORN	AQUARIUS	PISCES

And, unlike a pure Aries, you're still basically secretive and not at all attention seeking. You can scarcely control your strong emotions once they're all fired up. Self-restraint could make you happier!

Blocked and frustrated, you overflow into explosive outbursts. As kind and caring as the next Pisces, your Aries influence also pins your heart onto your sleeve, and you can get very hurt in love affairs. What do you do? Go back for more! Aries' courage plus that Pisces lack of self-control produces a dangerous level of risk-running, and without a true tough outer skin, you'd do better to stop putting your heart on the line with new friends and would-be lovers.

You won't admit it, but travel, thrills and fresh starts attract you more than the real business of finding a life mate. So your early lovelife is full of mishaps and mis-timings. Sensitive, perceptive and full of do-anything drive, moodiness can leave you in a muddle. But generally Pisces' gentleness gets opportunity-grabbing ability from aggressive Aries.

Sun sign Pisces/rising sign Taurus

While Pisces' waves of worry send ripples all through your life, Taurus is a safe, secure shore, a refuge from life's storms that's always calm and solid. So your sign combination makes you creative and cash-conscious, emotional yet down to earth, and a friend in a million.

Of course, having two halves of such different signs isn't without its problems. You get a double helping of romance capacity that makes you one of the most thrilling, and addictive, lovers around. And you've a basic nature that's patient, caring and so sweet without verging on the sickly.

But you may feel torn two ways when Pisces pushes to follow intuition and Taurus insists on facts, facts, facts. And in a crisis, Pisces' panic can erupt before Taurus' calm organisation can kick in. Avoid rushing into decisions, or relationships, however, and you can turn your powerful pairing to the positive. Pisces' creative energy isn't wasted but channelled into practical plans that can even make you money, and Taurus' inborn common sense shields your so-fragile heart from damage.

You're a home-lover who attracts love and friendship everywhere you go and you stand out because of your genuine interest in others and desire to help. Honest, patient and with huge reserves of inner peace and strength even you haven't fully tapped, you make the world a more wonderful place just by being in it.

Sun sign Pisces/rising sign Gemini

With your vitality, charm and warmth, plus that silver tongue inherited from your smooth-talking rising sign, there are few people you can't persuade to do what you want. Though you're far too basically sweet-tempered ever to take unfair advantage!

Restless Gemini marks you out as even more of an ever-changing personality, highly adaptable and prone to fit in with the last person you saw. You've a mental agility that helps you think on those nimble Pisces feet, but you have trouble spotting where fascinating facts end and far-fetched fantasies begin . . .

You can't resist letting your sex appeal do a lot of the work for you, either. This could land you in deep water with lovers who wonder what games you may be playing at work for ambition's sake. But because of your rising sign, they should also realise that you need a lot of freedom in relationships and that you must feel respect for the person you fancy if love is to last.

In fact, you'd prefer your partner to be brainier than you, which helps you overcome a lazy streak and pushes you to study, at any life-stage.

Gemini makes you appear more self-assured and self-reliant than you really are, chasing constant mental challenges and love risks. But your air and water blend of intuition and emotions makes you one of the most popular Pisces around.

Sun sign Pisces/rising sign Cancer

Imagination can run away with you all too easily! Your doubly emotional water sign blend can make you almost too sensitive and lead your heart right out of its depth. You're the sign combination most likely to hear wedding bells when a stranger gives a half-smile – and yet be far too shy ever to get your dream off the ground by introducing yourself!

Yes, you're an incurable romantic. But Pisces' indecision isn't helped by Cancer's timidity, so your ebbing moods blow hot and cold and your biggest love affairs stay locked in your own mind. Sentimental about the past, traditional Cancer also gives you staying power in the present. You take ages to decide, but when you do, not much can move you!

You do tend to over-dramatise small hitches, turning on the waterworks when things go wrong. You can wear lovers out with emotional demands, engineered 'scenes' and obvious tricks to get attention. So you may leap into too-early, stick-in-the-mud relationships, but without a partner you are completely lost. You'll never stop hoping, even when you've been repeatedly hurt.

Home-loving, sympathetic, reserved and shy, all you ask is to be held, stroked and loved. Since you're one of the most responsive characters around, there's a good chance your wish could come true.

Sun sign Pisces/rising sign Leo

Those fluid Pisces emotions are deepened by sincerity and warmth from hot-blooded Leo. Quiet confidence and a far greater talent for practical action than most Pisces are among your other gifts. Romantic, gentle, artistic and with a heightened feeling for others' suffering, you sound perfect! But without true Leo leadership qualities, you can shoot off at some odd angles, chasing all sorts of strange goals. Concentrate on just one project at a time and resist all temptations to sidetrack.

You also freeze when you come up against concrete walls at work or in your lovelife. When you can no longer hide, you panic! Luckily, you're super-popular, with many protective friends who want to shield you.

Leo gives you more hidden strength and endurance than you realise – if you'd bother to dig it out. Loneliness makes you rush into relationships and many of your love links never survive the early stages. But you're an understanding, forgiving lover who is ever aware of your partner's vulnerability, as it reflects your own tender centre.

Workwise, Leo's moneymaking ability and Pisces' fiction flair can mean success in business or writing – but watch that gambling streak! Like all Pisces, you're searching for a beautiful dream – Leo's creativity, vigour and sense of drama can make it come to life!

Sun sign Pisces/rising sign Virgo

Responsible, conscientious, practical. That's you – on the face of it! Actually, you're far softer and much kinder than your rather intimidating image suggests. You've more than your fair share of critical Virgo, but the Pisces softie in you ensures that you try hard to make only fair, positive suggestions.

Your rising sign gives you a cool cover-up for your sensitive inner soul. You make a great friend and loving life partner – but you can be tough to work with! You're quite a complex kettle of Pisces fish.

Flapping at trivial troubles, you mysteriously stay rock steady and perfectly able to cope in a real, giant crisis. Because of your cautious rising sign, you have to feel 100 per cent sure of others' actions before extending the hand of friendship yourself. With Pisces making you fickle and Virgo keeping you aloof, love affairs can soon develop into a war of nerves!

Once you do take the plunge, however, you're a devoted lover. But if vital trust is shattered, you'll never get together with that person again, be they business or bed partner. Self-pity and over-involvement in work are your worst faults, but you're gentle and good-natured, an excellent counsellor and carer. Yours is a constructive water-and-earth combination of impossible dreams and practical action.

Sun sign Pisces/rising sign Libra

Strongly fair-minded, loving and giving, yours is a very warm-hearted combination. You're able to express your feelings easily and relate to a large, varied circle of people, largely thanks to so-sociable Libra. But one black spot is that both your signs join forces to make it almost unheard of for you to ever, ever, make a decision.

Gentle, refined and very sensitive, you have the best of intentions, but can sometimes appear to be one of life's great lookers-on. Fun-loving but considerate – you'd never slam car doors after a late-night party – you must have pleasant, peaceful surroundings. People's voices matter a lot to you and you're bound to pick a partner who's easy on the eye and ears.

Pliable Pisces and laid-back Libra make you an easy-going lover, but one who could fall in love with a face in a magazine! You have energy, but it flows in fits and starts as if you've got your batteries damp.

Libra makes you suddenly pull the plugs and Pisces lets you drift away into dreamy idleness until loved-ones get worried. You're the icing on the cake in any work project, providing occasional creative inspiration, but not the reliable bread-and-butter type! Over-indulgence beckons from both your signs and weight could be a lifelong struggle. But no-one moves through life with more grace and charm than you.

Sun sign Pisces/rising sign Scorpio

Most Pisces would rather shut up shop and do a runner than put up their fists when trouble threatens. But with Scorpio as your rising sign, you're a piranha fish with pointy teeth, not a shy flounder desperate to hide away in the sand. You take on disputes before thinking them through and often land in hot water.

You're basically loving and romantic, but gain a passionate intensity from your rising sign. And although you're every inch as creative as the next dreamy Pisces, you're also so sporty it could even earn you money.

You adore going out and enjoying yourself, and can easily give in to over-eating and drinking! And your strong sex drive can send you into some disastrous relationships that satisfy your body but not your mind.

If you feel rejected, you can turn very nasty indeed, as Scorpio slips you a jealous, possessive streak. You like love to be all sewn up and may marry or have a live-in lover very young. Sensitive, relying on intuition rather than intelligence, you tune into people easily and can learn anything.

You throw yourself into the deep end of life but, with a lifejacket of Scorpio self-control and self-awareness, you'll always swim to safety and never sink. Painstaking Scorpio dedication and artistic Pisces creativity makes for someone who gets things done, and whose natural home is among the famous.

Sun sign Pisces/rising sign Sagittarius

You seek adventure and travel, but don't stray too far because your basic Pisces self likes home too much. Still, fancy-free Sagittarius sparks a wonderful image of yourself as the great explorer, and you just have to live up to it!

Your rising sign also makes you very cheerful and popular, and you love having friends round to your place. But you often end up with uninvited guests sleeping on your floor for weeks on end. And you get pushed into inconvenient trips you didn't plan because your too-soft sun sign hates saying no!

Kind, friendly and very warm, but not terribly sensible, that's how your mix measures up. You could profit from being a bit more devil-may-care, because there's a free spirit fighting to be released from the genie's magic lamp inside you. Yet no matter how lonely you feel, you fight against meeting strangers or taking up with new lovers.

You also find it hard to settle down and are terrified of falling out of love with the person you've picked. You may prefer romantic daydreams to down-to-earth reality when it comes to sex.

You feel others' troubles like your own and try to help people less well off. You're impractical, yet have a wonderful talent for making those around you laugh, even in the gloomiest of circumstances.

Sun sign Pisces/rising sign Capricorn

Normally life's knocks make Pisces reel, roll up into a tight ball and stay there! But Capricorn's surface toughness helps shield you from some of the emotional heat you find so hard to handle. It can't stamp out Pisces' tendency towards slithery dithering altogether, but Capricorn does make you more determined, and successful in the long term.

Sociable, helpful (you're such a protective friend) and consistent, you're a fine mix of sun sign caution and rising sign persistence. And Capricorn gives you a stainless-steel edge so that you can put up with poor working conditions and uncomfortable home circumstances better than any other Pisces.

You're not the fragile hothouse creature your sign's generally cracked up to be. You're not put off by obstacles but can become a full-time fretter, especially about your health. Marriage and other long-term links don't always appeal, yet you're best off with a mate who will help you keep your sense of proportion.

Deep, thoughtful and always there for everyone, you're a soft touch behind a businesslike front. Now and then, bossy Capricorn links hands with your over-emotional and involved sun sign to make you meddle, but you really do care about other people. Social services work would be perfect for you. Compassion plus calculated logic could really lighten the world's problems.

Sun sign Pisces/rising sign Aquarius

You're chock-full of deep feelings but also pretty keen on grabbing life's goodies – hardly the head-in-the-clouds character that Pisces is supposed to be. Aquarius rising gives you a mental coolness that offsets your sentimental side. And you've such a brill business brain that you can add up a bill in seconds and always know what your work's worth, down to the last few pence.

You also want to help people, although you're more interested in close friends than the population in general. And your mind-reading skills combine with your sympathetic nature and originality to make you a particularly understanding and helpful pal.

Firm-willed and fixed in your views, you find mental U-turns hard to manage. But in your lovelife you're quite the reverse, reckoning that anything, and anyone, is possible.

Bubbly, sociable and full of strong affections, you still fear commitment and can put off finding a mate for years. You like the idea of an artistic career but it's likely you'll end up balancing the books in the box office or fund-raising, rather than being out front under the bright lights!

'Try, try again' is your motto. You learn by absorbing rather than by conventional teaching and are brilliant at passing knowledge on to others. Tolerant and inspiring, you make the world a better place!

Sun sign Pisces/rising sign Pisces

It's no good, you can't help it. You're just a hopeless, incurable romantic with rose-coloured glasses fixed permanently on already starry eyes. As easily moulded as soft white clay, gentle as a giant gorilla, you're childish – in the nicest possible way!

As you blunder happily through life, often the only thing between you and total disaster is your natural good luck. Fortunately you bring out the best in everyone, so you lead a pretty charmed life. A no-hoper in business matters and personal finances, you are lucky to have genned-up protective pals who shield and advise you.

You're very indecisive and can dither until the cows come home over which bus to board and whether to put milk in your coffee or not. Life's trivia can be a trial to you. You're oddly secretive, too, and weave a fantasy version of every story, even when there's no point!

Your greatest fault is an unhealthy fascination for vice in every shape and form, which can drift you into the lower depths of life. Not very ambitious, you tend to live from hand to mouth and need to take your working life in hand. Sex and emotions top your bill of priorities, and disasters here hit you very hard.

Beware of abusing your body and permanently wrecking your health. You hate washing former loves out of your hair and prefer to keep them as friends forever. Highly talented, you can find fame if you quit cloud-cuckoo-land.

PART THREE

Stars in the Family, Stars for Life

Growing up with your sun sign from baby to parent, and the family relationships that shape your life

ARIES
Stars for Life

STAR BABY

The Aries baby loves the sound of his (or her*) own voice – especially the way it has parents and other adults giving him exactly what he wants. He is demanding and energetic, but those dazzling displays of tonsils don't last long – one minute Aries is yelling fit to burst, the next flashing that special smile that charms the hardest heart.

Thriving on attention but needing independence too, Aries isn't an easy baby – he's too full of frustrated desires and over-ambitious efforts. No sooner has he mastered sitting up than he's desperate to crawl, to walk, to run, to jump. Help him to conquer these physical challenges, and cuddle him when he fails or falls, and you'll be Aries' friend for life. And that's a very special reward for, although Aries baby is smiling and sociable to most, he saves his true trust for only a favoured few.

In all the hurly-burly of his life, Aries needs quiet moments to wind down, to share a special cuddle or a favourite book. Talking, singing and playing lots of games provide the stimulation his free spirit needs – but do try, wherever possible, to let him lead the way and set the pace. Efforts to steer Aries baby in the wrong direction or at the wrong speed (usually too slowly) will only set off this mighty wailer!

Give him as much freedom as you can to explore the world by Aries-proofing it, as far as possible, and watching

*'He' is used to cover he and she for Aries child.

him the whole time, especially around hazards like fires, knives and kettles. And save scoldings for the times he's really done wrong. Too much criticism could make Aries baby retreat back inside himself and dampen his natural spark.

FIRST STEPS FOR ARIES

One word toddler Aries learns early is 'No'. By the time he's up and running on his own two feet, he's heard it often enough. Yet he just can't resist trying to open that fridge one more time, or putting Mum's shoes in the loo just to see what happens. It's all part of his natural fascination with life. Shouting and smacks will only make him more determined.

The way to win Aries toddler over is to match him for charm with a friendly smile and a tempting alternative offer. If all else fails, try tickling him. Aries may stamp and scream, but secretly he likes to know who's the boss because it helps him feel more secure.

The next word he learns is 'Why?', bombarding you with questions from 'Why do I have to go to sleep?' to 'Why is the sky blue?' With a whole world out there to discover, Aries wants answers, and he wants them immediately. He also adores physical challenges and will fall off his trike countless times without losing his determination to 'do it myself' – and start your heart racing by suddenly shouting 'Look where I am' from the very top of the slide.

Fiercely independent, he'll never ask for help, and any given must be very carefully disguised. But that beaming smile that spells success makes it all worthwhile.

Aries' competitive nature can turn into aggression, especially when surrounded by more 'wimpish' toddlers who either can't handle his rough ways or happily let born-leader Aries whip them up into a frenzy of excitement.

Yet underneath that rough, tough, me-first surface, little Aries has a tender heart and wouldn't dream of hurting anyone on purpose. He's first to offer his last biscuit to a sobbing little friend – even if he's caused the tears in the first place.

Being best at everything is a serious business to Aries, even at this tender age. He'll give 110 per cent in the sack race or painting competition and be shattered if he doesn't end up the winner. That's when Aries' vulnerable centre shows and he needs plenty of cuddling and reassurance.

He may sometimes seem almost too self-confident, but in fact toddling Aries is desperate to be liked and accepted and can be permanently hurt by even a chance thoughtless remark. He needs calm, careful, consistent handling, and should be shown how to deal with other people so that he can follow your good example. That way Aries' vivid imagination and sheer excitement at life will survive everyday knocks, mocks and shocks to light up the future.

SCHOOL RULES FOR ARIES

Aries child would adore going to school – if only he could be the headmaster. His inborn need to lead, and reluctance to follow, mean that he may take to classroom discipline and routine like a duck to treacle, and end up showing his frustration by being cheeky, lazy or disruptive. He needs help and encouragement to adapt and fit in with other people now – it will be a valuable lesson for the future.

It's partly his bright intelligence that causes the problems. He'll barrel ahead leaving less advanced classmates far behind, then get bored with a task just before it's finished – and leap on to something else. Steer him towards tackling just one job at a time and try to balance his need to be always starting projects with an effort to finish at least some of them.

Quick to lose interest, Aries can appear lazy, but he'll soon stir himself if you whisper that he's lagging behind. The only place for Aries to be is at the top of the class. If all else fails, resort to bribery. He can never resist a tempting offer, and will see it as fair reward for his efforts.

Still buzzing with pent-up energy, by now Aries will hopefully have found a physical activity or sport to burn some of it off. Fuelling that fertile imagination needs constant input too – young Aries loves stories about giants and heroes, and will enjoy making up his own fantasies with guess who as the hero!

He may exaggerate but he'll never lie – not because he doesn't want to, but because Aries' basic honesty makes him choke on fibs. So don't ask what he thinks of your new outfit unless you're prepared to be told 'It's absolutely awful.' And beware of confiding any juicy personal secrets to him – you could hear young Aries blurting them out to the vicar.

Full of enthusiasm and ideas, Aries will make you shake with laughter one moment and with fury the next. Yet his kindness, generosity and absolute trust in you are a once-in-a-lifetime gift. However brave and self-sufficient an Aries child seems, he still needs his cuddles, even though he'd die rather than ask for them. Life in the fast lane can be lonely; show him that slowing down sometimes isn't just for sissies.

TEENAGE TAKE-OFF FOR ARIES

No running with the crowd for teenage Aries. Always an individual, he'll be the one wearing black when bright colours are in fashion, or taking up hang-gliding when all his friends are learning to ski. He's first to defend anyone's right to be different – especially his own – and accepts people just as they are.

From saving the whales to saving milk bottle tops for charity, Aries supports countless good causes and is quick to stand up for the underdog. But it's actions, not words, that win Aries' heart – his pet hate is people who moan and groan but aren't prepared to change their lives.

'Anything is possible' could be Aries' motto. He spends most of his life chasing challenges and trying as many new activities as he can. He needs to be subtly guided towards the ones he has a true talent for, especially any involving his powerful imagination. Science and numbers are perhaps best left to more organised star signs.

His bubbling optimism and basic love of living can lead idealistic Aries down some dark alleys. Always believing the best of people, he's likely to be disappointed many times. And having his way-out ideas ridiculed can leave him dejected and depressed. Boredom, too, takes its toll on teenage Aries. Without enough, or more than enough, to do he can become irritable – and irritating.

By now, Aries will have learned to hide his impatience behind a mask of humour and wangle his own way eventually. But there's a danger he may also cover up any hurt feelings under an angry, arrogant front unless encouraged to spell out exactly how he's feeling.

Temper tantrums, slamming doors and shouting matches over curfews or clothes are inevitable with an independent Aries teenager in the house. But he'll never sulk or bear a grudge and his snarls soon change to smiles.

He's strong-willed and sharp-witted, often infuriating but always entertaining, and his electric personality is like a magnet to the opposite sex. Oblivious to his own attractiveness, however, he'll keep his admirers as friends until the right one comes along and passion strikes. Then, like everything else in his life, Aries will fall 110 per cent in love. But it probably won't last long – this sunny, funny livewire has far too much living to do.

STAR PARENTS

Aries child with an Aries mother

One minute this dynamic duo are shouting and slamming doors, the next sharing a private joke together, or plunging head-first into a daunting joint challenge that leaves lesser signs shaking.

For both of them, life's a list of goals to be achieved, and heaven help the young Aries who doesn't match up to Mum's energy and strong will.

This mother's respect for individuality and independence mean her Aries offspring will have all the freedom he craves, and then some! No living through her children for this mum. She's far too busy getting on with her own life – and expecting Aries junior to do the same.

This free-and-easy approach could cook up trouble later, though, with an adolescent Aries accustomed to pleasing himself. However difficult she finds it, Aries Mum must establish set rules and discipline, and stick to them. She's strong on encouragement and enthusiasm, weak on patience and tolerance, and loathes it when young Aries is ruthless or selfish, for that's a little too close to home for comfort. And when both want to lead, look out for frustrated tantrums.

A risk-taker herself, Aries Mum welcomes her child's chance to go camping, caving or climbing, but her own lack of caution makes her underprotective and quite unable to encourage junior to look before leaping.

Full of fun but allergic to failure, Aries Mum must try to soften up. She should create a few minutes of peace in her hectic life to talk things through with her Aries child, before worries get swamped by the megawatt power of two larger-than-life personalities.

Aries child with an Aries father

There's never a dull second with an all-action Aries dad, and Aries junior will thrive under the wing of someone with so many interests, from sport to DIY. When this twosome aren't rough and tumbling around the garden, they're off on an expedition together or trying out the latest game Aries Dad has dreamed up.

The trouble is, Dad can set standards that are impossibly high and although little Aries will give his all to please, his inner drive could be damaged for life by never reaching Dad's success levels, so a sprinkling of realism is essential.

An Aries father would rather face a stampeding herd of elephants than the simplest emotional issue. If little Aries seems upset, he'll drag him off to the fair or the swimming pool rather than sit down and swop confidences or cuddles.

He also quickly gets impatient and angry with a cheeky

Aries child. Although he adores his family, an Aries father isn't prepared to give up everything, or sometimes anything, for them.

Both Aries senior and junior are tough, proud and competitive, and this dad offers little of the calm, caring understanding that could help soften his Aries child's hard edges and natural aggression. At least, not without a huge effort. But with a shared talent for creativity and charm, these two are sporty, spontaneous and able to give each other the space they so need. So what if extravagant Aries Dad can't show young Aries how to save – he'd rather learn how to spend anyway!

Aries child with a Taurus mother

Taurus Mum is like a loving, giving safety net to her adventurous Aries child. Through all Aries' daredevil feats and death-defying stunts she waits patiently in case her poppet, or his pride, should take a fall.

But trouble's ahead if a Taurus mother tries to tame her livewire Aries child and keep him close to the home she adores. This is one youngster who won't be moulded into shape or treated like a precious possession.

Although Taurus' natural stability can help Aries keep at least one foot on the ground, too much organisation, comfort and routine are as indigestible to this freedom-loving fire sign as the old-fashioned puddings Mum serves up.

Dreaming, ducking and diving, Aries' sights are set way above everyday life, and try as she might, Taurus Mum finds it impossible to join her offspring at such heady heights. Still, she can help and inspire her Aries child without understanding him – by doing the opposite of what instinct tells her and slicing through those apron strings.

There are plenty of pluses on her side, including patience and her ability to listen. Sometimes the fiery temper and strong will of her little Aries are almost frightening – and, hating confrontation, Taurus Mum backs down and lets Aries get away with murder.

But peace for the present simply stores up problems for the future. Firm discipline and a sensible set of guidelines will save Aries from his shockingly selfish self, and help him realise that life has to be lived with other people as well.

Aries child with a Taurus father

Taurus Dad loathes change and his Aries child loves it – which sums up a relationship that will have more than its share of storms, but plenty of sunny spells too.

A challenge-loving Aries child will take delight in shaking the secure foundations of his Taurus father's routine-based life, from wearing outrageous clothes to following every food fad around.

Desperate to explore life for themselves, Aries children thrive on the risks Taurus hates and wriggle out of any sort of responsibility. And when fiery Aries runs into earthy Taurus Dad's opposition, wham! It's like hitting a rock face. No matter how much coaxing and cajoling, ranting and raving Aries does, Taurus stands firm – and if pushed long enough will unleash his terrifying temper.

The danger here is that, although Aries desperately needs guidelines for life, being crushed once too often could turn a normally bubbly nature bitter. Even Aries can only bounce back so many times, so Taurus Dad must make an effort to be flexible. Some of his common sense is sure to rub off on impulsive Aries and be a bonus for the future.

Materially minded Taurus must avoid trying to buy Aries' affection with cash or treats, even if it is an easy way to keep the peace. It's the first step on the slippery slope to a horribly spoiled child. Aries, meanwhile, should make an effort to accept Dad's 'stick in the mud' nature – at least he's no competition in the energy stakes.

Aries child with a Gemini mother

Gemini Mum and her Aries child get on beautifully. They've got so much to talk about – and share the same playful love of life. They're both out to keep themselves entertained, which spells a lot of laughs in this hectic home. But Gemini can get fed up with Aries' bossiness as Aries will always want to take over the show and run it. Mum usually wants to be in charge – but in the case of exuberant Aries, who's a natural leader, it's easier to let him have his own way.

But she doesn't let him get away with everything – she has always got a quick reply to his cheekiness, and she doesn't put up with his fiery outbursts, either. She is smart enough either to laugh them off or simply ignore them. If pushed, she'll snap and hit back with a sharp remark that will put him in his place double-quick. But all is quickly forgiven and forgotten and the pair will soon be friends again.

The Aries child makes his mum feel extra-young and energetic. They often behave like a couple of kids when they're together, and really do enjoy each other's company. She'll encourage her child to make friends, join youth organisations, learn to swim early and generally make the most of life. The only problem could be her mood swings, which her open and optimistic Aries child will find confusing. And even sociable Aries will find her constant social whirl hard to keep up with.

But she'll teach him to analyse people and situations. And she'll have him speaking, counting, reading and writing as early as possible, preparing him for his rightful future role as top of the class. With this mother's help, young Aries will develop a superstrong mind of his own, able to express well-thought-out opinions with confidence.

Aries child with a Gemini father

Gemini Dad is best pals with his playful little Aries, as long as everything remains sweetness and light. He enjoys his child's active, fun nature – but only if there are no tearful outbursts or boring practical problems to sour things.

Gemini fathers like to be free to go down to the pub, work all hours, or head out into the country without spending hours making preparations. Aries is a freedom-loving, spontaneous and rather selfish little soul too, so at least he and Dad can understand each other.

Young Aries loves lively rough-and-tumble sessions with his Gemini dad. And Dad has good, fast reactions that match his child's physical speed and strength. He's good at stimulating Aries' active mind and imagination, too, with new and exciting games to play and a fund of unusual and interesting facts and stories. Aries will admire Dad for his lightning-fast brain.

Emotionally, though, Dad stays a little detached. And he can't resist indulging in playful teasing and manipulation with his child, secure in the knowledge that he has the intellectual edge.

Geminis find emotional scenes uncomfortable and altogether too serious, and the father of an Aries child will find his tantrums a pain. He'll leave it to Mum to handle any strife, although his emotional detachment will make it easier for him to talk tough when some discipline is needed. He can be very strict at times, but his Aries child will respect the fact that he knows exactly where he stands.

Aries child with a Cancer mother

Cancer Mum showers love by the bucketful over little Aries. The only trouble is that Aries sometimes feels he'll drown in it! The Aries child enjoys being loved. But he also yearns to be free to do what he wants, to be the reckless and adventurous little pioneer that he is. This mum wants him to calm down, to relax and enjoy family life, to stay at home and share the emotional closeness she so enjoys.

Aries' sudden rages stun and hurt vulnerable Cancer. If she's tired, she'll just let him get on with it rather than risk a further confrontation. But if she's feeling emotional, she'll give as good as she gets and punish him harshly. Either method can lead to more noisy nonsense from full-of-beans, wayward Aries.

Mum must learn to laugh at her speedy child and let him get on with being himself. Yes, he leaps into action without thinking, while she plans ahead. And yes, he seems to lack sensitivity, while she feels everything very deeply. Her child is a little bossy boots, bursting with the confidence that Mum feels she lacks. And he's always on the move, while Mum enjoys her restful peace and quiet.

But none of these need be bad qualities – and as Mum learns to appreciate her bouncy adventurer, she'll be swept along by his energy too. She will learn to enjoy life more and take advantage of all the opportunities it has to offer, while young Aries will try to be more caring, loyal and kind to please Mum. They'll both win if they handle each other the right way.

Aries child with a Cancer father

Cancer Dad is very kind and caring at heart. But he can have his stormy days. And when his swirling emotions get the better of him he may well take it out on the kids, acting the big boss to show who's in charge. Dad will expect obedience – even when he's ruined the family's day out by getting cross, packing everyone back in the car and storming home.

Aries is short on sympathy for moods so there are inevitable clashes as Dad sees his child going his own seemingly uncaring and defiant way. Aries feels his free-and-easy spirit is in danger of being crushed. And Aries is not willing to allow that to happen.

Cancer is happy to ferry his child around and pay out for his latest craze. But he'd like a word of thanks sometimes! Aries is too wild and free for the calculated routine of polite behaviour and there will be more noisy scenes as Dad tries to teach him manners.

Yet both admire each other. Aries likes the way Dad goes all out to achieve what he wants – he's full of determination. And Cancer is delighted that his child isn't an idler. Both are hard workers and, when the chips are down, father and child know they can rely on each other.

Although Cancer will always be basically homeloving while Aries is an adventure-seeker at heart, they have much to learn from each other.

Dad will help Aries with the background work and detail he's usually so lax about. And the Aries child will lighten his father's life and do all the things Dad secretly dreamed of doing but never had the nerve to try.

Aries child with a Leo mother

There is a warm and strong bond between Leo Mum and her Aries child, for she instinctively understands him. Both Mum and child share an outward-going, optimistic and humorous nature and between them they've got enough energy to conquer the world.

Mum's dramatics simply make Aries laugh – he enjoys her attention-grabbing ways and will even copy them himself. He also likes being part of her speedy social whirl – it makes his young life a lot more interesting.

Leo Mum will push Aries to succeed and all will be well as long as things go according to plan. Failure is something she can't accept and poor marks or a failed exam will leave Mum distraught, an experience that could scar a lesser child for life.

Aggressive little Aries will usually succeed once he sets his mind to something, but he is equally keen to do his own thing, and Leo Mum won't be allowed to push him on to a career path he doesn't want to go down.

Clashes will occur whenever Mum wants to do one thing and Aries another – and both signs hurt easily and complain loudly about it. Generally, though, the Aries child will bask in the glow of his warm-hearted mother's love and will rely on her to give him a stable base and deal with the practical side of life, as well as to share in his excitements and enthusiasms.

He'll always understand when his mum is a bit down, knowing how sensitive she is under that brave front. And she knows he's not quite the little toughie he makes himself out to be. Between them they'll enjoy a rewarding and exciting relationship. And young Aries will delight in knowing he's got a full-of-fun mum who can keep up with him.

Aries child with a Leo father

Aries looks up to his strong Leo father, who's very much the boss when it comes to home and family. A Leo father is someone Aries respects enough to allow him to take charge, for he knows he'll never beat Dad – unless it's by gentle flattery or by listening patiently and being smart enough not to argue, whatever he really thinks.

Leo is proud of his go-ahead youngster and loves being praised for having a clever child – but he mustn't be too clever. Any suggestion that Aries is smarter than Dad and he will be put firmly in his place. Competitive Aries will resent this because he hates being put down and likes to think of himself as a successful leader too.

Aries will find his imposing dad's demands for total obedience hard to handle as he grows older, and his respect for his father will become tinged with rivalry. Eventually Aries will discover his larger-than-life father makes mistakes like everyone else and isn't perfect after all. And there's a risk then that Aries will try to get his own back for the past.

Yet the bond of affection and understanding will stay firm between these two fire signs. Aries will adore his Dad for being warm-hearted, kind and supportive, while Dad will feel secretly very proud to have produced a strong child who knows his mind.

Aries child with a Virgo mother

Control is the keyword to a Virgo mum. She likes her family to behave in a certain way, and her home to be organised and tidy. But there's not much chance of that orderly quiet life with an Aries child. His unpredictable behaviour and natural exuberance could leave her ordered life in chaos.

She'll never understand why he has to rush into things without thinking, rather than following her example and carefully weighing up everything before acting. But she admires his vitality and enthusiasm and is secretly pleased when he knocks her tidy life off the rails now and then. She likes his directness and his practicality, too, and she's glad that he gets on with things without wasting time.

Virgo wishes she could be as tough and assertive as her Aries offspring, but sometimes worries that he is misdirecting his energies. She is quick to offer advice and suggestions on better ways of doing things. Aries pretends to listen – then does things his way. No-one tells him how to run his life!

Aries is always keen to get things moving and thinks his mum spends far too much time tidying the house. He thinks she wastes time on finicky points instead of getting on with living life in the here and now.

Virgo can deal with Aries' temper – when cross she gives as good as she gets. But she must curb her tendency to criticise him for being reckless. Too much disapproval could crack Aries' confidence. Instead, she should praise him for being bold, fearless and adventurous. He needs her encouragement – if he gets it he'll lighten up her life with laughter and whirlwind energy.

Aries child with a Virgo father

Just as Aries is confident that all his plans will work, so his Virgo father worries himself silly that everything will go wrong.

Aries may find this father far too controlled. Dad lacks his warmth and enthusiasm. Aries needles him and longs for the day when Dad really loses his temper and shows just what's going on inside his head.

Yet this child learns a lot about patience, manners and decent behaviour from his Virgo father. Aries in turn reminds his Dad to have more faith in his own abilities.

This father will do everything in his power to give his child a good education and a stable and secure homelife. But he isn't one for hugs and kisses and it can often seem to the young Aries that his father doesn't really care. Quite untrue, of course. But Aries can turn sullen and uncooperative if he's not absolutely certain he's loved.

Virgo father can get irritated when Aries digs his heels in and rebels against the ordered and predictable way of life Dad so cherishes. The child's boundless energy, noisiness and disruptive spark will find him on the sharp end of Dad's tongue, and there is likely to be a war of words, particularly during the stormy teenage years.

Dad would love his Aries child to share his interests, like fishing or cricket. But Aries is far too active to sit alongside Dad when the going is slow. Instead, Dad needs to take an interest in the child's all-action hobbies and let him take the lead sometimes.

Virgo will have to grin and bear it, too, when money burns a hole in the young Aries' pocket. He'll never turn the child into a careful saver like himself.

Aries child with a Libra mother

Easy-going Libra Mum reckons her little Aries must be hyperactive. He's always on the go and never seems to need much sleep – what other reason could there be? Mum likes nothing better than to put her feet up, recharge her batteries and mull over what to do next. She has no intention of expending time and energy unless it's on something worthwhile. Meanwhile, her young Aries has raced on to the next project.

Yet there are times when Aries loses his way. These directionless moments can find him uncharacteristically sullen and fed up. This is when he needs help to get him back on track. But the chances are that Libra Mum is so relieved he's taking it easy for once, she's tempted to leave him alone.

She finds it hard enough to decide on a course of action for herself. But she wants to help others – particularly her child. And she can give him good guidance and advice when she collects her thoughts.

Aries child is amused by the way Libra is always changing her mind. At least Mum is challengingly unpredictable – so much better than being boring, in his eyes. He finds her bright, friendly and fun, while she admires his courage and drive – although she can find him upsettingly self-centred and reckless, too.

They will have rows, but any bad feeling will be short-lived. Aries is explosive, and though Libra may seem calm, she does keep things simmering under the surface. Once her temper erupts, Aries will know all about it! She gets especially cross when Aries sounds as if he's making a demand for something – whether he means it that way or not.

But they are deeply drawn to each other by strong bonds. She will influence her child to become gentler, kinder and more tolerant without denting his energy and confidence. He can teach her to make decisions more quickly and to rev up her energy levels too.

Aries child with a Libra father

The Libra father's moods swing from happy to anxious. Aries, with his straightforward and open approach to life, finds this irritating. But Aries' uncomplicated outlook can be an inspiration to his father, as this impatient child gets straight to the point while Dad is still dithering.

Aries knows how much appearances matter to his father, who expects his child to be a credit to him in public. The teasing and cheeky nature of the Aries child will find him playing up wildly and getting his dad in a state over what people are thinking of them.

This dad can confuse and upset Aries in turn by covering up family problems and pretending everything is all right, instead of facing them head on. Direct Aries would much prefer it if Dad came clean about any major worries. Aries can't understand why anyone would hide the truth from him.

But father and child are basically in tune and understand each other well. Libra loves the playful energy of his Aries child and will readily arrange days out, trips and games to keep pace with the child's busy mind.

Libra treats Aries on almost equal terms, which is what he craves. But Dad will try to calm his rather reckless and determined child by explaining any do's and don'ts. Although Aries won't enjoy having common sense slung at him, it will make him stop and think – and will help to control wildness in later life.

This dad will spend time and money giving his child a good start in life. He won't dictate to him, though he may be a bit too possessive at times. The danger is that Aries may take advantage of Libra's kindness and end up spoiled. So Dad must sometimes force himself to be firm and not give in.

This will be a relationship that will produce a confident child, able to express himself and unbowed by attempts to stop him being his own true self.

Aries child with a Scorpio mother

Scorpio Mum has a high energy level and will be a fair match for her little Aries. She's all in favour of him taking up hobbies and interests and is delighted by his determination and enthusiasm for anything he tries. She'll do all she can to encourage him, buying equipment, giving him lifts, reorganising her schedule to fit in with his.

She's excellent at helping her Aries-born to find direction in his life, something he needs if he is not to become bored and disruptive. Both share a high degree of enthusiasm, which means Aries will get a lot of encouragement and support.

But there is a very real danger that Scorpio Mum will push her child too hard, or attempt to get him to fulfil her own frustrated ambition. The result will be that Aries will soon lose interest and try to resist her attempts to dominate him.

He may also feel that his Scorpio mum interferes in his life a bit too much and will try to distance himself. She needs to understand her child's nature – not an easy task for her as she can't remember how she felt at that age.

Scorpio is keen to maintain her privacy, and her natural

secretiveness and rather scheming nature can be upsetting to open, uncomplicated Aries. However, she'll teach him not to trust people too much, which can be an Aries weakness.

Scorpio can become snappy with Aries' impatience, and there will be big clashes when either loses their temper. When it's all over, Aries will quickly forgive and forget. With Scorpio, that's not so easy. She hates to lose an argument, for it shows an unacceptable loss of control. She has far more complex emotions than her straightforward Aries child, and he will often find her hard to understand.

On the plus side, she will encourage her child's business sense by being happy to pay him for chores, and will help him to find a Saturday job, supporting him in his efforts to be more independent and adult.

Basically, whilst encouraging her child, Scorpio Mum will want to remain in control, for this way she thinks nothing can go wrong. And Aries will struggle to be free of her domination, believing that luck and enthusiasm will win through. Both need to do some compromising.

Aries child with a Scorpio father

A Scorpio dad will spend long hours at work, away from his family, but his Aries child won't mind too much. He appreciates that others have their own lives to lead – as he does himself. Scorpio Dad may mistake this attitude for selfishness, though, and see Aries' spontaneity as thoughtless action.

There will be some rows in adolescence. Although they are drawn by each other's strong personalities, Aries will be on the defensive and Scorpio on the offensive, making cool, stinging remarks to pierce Aries' warm heart. Although Scorpio thinks criticism helps, he must be careful not to undermine his child's confidence. Neither of them will ever give up in an argument, or compromise their ideas, so head-to-head rows do need to be carefully rationed.

Competitive Aries refuses to be changed and does his very best to resist his father's power. Serious-minded Scorpio finds his child flighty, while young Aries, scared by, yet defiant at, his father's temper, is ready to fight back. He must learn to treat his father with respect, and try not to antagonise him, while Dad must relax, and not always be on the lookout for faults.

Scorpio can teach Aries a lesson in stability and staying power, while Aries can help his father become more flexible and open. Scorpio secretly admires Aries' free and warm approach to life and would love to be more like that himself. This powerful pair share a stimulating and exciting relationship. And life will never be dull.

Aries child with a Sagittarius mother

Sagittarius Mum will match her young Aries for enthusiasm and optimism. She'll treat her child as a friend, including him in her many activities and introducing him to all her fads and fancies. And there'll be plenty of them.

Aries is always on the lookout for new ideas, trends and hobbies, so he'll find this mum dazzling, stimulating and great fun. And she will love having a child with the energy to keep up with her. Just sometimes, though, it would be a good idea if she slowed down and explained what she was doing more clearly to Aries.

This mother puts a lot of effort into bringing up her child, spending hours teaching him and encouraging him. She creates a secure background in which Aries can develop his strength and confidence and teaches the child to see other people's point of view – a valuable lesson for the single-minded Aries.

Unfortunately this mum is not so good when it comes to emotions, ignoring even her own feelings if they become troublesome. Aries may appear tough but can be easily hurt by his mother's straight talking. In fact, all she wants is for him to be happy. She doesn't mean to say the wrong thing, it's just that tact isn't really in her repertoire.

She'll keep her child's energy and enthusiasm on a high, and find new diversions when he's down. However, her tendency to leap from one thing to another can disorientate Aries, who needs to check himself into one interest at time.

This mother is very good at dealing with her Aries child's quick temper. She simply throws back one of her blunt, forceful answers – often peppered with humour. She's also clever at finding outlets for her child's aggression and active energy, channelling them into a sport or an absorbing hobby.

These two fire signs look at life in a straightforward way. They are impatient pioneers, full of confidence, with a love of adventure. But they are both a bit reckless with money.

Sagittarius sets Aries a good example by being more warm and caring than her little go-getter. She keeps him on the go and encourages him to think and speak for himself. Meanwhile, Aries encourages his mother to turn some of her endless bright ideas into reality. With his lively Sagittarius mother, Aries will enjoy life and will learn to get along with others.

Aries child with a Sagittarius father

These two will have a wonderful relationship. Sagittarius knows how to capture this child's imagination and inspire him to greater things. Aries sees ways to put his dad's schemes into action – instead of picking them to pieces, as most people do. He'll help to make his dad's dreams come true.

Both love staying up to all hours. Dad won't pack his little Aries off to bed if there's something good on TV, and may let him stay up even later to talk about it. Aries admires his Dad's honesty, but can be shocked by his bluntness. Aries hates to hear any home truths about himself, though he can laugh when they're directed at others.

They are a compatible pair – confident, always on the move and with a noisy lust for life. Father can't stop talking and dreaming, and child can't help leaping into action. Sagittarius thinks fast, and stimulates the young Aries mind. Aries warms to his father's optimism and the way he spontaneously says what he thinks. He sees his dad as a marvellous, imaginative adventurer.

Dad may be too good at repressing real feelings and may try to avoid dealing with emotions. He'll shout back at Aries' tantrums though. But any rows will soon be over and forgiven. Generous Sagittarius will remind Aries not to be too selfish, and teach his child to enjoy his freedom without trampling on the needs and feelings of others.

Aries child with a Capricorn mother

A Capricorn mum wants her child to get to the very top and can put him under strong pressure to succeed. Aries is clever and capable and ploughs energy into anything he undertakes – but he doesn't like to be told what to do, or forced in the wrong direction. He'll only respond well if it suits him, and will rebel noisily if she pushes him too hard. But if Capricorn and Aries agree on ambitions, the child will benefit a lot from her strong encouragement.

If Aries loses direction, Capricorn Mum will quickly put him back on track. But she will become exasperated when her child's enthusiasm wanes and he wants to move on to something new. She wants him to stick at things and to fit in. She's upset by his determination to go his own way.

Capricorn finds Aries hard to control and will use all of her heavy-duty discipline on him. To her, routine and order are vital and it's hard to understand Aries' spontaneity and yearnings for freedom.

She finds him aggressive and headstrong, even ruthless and selfish, and will attempt to change him. Aries will fight back and she'll be shocked by his temper, unable to forgive and forget as quickly as her child.

Capricorn tries to encourage Aries to be more caring and considerate. She will teach him to calm down, be less impatient and reckless, and to consider his options before making a decision. She'll stimulate his inbuilt business sense, too, by paying for any work he does around the house.

Aries' love of risk and excitement isn't Mum's style at all.

And she's rarely as energetic as him, either. Yet she must learn to accept her child's need to live life at a different speed. She should realise, too, that she can learn from her enthusiastic child how to make life less of a chore – and a lot more fun.

Aries child with a Capricorn father

Capricorn Dad can seem a little too staid and sensible to his sparky Aries child. Dad secretly wishes he had Aries' courage, energy, enthusiasm and zest for life, while Aries appreciates how much Dad has achieved through his hard work, especially if it means that the family live a stylish life. What he won't understand is why Dad had such a rough time getting there. To Aries, there's always an easy route.

Capricorn Dad plans ahead and loves to gather fine things around him, which show everyone how well he's doing. Aries enjoys the here and now and is less materialistic. And they have the opposite approach to problems – Aries all or nothing, Capricorn one step at a time.

Both are tough and selfish. Aries can be thoughtless and Capricorn may be too ruthlessly determined to get his own way. There could be problems in the teenage years if both don't learn to compromise, and fast. Obedience, duty and conventionality are the watchwords of Capricorn. Dad will make Aries feel strongly disapproved of if he doesn't go along with these ideals.

Capricorn is rational and thinks along very straight lines. This child, with his openness and sense of freedom, will constantly challenge his authority and opinions and Dad may try to retaliate with sterner discipline, yet it would be smarter to accept that his child is entitled to his own outlook on life.

Some Capricorn fathers spend so long at work building the security they value that they miss their offspring's childhood. And the fact that they rarely show affection can lead to a growing sense of distance. This can be bridged, but to do so Capricorn must learn to unwind and live a little with his enthusiastic Aries child.

Aries child with an Aquarius mother

Aquarius wants her child to be fair and thoughtful towards others, and will do her best to shunt her self-centred Aries youngster in that direction. Yet worrying about other people's misfortunes really isn't his style.

She may find her child's tough, competitive streak a bit too much. Her own ideals say there should be no winners or losers in life, but natural want-to-win Aries will never see it like that. This mum loves the way Aries speaks his mind. She encourages him to question everything and everyone, which suits Aries, who hates being told what he should think. Yet she can let him get away with too much. Aquarius hates having to impose discipline, but must make the effort to stop Aries getting too wayward and bigheaded. She should use her skilful persuasion, rather than orders, to gradually tone down his excesses and teach him how to behave socially. The Aries need to be first will then become an ability to take charge without offending anyone. In return, she will enjoy his energy and warmth.

Aquarius is fairly cool emotionally, so Aries won't get a dramatic response to his wilder outbursts and schemes. In fact, he may find himself needling Mum to make her react. She may need to talk about her feelings just a touch more.

She does understand her child's need to get ahead, though she can find it hard to match his high energy level. But she believes in the right to freedom and independence, and this is the basis for a good relationship.

Aries child with an Aquarius father

These two will enjoy a cheerful, open and lively relationship. As a father Aquarius is kind and fair, but Dad can sometimes seem a little remote. Aries would like more time with him for rough-and-tumble play, which Aquarius isn't so keen on.

Aquarius finds it hard when young Aries doesn't match his idea of how a perfectly raised child should behave. But he hates fights, so he's unlikely to do much about it. Yet

Aries will wish his father stood up to him a bit more.

Dad lets Aries get on with being his exuberant self, but throws in some smart advice on how to get along better with other people. He loves Aries' warmth and enthusiasm and is pleased to have such an openly affectionate child.

This pair feel a strong bond of trust and can talk to each other easily. Aries doesn't mind Aquarius' sometimes eccentric ways. He admires Dad's originality and courage to be different. And Aries learns to enjoy reading and develops concentration, inspired by Dad's love of books.

Both love anything new, and like to dream up all sorts of crazy schemes together. And they accept each other's differences. Aries likes to live for the moment, while Aquarius leans towards the future. Dad is cleverly controlled, while Aries works on instinct.

Aquarius sometimes tries too hard, and too long, to convince his child to be sensible through logic, when an occasional straightforward order would work better.

Aries child with a Pisces mother

This mother is an easy touch for Aries. She adores and indulges her child and asks for nothing in return but his love and affection. It's too easy for self-centred Aries to take advantage of her gentle nature and kind heart.

However, Pisces is an inspiring parent who puts a lot of effort and commitment into her child rearing. She's imaginative and playful and is keen for her children to be themselves, which suits Aries.

But she could have a habit of ignoring problems, hoping they'll go away. When they don't it can lead to misunderstandings. Aries may even feel it's his fault and turn cross and violent in response. This mother must learn to explain more and face up to her difficulties.

Aries finds his Pisces mum relaxing. She rarely loses her temper with him, except when he pushes her to the limit and she snaps under stress. Yet Pisces can feel that energetic Aries is more than she bargained for when she decided to have a child. He's so loud and dominant – even when she's trying to rest, he's still making a noise. She knows he needs to keep active, but the question is, can she keep up? One of the smart ways is to share her own quieter creative talents, and get him to paint and write down his dreams and adventures instead of always having to noisily act them out.

She does accept his need for spontaneity, change and excitement and would never try to crush his free spirit. But she should resist becoming a martyr Mum and needs to show some of her own strength to keep the relationship fresh.

Aries child with a Pisces father

It's hard for an Aries child to know where he stands with a Pisces father. Aries is very direct and single-minded, while Pisces is a-flexible thinker and may secretly wish he could be as assertive and determined as his lively child. And that is what Aries wants too.

Pisces' gentleness, his desire to fit in and make others happy, encourages this aggressive and spirited child to try to provoke him. And Aries thinks Dad should always mean what he says, too. Aries is so straightforward, while Dad says he'll do things then seems to forget, or does something else.

However, Aries does hide a soft and vulnerable centre. Like Pisces, he hates to be hurt. The difference is that Aries will do his best to avoid being hurt and will retaliate if he is. Pisces is less quick to defend himself and deals with pain by retreating inwards. If Pisces takes some of the cunning that can make him a smart business operator and uses it on his child, the relationship will improve.

Pisces father finds his Aries child lovable – but so rough, tough, selfish and assertive. Tempers could flare as Pisces is pushed too far by his dominant child. Yet, they do have a strong bond and a deep sense of affection for one another. Pisces will stimulate his child's imagination and creativity, which less intuitive signs may not even realise are there. And Aries can teach his father to stop worrying quite so much and start enjoying life a lot more.

TAURUS
Stars for Life

STAR BABY

A calm bundle of beaming smiles, Taurus will lap up all the love you can give her (or him*), and cry only when her security feels threatened – or she's hungry.

She adores snuggling up, whether to bare skin or a teddy bear, and those fingers are forever reaching out to explore the world and experience new sensations. Plenty of tempting new things to touch will keep her fascinated for hours.

Under that Taurus soft surface, however, is a will of steel, which soon starts to show should she feel forced into doing something she doesn't fancy. Sunny smiles suddenly vanish behind a thundercloud of stubborn temper. She'll spit out her mother's lovingly prepared lentil purée until she gets her favourite fish-fingers, or bawl and bash her head until you bail her out of the bath if she's not in the mood.

Ignoring her won't work, shouting just makes her worse – but kisses and cuddles will easily distract Taurus, so scenes can be cut short by a well-timed tickle and hug.

Rather cautious, Taurus needs plenty of time and encouragement when it comes to walking and talking. She's far happier if allowed to progress at her own sedate pace – but once she finally finds her feet and her voice there's no stopping her!

This isn't a baby who copes well with constant change.

*'She' is used to cover he and she for Taurus child.

She's happiest meeting new people on her home ground and when she does venture into the outside world, she'll want to take a favourite toy along for company.

Her life revolves around familiar routine and she's super-sensitive to dirt and discomfort – no playing for hours in a dirty nappy for baby Taurus!

She's no fan of rough-and-tumble fun either, so forego energetic games in favour of gentle ones and soothing snuggles that help give baby Taurus the comforting glow of security she so needs to thrive.

FIRST STEPS FOR TAURUS

As she reaches toddling age, Taurus will be testing out that famous sun sign stubbornness in temperamental, foot-stomping tantrums over anything from her fork being in the wrong place to wanting to wear her right shoe on her left foot.

Don't waste time losing your temper. Instead, shock her into surprised silence with a loving hug and a reasonable alternative.

Born bargainer Taurus is always open to offers! To stop her stuffing sweets between meals, give slices of apple or some chewy raisins. If she refuses to walk to the shops, say she can ride her trike there instead.

When it comes to major issues like toilet training, a system of rewards works best for rather materialistic Taurus junior, plus plenty of praise, of course! But don't offer a reward for effort and fail to come up with the goods, for even a tiny Taurus will never forgive or forget.

With her basic bond to home and all things familiar, Taurus tends to be a bit wary with children she doesn't know, but soon relaxes. She's happiest, however, with a small circle of trusted friends and quiet, 'hands on' activities like digging in the sandpit or splodging paint onto paper, rather than noisy outdoor games where she might get dirty or, even worse, hurt.

Since Taurus' lazy ways can start at any age, do try to

encourage her in some non-competitive exercise like walking or swimming to counteract her passion for food!

An extra portion of patience is essential for parenting a young Taurus since she hates to be rushed in anything, and will drive you mad by dawdling even more if she suspects you're trying to hurry her.

Very possessive, what's hers is hers, and woe betide the child who tries to swipe her sweeties or the parent who thinks they can sneak her tatty old teddy bear off for a wash without her noticing!

More than any other sign, a Taurus toddler does need security, so any sort of upheaval like a house move or marriage breakup will be extra upsetting to her. She'll need lots of cuddles and loving confidence-building to cope.

Beware of letting her turn to food for comfort too often, as that's how the weight problems that plague many Taurus adults start.

SCHOOL RULES FOR TAURUS

'Slow and steady' is the Taurus school motto, and although she may not often win the race, she'll turn in a hard-working performance that rates high in concentration. And her sweet smiles and gentle nature make her Miss Popularity with the teachers!

Although she can be slow to take things in, once facts and figures are lodged in Taurus' practical head they'll stay there forever and a day.

Too much talking is Taurus' main learning bugbear. She's easily bored by over-academic teaching and is far happier relating lessons to everyday life by making models or going out on school trips.

Taurus' favourite subjects are likely to be music and art, although cookery also appeals to her 'foodie' side. But even if it's a subject she doesn't enjoy, she'll always do her best, and her inborn common sense and fairness mean she'll be a popular choice to lead any teamwork.

As Taurus sees it, what's the point of working if you can't

have some fun at the end of it, so make sure she has the time to do something she enjoys after the homework's done – even if it's just splashing in a bath of bubbles or stroking the family cat.

It may seem that young Taurus spends rather too much time dreaming, but that's an essential part of her personality development. She also tends to bury her secret insecurities deep below the surface, and occasionally they pop up and push Taurus into a stubborn, sulky silence, out of reach of reasoning. She needs gentle help and reassurance that it's all right to show her feelings of anger and disappointment as well as of happiness and excitement.

It's hard for Taurus to accept that the whole world isn't as honest and trusting as her, and frequent hurts are inevitable unless you can teach her how to stand up for herself, and show her you'll still love her even when she's made a mistake.

She may screw up her face and scream if you make demands or shout at her, but cuddles and common-sense explanations will soon calm her down.

As Taurus dips her toe into the vast unknown ocean of the outside world, she needs more than ever to know you're on her side – and always will be.

TEENAGE TAKE-OFF FOR TAURUS

Taurus' tantrums tend to be long gone by the time she reaches teenage years, much to her parents' relief! Although happiest on the sidelines rather than in the spotlight, and possibly the last choice for life and soul of the party, Taurus is quite sociable and enjoys outings with a select group of friends.

Well-mannered and mature for her age, Taurus manages well in adult company as long as she is allowed to make approaches in her own time, and isn't rushed into things. She's practical and stable, growing up gracefully without causing too many troubles along the way.

Looking in the mirror can be a problem, however, as

Taurus tends to be very self-conscious about her appearance. A bathroom cabinet bursting with spot cream, hair gel and herbal remedies is a sure sign there's a Taurus teenager in the house!

She's likely to opt for a unique style of dressing, too. Whatever you do, don't laugh, or Taurus will never forgive you!

Just go on building her confidence with endless loving support. Taurus may like to be bargained with for favours, but it certainly won't work the other way round. Nothing short of 100 per cent devotion will do.

Taurus will no doubt be exasperating, lazing in bed for hours, spending a month's Saturday job money on a single pair of new shoes, or refusing point blank to leave home and set up on her own.

But she'll also bring you surprise breakfasts in bed, cook Sunday lunch for the whole family without being asked and sit for hours helping you work out your tax return.

She's warm, reliable and sensible, with a heart of solid gold and unstinting loyalty towards those she loves.

Her laid-back approach could even teach her parents a lesson in forgetting their troubles for a while and enjoying the simple pleasures of life. All too soon little Taurus will be setting up her own home and becoming a parent herself. Then you'll realise just how much all-star sunshine she brought into your life.

STAR PARENTS

Taurus child with an Aries mother

Speedy Aries Mum often starts her family young and isn't keen to give up work and her lively social life. But she may have to find a happy balance when it comes to caring for Taurus, for she won't take kindly to being looked after by others – at first, anyway. She'll get used to it eventually, but it's a good idea for Aries Mum to introduce her little Taurus gradually to being cared for by a childminder or nanny if she does decide to go back to work.

Mum has endless energy and may think her slower moving, home-loving Taurus is lagging behind as she drags her off to endless parties, playgroups and family gatherings. Socialising actually does Taurus a lot of good, as long as she knows Mum's there to give her a reassuring hug whenever she needs one.

Aries is much more up to date than tradition-loving Taurus. It'll be Mum taking the risks while Taurus frets at the sidelines. This child can find Mum a bit too unconventional at times!

More than anything else, Aries Mum wants her child to succeed. Taurus goes at things like a bull at a gate and, if her heart is set on success, she'll make Mum proud. But she's not such a quick learner as Aries and hates feeling pressured. Mum must make sure Taurus has a thorough grasp of a subject, then she'll be unstoppable.

Stubborn young Taurus won't stand for it if Mum becomes domineering and tries to run her life for her. Taurus hates feeling Mum wants her to be someone she's not. Yet she likes to know exactly where she stands, and benefits if Mum can create some kind of reliable routine and delays forcing her to be independent too soon.

Mum will be irritated that Taurus takes so long to get ready and isn't as tough and assertive as she is. She must take the time to teach Taurus to stand her own ground and express her needs and emotions. Remember, Aries, that Taurus needs reassurance and help to build confidence, and that she should never be laughed at for being herself.

Here's a child who isn't an attention grabber, the way Aries is. But she's got a lot of wonderful strengths of her own and Aries Mum could take a few tips from Taurus' ability to relax.

Taurus child with an Aries father

Action man Aries isn't sure what to make of his stay-at-home child. Dad is constantly on the go and full of energy. He loves sport and always plays to win. Cuddly Taurus is quite happy to curl up with a book, or colour pictures while listening to relaxing music. She can't stand anything too strenuous or competitive and adores sweet things, so she may be on the plump side compared with her lean and lively dad.

Perhaps Dad can find a way to help her share his great interest in sport. Swimming may appeal, and walks in the countryside can help stir her. But Dad must remember that Taurus needs to develop in her own way and should encourage her if she shows an interest in acting, art or music. She loves the finer things in life and active Dad should make sure she gets plenty of chances to be herself.

Aries Dad is very much in charge. He can be a bit of a lad, acting the fool, and is a lot more spontaneous than his slower-paced child. But if Taurus dares to be naughty she'll probably get a smack before she's had time to explain. Quick-tempered Aries can put more blame on Taurus than she deserves. His sudden changes of mood can unsettle this security-loving child, so he should try to stop and think before he says something that might upset her.

Taurus in turn is a stubborn little soul if she wants to be, so it's important to avoid too many confrontations, otherwise father and child could find themselves at loggerheads. A cuddle always works wonders with Taurus, so Dad should give her a friendly hug and make up fast.

Taurus likes to take her time and be sure of her footing. She's uncomfortable when forced to be independent in the way Aries expects, so he mustn't push her to develop at his rapid pace. If he remembers her need for support, admires her patience and shows her what's expected of her, he'll have a happy little Taurus on his hands.

Taurus child with a Taurus mother

Little Taurus adores the comfy, cosy home her Taurus mum creates. The atmosphere of secure domestic bliss makes Taurus junior feel loved, protected and at peace. She's delighted, too, that Mum is so traditional, conventional, solid and reliable. She feels she knows just where she stands, and that Mum is happy with her just the way she is and will never expect her to shine the way other parents might.

Taurus Mum creates a stable routine that makes young Taurus feel secure in her world. She understands her child's emotional needs, and shares her love of physical contact and the comfort provided by material possessions.

Taurus Mum teaches manners, honesty, kindness and consideration. She's a sensible realist and in young Taurus she finds a child who laps up her lessons in good living without any resistance.

But it's not always sweetness and light and there can be problems when a row erupts. Two bellowing bulls charging at each other can be a worrying sight. And neither of these stubborn Taurus types would ever consider backing down. Taurus Mum must learn to help her youngster express her needs and emotions so that these blow-ups rarely happen. She needs to achieve a balance between being overplacid and over-explosive to avoid a build-up of frustration in herself, too.

When it comes to food, Taurus Mum is a good cook – which is just as well as young Taurus will finish everything on her plate and come back for more! Mum's home cooking, plus the sweets young Taurus is bribed with so successfully, could result in a rather plump child, so beware.

Young Taurus is glad Mum doesn't force her to go out all the time, and doesn't care that she's not sporty, although she does encourage her child's love of the arts. There is a risk that Taurus won't push her child enough, but this youngster will at least grow up with a feeling of warm security. She loves her mum's comforting hugs, her patience, kindness and understanding – and most of all her acceptance of little Taurus just the way she is.

Taurus child with a Taurus father

The Taurus father is usually a placid fellow who loves his children dearly. But he's got a special soft spot for young

Taurus, a child who's so very much after his own heart.

He won't put her under pressure to do well, though he's very encouraging when she does get good marks at school. And he won't push his youngster's development either. He's in no hurry to see his child grow up, preferring to offer love and security, an organised way of life and a stable home. Young Taurus appreciates this tremendously, which is all that Dad really wants in return. So everyone's happy.

There are times, though, when Taurus Dad loses his cool and explodes in impatience at his slow-moving child. Yet he knows inside how much these explosions can hurt his sensitive youngster, and should try hard to keep his temper well under control. Dad also knows how difficult it is to resolve a row with stubborn little Taurus. Neither forgive or forget easily, so arguments are well worth avoiding.

Taurus Dad favours the old-style way of bringing up his family, choosing traditional schools for them, where discipline is firm but fair and standards are high. This suits Taurus junior perfectly, and she is happily in tune with Dad's strict teachings on right and wrong.

Both love trips out into the country, gardening and nature study, so Dad can motivate Taurus junior to get out and about in a way that other parents might not.

Both have strong constitutions and hate wasting their efforts, so they choose carefully what they will and will not do, leaving plenty of time for rest and relaxation in between. Neither likes getting wet or physically uncomfortable in any way. They could seem a bit soft to other signs, yet they understand each other's preference to be in front of a cosy fire instead of getting soaked on some hare-brained adventure.

This lovable pair share a jolly sense of humour. Dad will happily spend time with Taurus, listening to her and helping her with her homework. Both love reminiscing and looking backwards – they're hardly risk-takers. Dad will encourage Taurus to make steady progress and will be glad she's not too noisy and demanding. And Taurus will love all those cosy cuddles with her big teddy bear of a dad.

Taurus child with a Gemini mother

Whizzy Gemini can't help but run rings round her Taurus offspring. Gemini lives life in the fast lane, while down-to-earth Taurus prefers a more leisurely pace. This child loves plenty of time to relax, and moves at a steady, practical pace. Taurus will keep her nose to the grindstone, getting there in the end, long after Gemini Mum has become bored and raced off to do something more interesting and fun.

Gemini is highly sociable and loves to have an audience. She delights, too, in playing tricky little games with words that confuse and upset straightforward Taurus. Here's a child who needs everything to be as it seems. She hates deceit and wants to be able to trust her mum to say what she means and mean what she says. Mum can fast-talk Taurus into anything – and frequently does.

Young Taurus would certainly like to be as free and unworried as her Gemini mum. She would feel a lot more settled if Mum would just slow down a bit, adjust herself to her child's speed and provide more of the warm sense of security Taurus craves.

Mum's best bet is to rely on cuddles to make young Taurus feel loved and wanted. This child adores a great big hug and if Gemini fails to give such affection Taurus can become stubborn and unresponsive. Warmth will make everything right in her world.

Taurus will need extra reassurance when it comes to moving house. Gemini is always on the move, becoming bored if she stays in one place for too long. Taurus adores stability and would be happy to live in the same house all her life, so she'll need to be introduced gently into any new environment.

Gemini Mum needs to develop her own interests, otherwise she'll find herself taking over Taurus' world and trying to steer her in a direction that may not suit her. Little

Taurus isn't a fast developer the way Gemini was and may be a late talker, which confounds Mum. But Taurus will get there in the end and Mum can be assured that time spent teaching her child won't be wasted. As long as Mum doesn't push too hard, everyone will be happy.

Taurus child with a Gemini father

Gemini Dad is clever with words and can quickly baffle young Taurus. Dad loves arguing just for the fun of it, while Taurus takes it all terribly seriously and is easily hurt, retreating sadly to lick her wounds.

Taurus reckons Dad's fine words and fancy ideas are a waste of time. She thinks shopping for new clothes and toys is much more interesting than talking at the top of your voice.

In fact, quiet Taurus wishes Dad wouldn't talk quite so much. He's always changing his mind and coming up with new plans for the family, which is most unsettling for placid Taurus. She also wishes Dad would stick to the truth. He tends to exaggerate and distort things at times, which can be too much for the slower-thinking child. Yet Dad's charm always wins the day, especially when it comes to bedtime. He's a genius at telling a good story and sending Taurus off to sleep with a smile on her face.

But Dad gets easily bored with the ways of children and will suddenly lose interest in playful games. Taurus prefers it when Dad sets aside a certain time for play, giving Taurus warning of when it's time to stop.

Gemini may act in a cool, rather off-hand manner a lot of the time, then turn over-strict all of a sudden. Taurus doesn't mind firm discipline, if it helps her know where she stands. But she doesn't like it when Dad chops and changes – stability is vital to her. If Dad can acknowledge this, and treat her in an even manner, little Taurus will feel far happier.

Dad usually thinks he knows the best way of doing things and is quick to point this out to Taurus. She won't necessarily agree and will dig her heels in and insist on doing it her way if Gemini pushes her too hard. It's best if Dad can let her find her own way round problems and projects, providing a helpful, guiding hand only when it's really needed.

Dad mustn't neglect his own need for change, freedom and excitement. He must find a way of meeting them, while still allowing time to devote to Taurus to help create the stability she craves.

Taurus child with a Cancer mother

Cuddly Cancer Mum adores her little Taurus, who fits so happily into her cosy home. Taurus loves Mum, home and Mum's meals more than anything else in the world and makes Cancer feel loved and appreciated for being such a caring mother. These two fit together like jigsaw pieces. They feel wanted and safe together and will stick up for each other till the end.

Cancer Mum loves to create a stable, warm and secure home – just the sort of place where security-seeking Taurus feels happiest. Mum's delighted that her child is in no hurry to grow up and leave, and makes Taurus feel perfectly relaxed about being a slow developer. Cancer doesn't like her children to act like mini-adults anyway. She prefers to baby them and lavish them with affection.

Taurus is delighted that Mum prefers staying at home to socialising. But Cancer must be careful not to turn into too much of a recluse. Even Taurus benefits from getting out and about. Seaside trips and walks in the woods will keep both happy – and healthy.

Cancer provides a safe haven when Taurus is haunted by worries, or confused by the speed that other folk seem to live at. Mum understands her need for relaxation and won't accuse her of being a lazybones. She knows Taurus needs to constantly recharge her batteries.

Both like to nurture and, given half the chance, Taurus will grow plump and happy on Cancer's delicious home cooking. Take care, though, for Taurus will slump into complete inactivity if she gets too fat.

Mum is delighted that she and Taurus share an emotional closeness – it's what she's always longed for in her relationships with her children. The Taurus child loves nothing better than Mum's comforting presence and will spend happy hours curled up beside her, watching TV or enjoying a book.

But Cancer must beware that she doesn't get too involved in the life of her child. She must leave Taurus space to find her own way, and should take up interests of her own so that she doesn't feel too alone when her child finally ups and leaves. Mind you, Taurus will be back often enough for more of that home cooking – she can't keep away for long!

Taurus child with a Cancer father

Cancer father is devoted to his child and will gladly make sacrifices to see she gets the best start in life. He'll encourage her interests and ferry her around to dancing and music lessons, making sure she doesn't miss out. Dad does his best to provide all the stability Taurus could need. He offers comfort and reassurance and will patiently listen to his child, which does Taurus a power of good.

But sometimes placid Taurus finds Dad hard to understand, for this is a father who is prone to mood swings. Dad also likes to show he's firmly in charge and expects Taurus to obey and never to criticise his changeable ways. Taurus' stubborn streak means that if she doesn't think Dad's right, she'll dig her heels in and refuse to be moved until he sees things her way. Dad can be put off his stroke by her attitude. He's not as confident of his authority as he pretends to be and doesn't much like to be challenged.

Cancer loves his home and is delighted to have a child who shares his enjoyment of material possessions. Taurus feels well looked after at home, which is just what she wants. She doesn't find the Cancer household the least bit repressive, the way some more independent signs might. Sometimes, though, she could do with more of a push to get her moving and stop her being lazy. Cancer Dad can be too accepting of her need for relaxation, her avoidance of change. He is actually more of an innovator than his tradition-loving youngster.

Young Taurus is there to cheer Dad up when those Cancer emotions start to get him down. She'll share her sweets with him and jolly him along till he forgets his blues.

Both are good savers who like to splash out only on quality goods that will last, so once Taurus is old enough she'll have fun discussing family purchases with Dad.

Both travel at a similar pace and feel no need to push each other along. They're happily set in their ways and almost never bothered by each other. Together this pair are unlikely to conquer the world. But Dad will be very pleased with his child, and Taurus will show how much she appreciates Dad, which is all Cancer wants in return for his efforts.

Taurus child with a Leo mother

Warm and loving Leo Mum envelops Taurus in affection and hugs. Leo is very well in tune with the way her child thinks and understands Taurus' emotional needs. She'll try to provide Taurus with the lovely room she wants, sharing her child's pleasure in the finer things in life. Taurus loves to feel well provided for, and Leo will delight her as much as she can with little presents, meals out, holidays and a warm, smart home. All Leo wants in return is to be idolised, told what a wonderful mother she is and frequently thanked.

So far, so good, but Leo tends to see her child as an extension of herself to be moulded to suit, and propelled forward to fulfil ambitions Mum never managed to achieve. Taurus will not appreciate the way Leo tries to take over her life and won't stand it for long. She's not as extrovert and noisy as Mum and will undoubtedly have her own ideas about where she wants to go in life. So Mum had better not push too hard or stubborn Taurus will dig in her heels and refuse to go anywhere.

Best if Mum can back off and allow Taurus to have her own patch of territory. Otherwise that adulation Leo so loves will not be forthcoming. Leo must remember that Taurus enjoys a bit of praise and encouragement, too, so she shouldn't just think about herself. Make Taurus feel she's wonderful and she'll return the compliment.

Leo loves to be centre of attention in any crowd or party, while Taurus is happy to keep a low profile and enjoy the food. In fact, Taurus much prefers to stay at home pursuing her quieter interests – reading, knitting, gardening and watching TV wildlife programmes.

Mum may despair that Taurus will never be as flamboyant, optimistic and spontaneous as she is. It's important for her to realise that this is a child who is more earthbound, who prefers the quiet life and rarely wants to grab the limelight. Traditional Taurus doesn't like to be embarrassed by Leo's occasionally wild dress sense, either.

Both love delicious food and Taurus will admire and praise her mum's cooking skills.

Leo's friendly warmth and generosity make Taurus feel snug and happy inside. And that counts for an awful lot where young Taurus is concerned.

Taurus child with a Leo father

Powerful Leo gives his Taurus child every bit of support he can. He's set on seeing his offspring succeed, mainly to prove what a wonderful man he is to have produced such clever children.

Taurus will take life at a slower pace than Dad, though, and seek success in different ways. She plods – yet she gets there in the end while others fall by the wayside. It's important that a Leo father learns to appreciate her for this and is not constantly goading her to go faster.

Frivolous Leo brings fun and laughter into serious little Taurus' life and fires her imagination. Maybe Taurus won't be quite as solid and respectable as she was planning to be after a childhood spent with wild and wonderful Leo Dad, who teaches her to break out and make the most of life.

Leo expects his children to think he's marvellous – no ifs or buts! He acts the part of the perfect parent, an all-powerful figure whose word is law at home. Sometimes, Taurus will be obstinate and refuse to go along with Dad's plans. And however hurt and cross Dad may be, Taurus won't give in. Proud Leo may have to learn to bend and respect his child's views. A little affection and a cuddle will help to put the smile back on her face.

There's bound to come a time when Dad will slip up and reveal himself to be less than perfect, something that will shock young Taurus, even though she's down to earth enough to have suspected it all along. Even if Leo Dad isn't perfect, Taurus is full of appreciation for the way he always stands up for her – he's very protective of his young and this helps Taurus to feel more secure, stable and cared for.

Taurus knows, too, that there is a more serious and reliable side to Dad, which she's very glad about. She values his advice, knows he wants the best for her, and appreciates that he teaches a moral code that matches her own. She loves his generosity and deeply values their shared sense of understanding.

Taurus child with a Virgo mother

Solid young Taurus loves the stability and security offered by her sensible Virgo mum. She keeps a tidy house where all Taurus' needs are efficiently taken care of, and she's always on hand to help with homework, put out fresh clothes and dish up delicious meals – which suits Taurus fine.

Virgo admires her Taurus child's stamina and purposefulness once she's set her heart on doing something. But she does hate it when Taurus digs her heels in and refuses to admit she could possibly be wrong about anything. Taurus is deaf to Mum's well-meant advice until she eventually concedes Virgo may have a point.

But Mum is delighted that Taurus has her feet on the ground and sees life in much the same way as she does.

Taurus enjoys being at home, just the way she does, and this child doesn't make Mum feel guilty for being such a stay-at-home – Taurus isn't the world's greatest socialiser either – though Mum will make sure her child gets out enough to learn to mix.

Mum is glad Taurus isn't reckless. But she does wish she'd be slightly more adventurous sometimes. When it comes to moving house, adaptable Virgo will get exasperated with stay-in-one-place Taurus. Mum's all set for pastures new while Taurus will resist change right up until the removal van is loaded!

Mum will enjoy taking Taurus out on educational trips to broaden her mind – historical houses are a favourite with both. But Taurus may have to plead with her mum for her longed-for ice-cream at the end of the day. Mum tries hard to keep Taurus on a healthy diet – which is hard with this little piggy.

Virgo tries to smarten up sloppy Taurus, too. This child loves what's comfortable, never mind how old it is, while Mum will insist on what's neat and presentable.

Otherwise this pair get on very well. Taurus is quite happy to go along with Virgo's lessons in manners and good behaviour and admires Mum's wish to help others. She may not give quite as many hugs as Taurus would like – Taurus is a particularly cuddle-loving child. But Mum will surround her with security, and that's the main thing Taurus wants from her.

Taurus child with a Virgo father

Virgo Dad likes to be in charge and Taurus enjoys an atmosphere of firm order, where routine matters. Occasionally, though, stubborn Taurus will feel compelled to stamp her feet and refuse to go along with Dad's wishes. You can't expect Taurus to be too compliant – being obstinate is part of her nature. At these times, Dad should bear in mind that basically she's a good little soul, who agrees with his ideas on manners, money, morals and old-fashioned hard work.

Virgo Dad takes a traditional view of life – just like Taurus does. Neither tends to dream about the future much, preferring to look back over the good old days, distrusting new ways and new ideas.

Virgo will try hard to find a good, traditional school that will suit Taurus, who benefits from an education that includes discipline and plenty of sensible study. Virgo will also enjoy teaching Taurus himself, encouraging her interests and accepting that she might not be as lively and outgoing as some other children. He'll love her for her qualities of strength, tenacity, confidence and bravery.

Young Taurus thinks her dad is wonderfully clever, quick-thinking and good with words. But she can find him a bit too picky sometimes, obsessed with health and getting things just right. This seems like a waste of energy to Taurus, who would rather relax than keep constantly busy like ever-active Dad.

Yet they have a happy, friendly relationship, and feel comfortable together. They both enjoy walks in the countryside, wholesome food, reading good books and acquiring lovely possessions. However, Virgo is more thrifty than Taurus, and Dad will think hard before splashing out on something really expensive. He won't mind spending money on Taurus, as long as what he buys has some educational value.

Taurus child with a Libra mother

This friendly pair, both Venus-ruled, feel happy in each other's company. Mum is a real charmer who tries to get on well with everyone, makes lots of friends and loves all things beautiful. She admires Taurus' kindness to the people she cares for, her reliability and loyalty, and they share an enjoyment of possessions and people. In fact, Taurus thinks her mum is lovely and doesn't mind showing her she cares with hugs and kisses, which makes Libra Mum feel warmly appreciated and loved.

Libra is demonstrative in her affection, which pleases

Taurus, for she thrives on physical warmth and fades if she doesn't get regular cuddles. Then she can easily turn super-obstinate to show there's something amiss in her life.

Caring Libra will see that young Taurus feels well balanced. And Taurus will balance Mum, too, as her down-to-earth approach helps Libra keep her feet on the ground and stops her pondering and weighing things up all the time. Taurus does not share Libra's indecision and has no time for ifs and buts. She has a far more relaxed approach to life, taking each day as it comes without fretting over every decision that has to be made.

Mum likes to debate matters, and enjoys proving a point. But steady Taurus can't be bothered with arguing just for the sake of it – she prefers a quiet life where things are stable and unchanging. She finds Mum's logical reasons as to why she should or should not do something tiresome, and suspects Mum thinks about things too much.

Libra Mum is more sociable than her little Taurus, and is always dragging her off to parties and gatherings, trying to draw her out and give her some social confidence.

Taurus is not the witty chatterbox her Mum is – in fact, she can be a slow developer when it comes to speech, quite different from Mum, who loves to talk.

Libra must be careful of what she says to Taurus, who is easily hurt by harsh remarks, hiding wounds under a bluff exterior.

When it comes to choosing a career, Libra offers sensible advice, wanting the best for her child. And Taurus will launch into life having benefited from the way Mum has opened her eyes to culture, freedom of choice, cooperation and friendship.

Taurus child with a Libra father

Optimistic Libra Dad jollies his less positive-thinking youngster out of any hint of gloominess. Libra thinks life is to be enjoyed. There are friends to be made, parties to be arranged – and he wants Taurus to fit in with his social whirl. Taurus is a bit of a stay-at-home at heart, who loves to have Mum and Dad all to herself and prefers just a few close and quiet friends to a big, noisy crowd. So she might take some adjusting to Dad's sociable lifestyle.

Libra is well in tune with the way children think and he will be happy to let Taurus be herself. He'll spend ages talking with her, and listening too, developing her verbal skills, which can need some help, especially in the early years.

Libra teaches her to be less clumsy with people's feelings, and more prepared to share her strengths – her quiet reliability and her supportiveness at difficult times. Dad stimulates earthbound Taurus' imagination too with brilliant bedtime stories and witty observations when they are out together. He shows her how to get enjoyment out of life – Libra is a great teacher to have as a parent.

And Libra reckons young Taurus certainly needs teaching. She is a practical soul who takes life at a slow, less spontaneous pace than Dad. Libra treats his children as young grown-ups, yet Taurus is in no hurry to grow up – she feels uneasy if she's expected to be independent too soon.

Dad should try not to push her too much, and let her take her development at a slow, yet steady speed. She'll get there in the end, and her sense of security and stability will still be intact, without the worry that she's not up to living life in the big outside world because she's been pushed out too soon.

Patient Libra smooths over troubles at home. He doesn't often trigger an attack of Taurus' stubbornness, except by being over-logical at times and not letting his child have the quiet periods of rest that she so needs.

Dad does tend to hide problems, occasionally exploding as tensions mount inside. Taurus wishes he was placid and consistent like her, yet she knows he's opened her mind to life in a way no-one else could, and is glad of his support and understanding, and of the secure home that his harmonious ways have created for her.

Taurus child with a Scorpio mother

This powerful pair can get on really well – if they try. But they're both determined types who won't be budged, so watch out for stubborn little arguments that go on and on. Mum must be prepared to soothe troubled waters and remember that her child is just a child. There's nothing to be gained by digging her heels in as well – try cuddles instead to jolly Taurus out of one of her obstinate moods.

Remember too, Mum, that Taurus hasn't got your high level of energy. She likes to plod along at her own pace, taking breaks when she feels like it. But she'll get there in the end and probably do all the better for not being rushed. And yes, she does want to succeed – especially if it will bring her material security. So when it comes to teenage exam time, she'll work extra hard if you remind her she'll be able to get a better job if she does well.

Scorpio will be there right behind her child, pushing her all the way to reach her goals, wanting her to be best of the bunch. In fact, she'll want her youngster to be just like her, and to achieve all the things she never managed to. This is a heavy burden for Taurus, who has a slower style and is unhappy pushing herself forward. She enjoys staying at home, and hasn't Mum's drive to be in control of everything, or her need to keep busy in pursuit of success.

However, once Taurus does set her heart on doing something, you'll be amazed at her determination. She'll sweep obstacles out of the way as she bulldozes ahead to her goal. Mum's help in encouraging her towards her ambitions can give her a big boost. She must make sure they are Taurus' ambitions, though – and not Mum's.

Taurus loves the stability that Scorpio provides. This home is one where security, routine, order and sensible behaviour are highly valued. Taurus feels she knows just where she stands – most of the time. That's unless Mum is in one of her secretive, plotting and manipulative moods. Then Taurus can be confused and upset by her controlling ways. Taurus prefers everything to be out in the open and easy to understand. Anything that's going on which is hidden from her will make her feel very uncertain indeed, and fearful for her much-prized security.

Scorpio admires her child's amazing calmness – she wishes she could handle her own swirling emotions in a crisis the way Taurus seems able to. But she can be irritated by Taurus' complete refusal to budge sometimes. Yet this pair can give each other a lot of support. Just remember, Scorpio, not to push Taurus too hard, and you'll have won your child's warm love and affection for life.

Taurus child with a Scropio father

Strong Scorpio expects his word to be law at home. Young Taurus laps up the security and stability he provides, but there can be clashes of will when this child wants to go her own way and refuses to cooperate. Scorpio Dad will doubt he'll ever win Taurus round, such is the strength of her stubbornness once she gets going. Yet usually Taurus is fairly happy for Dad to tell her how to run her life. She likes knowing what's expected of her, being told how and when to do things and being firmly shown what she shouldn't do.

Taurus admires Dad's effectiveness, his lively mind and his protectiveness towards his family, home and possessions. She also thinks Dad has the right attitude to money. To both it's vital to earn cash. Scorpio sees it as a means to exercise more control in his life, while Taurus sees it as a way of buying more security, in terms of pleasant possessions. Watch Taurus save hard for something she really wants. Piggy banks were designed for her.

Neither likes change much, so there won't be many house moves in this family. Scorpio distrusts new ideas, worried that he won't be able to control what he's not familiar with, while Taurus loves the comfort of her familiar teddy, her small band of close friends, her favourite sweater and the dear old family dog. Not much call for anything new around here – unless it's a luxury item that will make Dad feel even more in control, and Taurus even more comfortable and relaxed!

Sometimes placid Taurus will lose her temper after bottling things up for some time. Perhaps she's cross at the way Dad issues orders or won't listen to her point of view, or perhaps she thinks he's being too strict. Dad feels even more powerful when people get angry, for as they lose control, he gains it, so it's hard for Taurus to win. Dad should give her a hug and let it blow over, or risk Taurus becoming stubborn and sullen. After all, she's just a child and Dad is firmly in control anyway – there's no need for him to prove it more than is necessary.

Father and child have a shared love of tradition that will bind them together. And Taurus will be loyal to her dad till the end if she feels she can trust him to show her the consideration she needs.

Taurus child with a Sagittarius mother

Slow-speed Taurus has to buck herself up to keep pace with her racy Sagittarius mum. Sagittarius lives life at the double, likes to stay on the move and enjoys a changing scene. Taurus loves her home comforts, prefers to stay in bed curled up with a book and doesn't relish being dragged here, there and everywhere in pursuit of busy-bee Mum. It's best if speedwise they can meet somewhere in the middle. So slow down a bit and explain, Sagittarius – you're going too fast for your little Taurus. And Taurus, some fast living will stop you getting stuck in a rut.

Sagittarius is full of curiosity about life, bursting with new ideas and playful energy. Taurus takes a more serious approach to things and has little time for bright ideas and whizzy schemes. She feels safest with what she knows and can't see the point of change.

Sometimes it's not clear who is the grown-up and who is the child in this topsy-turvy relationship! Taurus looks at what can go wrong with Mum's latest plan, while Sagittarius always looks on the bright side. Her schemes may be full of holes, but they're also full of fun and enjoyment.

Because of this, young Taurus can't help but admire her

mum, but sometimes she thinks Sagittarius goes over the top. Then she'll soon have her acting sensibly again by reminding her of her responsibilities.

Both like each other's honesty and integrity, although Taurus can be hurt by blunt Mum's spur-of-the-moment remarks – she can't help but blurt out the truth. Taurus won't say she's upset, but will go away and brood in a corner. Cuddles are the order of the day, Mum, to set things to rights.

The priceless gift that Sagittarius Mum will give her little Taurus is a positive and optimistic view of life. Sagittarius will teach her child to see life as an adventure, rather than in terms of possessions and money. Taurus would like Mum to be more organised and reliable, but she can't help but love her for her enthusiasm, dreams and fun.

Taurus child with a Sagittarius father

Playful, sporty Sagittarius Dad is a bundle of laughs and does his best to share his optimistic outlook with his more serious-minded child. Taurus could do with some inspiration in her life and Dad's dreamy bedtime stories and inventive days out do her the world of good, if only she'll admit it.

But Dad will have to remember that she doesn't like whooping it up the way he does. She's a quieter type who loves making things with her hands, playing with puppets and reading. She loves stroking and petting animals, and in Sagittarius she's got a father who will let her have a pet – he's mad on animals too.

Taurus will probably find that Dad is way ahead of her when it comes to keeping up with the latest trends. He loves anything new, while she's happy with things the way they are. Change unsettles her as she yearns for certainty, not surprise about what's around the next corner.

In fact, Taurus often wishes dear Dad provided more security – he's always dashing off in pursuit of his latest scheme. And he finds it hard to slow down and take time to explain to her what's going on. He's not very organised about the practical necessities of life either, so she can be stranded without her fare home or her swimming gear when she needs it.

Sagittarius can get cross at Taurus when she doesn't take up the suggestions he makes for new hobbies or ways to steer her school career. Stubborn Taurus certainly won't live life the way Dad decides it should be.

And Dad can run into more problems because, although he loves the idea of children, he loses interest in the reality. Taurus needs lots of love and reassurance as proof of security, so it's no good if Dad opts out when it comes to childcare. Taurus needs total involvement or she'll feel insecure and be extra-obstinate because of what she sees as lack of love. She doesn't want to be pushed to be independent too soon either. Slowly does it is the best way with Taurus, who likes to take her time over everything.

Despite all this Dad loves her very much, and she knows it inside. He'll show her how to enjoy life more, and she'll show him how to take time out to relax and unwind, instead of living life at the double.

Taurus child with a Capricorn mother

These two share a similar outlook on life. Mum's delighted that young Taurus never gets too excited or unrealistic about anything, just like serious-minded Capricorn.

Both agree it's not good to blow your own trumpet in public. They prefer to stay quietly in the background. Yet this pair know exactly where they're going and won't let anything stop them getting there.

Capricorn Mum will be pleased with Taurus' slow but steady progress from toddlerhood through school. And Taurus herself will be delighted to have a mum who accepts her the way she is. She hates to be rushed and Capricorn lets her take her time, understanding that putting the pressure on too much will only undermine Taurus' confidence.

Yet Capricorn is ambitious for her child all the same and won't let her slack. Mum teaches that if Taurus wants the security in life she craves, she'll have to work hard for it. Taurus takes the point, for she knows that nothing comes for free.

Both of them like to feel that they've got a stable and comfortable home around them, that life is predictable and unnecessary change avoidable. Capricorn does enjoy a bit of progress, however, while Taurus is happy to keep things as they are.

Taurus is delighted that Mum has created such a pleasant home. This child is more concerned with the comfort and security it provides, though, while Capricorn likes the status a nice house brings.

Mum helps Taurus to feel very secure indeed, and the only area where she might fall down a bit is in showing affection. Taurus longs for plenty of warm hugs to make her feel loved and happy, but Capricorn is a rather cool sign, not given to open displays of affection, however strongly felt. Mum will have to loosen up a bit and remember that this is a child who can't do without demonstrative love.

Taurus can act much older than her years sometimes, just like Mum did when she was a child. In fact, Capricorn will have developed younger attitudes as she's grown older, so she'll feel plenty in common with her child.

Mum loves Taurus' solid sense of determination and admires her for her strong will, even if it leads to confrontations sometimes. Taurus is thrilled her mum seems to understand her so well.

Taurus child with a Capricorn father

Little Taurus looks up to her tough Capricorn dad, who is a real pillar of the community. He's usually a great success in his job and surrounded by expensive possessions that show just how well he's doing. He proves to her that hard work can get you somewhere and that her steady efforts are not in vain. Dad's first present will probably be a piggy bank, followed by a savings account book!

Dad is very family-minded too, though he may be slow to

show affection, which can bother Taurus. But he believes that his home and loved-ones are the foundations on which his whole life is based. So he puts money into making his home a haven and making sure his children are well fed, well dressed and well educated.

All this suits Taurus, for she loves to be cosseted – especially with cash. She adores a warm, cosy, comfy home where she's made to feel secure, and she'll do well with the old-style education Capricorn is sure to choose for her. He understands what she needs, and being the responsible father that he is, does his best to provide it.

What Capricorn does especially well, in Taurus' eyes, is to provide a firm framework in which she can live. He encourages routine, rules, honesty, conservative behaviour and teaches what's right and what's wrong. Although Taurus may sometimes be stubborn and flout his rules, she basically appreciates the steady base he provides for her, delighted that here's a dad who lets her know exactly where she stands. If there's one thing Taurus hates, it's being uncertain about what's expected of her, but with Capricorn Dad she knows what's what.

These two share a dry sense of humour, making little asides to each other that no-one else would appreciate. Both like to make fun of people who are full of big ideas and don't seem to have their feet on the ground. There's no chance of this pair doing anything they haven't thought out from top to toe – their feet are cemented into the ground up to their ankles!

Capricorn enjoys having a child who appreciates all the things his hard efforts buy for her, while Taurus is warmly happy to have such a stable and successful provider as Dad.

Taurus child with an Aquarius mother

Aquarius Mum has a dreamy, otherworldly quality about her while solid young Taurus' feet are firmly on the ground, with not a dream in her sensible young head. Not surprisingly, these two can find each other a puzzle at times.

Taurus worries whether Mum's going to drift back down to earth in time to cope with the practicalities of life, like making the lunch, pressing her favourite dress or putting clean sheets on the bed – Taurus can't do without her home comforts. Mum, on the other hand, is more concerned with intellectual matters – politics, social issues, current affairs – never mind the washing-up!

This mum is at her best in a group, helping it to function well and bringing out the best in the people involved. She loves to have plenty of friends with whom she can bounce ideas around, and plenty of interests to keep her creative brain buzzing.

Taurus just wants Mum all to herself! She isn't one for crowds and, although she enjoys the excitement and stimulation that Mum's friends bring into the house, she yearns for more quiet times when she can curl up with her mother and have a really good cuddle. Taurus thrives on cuddles, yet Aquarius isn't keen on too much physical contact. Words and ideas are her way of communicating her love.

Taurus distrusts flowery speakers and likes sentiments kept simple and easy to grasp. To Aquarius, she can seem sulky and moody sometimes, digging her heels in and refusing to be excited by Mum's ideas.

There's a danger that Taurus can feel Mum is critical of her, just because she doesn't go in for group living the way Aquarius does. Mum must remember to reassure her often, for security and warm affection are absolutely vital to Taurus.

Aquarius likes children to grow up to have minds of their own and act independently. Yet she mustn't expect this of Taurus too soon. Taurus needs to develop at a slow and steady pace. Rush her and she'll feel undermined and scared. Pat her and reassure her and she'll carry on her steady progress till she's ready to show Mum just how grown-up she finally is.

Taurus child with an Aquarius father

Aquarius Dad is full of life and bounce. He's accepting and kind, friendly and fair. But there are days when he seems caught up in his own world of grown-up interests, remote from his needy little Taurus, who wants his hugs, his company and his time. Dad must try to remember not to be remote when Taurus is around. It'll undermine her shaky sense of security and he could find her becoming stubborn and difficult in response, instead of being the cooperative, bright, peace-loving and idealistic child he so wants her to be.

Taurus is puzzled or just plain embarrassed when Dad acts unconventionally – as is his way. She feels best when he toes the line, acts like all the other dads and can be classified as perfectly ordinary. While this might not appeal to Aquarius, to Taurus it's important to be like everyone else. It all comes back to her quest for security. She's lost without it.

Dad doesn't really mind a bit of stubbornness from Taurus – and he's bound to get it! Aquarius takes the view that she's expressing her own will and learning to stand on her own two feet. He's unlikely to tell her off, either. He'll get Mum to do it, as Aquarius doesn't enjoy direct confrontation.

He does feel it's important for his child to learn how to get on with others without upsetting them. Being part of a group is vital to him and he wouldn't like his child to feel excluded. Both have very different ideas of what it takes to belong. Taurus thinks it's all about conforming, while Aquarius believes it's contributing new ideas and maintaining the peace.

What Dad must realise is that his approach to children allows too much freedom to an earth type like Taurus. These children yearn to be told what to do, and shown how to do it. They want to be reassured that what they're doing is right. They worry if they think too much is expected of them and get in a panic if rules aren't clearly enforced and routine maintained.

You may love your freedom, Dad, but Taurus doesn't. Think about her needs. You're so good at teaching what's right and what's wrong, if you put your mind to it. Here is a child who's prepared to listen.

Taurus child with a Pisces mother

Soft-hearted Pisces Mum weaves a web of love around her Taurus child. She'll soothe her when she's down, give her cuddles galore and teach her to dream. She organises fun outings, draws out Taurus' artistic abilities – and lets her get away with murder!

And that's the big problem. Pisces finds it impossible to be firm, so discipline goes by the board and Taurus is hopelessly indulged, which she loves! But to feel truly secure, she needs to be taught what's right and wrong, and Pisces can't bear a confrontation. So, she'll avoid laying down the law in case it causes a scene.

Young Taurus can grow up to be overdemanding if Pisces doesn't make a stand sometimes. Eventually Mum will – but only when she's driven to the absolute limit. Pisces can get very cross if she really feels under pressure.

Mum will find Taurus' stubbornness hard to deal with. She's such a flexible, flowing creature herself, moulding herself to every new situation, that it's hard for her to fathom a child who isn't prepared to adapt and simply digs in her heels. It's unlikely that Pisces has ever done such a thing in all her life, preferring to make herself scarce when problems loom.

Taurus thinks that her Pisces Mum is very caring, but a bit of a dreamer, full of impractical ideas and impossible to pin down. This child sets herself the mission of bringing Mum back down to earth where she can keep her under control, and will throw in little remarks designed to pop Pisces' balloon every time she looks like drifting off again.

Taurus likes everything solid and real, reliable and sensible. She wants to know where she stands and where everyone else does too. She can't bear uncertainty and likes to live her life surrounded by the things she loves, and following a strict routine.

But Pisces doesn't go for this structured way of life at all. She hates to be tied down to any routine – or to material possessions – preferring to be free to follow whatever new option comes along.

These two are going to have to meet halfway. Mum must make sure that she allows space in her life for her own interests, then try her best to stick to some sort of routine for Taurus' sake. She'll find herself with a much happier, more cooperative child on her hands.

Taurus child with a Pisces father

Kind Pisces Dad has all the time in the world for young Taurus. He loves coming down to her level to play childish games, especially when it means messy painting or making shapes with plasticine. He shares his child's love of touch – whether it's a soft pillow, a fluffy towel or a cuddly kitten.

His imaginative outlook helps Taurus, for he can stir her from her stolid view of life to see deeper than her usual practical and sensible level, stimulating her creativity. Both also enjoy the luxury of fine food – and share a tendency to put on weight. So watch out for diet problems, you two!

Dad thinks young Taurus is rather narrow-minded. She refuses to do anything too wacky or adventurous and Pisces may sometimes give up hope of being able to keep her amused. Yet he admires her for her determination, patience and stamina. He knows, too, that under that tough little exterior there's a warm and sensitive heart, a child who's generous and caring when she's given the chance to be.

Dad finds her very materialistic compared with himself. She seems to value everyone according to what they own, while he values people for their imagination, free spirit and creativity. Taurus seems obsessed with money, ambitious to earn it as soon as she can, while Pisces finds it hard to deal with anything as mundane as cash and doesn't put much effort into securing his future. He thinks that money will take care of itself and only worries about it when he realises he hasn't got enough.

Taurus feels at her best when surrounded by signs of wealth, security and certainty. Dad had better bear this in mind and force himself to sort out his finances for her sake. She really does feel shaky without obvious signs of stability around her.

This child also feels her father doesn't face up to life the way she does. She looks problems straight in the face and doggedly overcomes them, while he tends to skirt round difficulties and avoid confrontation. Yet she's glad of the inspiration he brings into her life. She knows it's not good to be too down to earth all the time. And she's got Dad to thank for lifting her feet off the ground now and again.

GEMINI
Stars for Life

STAR BABY

Gemini grabs your attention with eyes that are bright, alert and wide awake, taking in every tiny detail of this fascinating new world he (or she*) finds himself in, and focusing in wonder on the faces of his parents who are putty in his tiny hands from the start.

He adores being talked to and even at this early age communication is two-way for this most silver-tongued of the star signs. Be sure to leave him time to reply, whether it's by blowing a thoughtful string of bubbles, or pulling a funny face!

Before Gemini can even sit up he'll be struggling to master speech, babbling away fit to burst and trying to twist his tongue round real words. Silence may be golden, but unfortunately no-one told little Gemini.

Beneath the charm and chat, however, is baby Gemini's secret side. Nervous and unpredictable under that smiling, beguiling exterior, he needs constant reassurance and cuddles to keep him on an even keel. He's also restless and fidgety, and so active he resists all Mum's desperate attempts to establish a routine. His attention span is tiny, so keep a large supply of activity toys to hand and be prepared to sacrifice lots of time to keep Gemini amused! But when you're rewarded with one of his dazzling smiles, it will all seem worthwhile.

*'He' is used to cover both he and she for Gemini child.

Gemini is brilliant with his hands and loves stacking bricks and playing games like 'Round and Round the Garden' and 'This Little Piggy'. After all that activity, you'd think Gemini would simply fall into bed – but not a bit of it! Persevere with a calm, regular routine, and take time to help him wind down for an hour before bedtime. Eventually, he'll run down his natural superenergy long enough to go to sleep!

Once Gemini can get about, he's really in his element, able to explore the world for himself, and how! He won't stay still for a second, struggling up on to sofas, crawling under tables, hiding in the cupboard. Secure the house with safety catches and gates, and give him as much freedom as you can to explore – too many rules will only end in tears! And when your chatty little Gemini is suddenly silent, investigate – he's bound to be up to mischief!

FIRST STEPS FOR GEMINI

Joining a toy library is probably the best bet with a Gemini toddler in the house – you'll never be able to buy enough toys, books and puzzles to keep him busy! Start early to try to help Gemini concentrate on one thing at a time, for you'll find that no sooner has he started than he'll want to move on to something else. Setting time limits for activities, with plenty of variety, could be the solution.

Gemini also needs plenty of loving patience. As his talking improves you'll be bombarded by questions – why this, what's that, who's he, where's she? Thankfully little Gemini picks things up so fast you'll soon see a return for your patient replies, and when he's still a tot he'll be sharing long conversations with you about anything and everything. He has a tremendous imagination and adores making up little stories about what's been happening to him. Sometimes he convinces himself and has trouble recognising the truth!

Where less adventurous toddlers thrive on routine and repetition, Gemini adores anything new and exciting. It doesn't need to cost much or take a lot of time, but his ever-eager mind eats up new experiences, and squirrels them away for the future. Make sure he has his quiet times as well, or he may be too stimulated to sleep.

Toilet training will be as stop-start as any other Gemini activity, partly because his mind's always so occupied he forgets to ask to go. Work out some tricks together to help him remember.

A born mimic, copycat Gemini mirrors your words, gestures and ways. But that's just his way of looking at the world and finding out who he is. He can chop and change from cheeky to charming, helpful to horrid, but never for very long!

He finds it hard to let others get too close, and needs help, and hugs, to open up about his feelings. It's all part of his desperate desire to please, and for the same reason he'll often say what he thinks you want to hear rather than what he really thinks. Help him see he has nothing to fear from the truth, good or bad, and you'll put your Gemini toddler on the right life-track.

SCHOOL RULES FOR GEMINI

Ask your junior Gemini what he did at school today and you'll probably hear all about the tiger he shared his sandwiches with and the magician who turned his pencil into a magic wand! Gemini's mind is so hyperactive he's always inventing stories. It can be hard for him to tell truth from fantasy and anyway, especially if real life's a bit dull, he'll be only too happy to spice it up! The problem is, your young Gemini has such a way with words he's superpersuasive and full of plausible reasons, so he could even end up convincing you. Try not to slap down his imagination, especially if it isn't doing any harm. Instead, encourage Gemini to use it in story-writing.

Gemini's incessant questions and non-stop chat will keep his teachers on their toes. At least you're getting a break at last! He's brilliant at taking in information, but his busy mind does tend to flit about from fact to fact, and concentration is a skill he certainly isn't born with.

Information combined with entertainment and/or action suits him best – disco tapes that teach the times tables, for example, or a country walk to learn about the changing seasons.

Very popular and likeable, Gemini may still prefer imaginary friends to real ones and find it difficult to form deep friendships. Tuned in more to thoughts than feelings, he finds it hard to share his secret hopes and fears. Show him by example that opening up makes him less, rather than more, vulnerable and he may learn to be more trusting.

Above all, young Gemini is an individual, and will do anything to stay that way. He hates being labelled, whether it's 'bright', 'difficult' or a 'daydreamer', and if he thinks you've put him in a pigeonhole, he'll stop at nothing to fight his way out, even being slapdash and disappointing at school to prove a point. The recipe for success with young Gemini is plenty of praise and the freedom to be whoever, or whatever, he wants.

TEENAGE TAKE-OFF FOR GEMINI

Teenage Gemini is often bored, but certainly never boring! A chatty, scatty fun-lover, he fits in anywhere, but especially enjoys being among grown-ups, from whom he can glean all sorts of new ideas and information while also enjoying heated discussions on his thousand-and-one interests, from *EastEnders* to Shakespeare, rap to opera.

With so much action between his ears, it's no wonder Gemini finds it hard to choose just one career path. If he asks for help making a decision, point him towards something involving communication and as little office-based as possible. But never try to force, tease or threaten him into doing what you want! Freedom fan Gemini hates being manipulated and far prefers to hear things straight. Now's the time to take Gemini aside and point out that the rest of the world may not be as straightforward as him, however.

He can be a real little gossip because he can't help blurting out any secrets he's picked up – he likes causing a stir with what he knows, hoping it will make him even more popular. So unless you want the whole street to hear about the sexy underwear you've sent for, or how much your new car cost, point out to your Gemini that it often pays not to say too much!

Reaching adolescence, Gemini may be pulled between his need for private space and his love of being surrounded by admiring friends. He may seem to shut off and be rather sharp when he's under strain, when in fact he's just trying to sort out his feelings before he decides whether to share them or not.

He'll have plenty of friends of the opposite sex, but won't want to get serious until quite late in his teens. Love is something that doesn't rate high in his logical Gemini mind, until his hormones take over! Then there'll be a stream of dates and steam rising from the phone as he practises his natural chat-up technique for hours on end.

Just grin and bear it – Gemini's charming, disarming presence in your life more than pays you back!

STAR PARENTS

Gemini child with an Aries mother

Buzzy Gemini thinks his Aries mum is wonderful fun. She's got so much energy and enthusiasm and she thinks up brilliant things to do whenever he starts to feel bored. They are both determined to enjoy life – and that's exactly what they do when they're together.

Aries will take Gemini on fascinating outings that will stretch his active mind. She's glad to have a child who can keep up with her own lively style, and she's proud that he's so brightly talkative and interested in everything. Gemini is hard to stop once he gets going.

Both enjoy sticking up for what's right, whether it's a worthy cause or their own sense of freedom. But they'll only stay with an argument as long as it entertains them to do so. Gemini particularly won't do something that doesn't amuse him. They're both in search of anything new and exciting, more interested in what lies around the next corner than in the past.

These two treat each other like best friends. Sometimes Gemini thinks Mum is too bossy as she wants to be in charge all the time, while Gemini wants to have his say on what they do next. And he doesn't like her sudden outbursts either. Yet Gemini can be just as volatile in the wrong mood. At least both are fast to forgive and forget.

Mum isn't keen on Gemini's razor-sharp remarks. He's clever with words and sometimes uses them to wound. She's not always fast enough with a smart reply to put him in his place, and gets cross instead. But these two are quick to make their peace, for they don't want to miss out on the fun they have together.

Mum accepts the way Gemini likes to do several things at once. She understands his high-energy approach to life, but she thinks he ought to put more of his ideas into action, the way she does. Gemini prefers to spin wonderful webs with words. Making ideas a reality rather spoils them, in his view.

On the whole, Mum understands her Gemini very well and allows him the freedom to live his life as he wants to and have a whale of a time. And Gemini doesn't stop Mum from living her own life, either, being the independent little person he is. Above all, they have great fun together and make each other laugh.

Gemini child with an Aries father

Conversational Gemini loves his lively dad, who really knows how to live every second to the full. Dad is great at making things happen – life seems a whirl of excitement when he's around. And as Gemini's main aim is to stay amused and avoid getting bored, this suits him perfectly.

In fact, Gemini gets bored quite often because his mind works so fast it's difficult for others to keep up with him.

And because he likes to do more than one thing at a time, he sometimes runs out of things to do altogether! But Aries Dad always has bright new ideas to occupy his child's busy brain.

Aries may not be as speedy-minded as Gemini, but he's got the energy to beat him hands down. He'll often suggest a run round the park or a game of football in the garden – anything to stay active. This helps Gemini, who needs to exercise physically as well as mentally to keep a sense of balance.

Dad keeps up with the times too, which pleases Gemini who hates anything – or anyone – old-fashioned. And Dad is glad that Gemini is not an emotional type – Aries starts to get uneasy when anyone pours out their feelings.

Gemini child likes the fact that his dad tries to see a project through to completion. Gemini bobs between so many things he often doesn't manage to finish even one of them. Dad can lend a helping hand in encouraging Gemini to stick at it, but he shouldn't expect him to complete one thing at a time – it's not Gemini's style.

Aries is usually a very busy man, caught up in his work, social life and sporting hobbies. So he's pleased to have a Gemini child who doesn't make too many emotional demands on him and lets him get on and live his life. He'll have to spare the time to answer all Gemini's amazing questions, but Aries will find this stimulating and fun, so he won't mind a bit.

Aries is proud to have such a bright youngster and these two get along very well. They rarely get each other's back up – except when Gemini says something really needling, or Dad keeps butting in when Gemini's talking. On the whole, they find each other lots of fun and good company.

Gemini child with a Taurus mother

Speedy Gemini runs rings round his plod-along Taurus mum. And much as she loves him, she wishes he would slow down a bit sometimes to let her catch her breath. Gemini loves to do six things at once, while Mum is always telling him to concentrate on one at a time. She'll just have to learn to live with his whizzy ways – there's no other way of being a Gemini.

Taurus isn't a big talker, while Gemini rattles away nineteen to the dozen, making Mum feel tongue-tied in comparison. And has she got the energy to answer all those endless questions? Well, she tries her best, but it certainly takes some doing.

Taurus Mum can teach her child a thing or two, though – there's stamina and determination to keep going until he achieves his goal, patience, consideration for others, calmness, stability and a sense of valuing what he's got. Gemini has little patience, loves change and wishes Mum would break out and do something spontaneous, new and exciting. He loves ideas and conversation so much, but she seems to prefer her furniture and material possessions to what goes on in anyone's mind.

Sometimes Taurus is irritated by her fast-talking Gemini and her patience will snap with an almighty explosion. Gemini child must learn that cuddles work wonders to keep Mum sweet. This child is not given to great shows of affection, but it'll make Mum feel warm and appreciated if he gives her a hug now and again.

Sometimes, Mum would like to be as speedy and fun-loving as her amusing Gemini. She does her best to give him a secure grounding in life and lots of love, but she must avoid trying to fence him in. Gemini thrives when he feels accepted and free.

Gemini child with a Taurus father

Taurus Dad is a kind father who does his very best for his little Gemini. He may get laughed at by his impish child for being behind the times, but there will come a day when Gemini will thank him for always being there, for being an immoveable rock on which quick-thinking Gemini has been able to depend.

Dad loves to be able to rely on things. He wants to build a solid, stable home where there is a sense of comfort, cosiness, warmth and love, which is all to the good for Gemini. But Dad can be a bit too controlling and hates it when his child threatens the never-changing routine of his lifestyle. He's going to have to adapt to cope with go-ahead Gemini, who loves to turn everything upside down and force people to think again. Change is Gemini's watchword and there could be some clashes with traditional Dad over his love of the new.

Taurus will enjoy sitting down by the fire and relaxing with his feet up. He'll be irritated by Gemini always buzzing around, fidgeting and fiddling, unable to keep still. Best if Dad can set Gemini a project – or three! – to focus his attention.

Taurus Dad is very good at directing Gemini's nervous energy, and can eventually help him make a good career choice. Dad teaches sensible consideration of all the options, helping to ground Gemini's wilder ideas and bring him gently back to achievable reality.

Gemini child with a Gemini mother

These two are full of ideas. They chat all day and keep each other amused. Mum is brilliant at bringing out Gemini's verbal skills. She'll have him talking, counting and reading from an early age. They're both bright as a button and charm everyone, quickly making lots of friends, if only on a fairly superficial level.

Here's a mum who can keep up with Gemini's speedy ways, understand his love of change and his need to do six things at once to keep happy. She's got the energy to answer all his questions, the perception to see through his amazing excuses and can dream along with him as they share big ideas. Neither really wants to turn their schemes into reality – it's talking about them that's the real pleasure.

They feel comfortable with each other, though sometimes each could do with someone quieter to calm them down.

Gemini child is as excited by moving and change as his mum, so he won't mind a bit when she decides it's time to up and move house.

Gemini is glad his mum is as sociable as he is. And she's pleased he's not too emotionally dependent. She likes to feel free to chat and joke when she's out and doesn't want a tot clinging to her ankles. Yet it's important that they both find time for cuddles – even Geminis need them.

Sometimes they'll argue, for Mercury-ruled Gemini people love picking holes in things and enjoy a row. Yet they'll be best of friends too, understanding each other like no-one else can.

Gemini child with a Gemini father

Gemini Dad makes his child squeal with laughter at his tricks, crazy stories and fun-filled games. He's full of energy, just like Gemini, and both are dead-set on getting amusement out of life, putting their own need for enjoyment above almost everything else.

In Dad's case, this can mean that he spends too much time playing squash, mending his motorbike or following his career. It's important for him to realise how much time little Gemini needs to bring out the best in him. His bright mind demands answers to all sorts of questions, and Gemini Dad is often the best person to provide them.

When Dad's reading the newspaper, he'll share titbits of information with his child, and he'll take him on adventurous and exciting days out. He's always springing surprises and young Gemini adores him for it. Geminis can't stand being bored, though they often are. At least this pair will never complain of feeling bored when they're together.

Dad may have to learn to encourage young Gemini to complete tasks. They both tend to scatter their energies and leave things unfinished. Yet Gemini Dad will enjoy seeing his child develop so fast and little Gemini won't mind his father's rather disorganised lifestyle. They love each other's vivid imagination and way with words. And both are great at perking the other up on the rare occasions when they feel down.

Gemini child with a Cancer mother

Cosy Cancer Mum loves to surround her Gemini child with love and affection, but she must try to be sure she doesn't make him feel too hemmed in. Cancer can be very possessive, living life through her children, while Gemini likes to feel free as a bird.

Protective Cancer frets at the way he tries to do so much and is sure it'll all end in tears. But she shouldn't worry. Her Gemini child is just much more outgoing and restless than she is and loves adventure and gossip. Mum mustn't be disappointed if she doesn't share a sense of total emotional closeness with him, for he's far less feelings-based than she is and doesn't crave her strong family ties. Gemini is quite happy as long as he's accepted for the way he is and is free to have fun.

Cancer Mum may try to control Gemini's life and keep him at home too much. Neither would be a good idea. Gemini needs to be allowed to circulate. He thrives on new people and new situations. Cancer will have to be prepared to be a lot more talkative when he's around, too, for he needs replies to those endless questions.

Gemini will love the sense of stability Mum gives him. He may like change much more than she does, but nothing beats Mum's home cooking and her comfort when he's down. From her, Gemini will learn to look before he leaps, to be more patient and to finish jobs he's started. He'll learn that sometimes it's better to hold his peace rather than speak out. And Mum will learn from him that life is for enjoying, not for worrying about or wasting.

Gemini child with a Cancer father

Cancer Dad loves his whizzy little Gemini child and wishes he had his energy. He envies all that get-up-and-go, yet wouldn't want to trade his own solid sense of security for

Gemini's style. He'll be making a big mistake, too, if he expects Gemini to become more like him – home-loving, emotional, sensitive, traditional and family-minded. With all that speedy Mercury energy in him, it's hard for Gemini to stay still, tie himself to people and stop seeking change. It's better if both can accept each other the way they are.

This father is prone to moods and sulks as he battles to keep down those watery Cancer emotions. He's bound to explode from time to time, which Gemini won't enjoy. And in a bid to control, he sets harsh rules which Gemini will promptly try to break. But Gemini has a knack of charming Dad out of his moods and Cancer will end up smiling as witty Gemini entertains him with another tall tale.

Gemini would like Dad to play and talk all day long, but Dad needs his quiet times. He finds life a battle and some days simply wants to retreat and read with his feet up. Busy Gemini won't give him much peace, so Dad should try to grab rest while Gemini is otherwise occupied, and plan time to spend with his busy-minded child.

Gemini knows kind-hearted Dad will always agree to take him out and share his interests. Cocky Gemini may need reminding to say thank you, and he may poke fun at Dad for being old-fashioned during those difficult teenage years. But when he grows up he'll see that Dad always had his best interests at heart. He'll remember his common-sense advice and be glad of the way Dad always bucked him up when his schemes and dreams fizzled out.

Gemini child with a Leo mother

Gemini child thinks his Leo Mum is great fun and certainly never boring. She takes him out to meet new people, springs surprise treats on him, loves a gossip and shares his enthusiasm for life. Gemini thinks she's marvellous.

Leo Mum is loving and generous and understands her child well. She radiates warmth, which Gemini responds to, and his happy smile and cheeky conversation are all Leo wants in return. She enjoys the rapport they have, and

Gemini always makes her feel special.

Mum feels very proud of her Gemini child for being so bright and articulate, so curious and intelligent. And she basks in the reflected glory when he does well at school. She should take a lot of credit for having put so much energy into teaching him to read and write. With her outgoing spirit, she will have encouraged her child's desire to find things out, make connections and understand his world.

However, she must watch that she doesn't dominate and direct her child too much. Gemini needs to feel free to make some of his own choices if he is to become the confident person he can be. And Mum must try not to lose her fiery temper at the way he never gives anyone a moment's peace. It's all part of his charm. He must never be allowed to play little games with the truth, though. She has to tell him straight that he mustn't ever lie. Leo sometimes thinks Gemini is all talk and no action and she will help him turn useful ideas into reality.

Gemini child with a Leo father

Leo is big and boisterous and young Gemini is absolutely delighted by him. He sees that Dad is the life and soul of any party, and wants to grow up to be just like him.

But Gemini is rather different from Leo. His Mercury energy sends him scooting around in search of entertainment, while Leo loves to stay where he is and be the radiant centre of attention. Gemini is even more of a talker than his dad, and a great socialiser, but he lacks Leo's sparkly warmth and generosity, and his ability to spread enthusiasm. Instead Gemini loves to gather and share information.

Gemini loves the fact that his dad has so many friends – all the more people for him to meet and learn from! Gemini will pick up information from anywhere and everywhere and Leo has a lot to teach him. Neither father nor child are emotionally clingy, and they will enjoy a happy, undemanding relationship.

Dad's style of discipline will sometimes seem too harsh to

liberal Gemini, who loves to feel free. Dad wants to be in firm control of his family and can set tyrannical rules. Better in Gemini's case to give good explanations why – he'll be kept in check more easily then.

Gemini feels loved and protected by his strong dad. He's amused by Leo's little eccentricities and flamboyant style of dress. And he doesn't mind that the spotlight is on Dad more often than on him. As long as Gemini's got someone to talk to he's happy. And he's in for some fascinating conversations with his magnetic, imaginative dad.

Gemini child with a Virgo mother

Lively-minded Virgo certainly has the brain-power to keep up with Gemini's constant questions. But does she have the energy? Both are Mercury-ruled with quicksilver thinking, but Virgo is much more down to earth and her nervous energy often tires her out. In Gemini, it drives him on – he's always restlessly on the move and has to be kept extra busy.

Mum reckons that Gemini changes his mind too much and thinks about himself all the time. She's perturbed that he lacks her need to serve and seems chiefly concerned with his own amusement. She must curb her urge to nag, though. They are both critical and will have hours of fun picking holes in others. But if they turn their dissecting tongues on each other things could get very snappy. Best if Virgo accepts their differences for the sake of harmony.

Virgo spends a lot of time worrying whether she's done the right thing, while Gemini couldn't care less. He does what pleases him, never mind anyone else. But one thing he's good at is getting Virgo talking. He's such a chatty child, it's infectious. Virgo loves words too, but is usually better at writing them than speaking. With Gemini, she'll discover the true art of conversation.

Gemini loves the way Mum cares for the welfare of others – especially him. And Virgo enjoys her child's bright curiosity and winning ways. She'll certainly end up feeling very proud of him.

Gemini child with a Virgo father

Virgo father likes to run a tight ship and expects Gemini to do what he's told and always tell the truth. Gemini's clever way with words means that he often twists things round slightly, just for fun. Virgo Dad will insist on absolute honesty – he won't stand for anything less.

Gemini is brilliant at thinking up bright ideas – but he's such a scatterbrain he rarely puts them into action. Here's a Dad who can turn his child's thoughts into solid reality, much to Gemini's delight.

Neither are emotional types and both think soppiness is a crime. Yet Gemini knows he can always rely on his father to help him. And Dad enjoys answering his child's constant questions, for Virgo is as inquiring as Gemini and loves flexing his brain cells.

Virgo is glad Gemini is fairly tidy, but despairs of his lack of money sense. Gemini wishes Dad craved his need for excitement and change. Virgo can adapt to change, but he's more earthbound than Gemini and values a sense of security and reliability. Gemini can find Dad's routine too restricting, for this is a child who wants a flexible lifestyle with endless variety.

Dad is also less sociable than Gemini and so must make the effort to see that this child has plenty of opportunity to get out and meet people. Conversation is lifeblood to Gemini.

Virgo will take delight in having a child who is so eager to be educated. He'll provide Gemini with an ability to dream up workable schemes instead of hot air, something that will serve him very well in future years.

Gemini child with a Libra mother

Sociable Gemini child loves his talkative Libra mum. She's so good at making friends, it makes him feel quite envious. Somehow she has the knack of getting on with everyone, and while Gemini is great at making superficial pals, Libra seems to know how to make friends who last.

Libra spoils Gemini with new toys and nice things for his room. He loves getting surprise presents and can twist Mum round his little finger when it comes to buying him things. Gemini is such a charmer he can always get his way.

Yet Libra will say 'No' when he pushes her too far – even indulgent Libra Mum won't be put upon. She finds it amusing that he's always changing his mind as new and even more exciting possibilities grab his attention – she can never make up her mind about anything! Gemini can be good at showing Libra the way forward, for he's so impatient that he pushes her into making decisions.

Both love words above all else. Libra is delighted that Gemini starts talking so young and, before you know it, these two will be enjoying long conversations.

Mum can find Gemini's critical streak hard to handle – he's far more analytical than she is. And his speed is hard for her to keep up with. But their strong bond of communication will see them through anything. These two just love being together.

Gemini child with a Libra father

Both air signs, these two understand each other well. For a start, they're always talking. Libra isn't bothered a bit by Gemini's endless questions and habit of voicing all kinds of opinions. Dad is delighted to have such a bright-brained and expressive youngster – a real chip off the old block.

Gemini is much keener than Dad on new ideas. Libra loves a quiet life where everything goes along steadily and nothing rocks the boat. Gemini is always on the go, looking for something to entertain and amuse him. There are times when Libra wishes he'd stop fidgeting and learn to relax.

Gemini usually feels accepted and free to be himself around Libra. Most Libra fathers believe children should not be forced in any direction they don't want to go – just gently guided to make suitable choices. Gemini likes this hands-off approach, for he hates undue interference.

Both share an optimistic outlook and like discovering the

nuts and bolts of things. Dad would rather avoid an argument, repressing his feelings instead of starting a row, while contentious little Gemini thinks arguing is great fun.

Libra treats his child as a young adult, which delights Gemini and helps him be more responsible and less frivolous. He loves the way his dad always listens to what he has to say. These two certainly keep each other amused and enjoy a happy, balanced relationship.

Gemini child with a Scorpio mother

Talkative Gemini will have Scorpio reaching for the earplugs with his constant chatter, for she can only take so much. Yet she loves her bright-eyed child for being so clever and lively – he's a real credit to her.

Both are well supplied with energy, and Mum can easily keep up with Gemini's wayward behaviour. The only time she gets worried is when he seems to be wriggling out of her control. Scorpio Mum likes to know that she's firmly in charge and she won't let precocious little Gemini say otherwise.

Problems can arise because Gemini likes to feel free. Mum must find feasible ways in which she can extend his freedom but keep him within limits. This will prevent Gemini becoming frustrated and cross, making Mum even angrier. Mum must understand that he craves excitement, novelty and change, and allow him his quota.

Scorpio Mum likes an ordered home, run according to routine, where rules are observed. Gemini finds it hard to keep any rules that aren't fully explained to him. He's bored by routine and prefers an atmosphere where there is room for spontaneity and fun. They'll have to meet each other halfway if both are to be happy.

Scorpio will secretly love her child's playfulness – it lightens her heart and stops her taking life so seriously. Gemini can learn a valuable lesson from his mum's staying power – and he'll be glad of the real achievements he can make with her solid backing.

Gemini child with a Scorpio father

Commanding Scorpio father issues orders that will unnerve Gemini. Fast-talking Gemini will do his best to reason with Dad about his strict rules, but Scorpio is determined to be in control and hates to have a rebellion on his hands.

Yet Scorpio loves his little Gemini dearly and will gradually come to learn that this child needs to be allowed to express himself more freely than Scorpio would like. It would be a shame to crush his enthusiasm and zest for life, and Scorpio must tread carefully, explaining rules and letting Gemini have his say.

Gemini will always want to be more independent than Dad would like, and a wise father will train this child in self-reliance. He will have to admit his own life often gets so complicated it's best if his child doesn't get too caught up in it.

Scorpio is very positive when it comes to encouraging Gemini's many interests and talents – even if he does get fed up with Gemini always chopping and changing. He helps him to stick to manageable hobbies and gives him useful lessons in how to succeed. But Dad must watch that he doesn't push his child more than is needed. Remember, Gemini thrives best when given freedom and choice.

These two can be very cutting about other people when they get together, but they'll have some fine conversations too. They'll argue over change – Gemini wants it and Scorpio doesn't. And Gemini will wish Scorpio could laugh more and accept his love of adventure.

Scorpio will hide his feelings, while Gemini needs help locating his. And Scorpio will certainly be more manipulative than Gemini could ever be. Yet they'll come to terms with each other's differences. Scorpio will learn to smile and gossip, while Gemini will learn that sometimes life should be taken less lightly.

Gemini child with a Sagittarius mother

Sagittarius Mum is full of energy and enthusiasm for life, so she doesn't mind at all that Gemini is constantly asking questions. In fact, she thinks it's fun and a challenge to her considerable mental powers to think up interesting, stimulating answers.

She's good at teaching her budding little genius and he'll quickly learn to talk, count, read and spell with her lively help. Mum is delighted to have a child who's so bright. She understands how his mind works and realises that you have to make things fun if they are to appeal to a Gemini. And that's something she's very good at doing.

Mum thinks up inventive outings which impress Gemini's friends, and she loves taking him on action-packed holidays. She's always joking with him – he quickly develops a talent for clever replies – and she shares his optimistic outlook. Life is for enjoying – and it mustn't be wasted. Everything will work out if you have faith.

Sagittarius is more public-spirited than Gemini. Mum likes to help people, especially by spreading useful information, and is an idealistic soul at heart. Gemini's main aim in life is to keep himself entertained, using his analytical brain to see where he can get the maximum fun.

Despite their differences he'll be delighted with his Sagittarius mum. She's never boring, provides him with change and excitement and is almost as good with words as he is.

Gemini child with a Sagittarius father

This busy pair just love to talk. Gemini adores the sound of his own little voice, while Sagittarius Dad gets all fired up about new ideas, things he's read – in fact, any good titbit of information – and likes to share his pearls of wisdom with his bright youngster.

In Gemini he has an eager audience. There will be a lot of banter back and forth between this pair. Gemini loves having a dad who's clever at word games and tongue twisters, just like he is. They also have a wonderful time tossing big ideas and dotty schemes around. As for making workable plans – why bother? It's the talking they enjoy!

Sagittarius is rather more serious-minded than Gemini, if no less fun-loving. If he's interested in motorbikes or computers, he'll buy every magazine on the subject and spend days reading them. Gemini manages to sound knowledgeable, despite the fact that he skims over most things, changing hobbies at an alarming rate. Gemini reckons he'd get bored silly if life wasn't packed with variety.

Sagittarius Dad has to admit that he's tactless. Gemini may have a sharp tongue, but he usually knows how to avoid offending people. Dad marvels at Gemini's ability to charm, but thinks he manipulates the truth at times – and Dad doesn't approve. He accepts his child's need to do six things at once and is great at thinking up activities to keep him amused.

This wise dad can offer good advice to help Gemini keep his feet on the ground and actually get things done.

Gemini child with a Capricorn mother

Sensible Capricorn Mum finds it hard to keep up with chatterbox Gemini. He's constantly talking, pestering her with questions, singing little rhymes and being generally noisy. He may be funny and adorable but she wishes she had more energy to cope with her little livewire.

Mum wants Gemini to do well. And while he may be tiring, no-one can deny he's bright, which pleases her. She'll push him to shine at school, helping him to apply himself and reach his potential. But Mum must watch that she doesn't push too hard and dim his spontaneity and spark.

Switching subjects when he gets bored is natural to Gemini. But this mum is a stickler for thoroughness and gets cross if it seems to her he's frittering away his time.

Gemini loves ideas, words, non-stop talk and fun, while Capricorn is much more into solid hard work and being well thought of in the community. Mum will have to accept that Gemini has a faster, lighter way of doing things and simply doesn't care about what anyone thinks of him.

She's more conventional and is wary of new fashions and

ideas, both of which Gemini loves. And her dry humour may not always mix with his rapid wordplay. Yet Mum will admire her little Gemini for being so full of go and curiosity about life. She likes his social confidence and courage, and his verbal powers amaze her. Yet she won't stand for any distortion of the truth.

She'll keep Gemini firmly on the rails, showing him how to turn his best ideas into reality, and how to concentrate enough to be a real success.

Gemini child with a Capricorn father

Business-minded Capricorn Dad hopes his child will be a chip off the old block – serious, hard-working, successful and rich. Gemini may do very well indeed – he's a born media person, being such a wizard with verbal communication – but he's unlikely to be an ambitious slogger like his father. Gemini's main aim in life is to have fun – the more the merrier.

Dad has to accept that Gemini sees things in a different way or there could be big clashes between them. This child likes to flit from hobby to hobby, leaving projects unfinished, always reaching for something new. Capricorn thinks you should stick at things to the end, and has no great interest in the latest trends.

Capricorn loves home best and will defend it to the end, even if he can seem rather cold and off-hand at times with his family. Gemini loves to be up and out, meeting people, enjoying a busy social life and the warmth of lively conversation. To Capricorn, his social life is merely a way to enhance his reputation. He most enjoys civic or company functions, anywhere where he can climb another rung up the social ladder.

Neither is very emotional, so it suits them that they aren't given to big shows of affection or loud scenes. But if there's ever something on Gemini's mind, Dad would do well to coax it out of him. Gemini likes to pretend he doesn't care and hasn't got feelings, but he has.

Gemini needs to be acknowledged for his wonderful imagination, the inventive stories he makes up, his wit and way with words and his sense of adventure. If Dad allows him to be himself, life will be enjoyable for both of them.

Gemini child with an Aquarius mother

These two are more like chatty friends. Both like to talk and dream, but Mum's also happy to sit back and play amused audience to verbal Gemini as he performs tricks with words. She's generous, too, and Gemini is delighted with her surprise gifts of new books or toys to keep his busy brain occupied.

Mum will happily pass her love of books and learning on to her child. She's likely to be far more interested in social issues and politics than he is, and Aquarius likes her children to have a social conscience, too. Gemini, however, tends to put his own needs before anyone else's – keeping amused and avoiding boredom are his top priorities.

Both are mind-orientated and rarely feel strong emotions. And neither is keen on big shows of affection, although they're certainly very fond of each other. Aquarius likes the fact that Gemini leaves her free to work on her campaigns and projects, while Gemini is glad Mum accepts his need to circulate, to talk and chat to whichever pal will listen.

Like Gemini, Aquarius is very sociable, although she prefers being part of a group and tends to do things with the welfare of other people in mind, while Gemini simply enjoys having a group of friends to shine among. These two share a love of anything new and adapt easily to change. Both like thinking up bright ideas, though it'll be Mum who's quickest to turn her dreams into reality, and she'll help Gemini see which of his ideas are workable.

Aquarius admires Gemini's ability to explain things clearly and doesn't mind that this child seems to like arguing so much – she finds it entertaining to debate. But she wishes Gemini would stick to the truth the way she always does.

Still, she feels thrilled and proud to have such a bright-minded child, and Gemini thrives on the feedback he gets from his equally lively mum.

Gemini child with an Aquarius father

Inventive Aquarius Dad will delight his Gemini child with his bright ideas for things to do, places to go, people to see. Dad is very original, sometimes even quirky and eccentric, and Gemini loves it – so much better than having a father who's boring!

Aquarius helps to stimulate that clever Gemini imagination, getting him to write stories, draw and paint. He'll encourage the development of Gemini's verbal skills by spending time talking with him. And, as any Aquarius house is sure to be full of books, Gemini will have a head start when it comes to reading and learning.

Sometimes Gemini can be contentious and awkward, but Dad doesn't mind a bit for he sees it as a sign his child is growing up and learning to think for himself. Aquarius thinks that children should develop naturally without the imposition of harsh discipline, and Gemini is very pleased that Dad seems to accept him the way he is.

Aquarius will have to watch that Gemini doesn't take advantage, however. He's a cheeky little devil who'll bend the rules – and the truth! Aquarius knows how to explain to children what's right and what isn't, so there should be no problem.

Gemini is proud that his dad keeps so up to date and seems to know so much. This child has such a curiosity about life and Dad seems to have a lot of the answers. Aquarius loves clever children and will take delight in filling his bright little Gemini with fascinating facts.

Gemini child with a Pisces mother

Loving Pisces surrounds Gemini with warmth and security. But the way he's always moving, talking, thinking and racing around makes it seem as if he's constantly slipping through her fingers. Gemini seems too busy to have much time for her cuddles, so Mum can be left feeling high and dry instead of deeply bonded – the way she wants to be.

Yet little Gemini loves her very much deep in his heart. And Mum is such a good listener she's the perfect sounding board for all his big schemes and bright ideas.

Mum is a lot more emotional and intuitive than logical Gemini. But despite their differences, Pisces always allows him to be himself – to think, talk, create and keep busy. And this is vital to Gemini. There are times, though, when his persistent questions tire her, so she'll shut herself away to escape his chatter and get some peace.

Mum usually laughs along with Gemini's childish ways and enjoys joining in the fun when she's got the energy. But she hasn't got the speed to keep up with his verbal acrobatics and hates it when he uses his sharp tongue on her. Pisces is very sensitive to hurt and doesn't always know how to stand up to her clever Gemini child.

At times she can find him too much of a handful, particularly as she avoids imposing discipline. Yet she'll have to learn to draw the line sometimes if he isn't to take over. Gemini will respond well if he's set sensible rules and understands the reason for them. Pisces mustn't let grouses build up, or they'll both turn snappy with each other.

Sociable Gemini admires the way his Mum seems to fit in so well with people. And he's glad she thinks up such exciting things to do, teaching him about life in a broad sense, which is just what he enjoys and needs.

Gemini child with a Pisces father

Pisces Dad looks forward to having children – but livewire Gemini can be rather more than he bargained for. Gemini is so full of questions and energy, always dragging Dad by the hand out to play, that Pisces finds it hard to keep up with such a whirlwind of activity.

Pisces excels when it comes to stimulating Gemini's marvellous imagination. Pisces is very artistic and creative and these two can have hours of fun painting, modelling, dreaming up stories, playing make-believe and making music.

Dad wants the best for his child so he'll spare the time to see that Gemini takes part in interests that work off some of that excess nervous energy. He'll never fully understand his child's analytical quest for information, novelty and new ideas, though. Dad takes life much more sedately.

Gemini thinks Dad can be too vague and stick-in-the-mud, preferring what he knows to anything new. Both appreciate they're not the most straightforward people in the world, even if they never mean any harm. Dad forgets promises – what's said yesterday may not apply today. Gemini has such a vivid imagination he'll make up whoppers that simply confuse Dad. Neither will ever be sure that the other really means what he says.

Pisces secretly envies Gemini's energy and fast mind, while Gemini often turns to his father for inspiration. Dad encourages Gemini to go out and make friends and doesn't impose things on him that don't suit him. Which is all absolutely fine by Gemini!

CANCER
Stars for Life

STAR BABY

There may be more tears, but there will be countless smiles too. For baby Cancer is ruled by the moon and so is a slave to her (or his*) emotions from the start. One minute she'll be drowning in floods of tears, the next a giggling bundle of fun who'll melt even the hardest heart.

Full of affection, at baby Cancer's centre is a core of vulnerability that will bring out protective instincts in her parents they didn't even know they had. She's open and giving, with a range of facial expressions that say what she thinks better than any words, and eyes that communicate from the first moment she warily opens them to face the world. They light up when she smiles, darken in pain or fear, and cloud when tears are near, for Cancer will never, ever be able to hide her feelings.

From the start, she'll soak up scents, tastes and sights and very soon realise that safety lies in the security of her parents' arms, or wrapped up snug in her pram. She won't like being left with someone she doesn't know well, or handed round from person to person like a parcel.

She is likely to favour the slow and steady approach to life – no running before she can walk for cautious young Cancer! But give her plenty of time to get used to new faces and places and her confidence will grow, as she knows you are near.

*'She' is used to cover he and she for Cancer child.

Cancer adores all things sensual – different tastes and textures of food, bright picture books and toys to stimulate her vivid imagination. But the best plaything of all for baby Cancer is water, whether it's a paddling pool, a splash in the bath, or a bowl of water. With water around she's literally in her element. So after she's had her vaccinations, head for the local swimming pool and watch your water baby blossom.

FIRST STEPS FOR CANCER

Life's something of a seesaw for toddler Cancer – up one minute, down the next, but never stopping in the middle for very long! Tantrums are a constant threat because of her moodiness, but they can be diverted with a little forward planning. Give Cancer all the cuddling, compliments and coaxing she needs, and remember that the happy face she often wears is just a mask over the still, deep waters of her powerful emotions. Cancer needs handling with care!

Overprotecting her isn't the answer, though, however tempting it may seem, because that way she'll never learn to manage without her security blanket! Constant criticism sours her into a snappy, snide child, so aim for a firm, fair approach that's flexible enough to accept her mood swings and insecurity.

A born parent, little Cancer will soon be practising her caring skills by treating her toys like children. She's delighted to 'help' with the chores, and must be allowed to, even if it means everything takes twice as long. Feeling useful and helpful is essential to her inner harmony.

Cancer is very attached to home and family and will do anything to protect them, and herself. Her bond with her mother is central, and she may even seem suffocatingly clingy. But all she needs is a few pointers towards developing her own personality, rather than being an imitation of someone else's. Make sure she has plenty of other strong ties, with her father, grandparents, relatives and friends, so she grows up with more than one person to copy, or criticise!

Cancer also needs encouragement to be selfish sometimes. Make sure she sits and plays with her toys rather than helping to vacuum the lounge, or get her to admit she's tired rather than let her try to keep going.

Her sweetness can be mistaken for stupidity sometimes, and she does tend to take life rather seriously. But there's always that wacky streak of humour that will have the whole family in stitches! Helping little Cancer loosen up and relax will make her life a lot easier.

SCHOOL RULES FOR CANCER

By the time she starts school, Cancer's imagination should have burst into bloom. She'll lap up stories (the more outrageous the better) and even make up her own to tell to her toys. Both Cancer boys and girls love playing house more than anything else and will happily make elaborate pretend food 'for Daddy' or play at washing-up for hours on end. More physical play, like bouncing a ball or skipping, would help Cancer develop faster, so do encourage her.

Cancer is a terrible hoarder, jealously guarding each tiny bit of 'her' Lego with her life, and keeping every birthday card and school drawing she's ever done. But it's part of life to let go, so encourage her to loosen her clinging grip and accept she can't hang on to everything. It will help her later to learn that it's possible to let go of people, as well as possessions, without it being the end of the world.

She'll never be one for crowds of friends, preferring a well-chosen, trusted few. Although she'll seem shy at first at playgroup or school, once she's built up these bonds they'll never be broken. She may well keep these friends for life!

Traditional education suits her best, with a set routine and well-behaved, quiet classes, otherwise shy Cancer may never get a chance to speak. She'll thrive if she feels close to her teacher, so keep an eye on this relationship if young Cancer doesn't seem to be progressing too well.

Cancer is a born worrier and will clam up if anyone tries to find out what's wrong. She can take even the most innocent remark to heart and fret over it for days. Supersensitive and with the thinnest skin in the zodiac, she'll spend a lot of her early life feeling hurt and confused.

She needs help to learn how to cope with life's less than wonderful moments, and get them in perspective. Showing her by example that thoughtless remarks or actions may shake a bond but never break it is one way – trying not to laugh when she jumps out of her skin or is scared to try something new is another.

She's blessed with a world-beating memory, but does best when a school subject appeals to her emotions and strong imagination. Don't look for a stream of curious questions from a Cancer child. She prefers to absorb impressions and information and make sense of it in her own time. But she's likely to take a special interest in history, especially when it's brought to life by a costume drama on TV, or Granny reliving memories of her childhood.

TEENAGE TAKE-OFF FOR CANCER

After a childhood spent picking her way gingerly through the minefield of booby-trapped emotions, many Cancer youngsters come into their own in their teens. So don't despair if she's underachieved at school, for further education may be Cancer's forte!

By now young Cancer has come to terms with her fluctuating moods (although she's still likely to get emotional and rebellious around the time of the full moon) and has blossomed into a hard worker with a genuine interest in other people and a heart of solid gold.

She still needs gentle praise and back-up to make the most of her talents, and gentle guidance to do better next time when things go wrong. Harsh criticism just cuts her tender heart into tiny pieces! But it could be difficult to bite your tongue as teenage Cancer experiments with new ways of shocking and surprising you, from all-night parties to all-day lie-ins when that legendary Cancer laziness takes over.

She may seem vulnerable and easily led, but in fact your

Cancer teenager has a strong will under all that softness, and a great deal of common sense, developed over the years with your help. So she must make her own mistakes and test her own boundaries. It's all part of her natural, gradual growing away from you and towards independent adult life. Try not to suffocate her with worry and she'll always come home to share hilarious stories of her adventures.

All too soon Cancer is yearning to settle down in a home of her own which could lead her to fly up the aisle far too young and for all the wrong reasons. Friendships with both boys and girls, and livelier types who'll show her just what she'd be missing by marrying young, will keep her fun-loving side to the fore. She's sure to be very popular and most friends she makes will last for life.

When it comes to career choices, steer Cancer towards any work connected with water, counselling, catering or the health service. And later, when she becomes a model parent herself, you can sit back and feel privileged and proud to have helped Cancer find her way in life.

STAR PARENTS

Cancer child with an Aries mother

Energetic Aries Mum feels like putting a rocket under her Cancer child sometimes, for Cancer never springs into action at Mum's speed. She'll take ages over buckling her shoes and putting on her coat while Mum impatiently chivvies her along. But there's nothing to be done. Cancer will travel at her own pace whatever Mum says.

Aries Mum charges round in a buzz of activity while Cancer lives in the world of emotions, slowed down by her need to deal with strong and subtle feelings as they arise. Quick to take offence, watch her brow furrow when tactless Mum says something that sensitive Cancer takes to heart. She'll brood and mope, moodily mulling things over. Mum must try to tread gently, to soothe and reassure.

Aries prefers being out of the house without chores to tie

her down, while Cancer loves the cosy atmosphere of home. She'd rather retreat to her room or snuggle up by the fire feeling safe, protected, secure, than be anywhere else.

With a Cancer child, Mum must watch her tendency to push her youngster too hard, expecting her to grow up quickly and be less of a tie. Cancer needs affection, reassurance and encouragement to build her confidence. She hasn't got that inborn feeling of strength and superiority which is within every Aries. So take it slowly, Mum – don't force her to be independent before she's ready.

Cancer tries hard to please and hates it if anyone gets angry with her. She'll play up if she senses tensions just to get Dad or Mum to blow up and end the suspense. And Aries blows up quite often! Cancer is relieved that, with Mum, it's usually all over in a flash and life can go back to normal.

If Aries is feeling cross, she must try to explain her reasons. Cancer thinks she intuitively knows what's going on in the heads of others, but sometimes she gets it wrong and believes things are her fault when they're not. Slow the pace, Aries, and be straightforward with her, to help her feel more secure.

Rest assured, Cancer will be thrilled to have a mum who's so effective, so good at standing up for her, so strong and in charge. And Aries will learn to be gentler, kinder, more in touch with her own feelings through having brought up a Cancer child.

Cancer child with an Aries father

Aries Dad is always on the move, caught up in a hectic business and social life. He's adventurous, successful, a good leader and much admired by his little Cancer child. But she does wish he could spend more time at home with her. Cancer can be possessive and want Dad all to herself. And while he loves her dearly, he refuses to be tied down by anyone, even his adorable young Cancer. But it is important that he sets aside some time to spend with her. It will help her grow into the secure and confident person Aries wants her to be.

Aries has high expectations of his children and likes fast developers, seeing their success as a reflection on himself. Cancer may take a little longer than he'd wish to reach those important milestones. She likes staying close to Mum and doesn't enjoy drawing attention to herself. Cancer lacks the strongly competitive spirit of Aries – but give her time, Dad. One day she could turn out to be a very successful business person, as Cancer is excellent with money. Give her a chance, and she could make Dad very proud indeed.

If Dad behaves as if she's not meeting his high standards, he could seriously undermine her confidence and set her brooding that she's let him down. She needs to be built up all the time, praised, hugged and told how wonderful she is. Give her space to talk about her feelings. Don't expect her to be boisterous and outgoing like Aries, but value her strengths, particularly her caring qualities and her ability to understand and sympathise with other people's feelings.

She has wonderful intuition, reading a situation instantly. Aries' intuition works in a different way, allowing him to spring into effective action without having to sit down and think things out beforehand.

Dad enjoys short bursts of lively play with his children and expects them to be as adventurous and risk-taking as he is. Cancer is far more cautious and enjoys quieter, creative play. However, Dad will be amazed at her determination. Once she's decided to do something she'll stick at it and win through.

She'll enjoy keeping to Dad's rules, but only once they've been properly explained to her. And she'll be glad that Dad's so full of ideas for things to do. His full-of-fun attitude to life will draw her out of herself and inspire her to reach her potential.

Cancer child with a Taurus mother

This cosy pair really enjoy each other's company. Home-loving Cancer adores the comfy nest clever Taurus has created and feels safe, warm, protected and happy with this reassuring mum around. Mum is delighted to have a child who respects her values, helps take care of her lovely home and tucks into her delicious cooking.

Taurus is always there with a shoulder to cry on when little Cancer looks blue. Mum may seem blustery on the surface, but she's well attuned to her child's sensitive feelings and can see when she needs to talk and be cosseted. She knows little Cancer finds life a struggle sometimes and is there to soothe her better. She understands her child's moodiness, too, being prone to it herself, and will always try to gently jolly her out of it.

It's not often that these two will fight, but when they do it's bound to end in a sulk which Taurus can keep up for hours on end. Cancer will win her round with affection, for Taurus can't stay stubborn and cross for long after a hug.

Taurus is even more money-minded than thrifty Cancer. Taurus values what money can buy – it gives her a feeling of security to have lovely possessions around her. Cancer's main source of security is Mum herself and she can be clingy and slow to develop confidence. But Taurus doesn't mind. She likes her children to act like children and doesn't expect them to be independent until they are good and ready.

Cancer is very glad that Mum shares her home-loving values, though there are times when she could do with more push and challenge. Taurus shouldn't underestimate her child's capabilities. Mum should get her involved in activities which gradually stretch her to do more and more. Taurus Mum is very good at giving encouragement, once she sees the need.

These two love sharing little secrets and jokes, and they'll offer mutual comfort and support if anyone has done or said something that has hurt the other. Mum feels she's got a real little friend in Cancer, and Cancer feels she's got just the mum she wants – one who's always there to offer the protection and love she needs.

Cancer child with a Taurus father

A kind-hearted Taurus father will put himself out for his loving little Cancer child. Here's someone who shares his appreciation of home comforts and doesn't want to be always on the move. These two like pottering around the house doing little chores and Cancer will happily follow Dad into the garden, ready to help with the weeding. She really enjoys being useful.

Taurus sees himself as a traditional breadwinner and enjoys spending the money he earns on special treats for his child. But he must take care that he doesn't try to buy her love, making up for the times he's not around by plying Cancer with sweets and toys. What she really needs is Dad there as often as possible. She's possessive, just like her father, and she desperately needs to feel secure. She won't feel secure if Dad is always away working, no matter how many toys he buys her.

Yet Cancer does appreciate the lovely home Taurus has created with his hard-earned cash. And she knows Dad's always there behind her, encouraging her to develop her strength, stamina and determination. He'll give her confidence and show her how to win, without minding too much when she doesn't.

Sometimes Taurus can be very strict, especially if he thinks he's losing control of his child. But he must avoid being too harsh with Cancer. She's quick to blame herself, even when nothing's been said, and she'll start worrying if she isn't getting approval. Taurus can be gloomy, but Cancer can be supermoody. Reassurance will soon set her world to rights.

Watch her at mealtimes too. Like Taurus, food is important to her and, if she's worried, she could either go off her meals or indulge in comfort eating and pile on the pounds. Try to encourage healthy eating in your household so that when she does gorge herself, she does it on wholesome food, not chips and puddings.

In years to come, Cancer will be grateful for having had

such a close relationship with her dad. She'll be glad of the security, peace and order he offered, happy to have grown up in a warm and secure Taurus home.

Cancer child with a Gemini mother

Quick-witted Gemini runs verbal rings round her slower-paced Cancer child. Cancer is caught up in the world of feelings and emotions and her reactions are not as fast as those of her mum. Cancer's responses emerge from inside, taking time to appear, while with Gemini everything is on the surface. She doesn't feel deeply about anything much – but she can think at the speed of light.

Cancer finds it hard to keep up with Mum as she changes her mind a dozen times a day, and chatters on to anyone who'll listen. Cancer isn't sure what to make of the things her mum says. Gemini seems to love using words for the sake of it, and Cancer doubts if she can rely on everything she hears.

Yet she can't help but love and admire her mother for her urge to discover everything new and exciting. Cancer wishes she could be as dynamic and sociable, but fears her world might fall apart if she tried to be what she really knows she isn't.

Gemini will draw out Cancer by taking her to visit friends and teaching her how to relate to others. Friends are the mainstay of Gemini's life, yet Cancer isn't a lover of crowds and would often prefer to stay at home. Cancer would like Mum all to herself and finds it hard to keep up with Gemini's social whirl.

She's amazed, too, at how ahead of the times Mum is. Gemini knows more about the latest trends than young Cancer does. And she also seems to know the secret of how to get enjoyment and amusement out of everything life has to offer. Cancer is too often swept away by tides of emotion to enjoy every minute of the day.

Gemini doesn't understand her child's brooding spells, even though she can switch moods at a confusing rate. Still, she has the knack of getting Cancer to laugh her way out of her miseries and teaches her that life isn't worth getting upset about.

With a Cancer child, it's important that Gemini curbs her critical streak. Cancer is easily hurt, a sensitive child who thrives on encouragement and praise. So Mum should concentrate on boosting her confidence. If it's knocked, she could take a long time to find her feet again. And if Gemini must criticise, she should do it with gentle humour and a hug.

Gemini should appreciate Cancer's caring nature, and learn from her how to put others' needs before her own.

Cancer child with a Gemini father

Buzzy Gemini Dad is alive with ideas and could talk the hind legs off a donkey. He'd like Cancer to be as hooked on words as he is and tries to get her interested in books from an early age. Cancer certainly benefits from all the stimulation, but it may be some time before she can keep up with Dad's rapid-fire style of talk.

Gemini must let her take her time and not show disappointment when she doesn't develop at the speed he'd like. She may have a slower style, but she's as bright as a button and one day she'll amaze him with her brain-power, particularly when it comes to money. She'll surprise him, too, by thinking up schemes that actually work, while most of his are nothing more than a lot of hot air.

Dad delights young Cancer with his bedtime stories, setting off her strong imagination. She'll love his sense of humour too, and they'll share many a laugh together. But she won't be a risk-taker like Gemini, being altogether more cautious. And she won't be attracted to social life in quite the way Dad is, so he must dedicate some time just for her. She needs reassuring that she's important to help her feel secure, and she'll be hurt if Dad's always too busy.

Don't expect Cancer to follow rules that she doesn't understand. She'll feel hemmed in and unhappy unless someone explains how rules can help people, and they are likely to be important in the family as Gemini likes to feel he's in control.

Remember that Cancer needs help to develop some strength of personality. Her confidence needs building up and it won't be helped if Dad criticises too much, is over-strict, or stops her making her own decisions.

Emotional and sensitive Cancer needs consideration, not shouting matches or being sent to bed as Dad tries to assert his authority. But in his better moods, Cancer will find Dad full of fun. And she'll certainly benefit from his positive outlook, which will help to stave off her gloomy spells.

Try to get Cancer to talk about her feelings whenever she looks down in the mouth. She clams up if she's hurt, but patience and kindness can draw her out. If Gemini respects the fact that she feels things a lot more strongly than he does, he'll be three-quarters of the way to understanding and appreciating her.

Cancer child with a Cancer mother

These two would stay in all day, given half a chance. They both love their home more than anything in the world. Young Cancer will happily trot round after Mum as she does her chores, and will be itching to help once she's old enough. Cancer Mum is glad to have a hand from her domesticated child. Long may it continue, she thinks, as she feels put upon by less considerate children.

Cancer child is delighted that her Mum is caring, kind, affectionate and warm. She gives her the love and support she needs. But these two are often moody and there will be times when they're both feeling low and neither has the energy to cheer the other up. Mum must watch out for the warning signs, then forget her own cares and sort out her little one's woes.

Mum is a bit of a worrier – and little Cancer keeps all sorts of secret fears to herself! It's hard for Mum to give her child the confidence that will stop her worrying so much, for both are always fretting about something. They need someone positive in their lives to take them in hand.

When they're both feeling low, Mum and child can be crabby and snap at each other. They'll take each other's every remark to heart and retreat moodily to tend their wounds. Of course, it's really up to Mum to put things right. She should allow herself plenty of rest to recharge, so she's better equipped to cope with the cares of motherhood. Then she can spring back to being her loving, nurturing self – the side that young Cancer adores.

She thrives under Mum's protective care and warmth, loves the cosy home she's made and enjoys Mum's sympathy when something's gone wrong. She trusts Mum completely.

Mum may need to make a special effort to help young Cancer become more independent as she grows. She'll be happy to stay close to Mum, and Mum will be happy to let her stay there, dreading the day when her child leaves home. With a Cancer child it's important to help her take those first steps into the world by building up her confidence. Cancer Mum should encourage any interests her child has, and be prepared to put herself out to help her follow them.

Cancer child with a Cancer father

Cautious Cancer Dad is glad his child isn't noisy and over-confident like some children. He likes his child's more sedate style and understands her need to know what's round the next corner. He feels very protective towards her and will stick up for her loudly against any over-harsh teacher or the parent of the school bully.

Cancer Dad likes the fact his child appreciates the home he's worked so hard to build. He's happy to do all he can to give her a good start in life, taking the time to expand her education and interests. And he's pleased that she shares his love of nostalgia. They both like nothing better than reminiscing over old photos. These two share a yearning for an idyllic past – the present never quite seems to come up to their expectations.

This father can sympathise with Cancer's shyness and her tendency to be moody. He understands that she's sensitive like himself. But she finds it hard to cope when he gets one of his crabby days. Cancer can be cross and commanding under the pressure of his swirling emotions. He'll take it out on his family and expect them to simply put up with his bad temper.

Moon-child Cancer will burst into floods of tears and run to her room if Dad snaps at her. He must try to remember what a loving and caring person he can be if he tries, and turn the charm back on. Sensitive Cancer child will sulk for days if he doesn't give her a reassuring hug to show he's not cross any more.

Yet she will understand Dad's need for rest and retreat, as long as he remembers to set aside enough time to play and talk with her. She can become very inward-looking if deprived of attention.

On his happy days, though, they'll both be delighted by each other. Dad loves trips out to the sea or a walk by the local river. And Cancer child, being a water baby, will love these special days, too.

Dad will be delighted his child doesn't squander money. And he'll be pleased she shows gratitude for all the things he's done for her. It's important to Cancer that he's appreciated for being a caring and thoughtful parent, and his Cancer child will make him feel glad he made the effort.

Cancer child with a Leo mother

Lively Leo is a star among mothers, making everyone happy and willing to work together with her radiant smile and energetic attitude. Young Cancer thinks Mum is marvellously positive and optimistic, but sometimes she wonders if she can ever live up to her example.

Cancer is shyer, more self-effacing and lacks Leo's dramatic boldness. She knows she can be moody and pessimistic and would much rather stay in the background. She can't understand how Mum is always so jolly and bright.

Kind-hearted Mum will want her child to have her share of the spotlight. She can help by making Cancer feel good about being the caring little person she is. Cancer's confidence needs building up, so praise her for her intuitive wisdom, her thoughtfulness, her willingness to listen and help, her warm-hearted wish to cheer people up when they're down. They're all marvellous qualities and Cancer needs to know she's valued for having them.

Mum will love Cancer's affectionate nature – Leo feels really special when Cancer gives her an appreciative kiss on the cheek. And Cancer especially loves Mum for her generosity, buying her lovely clothes and pretty things for her room.

Mum will be glad she has a child who is willing to help at home, leaving her more time to do the things she enjoys. But she'll wish she could help Cancer to stop worrying. It's hard for her to understand that Cancer hasn't got Leo's inbuilt confidence.

Leo is very proud and feels most put out if Cancer makes a snappy, crabby remark, which she will do if she feels under attack for any reason. Leo must try to look at what's behind this sensitive child's sudden change of mood. Maybe a chance remark has hurt her without Mum realising?

Fiery Leo must tread softly when it comes to telling Cancer off. She's very sensitive and needs to be reassured that she's not being rejected if Mum's cross.

Leo likes to achieve personal ambitions through her children and must be sure not to push this child too hard in any direction she doesn't want to go. She must remember that Cancer is very different from her and should be allowed to be herself. In return she'll love Mum forever.

Cancer child with a Leo father

Forceful Leo Dad seems like a giant to small Cancer. He's big, brash, loud and boisterous, and everyone seems to love him. Dad shines like the sun in any crowd, drawing people to him like a magnet. Young Cancer is very proud to have such a powerful, invincible father.

Leo Dad laps up her devotion. He thinks of himself as kinglike, and his children are expected to idolise him. But Cancer does have a critical streak and one day she's bound to say something that will knock him down a peg or two. It's better if Dad doesn't pretend to be perfect all the time, as he'll feel silly when Cancer finally rumbles him.

Leo must make an extra effort to see that Cancer gets the attention she needs to build her confidence and make her believe in herself. Dad should try to take an interest in the things she enjoys doing. She's unlikely to share his particular interests, unless she's taken up something just to win his approval. It's vital that Leo validates her right to be an individual and to make her own way in life.

Cancer will enjoy Leo's protective guidance and, if he can find caring ways to help her, she'll start to feel a very close bond with him. Above all Cancer loves to feel protected, and with a big strong dad like Leo around she does. But he must take care with his temper, for if he gets angry for any reason Cancer will be convinced it's all her fault.

Leo must always explain what he's cross about, and make sure that any rules he sets are clearly understood. Cancer is far more sensitive than he is to harsh words and confusion. Her world revolves around her strong emotions and these can cause her a lot of anxiety unless she's encouraged to talk about and sort out her feelings. Sit down with her and give her time.

Leo will be proud to see how warm-hearted and caring Cancer is. He's a very warm person himself, who loves to spread happiness around. She may not help people on his broad scale, but those she chooses to love will feel the glow of her protective, nurturing ways.

Cancer child with a Virgo mother

Hard-working Virgo Mum does everything she can to make sure her sensitive and caring Cancer child is happy. She enjoys the fact that they're such good friends. They understand each other and can really make each other laugh. And when Cancer gets worried, or wakes at night from a bad dream, Mum is always there to soothe and comfort, for she knows what it's like to worry.

Virgo likes to be of service to others, and so she respects Cancer's willingness to nurture and protect. She loves her affectionate nature, too. Virgo finds it hard to be physically warm and is touched by the love Cancer shows her.

Virgo is too practical to fill her own head with dreams and fairytales, so she's amused and pleased to have a child who can weave webs of fantasy. It will probably be little Cancer telling Mum bedtime stories, rather than the other way round!

But Virgo encourages Cancer to be practical, too – she wouldn't want her to be all dreams and no action. Cancer lives in a world of emotions and can seem out of touch with reality sometimes, so she needs Virgo to help her get to grips with the nitty-gritty of life.

Cancer feels so at home with Virgo that she'll come out of her shell and be really chatty when usually she's more reserved. Virgo is a great house-cleaner and enjoys it when Cancer tags along with her duster at the ready. This child is tidy and careful – both qualities that Virgo rates highly.

But Virgo must watch her critical tongue. Cancer takes things very much to heart and will be wounded by any sharp words. Mum may just be trying to help by pointing out weak spots, but Cancer only thrives on praise. Virgo should look out for things she does well that she can compliment her on.

Cancer likes the security that Virgo provides. She loves a stable home, where not too much is expected of her, and as Virgo enjoys her home, too, they should have a fine time exploring the world from their kitchen.

Cancer child with a Virgo father

Virgo Dad is glad that his Cancer child listens when he explains his views on manners, morals and good behaviour. He likes well-behaved children and an orderly home, and luckily Cancer feels best when things run according to routine, so both are happy.

Virgo must be careful not to set rules without explaining why, for Cancer will rebel unless she's clear on the facts. She's not being difficult, she simply can't conform if she doesn't understand. She's good-hearted and wants the best for everyone, and once she's clear on the reason for rules, she'll toe the line.

Both Cancer and Virgo run on nervous energy and there are times when they'll get tired of the battle of life and will need a rest. Fortunately for Cancer, her Virgo parent will understand her need to retreat to her room, avoid people and recharge her batteries.

But Virgo must also make a point of helping Cancer to develop her more outgoing side, encouraging activities that will gradually build up her confidence and so help her to keep cheerful and not start worrying. Virgo is a worrier himself, so it'll be hard for him to shake her out of a gloom.

Cancer needs help, too, to become physically stronger. Not naturally sporty himself, Virgo Dad is unlikely to set an active example and finds it hard to push his children to do things he's not personally interested in. But he should encourage her to take up gentle exercise and gradually build up her stamina. Virgo will be pleasantly surprised at how hard Cancer works to achieve goals, once she's set her heart on doing something. She's full of determination.

Little Cancer will love her dad and be ready with a sympathetic smile and cuddle when he's feeling down. She enjoys cheering people up or giving them a helping hand, and Virgo Dad will admire her for her selfless ways. He should try to show her she's also valued simply for being herself, as well as for all the love and caring she offers others.

Watch out when a little sister or brother is born. Dad will have to try extra hard to reassure Cancer she's still loved as much as ever, otherwise she could become resentful towards the new arrival. Cancer hates change or any threat to her security.

Attention is the key. Virgo must bear in mind Cancer's strong need for emotional reassurance. All will be well if he reassures her regularly, as well as dealing with the practical matters he's so good at handling.

Cancer child with a Libra mother

Laid-back Libra loves her dreamy Cancer child and the two of them usually get on famously. They will treat each other with consideration, although it's hard for Libra to understand Cancer's deeper emotional side.

Libra is an outgoing, sociable soul who loves to gather people around her and create a sense of community. Cancer, on the other hand, is more inward looking and imaginative, full of deep thoughts and feelings.

Libra Mum is a logical soul who thinks such sensitivity makes Cancer a little too self-centred. She tries her best to haul her out of herself, taking her out to socialise and telling her to cheer up when the moon child's tears come. But she'll find that Cancer's a hard one to change.

However, Libra really appreciates the way Cancer sticks at things once she's set her heart on achieving something. She loves Cancer's sense of fairness, her artistic and poetic streak, her ability to make up wonderful stories. And she's charmed by Cancer's displays of warm affection and sunny smiles. This child can be very rewarding indeed for Libra.

Cancer can be possessive and clingy sometimes, especially when Mum wants to be off making friends and mixing. She expects Cancer to act in a more adult way as she hasn't much time for childishness. This unsettles Cancer, who needs to be reassured that she's loved and wanted and that she's not expected to be independent before she's ready. Libra must make a big effort to show her affection and to build her sense of security.

Libra will be impatient with Cancer's tendency to fret. Mum takes a more relaxed view of life, enjoying the beauty of things around her and pushing worries and decision-making to the back of her mind. She suppresses emotions too, unwilling to face problems until she has to, so different from her child who swings from one feeling to another. Both can be moody, for very different reasons.

Cancer can sometimes find Mum indecisive, and this again can undermine her sense of security. Mum must use all her powers of sensitivity to try to tune into her child's needs. Caring Libra can certainly offer the security Cancer craves, if she puts her mind to it.

Cancer child with a Libra father

Optimistic Libra Dad tries to teach his Cancer child to have a positive outlook on life. It's a useful lesson for young Cancer, who can become glum as her emotions buffet her around.

Yet Libra Dad can be moody, too. He tries to stay in a happy state of balance but, like the scales that represent him, his feelings can swing and change. This pair just have to hope they're not swung by emotions at the same time. Somebody's got to stay in a reasonable mood to get things done!

Libra Dad works hard to earn the money to make a pleasant home for his Cancer child. She's delighted at the cash he's prepared to spend on making her room perfect and at the pretty clothes he'll let her buy. Dad likes to see his children looking smart, and Cancer adores dressing up.

Dad can be very kind and indulgent. In fact, he's a real softie and there are times when Cancer will take advantage of this. He must pull her up if she goes too far. But if he gets too annoyed with her, she'll burst into floods of tears and he'll end up feeling guilty. She'll take everything he's said to heart too, and will need lots of pacifying to make things better.

Libra Dad is very good at wheedling secrets out of clammed up Cancer, getting her to talk as few others can. Cancer needs help to reveal her emotions, so it's worth the time it takes for her to express anything that's worrying her. She may seem over-emotional to Libra, but it's vital that she's given the space to air her concerns.

Libra is amused by talkative, sparky youngsters who act like grown-ups from an early age. But Cancer mustn't be pushed to behave like this. She'll cling to her parents and refuse to go along with their efforts to make her more independent. They must accept that she'll spread her wings only when she's good and ready. She'll be much happier for it.

Cancer child with a Scorpio mother

Cancer child respects her protective Scorpio mum and is delighted to have such a powerful person to look after her, while Scorpio is thrilled to have a child she feels so at home with. Both are water signs and understand each other's need for self-protection.

This pair will reveal their innermost secrets only to each other. And they will stand up for each other against any attack, snapping back with stinging replies. Sometimes Cancer will turn her snappiness on Mum, but, being a powerful, effective Scorpio, she'll be quick to put young Cancer in her place. In fact, she thinks Cancer is a bit of a cry-baby who needs toughening up. Even though Mum is emotional, she prides herself in being able to keep her feelings under control and thinks Cancer should be able to mask her emotions from the world the way she does.

Cancer will be very hurt if Scorpio acts harshly, for she feels things deeply. Hopefully, their shared sense of understanding will help Scorpio curb her tougher tendencies. In fact Cancer can teach Scorpio to be more caring, kind and diplomatic – and less stinging. Cancer needs drawing out with trust, support, love and encouragement. It's up to Scorpio to do her best to develop her child's confidence, and never crush it.

Scorpio is driven to control, so it's easy for her to be critical and to manipulate with fear. Mum must remember that Cancer needs gentle handling to bring out that marvellous imagination, creativity and intuition. Cancer can be very good at expressing herself if encouraged. She tells wonderful stories and is a great little actress if given the backing. She's got determination, too, which Scorpio will admire.

Scorpio is keen to encourage her child's interests, but must watch that she doesn't try to fulfil her own ambitions through her children. She may try to take over every aspect of Cancer's life, and Cancer is certainly easy to control. But it won't do her any good. What she needs is gentle help towards achieving more independence, and acceptance to help curb her moods. Above all, she needs love to give her a feeling of security. With a little effort, Scorpio can be a wonderful mother for her Cancer child.

Cancer child with a Scorpio father

Cancer feels secure in the stable home that her Scorpio dad creates. Dad likes a well-disciplined and orderly atmosphere in the house, with everything under his control. He won't stand for any nonsense and can be very bossy with anyone who steps out of line.

But Cancer hates his occasional harsh tellings off. She'll retreat to her room and refuse to speak or come out for hours. She's sweet and sensitive and simply hasn't got Dad's power and strength, although that's not to say she won't stand up for herself with cutting remarks when she feels unfairly attacked. Watch out, Scorpio, for you won't like being criticised by someone only half your height!

This secretive pair will let each other in on their hidden thoughts and feelings, although there will be times when Cancer wants her privacy. Dad likes to know everything that's going on in her life and at times she'll feel that he's not being fair. She won't be happy if Dad plays with her emotions by being too dominating, either. She needs spontaneous shows of affection, laughter and fun to keep her cheerful and optimistic. The trouble is that Dad isn't very demonstrative and has a serious side that tends to warp his own suppressed emotions until they resurface in the form of manipulation and revenge-taking. Cancer will have to grow up pretty quickly and learn to steer clear of Dad's complicated life. For Scorpio is often busy hatching plots and schemes in which children have little place.

Young Cancer is very dependent on Dad, though. She desperately wants his approval, which he may not always give. She'll cling and be possessive and the only way to help her break free is to give constant, gentle support. Dad must never push her too hard in a direction she doesn't want to go, and should always be there when she needs help.

Dad seems marvellously effective, powerful and protective to young Cancer. She wishes she could inspire people with awe the way he can. But Cancer is a more cautious type who'd never take the risks with people that Dad will. She's always more concerned about protecting herself.

Scorpio Dad will be relieved that Cancer isn't too adventurous or difficult. But he'll have to face the fact that one day she will rebel. He must learn to be pleased she's showing some spirit!

Despite his complex nature, Scorpio will feel very at home with his moon child. He sympathises with her sensitivity, loves her imaginativeness and determination. He feels accepted by her, and protective of her.

Cancer child with a Sagittarius mother

Lively Sagittarius Mum brings lots of fun into the life of shy little Cancer. Mum always seems to be on the go, thinking up new adventures and making funny little jokes that send them both into gales of laughter. Even Cancer gets carried away with the jolliness of it all. Sagittarius really brings the child in herself out and Cancer hasn't time to get moody too often when she's around.

Sagittarius is impressed by her child's imagination and intuitive wisdom. She thinks she comes out with some marvellously clever remarks and she loves the way Cancer cares so much about the needs and feelings of others. Sagittarius is an idealistic sign and loves to be of help to people, so Mum is pleased to see such good-heartedness in one so young.

Mum can't help but say the wrong thing sometimes – Sagittarians are very blunt. Cancer will snap back in surprise, then rush off to her room to sulk. But Mum has ways of charming her out of her mood. Her positive attitude is infectious and she stops Cancer from being gloomy about life. Sagittarius is exciting to be around and she opens Cancer's eyes to all sorts of joys.

Cancer thinks Mum is a spendthrift, while Mum thinks Cancer should loosen up and spend some pocket-money to enjoy life. Mum may seem a bit hare-brained, yet she's capable of giving very good advice that can be of great help to Cancer. Nevertheless, Cancer wishes Mum was a bit more settled.

Cancer prefers to stay in one place, while Sagittarius likes to be on the move. And Sagittarius doesn't relate to feelings the way Cancer does, so Cancer may not feel she has the deep emotional bond she wants with Mum, to make her feel fully secure.

Yet Sagittarius will certainly do her best to create a good home and a happy life for her Cancer child. She'll teach her that life's too short to waste by worrying and will help her to develop a more positive outlook. Life will never be boring with Mum around and Cancer will be treated like a best friend and allowed to be herself. Sagittarius never talks down to children.

Mum may not be too hot on dealing with the practicalities of life, which she finds tiresome. But if she offers Cancer plenty of reassurance, affection and fun times, they will have a happy relationship.

Cancer child with a Sagittarius father

Warm-hearted Sagittarius Dad shows Cancer that life is for enjoying. He loves reading to her and will dream up marvellous stories to tell her. This pair love dancing and skipping, hopping and jumping. And if Cancer ever looks down in the mouth, Sagittarius will simply make a funny face to start her laughing again.

Dad helps to bring out Cancer's creativity by encouraging her imaginative skills and artistic talents. He will try to help her to express her feelings, too, which she certainly needs. His direct attitude will help Cancer to focus outwards, instead of getting lost in an emotional maze. Sagittarius thinks that childhood should be enjoyed, not cried over. Yet without realising it, he can fail to offer the emotional security Cancer needs to feel truly happy.

Sagittarius likes to feel free and hates being tied down. He's always off on a business trip or venture while Cancer wants him all to herself, at home and giving her his total attention. Sometimes he will say the wrong thing and upset Cancer, or decide he's had enough of emotional problems and act off-hand with her.

Sagittarius will have to compromise and devote sufficient time to Cancer to help her develop confidence and stability. Above all he must not rush her into being independent before she's ready. Cancer needs acceptance and support to gradually step out into the world. She needs encouragement to take up activities that will build up her belief in herself. And she needs to know Dad is there, supporting her, and that he won't be cross or too disappointed if she fails sometimes.

Dad must spend enough time on practical matters that need taking care of, like guiding Cancer gently towards the right career, sorting out bills and dealing with day-to-day problems. Sagittarius is often too busy trying to keep himself free to take the responsibilities of fatherhood really seriously.

Cancer will find Dad a marvellous source of information. He can't keep things to himself the way Cancer can – he just has to tell someone! Cancer will be amused and enlightened by his pearls of wisdom and he'll love her for her marvellous imagination and intuition and her caring attitude to other people.

Cancer child with a Capricorn mother

Low-key Capricorn Mum offers Cancer the stability she needs. Home is a haven where everything runs according to rules and routine. A hearty dinner is always on the table at the same time every day and everything is kept neat and tidy, the way they both like it.

On an emotional level, though, Capricorn Mum can seem rather remote to the more sensitive Cancer. She tries hard to conform to the image of a perfect loving mother, yet her affection level isn't high, however strong her bond with her child. Capricorn has great difficulty in showing warmth.

Cancer needs as much emotional closeness as she can get. She's very dependent on Mum and Capricorn must try to be as open and demonstratively loving as she can. Little Cancer's confidence needs building up gradually, with plenty of hugs and reassurance.

Don't tease her too much – she takes everything to heart. And don't criticise too harshly when she fails to meet your high standards of achievement. Cancer will be crushed and mortified. Never underestimate the amount of encouragement she needs, and lighten difficult situations with the gentle humour that Cancer appreciates.

Capricorn wants Cancer to grow into a solid, respectable citizen just like herself. But it's vital to allow Cancer room to develop her dreamy, intuitive side, her creativity, and her artistic and musical gifts. Capricorn will be rewarded as she sees her child's blossoming talents.

Mum is glad that Cancer is so home- and family-loving. Capricorn too thinks that home is the lynchpin of life, and both will stick up for the family fiercely against any attack. Capricorn can help Cancer to find direction in her life, but she must watch that she does not force her to follow a path that is not of her own choosing.

Gentle guidance is the rule where Cancer is concerned. Capricorn mustn't be too controlling, or try to push Cancer to grow up before she is ready. She must be allowed time to rest and recharge her batteries. If Mum accepts that Cancer sees life through far more emotional eyes than she does, and lets her be herself, they'll both be happy.

Cancer child with a Capricorn father

Hard-working Capricorn father admires his little Cancer child's determination. She always sticks at something once she's set her heart on it. And being ambitious himself, Dad sees this as an excellent quality.

Cancer thinks Dad's aura of cool control is impressive – he really knows how to get to the top. But he doesn't seem to understand her emotional outlook on life. He simply doesn't feel things as deeply as she does, and thinks she wastes a lot of time getting bogged down by her emotions.

Dad must learn to warm up around Cancer and be more open and encouraging. It's easy for him to dominate a quieter, more sensitive soul like Cancer, and he must be aware of his responsibility to draw her out, build up her confidence and help her to achieve the things he knows she's capable of. In turn, she will help Dad to develop his sense of humour and warmth in response to her affectionate and playful ways.

Although Cancer enjoys gentle discipline and routine, she'll be upset by harsh tellings off and high expectations. Sometimes Dad will have to accept the fact that she's bent the truth a little. Capricorn wants his child to be completely honest, while Cancer sees the truth as something more fluid.

Dad can give Cancer a boost and help her confidence by paying her for the chores she so willingly does. She also needs a hobby like art or music to help her to express all those complicated emotions in a positive and inspiring way.

If she doesn't have some way of expressing herself, or if she fails to receive the love she needs, Cancer can become snappy, withdrawing into her own world. She may even give up trying to be herself at all if Capricorn ever crushes her emotional nature. It is vital that she is allowed to be the person she is, if she is to develop strength and resilience. Dad must take care not to issue warnings to her all the time.

She's cautious enough as it is and needs Dad to believe in her.

Usually, though, she'll be delighted with her protective Dad. And Capricorn will be pleased to see how caring she is, and be glad that she doesn't want to fly the nest too soon. She'll encourage him to try to be more flexible and kind – he can learn a lot from his imaginative and intuitive child.

Cancer child with an Aquarius mother

Sociable Aquarius Mum loves to take her Cancer child out to see friends. She tries her best to expand her youngster's mind and to make her more socially aware, all of which does Cancer good.

But Mum must never forget that Cancer's a homebird at heart. She's not the type to grow up fast and should not be pushed to be independent before she's ready. Aquarius may find her clingy, hiding behind Mum's skirts when meeting new people. She needs lots of support from her mum before she's ready to embark on anything new. Give her time!

Aquarius likes Cancer's sensitive, intuitive and caring nature. Yet she has to make a big effort to offer the heart-level affection that Cancer needs. Aquarius is a logical and rational thinker, who likes to be involved in social issues and world-changing campaigns. She doesn't want to be slowed down by complicated emotional demands.

Yet Cancer lives life through her emotions. They colour everything she does, and strong emotional connections are as vital as air to her. Aquarius must try to understand the nature of her child and provide affection, play, listening and time to help her feel secure.

Mum is a great believer in universal love and understanding. It's harder for her to apply her theories on a personal level, but she must for Cancer's sake. Any cool criticisms can knock her sensitive youngster for six, and set her sulking for hours. Aquarius won't understand what all the fuss is about and will wish that Cancer was more logical. In fact, all Cancer probably needs is reassurance that she's still loved.

Mum must try to create some sort of routine for Cancer, even though it's not in her nature. She is more likely to be off chairing a meeting when Cancer wants her tea! And Aquarius mustn't condemn Cancer as self-centred when she shows no interest in Mum's campaigns. She'll just have to accept that she works on a broader scale, while Cancer is busy on the cosy home front caring for her dolls, the cat – and Mum.

Aquarius is excellent at giving children room to develop naturally, without imposing too many demands on them. With Cancer, Mum needs to remember to show her every day just how much she cares.

Cancer child with an Aquarius father

Unconventional Aquarius Dad seems full of surprises to staid little Cancer. He'll suddenly decide on a trip out or start acting the clown – and she'll wonder what's coming next. Yet despite his fun outlook, Aquarius can be moody and get that faraway look in his eyes just as often as Cancer does.

In fact, these two have got quite a lot in common. They've both got very caring natures, except that Dad always seems to be caring about helping other people, while Cancer wants him to care only for her! She finds Dad fair-minded when it comes to rules, because he takes the time to explain why they are necessary. As long as she understands, she'll be content.

Dad gets exasperated with Cancer when she's snappy. He wants her to fit in with people when she grows up, the way he does, but he fears she's far too crabby and emotional. He also wants her to broaden her outlook and learn to question government and other decision-makers and to work things out for herself. Yet she doesn't naturally think in these terms, preferring to base her life on Mum and home. Learning to think in this way may well help her later, so she should be prepared to try.

Aquarius Dad is often more up to date than his Cancer

child. She will always prefer what's tried and tested, but Dad is an innovator who thrives on exciting new ideas.

Sometimes Dad will retreat off into his own world, losing interest in the childish things that keep young Cancer busy. This will worry her, for even though she has a similar need for retreat, she wants to know that Dad is always there when she needs him. It will be better for all concerned if Dad can show more of the affectionate side of his nature with his Cancer child, as this will give her reassurance that she's loved and secure, and will stop her feeling rejected when Dad wants time to himself.

Aquarius broadens Cancer's mind with books and conversation, explaining what's happening in the world in terms she can understand. Dad will do best at this when he relates issues to people's emotions. As long as he remembers that Cancer's world is one of feelings, he can find a way of communicating that will really get through to her.

Cancer child with a Pisces mother

These two get on well, for Pisces offers boundless love and affection and Cancer feels snug, secure and wanted. Pisces in turn is glad to have a child who is not too aggressive, returns the love she gives and thinks in the same intuitive, imaginative and responsive way as herself.

Their strong bond and emotional affinity helps to boost Cancer, but Mum is unlikely to offer the sort of routine that Cancer thrives on. Pisces avoids structuring her life too much, preferring to be open to new opportunities that come along, so she may not have created the reliable home base that, ideally, Cancer likes best.

Mum doesn't plan ahead much, which can leave Cancer feeling all at sea. When she doubts her stability, Cancer can become moody – but Mum is also prone to moods when feeling wound up, so both should take care. There could be quite a blow-up if they coincide!

However, their closeness will see them through almost anything. Both are emotional water element types, which means they have strong intuitions and can sense when the other is feeling down or hurt. Both take on the pain of each other, so they'll each need time to retreat and recharge, to find themselves again when they've absorbed more than they can cope with.

The result is that Mum can seem a bit distant as she retreats inwards to rebalance herself, which Cancer may not understand. And Cancer will feel cross when dreamy Mum tells half-truths or changes her mind too often – although Mum would accuse Cancer of doing the same thing.

Pisces spends ages playing with Cancer and happily organises days out, painting sessions and musical mornings. But she may be too much of a softie and not firm enough with discipline, allowing her children to take advantage of her. Even sensitive Cancer must know Mum's limits if she is not to grow up selfish and demanding.

Cancer is a worrier and so is Mum, although Pisces is a good listener and can draw out Cancer's secret worries. What Cancer needs is to feel that Mum believes in her, which will help her gain confidence. Cancer will give Mum the love she wants in return for all her efforts. And this affectionate child will go on showing how much she cares.

Cancer child with a Pisces father

Pisces Dad loves to spoil his Cancer child. He'll grant her any wish, buy her all the toys he can, give her endless love and support. The result will be that Cancer feels more secure with Pisces than with most others.

These two are on the same emotional wavelength, but although Dad understands the way little Cancer is swirled around by her emotions, he can find it hard to keep a check on his own. He tries to repress them, but they have a habit of welling up and putting him in a bad mood. He can be just as snappy as Cancer, and both will end up sulking.

Dad will love little Cancer's intuitive ways, her closeness to home and family, her protectiveness and her caring attitude to all those she loves. He feels he understands her, and he's excellent at inspiring her to develop her imaginative and creative side. He's impressed by her ability to stick at things and understands her need for rest and quiet times.

Pisces must take care when Cancer's around not to show the worry he sometimes feels. Any excuse and she'll start feeling anxious herself. Instead, Dad should show her what faith he has in her abilities. That way, she'll feel buoyed up and able to take on more than she ever thought she could.

Sometimes Dad forgets promises he's made, which bothers Cancer. He's rather dreamy and doesn't always remember what he's said. He finds her defensiveness irritating – the way she puts up the shutters and scuttles off if she feels under attack, making snappy little remarks as she goes. He'll find her changing moods hard to deal with sometimes, too. He doesn't like bother and wishes she wasn't such a cry-baby.

Dad is great at channelling Cancer's strong emotions into creative outlets. He'll broaden her mind, sympathise with her and adore her. And she'll return his love with all her heart.

LEO
Stars for Life

STAR BABY

Leo likes to start as he (or she*) means to go on – as the centre of attention – and this born charmer does it with his dazzling smiles, spontaneous affection and lucky, plucky character.

He's an individual from the word go, with a yell that sets him apart from the rest because it's so loud! Patience isn't something baby Leos are born with, as the parent who keeps him waiting for his food or his fun will discover. He'll soon let you know he wasn't born to wait.

If your eardrums can stand it, try not to jump every time little Leo shouts, or all too soon you'll find yourself a slave to his every whim. At some point, he has to realise that the whole world doesn't revolve around him – although some Leos never get the message!

Unusually alert, curious and active, baby Leo loves being jogged up and down on Daddy's knee. His concentration levels are high, too, so he'll happily spend half an hour trying to put the lid back on a plastic teapot or examining every tiny part of a fascinating pine cone. He needs constant stimulation and company – he's certainly not one of those babies who'll happily lie in his pram and gurgle the day away!

Leo's inborn love of life means he may be reluctant to leave it at night, so sleep problems could crop up. Stick to a calm, regular routine and always be loving but firm, and little Leo will eventually manage to let go. However bold and

*'He' is used to cover he and she for Leo child.

independent he seems, he still likes to know his life's securely protected by a set of safety rules.

Older baby Leo needs lots of space to roll and wriggle around, with a toy box handy so he can choose what he wants to play with. To avoid later tantrums, start giving him some say in his life now, from choosing which teddy to take to bed to feeding himself – even if it is a messy business!

Never forget that under that confident exterior beats an insecure little heart that needs the constant reassurance that you will always be there and always love him. So make time in every all-action day just to cuddle your little Leo quietly and tell him he's the greatest!

FIRST STEPS FOR LEO

All the world's a stage to toddling Leo, with you and everyone else his willing audience! Whatever he gets up to, he'll keep checking just to make sure he has everyone's undivided attention. He'll clown around and shamelessly applaud himself for every new stunt or antic.

Generous and golden-hearted, little Leo loves company and loathes being left alone, even for just a few moments, so take him with you wherever you go. He'll thrive on being out and about, meeting new people and exploring new places, as long as he knows you are there to kiss him better when he falls. Busy and brave, if Leo does take a tumble he'll be up and at it again in no time. No setback floors his determination for long, and he's a natural at cheering others up. But never take him for granted!

Praise is like oxygen to little Leo – he can't survive without it. But it has to be sincere and from the heart. False flattery may make him do what you want the first few times, but if he finds out it's fake, he'll never forgive you. And he'll have trouble believing anything else you later tell him as well!

Frustration at wanting to tackle everything in the world at once can lead to spectacular Leo tantrums around the two-year-old mark. And like everything else in his life, he won't do them by halves! Smooth his path by giving him as many choices and as few rigid rules as possible, and when a rage does erupt, either leave him alone to work it off or try to laugh him out of it. Leo never sulks or bears a grudge, and once the bad mood's passed he'll be back to his smiling self.

Leo will use his vivid imagination to make life match up to his magical vision of it. He'll act out fantasies with guess-who as the star, tell you incredible stories and probably have an imaginary friend who adores him (of course). Before he gets too carried away, let him see that the plain, unvarnished truth will always be enough for you.

More than anything else, Leo needs his independence. Never bundle him into the buggy if he can walk under his own steam, and encourage plenty of physical exercise to use up his energy. Sociable and charming, he'll adore a playgroup or nursery and soon have all the other children organised to play the game he wants. And he'll thrive on outdoor play, splashing in the paddling pool or rolling downhill in the park. Fearless and strong, Leo is a sporting natural, so take him swimming early and let him tumble around at a baby gym.

As he grows older, Leo's main problem may be covering up minor hurts and worries until they become too much to cope with. Encourage him to tell you when something's wrong, and show him you don't love him any less just because he's not perfect all the time. Leo sets himself impossible standards, so just make sure you don't do the same!

SCHOOL RULES FOR LEO

Friendly, confident and kind, when Leo gets to school he'll probably be teacher's pet, as his try-anything nature and sunny disposition make him irresistible to all. But he could annoy other mums, because his basic need to be biggest and best makes him push classmates out of the way in a bid to be first out of the school gate or at the head of the dinner queue. The major lesson to learn here is never to undermine

Leo's dignity by telling him off in front of his friends – a few quiet words at home should do the trick. After all, he can't help being born a leader, not a follower!

Leo will need a few gentle pointers on how to behave at home or he'll be forever trying to take over, butting in on your conversations in his haste to make sure he's heard. Firm handling, plus a set time each day when he can talk to you to his heart's content, should help. But once he sees that good manners, combined with his natural charm, can get him even more of his own way, he'll be Mr Politeness himself!

Rebellion and a natural aversion to strict orders may make Leo seem out of control at times. The answer isn't to try to crush his fighting spirit, which could leave him sad and insecure, perhaps taking the wrong life path in search of the acceptance he so craves. Remember, however naughty he seems, Leo secretly longs to please you. The trick is making him do what you want, but making him believe he's doing just what he likes!

Always an individual, he hates to be seen as part of the crowd, and will set himself apart from others at school. He loves the limelight, starring in the school play or reading his latest story aloud, and can be overbearingly bossy until it's pointed out to him that the best leaders get other people on their side, rather than simply lording it over them.

Knocks and setbacks are inevitable, but Leo will bounce back with a smile if he is helped to find security within himself rather than seeking it from others.

TEENAGE TAKE-OFF FOR LEO

Testing, testing, testing – that's Leo when he hits his teens, still torn between his need to be loved and his equally powerful need to be in charge of his own life. And what a life! The centre of attraction at any after-school party, racing heart-first into all sorts of unsuitable romances, Leo's easy charm and warmth make him much in demand and he falls hook, line and sinker for the attractions of the opposite sex.

Needless to say, his schoolwork can suffer! That's because he throws his whole self into one major project at a time, abandoning half-finished homework if something – or someone! – more interesting comes his way. Appealing to his natural desire to be best can get results, but he also needs constant (but well-disguised, of course!) guidance so he doesn't rush work and get sloppy. It's in any parent's interest to keep Leo's nose to the grindstone at school. You're the ones who'll suffer when those exam results don't match up to what he expected, and he's overcome by shame and spends months mooching around the house.

As in all things, it's better to get Leo's cooperation than try to work against him. Setting curfews and restricting his free time will only make Leo more determined to escape. So aim for a balance of work and play, but without letting young Leo feel he has the upper hand at home. Otherwise he'll treat you like his personal slave, snapping his fingers to be picked up from sports practice or slumping in front of the TV expecting a silver-service supper!

Teenage Leo's likely to be part of an amateur dramatics group, and even offstage he'll be surrounded by an adoring crowd of fans lapping up his words of wisdom and laughing helplessly at his jokes.

He'll be supersensitive about his appearance, constantly checking himself in mirrors and shop windows. Often demanding, sometimes downright infuriating, but never dull, by 16 he'll have his own definite opinions on the world, and won't be afraid to voice them! If he does rebel, he won't do it by halves, yet his basic, brash bravado and magnetic personality mean Leo never loses his special place in your heart. Who else could make you feel so lucky to be a parent?

STAR PARENTS

Leo child with an Aries mother

These two are firebirds of a feather. Both share a bright and confident outlook, admiring each other for being so enthusiastic, effective and full of warmth and life. Mum's delighted that Leo likes to be in on the action and is determined to make his mark, though it's always Aries who'll leap in first. She's slightly faster off the starting block when it comes to turning ideas into reality. Leo's right behind her, but needs a little nudge to get going sometimes. He isn't quite as wildly spontaneous and pioneering as his brave Aries mum.

Leo knows he's got nothing to prove anyway. He has an innate aura of superiority about him, and even proud Aries is expected to pay homage to him. Mum will keep Leo happy with adoring words and looks, spending time answering his questions and holding back any criticism. That way Leo junior will behave more like a purring pussycat and less like the angry lion he can be without his daily dose of love, affection – and worship.

Mum may think she's best at everything, but young Leo will want his turn at being best too. Mum should praise him for his latest bright idea, but always make sure her kind words are sincere. Leo is easily flattered by praise and laps it up. In fact, she can get him to do almost anything by heaping on the compliments. But if she doesn't mean them, Leo will eventually realise and feel betrayed. So careful how you phrase things, Mum, and don't try to manipulate Leo too much.

This pair both see the vulnerable centre behind each other's show of bravado. Leo knows Mum isn't quite as brave as she makes out, and that she needs the support of others to stay on top. Aries sees that her roaring Leo is actually as tame as a tabby under the surface, with a tender heart that's easily hurt.

Both can reassure the other that there's someone there who'll always love them. They give each other the courage to carry on facing the world with their own special brand of honesty, directness and optimism.

Leo child with an Aries father

Aries Dad wants his child to be effective and successful, just like he is, and in Leo he's got a child he can pin a lot of his hopes on. Leo is outgoing, tough, driven to be first at school and the centre of attention in class. He may be slightly less of an adventurer than Dad, yet he's got that fire sign spirit, and Dad loves him all the more for it.

Both are up to date and love new ideas, believing that life is to be enjoyed, not fretted over or wasted. Sporty Dad will be delighted to have Leo to play football with in the park and slope off to cricket matches with – although Leo may not be quite as keen as Dad, having a stronger love of his home comforts and slightly less of a need to be always on the go.

Leo takes an expansive view of the world and is thrilled to have a dad who shares it. These two are out to have fun, and no-one's going to stop them. Dad thinks up wonderful trips, taking time out from his hectic work and social schedule to treat Leo to a day at the zoo, a boat ride, a visit to the safari park. With Dad, the day becomes a real adventure – one to add to Leo's other lively memories of childhood.

Dad's a fast-fire thinker and speaker, a little ahead of his slightly more thoughtful child. But Leo always insists on being heard too, and both of them are most put out if anyone else gets in the way of them running the show. Between them they've got enough drive and energy to achieve whatever they want. They can work well as a team as long as no-one comes along and tries to crush their excitement, or they don't start competing with each other and insisting on having their own way instead of cooperating. They will always need someone to handle details for them. These two think big and often can't see those all-important minor points.

From Leo, Aries Dad will learn that it can be enjoyable to give warmth and help to others, instead of always thinking of himself, and that life shouldn't just be a bid to get to the top. Warm-hearted Leo shows him to stop and think of the needs of others.

Aries can tend to be an absent father, too busy to care for his children properly. But with Leo there's so much fun to be had that Dad won't want to miss out on a minute more of his upbringing than he has to.

Leo child with a Taurus mother

Placid, cuddly Taurus Mum loves her friendly little Leo, though his imperious commands can drive her up the wall sometimes. She doesn't really mind acting like a servant to this regal youngster and patiently lets him get away with all sorts of things. But there does come a point when she feels pushed too far and will call a halt to being at his beck and call.

It's just as well she does put her foot down sometimes, otherwise Leo could grow up thinking people are only there to serve him. With Taurus, he'll learn to be more considerate and grow up feeling loved and secure in the cosy home she has created. Both these two like to indulge themselves, and they'll share a love of good food and little luxuries.

Mum must make sure that active Leo is stretched. Taurus tends to be on the lazy side, while creative Leo needs to be stimulated if he is to achieve his potential. So stir yourself, Mum, and take him on some educational outings. He's the busy type who needs his freedom, so don't stifle him with love and homelife, either. Push him to succeed – he thrives on encouragement.

Try to encourage his dreamy tendencies, for that's when he thinks up his best ideas. To Taurus, dreaming can seem a real waste of time. She's so down to earth she has no time for big ideas and schemes. Yet here's a child who needs to be free to let his imagination roam.

Help him if he shows an interest in art, writing or playing a musical instrument. These are creative outlets that will help him to express his true self. It's no good Mum expecting him to be a solid, sensible type like her. It's through his creativity that he becomes wise and Mum must accept that everyone has their own special way of making sense of life.

Leo can find Taurus' traditional home rather limiting as he grows, and he may accuse Mum of being old-fashioned during his rebellious teenage years. Yet she will have taught him to find stability within himself, and will have encouraged his integrity and thoughtfulness towards others. Taurus will feel pleased with her generous-hearted child and especially loves the special little presents he hands her. No-one else could give in such a warming and delightful way.

Leo child with a Taurus father

Steady Taurus father enjoys spending cash on his luxury-loving young Leo. These two will relish shopping sprees and material-minded Dad will make sure Leo is bought every comfort for his room. They both enjoy owning things.

Both love their comfortable home. Taurus makes sure it's warm, secure, and run to a regular routine. It's here that Leo is taught Dad's common-sense attitudes, conventional behaviour and how to become a moral and upstanding citizen. Sometimes, fire child Leo will want to break out of all this order and sensible living. Taurus must remember to leave him space to breathe, and try to avoid putting him down for being so full of ideas and energy.

Dad will find it hard to keep up with his Leo child and may be extra strict at times to mask his irritation at not being able to cope. He thinks Leo can be a bit too much of an attention grabber, a show-off who doesn't seem to understand the serious side of life.

Taurus has a far less light-filled outlook than his child. He is prone to spells of gloom and pessimism that drive Leo to distraction. This child has no time at all for gloom mongers and will do his best to jolly Dad out of his mood. Filled with optimism and a belief in himself, Leo thinks life is to be lived, not moped over.

Stern Dad may seem a toughie on the surface, but he's keen to help his child in any way he can, and will listen to his problems and give advice. Yet it's hard for him to be in tune with a child's mind, because his outlook is so much more responsible. He's often tickled by Leo's capers, though, and gives Leo presents that make him the envy of his friends.

Dad will teach Leo some valuable lessons in patience and turning his ideas into reality. He'll also teach his open and honest little Leo not to be so trusting with strangers, as well as how to reach his goal once he's really set his heart on something.

Leo child with a Gemini mother

This bright pair are full of ideas. Buzzing with energy, they'll be the life and soul of any playgroup, the jolliest combination at the school fete and the holders of the best children's parties in town. Gemini loves to socialise and will invite hordes of mums and tots round to keep her and Leo company. Of course, Leo loves this – as long as Gemini lets him be the centre of attention, shining out from the crowd as the radiant young host.

Fast-talking Mum sets Leo's head spinning with her endless plans and bright schemes. Leo loves people who enjoy words and ideas, but it's hard even for a fire type like himself to keep up with Mercury-ruled Mum. She can make words twist and turn, outsmarting her youngster with her verbal skills.

Sometimes she'll praise little Leo to the skies because she knows that's the best way to get him to do what she wants. But she'd better watch out! Leo may lap it all up, believing every word of it, but the day will come when he realises she was just manipulating him with her word power and he'll feel shocked and let down.

Gemini enjoys being the person she is, just as much as Leo takes delight in being the warm little individual he is. Gemini is one of the liveliest of mothers, always coming up with bright ideas for days out, fun games and sporting events. Leo needs to be kept busy, and he certainly will be with his Gemini mum. His stay-at-home side will soon be taken over by the full-of-fun playfulness she encourages. She'll constantly present him with new things to do and his childhood will be filled with excitement.

It is important that Gemini Mum finds some excitement of her own, too, for Geminis can too easily take over their children's lives. Mum should join an evening class, and keep her active mind as busy as possible. Leo enjoys his freedom, so she must be careful not to hem him in and remember that he likes to be the one in charge. Gemini will always give in to him, won over by his warmth, generosity and positive nature. Leo will enjoy Mum's enthusiasm and hectic energy in this lucky combination.

Leo child with a Gemini father

Up-to-date Gemini Dad is often way ahead of Leo when it comes to the latest trends. He certainly can't accuse Dad of being behind the times. He's light and bright, playful and fun, and Leo loves him because he's never a bore.

Just sometimes Leo wishes Dad would be a little more responsible and reliable. Leo is never completely sure he can bank on his changeable, fast-moving father to do everything he says he's going to do. Dad must try to make any schemes involving Leo match up to his big words. If they don't, though, Dad can reassure himself that Leo will forgive him. Leo likes people who aim high, and doesn't mind if they fail sometimes.

Dad does love to tease, and poor Leo, who takes words at face value, will feel mortified when he realises Gemini has made him look silly. Leo is proud and this is just the sort of thing that can undermine his confidence, which isn't as strong as it seems.

Gemini has a habit of insisting that he knows best when it comes to doing something. Leo will object as he has a strong drive to change anything he comes across for what he sees as the better. He certainly won't welcome Dad's know-all advice on how he should tackle his latest project. Gemini must leave it to Leo – he usually gets it right in the end.

These two have a great time discussing ideas. They'll happily talk late into the evening, although Dad does have an unfortunate tendency to suddenly find childish conversation boring. Then he'll walk off and leave Leo wondering what he's done wrong. And sometimes, too, Dad will turn bossy or critical – merely because he wants to prove he's in control.

Better for Dad to stick at what he's good at – encouraging Leo's creativity, his enthusiasm and generosity, his ability to dream and think up wonderful ideas. That way everyone will be happy.

Leo child with a Cancer mother

Loving Cancer Mum ladles out affection and will certainly make little Leo feel loved and wanted. She has to watch that she doesn't overdo it with this fire child, though. He loves his freedom and needs room to breathe. Leo won't be happy if he feels overprotected. He craves excitement, stimulation, brilliant ideas, laughter and fun. And he won't have much sympathy for his worrying mother, either.

Leo is usually outgoing, bouncy and bright, so he's not naturally drawn to the cosy, comforting, closeness Mum hopes for with her children. He'd prefer her to be a launch pad for his latest adventure, and will get frustrated when she tries to hold him back, even if it is for his own good. There are going to have to be a few compromises between these two.

Cancer Mum must arrange for her energetic fireball of a child to have his daily dose of excitement. Start with playgroup and move on to playgrounds, days out, seaside holidays and river trips, which will also appeal to Cancer's love of water. Once Mum has found something that she enjoys doing, she'll pass on her enthusiasm to receptive Leo and they'll have a great time together.

Cancer is a reserved homebird who centres her life on her family and her cosy nest. Leo likes his home, too, so he'll benefit from the comfy environment she creates, as well as from her good home cooking. He'll certainly be back for more after that traumatic (for Mum) day when he finally does fly the nest.

Leo thinks Mum worries too much, sticks to what she

knows for safety and frets about what other people think of her. She's so different from her confident offspring, who's sure everyone approves of him and positively brims with enthusiasm. Mum must watch that she doesn't dampen his spirit. Better to encourage and admire him for his bravery and brilliance.

If Cancer shows her Leo child that he's the brightest star in her universe, he'll burst with pride, for Leo thrives on being worshipped. She must look delighted when she's on the receiving end of that Leo generosity, even if she is only being offered a daisy. Mum will be touched by little Leo's sweetness, and he'll feel good about himself for having made Mum happy.

Leo child with a Cancer father

Cancer tries extra hard to be a good dad. He's prepared to make sacrifices to see his Leo child has only the best, and this suits Leo as he values quality. Dad's quite prepared to help Leo follow his wide range of interests too, ferrying him around in the car to classes and soccer matches. But poor Dad hasn't got Leo's energy, so he'll end up worn out.

When Dad gets tired he can turn snappy. He's actually a very emotional man, but he likes to hide the fact. He pushes down his feelings, only to be unable to fight them off when they bubble back up causing grumpy moods and cross remarks. He expects everyone else to accept that that's the way he is and still treat him as boss at home.

Proud Leo may not stand for Dad's moods and will tell him so to his face. There could be confrontations as Leo makes his presence felt. Nobody orders him around, unless they've done something extra special to win his respect.

Cancer is a traditional soul who likes what's tried and tested. He hasn't much time for Leo's love of anything new, or the child's excitement at bright ideas. Cancer wants Leo to act conventionally too, but Leo has an eccentric streak and may shock with his choice of clothes, friends and ways of expressing himself.

Leo is creative, adventurous and pioneering, even if he does still enjoy his home comforts. Dad should be glad that he treats his house well. He'll have to accept that Leo's got more zest for life than he has. He must never crush that bouncy joyfulness, for although Leo will become quiet if beaten down, he'll get his revenge in the end.

Leo is far more of a risk-taker than Cancer. To Leo, thrills and excitement are the spice of life, and he can't understand why Dad doesn't enjoy a challenge the way he does. If Cancer is honest, he admires his child's confidence and bravery, and mustn't put him down for it. In return, Leo will give Dad the benefit of his dazzling warmth, making his father feel he's more than got his money's worth for the time and cash he's gladly invested in him.

Leo child with a Leo mother

This vibrant pair like to make their presence felt. It will start with a grand entrance at playgroup, and they'll go on to steal the limelight at school sports day, probably with Mum's amazing hat and little Leo's time in the 100 metres. They both want to be the centre of attention, the shining stars in any crowd.

Problems can arise if Mum won't let little Leo have his turn in the spotlight. She usually gets round it by soaking up the reflected glory when Leo junior does well. And she'll make sure he's as much of a success as he can be. Here's a mum who pushes her children to do their utmost, and won't take kindly to failure. Leo is expected to get top marks and excel in every subject. And most likely he will, for this is a child who's strongly driven from within to be best.

Yet Mum must be careful not to push too hard. Leo hates to be ordered around and will one day rebel if every aspect of his life seems to be under her control. Yet he will have benefited from Mum's ability to keep him busy and supplied with bright new ideas. Creative Leos need stretching if they're not to become lazy.

Mum understands her youngster's need for admiration

and knows just how to heap on the praise. She'll get praise back, too, for he knows how to make her feel appreciated for being such a caring mum. Both truly admire each other's warmth and generosity. This outgoing, magnetic, lovable pair give out warmth to others too, spreading exuberance wherever they go. Everyone likes to have Leos around.

That's as long as they're not being too bossy! Neither will want to take any orders from the other and there could be deadlock if Mum gets fed up with little Leo's imperious commands and tells him to tone it down a bit. Cross words will follow from this fiery pair, and neither will want to apologise, slinking off instead in a huffy silence. It'll take some time before they're back to their warm, sunny selves again. Mum can speed up the thaw by relenting and giving little Leo a cuddle.

Most of the time Mum and child feel a sense of mutual trust, openness and friendship. They like being together and light up each other's lives as only sun-ruled people know how.

Leo child with a Leo father

Leo Dad has a rival for boss of the house in his Leo child. For Leo junior likes to take charge just as much as his father does, and will have his parents scurrying around to carry out his whims at an early age. Leo is the most imperious sign of the zodiac, and it's obvious from the start.

Leo Dad is the ideal role model for young Leo. This father loves being the focus of attention, the centre of any social gathering, leader at work and a matchless parent. He demands to be respected and admired. And young Leo will have nothing but admiration for him, hoping to grow up just like him. He'll make Dad feel really special and perfect. But Dad must beware, for although he may lap it all up now, one day the cracks will show and young Leo could feel disillusioned when he realises that Dad's only human after all.

For now, Dad provides all the fun, energy and inspiration young Leo could ask for. Dad likes to get the most out of life, living it on the grandest scale he can afford with treats and surprises to fill young Leo's life. Even on a shoestring, Leo Dad will manage to create an atmosphere of abundance and enjoyment.

Dad is delighted to have such a bright-minded child who shares his outlook. They enjoy each other's generosity and warmth and would defend each other to the end. Young Leo feels particularly grateful for his dad's strength and protectiveness – these two will take on the world together, given half the chance.

Little Leo thinks it's a real laugh when Dad dresses wildly or acts flamboyantly. Leos don't know the meaning of the word embarrassment and adore making grand gestures and turning on the theatrics. They will amuse each other endlessly, as long as Dad allows his child to have his turn in the limelight and doesn't try to steal the glory all the time.

Young Leo is delighted by his dad's optimism, and inspired by the way he always seems to believe in his own abilities. No obstacle is too great for Leo Dad to overcome. This pair will always make the time to share ideas, jokes and jolly games, for they are not only father and child but friends for life.

Leo child with a Virgo mother

Virgo Mum is stunned at the liveliness of her Leo youngster. He's always on the go, rushing here and there, while she trails behind trying to keep up with him. He's bursting with ideas and schemes and always wants to be at the centre of things. All rather different from Mum, who's shy, modest, practical and sees the flaws in young Leo's big plans.

It's better if Mum can keep her criticisms to herself, even though she's usually just trying to be helpful when she voices them. Leo thrives on being fun, boisterous and full of hot air. There's really not much point in pricking his latest bubble, for a deflated little Leo is a sorry sight. Better to let him have his fun. Leos are meant to live life on a larger scale than anyone else.

It will be hard for Mum not to keep harping on about minor points. She should try, though, for proud Leo needs praise, encouragement, warmth, affection and approval. Don't knock his haughty ways – his sense of pride is more fragile than it looks, and it's essential to him that it remains intact.

Mum is not a great cuddler, preferring to sort out the chores rather than attend to emotional needs. Yet Leo loves nothing better than a good snuggle, and Mum will enjoy it too, if she lets herself.

Leo can be an imperious little person, demanding drinks, sandwiches and clean clothes at the double. He thinks he's a little prince, and Mum's tendency to want to serve others makes her liable to end up being his resentful doormat. So Mum must put her foot down sometimes and tell him to stop being so bossy. It'll do him good in the long run, as there's a risk he could grow up taking everyone for granted.

Call on his generosity instead. He's warm-hearted and kind and doesn't want to hurt anyone. And Mum admires him for this, for it's rather like Virgo's drive to be of service. Virgo actually admires Leo's rather superior ways, though she hates to admit it. Deep down she'd love to be able to order people around without offending them, the way Leo somehow manages to. When he tells his classmates what to do, they all fall in with a smile on their faces. Mum will bask in the knowledge that he's going to be somebody big some day.

Leo child with a Virgo father

Sensible Virgo father sees his role as lion tamer when confronted with his ultra-active little Leo, bursting with energy and ideas. Virgo thinks it all needs directing, and Dad's just the sort of person who can help his child to channel his efforts into real achievements and encourage him to take up worthwhile interests.

Virgo must watch that he doesn't hem Leo in. He fears that all Leo's spontaneity will wreck the orderly routine of his home and so tries too hard to calm the child down. Better to allow Leo some measured freedom to express himself, for he'll feel frustrated if he's expected to be good all the time.

Yet the good manners and standards of behaviour that Virgo does teach will set Leo up for life. They will counterbalance his selfishness in thinking everyone else is just there to serve him. Virgo Dad will expect him to help with the chores, not leave it all up to Mum. And he'll be very cross if messy Leo doesn't clear up after him.

All Virgo wants is the best for his child. He'll work hard to give him everything he needs to further his education. He'll teach money sense, which Leo could benefit from learning, and he'll show Leo practical ways in which he can turn his clever ideas into reality. Dad has a lot to teach Leo about living in the real world.

Unfortunately, Dad will react badly to Leo's teenage rebellion, when he acts eccentrically and flounces off at the first sign of discipline. Virgo is concerned to keep order in his home and won't stand for Leo's imperious behaviour, so sparks are bound to fly.

Yet Dad will be of great help to Leo when it's time to sit those important mid-teen exams. Virgo will show him how to apply himself to study, how to finish one thing at a time and do things properly instead of rushing at them. Leo should pass with flying colours, thanks to Dad's advice.

Leo child with a Libra mother

Sociable Libra Mum creates just the right environment for friendly Leo. She's got lots of friends, which provides him with an instant audience. Leo loves to show off, and as Mum is keen to take him to see people as often as possible, he'll be able to bask in their appreciation to his heart's content. People rarely get tired of seeing little Leo. He seems to shine so radiantly they forgive him for wanting to grab the attention all the time.

Libra knows how to make Leo feel he's the most special child in the world. She praises him for being so good-hearted, and he laps up every word, glowing with warmth at the compliments. In return, he'll make Mum feel appreciated for being a super softie too. This pair really do admire each other!

Bouncy Leo rarely feels down, though Mum will see he's soon cheered up when he does. Libra tends to be far moodier and Leo will force her to snap out of any hint of gloom, for he has no time for dwelling on things. Leo thinks life should be lived to the full, with not a second wasted. His energy and positive attitude will soon cheer her up.

This Mum likes lovely things and doesn't mind spending her money to make sure Leo has a comfortable room, fashionable clothes and all the books and toys he needs. Leo loves all this as he feels he deserves to live in style! Mum must be careful not to indulge him too much, though, or he'll expect the best all the time, which could get expensive. Libra's so soft-hearted, she's easily bullied by forceful Leo into doing what he wants.

Leo's generosity will more than make up for his shortcomings. These two love sharing ideas and dreams, are optimistic and think life is to be enjoyed. Mum will give Leo the freedom to be spontaneous, creative, warm and funny, and she'll teach him some common sense too. They really make a great combination indeed.

Leo child with a Libra father

Libra Dad wants children to be proud of, especially when they're at a social gathering. He's very keen on creating the image of the perfect family and wants his children to behave impeccably at all times. In Leo he has a child who'll be admired by all for his bright sociability, his magnetism and warmth. Sometimes he'll slip up when it comes to manners though, cutting in and speaking out of turn. And his dress sense can be a bit eccentric, to say the least. But in the main he'll be a credit to his dad.

Most Libra fathers are home-lovers who put their family first. But there are those who are very self- and career-centred and neglect their duties on the home front. Leo will find it hard if Dad is always away, as he really does need lots of attention. His sense of self-worth needs encouragement in those early years by parents who help him to build up a sense of pride in himself.

Leo will be particularly hurt if Dad is critical of him. Leo will get his own back in the end, often using underhand means to do so. It's much better to fill his young head with praise. It won't do him any harm, and even if he gets big-headed he's got enough charm to carry it off without offending anyone.

Libra encourages Leo to be independent and to act responsibly. This child is destined to be a good organiser and the earlier he gets the chance to start taking care of things, the better. Let him have a kitten perhaps. He'll love being responsible for feeding it. Libra also introduces Leo to the world of culture and to a love of beautiful things, lessons that will last him a lifetime.

Leo is more fiery than Libra and will happily launch into an argument, while Dad does his best to avoid one, resorting to logic, which only makes Leo crosser. Sulky Leo will slink off if he loses and it will be up to Dad to restore balance and harmony – one thing he is particularly good at doing. Libra must be careful not to hide any family problems from Leo too often. He's more grown-up than he looks and prefers to know what's going on.

Most of the time Leo will keep his father entertained and amused. Libra enjoys his child for his assertiveness, effectiveness, warmth and energy. Leo admires the way his dad can sort out differences between people, and thinks his taste is wonderful!

Leo child with a Scorpio mother

These two are powerfully linked and love each other dearly. But they have some spectacular rows sometimes, for they are both strong signs who like to be in control. Mum, particularly, insists on being in charge of everything Leo does, and that's very hard for him. He's a natural organiser who has his own special ways of doing things, and he hates it when Mum pushes in and takes over, and all his efforts look like being spoiled.

Their huge rows will involve much stamping of feet and angry shouting. Both will march off in a huff and refuse to speak to each other for some time, but once they eventually make up they'll be the best of friends again. Mum can try to avoid these rows by holding back her urge to control. Leo is a commanding child who hates being told what to do all the time. Mum must respect his pride and let him have some say over the way he runs his life.

Scorpio tends to push her children – with the best will in the world, of course. She wants them to do well, to do all the things she never managed to, and Leo won't let her down. He is driven to succeed, to prove that he's the best, and he benefits from her encouragement when it comes to his interests and studies.

He could be stubborn, though, if pushed too far, and simply stop what he's doing so well. Then Mum must go easy on telling him what to do. He's a warm, generous and clever child – all he asks is that he's allowed to be himself.

Leo will be delighted that Mum has the energy to keep up with him. They both live life at speed, yet they also share a love of home and Leo will benefit from the order, stability and security Scorpio provides. She will expect him to act conventionally and thoughtfully around the house, so at times she will find his spontaneous enthusiasms and occasional laziness hard to deal with.

She'll be proud of Leo's creativity and the way he obviously believes in himself. She'll try to teach him not to be quite so trusting, telling him it's better to hold back like she does and keep some things about yourself hidden. But being such a radiant soul, he'll only half listen.

This powerful pair give each other love and strong support and know they can always rely on each other.

Leo child with a Scorpio father

Proud Scorpio Dad is delighted to have a little livewire like Leo to carry on the family line. He's full of admiration at the way Leo stands up for himself and says what he thinks. And he's proud that his child always ends up near the top of the class. Leo's a bright little sparkler, a real chip off the old block.

Both live life energetically, intensely – and both want to be acknowledged as being in charge. Leo seems to get support from others far more easily than Dad does when he takes command, which peeves Scorpio. How is it the whole family seem happy to do what Leo wants, while they usually resist Dad's suggestions, he wonders.

It would be wrong if Dad reacted by trying to beat Leo down. He'd only succeed in hurting his pride, and one day Leo would get his own back on Dad for denting his confidence so badly. There's no point in resenting Leo for being proud and strong. It's all part of his charm.

Scorpio Dad can be inflexible, convinced he knows the best way to do things, while Leo loves the freedom to go about tasks in a new or different way. Dad must respect that Leo is a person in his own right who, within limits, must be given the chance to run free. Dad's way may suit him, but Leo needs the space to experiment and find his own special style.

Leo likes Dad's lively way of thinking, the interest he takes in the world about him, and his effectiveness. They'll have some lively discussions together and Scorpio will broaden his child's mind. He teaches him attitudes that will help him make money and succeed in the real world. Scorpio admires his child's outgoing nature and thinks he's destined for big things.

He does feel that Leo neglects detail and can be lazy sometimes. He wants to drive him on to achieve his full potential, but it must be done gently for Leo to derive any benefit.

Leo child with Sagittarius mother

This bright, buzzy pair really like each other's company. Mum is a good teacher for her clever little Leo and keeps his active mind on the move. Leo's at his best when stretched and busy, and Mum enjoys answering all his questions and joining in his games. She's still a child at heart and loves any excuse to play.

Yet she's not so good at the serious side of life. Responsibilities bore her – she'd much rather be out having fun than doing the chores. Leo's glad she's so full of life and – being a self-sufficient creature – can cope with her lack of organisation. In fact, he organises her instead! He has to admit she outshines him sometimes with her humour, confidence and positive outlook. He does love his home comforts and Mum is forever dragging him out – just sometimes he'd prefer to stay in.

Both Leo and Sagittarius are cheery optimists who don't have much time for moaners. There are times, though, when Mum feels let down by the world, and Leo will have to learn that it's not him that's at fault when she loses her bounce for a while. Mum must remember to reassure him on these occasions, as his apparently strong sense of self is easily deflated. He's likely to take it on himself to cheer Mum up, something he'll manage in no time at all.

Leo loves new ideas, but not in the over-enthusiastic way Sagittarius does. Leo draws comfort from things he knows and loves, while Sagittarius enjoys launching off into the unknown. She'll teach Leo the joys of travel, with days out and holidays abroad.

Leo loves Mum for her flair, imagination, integrity and honesty. Yet there are times when she's too honest for his taste. She feels compelled to tell the truth, and will say that she thinks he looks spotty just when he's off on his first date. Proud Leo is cut to the quick by her blunt words. Yet she does him good, too, by knocking him down a peg or two. As long as she does it with humour, it won't hurt him too much.

When Mum does say something extra-nice, Leo can be

sure she means it and will be touched. Yes, there will be rows between this fiery mum and child. But they will be forgotten in the hours of fun and the many happy times that Leo will look back on and treasure.

Leo child with a Sagittarius father

Sagittarius father is a friendly fireball of energy, always full of bright ideas for things to do, games to play, places to go. Leo adores him for being so full of life and colour, and Sagittarius can't help but admire his child's knack of getting on so well with other people. Everyone seems to want to know his little Leo, while Sagittarius' foot-in-the-mouth ways tend to make people steer clear of him sometimes.

When Sagittarius does say something by mistake that upsets his child, Leo will go off in a huff. Neither will want to apologise, but eventually Dad will give in and they'll be the best of friends again. Nothing keeps these two cross with each other for long.

Dad wants his child to do well and to make the most of any chances that come along. Leo loves to prove he's the best at anything he tackles and will make Dad very proud. But this father's lack of concern with practical matters may mean he doesn't spend enough time with his child. Sagittarius likes the idea of children rather more than the hard slog involved in bringing them up and may opt out from time to time.

Luckily Leo is a strong character who believes in himself and can cope without too much practical back-up, even at an early age. Yet it's vital that Sagittarius does what he can to develop Leo's confidence, and takes care not to put him down. Leo needs building up if he's to become the self-reliant and powerful person he can be. He could interpret lack of concern as rejection, so Dad must do his best to take his responsibilities seriously.

These two will enjoy sitting down and sharing ideas, fantasising their time away with bigger and better dreams together. Neither is very interested in details – instead they'll stoke each other's enthusiasms and have a fine time planning their latest scheme. Both are realistic enough to know it's only fun, and that not many of their ideas will ever actually get off the drawing board.

Leo is impressed at the way his dad seems to know so much and can talk in such an interesting way. And he likes the way Dad copes with change, always looking on the positive side. Dad is glad that his little Leo is just as generous, original and open as himself. Here is a pair who really do complement each other.

Leo child with a Capricorn mother

Practical Capricorn Mum admires her little dreamer Leo. There's not a lot that makes Capricorn laugh, but Leo can bring a big smile to her face with his amusing antics and outgoing personality.

She thinks he's a daring, brave child and sometimes wishes she had his courage. Leo loves Mum for always being there, for being like a rock, someone he can rely on. Capricorn is thrilled to have a child with such an optimistic outlook, belief in himself and vivid imagination. Usually unwilling to be a servant to anyone, Mum doesn't mind treating little Leo like a prince and carrying out his every whim. His charm will win her over, even from the cradle.

As Leo grows, Capricorn will find it hard to understand how Leo manages to do so well, and win so many friends, without apparently trying. Capricorn is always telling her child not to be lazy. Yet Leo seems to have it all without lifting a little finger. He's a mystery to her, this radiant sun-ruled child, who attracts people and success like a magnet.

Yet there's no sense in Capricorn resenting Leo for being the centre of attraction. It's his natural state, and if he's knocked for it, his pride could be damaged. Mum mustn't try to compete, or be too tough on him either. While Leo benefits from the security of knowing what's expected of him, he'll feel trapped if he's not free to express himself.

This child needs to be allowed to act on the spur of the

moment, follow his enthusiasms, explore and discover the world in his own individual way. Capricorn tries to stop him taking risks, and wishes he would act like everyone else instead of being so unconventional. She thinks that if you conform, others will accept you, and fears that Leo will lose out in life if he steps out of line. What she doesn't realise is that people will always accept Leo for his warmth, generosity and sense of fun.

All he needs is the space to be himself, to be acknowledged as someone special and allowed to be leader sometimes. In return he'll bring happiness and sunshine into cool Capricorn's life, enriching it in a way no-one else can.

Leo child with a Capricorn father

Forceful Capricorn Dad is a sensible person who wants to pass his down-to-earth attitudes on to his children, and he enjoys the satisfaction of knowing he's been listened to.

Yet Leo is not a child who'll be told. He'll listen, yes, but inside Leo knows he has his own special way of handling things and that everything usually turns out for the best if he's left to get on and do it his way. So while he may seem insolent to Dad by ignoring his advice, Leo is simply following his own inner voice. Capricorn mustn't chastise him for it. Instead, learn to appreciate this creative, intelligent youngster.

While Leo feels pride in himself, Capricorn feels proud to be surrounded by expensive things that show the world just how well he's doing. Leo loves little luxuries too and shares his Dad's enjoyment of quality. Capricorn will also feel pride in having a child like Leo, who is driven to do well at school.

There's no point in Dad pushing Leo too hard to follow a path that he's mapped out. It's important to Leo that his motivation comes from within, and he's not one to be cajoled into doing well. Capricorn can help by appealing to his pride and dignity – why let anybody else outdo him? Once Leo takes that message to heart, there's no stopping him.

Capricorn mustn't expect Leo to uphold all his traditional views and values either. He's a little trail-blazer, bursting with creative ideas and a need to change things for the better. Dad must have faith that Leo may one day come round to his way of thinking. For now, let him be his flamboyant, theatrical and appealing little self. Do otherwise and he'll feel as if he's in a straitjacket.

Capricorn wishes he had more of Leo's sunshine. Ruled by chilly Saturn, it's hard for Dad to match his child's warmth. Yet he must try to offer affection to little Leo. The child loves cuddles, which reassure him of his worth and boost his confidence. Leos thrive if treated in this way, but can be difficult and rude if not treated properly. Dad's common sense will help him handle Leo for the best.

Leo child with an Aquarius mother

Leo is delighted that Mum lets him get on with his life without too much interference. He knows how he wants things done and hates it if people keep butting in and telling him to do it their way. Aquarius loves it when she sees Leo dreaming up his own ways of tackling situations. To her, it's important that children learn to become independent early.

Aquarius can find Leo rather self-centred and thinks he needs teaching to care more about others. To Aquarius it's important to direct your efforts towards the benefit of the group or unit you belong to, not entirely towards yourself. Leo follows his own whims and likes to be free to make spontaneous choices of his own.

If he's in a group, he likes to be at the very centre of it. And though he enjoys throwing himself into fun hobbies, the social and political issues Mum supports are unlikely to hold much appeal for him – that's unless he can lead the campaign, and there's not much hope of that with his banner-waving, idealistic mum around.

Best if Mum encourages Leo to pursue his own interests, which he will, for Leo loves to keep busy and he'll have all sorts of hobbies. He can become lazy if he's not being stretched, so Mum will be pleased to see him applying his mind and will help him all she can.

She hasn't much time for his attention-seeking ways, and will pull Leo away from the centre of the party if she thinks he's showing off. She believes in equality, which can clash with Leo's desire to be first and best. Yet this drive to shine is central to sun-ruled Leo's personality. If Mum crushes it, she'll end up with a dull child who could become even more imperious and selfish to get revenge for what's been done to him.

This pair love nothing better than talking together. Aquarius admires Leo for his creative thinking and enjoys his warmth and loyalty. And Leo loves his Mum's excitement at new ideas, her fairness and generosity. She will calmly cope with his teenage rebellions and he'll emerge a balanced adult with a deep respect and admiration for his Aquarius mother.

Leo child with an Aquarius father

Aquarius Dad is full of energy and new ideas that he loves sharing with his little Leo. Dad finds Leo honest, open and friendly, a fine little friend to take on jaunts or to one of those social gatherings he loves so much. Leo shines in a crowd and Dad will feel proud of him, as long as he doesn't hog all the limelight.

Dad enjoys talking with Leo, discussing everything under the sun until it's way past the child's bedtime. Both are forward-looking, kind, protective – and love springing wild surprises on each other. Dad is full of zany schemes that make Leo look quite conservative in comparison. This father loves to be different from everyone else and, while Leo will enjoy his originality, there are times when he wishes Dad would act like other fathers.

Leo is good at turning words into action, something that Dad admires, for although Aquarius is brilliant at thinking up ideas, he's less hot on making them work. Leo spurs him on to achieve his dreams. Sometimes, Dad does find his offspring too bossy, for Leo loves to take control and issue commands. Dad's sense of fair play won't stand for this and he'll soon knock his child down a peg or two.

Dad introduces Leo to the world of books, culture and politics. He involves himself in group campaigns and loves to get a debate going. Leo is altogether more frivolous and bent on enjoying himself. His way of making the world a better place is to spread warmth and enthusiasm, joy and laughter. He thinks Dad could get more fun out of life if he wasn't so set on changing the world.

Aquarius' home is a bit on the clinical side for Leo. Dad lines the walls with books, and wouldn't even think of buying comfy chairs or the cosy sofa Leo loves to curl up on. Aquarius would think it extravagant, yet extravagance is one of the great joys of little Leo's life.

Dad will love seeing his bright and clever child develop. And Leo will be thankful that ultimately he was allowed to grow at his own pace, in his own way, without any real interference. Dad will have taught him to cope with life and to make wise choices.

Leo child with a Pisces mother

Soft and emotional Pisces Mum needs to summon all her energy to cope with her bossy little fire child. Leo loves to order her about, organise her and tell her what she should and shouldn't do. Placid Mum doesn't usually mind, unless she's feeling really harassed. Then she'll snap back and put him firmly in his place.

Mum loves Leo's happy outlook, his warmth and generosity, his optimism and strong personality. This little powerhouse lends her the energy to sort out her own life. She's unlikely to have built much order into her lifestyle, but with Leo around she sees the necessity and is fired to create a comfortable home and a routine that will keep him occupied.

She'll forgive him anything because he's such a charmer, and she's a big softie for his affectionate hugs and kisses. All Pisces wants is to be loved by her children.

Pisces teaches Leo to tread a little more softly through life, to avoid saying things that hurt, to use his imagination and to awaken his creative talents. She's an arty type and will have him painting and cutting out shapes as soon as he can hold brush and scissors.

Sometimes she'll feel knocked for six by the way he rushes around the house, issuing orders and making a commotion. Leo isn't happy unless he's getting attention and making things happen, and there are days when Pisces simply wants some peace and quiet and can't cope with his loudness and brash enthusiasm. Then it's best if she can persuade Dad to take Leo out for a walk to work off that surplus energy, while she has a rest.

Pisces needs to learn to be firmer with Leo, otherwise he could grow up to be a real bossy boots, expecting everyone to serve him and do his bidding. It's vital that she teaches him that other people have needs that must be respected.

Yet as the years go by she'll develop a deep sense of understanding with her Leo. As a teenager, he can be a little tyrant and she'll have to work hard to avoid major clashes. Once those days are past however it will be plain sailing and these two will be close for life.

Leo child with a Pisces father

Pisces Dad tries hard to keep his swirling emotions well under control. But there are days when young Leo drives him mad with his boisterous energy and his self-centred ways. Then Dad will really blow his top and Leo will end up sulking. Yet it will have done Leo good to show him that there are limits to his behaviour.

This busy child likes to push things to extremes and sensitive Pisces finds him hard to keep in check. It's best if Dad can try to use measured firmness instead of losing his temper. Sensible discipline is what's needed, yet it's tricky for Pisces to be firm on a regular basis. One minute he'll be indulging his child and letting him get away with riotous behaviour, the next coming down on him for a lesser crime.

This Dad isn't the sort to create a regular routine, either. He has little order in his own life, preferring to be free to follow the latest opportunity that comes along. He hates feeling too tied down. Leo would like a little more routine and normality in his life than Pisces Dad provides. He may be a creative fire child who loves his freedom, but he's also a homebird who loves the cosy feeling of comfort he gets from knowing he's safe and secure in his warm, reliable home.

Leo's not keen on the way Dad is always changing his mind, either, following new projects and leaving things unfinished, forgetting promises he's made. He does enjoy his father's ability to play, to chat and to dream with him. Pisces teaches Leo to take more notice of the world around him, to delight in nature as they go on walks. Dad seems able to open Leo's eyes and ears, and to help him translate what he's seen into clever, artistic creations.

Pisces envies the dramatic and daring way his little Leo lives life, wishing he had his courage. And because Leo is so affectionate, Pisces will forgive him his domineering ways. But Leo must try to tread gently with his sensitive father, and Pisces should remember to show his appreciation of Leo's unique personality more often. That way they will enjoy a happy relationship.

VIRGO
Stars for Life

STAR BABY

Virgo will only reward you with her (or his*) gentle, heart-melting smile when she's quite sure she can trust you to feed her and change her on time. She's a baby who'll need plenty of affection too, and extra reassurance that you love her just the way she is.

It's the first signal that she's a child who'll only thrive with endless encouragement and sweet words. It will never go to her head, as young Virgo rarely feels confident about herself. Instead she'll take the tiniest criticism very much to heart, and need all the praise you can give just to keep that sweet smile on her face. And although baby Virgo will rarely make the first move for a cuddle, physical closeness also helps her self-confidence develop. But keep it gentle – no rough and tumble stuff for this little lady!

She may have an extra share of digestive problems and feeding can take longer than with other star signs. She just needs time to get used to life in the big wide world. If you don't sort out her needs fast, she'll get in a state, screaming the place down. But once changed and tucked up comfortably again, she'll be as good as gold.

FIRST STEPS FOR VIRGO

Virgo turns into a busy explorer who hates staying in one place for too long. But she can be wary about wandering far, as she worries about having an accident or being told off for doing something naughty. Encouragement keeps her on the

*'She' is used to cover he and she for Virgo child.

straight and narrow much better than warnings and tellings-off which cut too deep, though you will have to issue them sometimes.

Virgo will be early to talk and will want you to name every object she points at with her demanding finger. You're going to need patience! Best of all she enjoys being lifted up on your knee and cuddled while you look at a colourful storybook together. She loves animal stories, although fairy-tales don't appeal much to this down-to-earth child.

Building blocks and alphabet shapes keep Virgo happy, and she'll soon be sorting her cuddly toys into neat rows, pretending she's teacher. She'll adore kittens and puppies, often preferring them to people. If you do eventually decide to buy her a pet, you need have no fears about her looking after it properly.

Toilet training usually goes smoothly, unless finicky Virgo gets it into her head that it's embarrassing. Take your time with her, explain that she'd be more comfortable out of nappies. She'll soon take your point and she's always eager to please and to do well. But don't get cross about the occasional failure – it will set her back.

Virgo will be forever asking you questions. It's the start of a lifelong habit, for Virgo wants to find out how everything works and make sense of her world. She needs to feel she's understood everything and has it labelled in her mind. She will either be very tidy, or the complete opposite, but even the untidy sort has a place for everything, although no-one else can make head or tail of the mess in her bedroom.

Virgo loves to help her mum and will enjoy putting away shopping or hanging up clothes when she's old enough. Of course, she can sometimes be more of a hindrance than a help, but don't be tempted to put her off. She wants you to love her and think she's perfect, and helping you is one way she tries to win your approval. But be fair about it. She'll feel resentful if you tell her to do the chores while little sister or big brother is allowed to sit with their feet up watching the TV. Allow her plenty of time to play, and encourage her to take time off from being helpful. She needs to know she deserves to have fun – Virgo can think that work is all she's cut out for.

Virgo may seem quite capable of coping with life, but she'll still be thrown by big upheavals, especially if a new baby arrives. She won't sleep well and will become nervous and edgy as she tries to assess what her new role will be. She needs to share these worries – otherwise they will fester into a resentful panic.

Virgo often prefers to play quietly with a few like-minded pals rather than chasing around with a big gang. She enjoys time alone playing games that exercise her brain. But when she's quiet she'll start thinking and may well fall into the Virgo trap of worrying that she's not as perfect as she thinks others expect her to be.

Do reassure her that people love her just as she is – she desperately needs to feel she has your acceptance. And if you do have to tell her off, remind her she's still your favourite girl. It's so easy for her to feel rejected.

SCHOOL RULES FOR VIRGO

Virgo may find the hurly-burly of school hard going at first, until she discovers that her bright mind puts her ahead of most of the class. But she'll dread even the smallest telling-off, building it up in her mind till she can think of nothing else. The worry may give her nervous tummy aches or sickness, or she may stop working as hard. Ask her always to tell you if anything's on her mind.

Try to find ways to help Virgo to stand up for herself and believe in herself. There's every reason why she should, but it's hard for her to accept this. Explain to her exactly what is and what is not expected of her and that it's normal to fail sometimes. Give her plenty of praise when she does do something well, and make it a rule to watch for the signs that she's worrying and find ways to reassure her.

Unfortunately, when Virgo gets too relaxed and sure of herself, she can become a bit too critical, turning her sharp mind away from her own failings and on to those of others. Watch out for that cutting Virgo tongue. It can be unkind, even in one so young, and can alienate people. Remember that Virgo will always be harder on herself than on anyone else, so don't get too cross with her. She's not a spiteful child.

She is very critical about food, with strict limits on what she will eat. However hard, try not to make an issue of it – this phase will pass, and quarrels could give her digestive problems.

TEENAGE TAKE-OFF FOR VIRGO

As she gets older, Virgo is forever changing. One minute she's an awkward complainer, the next sweet as pie. You can never be quite sure where you stand with her, which is enough to drive even the most patient of parents and relatives to distraction. But often these wild swings are just as baffling to young Virgo herself, so there's no point in lecturing her. Just remember she's well-meaning and unassuming underneath and can't help her contrary ups and downs. Try humour on her. She's usually quick to see the funny side of any situation.

Teenage Virgo wants everything to be right in her world and can get very pessimistic if things go wrong. She needs reassurance that setbacks are natural and that life's like that for everyone.

She can be very self-contained at this stage, backing away from more extrovert schoolfriends and finding fault with them. It's more likely that she secretly admires their flamboyance and wishes she had more of her own.

She's unlikely to be a rebellious teenager, or to race after the opposite sex in a hurry. Instead she can retreat into her own world too much, perhaps studying too hard. Remind her how people value her bright mind, her subtle sense of fun, her hard work and her thoughtful, helpful nature. Tell her that she's special and, above all, that you love her very much.

Virgo child with an Aries mother

Young Virgo can't believe how energetic her Aries mum is, the speed at which she gets things done and how she always seems to know how to make everything turn out right.

Virgo likes to keep busy, but doesn't even try to go at Mum's pace. She prefers to think out the details of what she's going to do and make sure she's chosen the right way of doing it. Aries does something the moment it comes into her mind, and never considers things might go wrong, the way young Virgo does.

Virgo child wishes she was as forceful and direct as her powerful mother, but realises that's not her way of doing things. She'd like to stop worrying, too – Mum never seems to worry much about anything. There are times, though, when Virgo is sure she knows a better way than the spur-of-the-moment methods Mum uses. Aries may agree that her clever child has some bright ideas, but she wishes she'd live more for today instead of always fretting about tomorrow.

Aries is keen to encourage Virgo's interests, although there's a danger she'll either take them over or get so caught up in her own busy world that Virgo will be left behind. These two are best when they've got a project to work on together, like making a birthday surprise for Dad or a costume for the school play. Mum's very up to date and will often be well ahead of conservative Virgo in her thinking.

Mum will put pressure on Virgo to succeed, to be as effective as she is, to do all the things she wishes she had done. This is pressure Virgo could do without as she feels unsettled by demands on her to become independent before she's ready. Aries wants her to be responsible for herself, outspoken and assertive. Virgo prefers to act within fixed limits, know just what is expected of her and follow her own slower path, the one she's sure of. Too much pushing to be bold and outgoing can make her feel self-critical and insecure. She'll never be an aggressive go-getter like mum.

Virgo's critical nature can activate that famous Aries temper, although it will all be over in a flash. Aries basically does everything for herself and she can't fathom the way Virgo wants to help others all the time, instead of promoting herself. Yet she can't help but admire Virgo for it, and Virgo benefits from the energy, strength and enthusiasm she gets from her mum.

Virgo child with an Aries father

Aries father is in a rush to be a dad – just to prove he can do it – so it's likely he'll be young and full of energy when Virgo is born. Dad's very sporty and overwhelmingly full of life, while she's gentler, prefers quiet pursuits and tends to get tired easily. Despite their differences, Dad will encourage her to have fun and make the most of every day, to stop worrying and get on and do things rather than holding back from even trying.

Many Aries fathers spend a lot of time away from the family, busy with work, socialising or playing a sport. Virgo would like Dad to be at home more because she loves the cosy feeling of the whole family being together, with everything in its place. When he is at home, Dad goes in for spontaneous bursts of play and affection which amuse Virgo, yet make her feel uneasy. She prefers a comfortable routine and likes to know what's around the next corner.

Aries can be irritable and snap at Virgo when she suggests a better way of doing something and she'll take his sharp words deeply to heart. Virgo needs lots of encouragement and love if her confidence is to develop. Aries believes in treating his children quite roughly to toughen them up and make them ready to cope with the harsh world. He thinks emotions are for sissies, while little Virgo longs for cuddles and kind words. She hates it when she's expected to join in the family rough and tumble.

Dad is very competitive, too, which Virgo certainly isn't. He wants her to do well, to prove she's worthy of his pride in her, but his pushing can make her miserable. She needs gentle handling and Dad's acceptance that she's a busy worker bee and will never be the queen.

Aries is a natural leader and it can take some time for him to realise that Virgo prefers to be a follower. His encouragement, if properly handled, will help her to fulfil her potential, as Virgos tend to underestimate themselves. If Dad can show her she's worth a lot more than she thinks she is, the sky's the limit!

Virgo can seem a prim little soul to expansive Aries, but he admires her bright mind and enjoys answering her curious questions. She's a good conversationalist and forward at reading and writing so she'll do well at school and Aries, who wants children he can be proud of, will be thrilled.

Virgo child with a Taurus mother

These two are as comfy as an old pullover. Mum and child enjoy all that's solid and sensible and would never get carried away with big ideas. They're both much too practical. Virgo likes nothing better than being at home, with Mum in the kitchen cooking up something delicious while she is neatly setting the places at the table.

Taurus is delighted that Virgo is such a homebody, someone who really appreciates her comfortable surroundings. Home is very close to the heart of Taurus and, within her four walls, Mum will give all the love and security sensitive Virgo could want, understanding her unspoken need for stability and reassurance.

She's such a good little scholar, too, scoring top marks in reading and writing. She may not push herself forward the way some other signs might, but Taurus is quite content to let Virgo take life at her own pace, accepting her just the way she is.

Taurus has all the patience in the world for Virgo's endless curious questions. The child's perky, friendly ways make Taurus feel warm and glowing inside. But she will be wounded more than she shows when Virgo turns her critical powers on her mum. Taurus will be distraught if she feels all her efforts are not being appreciated, but she should be comforted by the fact that Virgo is always most critical of herself. There's really no point in getting too het up with her – it's reassurance that Virgo needs more than anything else.

Taurus is good at showing Virgo just what's expected of her, and it makes Virgo feel so much more confident if she knows exactly where she stands. In fact, Virgo puts herself down far too much, but sturdy Taurus will bolster up her sense of self-worth. Taurus praises her for her hard-working ways – this child is far more of a busy bee than her rather lazy mum – but she can get so caught up in the details of life that it will take Mum to unravel her.

There will be rows because Taurus is sometimes too obstinate to see Virgo's viewpoint. And Taurus, who thinks her child is her own personal property, will be devastated when Virgo suddenly grows up and flies the nest.

But Mum can rest assured that Virgo will never forget the love and kindness she received at home and will be a regular visitor.

Virgo child with a Taurus father

Virgo knows she can rely on her steady and solid Taurus dad. She appreciates how hard he works to keep her well dressed and well fed, for this generous dad wants only the best for his loving little Virgo. He's so glad she shares the same conventional values that he holds so dear, and that she loves the happy home he's put so much effort into creating and the good things in life he's worked hard to achieve.

This dad always thinks hard before he does something. And he's convinced that his way is the best. He'll mull it over when Virgo suggests a more effective course of action and, if she turns out to be right, he'll give her a pat on the back for her cleverness. But if Virgo starts to argue or criticise, Dad will get very uptight and insist she sees things his way. He hates any sort of rebellion and can become overly strict, which will give sensitive Virgo a shock. She can't cope with heavy-handed treatment – it knocks her confidence for six. Taurus' normal gentle discipline suits her perfectly and Dad should strive to keep to it.

Young Virgo is a real busy bee who can't sit still, compared to her slower-moving, somewhat lazy father. But he'll be happy to take Virgo on fun days out in the country-side, for they both enjoy nature and wildlife, as well as craft work. Taurus is delighted that his little Virgo is always so nice and neat, and that she's good with money and ever helpful when it comes to chores. She's almost perfect in Dad's eyes.

Some Taurus fathers are away from their families too much in their quest for wealth. And when they do come home, laden with gifts, they expect to buy their way back into their children's affections. Virgo would much prefer Dad to be there regularly in her day-to-day life than to be absent and then attempt to bribe her with sweets or toys.

Being an earth sign, Virgo thrives on stability and loving attention, recognition and approval. Many Taurus fathers have a strong, protective streak and give Virgo the care she needs. In return, Virgo gives Taurus what he needs – admiration and appreciation that will make him feel he's the best dad in the world.

Virgo child with a Gemini mother

These two may love and understand each other, but there will be arguments. They're both full of Mercury energy and spend endless hours discussing and analysing everything they do. Both are critical and the rows will arise when they turn their needle-sharp wit on each other. Gemini Mum will always win for she is faster with words than Virgo, who is better when she communicates in writing.

Gemini's words spill out before she's had time to think and she's usually criticising the way Virgo is doing some-thing. Virgo could retaliate in the same way to Mum, and often does, but inside she's very hurt for she takes harsh words more to heart than most other signs.

Gemini is moody and changeable, and can be distant sometimes, too, which confuses and upsets Virgo, who takes everything personally. Gemini must make more use of her vivid sense of humour to help defuse potentially upsetting situations.

Still, if they can avoid criticising each other, Virgo and Gemini will have lots of fun together. Mum is very active and dreams up all sorts of wonderful things to do. She'll join Virgo in the swimming pool or take up the flute alongside her, with the aim of encouraging Virgo. Trouble is, Mum will get so involved in their shared hobbies that Virgo may feel Mum's taking over and she's being squeezed out. It's important that Gemini develops her own interests and leaves her child space to find and enjoy her own interests.

Gemini is very sociable and encourages shy Virgo to make more friends than she otherwise would. Mum is delighted that Virgo is so bright and asks so many interesting questions. Being a good communicator, Virgo is excellent at reading and writing and responds well to Mum's pre-school lessons. Gemini will enjoy having a child who loves words as much as she does, even if Mum prefers speaking them. In fact, Gemini can be so busy bringing out Virgo's mental abilities, she sometimes forgets the child's emotional needs. She should spare time for cuddles, listening and reassurance, too.

This whizzy mum is way ahead when it come to trends and new ideas, leaving more conventional Virgo behind at times. Virgo is neat and reserved and loves looking into the detail of things. Gemini is more interested in talking about new ideas and information and doesn't much care about the mechanics of them. These two intrigue and stimulate each other and if Virgo turns out to be a writer, she may well have her mum to thank.

Virgo child with a Gemini father

This dad is so up to date Virgo finds it hard to keep pace with him. He's always the first to hear new ideas and tells

Virgo excitedly what's going on in the world. He'll be disappointed when she doesn't immediately share his fascination, but she prefers to get the full picture, down to the last detail, before she can get excited about anything.

If he criticises her for it, she'll be very upset. Virgo's criticisms may bounce off Gemini, but cutting comments from Gemini will give Virgo's confidence a hard knock. Mind you, they enjoy criticising other people together!

Dad loves seeing Virgo's clever little mind develop, but he's easily bored by children and Virgo can take this as his rejection of her. Gemini's at his best when they share a hobby – even if it's just reading, walking or watching the television together. Then he's got time to explain the ideas he loves in more detail. Virgo will be stimulated by all this and encouraged to be more outgoing.

The atmosphere at home won't be quite as secure as Virgo would like, and Virgo won't be as lively as Gemini would like, but there will be a lot of understanding between them. Virgo will grow up with a much wider vision of the world, and with well-developed powers of communication, thanks to Dad.

Gemini is often very caught up in his own work and social life and may not have as much time for Virgo as she would like. It's important that he gives her the warmth and reassurance she needs when he's about. His energy tends to come in bursts and Virgo will forgive him when he flags and wants to go on to something else. As long as she has his company and attention, she'll be happy.

Sometimes Gemini Dad uses his skill with words to play verbal games with innocent Virgo. She hates this as she's an earth child who needs to know exactly where she stands and what people are up to. She dreads having to deal with Dad's joke words that baffle her practical, straightforward young mind.

Yet she thinks it's marvellous that Dad has such a quick understanding of things and would love to be able to think up brilliant replies to people the way he always does. She's going to have to face the fact that even though her brain works pretty fast, she's never going to reach the speed of her quicksilver Gemini dad.

Virgo child with a Cancer mother

Virgo feels snug as a bug under the wings of protective Cancer, who is everything she thinks a mother should be. Virgo particularly benefits from Cancer's caring ways because she needs so much reassurance and praise to beat the self-critical streak that dogs her. Cancer Mum can make her feel warmly loved, valued and secure.

But Cancer can worry so much about her child that her anxiety is transferred to Virgo. She is also very possessive and doesn't encourage young Virgo to seek independence. In fact, Virgo is a slow developer who'd rather be at home than anywhere else so she's quite happy with Mum, although she could sometimes use a little push to be more adventurous.

Cancer wants her children to have a good all-round education and she'll encourage out-of-school activities, which will meet Virgo's need to be busy. Unlike most people, Virgo is good at getting Mum talking and their conversations will bring them very close.

Cancer will encourage Virgo to use her imagination and intuition, which will help develop her often strong talent for writing. Both seem to bring out the best in each other, though on rare occasions an argument will blow up. Then Virgo will usually get the better of Cancer, for she's much faster with words – especially cutting ones.

Both like to serve others. Virgo prefers to be of service to a group or cause, while Cancer likes to devote herself to one person. Virgo will be delighted if it's her who's the focus of Cancer's warmth and love, for she thrives on Mum's comforting support. But Cancer must remember that Virgo needs contact with other people, too. Once a balance is achieved, Virgo will show all the appreciation Cancer needs. She'll bring her troubles and secrets to her, as well as all her joys.

Cancer is pleased that Virgo helps around the house and that she appreciates the comfortable home Mum has created. In fact, Virgo may live at home for longer than is really good for either of them. But when she does finally leave, she'll do it gently and make the break as easy as possible for Cancer, who hates to let go.

Virgo child with a Cancer father

These two are a pair of hard workers who get so involved in a project, whether it's weeding the garden or building a boat, that they'll forget all about tea unless Mum repeatedly reminds them it's time to eat. In fact, they're both so hooked on hard work, it's good if someone does remind them that life's about relaxing and having fun, too. All work and no play makes Cancer and Virgo a bit dull, even if they do get a perverse sort of pleasure out of it.

Cancer Dad works hard to see his children have everything they need, that they are taken to all their clubs and swimming lessons and that they have a cosy home to live in. All this is especially important for Virgo as she needs security more than anything else.

Both love mulling over the past – they could hardly be called forward looking. A box of old photographs from Dad's childhood will keep this pair engrossed for hours. Both enjoy being at home, though Cancer will make sure Virgo gets plenty of fresh air, probably with regular trips to the seaside as he loves water.

Touchy Cancer can be crabby when he's tired, which upsets sensitive Virgo. She takes any telling-off far too seriously. Likewise, Dad will be hurt when Virgo criticises him, though she'll be less harsh on Cancer than on most. Importantly, Dad understands her tendency to turn that critical streak on herself and comforts her when her world looks bleak.

Often Cancer is a retiring sort of person who finds Virgo's slightly livelier outlook on life exciting and stimulating. He's not as chatty as she is and his moodiness can puzzle rational

Virgo. But Cancer can help Virgo come to terms with the emotional side of life, while Virgo helps Cancer relate better to the down-to-earth matters that everyone has to face.

Above all, Virgo loves knowing that her Cancer dad really cares for her. She honestly believes she could ask for nothing more.

Virgo child with a Leo mother

Generous Leo lavishes love and understanding on young Virgo. She gives tremendous confidence and back-up to this rather shy child, teaching her how to make friends, have fun, be brave and do well.

Leo sees her children as an extension of herself, and if she has any thwarted dreams she may well try to get Virgo to fulfil them for her. In doing so, she could put too much pressure on Virgo to succeed.

Virgo has a very different personality from her mum. Leo seeks the limelight, while Virgo prefers the shade. Leo is eccentric and flamboyant, and conventional Virgo just wants to hide when Mum starts showing off.

Leo can threaten to outshine her child, and if she does try to live out her dreams through Virgo, there could be trouble ahead. Leo will take it personally if Virgo doesn't come up to her high expectations, and poor Virgo expects so much of herself that, if Mum criticises her, she'll be mortified. It's far better if Leo leaves her to discover her own path through life, her own hobbies and strengths. Of course, any encouragement Leo can give will be greatly appreciated, but it must never be heavy-handed.

Leo must sit down and listen to her child, acknowledge her opinions and not be a know-all. This child has a curious mind and will enjoy exploring places with Mum, discovering details of an area's past and wandering round historical buildings.

Mum can encourage Virgo to channel her tense, active energy into a range of interests. Her positive personality will help Virgo to stop worrying and underestimating herself and to get on with life, discovering what she's capable of. Leo enjoys Virgo's talkative ways and is usually very proud of her, for Virgo is likely to be a high achiever at school as she works so hard and takes her studies seriously.

Leo teaches her to be more generous and less tightfisted. And the deep love bond Leo has with her child will teach Virgo to value herself more than she ever thought possible.

Virgo child with a Leo father

Sun-ruled Leo fathers radiate love and warmth and young Virgo enjoys basking in this glowing presence. She adores her big strong dad, who seems to know the answer to everything and can protect her come what may.

Leo certainly has a very soft spot for his young Virgo, even if he thinks her busy little outlook is rather narrow compared to his grand view of life. And despite her love for him, Virgo thinks Dad is a slapdash big thinker with no eye for detail. Yet these two share a deep understanding, making each other feel extra special.

Dad loves to be the centre of attention and laps up the adoration Virgo pours on him. She's thrilled by his dramatic flourishes and frivolous, eccentric ways. Despite being so prim and proper herself, she thinks it's wonderful to have that confidence and belief in yourself.

It's vital to Leo that his children succeed, proving what a wonderful father he is to produce such clever offspring. Virgo will certainly work hard, but tends to underestimate her own abilities. Leo will try his best to build her up with good advice and help to stop her worrying, but if she really is happiest in the background of life, Leo will be disappointed and show it. Virgo takes criticism so seriously she can be completely floored by it. Dad must not have unrealistic expectations of her. He can certainly push her, but he must know when to stop and remember to praise her to the skies every time she does well. She can't get enough encouragement as it's easy for her to put herself down.

Leo issues orders that must be obeyed and his word is law

at home. Virgo can be quietly resistant to harsh orders, dragging her feet and refusing to jump to it. However, if Dad's fair, she will benefit from gentle discipline that helps her know just where she stands. But it must always be tempered with love and consideration to get a positive response.

Leo only acts tough because he thinks it's the way to produce the ideal child. Virgo will feel far from ideal, though, if Dad doesn't build up her fragile confidence.

This father is a real show-off who may grab all the attention, leaving little over for young Virgo. He must remember to share the glory, and to use his sense of humour to help Virgo feel included. And though she admires Dad for being so big and bold, he must never embarrass her by acting too theatrically at the next parents' evening or in front of her friends!

Virgo child with a Virgo mother

This pair are like a mutual admiration society. Virgo junior thinks Mum knows how to do everything properly. She cleans the house to perfection, cooks super food, has a demanding job, yet seems to juggle her life so that young Virgo never feels neglected. There are always freshly ironed clothes in the cupboard and tea is on the table when it should be. Never mind that Virgo Mum spends her time racing around trying to achieve this perfection. Rest assured, somehow it will be done.

Virgo child has nothing but gratitude for Mum's efforts. And Mum is delighted to have a youngster who's a real chip off the old block, applying herself conscientiously to her schoolwork, folding her clothes neatly before she goes to bed, helping with the chores when asked and keeping her room tidy. What a perfect little angel!

Of course, no-one can hold a candle to these two paragons of virtue and they'll have great fun criticising others for being sloppy, late, untidy or lazy. No-one escapes the sharp tongues of two Virgos!

Things can turn nasty, though, when their barbed comments are directed at each other. Both hate to be criticised and will take it to heart and lose confidence. Virgo Mum particularly must remember that little Virgo thrives on praise and will pale under criticism. And little Virgo must remember that Supermum is not always as confident and capable as she constantly tries to prove.

Their great strength is that they love to be of service to others. Mum will help bake cakes for the bring-and-buy sale at school. Together they'll keep an eye on an elderly neighbour and make sure he gets his shopping and eats the meals they've provided. And they'll help anyone in the family with reassuring advice if something goes wrong.

Virgo Mum frets so much herself she'll find it hard to help her child to stop worrying. And she's unlikely to teach Virgo to push herself forward more, as she's just as retiring when it comes to taking a turn in the spotlight. But Virgo Mum is a wonderful teacher, bringing out her child's innate skills at reading and writing, brightening any trip by pointing out new and exciting things, educating her child along the way. She encourages Virgo to be polite and patient, to have a full range of interests and to make good use of her time. Importantly, she makes her feel cherished for being the bright and helpful little person that she is.

Virgo child with a Virgo father

Lively-minded Virgo Dad makes sure his little Virgo is kept as busy as a bee. Father shares his child's curious outlook on life and understands her thirst for information. So he'll take Virgo to stately homes and tell her stories of the amazing events that took place there. He'll point out details about the animals in the local wildlife park, and when they're back home, he'll find books to share with her that tell her more about what she's seen. He's traditional yet open to new ideas, testing them out in detail to make sure they'll work before he accepts them.

At home Dad likes to be in control and in Virgo he has a

child who won't challenge his authority too often. She's tidy, helps with chores, dresses nicely and is as rational and unemotional as he is. If he understands himself well, he'll know that she too reacts badly to criticism, that her self-confidence needs a lot of bolstering and that she responds best to praise, even though she often doubts that it's really meant.

Both are full of busy energy, yet need plenty of rest from life's struggles. They prefer routine to risk-taking as they'd much rather know what's around the next corner – it saves worrying. And they certainly are a pair of worriers. Virgo father will worry even more on behalf of his child when he sees this trait coming out in her.

Little Virgo needs drawing out and Dad should make the effort to get her out and about to socialise. Virgo will also see that his child needs encouragement to believe in herself and to stop under-rating her abilities. He'll sympathise and try to help her avoid feeling too depressed when she doesn't live up to her own high standards. Dad may well have the same attitude and will need to make a special effort to help her develop a sense of achievement. She works so hard, she certainly deserves to think well of herself.

Both are at their best when they've thrown themselves into a project together. They like learning about each other's hobbies and enjoy bright and lively chats. But this pair can be overcritical when it comes to others. Young Virgo needs to be taught that people should be allowed to be the way they are. Picking holes in others may just be harmless fun to her, a way of exercising her analytical brain, but it can be very hurtful to the person it's directed at.

Virgo child with a Libra mother

Loving Libra is soft and kind, encouraging, often indulgent and spoils her sweet little Virgo – which is just what this child needs. Virgo can hardly believe it when she is praised for her hard work, her neatness and cleverness. But when encouraging words come from Libra, Virgo knows they are meant from the heart.

Libra is determined to enjoy being a mother and lays on all kinds of treats, from trips out to parties and games. This not only keeps Mum amused, it stimulates that active Virgo mind.

Friends are vital to a Libra mum, who needs to feel she's involved in the community, drawing people together. Virgo is more retiring, preferring to work on her own projects than go to Libra's coffee mornings and clubs, which she thinks are a waste of time. She loves her privacy, her routine and her little rituals. Virgo benefits from sociable Mum's approach for it helps to encourage her to be more outgoing and diplomatic, less critical of others. She fits in best when Mum can arrange a way she can be of service to those around her, helping out with children or old people, even looking after the neighbours' cat when they are on holiday. Virgo feels so much more comfortable with people when she knows she's being useful to them.

Mum can be a bit of a nag sometimes, which upsets Virgo who feels she always tries her hardest to get things right and doesn't need to be told to try harder.

Libra needs to feel appreciated. She'll do a lot for her children, and she hates an argument, but there's a point beyond which she won't tolerate cheek or Virgo's over-frank opinions and criticisms. And she certainly won't let Virgo have her own way all the time. She uses logic instead of anger when telling Virgo off, which is better for a child who cringes at harsh words.

Libra introduces her child to art, music and the theatre, and is delighted that she has the capacity to enjoy the finer things in life. Virgo feels that here is a parent who treats her like the almost grown-up person she is.

At times, though, she wishes her imaginative and dreamy mum would be more decisive and firmer in her instructions. But she's very glad to have a parent who basically lets her be herself.

Virgo child with a Libra father

Kind Libra Dad is happy to spend his hard-earned cash kitting out Virgo's room, and buying fashionable clothes for her. Libra takes delight in things that please the eye and loves to see his children looking their best.

Dad is full of encouragement, which suits Virgo as she needs endless reassurance to stop her doubting herself. He loves her bright mind and her clever way with words but it can be tough for both of them when it comes to decision time. Virgo has difficulty in making up her mind because she gets so bogged down in detail. Ideally, she needs help from Dad, but he spends so much time weighing up the pros and cons, she's left even more unsure.

However, his heart's in the right place and eventually he will steer Virgo towards the right decision, based on her abilities and the situation she faces. He won't push her to go in a direction she doesn't want to take.

Virgo enjoys being treated like a grown-up by Dad. But being sociable, he's irritated when she digs her heels in and refuses to go to a party, or takes a sudden dislike to someone for reasons he can't fathom. Libra wants to look good in public and would like Virgo to be a bit more gregarious. But he's glad that she always looks smart and doesn't behave in a silly way or embarrass him. They're both as cautious as each other about making fools of themselves.

Sunny Libra loves sitting down to answer curious Virgo's questions, but he can't quite get to grips with the way she wants to know all about everything down to the last detail. He thinks it must be boring to always make such hard work of everything. Virgo is such a busy little bee she finds Dad lazy in comparison, spending all his time chatting instead of getting on with things.

Some Libra dads, depending on their rising sign, are tougher fathers who put their own needs first and speak harshly to their children when they get in the way. This sort of father will frighten fragile Virgo and, when his mood swings wildly, she will think she's to blame.

But most Libran fathers are devoted to their children and give them a very happy childhood. One thing they must learn is not to conceal problems. Virgo will sense if something is wrong and worry herself into a panic. Gentle reassurance will keep her happy.

Virgo child with a Scorpio mother

The stable home Scorpio Mum creates will give Virgo a lot of the security she needs. Scorpio's world runs according to a strict timetable, with everything in its place, well organised and under control. Earth child Virgo feels safe in such a predictable environment.

Yet to help Virgo feel truly secure, Scorpio will have to make some allowances for the differences in their temperaments. Virgo may seem reserved and self-sufficient, yet she really needs lots of affection and warm words to develop her self-image. Scorpio is not the most sensitive of creatures, except when anyone attacks her, so she's unlikely to sense Virgo's hidden emotional needs. Scorpio must bear it in mind that what Virgo needs most is reassurance that she is indeed a worthwhile and lovable person.

Scorpio has a wonderful imagination, and her amazing bedtime stories stimulate earthbound Virgo to be a little more fun-loving, a little less the practical realist. Both love to find out about things in great detail and always want to get everything correct. Scorpio is pleased that she can rely on her Virgo child to do things properly and that she has a sense of duty and wants to be of use. They'll work well on many a project together.

But Mum thinks Virgo is a bit too picky and gets cross when this rational and frank child sees something amiss in her plans and points it out, or tells Mum to stop interfering all the time. Scorpio takes criticism badly and can lash out at unsuspecting Virgo. Scorpio will have to make a special effort to understand just how sensitive her child is. Virgo may be critical of others but she's far more critical of herself. She'll need lots of hugs after any cross tellings-off.

Virgo is usually only too willing to obey Scorpio's rules, having a great respect for authority. But she won't have much time for Scorpio's secrecy or manipulative intrigues. This child wants everything honest and open.

Scorpio should learn to listen to her wise youngster, to spare the time to acknowledge how bright and clever she is. And she must learn, too, not to expect Virgo to fulfil her own thwarted ambitions. Here is a very different and less pushy personality who is unlikely to have the same sort of goals.

Virgo child with a Scorpio father

Scorpio Dad is the strongest person in the world to young Virgo. He's tough, powerful and in complete control – the kind of person Virgo would secretly like to be, but knows she never could. Virgo loves to help her dad and throws herself into tasks he sets with enthusiasm. He'll often give her a little pocket-money as a reward and incentive, which gives her self-esteem a much-needed boost.

Dad will certainly keep Virgo busy, which is just what she needs, although there is a risk he'll find her so handy he'll give her more responsibility than she can really handle. He'll encourage her to have a wide range of interests and will be pleased at how she applies herself – he can't stand laziness. But at times he can put too much pressure on her. Even Virgo needs her restful moments and she may just want to read a book while Dad thinks she ought to be out practising her netball goal-scoring technique. Scorpio must remember that Virgo needs gentle handling and she'll be upset if she feels misunderstood.

Young Virgo will back away when Scorpio's temper shows itself. Dad seems so cool and collected, but inside he's a swirl of emotions, always threatening to erupt. Virgo is much less emotional, preferring logical discussion to big blow-ups. Her passive nature can't stand up to Dad's tough discipline, either. If only he'd take it a little more gently, she'd benefit greatly from his ordered upbringing, where she knows just what's expected of her.

Scorpio wants the best for his child and loves her dearly, but he must learn that his way isn't always the best way for her. The problem is, he's determined to stay in control of his family, come what may, so it's hard for him to let go and allow his children to be themselves, especially in the face of change. He thinks they'll make the wrong decisions or waste their talents without his firm guidance.

Virgo is not interested in Dad's power games and enjoys facing change and finding her own solutions. Yet basically, these two communicate well. If Dad can soften his approach a little, he'll have a good relationship with his little Virgo.

Virgo child with a Sagittarius mother

Lively Sagittarius Mum shows Virgo that life's for living, not for worrying about or avoiding. She thinks the way Virgo frets over details and worries about what everyone else thinks of her is silly.

These two love to talk and Mum's frankness is a match for Virgo's criticisms. They both upset each other but you can't stay serious with a Sagittarius mum for long, and this pair will end up laughing. Mum must realise, though, how sensitive Virgo is and watch that her rather blunt manner doesn't upset without her realising.

Virgo will encourage her bubbly mum to be more sensible, patient and practical, while Sagittarius will help her child to be more tolerant, generous and accepting. Her warm, loving attention will thaw careful Virgo's heart and bring her happiness. Sagittarius will give Virgo praise and encouragement in her drive to help others, which Mum sees as very noble.

Mind you, Virgo isn't entirely perfect and enjoys deflating some of her mum's wilder ideas. Yet as she grows, she'll find ways to make Mum's ideas a reality and both will appreciate each other even more.

Sagittarius is full of bright new ways to stimulate and educate her clever Virgo child. She loves answering Virgo's stream of questions, and will happily sit down and play with her. Mum is less strong when it come to practical matters, though, which is disconcerting for Virgo who likes to feel that her life and home are ordered and under control. This may not be the case with a Sagittarius mum, who often forgets things like the ironing and tidying up because she'd rather spend the time with her child, discovering new things to do and having fun.

Although Sagittarius enjoys spending time with Virgo, she may not sit down long enough to help her with her choice of exam subjects or decide on a career path. She thinks everything will turn out all right in the end, so why worry about the details? But poor Virgo frets and frets if the nuts and bolts of her life are not fully worked out. And it's a pity because Sagittarius can give very wise advice if you catch her at the right moment.

Sagittarius may expect Virgo to be independent and adventurous before she is ready. She must remember that Virgo is quite serious and hesitant and needs time to mature. Virgo will certainly be livelier for having been brought up by Sagittarius. Some of Mum's infectious enthusiasm will replace her worries and doubts and she'll be all the better for it.

Virgo child with a Sagittarius father

Playful Sagittarius Dad is great fun and even reserved little Virgo will delight in his bursts of energetic play. They'll spend hours dreaming up adventurous things to do, and Dad will inject energy into his less lively Virgo. In this relationship, it will be boyish Dad who's yearning to have a puppy or kitten, not neat and finicky little Virgo who thinks they're too much trouble.

Sagittarius has a close understanding with his Virgo child. Yes, they row sometimes because she's too critical and he's too blunt, but they're both very adaptable and all will be quickly forgiven and forgotten.

Dad's a lot more sporty than his Virgo child and may be disappointed that she doesn't share his love of physical activity. However, she's got a brain that's bright and fast enough to keep up with his and they enjoy lively conversations together.

Dad would like Virgo to act more on the spur of the moment, the way he does. He's irritated by the methodical way she does things, for her patient plodding seems to leave no room for the brilliant flashes of insight he so enjoys sharing. He must learn that Virgo's mind works differently than his and while he takes in everything with one sweeping glance, she likes to see something in all its detail, no matter how long it takes.

Dad's imagination is wide-ranging and vast, and it has to be said that Virgo's imagination is pretty limited. She takes a practical view of life and thinks Dad is a bit of a dreamer. His endless bright ideas unsettle her because he always seems to want to be on the move and changing things, while she's quite happy for everything to stay as it is.

Virgo thinks Dad's wonderful for being so kind and helpful to others and admires his good-hearted nature. He's the perfect role model for her helpfulness, reminding her of her own need to serve others.

Sagittarius Dad must watch for a tendency to be over-disappointed when Virgo fails or makes mistakes. Virgo will be particularly hurt if Sagittarius reacts in this critical way. She needs lots of encouragement and reassurance that she is accepted for being who she is, however she does. She's not helped, either, if Dad's idealism makes him moody every time life lets him down. Sensitive Virgo will think it's all her fault and worry unnecessarily. Instead, Dad should concentrate on spreading his love of life to his child. That way these two will be friends forever.

Virgo child with a Capricorn mother

Virgo feels very much at home with her Capricorn mum for they are similar in all sorts of ways. They both like to be thought of as normal, respectable, dutiful and responsible. And both would curl up and die if anyone poked fun at them. They're full of common sense, careful with money, like staying close to home and dislike bold, brash types. Both are pessimistic, cautious, neat, organised, value their belongings, respect authority, and have no time for idle dreamers. They work hard, share a dry sense of humour and believe that everyone and everything has its place. Both take life very seriously indeed.

Where they differ is that Capricorn Mum is more driven to be a success than her shrinking violet of a child. Capricorn knows she deserves to be highly successful, and she thinks her child should be up there with her. She's glad Virgo works so hard and she encourages her desire to get things just right. Others might call Virgo obsessive, but to Capricorn her perfectionism is a virtue because it can help her succeed. In return, Virgo only has to look at her mum and the comfortable lifestyle she has achieved to see that hard work can bring its rewards.

While Virgo is often humble, happy to serve and shy about pushing herself forward, Capricorn never is. She knows just what she wants and how to get it. And if she wants Virgo to be a success or to fulfil thwarted ambitions of her own, Capricorn can become a bulldozer, forcing her child in the direction she has set for her. Virgo needs much softer treatment for she'll feel guilty and inadequate when she fails to match up to the standards Mum seems to expect of her.

Capricorn must realise that any pushiness on her part has to be tempered with warmth and reassurance. Ruled by cold planet Saturn, Capricorn finds it hard to show real affection, yet she has to if she's to help Virgo overcome problems of self-esteem and give her a sense of self-worth that will enable her to do as well as Capricorn wishes.

Virgo needs a firm structure behind her and Capricorn is just the person to provide it with her drive and direction. And if Virgo chooses to veer off the path Mum's set, Mum must realise it's not the end of the world. Instead, she can reassure herself that whatever Virgo chooses to do in life, she'll achieve far more for having had such a powerful, directing force behind her.

Virgo child with a Capricorn father

Capricorn Dad is hard working, well respected and very much in charge at home. Virgo wishes he was more affectionate and showed his approval more often, yet basically she knows the two of them are in tune. Virgo looks up to Dad for the sensible and positive way he acts. She admires the status he has achieved and finds it hard to think that she could ever do better than him – should she even have the courage to compete.

Virgo likes being Dad's back-up when they're working together on a project, although she finds him rather strict. He thinks that toeing the line brings you status and security and acting eccentrically or going against the grain will lead to universal disapproval. He's preaching to the converted with Virgo, who would much rather obey and conform anyway. Dad should use more of his wonderful dry sense of humour with Virgo, to lighten her rather serious nature.

Virgo could become narrow-minded if Dad is too focused on all things rational, practical and sensible. Although the stable background he provides for Virgo is ideal, she needs a wider view of life if she is to attain her potential. Fewer set ideas and more emphasis on relaxation and fun will stimulate her imagination and bring out her hidden talents – she's particularly good at writing.

Work-obsessed Capricorn finds it hard to show emotion, but Virgo needs reassurance that she's loved and valued to help her develop the confidence she lacks.

Dad will praise Virgo for being so neat, well behaved and helpful. And he'll pay her for doing chores, which will encourage and please her. But secretly, he thinks she's a bit silly for being so keen to serve others. He believes it pays to help yourself and thinks that Virgo spends far too much time running round after other people. It's actually her way of showing she cares, and Dad should remember that. He enjoys giving her advice and she's a willing listener. This may be good for his ego, but sometimes Virgo thinks he's a bit of a know-it-all!

Capricorn is delighted Virgo does so well at school through sheer hard work. He'd like to see her push herself forward more and Virgo will be inspired by her father's success, eventually making her mark on life in her own individual way. One day Dad will look at her and realise she's a child he can be very proud of.

Virgo child with an Aquarius mother

Forgetful Aquarius puzzles sensible, organised Virgo. Mum seems to live in a dream world, and Virgo would much prefer her to be more in the here and now, handling the practical matters that are so important to this child's security. Although both are coolly unemotional and logical, Aquarius isn't set on imposing order on the world in the way that Virgo is.

Aquarius is happy to launch her children into life early, allowing them to be themselves and develop naturally without any undue interference. Yet in Virgo, Mum has a child who could do with some intervention. She likes to feel there is a stable, ordered framework around her, giving her protection and clear guidance.

Aquarius encourages her children to question everything. Virgo likes asking questions, but her aim is to gather information, not to challenge the status quo. Her style of criticism is more personal and she would never question authority the way rebellious Aquarius does. She'll benefit from the way Aquarius teaches her that it's healthy to question decisions made by government and teachers, or to challenge views put over in newspapers. Virgo could do with being more free-thinking and needs help to realise that her actions and ideas can, indeed, influence others. But Aquarius must expect Virgo to pour cold water on her idealistic views sometimes, preferring to retreat to her own more earthbound safe outlook.

Aquarius is keen that Virgo should learn to get on well with others, to cooperate and act honestly. Diplomatic Mum will teach her how to say things without offending people. She hates violence, so is unlikely to shock sensitive Virgo with smacks, preferring sensible persuasion. She's non-competitive too, which suits Virgo, who hates to be pushed to achieve by an aggressively ambitious parent.

This mum is very fair and will make sure helpful Virgo isn't left doing all the chores while the rest of the family watch TV. Sociable Aquarius draws out quieter Virgo and helps her to make friends, encouraging that bright little Virgo mind to see the world in broader terms and introducing her to books, politics and social issues.

These two will share a stimulating and satisfying lifelong relationship.

Virgo child with an Aquarius father

Aquarius father seems to be a lot of people rolled into one. He's unpredictable, eccentric, full of ideas, energetic and so enthusiastic. This can be daunting for more conventional Virgo, who likes to know just where she stands with Dad – and exactly who Dad is!

Being traditional, Virgo finds it hard to make sense of Dad's forward-looking views and wonders how on earth he could ever put all his bizarre ideas into practice. He's way ahead of his time and, although Virgo has a lively mind, she prefers the reassurance of looking back to the past. Too many new experiences unnerve her.

Fairly thick-skinned, Dad can laugh off Virgo's inevitable little criticisms. He doesn't mind hearing the truth – it doesn't hurt him as he won't take it too personally.

This father lives in his head, fascinated by all things scientific, political and sociological, and he's delighted that Virgo's such a bookworm. But he can get so caught up in his own world, he neglects the hidden emotional needs of his child. Aquarius must offer support and encouragement at all times to Virgo, and not expect her to be self-sufficient and independent as some other signs can be. Self-doubt can cripple her unless she's given positive back-up throughout childhood.

Aquarius is good at listening to wise little Virgo and won't force her to accept his views without question. In fact, he's delighted when she does come up with arguments – it shows she's growing up and learning to think for herself. He reassures her that it's good to have a social conscience, to think of others and to know what's right and what's not. Even if he seems a bit batty in some ways, at least his attitude helps to create some stability for his sensitive child.

Virgo will love and look up to her Aquarius dad and he must remember how much security and stability she needs. With care and consideration, these two will always get on swimmingly.

Virgo child with a Pisces mother

Pisces the dreamer seems to her practical, down-to-earth Virgo to have her head permanently in the clouds. Why can't Mum be more sensible, organise a proper routine and keep the house in order, wonders critical little Virgo. But she can't complain where love is concerned, for Pisces is a devoted mother who'll do anything for her child and protect her with her life.

Young Virgo is a sensitive creature who's easily hurt, often criticises herself and finds it difficult to believe any praise that's directed at her. So Pisces' cosy affection and endless encouragement is good for her.

Ideally, though, Virgo feels most comfortable with a more solid and stable upbringing where everything is organised down to what time tea's on the table. Pisces is unlikely to be very organised, because she doesn't believe in structuring her life too rigidly. Yet these two are an adaptable pair and both will try to alter their behaviour to match each other's needs.

The fact that Pisces doesn't provide firm discipline won't really matter as Virgo keeps herself in check and rarely misbehaves. Pisces is very proud of Virgo's good manners in public.

Pisces responds to life with her feelings, which are deep and complex, while Virgo takes a more practical and analytical view which seems surprisingly cold to Mum.

Pisces often finds it hard to deal with the noisy demands of children and she'll be glad Virgo is rather quiet and doesn't disturb the peace too much. Only when driven to extremes will Mum explode – she hates an argument. Virgo doesn't mind the chance to let off steam once in a while, but will take it to heart if anything too harsh is said, even though she's usually quick to forgive and forget. The trouble is, Virgo herself says such cutting things sometimes, it's hard for sensitive Mum to forget that quickly. But a few cuddles will put everything right.

Sometimes Mum will act the martyr and make Virgo feel guilty for allowing her to do so much for her. But mostly these two respect each other and Virgo is happy to give all that Pisces wants in return for her tender care – a little bit of gratitude and lots of love.

Virgo child with a Pisces father

Changeable Pisces Dad confuses sensible young Virgo, who likes to know just where she stands and what lies ahead. Pisces is always dreaming up new projects, refusing to live a settled lifestyle, still acting the teenager.

Virgo wishes he'd settle down, stay in one place and be normal and ordinary like all the other dads. Yet in some ways she's glad he isn't, especially as he's so kind and caring to her and seems to understand her in a way a lot of other fathers wouldn't.

He loves sitting down and playing and talking with her and helps her to develop her inbuilt powers of communication. He introduces her to art and music and encourages her to do well at school. He listens carefully to what she has to say and understands immediately. But sometimes life gets too much for him and he'll close up and retreat from the world. Virgo will find this very baffling and thinks it must be her fault.

And Pisces' moods will confuse Virgo too. He'll try to repress his strong emotions but will end up having cross outbursts from time to time. He reacts too harshly, unable to handle his swirling tide of feelings like cool Virgo can, and inevitably upsets her. Pisces will do anything for a quiet life and finds it hard when Virgo becomes argumentative and outspoken. She's a lot less diplomatic than he is.

Pisces ladles affection on Virgo which could spoil other children. Yet self-doubting Virgo needs every bit of it. Pisces wants his child to fit in with others socially and is pleased Virgo generally treats people with consideration. But he may find it hard to provide the guidance that will help Virgo find direction in her life. He's still trying to find it himself!

Pisces also finds it difficult to be consistent and changes his mind so often Virgo feels he's just a mass of indecision. It's hard for her to see disorganised Pisces as the firm and reliable parent she wants him to be. He doesn't exercise strong authority, preferring to be a friend to his child. Virgo certainly feels better when he does make a special effort to be more organised. But despite his shortcomings, the main thing is that she knows how much he loves her, which is vitally important to a Virgo child.

LIBRA
Stars for Life

STAR BABY

Libra is a contented baby with a happy smile, who starts cooing conversation with his adoring parents from the word go. He (or she*) murmurs and looks lovingly up at Mum, who can't get over what a little charmer he is. Libra loves to form close relationships with others and will be thrilled by a warm welcome into the world.

This child likes things done just so. Bottles must be warmed to the correct temperature and bedtime has to be at the usual time with his favourite tune playing on the cot mobile. Keep major upsets to a minimum by anticipating his needs and feeding and changing him the moment he cries.

Libra soon turns into a choosy child, who enjoys mulling over what romper suit he should wear that day or which teddy deserves his special hugs. He needs this practice at learning to make decisions, so try not to tear your hair out as he endlessly hums and hahs. Teach him gently how to make up his mind that little bit faster.

Family celebrations delight this little socialiser. He loves nothing better than a visit from Granny and Grandad, when he's in the spotlight, showing how fast he can run and practising his first words. He'll be quick to speak because he so much wants to talk with others and share in their world.

FIRST STEPS FOR LIBRA

He's quick to make toddler friends, so take him to a mums and tots group as soon as you feel he's ready. Libra loves to

*'He' is used to cover he and she for Libra child.

get out and about and needs daily social contact. Soon your house will be filled with his young pals. Other mums see little Libra as a nice child for their youngsters to play with. He doesn't push and shove, sees that everyone gets a turn with the toys and rarely throws a tantrum.

But Libra can run into a few pitfalls. He tends to judge himself by what his friends are doing. If one is taller, more talkative or a better runner, Libra can feel uneasy and back away from them. He feels best with people he knows he has a lot in common with. Reassure him that it's okay for people to be different from him and teach him to accept others as they are. Then tell him what a great person he is and he'll swell with pride, forgetting any worries about his progress.

Libra will settle in well at nursery school. He thrives on lively company, but can become defiant, loud and stubborn as he finds his feet in a crowd. It's good that he's learning to stand up for himself and become more independent, but he needs teaching what the limits are. At this stage he will push you to find out how far you will let him go. Be firm but fair if you want to bring out his loving and caring side. Libra can be an awkward little so-and-so if you let him become spoiled.

This child is easily bored now and will always be demanding new toys and activities. Help him learn to concentrate and get the most out of what he's doing by encouraging him and praising him for the things he does well. Libra loves to please you and will respond well to logical explanations about why he should or should not do something. Harsh tellings-off don't suit him at all, as his behaviour just becomes disruptive and angry if he feels strongly disapproved of.

SCHOOL RULES FOR LIBRA

Libra loves being surrounded by people and hates being left out, so he'll fit in well at school. He'll invite classmates home for tea – plus a lively session of chasing, painting and climbing all over the furniture.

Don't discourage him too much, unless your home is

being wrecked. He loves to have friends around and can feel at a loose end when on his own. For some peace and quiet suggest he does something useful with his pals – like cleaning the rabbit hutch or feeding the fish. Libra is very caring and loves to have a pet. He likes sharing his enjoyment of small animals with friends too.

Libra can seem very grown-up for his age, a clever talker who is polite in company and, usually, obedient. But he can need pushing to achieve his best. Libra is not as sure of himself as he looks and can secretly feel he can't live up to the expectations others have of him. He needs a lot of love and encouragement, as well as praise whenever he does something well.

Make sure that the school he attends suits him, too. Libra loves a peaceful, harmonious atmosphere and can be thrown off balance by noisy, unruly types. It's only in a structured, ordered and organised classroom that Libra's artistic, musical, dramatic and academic talents can flourish.

He works best on straightforward assignments that involve subjects in which he takes a special interest. You can help him by setting special times for homework – this will overcome his tendency to be lazy and slouch in front of the TV. But bear in mind that Libra laziness is often a way of restoring balance after a spell of hard work and Libra needs rest in big doses.

Try to make his room as pleasant as possible for him to be in. Libra loves harmony and hates a mess. Teach him to be tidy and allow him to have some say in the decorations. He'll go for gentle, restful colours that will help to soothe and recharge him. But try to help him with his choice. As he grows older he'll still be plagued with the Libran tendency towards indecision.

What he really fears is making the wrong decision, being stuck with things he doesn't really want, or upsetting someone through his choice. Try to teach him that most choices are not matters of life-and-death importance. Help him to relax and never rush him into decisions.

Teach him, too, to sort out what he actually wants. He's easily swayed by friends and fashion and needs to learn to think for himself – but it can be a slow process. Yet once he's finally made up his mind, his determination to reach his goal will amaze you. He'll bulldoze obstacles out of the way – just watch that you're not one of them. Libra must be taught that trying to manipulate others doesn't pay. He still needs those regular lessons in how to behave.

Libra likes to talk around a subject and will enjoy a lively debate with you. He's a young thinker who sees the other person's point of view as well as his own and can have some interesting insights into life. He wants to please you and enjoys keeping rules once he understands them. He's a conservative soul at heart and may try to do what he thinks is correct and neglect his true desires. Help him to discover his own wishes and follow his own interests.

When he does encounter problems in life, there's a danger he'll hide them inside, while pretending outwardly that everything's fine. Help him learn to unbottle his feelings. Explain there's no shame in finding life hard to cope with sometimes and reassure him that you're there to help him.

Libra hates to cause what he sees as trouble, is frightened by his own temper, and can think it's wrong to get angry anyway. He can wind himself up into tension and confusion, so it's vital that you learn to spot when something is wrong and give him the chance to unburden himself. Otherwise he'll bottle things up, pretending on the surface that everything's fine, until one day he explodes with frustration, the problem having become far too big for him to handle.

Also remember that he'll prefer to hear you being positive about other people. Libra values fairness above everything else and recoils from unnecessary vindictiveness. He'll fight for those he believes are in the right, even though he usually hates confrontation.

TEENAGE TAKE-OFF FOR LIBRA

Teenage Libra will be a busy young partygoer. He revels in

having lots of friends, is always on the phone and is out more often than in. Remind him to concentrate on his schoolwork as well as on his social life. It would be a shame to miss future opportunities just for a bit of fun now. But you'll have to be tactful. Libra can be rebellious at this stage, determined that he knows best.

Libra will be on the lookout for a girlfriend early. But once he finds one, she's unlikely to stay on the scene for long. Libra loves to experiment with relationships at this stage and quickly moves on. He may get sex and love all mixed up in his mind. But he's a careful youngster who will not take undue risks, as long as he's been given appropriate advice somewhere along the way.

He loves to help people and often lends his shoulder to cry on. Encourage him, too, to focus more on himself and his personal needs. He can be so busy thinking about others and how he can relate to them that he forgets to keep his own goals and secret wishes in mind. He loves bringing peace, goodwill and harmony to others. Teach him how to find fulfilment for himself, too.

STAR PARENTS

Libra child with an Aries mother

Active Aries is bursting with energy and has to keep busy. Libra likes to have a break sometimes and wishes Mum could slow down a bit, although all that activity does him good. He needs a kick from behind to help him make the most of his potential.

There's a hidden adventurous side to Libra that's just longing to break out and make new discoveries, and pioneering Aries is the ideal person to bring it out. She can spark his enjoyment of trying new things with her inspiring enthusiasm and zest for life. Libra will never be lazy with this mum around.

Aries is sociable and delighted that her Libra loves to mix too. He adores social gatherings and quickly makes new friends. Mum has to admit that Libra thinks of other people more than she does and has a more pleasant and easy manner. He's more diplomatic than she could ever be, too. Mum is motivated by a need to stay active and amused, while Libra enjoys bringing others together and creating groups of people he can charm and please.

These two differ even more when it comes to decisiveness. Aries leaps into action as soon as she's decided to do something, but Libra weighs up the pros and cons and avoids decisions for as long as he can, frightened of offending anyone by making the wrong move. Mum would prefer to see Libra direct his energy in more positive ways.

Libra needs plenty of love to keep his emotions balanced and Mum must take time out of her hectic schedule to make sure he gets all the affection he needs. At least Aries isn't likely to tip the other way and spoil him. It does Libra good to live with the firm and consistent style of discipline his Aries mum imposes. He can turn out to be rather soft unless his tougher side is developed. But don't be too harsh, Mum. Your little adventurer always needs a balance of love and firmness. Get it right and he'll grow up happy and confident.

Libra child with an Aries father

Sporty Dad will be delighted if his little Libra turns out to be the sort of child who enjoys games. Not all Libras do, but those who are sporty will have a whale of a time from toddlerhood onwards, kicking a ball around in the garden, then graduating to the school team, egged on all the way by cheering Aries Dad.

Here's a father who is active, busy and full of enthusiasm. He'll have no patience with Libra if he slumps in front of the TV instead of getting on with his work. Aries wants his child to be effective and successful and hates it when Libra puts things off in favour of a rest. But Dad must give his child enough time to recharge, for Libra genuinely does need quiet spells.

Aries has a rapid-fire temper but it's over in a matter of

minutes and all is quickly forgiven. Libra can be bossy and temperamental at times, and he tends to hang on to hurts and worry, hiding his feelings when anything is wrong and pretending life is fine.

Dad hates to deal with emotional problems. He's always direct and open about what's on his mind, and he must take time to ask Libra gently what's wrong if he senses something amiss. Libra must be taught there's no need to bottle everything up so much.

In an Aries home, the more assertive side of Libra will be brought out. Dad will teach this child to stick up for himself and will expect him to do well. Aries will jolt Libra into trying hard at school and will encourage him to be more competitive. But Dad must not be too hard on him if he doesn't always live up to those high Aries expectations, for that could crush Libra's confidence. And he should see that the imaginative, artistic and creative side of Libra gets a look-in, as well as the sporty and adventurous side that appeals so much to Dad.

This pair will enjoy a go-ahead relationship and Libra will benefit greatly from Aries Dad's enthusiasm and energy.

Libra child with a Taurus mother

Warm Taurus mother is loving and protective and doesn't mind at all if Libra wants to be lazy once in a while. She enjoys a good rest herself. But she's quite a tough disciplinarian under her cosy exterior, so Libra won't get away with anything for too long and she'll make sure he knuckles down to his schoolwork.

Taurus hates confrontations and will cringe when Libra throws a little tantrum. Yet she knows she can beat Libra hands down when it comes to stubbornness. She'll see he follows her orders in the end, and he's unlikely to grow up soft and spoiled.

Libra may not be as adventurous as he could be with this mum around. She's cautious and sensible and centres her life around her home. She cooks wonderfully and must watch Libra's weight as he shares her tendency to over-eat.

Taurus sets up a routine that leaves nothing to chance. This will add to Libra's sense of security, as well as help him organise his schedule and make sure he gets his homework done. However, Mum must watch that she doesn't hem him in too much. Social life is as important as air to Libra, and he simply has to get out and meet people. Usually he's a charmer, which pleases Mum, but she will lose patience with him when he takes strong dislikes to people or is bullying or manipulative. Mum insists on traditional good behaviour and will give Libra a stern ticking off.

Her sensible lessons in life and her good example will be of great benefit to sociable Libra as he grows up. Mum provides a secure and caring home from which he can start his adventures into society. And even when he's flown the nest, she'll find he won't be able to stay away from his Taurus mum's home cooking for long!

Libra child with a Taurus father

Taurus Dad likes an ordered and traditional life. He adores his home comforts and loves to relax, and while Libra enjoys a relaxing time, too, he can sometimes turn rest into an excuse for laziness. Dad must watch he doesn't set him too laid-back an example. It's important that Libra is pushed to get up and move, to circulate and meet people.

Taurus is kind and caring towards those he loves, but he can seem gloomy or grumpy to those he's not so keen on. Libra, on the other hand, is a picture of charm to almost all he meets. He's got a pleasant manner and a friendly smile and wins friends easily. It's only occasionally that he refuses to turn on the charm.

Like his Taurus dad, Libra dislikes confrontations and often hides upsets, carrying on as if everything is fine. Dad is more sensitive to his child's emotions than he seems. He won't find it hard to give Libra a hug and gently persuade him to talk about anything that's worrying him.

Libra likes to mull over any decision before he makes it

and never does anything in a hurry. Taurus thinks things through, then makes a firm decision and gets on and does it, and can't understand why Libra takes so long to make up his mind. He'll do his child a favour if he can pass on his common-sense attitudes to him. Libra needs to learn how to make up his mind and patient Dad is just the person to teach him.

Here's a father who enjoys buying lovely things for his home. Libra likes objects of beauty too, but doesn't have Dad's strong desire to own them. Libra can appreciate things without feeling desperate to possess them.

Libra is happy in the warm and comfortable home Taurus works so hard to create. During his rebellious teenage years, he may think Dad is a bit of an old fogey with no time for new ideas. But he'll grow up to appreciate his father's warmth and wise advice, his loyalty and his values.

Libra child with a Gemini mother

This talkative pair are best friends. They understand and amuse each other and Gemini is thrilled to have such a chatty, bright and friendly child. Here's a mum who can easily get bored with domestic drudgery, but with light-hearted Libra around there's not much chance of that!

Gemini is delighted, too, that Libra is such a sociable soul. Mum loves to get out and meet people and, in Libra, she has a fun-lover who talks as soon as he toddles and makes friends as fast as she does.

Neither are particularly emotional and both prefer to bat ideas around rather than get bogged down in feelings. When it comes to decision time, though, there can be pitfalls. Gemini makes up her mind in a flash and changes it just as quickly. Libra takes ages weighing things up and is puzzled and confused when Mum changes her mind.

Libra needs help to learn to make decisions and Mum must slow down and show him how. And she must watch that she doesn't try to take over his life, making every decision for him. Lazy Libra will let Mum get away with it, but it won't do him any good. He must be encouraged to think for himself.

Mum is bubbling with energy and she'll see that Libra doesn't stay still for too long. She'll get him up and going with bright ideas for things to do, although she must remember that he needs his rest to recharge.

Both find each other fun and the source of many happy times. This is a relationship that will be rewarding for both mother and child.

Libra child with a Gemini father

Gemini Dad is full of bright ideas which he loves to share with little Libra. He'll fire Libra's imagination, and teach him common sense, too. Gemini helps Libra discover all the interesting things life has to offer and this child will never be short of something to do when Dad is around.

Both like to think and talk, but Gemini must watch he doesn't race ahead of Libra, who can't always keep up with Dad's quick-fire wit. Libra prefers to charm people with his easy, relaxed manner. He's alarmed when volatile Dad becomes bad-tempered. He prefers peace and harmony, and though he likes a logical argument he doesn't enjoy a big flare-up. Dad must reassure him that he's not always as cross as he seems, and that any family arguments are not the fault of sensitive Libra.

This father is keen to move house or job often and, while he finds change exciting, he must remember that Libra can be upset by the upheaval and needs more stability than Dad does. It helps Libra to know that some things in life are constant, so that decision-making is less difficult and less necessary.

There's little risk that Gemini will spoil Libra. Dad will try to prove he's in control by being strict and behaving in a rather detached way. He'll do his best to bring out Libra's assertive and determined side, and won't give him a chance to become lazy and soft. But he should accept that Libra needs a few luxuries in life. He's a generous, outgoing child who deserves rewards. Dad is more self-centred and mainly concerned with keeping himself entertained.

Gemini has a way with words and will make Libra laugh often, and Libra loves Dad's jolly bouts of play. He'll benefit greatly from his Gemini father's influence. Dad will bring out the child's creativity and imagination, and develop his ability to speak up for himself.

Libra child with a Cancer mother

Loving Cancer mother creates a warm atmosphere of security for little Libra, but she must watch she doesn't spoil him. It's all too easy for Cancer to let Libra get away with being naughty and feel it's not worth the trouble of disciplining him. Yet Libra needs firm guidance if he's to become assertive and adventurous instead of lazy and soft.

Libra can be temperamental if things go wrong, putting the blame on others, and Cancer will find him very hard to stand up to. Cancer is much more emotional than her child, and logical Libra won't understand why Mum takes it so much to heart when he gets cross, especially as she can get snappy herself when she's tired. Libra will try to charm his way back into her good books, and he'll usually succeed!

Mum creates a routine that gives Libra stability, but she's possessive and must watch she doesn't try to run his life. Libra needs to find his own direction and especially needs to learn to make decisions on his own. It won't help if Mum tries to keep him dependent on her. She must let him be his own person.

Libra needs to get out and socialise, for he's at his best in company. Shy Cancer prefers to stay at home and must make sure Libra gets plenty of chances to meet people. She should start by taking him along to a playgroup.

Caring Cancer Mum wants emotional closeness with her child but Libra lives in his mind and strong affection is not a great priority with him. Mum mustn't worry if he seems a little cool. It doesn't mean he doesn't love her. She must allow him to strike out on his own sometimes, still under her guiding eye. He should be confident and sociable, so she can let him fly a bit!

The result will be a happy child, and a proud mum.

Libra child with a Cancer father

Cancer Dad is a lot more emotional than his logical and cool Libra youngster. Dad tries hard to hide it, putting on a strict and bossy front to appear tough. Firmness never does Libra much harm, as long as it's fair and not haphazard. It helps Libra to build up his own character so that he is better at decision-making, more assertive and less of a lazy charmer.

But Dad must be fair and consistent. He'll often ignore bad behaviour if he's feeling quiet and not up to coping with a scene, then blow up if he's feeling irritable. Libra dreads upsetting his dad and tries to do what he hopes will please him. He'll be confused if he gets a different reaction at different times.

Libra is usually carefree, optimistic and interested in new ideas, while Cancer worries, is often pessimistic and much more interested in the tried and tested than in anything new. He's not as light-hearted or charming as his Libra child. Cancer certainly finds it more difficult to get on with people and make friends than pleasant, smiling Libra.

Dad needs to retreat frequently to recharge his energy. He gets so worn out because he tunes into other people's emotions as well as dealing with his own, often turbulent ones. Libra understands his need for rest. This child gets worn out, too, trying to weigh things up before making any decision, and needs his own lazy, quiet moments.

One thing Libra knows he can rely on is his father's love, however erratically Dad may act. And Libra benefits greatly from Cancer's kindness. Libra needs a lot of interests to keep lazy moments from becoming a habit and Cancer will be quite happy to ferry him around to take part in anything he wants to. Together they'll enjoy a rewarding relationship.

Libra child with a Leo mother

Warm, generous Leo Mum is good at making Libra feel secure. There may not be a lot of routine in the Leo home, as Leo loves a life of surprises, but there will be firm, fair discipline, which helps Libra learn to become assertive and better at making decisions. Imposing Mum teaches her child to be strong and active. She has no time for a charming lazy-bones.

Leo will push Libra to achieve the things she never managed to. But Mum must watch she doesn't force him in a direction he doesn't really want to go. Libra can suppress his own wishes out of a desire to please Mum, to be appreciated and loved. Leo must reassure him that he is loved, and gently help him to discover his true ambitions.

This pair both love life's little luxuries. They enjoy holidays too – Leo loves soaking up the sun and Libra likes nothing better than lazing on the sand.

Leo Mum thinks it is important to win, to be the best and the centre of attention. Libra would like everyone to be equal and happy. He is nowhere near as ambitious and is happy if he's a success socially. Both enjoy getting out and meeting others, but Mum must watch she doesn't hog all the attention.

Leo will be firm if Libra shows any sign of becoming moody, bossy or rebellious, and she'll admire the way he tries to make peace between people. Leo will broaden her child's horizons and stimulate his imagination. The world will be an exciting place for Libra under the guidance of his bold Leo mum.

Libra child with a Leo father

Leo Dad won't stand for any nonsense from his Libra child and will be very firm if Libra is temperamental. At his best, Dad can help his child become tougher and more adventurous. He can bring out his leadership qualities and jolt him out of any laziness. But Dad must always be fair. If Leo lays down the law too much, it could backfire and simply make Libra anxious to please and scared to speak his mind.

Dad may love to see Libra's lively intelligence develop, but Libra may have a struggle to make himself heard as Dad likes to be the star and anyone who tries to grab the attention will get a firm rebuke. Leo must try to be a little less self-important when Libra is around. His confidence and sense of independence need nurturing, and that will take time and effort.

Leo is good at thinking up entertaining ways of educating Libra and keeping him busy. He's good at giving practical advice, too, which can help Libra find his feet when it comes to decision-making. In return, Libra will charm and flatter, making Dad feel respected and adored, which is exactly what every Leo wants most.

Libra loves luxury and beautiful things. Successful Dad will see he has what he wants and lives in comfort, and Libra will be thrilled with Dad's generosity. Both enjoy sharing ideas and appreciate each other's outgoing nature.

Leo believes in his own abilities and can inspire Libra to do well, too, but Dad must watch he doesn't push Libra to take on too much responsibility too soon. He must also watch that he doesn't expect his child to be perfect and that he's not too harsh when it comes to Libra's teenage years. Leo should not impose things on Libra. Encouragement and confidence are the best gifts Libra's warm-hearted father can give.

Libra child with a Virgo mother

Virgo the perfectionist wants everything done well – and now! Relaxed Libra won't be rushed into doing anything and Mum will despair sometimes at her child's lazy ways. Young Libra likes to maintain an inner sense of balance and harmony and tough talk or family arguments can upset him. Reassurance that he's loved and that rows are not his fault will make him feel more secure.

Mercury-ruled Mum loves words and she'll enjoy conversations and discussions with her child. Libra gets on much better with people than his mum does, for she is shy and tends to worry too much about what others think of her. She's pleased to see that Libra is so at home in company, though she warns him not be too trusting. Mum must be sure she takes Libra out and about often, as he's unhappy cooped up at home.

Virgo teaches manners and patience and will make Libra apologise if he hurts another child or tries to pin blame on them for something he's done. And she won't stand for any laziness. She expects effort and high standards and Libra will benefit from a push to keep him achieving.

Mum insists on tidiness and, while Libra likes pleasant surroundings, he can be lazy when it comes to tidying up. He may hope he can charm his way out of doing chores, but there's no chance of that with tidy, fussy Virgo Mum around! It's unlikely that firm Virgo will spoil Libra, either, but she must remember that he needs lots of affection. Mum can get tied up in routine and forget all about cuddles.

Libra will benefit greatly from the stable start she gives him and will learn from her the valuable lesson of not putting off till tomorrow what he can do today.

Libra child with a Virgo father

Practical Virgo Dad likes an ordered life and expects young Libra to learn manners and good sense. He will give undecided Libra more direction in life, guiding him firmly towards workable goals. Dad will encourage Libra to fulfil his potential and will give him a good shake if he thinks he's getting lazy.

Dad will enjoy organising Libra but he must watch that he doesn't run the child's life too much, making every decision for him in the name of efficiency. Dad can't bear dilly-dallying, but if he's not careful Libra will never learn how to make decisions and will be lost when Dad isn't on hand to help him. He must let Libra do things for himself sometimes.

Libra's adventurous side should be encouraged and not repressed by cautious Dad. On the plus side, Virgo's stable lifestyle will create a firm base for Libra, making choices easier and helping the child to become strong and positive, instead of weak and indecisive.

Virgo is not a very emotional sign and Dad is not given to big shows of affection. But Libra loves lots of hugs, and Dad mustn't push him away or tell him not to be soppy. He mustn't laugh at Libra's big ideas, either. This child is more imaginative than Dad and needs help, not scorn, to develop his ideas until they are workable.

This pair love talking together. Dad is great at explaining things in detail and Libra loves to listen, although Dad should make sure he listens to Libra, too. There's a lot he can learn from his child – how to relax more and laugh about life, how to get on easily with people and how to be inspired by new ideas. In turn Libra can learn common sense, and how to put ideas into action and make real achievements. These two have much to offer each other.

Libra child with a Libra mother

Libra Mum takes pride in seeing her child look smart, and Libra loves having a mum who spends so much on his appearance. He laps up her encouragement and kindness, and knows just how to get round her with charm and smiles. He knows she's just a softie at heart and she'll always give in to his demands.

This pair take ages over any decision, weighing things up for so long it's a miracle anything ever gets done! Young Libra needs a lesson in decisiveness and some firm guidance if he is to strengthen his character. There's a risk that indulgent Mum can spoil him and allow him to become demanding and lazy. Usually, though, the Libra sense of fairness will come into play and Mum will call a halt if he becomes too obnoxious.

Fun-loving Mum socialises a lot, which suits Libra who needs to get out and meet people. Neither are very emotional and both like to be pleasant and light-hearted to all they meet. They much prefer talk to action so Libra

Mum will be delighted that her child speaks well from an early age.

But both can suffer from moods, and chances are they'll never be in harmony, with Mum exhausted just as young Libra is raring to go. But at least the lively one can cheer up the one who's feeling down.

These two share a love of art and music and Mum will help bring out her child's creative potential. Both can be lazy at times, yet they love each other's optimism and friendliness. They'll enjoy a chatty, fun relationship full of love and laughter.

Libra child with a Libra father

Cheerful Libra Dad loves talking about new ideas with his bright-eyed youngster. In fact, this pair can talk for hours without stopping, and Dad particularly likes thinking up answers to Libra's intelligent questions. Dad is proud of his youngster's early verbal abilities. He thinks Libra is a real bright spark and enjoys their lively debates.

Both are outgoing and gregarious and make lots of friends wherever they go. Libra junior is sure to get the lively social life he needs with this sociable dad about. Libra will make Dad proud in company, too, for Dad thinks that how he appears to others is very important. Libra understands this and won't ever deliberately let him down.

The trouble is that cautious Libra Dad's wish to keep up appearances can sometimes lead to emotional muddles at home. Dad conceals problems, repressing them until they build up and erupt. Young Libra would rather have a clear idea of what's going on. He feels more secure if things are explained to him and needs to be reassured that any family rows are not his fault.

This pair love finding out how things work and will share common interests. Dad will do his best to let Libra choose his own path in life. He thinks a child should be allowed to develop naturally, without being forced in any particular direction. But he must remember that Libra will need help in making decisions. He mustn't always make them for him, just guide him towards the right choice.

These two will find their own balance to create a caring and loving relationship.

Libra child with a Scorpio mother

High-energy Scorpio Mum wants her child to succeed and will keep pushing Libra not to be lazy. Libra likes Mum's encouragement, but won't be pleased if she pushes him too hard. He's not as openly ambitious as she is and needs to find his own way in life. Well-meant guidance is what he needs, not a takeover bid on his life. Libra needs to learn to make decisions and he never will if Mum makes every choice for him.

Scorpio creates a stable home where everything is in order and runs according to routine. This can help Libra because it cuts out the need for too many decisions and makes those he has to make easier. He benefits from Mum's traditional lifestyle, too, as long as it doesn't become too restrictive.

On the minus side, manipulative and controlling Mum can pry into Libra's life too much and blow her top if she finds he's doing something he shouldn't. She must respect Libra's need to develop a sense of independence and allow him some space.

Mum is pleased to see that Libra is cautious and weighs things up before making a decision. Scorpio always thinks hard before she does anything, too. But she'll find Libra far too open and trusting. Mum thinks it's better to keep things to yourself.

She'll be irritated by the way Libra often changes his mind, as she likes everything decided and firmly under control. Yet Libra's warm hugs will soften his Scorpio mum's heart. This pair are very much drawn to each other and will love each other dearly, despite their differences.

Libra child with a Scorpio father

Bossy, ambitious Scorpio Dad rules his family firmly and won't let Libra charm his way out of anything. Dad's well-meant toughness can actually have a good effect on the child, bringing out his more assertive and adventurous side and helping him to become a true leader. But Dad mustn't overdo the strictness as it can also bring out the rebel in Libra, who'll become slapdash and idle in defiance.

Libra gets on well with everyone he meets. He's always got a smile for people, and they find him pleasant, humorous company. Scorpio can be a charmer too, but it's a mask he wears to manipulate others. Dad is a master at hiding his true feelings and makes enemies easily. Libra needs to grow up fast and learn to stay out of Dad's complicated life. This child will be out of his depth when it comes to Scorpio's intrigues.

Yet Scorpio wants the very best for his child and will treat him to generous gifts. Dad must remember to be as generous with his affection, too. Both love talking about new ideas and Libra will enjoy Scorpio's in-depth answers to his questions. Dad's intuition will always let him know if Libra is hiding a problem, for he's good at reading his child's mind.

Dad can force his own views on his child too much, believing that his way is the only way of doing things. What Libra needs is encouragement to find his own way and to make his own decisions. He'll benefit, though, from Dad's enthusiasm for any interests he develops. His encouragement and guidance, when gently given, can help take Libra to the top.

Libra child with a Sagittarius mother

This outgoing pair of optimists will charm each other with their fun conversations. Never bored together, they'll get on extremely well except when Mum's blundering insensitivity lands her in hot water with her child. And Libra's reasoned arguments about why he should be allowed to do something can drive Mum mad!

Both will make lots of friends wherever they go. Sagittarius will be delighted to have such a lively little charmer in tow, and Libra will love having a mum who dreams up such exciting things to do.

Playful Mum may be, but she's not so hot when it comes to responsibilities and discipline. She prefers fun and games to the serious side of life and Libra needs some sense of structure to feel secure. Fair discipline stops him becoming lazy or trying to get away with everything through charm, and also develops his positive and active side. Mum must set a few well-explained rules to put him on the right track, and keep him there.

Libra will certainly need Sagittarius' help to make decisions, so Mum must slow down and help him make up his mind. But she mustn't fall into the trap of choosing for him, because he's got to learn to do it for himself.

This duo both love to travel, but while Mum wants to be exploring and on the go, Libra prefers lazing in the hot sunshine. Sagittarius should concentrate on bringing out Libra's adventurous side and teaching him to take the occasional risk instead of being so cautious all the time.

These two get a lot of fun out of life together. Kind-hearted, enthusiastic Mum makes sure there's plenty of action and play to keep Libra busy. She broadens his mind and passes on wisdom too. Libra can't lose with this mum around.

Libra child with a Sagittarius father

This playful dad loves sport and will be pleased to find that Libra joins in with enthusiasm. Dad will enjoy sharing endless new ideas with his chirpy little Libra, too. Libra will be only too happy to encourage Dad's dreams and Dad will enjoy building castles in the air for Libra's amusement.

Creative Sagittarius is good at bringing out Libra's artistic and musical talents. He encourages him to read a lot as well, and keeps his child busy and occupied with new things to do. Libra won't have much time left for laziness.

When a row occurs, carefree Dad is quicker to forgive than Libra. Sagittarius rarely hangs on to grudges, while Libra broods. But Dad will quickly bounce him out of his mood, for he's never miserable himself except on those rare occasions when life gets him down and he loses his cheery optimism for a while.

At those times Sagittarius must reassure Libra it's not his fault he's feeling down in the dumps, otherwise Libra's confidence may be shaken. Libra so wants to please and dreads upsetting anyone. Dad must also take care not to demand too much of his child, or to get too annoyed if Libra chooses not to follow his advice. Libra needs encouragement to make some independent moves. It's all too easy to let Dad do his thinking for him.

This father's adventurous spirit helps bring out the brave streak in Libra. The time Dad spends talking with his child will develop Libra's confidence and verbal skills, and their joint sense of optimism and enthusiasm will inspire Libra to become the smiling, sharing, caring person he can be.

Libra child with a Capricorn mother

Ambitious Capricorn Mum won't let Libra live the easy life. She'll push him to achieve and behind that quiet exterior she's strict and very much in control. Libra can't dodge chores or homework with a charmer's smile when this mum's around. She makes sure he gets things done.

Once Libra has actually made up his mind to do something, Mum will be proud of his determination. She must watch that she doesn't make his mind up for him too much, though. Libra has to learn to think for himself.

Capricorn admires Libra's love of art and music, which appeals to this practical mum's hidden creative streak. She'll be pleased, too, that Libra gets on so well with people. Capricorn can be reserved and cool with others, while Libra quickly makes everyone feel at ease, although Mum will take pains to warn him not to be too trusting with people he doesn't know well.

Mum secretly wishes that she had Libra's humour and lively personality. Her wit is much drier, and though she has plenty of energy for work, she could hardly be called a live-wire. She'll get annoyed when she thinks Libra is being lazy, mistaking his need to flop and recharge his batteries for sheer idleness.

This child needs to know he's liked and loved, so Mum must show him affection. One day Libra will thank her for teaching him to be responsible and assertive, instead of just plain charming. He'll be tougher and more of an achiever for having grown up with no-nonsense Capricorn.

Libra child with a Capricorn father

Decisive Capricorn Dad knows where he's going and offers Libra lots of sound advice. He wants Libra to be as successful as he is, and mustn't be disappointed if Libra follows a less conventional path than his own. Success can take many forms, and at least Libra will have learned to be organised and disciplined from Dad's good example.

He may not actually have Dad's strong drive to get to the very top in his chosen career. Libra likes the idea of a world in which everyone is equal and would rather get on with people than be the boss and have to be ruthless or make vital decisions. There are, however, some Libras who turn out to be excellent leaders, adventurous and powerful, and Capricorn's firm style of upbringing will certainly add strength to these children's character.

Status-conscious Capricorn wants to own things that show how well he's doing and Libra will enjoy using Dad's expensive possessions. He'll be upset if Dad is always saying 'Don't touch', or spends money himself and forgets to buy junior something too. Dad must remember not to put outward appearances before the needs of his own family. Libra has to know that he's loved, and special presents will touch his heart.

Libra is friendlier than Dad and a lot more open. But Dad thinks Libra can be a moody little so-and-so at times, and

Libra hates it when Dad's stubborn streak results in an argument in the family.

Libra is proud of Dad's success, but he would like him to be more spontaneous and light-hearted sometimes. Dad is great at providing an organised life for Libra but must remember that this child needs an occasional taste of freedom too.

Capricorn often dismisses Libra as just an amusing dreamer, full of silly schemes. Libra wishes his stern dad could share the joy of dreaming for the fun of it. Yet despite their differences, there's a lot of affection between these two and they can get on very well if they both try.

Libra child with an Aquarius mother

This pair love to talk and dream together, although Mum is slightly more practical than Libra and will happily pick holes in their big plans. Libra likes an idea for the sake of it, while Aquarius enjoys seeing how she can turn it into reality.

Mum loves her child's idealistic views on fairness and equality and Libra respects Mum's wish to change the world for the better. But Aquarius likes to work with large groups, getting involved in politics or campaigning for charities. Libra prefers to spread sunshine on a smaller scale, helping his neighbours and giving a cheery smile to perk up anyone who looks down.

Aquarius and little Libra both feel suffocated if they're not allowed their freedom, so this mum will never hem her child in. She'll enjoy seeing him spread his wings naturally, without being pushed in any direction he may not want to go. She must try to provide some order and routine to give him confidence and a feeling of security, though. He has trouble making decisions and a regulated life makes the process a little easier for him.

This duo are rarely emotional, although Libra is more likely to start an argument than his mum. Aquarius doesn't really mind as long as he's putting his point logically, for she's pleased to see he's learning to speak out and think for himself.

Best of all she loves his enthusiasm, his optimism and the friendship he offers. Together they make a popular pair.

Libra child with an Aquarius father

Energetic Aquarius inspires Libra to take up all sorts of interests. There's no opportunity for laziness with this dad around. Aquarius has an imaginative, creative mind and Libra loves sharing new ideas with him.

Libra will thoroughly enjoy Dad's spontaneous attitude to life. He never knows what to expect next from his unpredictable and, at times, eccentric father. Dad must just watch that he doesn't behave too strangely in front of Libra's friends. Libra is far more concerned about keeping up appearances than his dad.

Free-and-easy Aquarius must be aware that Libra needs a certain amount of firm discipline to strengthen his personality and encourage him to be more adventurous and decisive. A Libran who's been spoiled or allowed to get away with too much will become a lazy charmer who can't be bothered with achieving anything. Dad must make the effort to channel Libra in the right direction, which means firm, fair guidance.

This pair both love to travel, though Dad likes to explore while Libra prefers to laze on the beach. Both are forward looking and imaginative, and neither is particularly emotional. They'll be sociable and friendly with all they meet, if a little detached. Lucky Libra certainly won't suffer from a shortage of social life with Dad around.

Aquarius can get so caught up in political, scientific or social issues that he becomes distant from his own family. Too much coolness will sting Libra, for he needs to know he's loved, so Dad mustn't forget those hugs.

Dad encourages Libra to read a lot and do his homework, bringing out his child's creative side and stimulating his imagination. He teaches Libra how to have the confidence to be himself, instead of trying to please others all the time, and how to discover what it is he really wants out of life, then make decisions and stick with them.

Libra child with a Pisces mother

Libra loves snuggling up to his soft-hearted Pisces mum and she makes him feel warm and adored. Mum must watch that she doesn't spoil him or he will start to take advantage and become demanding. He needs firm but fair discipline, as well as some pushing, if he's not to become lazy.

Neither of them like a row, although there can be tiffs if they are feeling stressed. Mum prefers to disappear if an argument is brewing and Libra's desire for harmony at home will mean he'd rather bottle things up and hope his intuitive mum will notice there's something wrong.

Pisces doesn't like to make firm plans or be too settled, which can leave Libra feeling all at sea. He needs some sense of reliability in his surroundings to help him build confidence and learn to make decisions. Mum should do her best to create some routine and to act in a consistent way. She should get Libra organised, too, and see that he does his homework on time and doesn't charm his way out of chores.

Mum loves her child's warm, caring personality, which makes all the hard work he causes worthwhile. She's amused by his humour and understands his need for rest, for she needs rest too. But she does find it hard to cope when he tries to get his own way by bullying. And once Libra has actually made up his mind, nothing will stand in his way. Poor Mum's likely to get trampled in the stampede.

Creative Pisces brings out Libra's musical and artistic talents, and she dreams up endless things to do to keep his mind busy. With his Pisces mum, Libra's imagination will grow and this pair will share many happy days.

Libra child with a Pisces father

Kind Pisces Dad understands what it's like to be a child and will open up a whole world of painting, writing and music to spark Libra's creative imagination. Both love beautiful things and will enjoy visiting art galleries and museums. Dad wants to be loved and will be indulgent with Libra, letting him get away with a lot. Pisces needs to learn to set limits to stop Libra becoming manipulative and too cheeky. Libra does so much better if offered firm discipline and fair rules.

Sometimes Dad's swirling emotions overwhelm him. Libra thrives on an atmosphere of peace and harmony and can be thrown off balance by Dad's outbursts. Libra will blame himself and feel guilty even when it's not his fault. Dad must reassure him that he's blameless and loved.

Pisces must remember that Libra loves to lead an active social life. Libra enjoys finding out what he has in common with others, and likes being with people. Pisces, meanwhile, soaks up the emotions of others and will try to act like the people he's with. This eventually tires him and he often needs to retreat for rest. Libra needs rest too, but it's usually only necessary because he's overdone things.

Young Libra feels he can never quite pin his unusual dad down. Dad sometimes forgets what he's said and doesn't always give straight answers, which makes Libra feel uneasy. This child needs some sense of solid stability behind him to help him learn to handle the world.

Pisces should try to be straight with his child, dealing with problems as they arise instead of ignoring them. And he should try to create a stable lifestyle, mixed with enough freedom to keep Libra feeling buoyant and positive.

As for fun, Pisces will provide plenty of that and Libra will remember childhood as a magical time, made even more special by his caring father.

SCORPIO
Stars for Life

STAR BABY

Scorpio is a real howler who certainly knows how to get what she (or he*) wants. She opens her cute mouth and yells for it! Her smiles are a joy, but most of the time she's straight-faced, looking curiously – and slightly suspiciously – about her.

She won't be quick to hand out too much love, either. She likes to feel her way in the world, and wants to make sure you can be trusted to tend to her every whim before she truly gives her heart. Her natural reserve at this stage will make you want to handle her with care. She's not a baby who enjoys being thrown up in the air or played with at all roughly. She wants to know she's respected as an individual with her own rights. She hates any threat to her security or disruption of her precious routine.

Love, reassurance and cosseting cuddles keep her happy. Even at this early stage, Scorpio likes to feel she's in control of her life and her surroundings. Gradually her somewhat alarmed look gives way to beams of delight and a desire to explore as she begins to trust in her world – and in you. That early wailer turns into an extra-good baby, who simply wants to please.

Be sure that she is expressing her own wishes, though. Scorpio can be very secretive and hides her true feelings

*'She' is used to cover he and she for Scorpio child.

under a calm surface. She's a very emotional child, much more sensitive than she looks. Constant reassurance is essential, even if she appears to brush it off. Unless she feels truly accepted, negative emotions can begin to take root. Jealousy of a sister or brother, or small resentments she finds hard to let go, can blight her mind. Try to keep her bright by making her world a happy place to be in.

FIRST STEPS FOR SCORPIO

Once on her feet, energetic Scorpio will race around enthusiastically. She's curious and wants to get into every corner. Out in the garden she'll be rooting around for stones, oblivious to your pleas to keep clean. And on a sunny day she'll love nothing better than a paddling pool to splash in. Being a water sign, she really adores getting wet. She loves modelling too, and will prefer Plasticine and Playdough to a mountain of less adaptable toys.

Toddler Scorpio is quick to turn her baby babble into real words. She'll be full of questions to which you must provide the answers to satisfy her deep and mysterious young mind. She may not be the most sociable of children and takes time to make friends. Help her by formally introducing her to other children, thus reassuring her that you trust them – and she can, too.

She'll sulk if you try to order her about. So when it comes to toilet training the best thing is to take it gently, explaining what's needed and then allowing her time to respond. Don't make a fuss about 'accidents', or Scorpio could turn tearful and angry and you'll be back where you started.

Toddler Scorpio will be determined to get her own way. She'll flash a fiercely reproachful look at you and refuse to budge an inch if she doesn't want to do something you're insisting on. There are times when a stern talking to is required. But always temper tough words with love and logic, to make her see the sense of your actions. Punishments she doesn't understand will just lead to brooding, resentment, even the plotting of revenge. And Scorpio can be merciless when trying to set straight what she sees as an injustice.

But Scorpio will appreciate knowing who's boss. She likes to feel that there is order in her life and that someone is in control. It gives her a feeling of security to know her limits and that wild behaviour will not be tolerated. You'll know she's got the message when she suddenly brightens up in the middle of a telling-off. She realises that enough's enough, which makes it easier to forgive her naughtiness.

Scorpio is a homelover who loves to know there's a place where she belongs. She needs routine, warmth and a pleasant, loving environment. Arguments within the family shake her deeply, although she may continue to act cool and aloof on the surface. She has difficulty dealing with the turbulent emotions she hides underneath and needs a lot of time and understanding to help her express her fears and worries.

She hates secrecy in others and always prefers to know what's going on. But she insists on privacy for herself and will enjoy having a room of her own where she can mull over her little problems in peace. The good news is that she'll cheer you up no end when you're feeling down, by being sensitive to your mood and giving you a loving hug to drive away the blues.

SCHOOL RULES FOR SCORPIO

Scorpio can feel overwhelmed by her first experience of school. She still needs her privacy and finds being one of a crowd difficult to deal with. She'll stay out of any rough and tumble, wondering if she will ever be able to join in. Reassure her and listen if she tries to express her feelings about school. She needs a lot more encouragment than she ever asks for.

The upheaval of starting school will cause a bubbling up of the deep emotions that Scorpios battle with all their lives. Eventually she'll get them under control and become expert at hiding her true feelings, letting out only what she thinks will get the response she wants. She needs to be told that it's okay to reveal her feelings. Help her by listening sensitively and never dismiss her fears by telling her she's just being silly.

Young Scorpio is fiercely loyal to the chosen few. Those she dislikes will come in for a fierce tongue-lashing instead. But she will stand by anyone she loves through thick and thin. And if they happen to be suffering in some way, she'll be the first to bring flowers and a smile to cheer them up. She can be very warm-hearted when she's not brooding about herself. Scorpio stays at her most positive when she feels needed, helpful and, above all, when she's busy.

She usually has a few close friends she can share secrets with, preferring one best pal to being part of a gang. But teach her some tact. She must learn to give her friend space and not to turn cool or angry if that friend's busy and can't play sometimes. And she must be taught not to boast so much. Scorpio likes to prove she's best, but her bragging can put potential pals off.

As she nears her teens she seems driven to achieve, though often she's just trying to match expectations she believes others have of her. Teach her it's okay to relax, be herself and have some uncompetitive fun.

TEENAGE TAKE-OFF FOR SCORPIO

Teenage Scorpio can be pretty obnoxious to her parents at times, yet underneath it all she'll feel a deep bond with them. She wants to be treated as a friend and expects them to be honest and direct. She hates it if they break their word or show her up in public. Scorpio still knows how to get her own way and will artfully persuade Dad to let her stay out late or increase her allowance. But she hates being bossed about and there could be big clashes if Dad tries to lay down the law.

At school, competitive Scorpio stands a good chance of coming top of the class if she keeps away from trouble. She may not be as outgoing as some, but she'll impress with her abilities. She works hard, secretly dreaming of reaching the very top. Being prime minister or head of a bank would suit her image of herself. Don't laugh at her big ideas – she's got the determination to succeed!

STAR PARENTS

Scorpio child with an Aries mother

This pair are bursting with powerful energy. Mum's always on the go and rarely thinks much before she does something. Scorpio's strong energy is more centred around her emotions. She needs to keep busy, to stop her feelings boiling up and overwhelming her. Active Aries is just the person to see she hasn't got a spare moment to fret or brood.

Scorpio is more cautious and complicated than Mum. This child always thinks hard before she does anything new. She is a secretive little soul who is slow to trust others, while Mum is open and friendly, if perhaps a little too self-centred.

Aries Mum loves to have her own busy life besides her family. Scorpio has emotional needs she may not show and will feel anxious if Mum is off doing her own thing too often. Aries thinks children should be independent at an early age and it's very hard for her to understand their emotional dependency. Scorpio needs lots of love and security to grow into a strong person and Mum must take time to show how much she cares, otherwise Scorpio will be clingy and grow up withdrawn and moody.

Here's a child who tries very hard at school. She's driven to succeed and Mum will be delighted to see her progress. Aries wants Scorpio to be as successful as she is and this child is more than willing to compete. She's good at games, and often top of the class. Aries' enthusiasm and drive will help her on to greater things.

Mum can sometimes be too spontaneous and volatile for Scorpio, who prefers people to be consistent. Aries wishes her child was more direct and open, less secretive. Yet she will make sure Scorpio has a lovely happy childhood, and

Scorpio will feel secure in knowing that strong, effective Aries Mum will always be there to protect her.

Scorpio child with an Aries father

Aries Dad and Scorpio child are both active and sporty and determined to get the most out of life. Dad thinks up lots of exciting things to do to keep Scorpio from turning inwards and brooding, but he must remember that Scorpio enjoys the intellectual side of life too. Aries should try to balance lively trips with activities that will stimulate Scorpio's mind.

Dad has a hot temper that cools in a flash. He never holds a grudge and quickly forgets hurts, for there's too much fun to be had to waste time fretting. Scorpio will allow an upset to linger until she finds the chance to exact her revenge – and it could be years later! Optimistic Dad finds this disconcerting. He's so candid, while Scorpio has hidden depths, concealing strong feelings under a placid exterior.

Dad hates to hear home truths about himself, and while Scorpio is very loyal to her loved-ones, she can make stinging remarks in self-defence. She also tends to analyse everyone she meets, while Dad takes them at face value. Scorpio is more of a thinker than her father and, although he's clever, he's more concerned with action, and she with feelings and thoughts.

Aries hates to be tied down, while Scorpio would like to keep him at home more. He's usually a busy man with an active career and can seem loud, assertive and overconfident to Scorpio at times. She wants him to be softer, more caring, to listen to her and to meet her need for emotional reassurance. Aries finds it hard to relate to feelings, but he'll find it's worth the effort when he does.

Dad must take the time to answer Scorpio's searching questions. He might not understand how anyone can think about things so deeply, but she does need to know all the answers. Aries will admire Scorpio's determination and she'll always look up to him for his effectiveness. If Dad can create routine in their lives and show the warmth he feels, he'll enjoy a happy relationship with his Scorpio child.

Scorpio child with a Taurus mother

Warm-hearted Taurus Mum gives Scorpio all the love and security she could wish for. Mum is completely in tune with Scorpio's hidden emotional needs and showers her with affection. But she can be overprotective and possessive and must watch that she allows Scorpio space to develop in her own individual way.

Taurus hasn't got Scorpio's high level of energy and can lose patience with this child's deep questions about life. Taurus prefers a quiet and gentle existence, centred on home and family. And while Scorpio is a homebird too, she needs constant activity to keep her energy channelled in positive ways. Mum must encourage her to take part in a wide range of interests. Anything scientific or historical will fascinate her, and sport will keep her fit. She tends to be greedy, like her Taurus mum, and will put on weight easily.

Here's a mum who hates confrontation, and Scorpio can be a real little foot-stamper. Soft Mum often gives in for a bit of peace and quiet, but she must learn to say no to stubborn Scorpio, otherwise the child will grow up full of demands and tantrums. Scorpio responds best to firm discipline and logical explanation of any rules.

Mum can lose her cool when she's really pushed. Scorpio may not show it, but she'll take it very much to heart and plot her revenge. She can't help this vengeful streak – it's part of her nature.

Sensible Taurus will help Scorpio to see logic, accept her feelings, and be more open with people. Mum will also show her how to handle her very strong emotions and grow up a happy and balanced person.

Scorpio child with a Taurus father

Good-hearted Dad creates a happy, stable home where everyone knows what's expected of them. Scorpio loves the emotional warmth, the stability and predictability. It makes her feel safe and loved. All Dad expects of her is that she behaves with consideration, and she will do most of the time.

But there will be days when Scorpio loses her grip on her strong emotions and erupts with tantrums. She'll be difficult and snappy and won't let go of an argument. Dad will lose his temper too, if pushed too far, and both will sulk until Taurus offers a big hug to make everything right again. Taurus is one of the few people Scorpio feels confident enough with to say what she actually thinks, not just what will win her approval for her. Dad is the sort of person this cautious child trusts.

Scorpio can become impatient with Dad's lack of get-up-and-go, and she needs activity to stop her becoming bogged down by her thoughts. It's a good idea to get her involved in sport or dance to help her work off some spare energy, so that she doesn't take things out on those at home.

Taurus distrusts anything too new, while Scorpio is rather more curious and enjoys novelty. In the teenage years she'll accuse Taurus of being an old fogey. Scorpio is into fashion, while Dad's happiest in his comfortable old clothes and can't be bothered with shopping.

Both value security. Taurus loves his home comforts and enjoys buying things for the house, while Scorpio is anxious to have emotional security. Dad is a comforting character who understands his child. He may be moody and pessimistic at times, but he's full of kindness and warmth. He'll make a perfect father for Scorpio.

Scorpio child with a Gemini mother

Lively Gemini Mum lives in her head, which buzzes with bright ideas. While Scorpio is equally energetic, life for her is coloured by her emotions and she expects people to take account of her feelings, which Gemini Mum often forgets to do.

It's hard for quick-thinking Gemini to understand the tidal emotions that sway her forceful child this way and that.

Gemini loves fun and laughter while Scorpio lives life far more seriously, and certainly takes any hurts very badly indeed.

Gemini doesn't even take the truth that seriously. She'll play games with it, which confuses Scorpio, who hates to feel anything is being hidden from her, although she'll frequently hide her own feelings. Above all, she can't stand jolly Mum's teasing.

Gemini hates to be bored and is always out socialising. Scorpio would prefer to stay at home more and have Mum all to herself. Yet she benefits from Gemini's outgoing personality and will learn a lot from her about communicating with others.

Scorpio will be glad of Mum's firm direction, although she'll sometimes wish Mum wouldn't try to run her life for her. Scorpio needs to find her own direction and Gemini must watch she doesn't try to live her own life through her child.

Gemini will enjoy conversations with her early-talking Scorpio and will be highly amused by her grown-up questions, thinking up clever and entertaining responses.

Mum can best help Scorpio by setting up a regular routine at home and remembering that her child has a strong need for emotional security. Lots of love and affection – as well as Gemini-style fun – will help Scorpio grow up happy and positive.

Scorpio child with a Gemini father

Restless Gemini Dad has to keep busy, which can be a good thing for Scorpio. She needs plenty to do, to stop her from brooding on hurts, plotting childish revenge and becoming pessimistic. She's full of energy, and can achieve so much if it's properly channelled. Dad is bursting with bright ideas and should apply his mind to keeping Scorpio active.

He's more likely to choose hobbies that exercise his mind. Scorpio needs a good balance of intellectual and sporty interests so that she gets the chance to work off that strong supply of surplus energy. Dad should make sure she gets both, and watch that he encourages her to finish what she starts. He's not very good at doing this himself, and Scorpio often gives up on things all of a sudden. Once she's really set her heart on something, though, she'll do everything she can to achieve her goal.

Gemini has an unpredictable temper and Scorpio will take his outbursts to heart, preferring people who aren't so volatile and changeable. She wants everything and everyone in her life to be under control. Dad loves springing surprises, which Scorpio doesn't always enjoy. She actually hates surprise and likes plenty of warning, especially about any changes that lie ahead.

Here's a father who lives for amusement and fun. Scorpio is more serious, but both share a great sense of curiosity and will have a lot of fun together discovering new places or finding out how things work.

Dad enjoys answering Scorpio's stream of questions, but can get bored all of a sudden. He should watch his step with sensitive Scorpio. She'll feel hurt if he shows that he's suddenly lost interest in her chatter.

Scorpio will benefit considerably from Dad's lessons in how to speak up for herself and get on with others. He may not be emotional in the way she is, but together they share enthusiasm and wonder about life, and Dad will teach Scorpio the important lesson of how to have fun.

Scorpio child with a Cancer mother

Loving Cancer Mum creates a protective environment in which her emotional little Scorpio child can thrive. Cancer is one of the few signs Scorpio is quick to trust. Cancer is certainly more generous when it comes to love than most other signs, and Scorpio will respond to her caring ways.

Mum tunes in happily to Scorpio's thoughts. Scorpio likes her privacy and would hate to think Mum knew all her secrets, but she's glad that Cancer can sense when she's hurt and offers a warm shoulder to cry on. Cancer can make

Scorpio reveal her feelings the way no-one else can.

Mum must watch that she allows Scorpio some space to be herself. Cancer can tend to live through her child and Scorpio will want to shake her off, insisting she finds her own individual path through life without Mum's rather heavy-handed interference.

Cancer admires Scorpio's determination and her ability to reach her goals. Mum is a much softer character who hasn't got Scorpio's sense of direction, so she'll probably need some help when it comes to guiding Scorpio towards a career. She may doubt her child's big dreams, but Mum should appreciate that Scorpio can get to the top through sheer determination.

Scorpio finds it easy to get her own way with her pliable Cancer mum, but Mum must learn to put her foot down or Scorpio could end up very spoiled. Sometimes Mum will erupt with anger when things really do get out of hand and she should watch for signs of brooding and sulking afterwards in Scorpio. She feels things deeply and is reluctant to let go of hurt.

Mum offers the kind of traditional upbringing that Scorpio needs, and Scorpio feels safe and loved with her. These two understand one another well and will have a strong bond indeed.

Scorpio child with a Cancer father

Emotional Cancer Dad may seem calm on the surface, like his Scorpio child, but inside this pair swirl with emotions. And while Cancer Mum often learns to accept her feelings and go with them, both Cancer Dad and Scorpio are experts at repressing them.

Scorpio particularly can keep a cool and collected front, but eventually her feelings erupt. The result will be tantrums, while Cancer Dad will be volatile and bossy. Dad should try to make sure his style of firm discipline is fair and consistent. This will help Scorpio feel safe and secure, and avoid him being bossy back in response. If Dad keeps changing his mind about the way he deals with Scorpio's behaviour, she'll soon doubt his strength and learn to manipulate him.

Dad can cool situations down by taking young Scorpio for an outing. These two are both water element signs and love a day at the beach or a walk by the river.

Both Scorpio and Cancer are cautious and very careful with money. They hate unnecessary change and favour traditional ways, particularly when it comes to education. Both tend to be pessimistic worriers but they can cheer each other up, Dad by offering care and support and Scorpio with amusing tales that make Cancer laugh.

Dad finds Scorpio's rather grown-up questions disconcerting, but does his best to answer them. He likes a child to act like a child and puts no pressure on Scorpio to grow up too fast. Scorpio is more likely to put pressure on herself to succeed and Dad will give her loving support, even if he thinks she is too competitive sometimes. He'll teach her how to be more caring and affectionate to others, and she'll be forever glad of the love and security he worked so hard to give her.

Scorpio child with a Leo mother

Warm Leo Mother is generous-hearted and affectionate and makes Scorpio feel very much loved and secure. She understands her child's feelings, even down to Scorpio's need for privacy, though she doesn't share this herself. Mum is more open and sociable and loves nothing better than being the centre of attention, surrounded by people.

Scorpio is less sociable and can be shy before she decides to trust others. She needs to feel safe with people before she opens up at all. Mum helps to draw her out of herself, although Scorpio often wishes she could have Mum all to herself, instead of sharing her with hordes of her friends.

Mum will push Scorpio hard to succeed, and will enjoy basking in the reflected glory her clever child brings her. Scorpio pushes herself anyway, for she secretly dreams of leading the world and will work hard to reach her goal. It does her good to have plenty to occupy her mind, as she can brood and be negative if left with little to do. With active Leo Mum around there will be no shortage of ideas for outings and pastimes.

Leo must watch that she does not become too dominant and try to run her child's life. Scorpio can throw tantrums or withdraw into sullen moodiness if she's denied the chance to find her way through life.

Impulsive Mum is a little on the unpredictable side at times for Scorpio. This child likes to know exactly what's expected of her and loves regular routine, but Leo enjoys the unexpected and will change her schedule at the drop of a hat to fit in more fun.

Mum is eccentric, original and humorous and there will be times when serious Scorpio won't feel in the mood for Mum's jokes. Yet she offers brilliant advice which will impress Scorpio with its sense. Overall, Scorpio will have an enjoyable childhood with her clever and witty mum.

Scorpio child with a Leo father

Magnetic Leo Dad is a powerful man who makes it clear he's in control. Scorpio likes to feel her parents are strong enough to look after her properly and she respects Dad for always knowing what action to take, although Leo must watch he doesn't become too domineering or tough with her. Scorpio can easily rebel, sulking in her bedroom until she's hatched a plot of revenge. And yes, she will eventually get her own back!

Dad must be careful that he doesn't expect too much of Scorpio. She has high expectations of herself and extra pressure from Dad could start her worrying. Scorpio enjoys the chance to help in decision-making so Dad should be sure to include her. She likes to feel she has some control over her own destiny.

Scorpio needs emotional reassurance and here Dad is very good. He's warm, caring and understanding and this pair can forge a very strong bond between them. As she grows, Dad will enjoy answering her many questions, proud to have a child with such a bright and curious mind.

This child is more reserved than her flamboyant father and can sometimes be taken aback by his behaviour. There'll be clashes of willpower, as both insist on having their own way and neither will want to back down. They have fiery tempers, too, and sparks will fly although love will see them through.

Leo enjoys being looked up to and Scorpio may use this, flattering him to get things out of him. Leo's confidence will rub off on Scorpio and help to make her feel more secure and happy. She'll be put out, though, that so many people are drawn to him and take up his time, as she wants to be the special person in his life. He'll find the time to show her she is, and in return she'll be totally loyal and will love him dearly.

Scorpio child with a Virgo mother

Hard-working Virgo Mum approves of the way Scorpio applies herself at school, believing that effort will get you anywhere. Scorpio secretly knows she's destined for the top, so she drives herself to achieve and she'll be glad to have such strong support from Mum.

Virgo is pleased that Scorpio takes a pride in her appearance and that she's tidy about the house, too. Mum likes their home to run according to a regular routine and is a believer in firm discipline, all of which suits Scorpio, who likes to know just where she stands and what's expected of her.

Both admire each other for their attention to detail. Mum enjoys using her lively mind to answer Scorpio's questions and, as both like looking into how things work, they'll have fun finding out together.

Mum is not a great one for hugs and kisses but Scorpio accepts her emotional reserve. Mum seems happy to help without making big emotional demands on Scorpio, who has enough trouble coping with her strong feelings without having to deal with anyone else's needs.

Mum will find it hard to understand Scorpio's likes and aversions, her moods, jealousies, desire for revenge and her powerful imagination. Virgo lives life on a more light-hearted level and lacks really strong feelings herself. And she hasn't got Scorpio's competitive spirit either. Virgo is happy to be second in command, serving others rather than striving for power, while Scorpio is dead set on achieving power and control. Whenever she helps others, she'll expect something in return, too.

This pair can both be very critical of others at times, and they tend to worry and set impossibly high standards for themselves. Mum will try hard to create a secure, traditional home for her child and will teach her good behaviour and common sense. She'll see Scorpio has an education that suits her, and while neither are good at creating fun and laughter, they'll enjoy each other's company. Scorpio will feel that her Virgo mum is someone she can truly rely on.

Scorpio child with a Virgo father

Virgo Dad is keen to keep order in his home, which is a real plus for Scorpio, who needs firm discipline to feel secure. She likes having a dad who is so predictable and reliable, and she laps up his lessons in money sense and how to behave towards other people. Even his career guidance makes good sense to her.

Dad is full of down-to-earth common sense, which reassures Scorpio. He helps her to feel safe and sure of where she belongs and what's expected of her. The organised base Dad provides improves her confidence and trust in life, but this serious pair can clash sometimes. Scorpio always wants her own way and if Dad thinks this might lead her into trouble or time-wasting, he'll act firmly to stop her. Scorpio will throw noisy tantrums until she realises she'd be better off using her other weapon – manipulation. She knows how soft-hearted Dad really is and will choose the right time to charm him round to her way of thinking.

Dad encourages Scorpio's educational interests, which keep her mind active and stop her brooding or being negative. He must encourage some sporty hobbies, too, to help work off some of that Scorpio energy. Virgo loves to see his child's lively mind developing and will take delight in her precocious questions as she grows. Scorpio thinks on a larger scale than Virgo, but she'll approve of Dad's talent for detail and getting things right.

Both are cautious and wary of strangers. They are careful with money, to the point of meanness, and both love home best of all. Dad will teach Scorpio to treat others more caringly and politely and Scorpio will entrance Dad with her imagination and her mysterious, secretive depths.

Scorpio child with a Libra mother

Sociable Libra Mum encourages Scorpio to stay busy and keeps her mind off negative thoughts. Scorpio is slow to trust others and is more of a homebird than friendly Mum, who has to be on the move. Scorpio is the sort to take instant dislikes to people, and Mum can teach her to be more open and welcoming to others.

Scorpio thinks Mum is a ditherer when it comes to making decisions. This child likes to press ahead determinedly with anything she starts and hasn't much time for people who keep changing their minds. She'd like Mum to be firmer and more definite about life because she feels safest with people who seem to have everything under control, and who can prove they're strong enough to protect and look after her.

Yet Mum's loving nature does Scorpio a power of good on an emotional level. Scorpio needs a lot of reassurance and Mum is always there with hugs and smiles to keep her feeling loved. Libra is generous, caring and sharing, while Scorpio likes to keep everything to herself. Mum will have to learn to live with Scorpio's secretive ways, as this child hates anyone to threaten her privacy.

Soft Mum indulges Scorpio and buys her all kinds of

treats. This delights Scorpio, who loves to show off when she's got something better than her friends. But she may not show the gratitude that Libra would like. Libra must learn to be firmer with her and not let her get away with so much. Scorpio really is better with firm but fair guidance. These two will enjoy a loving and fairly relaxed relationship, and Scorpio will benefit from her Libra mum's outgoing nature.

Scorpio child with a Libra father

Caring Libra Dad likes to treat Scorpio as a little grown-up, which makes Scorpio feel very proud of herself. Dad enjoys her precocious questions and is amused by her intuition and her amazing ability to turn up anything that's been lost. Libra is so absent-minded, Scorpio can be a real help!

Dad encourages Scorpio to be creative and to appreciate art and music. He helps her develop her intellectual abilities but must watch that he encourages her love of sport, too. She's more energetic than he is and needs to keep active to stop herself dwelling on things too much.

Libra believes in giving his child the freedom to decide what she wants to do with her life. Just sometimes Scorpio would prefer to be told – she likes firm handling as it makes her feel safe. Otherwise she will push poor Dad to the limit trying to get her own way, testing just how far she can go.

Sensible Dad will try to reason with her, and she'll see sense and stop her tantrums once she understands why she should. Above all she hates commands and shouting, as she's far more sensitive than she acts. Scorpio isn't an optimistic, sociable person like Dad and she can learn from him. She'd actually like him to be at home with her a lot more than he is. She likes everything to be in its place, reliable, predictable and under complete control.

Dad loves new ideas and enjoys lively debate. Scorpio is curious about anything new, too, as long as it doesn't threaten her sense of security in any way. Both think that how you appear to the outside world is important, which can make Dad hide any problems and carry on regardless, pretending everything is fine.

Scorpio's intuitive powers will soon tell her if anything is wrong, and she'll feel insecure and may start behaving badly or become withdrawn. Security is everything to her and it's far better if Dad can be open with her so she'll feel reassured that problems are not her fault. With Dad's ability to tune into her feelings, these two should enjoy a happy family relationship.

Scorpio child with a Scorpio mother

These two bounce through life with the same Mars-driven energy and ambition. Scorpio pushes her child like mad to get to the top, and Scorpio drives herself to be best of the bunch. It's unlikely she'll fail with Mum's enthusiasm and drive to help her, but Mum must watch she doesn't push Scorpio so hard she rebels. Scorpio child is determined to make her own way in life and won't be amused if Mum tries to use her to fulfil her own thwarted dreams.

This Scorpio pair must watch that they don't spark each other into rows and tantrums. With Mars constantly tweaking their emotions, there are bound to be flare-ups. Both want their own way all the time and will never back down in an argument. They are likely to sulk and put endless effort into manipulating each other emotionally. What they both need is to be kept active to stop themselves drifting into the less positive and attractive Scorpio traits – jealousy, brooding, plotting and a desire to control.

Mum has plenty of energy to keep up with her whirlwind Scorpio child. But she must watch as the child grows that she doesn't pry into her life too much. Scorpio wants to control everything that moves and Mum would hate to think her children kept secrets from her. She should understand that little Scorpio is a secretive soul who needs her privacy – just like her mum!

Mum will do a fine job in creating a secure environment for Scorpio to grow up in. Scorpio Mum likes order and routine. She imposes firm discipline, doesn't spring unwelcome surprises and likes life to be predictable, all of which makes young Scorpio feel very much at home and happy.

Neither are great sharers, so little Scorpio may seem a bit of a mystery even to her mother. Yet Mum will enjoy answering all her questions, and both appreciate each other's inquiring minds – as long as they aren't inquiring into each other's business, that is!

If they learn to respect each other's privacy, these two will have a happy time together.

Scorpio child with a Scorpio father

Scorpio Dad loves his lively little Scorpio child dearly. He's a devoted father at heart who wants the very best for his family, although he may not always act that way. Dad is usually a very busy man, often away on business, and he can live a rather complicated life, full of intrigues that have no place in the life of a child.

Young Scorpio will have to learn some independence, which can be difficult because she is secretly a very dependent child emotionally. She needs a lot of reassurance and love from Dad as she feels hurts much more deeply than she shows and can worry and brood when things don't go right. Dad should use his intuition to see how best he can help his youngster.

Dad must watch his tendency to be bossy. He enjoys exercising control over his child but should remember that Scorpio will take it to heart, despite her sometimes aggressive front. He should concentrate more on what he's so good at – creating an orderly, well-run home where little Scorpio knows just what's expected of her.

This pair hate change and are quite unwilling to adapt. Both are suspicious of new ways of doing things and like traditional methods best. Neither like to show their feelings and will try hard to control their emotions. It's when these repressed feelings build up that there could be clashes.

Yet Scorpio has an almost psychic ability to see the hidden feelings of others and to unlock their secret thoughts.

This skill, used kindly on each other, will help these two to avoid major clashes.

Scorpio child with a Sagittarius mother

Bouncy Sagittarius Mum likes to stay on the move while her child prefers a more sedentary life. Mum yearns to get out and about, meeting people, sharing ideas and having fun. Scorpio secretly wishes she'd stay at home more often, which is where this child thinks Mum belongs.

Yet Scorpio benefits from Mum's sociability and enthusiasm for life. Active Sagittarius will see that Scorpio is kept busy, which helps to stop her brooding, feeling jealous or plotting revenge for minor hurts. Scorpio needs all the help she can get if she's to be happy and positive.

Sagittarius loves to see Scorpio's mind developing so fast. She especially enjoys thinking up answers to the child's endless questions and will spend a lot of time talking and playing with Scorpio. She's not one for a strict routine, preferring to take life as it comes, and she's unlikely to be highly organised. She's unlikely, too, to be firm with discipline. Scorpio, however, likes a more ordered atmosphere where she knows what's coming next and exactly what's expected of her.

Mum is not the most tactful person in the world and Scorpio is a lot more sensitive than she looks. She broods when she's hurt, and will quietly vow to get her own back. Scorpio is far more emotional than Sagittarius and needs a lot of reassurance and affection, despite her cool exterior.

These two are different in many ways. Scorpio is secretive and needs her privacy while Mum is open and honest and loves to share knowledge, affection and fun. Sagittarius enjoys change and travel, while Scorpio is not so keen, unless her curiosity gets the better of her. Mum is full of little jokes, while Scorpio is more serious. And Mum takes risks, while Scorpio tags along telling her to be more cautious.

But Mum will teach Scorpio the very useful lesson of how

to direct her energy in ways that will bring happiness and prosperity. They will enjoy a busy, loving relationship and share a close bond of affection.

Scorpio child with a Sagittarius father

Playful Sagittarius Dad treats his Scorpio youngster as his best friend. Dad is full of energy and is delighted that Scorpio shares his lively love of sport. His encouragement to take up exercise can help Scorpio by channelling off her excess energy so that she doesn't have time to brood, fret or be pessimistic.

However, much as Sagittarius likes being a dad, he prefers the fun of fatherhood to the responsibilities. He should try to make an extra effort to give Scorpio practical and emotional support. Security is vital to her and Dad is such a free spirit that she can feel anxious about her stability unless he takes the time to reassure her.

Sagittarius must offer Scorpio plenty of praise for her splendid efforts at school. Scorpio is set on getting to the top and is often better than her father at directing her energies towards her ambitions. She'll do even better if she has Dad's approval.

Here's a father who enjoys teaching his child the fun things in life. He'll pass on the joys of singing, drawing and reading and help Scorpio to learn how to enjoy herself and not take life too seriously. Dad is open, optimistic and straightforward, while Scorpio hides secrets, holds grudges and won't back down in an argument. Dad can win her round with affection, although he's never keen on apologising either.

Dad will explain any rules he sets, which suits Scorpio as she resents commands. And he'll make her laugh her way out of a tantrum. Scorpio may sometimes wish she had a more predictable and dependable dad, but she'll never forget his valuable lessons in how to enjoy life.

Scorpio child with a Capricorn mother

Behind that gentle exterior, Capricorn Mum is a toughie who enjoys being in firm control at home. She's rather like her power-hungry Scorpio child, in fact, who appreciates the way Mum creates a solid base where everyone knows their place.

Scorpio feels happiest in this orderly and disciplined environment. Ambitious Mum offers direction and common sense, and though at times Scorpio can feel pressured to do her best, she's glad to have such strong family back-up. Scorpio is driven from within to succeed, but her emotions can be fragile at times and she's greatly encouraged by approval from Mum when she does well.

Capricorn can seem cool and unemotional and Scorpio won't show her feelings on the surface either. Yet she needs more affection than she'll ever ask for and Mum must learn to be warmer with her. Both share a dry sense of humour and love making jokes at other people's expense, although neither will enjoy it if the tables are turned on them. Scorpio will also brood on hurts and plot revenge – which she'll be determined to get, no matter how long it takes.

Scorpio respects Mum for being strong enough to discipline her firmly and therefore strong enough to protect her properly. But she'll rebel if Mum is too stern. Remember, Capricorn, that rules need explaining to Scorpio. She can't stand commands. Yet Scorpio always wants her own way and there will be major clashes in the teenage years when this strong-willed pair fail to see eye to eye.

Mum will make sure Scorpio has access to the wide range of interests she needs, and the traditional education that suits her best. And even when rows erupt, Scorpio will be clear in her mind that she has a strong and caring protector in Mum – someone she knows she can rely on.

Scorpio child with a Capricorn father

Sensible Capricorn Dad may not have Scorpio's energy or love of sports but he's just as competitive, although he keeps much quieter about it. Capricorn thinks his place is at the top, just where Scorpio thinks she should be. Providing Scorpio treats him with some measure of respect, Capricorn will back his child strongly to succeed, especially if it means Capricorn gets some reflected glory and status.

Dad is very concerned about his public image. He wants to be seen as a pillar of society, with well-behaved and hard-working offspring. He's glad Scorpio wants to study hard and conform as much as possible – both agree that conventional ways bring security and respect.

Capricorn enjoys giving fatherly advice, but he can be irritated when Scorpio asks for more details before accepting what Dad's said. Conversely, Dad is pleased to see that Scorpio always thinks about what she's going to do before leaping in. She's just as cautious as he is.

Scorpio has more imagination than Capricorn and is more intuitive. She has an emotional depth, mystery and subtlety, while Capricorn sees everything in simple terms of right and wrong. Both dislike change and agree that it's important to continue tradition. They differ in that Capricorn is geared towards accumulating material wealth, position and respectability, while Scorpio craves power and control.

Dad must show Scorpio love and affection. That may be hard for reserved Capricorn, but it's vital, otherwise Scorpio's boundless energies could take a negative turn. Jealousy, revenge, anger and pessimism all trickle from an unloved Scorpio. Given plenty of affection, she'll be fine.

Scorpio will be very grateful for the secure and safe home Dad provides, despite the unavoidable rows of adolescence when this wilful pair clash spectacularly. There may not be a lot of spontaneity and humour in a Capricorn home, but there is structure and life is predictable, which is just the way Scorpio likes it.

Scorpio child with an Aquarius mother

Absent-minded Aquarius is delighted to have Scorpio around

to find things she's lost, for Scorpio seems to have X-ray vision. She understands the way people are thinking too, and it can sometimes be disconcerting to have a little mind-reader in the family! But most of Mum's thoughts are highly commendable. She's always campaigning on behalf of those worse off than herself and is fascinated by politics and social issues.

Here she differs from Scorpio, whose world centres around herself. Aquarius thinks in terms of groups, bringing people together to act for the good of the whole. Scorpio isn't nearly so idealistic. All she asks is that she has a secure home, where everything is understood and in its place. Mum sometimes despairs at her lack of social awareness.

Scorpio wants Mum to concentrate more on her but Mum always seems to be off chasing new ideas. She'll try to make her child independent as fast as she possibly can, but Scorpio craves emotional reassurance, affection and the sense of a firm structure around her. Aquarius can be too free and easy and must try to remember that her child reacts sensitively to change and needs a regular routine and sensible discipline.

Logical Aquarius lives in her mind and is ill at ease with feelings. She can find it hard to understand Scorpio, who is emotional through and through, even though she does try hard to hide her feelings. Scorpio is very ambitious and believes she is destined for the top, and Aquarius may find it difficult to lend wholehearted support to her ambitions. She feels people should be as equal as possible and that working to better the lot of others is the highest calling.

Mum will explain any rules and is even understanding when Scorpio goes through her teenage tantrum stage, remembering her own. Scorpio will admire her mum's social skills and wish she could be that nice to people. Aquarius can teach her to think of others, but Mum must remember that to truly connect with this child there must be constant affectionate proof of her care and concern.

Scorpio child with an Aquarius father

Energetic Aquarius Dad is buzzing with ideas to keep Scorpio busy and stop her brooding. He's amazed at her thoughtful observations and questions and loves answering them. Dad is delighted to discover what a lively mind young Scorpio has and thinks she's very grown-up.

There's a real danger that he can think she's more mature and responsible than she really is. Scorpio doesn't want to be pushed to grow up. Inside she's a needy child who craves love and affection, even if on the outside she seems cool, detached and unemotional, like her Dad. Underneath she's bubbling with strong emotions that can burst violently to the surface at times. Dad can help her best by giving affection and reassurance. That way she'll gain self-confidence much faster.

Aquarius is many-sided and acts in unpredictable and sometimes eccentric ways. Scorpio feels more at ease with people who are consistent and behave in a way she can understand. She wants everything in her life to be under control and finds her good-humoured Aquarius dad a little too spontaneous and free-spirited at times. She has to admit he's fun, though!

Scorpio is more conventional than Dad and wants a traditional upbringing and schooling. Aquarius has futuristic ideas and lives in a world of books, science and social issues. Scorpio can feel he lacks heart, and it's important that Dad tries hard to show he cares. Scorpio thinks deeply, but she's no detached intellectual. She can't help but feel things deeply too.

Surround her with practical support and affection and she'll learn to enjoy Dad's wacky and wonderful ideas. Her horizons will be broadened and her hidden fears all but banished.

Scorpio child with a Pisces mother

Kind Pisces sometimes finds her energetic Scorpio child is more than she bargained for. Pisces Mum looked forward to having children but she didn't anticipate an energetic, foot-stamping little creature like Scorpio.

Yet there's a very strong bond between these two. Pisces Mum is brilliant at tuning into Scorpio's hidden emotions. She understands her child deeply – they're both water signs and life is coloured by their feelings. They both like to make decisions based on intuition, but while Scorpio puts a lot of work into hiding her feelings, Pisces Mum is more relaxed with hers, happy to follow where they lead. Mum can teach Scorpio to accept her emotions so that they become less overwhelming for the child.

Pisces often changes her mind and mood and lives in a dreamy world where everything shifts from day to day. This is something that bothers Scorpio. She prefers people to be consistent and reliable and likes to know just where she stands. Pisces avoids anything as structured as routine.

Mum can be irritable under pressure, which will unnerve sensitive Scorpio. And she isn't good at exercising firm discipline either, preferring to ignore Scorpio's wayward behaviour rather than have a row. There's a risk she'll allow Scorpio to become too demanding and spoiled, so Mum must try to be firm and consistent. It makes Scorpio feel safer and more sure of her limits.

Mum is a bit of a worrier and Scorpio can easily pick up the habit too. Sometimes Pisces seems distant, usually when she's recharging her batteries and is too preoccupied to give hugs and reassurance. But most of the time she showers warm affection on Scorpio, making her feel loved, secure and understood.

Scorpio child with a Pisces father

Pisces Dad feels a close sense of understanding with his little Scorpio. But he can be too kind to her as he loves his peace and quiet and will agree to anything to stop Scorpio bothering him. She always wants her own way and he knows there will be tantrums if she doesn't get it, so he gives in. He knows Scorpio won't back down, so he does instead.

He'd be wiser to get tough with her sometimes. She needs telling firmly what to do and feels much safer if she knows Dad has the reins and she doesn't have to take complete control of her life. Dad must learn to exercise discipline.

Sometimes Dad will be pushed into exploding and Scorpio will either go away and sulk or laugh to herself because she's managed to push Dad into reacting. Basically she wants Dad to be firm, reliable, predictable and strong, which are all the things Pisces tries to avoid. Yet he'll win her over every time with his caring heart. Dad ladles affection on Scorpio, so at least she knows she's loved and is reassured on an emotional level, which is important to her.

Dad sometimes says he'll do something then he often changes the way he acts to suit the circumstances. This disconcerts Scorpio, who'd prefer that he stayed the same all the time. Yet she benefits from the way he teaches her about art, theatre, music, poetry – interests that can stimulate that strong Scorpio imagination.

Pisces can be taken aback by Scorpio's probing questions, but he likes to investigate life too and enjoys finding out answers for her. He lacks Scorpio's energy yet his creative streak ensures he thinks up lots of interesting things to do to keep that powerful Scorpio mind occupied and happy. And though he might not be brilliant at providing a highly organised lifestyle for her, when it comes to love and affection he'll win hands down.

SAGITTARIUS
Stars for Life

STAR BABY

Restless Sagittarius is so packed with get-up-and-go it will be hard for his (or her*) proud parents to keep up with him. From the moment of his birth, his wide-awake eyes look at the world with a fascinated gaze. He wants to know about anything and everything, and that winning smile will reward anyone who takes the time and trouble to show him something new.

Bright mobiles over his cot will amuse him. Baby gyms will keep him busy, and gentle bouncing on Dad's knee will thrill him to bits. But prompt service when he howls is a must for little Sagittarius, who can get very grumpy if his needs are not met fast. Above all, he wants lots of warmth, laughter and cuddles, although he'll tell you clearly when he's had enough. Sagittarius enjoys feeling free and dreads being prevented from simply being himself.

FIRST STEPS FOR SAGITTARIUS

Sagittarius will make mammoth efforts to get moving. He's usually quick to crawl and is determined to get on his feet as fast as he can. Once moving under his own steam, life becomes an exciting adventure for this busy explorer. But watch him closely – he'll soon be fiddling with the TV, trying to work the video, pulling books down on himself and,

*'He' is used to cover he and she for Sagittarius child.

worse, reaching for the kettle or trying to work out what matches do. Try to make the house safe for him so that he can explore in peace. Too many warnings and tellings off will depress this little pioneer.

Toddler Sagittarius is an entertainer who loves to see you smile as he races round in circles, pops out from behind the sofa, or tries to stand on his head. He's usually pretty well behaved, except when bored. Solve his restlessness by taking him out as often as possible – he'll love anything new. At the same time, a secure home means everything to Sagittarius. With a loving family, he'll bloom into a happy and responsive child, a favourite with everyone. Let him take his time getting to know people, though. He likes to be formally introduced before he'll relax and play.

Sagittarius laps up whatever he's taught at an amazing rate and may well show signs of wanting to learn to read when he can barely talk. He adores picture books and children's videos. Try to make sure they're ones he'll learn a lot from, though. Sagittarius has a huge thirst for knowledge, so don't waste his time.

Make sure you talk to him as much as possible too. There's so much going on in that head, and so many corners to explore, that he needs encouraging to become more conversational – although once he does start to talk properly, you won't be able to stop him. And of course, it will be questions, questions, all the way, as he eagerly tries to make sense of life.

Toilet training can be tricky. Sagittarius thinks it's all a big game and is far too busy to take it seriously. But once he tires of nappies, he'll start to see the point of racing for the potty. Don't rush him, he'll train himself in his own good time.

Toddler Sagittarius loves bouncing on the bed, washing up in the sink, and splashing in a bathful of toys. He sees your home as a giant playpen, full of things for him to have fun with. And when friends come round he's quite willing to let them share in his games. He's not possessive about his toys and makes sure everyone gets a go.

Sagittarius hates being told what to do, and any over-tough discipline can knock the stuffing out of him. What he needs is firm guidance, with a touch of good humour thrown in, to keep him happy and bright. As he gets older, Sagittarius learns to put his foot down and insists on his own way. He certainly has a strongly assertive side to his character and he won't stand for anything he thinks is unfair.

He hates, too, feeling pushed to do things he doesn't feel he's up to. Encourage this little individualist to tell you what he does and doesn't feel he can do. Help him to feel all right about himself, and reassure him that it's fine to ask for help sometimes.

Sagittarius has a busy imagination and loves magical tales. Mermaids, monsters, talking bears, Mickey Mouse – all of them send Sagittarius off into a fantasy world with a delighted look on his face. But keep a check that he doesn't think all these stories are real. Sagittarius can get muddled and people his world with all sorts of strange creatures. Don't worry too much, though. He'll grow out of it – well, almost. Even an adult Sagittarius remains something of an imaginative child – it's all part of this sign's enormous charm.

SCHOOL RULES FOR SAGITTARIUS

Sagittarius loves to learn. So it's important that you find a school that's right for him. It must offer enough discipline to help him to concentrate – which he can find hard. Yet it must give him room to think creatively and imaginatively. Poor teachers or dull classmates will drag him down, and he could even give up trying if he feels he's in the wrong environment.

He's at his best when his interest is grabbed. He'll read anything he can lay his hands on if he likes the subject and works well on bite-sized assignments he can really throw himself into. See that he doesn't race through his work too fast, though, and make sure he finishes his homework. Busy-minded Sagittarius finds it hard to complete things when something new and even more fascinating has caught his attention.

Praise him for his successes and help him see what went wrong when he doesn't get the marks he was hoping for. Sagittarius often carries on on his merry way without analysing why he's made mistakes. He needs some advice on how to do even better next time, plus help to see he can't shut out reality forever if he's ignoring his reasons for failing. Be tactful, though. Sagittarius is at his best when optimistic and bright. Cast a shadow of doubt over him and he could lose his hopeful sparkle.

Emotions can be a tricky area for Sagittarius and he may well conceal hurts and upsets behind smiles and wisecracks. Once again, he's unwilling to face reality in case it doesn't live up to his idealistic expections. Sagittarius needs to be told that everyone has feelings they sometimes find hard to deal with, and that it's okay to talk about them. Let him know you love him just as much when he's sad as when he's happy-go-lucky, and that you're there to offer support when he needs it.

Sagittarius can be amazingly open and honest – in fact, downright tactless – when it comes to other people's feelings. You'll have to learn to live with his foot-in-the-mouth approach to life. He certainly never means any harm. It's unlikely he'll ever grow out of it, and his attempts at putting things right usually only make matters more muddled. You'll just have to let him get on with it and love him for what he is. In his favour, he's always very forgiving and his charming nature usually knocks people off their feet.

TEENAGE TAKE-OFF FOR SAGITTARIUS

Teenage Sagittarius loves to argue a point and is usually sure he's right. He'll throw himself into campaigning to save the rainforests or the African elephant. You'll think he's found a cause for life – when suddenly he's on to something else. And he's always changing his mind too. Just when you think he's definitely decided he wants to be a doctor, that's all off and he's writing away for information on how to become a journalist. He's still as hard to keep up with as he was in toddlerhood.

As a teenager, he'll be optimistic, full of ideas and fun. He'll rebel against you if you lay down the law without explaining any rules that you set. Sagittarius is keen to find his own way in life and won't be told what to do. Clamp down on his freedom and you risk losing his respect, as he desperately wants to feel he's trusted. But gentle guidance is welcome. Even he knows he can be a bit reckless at times.

A secure home and a loving family still mean a tremendous amount to Sagittarius. He knows you can't explore without a safe base to come back to, but he'll expect you to be as honest and fair as he is. He wants, above all, to be treated as an equal.

STAR PARENTS

Sagittarius child with an Aries mother

Although Aries Mum loves her Sagittarius child, she's pleased that he leaves her fairly free to follow her own interests. Even as a baby he's happy to be dropped off with babysitters while she gets on with her speedy round of activity. Sagittarius likes his world to be fast-moving and there's never a dull moment with this up-to-date mum around. Both are sociable, and love to have something new and exciting to do, although she does think he swops hobbies too often. He could achieve so much more if he'd only stick at it.

Aries wants Sagittarius to be effective, successful and top of the class, and perhaps to fulfil her own thwarted ambitions. Sagittarius is bright as a button when it comes to brainpower, but he hates being pushed to follow a path that's not his own, so Mum should leave him to find his own way in life. He can't help but benefit from all that Aries drive and enthusiasm, and from having a mum who loves life as much as he does. Aries may be in for a shock when Sagittarius ups and leaves home early. He is often fast to seek independence, while Aries often thinks her children can't exist without her.

Young Sagittarius fidgets when he's got nothing to do, but his Aries mum will come up with a torrent of ideas to keep him busy. Sagittarius is full of good ideas too and impressed that his mother knows just how to put them into action. He's amused at her spontaneity – she does something the moment she thinks of it, and it usually turns out well. He wishes he could be that effective.

Mum may appreciate how emotionally independent and advanced he is, but she may not give him the discipline he needs and could be in for a full-scale teenage rebellion. He must have well-explained direction from the start, not Aries-style outbursts of irritation.

Powerful Aries Mum organises all sorts of outings to places they'll both enjoy. She'll pay Sagittarius for any chores he does, teaching him that money is to be earned and doesn't fall out of trees. But she can be a spendthrift, so Sagittarius won't learn to save.

Aries likes Sagittarius' enthusiasm and his full-of-life straightforward nature. He's as direct and unworried as she is – and just as impatient and adventurous. Mum must try to be more generous and kind when warm-hearted Sagittarius is around. Sagittarius in turn knows Mum will always stand up for him and thinks she's the best.

Sagittarius child with an Aries father

These two have lots in common. They're both night owls who love to get the most out of every minute. They like discussing ideas and enjoy throwing themselves into high-flown causes together. Being a pair of fire signs, they'll stoke each other's enthusiasms into a blaze of action. But watch out – they're both accident prone and need reminding to look sometimes before they leap.

Aries loves Sagittarius' cheerful optimism, which is so like his own, and likes the fact that he's honest too. But he tries to dodge any blunt Sagittarius remarks aimed at himself, though he'll laugh when they're directed at someone else. Aries knows, however, that fast-talking Sagittarius just blurts out whatever comes into his head and never means any harm. Both hate to be tied down – freedom is essential to this pair.

Sagittarius is slightly less of a loudmouth than his forceful father. The youngster is able to calm down and see what's going on, while Aries leaps into action before thinking things out. Both are brimming with confidence and could never be accused of being boring, especially when they're together. Aries enjoys Sagittarius' yarn-spinning and wild exaggerations, and often wishes he had his child's way with words.

Busy Dad is not one to discuss emotions and may think that the best way to learn is through the school of hard knocks. Dad wants Sagittarius to achieve and to be as successful and tough as he is. And though the child may not be as ambitious as his dad, he is independent and a fast developer who can cope quite well with Aries' attitude.

Dad must remember that Sagittarius needs warmth and reassurance if he's going to keep trying and not give up and turn his attention solely to having fun. He may idolise his father and believe that he can never live up to him, so why even try? A little approval from Aries will go a long way towards keeping him on track.

Aries must help Sagittarius find direction in life by showing he respects his child's talents and achievements. And he should remember, too, the lesson that Sagittarius can teach him – how to give more thought to others instead of trampling them on the road to success.

Sagittarius child with a Taurus mother

Taurus Mum is warm-hearted, loving and protective, but she can find it hard to understand Sagittarius' need to live life on the wild side sometimes. Taurus can be very possessive of her child, thinking that because domesticity suits her, it will suit him too. Sagittarius can be left yearning for fun, laughter and excitement, while Taurus provides cosiness and a good book by the fireside. She loves routine, and needs to make a special effort if Sagittarius is to express the strong, impulsive side of his nature.

Taurus tries hard to understand her children and will spend hours listening to them. Yet coping with restless, changeable Sagittarius and his endless questions is quite a job for her. She's very traditional and settled, so his forward-looking, ever-active character is quite foreign to her. Sagittarius tries to haul his mum up to date and make her enthusiastic about new ideas, but she's not really that interested.

Taurus can't bear confrontation and tries to ignore young Sagittarius' fiery tantrums. She only loses her temper when his noisiness, casual appearance and spendthrift ways push her to the limit. Then it comes out like a thunderclap, leaving Sagittarius wondering what he's done wrong, for he rarely means to misbehave. He soon forgets any outbursts, although Taurus is slower to forgive. In fact she'd be wise to speak to him quietly and explain why she wants him to change his behaviour, rather than letting things reach blow-up point, or trying to set rules he doesn't understand and therefore just ignores.

Taurus can be highly amused by Sagittarius' playful sense of humour, and her hidden sensitivity understands his emotional needs. She helps him turn his schemes into reality and teaches him money sense, too.

Taurus tends to feed up her young and she should remember that it suits Sagittarius to stay lean and lively. She can over-indulge children with presents too, but usually her common sense will stop her handing over too much pocket-money to Sagittarius, who tends to spend cash freely.

Taurus provides Sagittarius with a solid grounding and a good moral training. She encourages his natural integrity and honesty by setting a fine example herself. Most of all she teaches him to direct that restless energy so that he can make real accomplishments, instead of frittering it away on idealistic dreams.

Sagittarius child with a Taurus father

There are big differences between these two, yet they can get along fine if they try. Both are good-hearted, but they don't see eye to eye when it comes to home and traditional values. Home is the centre of the universe for stolid old Taurus, while to Sagittarius it's just somewhere to hang his hat between adventures. Dad can get very cross as Sagittarius blazes a trail through the house, ruffling its neat and cosy atmosphere.

Taurus likes his children to be well behaved and grateful for all the love and care he lavishes on them. But Sagittarius won't feel grateful at all if Dad denies him the action and fun he craves. In fact, worried Taurus can lose patience and be extra strict to control his lively, wayward child. He would do better to appeal to Sagittarius' sense of logic. Sagittarius isn't deliberately naughty and will always listen to sense.

Sagittarius benefits greatly from the stable base Dad provides, and his common-sense approach will help Sagittarius sort out the workable schemes from the wild ones. But forward-looking Sagittarius knows his dad will never share his excitement about bright, new ideas. Taurus believes the old values are best – and sees Sagittarius as something of a revolutionary.

Slow-moving Taurus may not be able to keep up with Sagittarius' fast-moving mind, but he does offer support in finding direction and seeing things through, which is just what Sagittarius needs. Dad must take care not to dull Sagittarius' spontaneity and creativity, or fence him in. Kind-hearted Taurus understands children well, so once he realises the freedom-loving nature of his child he'll give him more rein. He responds warmly to the child's truthfulness and integrity, and to his desire to help others. Eventually Taurus might even decide to ask Sagittarius to work with him, for this is a match that, despite its differences, is starred to make cash.

Sagittarius child with a Gemini mother

This mother finds the bright and curious Sagittarius mind very stimulating. Even so, she'll need to set some time aside to concentrate on her own interests and friends, for being stuck at home even with sparkling Sagittarius for company can bore her.

Gemini will thoroughly enjoy the playful warmth and idealism of her Sagittarius child. She must take care not to start looking for fulfilment by taking over all Sagittarius' hobbies and talents, though. Freedom loving and adventurous, Sagittarius won't like it one bit. As he gets older, he'll tell her so, asking her to keep her nose out of his private life. He wants to be left to live as he chooses.

These two are energetic and enthusiastic and usually very loyal to each other. But Gemini thinks Sagittarius is a little too open and trusting and she soon teaches him to beware of strangers. Sagittarius is likely to talk early, which pleases communicative Gemini, who finds it fun to chart her child's development and is glad when he shares her love of speech, reading and writing. She also adores his bubbly personality and his lively enjoyment of life.

Some Gemini mothers can unwittingly dampen the bright spirit of little Sagittarius. From time to time, analytical Mercury, Gemini's ruler, can make her criticise too harshly. Gemini must remember that her child will do so much better when given positive praise rather than confidence-crushing criticism.

Mother and child are both restless if bored and need a constant stream of new things to keep them occupied. Gemini will always be taking her youngster out to socialise and she'll want to move home every few years. Luckily Sagittarius is extremely adaptable, although he'll find Gemini's frequent changes of mind about where they are going to live rather irritating. Sagittarius knows, though, what it's like to have endless ideas and not want to choose one for fear of missing out on all the others.

Gemini's lack of routine would disturb most other star

signs but Sagittarius can cope with it, not being one for boring routine himself. He does sometimes wish Gemini would control her outbursts – she's rather too volatile for happy-go-lucky Sagittarius. But he's glad that she thinks in the same quick, changeable and often inspired way that he does. These two will share many happy times.

Sagittarius child with a Gemini father

These two get along well, although there will be stormy moments. Quicksilver Gemini keeps Sagittarius laughing with his fast talk and tall tales. But Sagittarius can get muddled by Dad's blend of fact and fiction. It's a good idea for Gemini to let honest Sagittarius know when he's fooling, and when he's telling the truth.

Gemini loves having fun and so does Sagittarius. But sometimes Gemini seems so caught up in his own need for amusement he forgets to include Sagittarius, which leaves the youngster feeling crestfallen. And Dad's always bossing Sagittarius about and criticising, while this creative and original child would much rather be praised for having his own special approach to the world – and left to get on with it by himself.

But differences of approach are soon forgotten once this pair get together over some new and exciting venture that's caught their imaginations. Their high-energy conversations will help Sagittarius to find common-sense ways of applying his bright ideas, instead of rushing into half-thought-out schemes.

At bedtime Gemini will use all his powers of communication to dream up fantastic stories to catch Sagittarius' imagination. He's great at playing children's games, too, but Sagittarius will resist like mad when Gemini tries to manipulate him, and he'll feel rebuffed when Gemini suddenly gets bored and wanders off just when he thought they were having so much fun.

Gemini is often a busy career man with an active social life, so children may have to play second fiddle. Yet he'll take time to encourage Sagittarius to express himself well, to dream and think up endless wonderful ideas. He'll teach him how to handle people well, and he'll launch Sagittarius into life with good memories of happy times with a father who never lost his curiosity about life.

Sagittarius child with a Cancer mother

Shy Cancer loves to stay cosily at home, while little Sagittarius pines for fun and excitement. Cancer must make the effort to get him out and about and socialising, for he thrives on new and entertaining experiences.

Loving Cancer is an excellent mum. She instinctively knows when Sagittarius is feeling down and soothes him back to his bright-eyed self. But she may expect an emotional closeness with Sagittarius that can be hard to achieve. She shouldn't be offended by chirpy Sagittarius' bluntness, either. It's never meant to wound, although sensitive Cancer can't help but be hurt sometimes. Nor should she take it to heart when he scoffs at her love of tradition and correct behaviour. Unconventional Sagittarius cares a lot more about the future than the past and all its trappings. He'll behave exactly as he pleases, though he's more exuberant than mischievous.

Mum should try not to be too possessive or clingy. Sagittarius likes to feel free as a bird and will resist like mad any attempts to control him. Cancer must also accept that he likes to take risks sometimes too, and needs safe ways to express his strong sense of adventure. It's no good expecting Sagittarius to depend on Mum for ever, either. This is a child with a strong sense of independence, so Cancer must develop interests of her own, so that when Sagittarius finally flies the nest it's not too tough for her to take.

Cancer will expect bouncy young Sagittarius to be as tidy as she is, which is unlikely. She wants him to look smart, while he prefers casual, comfortable clothes. His zest for life can be rather squashed by her well-meant nagging. Sagittarius is never quite sure how Mum is going to react to his next bout of naughtiness. Sometimes she resignedly lets him get away with anything, while at other times she explodes in crossness as her repressed emotions well up and overflow.

Cancer is surprised at the very adult remarks Sagittarius sometimes makes. She prefers her children to be children, so he may not get much acknowledgment from Mum for being so grown-up. She admires him for being kind and adaptable and helpful to others, and even his tearaway spirit and optimism can be appealing to her. She knows she could never be that adventurous and hopeful, but part of her wishes she could.

Sagittarius child with a Cancer father

Much as Cancer loves his little Sagittarius, he thinks he's a bit big for his boots sometimes. He wishes he'd calm down and be easier to control, stop springing endless silly japes, and saying things that hurt without thinking. Secretly, Cancer wishes he was as bubbly as Sagittarius and less swayed by his up-and-down emotions.

Sagittarius finds Cancer's moods hard to handle, as he hates to be bogged down by anything emotional. He likes to feel free to play, run around and have fun. Cancer is unlikely to be quite the livewire dad that Sagittarius wants him to be, though he'll certainly try to give his child the very best upbringing he can.

Cancer doesn't trust people the way Sagittarius does and, while it's good to teach children not to be too open with strangers, Cancer must watch he doesn't put a clamp on Sagittarius' natural sociability. Dad will more than make up for any shortcomings by ferrying his youngster here and there to take part in his many interests, and he'll provide him with a wonderfully secure base from which to go exploring. Sagittarius is a good-hearted child, but there are times when he may take Dad's generosity for granted.

Cancer will find it hard to stand the pace as he's not as energetic as his whizzy fire child. However, he'll make the effort to provide plenty of days out for the two of them. The only ingredient that may be missing is an element of risk and excitement. Lively Sagittarius thrives on a little risk but Cancer doesn't approve at all, being a real worrier.

Cancer Dad will think Sagittarius is a spendthrift who wastes money on unworthy causes, while Sagittarius thinks Dad is stingy. In fact, Cancer will have given up a lot for his child, spending endless time and money on him, and he'll be most upset if Sagittarius flies the nest early with hardly a thank you.

Cancer must learn to let go, safe in the knowledge that Sagittarius will one day thank him for all the love, warmth and security he tried so hard to provide.

Sagittarius child with a Leo mother

Warm Leo Mum makes Sagittarius feel extra loved and cared for. She recalls well her own jolly days of childhood and loves nothing better than joining her playful child in his games. But there is a danger that as Sagittarius grows, Leo may make a takeover bid on his individuality, trying to fulfil her own ambitions.

Sagittarius needs to be given every encouragement to develop in his own way and at his own pace. If Leo can back-pedal on the pushiness all will be fine, for Sagittarius benefits greatly from Mum's sunny enthusiasm and willingness to help. And it's vital that Leo keeps up her level of support, for Sagittarius can give up trying if he senses Mum is putting her own needs first all the time.

Leo loves to feel proud of her children, and Sagittarius' ability to make friends, his sunny outlook and his bright optimism will please her greatly. Sagittarius adores travel and will be thrilled with days out and holidays – anything that triggers his imagination and gets this little wanderer out of the house.

Sagittarius learns from Leo's friendly ease in social situations. But Mum can rely on her own popularity more than Sagittarius can – for he's always dropping clangers! Even Mum finds his home truths very hard to take, but at least he knocks her off her pedestal with a touch of humour.

Sometimes even vibrant Leo finds it tough to keep up with ultra-lively Sagittarius. She loves her cosy home, while Sagittarius wants to be always on the move and free. When rows erupt between this temperamental pair there will be big sulks afterwards. Both hate to back down, and Leo's so proud it will have to be young Sagittarius who makes the first move, even if his apologies do make things worse!

Leo loves her child for his energy, humour, bright ideas, optimism, enthusiasm and playful spirit. Sagittarius is delighted by his frivolous, fun-loving Mum and very much helped by her sensible side, relying on her advice in many situations. This pair have much to offer each other.

Sagittarius child with a Leo father

Leo Dad wants to be adored by his children and Sagittarius is his number one fan. But in idolising Leo, there's a danger Sagittarius will get it into his head that he can never live up to his regal father and so give up trying before he reaches anything like his full potential. Leo Dad should make a special effort to show Sagittarius how much he matters and help him find direction in life, otherwise Sagittarius could fritter away his energies. With guidance, Sagittarius' bright mind is capable of great things. Leo should climb down from his pedestal and show Sagittarius some approval.

Dad wants Sagittarius to do well and can be horrified if the child ever fails at anything, knocking Sagittarius' confidence for six. Leo should back off instead and learn how to encourage.

Leo gets on best with children once he can hold a conversation with them and luckily Sagittarius is a bright little talker from an early age. Both share a love of things that are new and exciting. They'll enjoy many a lively expedition together, talking over their day for hours after they've arrived home. Leo admires Sagittarius for his integrity, truthfulness, and love of finding things out. But he expects him to always know his place, and Dad will become an angry lion if his child tries to make out he's a silly old fool. Sagittarius must watch his tongue. At least he won't complain about Leo's flamboyant ways and style of dress, for he would hate his parent to be boring and ordinary.

Many Leos are up to date and adaptable, like Sagittarius, but some are old-fashioned tyrants who think you have to be cruel to be kind. This approach won't suit Sagittarius, who will strike out for freedom whenever he can, especially in the teenage years.

On the whole, this pair will thrill each other, though. Sagittarius laps up the security and comfort Leo offers, while Leo loves the wit, humour, energy and wild ideas of his child. Together they will put the world to rights over and over again.

Sagittarius child with a Virgo mother

Perky Sagittarius will bring light and laughter into Virgo's life. He'll teach her not to care so much about what others think and to let go and have fun. She's got a few lessons for him, too, in being patient and polite and using his common sense instead of tripping into trouble.

This youngster will laugh at the way Virgo always wants to get everything right. He's impatient to move on to the next thing and can't see the point of fretting over details. He'll get especially annoyed if tidy Mum spends all morning scrubbing the kitchen instead of playing with him.

At least these two can talk, and they will do so all the time, chatting on the move as little Sagittarius trails around in the wake of Virgo as she cleans and polishes the house. There's a lot of basic understanding between them, and they are both likely to blurt out home truths. Neither is emotional or sentimental, and when a row does blow up both are flexible enough to fix things fast.

Idealistic young Sagittarius admires his mother's need to help others by baking cakes, offering advice, giving lifts to elderly neighbours. Sagittarius is faster to see the whole meaning of something, though, while Virgo gets bogged down in details. Both Mum and child are fast-thinking and Virgo will easily be able to keep up with her youngster's stream of quirky questions.

Virgo will make a great parent for Sagittarius if she learns to hold her peace instead of criticising him. Here's a child who needs lashings of praise, as often as possible. Virgo especially hates it when he makes a mess of her home, yet for Sagittarius, a bit of mess is a small price to pay for an afternoon of adventure and imagination.

Sensible Virgo has the ability to make Sagittarius' dreams become reality, so she should spare some time to help him sort out the practicalities, which she can do so well.

Sagittarius child with a Virgo father

Virgo father wants to be in charge at home and freedom-loving Sagittarius can't help but go his own sweet way, especially in the teenage years. Yet, much as he might not appreciate it at the time, he benefits greatly from Virgo's sensible upbringing, learning how to behave, to think before leaping into action, to channel his energies and be careful with cash.

Dad himself works very hard to make sure Sagittarius has a good start in life, offering him useful guidance when it comes to career time. He helps the youngster sift through his many ideas and find ones that will work on a practical level.

A very traditional parent, Virgo values discipline and order. He doesn't share Sagittarius' forward-looking view of the world, or his endless energy. Virgo needs his rest, but he doesn't begrudge Sagittarius his adventures, as long as they don't get him into trouble or force Dad to join the boisterous action.

Virgo sees himself as a parent-teacher and will encourage any interest Sagittarius has, as long as it's educational in some way. There is a danger he'll expect his child to do everything his way, instead of letting Sagittarius find his own pioneering path. Virgo mustn't hold him back. And he might actually learn something himself from his child!

Sagittarius' tendency to idolise his parents can make him take Virgo's needling remarks far more seriously than they are meant, which could cloud his sunny disposition. Still, even Virgo can't help praising the way Sagittarius grasps ideas so quickly. He enjoys seeing Sagittarius suddenly captivated by something new, colourful and exciting. Dad is delighted, too, by the child's bright confidence, his amazing perceptiveness and his way with words.

Sometimes Virgo gets fed up with the way his child has so many brilliant ideas that never come to anything. Yet he understands that dreaming up ideas is the most tremendous fun for Sagittarius, who doesn't really expect anyone to turn them into reality.

Sagittarius sometimes wishes his father would act more on impulse, while Virgo wishes Sagittarius wouldn't always rush headfirst into things, although he can't help but admire such enthusiasm. He also thinks Sagittarius exaggerates and takes too many risks, while Sagittarius wishes Dad was more sporty. But if both accept each other's differences, they'll get along splendidly.

Sagittarius child with a Libra mother

Libra Mum wants only the best for her Sagittarius child, which means plenty of clothes, a lovely room and more toys than he can ever play with. She'll take him anywhere he wants to go to further his education, too. There's a distinct danger that if she isn't careful, she'll spoil him, though honest Sagittarius would never take advantage of Mum's loving nature the way other signs might. But he can find her a bit too much of a softie at times, lacking his positive assertiveness, although he values her wise advice.

Libra is never short of bright ideas for activities to keep young Sagittarius amused. His only complaint is that Libra can be a bit of a nag at times. But she'll give him plenty of freedom and not tie him to her apron strings. Libra dislikes arguments and will dodge rows by diverting Sagittarius' attention.

Sagittarius is more of a risk-taker than Libra. He's trusting and open, full of life and unclouded by worries, all of which delights the more cautious Libra. Sagittarius admires the way Mum's always friendly and light-hearted with people. But lazier Libra will need a rest before she can keep up with her lively little Sagittarius, who loves to stay on the move.

Sagittarius always seems to be changing his mind as yet another idea, bigger and better than the last, pops into his head. This trait is balanced by Libra's need to weigh things up and her slowness to make decisions. She realises that Sagittarius sometimes needs firmer guidance than she can give to stop him being a jack of all trades and a master of none. Probably without realising it, she nudges him in the right direction by giving him the space to find himself and the freedom to breathe.

Sagittarius is quick to share Libra's love of art, beauty, good taste and culture. If he's got artistic talent, Libra will certainly help bring it out. She'll keep his feet on the ground too, yet never discourage him.

These two will have wonderful conversations – Libra especially loves listening to Sagittarius exercising his creative imagination. Sagittarius always rushes home to tell his mum what he's been up to and there will be lots of laughter in the telling.

Patient mother Libra even manages to get some unusually good behaviour out of her sometimes wayward youngster. Between them, they'll bring out the best in each other.

Sagittarius child with a Libra father

These two are the best of friends. Young Sagittarius is glad to have a dad who shares his sunny optimism and who likes to be on the move. Here's someone who'll listen and respond positively when Sagittarius unveils his latest plans to change the world. Libra believes bright ideas are the spice of life and, even if they come to nothing, this pair will have enjoyed themselves enormously discussing them for hours on end.

Friendly Libra adores his frank and fearless little Sagittarius. He admires and encourages his bright intelligence, laughs at his jokes and pranks, and picks him up when he falls. Libra is very much in tune with children, especially livewires like Sagittarius. He'll be especially delighted when Sagittarius starts talking early and will enjoy answering all his questions.

They can get on each other's nerves though sometimes, Libra because he's a stickler for reasoned argument and Sagittarius because of his insistence on revealing the truth, no matter how uncomfortable it might be for Dad. Sagittarius finds it hard if Dad hides things from him, building hidden tensions that confuse. Sagittarius would always prefer to hear the truth, no matter how painful.

Most Libra fathers adore their families and base their lives around them, treating their children on equal terms. This attitude suits young Sagittarius well. He's full of grown-up observations and Dad is someone who'll actually give him credit for them. Libra won't think Sagittarius is so grown-up when he shows him up in public, though. Libra always wants to keep up appearances and Sagittarius can be naughty just to tease.

Most of the time, these two get on famously. Sagittarius eases Dad out of indecisiveness and cheers him when he looks like getting gloomy. Libra is proud that Sagittarius is such a good mixer, a little bit of a show-off, and the life and soul of any party. Most of all, he's thrilled to have produced a child who is a real friend.

Sagittarius child with a Scorpio mother

Here's a parent who's got enough energy to keep up with wildfire child Sagittarius. Scorpio enjoys being active and they'll have some great times together, as long as Scorpio resists the temptation to push Sagittarius in the direction she wants to go, fulfilling her own ambitions instead of letting him discover his unique path in life. Sagittarius won't let her take too much control, which worries Scorpio who needs to be very much in charge of her family and feels anxious if she isn't.

Scorpio Mum can help Sagittarius do better than he ever would without her support. She gives endless encouragement and praise, and she won't be mean when it comes to buying Sagittarius the things he needs for his hobbies. Just sometimes, Sagittarius can feel Mum has too much control over his life.

Young Sagittarius' more wayward tendencies are balanced by the stable home and sensible routine that his Scorpio Mum provides. But Scorpio should watch she doesn't dampen Sagittarius' wonderful spontaneity. She admires his imagination and his ability to assert himself although she finds that trying to make him behave is an uphill task. Playful Sagittarius thinks Mum is too serious – he likes her best when she puts on a smile and plays with him.

Scorpio thinks Sagittarius is far too honest with people and takes risks she would never dream of taking. But if she attempts to stop him going out and about, he'll get very upset, for he loves to be on the move and no-one's going to stop him.

Sagittarius is glad to have a mother who's a good thinker, and is interested and curious about life, just as he is. He especially likes the way she puts her ideas into action. Her fierce commands may send Sagittarius scuttling for cover, but he knows he's loved, cared for and safe. If Mum can allow him his spontaneity, everyone will be happy.

Sagittarius child with a Scorpio father

Sagittarius is rather wary of his Scorpio dad for he makes it clear to Sagittarius that he won't tolerate him rushing off as and when he pleases, or acting selfishly. This is something of a burden for light and airy Sagittarius to carry, but this rather serious side of Dad is more than balanced by the obvious delight he takes in his growing child. He's willing to help Sagittarius in every way possible to do well and make something of his life.

Some Scorpio fathers act in such a powerful way at home that they scare their children rigid. Dad likes to be in total control, and will roar and snap orders. Dad should remember that Sagittarius is at his best when he's carefree and happy. He shouldn't loom over him like a black cloud.

Scorpio Dad is an inflexible chap who can't understand Sagittarius' need for constant change and freedom, or his love of all things new. Dad can become very upset and insist he's right if Sagittarius can't see things from his point of view. Scorpio would do better if he let his original and creative child find his own way of doing things more often.

Scorpio is desperate to be in control of his family. He thinks Sagittarius is far too open, and dreads that he is revealing family secrets that are supposed to be under lock and key. Sagittarius seems wise beyond his years – and Scorpio sometimes fears that he understands too much about whatever is going on.

Scorpio can react to young Sagittarius' perceptions with a stinging reply, but more usually he ignores him, which drives Sagittarius mad. However, if Sagittarius learns to use a little tact, he'll find he's got a dad who will stick up for him through thick and thin. Scorpio in turn will love Sagittarius for his energy, will learn to cope with his adventurousness and will one day feel very proud of his child's amazing understanding of life.

Sagittarius child with a Sagittarius mother

Sagittarius Mum knows how the world looks through a child's eyes, for part of her has never really grown up. She takes a special delight in playing with and teaching her Sagittarius child right from the very start.

She'll respond with wise and funny answers to all his curious questions and share his lively sense of adventure, thinking up all sorts of exciting activities. She admires his fast reactions and his grown-up way of understanding just what's going on. With young Sagittarius she'll rediscover a whole world of excitement, curiosity, enthusiasm and delight.

The only pitfall is that Sagittarius Mum doesn't like boring practicalities. It may have to be Dad who takes care of the mundane details of life, for even a Sagittarius child likes some sense of organisation and routine around him.

Mum must make a point, though, of helping Sagittarius with the important task of finding a direction in his life. It's easy for a Sagittarian youngster to scatter his energies and fail to find a satisfying field of work. Once he does, he'll put everything into it. He just needs help getting started.

Young Sagittarius finds it easy to talk to his broad-minded Mum. But both can take each other aback by being overhonest, although they'll usually see the funny side and have a good laugh about it. They enjoy each other's jokes and pranks and treat each other as equals rather than parent and child. Sagittarius doesn't mind if her youngster takes the occasional risk, within reason. She knows it's in his nature, just as it's in hers. And she's only too happy to provide the travel and outings he so enjoys, for she needs to be on the move just as much as he does.

These two never get bored with each other and Sagittarius Mum knows how to show the kindness, fairness and positive attitude that young Sagittarius thrives on. She's prepared to see his side of any argument, too, and is interested in his hobbies and activities, learning and teaching at the same time. A happy pair, these two complement each other perfectly.

Sagittarius child with a Sagittarius father

Sagittarius Dad is a little boy at heart and loves playing all sorts of sporty games and having fun with his Sagittarius child. He encourages Sagittarius to make the most of every second, although he isn't the most practical person when it comes to the responsible aspects of life.

Sagittarius Dad is straightforward and optimistic, and

shares his child's enthusiasm and energy. Both will act like a couple of kids, playing jokes on Mum, giggling together and generally having a great time.

There's a thoughtful, more studious side to Sagittarius Dad which will inspire his child. He's a great teacher, which stimulates the curious young Sagittarian mind, and will show the child how to learn. He'll provide many opportunities for young Sagittarius, and take him with him on his travels to satisfy his innate wanderlust. He'll be cross if the youngster doesn't show enough interest in what he's offered, but he's quick to forgive and forget when the occasional row does blow up. Usually it's when both insist their way is best and won't give in. Neither likes apologising – young Sagittarius would prefer a pat on the shoulder and a smile by way of an apology, rather than Dad actually saying he's sorry.

If young Sagittarius looks fed up, Dad will be quick to cheer him up by playing the fool. Or he'll take him on an adventure, to take his mind off his miseries. In fact, Dad will do anything to avoid emotional scenes and junior will have to learn to go to Mum with his troubles.

Some Sagittarius fathers are so busy following their many interests they don't leave much time for their children. Young Sagittarius may have to learn to be independent, although this won't be too difficult for him.

Dad is well prepared to cope with his child's boisterous behaviour, as both are as excited as each other about life. Dad also understands young Sagittarius' need to have rules explained, rather than just being issued with orders. He'll help to bring out his child's creativity, and develop his confidence and assertiveness. He'll teach him to speak up for himself and feel good about being such a direct, honest and warm-hearted little person.

Sagittarius child with a Capricorn mother

Capricorn Mum is very ambitious for her children and will feel proud of her bright and popular Sagittarius. But there could be friction as he skips through life in his own merry manner, instead of following Mum's orders. Still, she'll be charmed into forgiving him, for she can't help but admire his enthusiasm, honesty, energy and bravery.

Both love music and art, and religion too, although Sagittarius may follow a less conventional path than Capricorn. They work very hard to achieve the goals they've set themselves, but Capricorn's targets are often more clearly defined than her child's. He's easily distracted by his interest in anything and everything.

Success, duty and responsibility mean a lot to Mum, while enjoying life is Sagittarius' number one priority. Sagittarius doesn't care much about being seen to be successful, but Mum likes to have a nice house, good car, and, above all, status. Sagittarius sees all these things as burdens which take away his sense of freedom.

Capricorn will encourage Sagittarius to try hard at school, establish a routine, work towards a good career and take fulfilling his potential more seriously. Sagittarius is best motivated by his own enthusiasm, so Mum should try to spark his interest and not complain when he occasionally doesn't do as well as she'd hoped. Tellings-off, if too harsh, can make him feel like giving up, just to spite her.

Some Capricorns find it hard to express affection or create a sense of closeness with their children. Mum must make time to spend with Sagittarius to reassure him. It will make him feel far more loved than any present. Capricorn mums become more fun-loving as they grow older and are then more likely to be in tune with the busy, enthusiastic energy of Sagittarius.

Capricorn enjoys Sagittarius' grown-up way of asking questions, but she gets cross when he boasts. She can't keep up with his sporty side, but she'll try to encourage him to keep up his efforts to achieve. She'll be well rewarded when Sagittarius one day admits that he couldn't have done it without his mum.

Sagittarius child with a Capricorn father

Young Sagittarius would like to be as successful as his hard-working Capricorn father. But if he gets to the top, it will be through sheer brilliance, not hard work! These two certainly have a very different outlook on life.

Sagittarius is a little joker, although behind the laughs there is a wise and wistful side. Capricorn is serious through and through, although as he gets older, a more playful streak emerges. Young Sagittarius is a real daredevil, while Capricorn is cautious and will scold him for being so adventurous. Sagittarius loves talking and gets carried away with enthusiasm. Capricorn is quieter, observes before speaking, and refuses to get carried away about anything new, preferring the tried and tested.

Capricorn is interested in wealth, living comfortably and providing for his children. He'll show his love through material things, rather than the hugs that Sagittarius wants. Reserved and unemotional, when Capricorn does have something to say, he expects Sagittarius to listen to him. To his annoyance, Sagittarius is likely to disappear in mid-sentence having thought of something far more interesting to do.

Sagittarius loves to travel, while Capricorn prefers to stay at home. Dad likes to get everything organised and under control, while Sagittarius likes to keep his options open. Capricorn thinks patience is a vital virtue, while Sagittarius hates to be kept waiting for anything. Dad believes the way to a secure and successful life is to conform, but Sagittarius has a strong urge to be different and doesn't give a hoot for convention.

Despite the differences in their characters, Sagittarius knows that in many ways Dad's got it right. He realises that if he follows Capricorn's advice, he's likely to do better than he would otherwise. He understands Dad's point about not rushing into anything before thinking it through, and he wishes he always knew the right way to act, as his father seems to.

Although Capricorn would never admit it, he actually

admires the way young Sagittarius throws caution to the wind and has such optimism and vitality. He's determined to give his child the very best start in life that he can, and although Sagittarius may not thank him when he's young, he'll certainly appreciate Dad's efforts when he grows up.

Sagittarius child with an Aquarius mother

Aquarius Mum loves the energy and enthusiasm of her little Sagittarius and warms easily to his affectionate nature. She's happy to let him be himself and develop at his own pace. Aquarius is very pleased Sagittarius is independent and not clingy, with a lively, independent mind to match her own.

Aquarius Mum likes visiting friends and has lots of interests. Sagittarius will happily tag along, learning as he goes and surprising Mum with his perceptive observations. They won't have too many disagreements, although Aquarius may cause Sagittarius to blow up now and again, while staying cool, calm and collected herself. All will be quickly forgiven and forgotten, though.

Both believe in freedom and the rights of the individual. Some Aquarian mothers can be very political and expect their children to campaign alongside them. Sagittarius likes to help others, but often puts his own needs first, so if an evening's campaigning doesn't suit him, he won't join in.

Aquarius can teach Sagittarius to put his foot in it less often, and to direct his energy into real achievements rather than scattering it in all directions. Mum's fair and sensible way of explaining the rules suits Sagittarius, who hates being issued orders. He'll appreciate, too, how Mum tries to keep up to date with her thinking to match her forward-looking child.

In Sagittarius, Aquarius sees a kind and straightforward child, with integrity and imagination. She's delighted by his love of freedom and independence, his ability to go his own way with positive results. Above all, she's grateful to have a child who seems to understand her so well.

Sagittarius child with an Aquarius father

The very best of friends, these two look at life in an almost identical way. They're both full of fun, enjoy doing similar things and will spend hours batting around ideas, each as bright and inventive as the other. Aquarius Dad fully appreciates young Sagittarius' open, straightforward, warm and honest nature. He never puts on an act and Aquarius respects him for it.

This is a father who'll sit for hours answering Sagittarius' questions. He understands that Sagittarius will behave in a silly way one moment and a wise one the next. Sagittarius loves having a Dad who dares to be different and is full of surprises and schemes. In fact, both like each other just the way they are.

Aquarius laughs it off when Sagittarius puts his foot in it, and Sagittarius doesn't mind a bit if Aquarius draws attention to himself by doing something unconventional.

Aquarius appreciates Sagittarius' wish for independence and can teach him some sensible lessons in coping with it when it comes. He teaches the child always to be himself, which gives him a lot of confidence. Aquarius helps develop Sagittarius' love of learning, of gathering information and developing ideas. Dad's home is sure to be full of books on all sorts of subjects, which Sagittarius will enjoy reading.

Aquarius is always prepared to listen and won't push dogmatic views or harsh discipline at his child. In fact, he can err on the soft side, but Sagittarius is not naturally naughty and won't take too much advantage.

Dad will be useful to have around when young Sagittarius has to sit down and do his homework. He will gladly advise, suggesting ways Sagittarius can channel his energies for the most productive results. Dad will encourage him, particularly with languages, and the more interested Sagittarius turns out to be, the more Aquarius will want to help him.

Sagittarius child with a Pisces mother

Kind-hearted Pisces Mum will give Sagittarius lots of affection, take an interest in his hobbies, never expect him to help around the house and cuddle him every time he cries. She's always open to new ideas, which pleases forward-thinking Sagittarius, and she comes up with unusual and wonderful places to visit which leave him with happy memories of his childhood.

Pisces Mum is very artistic and will bring out Sagittarius' own creative abilities. Her strong intuition helps her understand the minute he's feeling down.

But at times, Pisces will find her boisterous youngster overwhelming. He's full of impulsive enthusiasm, and if ever a mother needed regular quiet times to herself, it's Pisces. She finds it hard to stand up to her child's fiery temper, too. Sometimes she'll let him get away with being cheeky rather than face a scene. But when she's driven to the limit she'll explode. Sagittarius rarely means any real harm – he's just a bit rash and clumsy. He also comes out with some painful truths without thinking, which can upset Mum terribly.

Pisces has a mystical, psychic element, with religious leanings. Sagittarius shares this religious, idealistic side despite his rough, tough image, and Pisces will appreciate this in her child. But Sagittarius' need to be straightforward can run into trouble with Pisces Mum, because of her unwitting tendency to embroider the truth or disguise problems under a protective web. Sagittarius can be bitterly disappointed when he discovers that things are not quite as Mum said. He'd much rather she was straight with him.

Pisces likes well-behaved children and will do her best to teach wayward Sagittarius good manners. But because she prefers to lead an unstructured life herself, she may find it hard to give Sagittarius the sense of direction his diverse nature needs. She'll have to make herself sit down and guide him towards a workable future.

Pisces will provide her Sagittarius child with the inspiration to make the most of his life. Above all, she will try to make him feel happy to be himself, a gift Sagittarius will greatly value.

Sagittarius child with a Pisces father

Pisces father loves his Sagittarius child dearly and will happily spend time talking and playing with him. Sagittarius loves all the attention and enjoys the understanding he shares with his intuitive father.

Pisces' emotional nature means he's a warm and loving father, but it also makes him prone to mood swings and noisy outbursts when Sagittarius unwittingly infuriates him to boiling point. Sagittarius is so rational, he can't understand why anyone would want to get so emotional about things. But he's quite capable of retaliating with a fiery response that will take sensitive Pisces by surprise.

Both Pisces and Sagittarius are fascinated by the way things work and young Sagittarius loves his father's lively-minded way of getting all the facts on anything that interests him. Both love talking about new ideas, but Sagittarius will be upset when Dad sometimes doesn't share his enthusiasm for some wild scheme or other. All Sagittarius wants is the fun of sharing ideas and he certainly doesn't want them clouded by a doubting Pisces pointing out why they could never work.

Pisces' quieter, imaginative and creative side fascinates Sagittarius, who yearns to learn all about music, art, books and the theatre from his cultured dad. Pisces happily stimulates Sagittarius' colourful imagination with inventive stories and painting sessions, although there are times when all Sagittarius longs for is a down-to-earth game of football or help mending his bike.

Pisces Dad always assumed any children he had would be quiet and well-behaved. Sagittarius shows him that this isn't always the case! But Dad admires his child's energy and ability to come up with bright ideas, even if a lot of it is pie in the sky. He likes Sagittarius' sense of logic and his confident way of expressing himself, too.

Pisces father and Sagittarius child actually enjoy the differences in each other's characters and will share many interests in their rewarding relationship.

CAPRICORN
Stars for Life

STAR BABY

Capricorn will surprise everyone from her (or his*) first moment, with her grown-up and knowing look. She seems old before she starts.

This child adores a cuddle and needs plenty of them to help her settle in to her new situation. She wants to know that Mum is with her all the time, ready and willing to look after her. Any threat to her security can make her feel very frightened indeed.

But with reassurance, she'll gradually find her feet. And when she does, the world will become an exciting place to be in. She adores her growing feeling of independence. Learning to pull off her socks, crawl and, most of all, walk become big adventures.

Soon Mum will have a little helper at the kitchen sink, and Capricorn's favourite toy will be the brush and pan. She loves to copy what you say and do – you'll find you have an echo every time you speak. She's learning fast and constantly asks questions, wanting to know all the details.

Toilet training is easier than with most as it's another way she can be like the grown-ups. Remember to give her plenty of praise for her progress. Her confidence needs a lot of bolstering.

She says grown-up things that surprise you and takes

*'She' is used to cover he and she for Capricorn child.

what she's told very seriously – so don't tease or mislead her, unless you make it clear you're joking. She'll make you laugh with her quirky sense of humour, but you'll be aware that you have a very down-to-earth and sensible child who won't stand for any nonsense.

FIRST STEPS FOR CAPRICORN

Capricorn loves her home routine. But when she does venture out, she'd prefer a trip with just the two of you rather than a noisy playgroup where she fears she may get lost in the crowd. But she does need to get out and meet other children to help her gain confidence for the day when she starts school.

Usually she'll make a few close friends she enjoys playing with. Quiet she may be, but she's perfectly content. Tell her stories about your own childhood, and fairytales to lift her earthbound mind off the ground a little. Explain everything to her so she can understand and feel pleased about her widening knowledge of the world.

Capricorn often has a favourite teddy bear or toy she takes everywhere with her. She'll have a special cupboard in her room for all her toys and won't be happy if you tidy it up without asking her first. At this age she's generally very well behaved, but there will be times when she gets cross, stubborn and bossy, determined to do everything her own way. When thwarted she turns grumpy, with the occasional angry outburst. In her mind she knows she's in the right, and it'll take some coaxing to bring back her smiles.

This child is a sensitive soul who feels frustrated and cross with herself when she fails to live up to her own high expectations. Nursery school is a bit of a trial for her at first. Capricorn is afraid to relax in case she does things wrong or makes a fool of herself. But eventually she may even become high-handed with her classmates, turning her critical eye outwards instead.

Help her to have a better opinion of herself – and others – by praising and reassuring her. She finds it hard to get close to others because she fears people won't like her, so she takes her time. But once she feels accepted she shows her warm and tender side. She's a caring friend indeed who tries hard never to let people down, especially if they need her help. Capricorn is full of hidden warmth below a cool and reserved surface. It's up to you to provide the care that will help her loving little heart express itself.

As she gets older, Capricorn gains in confidence. She's still a perfectionist who takes hours over small jobs, determined to get them just right. And she expects others to do their best at all times too. She starts to become more ambitious, determined to steal quietly ahead until she's doing better than her friends. But she does tend to take on too much. Help her see which tasks are important and which can be left till tomorrow.

Capricorn enjoys rules. It makes her feel secure to know what behaviour is expected of her – and she likes to know that the same rules apply to others too, so that she can predict how they are going to behave, or at least disapprove self-righteously if they step out of line.

She's serious, conventional and sensible, and you may well feel she can cope with more chores than other children of her age. But don't load her with this burden. Her childhood slips away all too fast and she should be encouraged to enjoy it while it lasts. She's far less confident than she looks and needs to know there's someone there to look after and protect her. So don't expect too much of her too soon. However, a few simple tasks around the home will boost her confidence in her abilities and make her feel grown-up, with none of the pressures.

SCHOOL RULES FOR CAPRICORN

Capricorn takes to the routine of school quite well. She works hard, but may need to hear things repeated before they really sink in. Her concentration is good and she performs well at exam time, though she can get anxious about whether she will pass.

She's very well behaved and a favourite with the teachers because she shows respect, listens and is a calming influence in class. She may still be shy and reserved, but her underlying drive and ambition will force her forward and she may well end up top of the class.

Gradually she'll make friends, who'll bring her out of herself. They're likely to be bright, studious and serious little pals. But she needs reassuring that she is liked for being her, not just for what she can do. She'll bring her friends round for tea, which will usually include a study session. Bookish Capricorn can't enjoy herself until she's got work out of the way.

Capricorn is very down to earth and knows just what she's capable of – and what she isn't. She's certainly more cautious and anxious than some of her more spontaneous classmates. But she's determined, helpful, thoughtful and kind. She hates to hurt anyone and often worries that she's said the wrong thing. And if she's criticised she goes into a whirl of worry, condemning herself for small faults which she needs telling don't really matter.

She loves to feel needed and valuable. But she's embarrassed to ask for help for herself. Just as she's so compassionate towards others in need of help, so she needs to learn to be gentle with herself. Teach her that such a caring and thoughtful person should value herself and that there's no need to punish herself for any tiny failings.

TEENAGE TAKE-OFF FOR CAPRICORN

Teenage Capricorn won't shirk during the vital years leading up to her big exams. She sets her goals high and sees herself as a future bank manager or businesswoman. She's driven to achieve and won't waste time on frivolous teenage behaviour.

In fact she may delay getting involved with the opposite sex, preferring to concentrate on her work. She fears rejection, as ever, and finds it hard to relax into relationships. But as she learns her own worth, which she will as she grows older, she'll find her way towards happiness and achievement.

Teach her how useful her practical nature can be, and how her hard work, kindness, integrity and common sense are prized. Above all, her caring desire to give and to be useful makes her a valuable person to have around.

STAR PARENTS

Capricorn child with an Aries mother

Energetic Aries Mum lives life at a whirlwind pace, while her slower Capricorn child tags behind, approaching things very differently. Capricorn likes to think ahead and make plans, then do things methodically and see them through to the end. Mum whizzes into action the moment an idea enters her head and is puzzled at why Capricorn takes so long to get going.

Capricorn likes routine while Mum hates it. Aries prefers change and excitement, and is determined to squeeze the most fun out of every minute of life. She's bored by day-to-day chores and tends to put her own need for entertainment and excitement before anything else. She must learn to consider Capricorn's needs, too. The child feels unsettled unless she knows exactly what time tea will be ready, and where Mum is if she needs her. Aries should keep to some sort of timetable for her child's benefit.

Aries Mum loves company and is keen on group activities, particularly sport, while Capricorn is shyer and prefers a few close friends to being one of the gang. She fears rejection, and it's important that Aries takes time out of her hectic schedule to help Capricorn develop self-confidence. Mum must also try to avoid angry outbursts, for Capricorn will take them too much to heart and become so upset or grumpy that Mum won't get a smile out of her for days.

Aries mustn't expect Capricorn to be as outgoing or bouncy as she is. She must be allowed to take life at her own cautious pace. Aries wants children she can be proud of, and Capricorn will one day justify Mum's faith in her. She'll stay in the background, suddenly emerging as an ambitious front-runner. She's likely to do very well indeed if she's given encouragement and not made to feel that being quiet is somehow wrong. Mum must accept her and reassure her with lots of cuddles!

Capricorn child with an Aries father

Action man Aries loves sport, socialising, staying up late and having fun. Capricorn is an early-to-bed child who takes care not to overdo it, hates games and always thinks ahead. She admires the energetic way Dad gets things done and the fact that he's so effective and fast to act. Capricorn may take longer but even Dad acknowledges she's an achiever who never gives up until she's finished something.

Dad must beware of pushing her too hard. Capricorn sets her own standards and is mortified if she doesn't reach them. What busy Dad can teach her is how to attack things more directly and achieve her objectives faster. He shows her how to live life with more imagination and teaches her it's not worth wasting time worrying. Life is to be lived right now!

Capricorn is not as open and trusting as Aries, so Dad should not expect her to have his wide circle of friends. She'll prefer a small group of close friends who she can relax with. Capricorn takes life far more seriously than her father, but she's warm and caring under that reserved surface. Her softer side needs careful handling to bring it out.

This child usually enjoys sticking to rules, because it helps her feel more secure if she knows just what's expected of her. But she'll suffer a blow to her confidence if Dad imposes Aries-style harsh discipline. He must accept that she means well and rarely misbehaves deliberately. She's an old-fashioned child, who doesn't share Dad's modern go-ahead outlook. This is an important factor to remember when it comes to choosing schools for her.

Dad mustn't expect her to grow up too fast. Aries likes his children to become independent early, leaving him more free time. Capricorn may seem grown-up and responsible, but she still needs a lot of love and reassurance. Given time and affection, all will be well.

Capricorn child with a Taurus mother

Capricorn child will feel snug and secure with her warm-hearted Taurus mum. Taurus tries to create a happy home where things run according to routine and cosy stability is the order of the day. This sort of world might seem restricting to some, but not to Capricorn. She loves her home comforts and enjoys feeling safe and well cared for.

Both are great believers in the maxim that the only way to get on in life is by hard work, so Mum encourages Capricorn's serious efforts at school. This pair have little time for frivolous dreamers – they're born under earth signs and are destined to be practical and efficient.

There are moments, though, when they allow a little off-beat humour to break through in the form of shared private jokes. And though they're both quite serious on the surface, warm hearts beat underneath. Both would do anything to help the people closest to them, and they share a love of animals.

Capricorn craves affection, but finds it hard to ask for. As Mum is a very demonstrative person, she'll soon warm that reserved Capricorn heart. Mum understands that Capricorn needs to know just what's expected of her, for Taurus likes to know where she stands, too.

These two admire each other's determination and sticking power, but Capricorn will kick up a fuss if Mum tries to impose harsh rules on her. She can be stubborn, too, if pushed too far.

Basically, Capricorn is very happy with Taurus' conventional style of upbringing. Mum will see that she gets the traditional education that suits her so well and she won't tease her for behaving in such a grown-up and serious manner. Capricorn will feel accepted and secure, and so pleased to live in a home where she's understood.

Capricorn child with a Taurus father

Home-loving Taurus Dad enjoys having a serious-minded Capricorn child who values comfort and security the way he does. And Capricorn is pleased he's as sensible, down to earth and responsible as she is, someone she can rely on. Dad is proud that Capricorn is so well behaved and that she takes her studies seriously. He feels very protective towards her and she, in turn, feels warmly loved and cared for.

Taurus loves routine as much as Capricorn does, but it's not a good idea for either of them to get in a rut. Dad should plan unusual treats to keep Capricorn guessing – she mustn't become too staid and stolid. Taurus must remember, too, that they both have low energy levels, and although Capricorn must be allowed her rest, Dad mustn't let her become as lazy as he can be! Exercise will help and Dad should set a good example by trying to keep in shape himself.

Like her Taurus dad, Capricorn has a good business brain and might one day make a fine addition to the family firm. She also shares Dad's interest in music and art, and both enjoy nostalgia – they love the past and distrust anything too modern. Another of their pet hates is loud-mouthed people. This pair prefer those who are reliable and reserved, like themselves.

Taurus helps Capricorn to develop her ability to apply herself and succeed. He provides all the security she could ask for, giving her the start in life she needs.

Capricorn child with a Gemini mother

Quiet Capricorn thinks her chatterbox Gemini mum is never silent – yet she can't help laughing at her gossip. Mum does her staid little Capricorn a power of good by showing her it's fun to talk and think up new ideas.

Gemini is good at enjoying herself and thinks that Capricorn should have more fun, too. She shows her that life doesn't have to be all work and no play, but Mum must remember to encourage Capricorn's hard-working streak. It's essential to her that she is praised for her efforts and not made to feel a boring stay-at-home swot. Help her to achieve a balance. She certainly doesn't want to be thought of as dull, but she must have time to herself for serious study.

Capricorn has a great need for routine and wishes her mother could be more down to earth and organised sometimes. But Gemini is constantly trying to break out of any domestic rut and will resent being a mother if she has no other interests to keep her busy brain occupied. She needs to get out and meet people every day, while Capricorn prefers a quieter life. She'd like to have Mum to herself more often, too, yet Gemini is always racing round making new friends and hardly ever seems to be at home.

Gemini loves anything new but Capricorn distrusts fads and fashions. This is an old-fashioned child who will want a traditional education. She's a determined little soul and Mum will feel proud of her when she does well at school. Capricorn plods along until she finishes every project she undertakes, while Mum only works hard as long as it entertains her to do so.

Mum is full of speedy Mercury energy, while Saturn-ruled Capricorn takes life at a slower pace. No matter – these two can learn to appreciate each other. But Mum must acknowledge Capricorn's need for security, routine and acceptance. Give her this and these two will enjoy a deeply satisfying relationship.

Capricorn child with a Gemini father

Hard-working Capricorn thinks her dad lives a hectic life. He's very tied up in his busy career and social life, follows all sorts of sports and keeps active all the time.

Sometimes she fears he is bored by her and her childish needs. And if truth be known, Gemini does hate to feel tied down and doesn't fall into the role of father easily. He must watch that he doesn't act the big boss at home to try to assert his authority. Capricorn is a well-behaved child who wants to please. Criticise her too much and she'll be mortified.

Capricorn finds it hard to keep up with Gemini's lightning mind. He's full of puns and practical jokes, and so clever with words he makes her feel she's a real plodder in comparison. It's important that Dad gives her credit for the things she's good at, like being a reliable, good-hearted and determined little person with the ability to do very well indeed. He must allow her to go at her own pace and spare some time to help her with her homework. She'll make him proud as punch one of these days.

This child wants everyone to be as truthful as she is, but she suspects Dad isn't always honest, even if his truth-bending is all done in fun. She wants to feel solid earth beneath her feet and can be frustrated by Dad's sometimes rather sly ways.

Dad admires Capricorn's determination and the way she sticks at something until she's finished. He's quite different, tackling six things at once, whizzing between jobs to avoid being bored by one. Gemini is also full of bright ideas, but it often takes down-to-earth Capricorn to show him which ones will work and which won't.

Although she secretly thinks he's full of hot air, Capricorn loves Dad's brilliant bedtime stories. His tale-spinning gets that stolid Capricorn imagination stirring. Dad will help her bring out her artistic and musical talents, too, and teach her that making friends is one of life's joys. He'll awaken her curiosity and broaden her outlook, helping her to enjoy childhood instead of worrying or working too much.

Capricorn child with a Cancer mother

Capricorn feels that her sympathetic Cancer mum understands her completely. This child usually fights shy of getting too close to anyone, but her fears melt in the warmth of caring Cancer's affection. Capricorn enjoys her mum's sweet sense of humour and the way she looks after her so well, making her feel loved, secure, wanted and accepted.

Cancer's world is coloured by her swirling emotions, family ties and the response she gets from others. She needs to retreat from the fray often to restore her sense of balance. Capricorn looks at life in terms of her ambitions and how she can achieve more recognition. She wants to be valued for being top of the class while Cancer wants to be valued for being so caring.

This mother is good at encouraging Capricorn to work hard at school and will give up a lot to see that her child has everything she needs to further her education. Cancer is delighted that Capricorn sticks at things until she has finished them. And she's glad her child isn't a noisy show-off. Cancer thinks it's far better to be a little reserved.

Mum teaches Capricorn how to show other people affection and to share her feelings more. Cancer's warmth makes Capricorn feel secure enough to be more open, yet she won't want to be smothered with love. She needs quiet times and space to herself, and encouragement to be independent and responsible. Mum dreads the day that Capricorn flies the nest, and though Capricorn adores home, she's so ambitious she's bound to leave sooner rather than later.

These two homebirds hate to go out a lot, but it's important that Capricorn gets a chance to develop her social skills, so it's worth pushing her to make the effort to get out and meet others. Cancer is quite happy to let Capricorn develop in her own time. This mum is not pushy and appreciates Capricorn's careful, plodding style and sensible, down-to-earth views.

Capricorn child with a Cancer father

Sensitive Cancer Dad is far more emotional than his cool young Capricorn child and will sometimes erupt with irrational outbursts caused by his tidal emotions. Capricorn will take this badly, for she prefers people to act logically so that she knows where she stands. Predictable behaviour makes her feel more secure. Dad likes to be boss and this, coupled with his volatile temper, can make Capricorn stubborn if she thinks Dad is issuing orders that are in any way unfair.

Yet Dad more than makes up for his moodiness by being a caring and concerned father who'll take Capricorn anywhere she wants to go and will give her efforts at school every encouragement. He'll choose a traditional education for her, which is just what she needs, and try his best to build up her confidence so that she can reach her full potential.

Neither is sporty and they understand each other's need for rest. They take time to trust others and prefer quieter types whom they feel they can rely on. Capricorn loves the security and routine of her dad's home, and Cancer is pleased that Capricorn isn't the sort of child who takes risks. She's just as cautious as he is.

This pair certainly couldn't be called forward-looking and they'll love to reminisce. Cancer will help Capricorn to choose a suitable career and will back her all the way, with warmth, love, security and acceptance.

Capricorn child with a Leo mother

Capricorn is fascinated by her Leo mum's outgoing personality and her ability to shine in a crowd. Leo is willing to give endless time and attention to Capricorn, which makes her feel warm, loved and wanted. In fact, Leo Mum is the centre of Capricorn's world.

This child finds her mum's eccentric ways and colourful character amusing. Capricorn is much more reserved and usually distrusts noisy people, but in Mum's case she envies her ability to be commanding and confident. She thinks her mother is brave and kind, too, and admires the large scale she always works on. Leo never seems to get bogged down by details.

Mum feels very much at home and relaxed with her stable and dependable Capricorn child. Capricorn doesn't make big demands on her, and they enjoy looking after each other, even though they are quite different.

However, Leo finds it easy to do well and may not offer Capricorn the praise she needs for all the hard work she puts in. And Capricorn can never be as warm and appealing as her mum. She's ruled by the colder planet of Saturn and takes a long time to warm up. Mum radiates warmth and humour – everyone loves her, while people can find young Capricorn reserved and difficult to talk to.

Capricorn does think that Mum should put more effort into things – and she's hopeless with money! Yet this child loves her mum's warmth and energy and admires her ability to attract attention and inspire people. She likes the fact that Mum has a more serious side too, one that gives good advice, love and support. She knows that Mum will take care of the practicalities when it comes down to it, and she feels safe and loved.

Capricorn child with a Leo father

Big, strong Leo father is like a god to his Capricorn child. Dad seems to know everything – and with so little effort too! Capricorn wonders how on earth he does it. Capricorn would like to be centre of attention and adored by everybody too, but she knows she hasn't got Dad's extraordinary presence and personality. She has to rely on hard work to get by, while he relies on sheer magnetism.

Dad wants his children to succeed and will be proud when Capricorn does well at school. But he can push this child too hard at times, then let her know how disappointed and dismayed he feels if she doesn't come up to his high standards. Capricorn usually makes the grade because she drives herself so hard, but Dad mustn't show his disappointment if she sometimes falls short of his expectations.

Capricorn wants to succeed and to be acknowledged for it. She wants everyone to know she's clever and will be so proud if her dad gives her some praise. It will help build her confidence, which can be fragile in the early years, though it will become stronger later if nurtured.

Dad must try to avoid always grabbing the spotlight and

let Capricorn have her turn as the centre of attention to help her learn to value herself. Show her, too, that her reliability and hard-working attitude are worthwhile, and that it's not only extroverts who make a useful contribution in life.

Capricorn may act like an adult from an early age, but she needs reminding to enjoy her childhood. Leo can teach Capricorn to use her imagination and have fun. He helps her to be more optimistic, forward-looking and adaptable, less stuck in a groove and more open to all the possibilities life has to offer.

Capricorn child with a Virgo mother

These two are sensible souls who want to be respected. They're careful with money and have a strong sense of duty and responsibility. Mum will be pleased her youngster tries so hard at school, helps with the chores and rarely disobeys her. Capricorn is like a miniature grown-up and Virgo is delighted to have a child she can rely on to bring brothers and sisters into line and make them see sense.

Capricorn respects Virgo's need for tidiness and is unlikely to be desperate to own a pet, which relieves her fussy mum. Virgo will concentrate on teaching her child how to do things on a practical level and make solid achievements. Capricorn is a fast learner – achieving comes naturally to her and Virgo will be delighted with her progress.

But Capricorn won't like Virgo's critical streak. Capricorn has her own high standards and will be desperately upset if she doesn't reach them, so she hates it if Mum adds her harsh words too. Mum should offer more praise to build up Capricorn's confidence. She can be very confident in later life, but in these early years her confidence needs boosting.

Neither is particularly given to displays of affection. Yet Capricorn will need reassurance, so Virgo should make the effort to show her she cares. In other ways Capricorn will feel very secure in Virgo's sensible home. Everything is neat and tidy and run according to routine, and Mum can always be relied on to organise things well and do what she says she's going to do.

These two share the same quiet sense of humour and will enjoy many little jokes together. They'll get on well on the whole and have a rewarding relationship.

Capricorn child with a Virgo father

Dad likes good-mannered, well-behaved children who want to learn. So he'll be thrilled with earth-child Capricorn, who is responsible and serious from the moment she first opens her eyes.

Capricorn is determined to be a success, and caring Virgo Dad will do everything he can to help her achieve her goals. In fact, Dad secretly admires his child's ambitious streak and wishes he had the same drive to get to the top.

Both are rather pessimistic, though Capricorn believes that if she works hard things will be fine in the end, while Virgo is never sure that his efforts will be worth it. Both are honest and down to earth and tend to look before they leap. Neither is the world's biggest joker, though they amuse each other with quirky little observations of life.

Capricorn could do with more fun to draw her out. She takes life too seriously at times, so Dad should try to organise treats and surprises to brighten her outlook.

Dad enjoys being helpful and useful to people. Capricorn secretly thinks he'd achieve more if he put his time and energies into making money. Virgo can cope with changes better than his Capricorn child and will have to prepare her well for any upheavals, particularly house moves or the birth of a new baby in the family. Capricorn hates anything that she sees as a threat to her security.

In the main, Capricorn will feel very secure with Virgo Dad. She knows she can rely on him and they share a similar outlook on life. Virgo never expects too much of his child and he gives plenty of support whenever it's needed. He shows Capricorn how to do things and satisfies her curiosity by sharing his deep understanding of how things work.

Capricorn child with a Libra mother

Libra Mum encourages Capricorn's artistic and musical talents. She loves beauty and harmony and her emphasis on the creative side of life brings brightness to Capricorn's rather serious view. She broadens her child's outlook on life, stimulates her imagination and encourages her to make wise decisions as she grows older.

Here's a mother who loves to socialise and make new friends, bringing people together to share interests and enjoy each other's company. Capricorn is more reserved and prefers a few close friends to a big gathering. She sometimes thinks Mum spends too much time with other people and not enough solely with her. Yet she benefits from Mum's outgoing personality, learning to mix and get on better with people.

Capricorn loves routine, but Libra isn't that keen on it. She can see the sense of being organised, but she prefers to go where life takes her and hates to be tied down by mundane chores. She thinks Capricorn is too staid and stolid sometimes, always thinking in practical terms. Capricorn doesn't seem to enjoy spinning intellectual dreams the way her chatty Libra mum does.

Young Capricorn is more decisive than Libra, which Mum admires. And Capricorn is very determined, always reaching her goal, even if she gets there by gradual steps. Mum is less directed and tends to be lazy, and Capricorn often wishes she was better at making up her mind.

Libra enjoys buying things for her youngster, and Capricorn is proud of the status Mum's extravagant gifts win her with friends. She's glad of Mum's encouragement too, although Mum must avoid nagging – Capricorn takes it to heart, and she's hard enough on herself as it is. Libra would like Capricorn to be more loving, but she must accept it's not in her child's nature to be highly demonstrative. But this mustn't stop Mum from showing affection. Even if Capricorn doesn't admit it, she needs lots of reassurance and will secretly love those hugs.

Capricorn child with a Libra father

Mind-changing Libra Dad can seem unpredictable to his Capricorn child, who likes to know what's ahead and how people are likely to behave. Libra loves to play at happy families and wants everything to be sweetness and light, and if Capricorn is bad-tempered after he's been in one of his moods, Dad will find it hard to understand why.

Libra is very sociable and loves a party, while Capricorn prefers to see just a few close friends and feels uncomfortable in a crowd. She concentrates her energies and will work very hard indeed to succeed. Libra will be proud of her for doing so well, but at times he'll feel she's too practical and seems incapable of debating things just for the fun of it. The difference is that she's earthbound and materialistic, while his head is filled with culture and concepts.

Capricorn likes the way Dad treats her as a grown-up. Of course, she's acted like an adult almost from birth, but Libra should watch that he doesn't burden her with responsibilities too soon. By all means give her little tasks to build her confidence, but make sure she has the chance to enjoy her childhood in a carefree way. She can be too serious for her own good.

Some Libra fathers rule the roost fiercely, while others are far gentler. Capricorn responds to kind handling as she's tough enough on herself without anyone else telling her what she's done wrong. She needs love, encouragement, time and acceptance.

Dad is usually patient and listens to what she has to say. He doesn't often impose rules without explaining why, which gives Capricorn less scope for stubbornness. He helps Capricorn to learn to think for herself and encourages her not to be afraid to speak out.

Libra Dad will bring out the best in his Capricorn child, as long as he gives her the time and understanding she needs.

Capricorn child with a Scorpio mother

Energetic Scorpio Mum encourages her children to do well and can sometimes push them too hard. But in Capricorn's case, there's no need to worry that she won't do her best. Capricorn is driven from within to succeed and Scorpio is sure to end up feeling proud of her. As long as Mum lets her go at her own pace, all will be well.

This pair are both secretive, though Scorpio will find it hard to resist poking her nose into her child's life and trying to make her reveal her feelings. Capricorn needs space to herself and hates to feel under pressure. However, she'll appreciate the secure and orderly home Scorpio creates for her, for Capricorn thrives on stability and a traditional upbringing and schooling. Scorpio will make sure that she gets all of these.

There will inevitably be clashes as Scorpio goes all out to show that she's in control. Stubborn Capricorn can be bad tempered if harsh rules are imposed on her without any explanation. She feels she's responsible enough to be left to make some decisions for herself, and she hates to feel she's being manipulated.

Scorpio must watch that she doesn't knock her youngster's confidence. Capricorn is not as sure of her own abilities as she seems and needs building up if she's to become secure and confident.

Both are money- and status-minded and Capricorn admires Mum's ability to get things done. Neither likes change, nor do they have a great sense of humour or fun. But they'll get on well. Mum will be relieved that Capricorn isn't a naturally disobedient child and that she shows plenty of common sense. And Capricorn will thrive on the security and settled routine her mum provides.

Capricorn child with a Scorpio father

Scorpio Dad creates a home where things are run according to a regular pattern, even when he's not there, which helps Capricorn feel she lives in a world she can rely on. However,

Dad is often away working and must be sure to make the time to give Capricorn the encouragement she needs.

Scorpio should try not to issue harsh orders or lose his temper too often. Capricorn is more sensitive than she looks and it could give her confidence a blow if she's not treated fairly. She'll simply retreat, bury her head in a book and feel miserable.

Capricorn senses that Dad often hides what he's thinking and it disturbs her when his life gets complicated and he has to fight battles that are way beyond her understanding. If Scorpio has helped to build Capricorn's confidence, she will be able to cope with the occasions when his actions confuse her. It's better, though, if he can keep her out of his intrigues.

Scorpio Dad loves his child dearly and wants the very best for her, but he finds it hard to really understand children or to grasp that his ways may not always be best for Capricorn. He should concentrate on creating an enjoyable and fun atmosphere for her so that she does not become too serious and work-focused.

Dad must help her to enjoy her childhood and listen to her when she puts her point of view. Offer her security and try to be straightforward with her, go easy on the discipline and give her lots of encouragement and praise, and she'll grow up happy with her Scorpio dad.

Capricorn child with a Sagittarius mother

Talkative Sagittarius Mum seems so full of life and energy to her Capricorn child. Mum is all action and loves anything new. She's always on the go and loves to talk, while Capricorn is quieter, more serious and studious. Yet she benefits from Mum's lessons in how to enjoy life. Capricorn certainly won't be allowed to become boring with this mum around.

Sagittarius is marvellous at opening up the world for Capricorn. She gives her child lots of attention and takes her to all sorts of places. Capricorn is more of a homelover than Mum, but it doesn't do her any harm at all to get out and about and learn how to make friends.

One thing Mum's not good at is creating a steady routine to help Capricorn feel truly secure. Sagittarius never likes one day to be the same as the next, so she's always changing the way she does things. This can confuse Capricorn, who hates the unexpected.

Mum can also be a bit insensitive, and so blunt she can make Capricorn cringe. Capricorn is more sensitive than she looks and is quite self-critical, so Mum must learn to praise her instead of being outspoken.

Capricorn will learn to shake off her pessimism when Mum's around. Sagittarius gives her the confidence to believe that everything will work out at the end of the day.

Sagittarius teaches Capricorn to enjoy travel and to take the occasional risk. The problem with Capricorn is that her determination to succeed overpowers her need to have fun. If Mum encourages her in the things she enjoys, like her schoolwork, she'll have a well-balanced little Capricorn on her hands.

Capricorn child with a Sagittarius father

Playful Sagittarius Dad enjoys a bit of fun but may move too fast at times for his slower Capricorn child. Dad seems very restless to staid Capricorn, who prefers to stay in one place rather than spend all her time rushing round. Dad thinks Capricorn is a funny little stick-in-the-mud, but he can't help but admire her determination and her ability to apply herself.

Dad teaches Capricorn to draw, play music and speak foreign languages. He encourages her to read and broaden her mind and makes learning fun, teaching her little rhymes and fun ways to remember things. Dad is really just a big kid himself and often Capricorn seems more adult and sensible than he does. One thing he does show her is that life is to be enjoyed, a lesson this serious little soul needs to learn.

Sagittarius always explains any rules and is very fair, which suits Capricorn who can be stubborn if she doesn't understand why she's being told not to do something. Dad helps her to be more outgoing, too, and to enjoy meeting people.

Sometimes, though, he expects too much of his child. He wants her to match his ideal and can be offhand with her if she doesn't. Dad must learn to accept his child as she is and to value her strengths, particularly her reliability in a crisis, her warm heart under that reserved exterior and her love of hard work.

Sagittarius Dad may not provide her with a sense of complete stability, but he'll teach her to think for herself, question authority more and express herself well. He's not brilliant when it comes to fulfilling all his responsibilities, but he offers inspiration, which will be an asset to Capricorn for the rest of her life.

Capricorn child with a Capricorn mother

Cool Capricorn Mum knows just how to help her child get the most success out of life. She's ambitious for Capricorn, who is desperate to do well. With this mum behind her, she'll climb to the very top.

Although Mum cares a great deal for her child, she can be a bit slow in showing it. This pair are both reserved and hate extravagant gestures of affection. Yet Capricorn will need lots of reassurance that she's wanted and accepted, so Mum must make an effort and show appreciation to build her youngster's confidence.

Capricorn is a good homemaker and creates an ordered environment where her child can feel secure and happy. Life runs according to the clock, so Capricorn knows what lies ahead each day, which pleases her. There won't be a great deal of fun and games, but Capricorn child doesn't yearn for laughs although they do her a lot of good sometimes.

Mum likes to be in control and this too can add to Capricorn's sense of security, as long as Mum doesn't become too domineering. Capricorn child likes to be trusted to make some decisions for herself, so Mum should give her credit for her grown-up and responsible behaviour.

This pair both love tradition and the past. Neither likes change though both like to improve their lot and gain prestige as time goes by. Mum will guide Capricorn towards a suitable career and back her all the way. Capricorn will look back on her childhood and be grateful for the solid base that Mum provided while she was growing up.

Capricorn child with a Capricorn father

Capricorn Dad is a dependable man who supports his family through thick and thin. He has a great sense of duty and he likes to be respected for his achievements.

Young Capricorn certainly looks up to him. She shares his work ethic and thinks he's marvellously clever. She loves the things he buys with his hard-earned money and feels very proud to have such a successful dad.

The trouble is he may spend a lot of time away working. Young Capricorn would prefer him to be around to add to her sense of security, and Dad must remember that children need love and affection as well as financial support.

Both are very traditional, and it's unlikely that Capricorn child will rebel as much as some might in those teenage years. But Dad may push his child a little too hard sometimes, not allowing enough scope for fun and relaxation. All Capricorns need encouraging to enjoy themselves, so they should both make time to have some fun together. The main reason Dad pushes Capricorn child is that he wants her to do even better than he has. It delights him to think that the next generation will win further respect and material success. And his hopes are bound to be realised by his ambitious Capricorn child.

Dad can be a tough disciplinarian and it's wise to go easy with Capricorn. She rarely misbehaves intentionally and she'll be mentally ticking herself off if she does something wrong. She doesn't mind rules as long as they are explained, but she can take harsh words to heart, becoming sulky and withdrawn in response. Dad should draw her out with kindness and praise instead. Encourage her and surround her with security and she'll be a very happy little Capricorn indeed.

Capricorn child with an Aquarius mother

Aquarius Mum is ruled by cool planet Saturn, just like little Capricorn. However, Mum loves a crowd and her reserved child definitely doesn't. Aquarius needs to be out and about, joining groups, campaigning for social change, helping those less well off than herself. Capricorn prefers a quieter life where her main aim is to work hard and improve her lot.

Capricorn wishes Mum would stay at home more. This conventional youngster thinks that's where mothers belong. But Aquarius hates to be tied by domestic routine. She's always dreaming up new projects to take part in and hates feeling trapped and bored. It's vital that she has time for her own interests in order to be a good parent, which is worth explaining to staid young Capricorn.

Stability and security are vital to Capricorn, who doesn't want to be pushed to be independent before she's ready, however mature she may seem on the surface. There's a risk that Aquarius may expect her to grow up too fast, offering responsibilities and freedom that Capricorn is not ready to handle.

Mum must remember that Capricorn thrives on sensible discipline and an orderly environment. She needs to be sure that practical matters are being attended to as well. She's also less of an intellectual than Mum. Capricorn functions in the here and now and doesn't have much time for the ideas, dreams and debate that Aquarius loves. They make her feel uneasy.

All Capricorn wants is a solid base to allow her to feel safe, cared for and confident. Mum should offer her as much love and stability as she can, accepting that this child has a different outlook from her own.

Capricorn child with an Aquarius father

This like-minded pair find a lot to admire in each other,

They are both honest, direct and fair, although Dad would like Capricorn to get on better with her fellow human beings and consider their needs as well as her own. He also wants to open Capricorn's eyes to social injustice and world affairs. He may not meet with a very keen response, but at least Capricorn's outlook will be healthily broadened.

Dad's love of books will be passed on to his child, and he'll encourage her to read, study and do well in exams. Capricorn wants to succeed at school and she's determined to get to the top one day, through her own hard work.

This child may lack her father's zany sense of inspiration – she's much more down to earth – but Aquarius will admire the way she sticks at things. He'll be only too happy to help her with her homework and show her new ways of tackling problems.

Aquarius is more energetic than Capricorn, but he understands her need for rest and retreat. He has a reserved side himself that allows him to be involved in life yet an observer at the same time.

He'll think she's a bit too mean when it comes to money, though. Prising cash out of her for the latest good cause he's supporting will be hard going. It will do her good to learn to give.

Dad is an easy disciplinarian and will explain any rules he does set, which suits Capricorn, who hates to be bossed about. But Capricorn sometimes requires firmer guidance than Dad gives to help her feel secure and know what's expected of her.

Aquarius believes children should develop naturally and be given plenty of freedom, learning to think and speak for themselves. Capricorn finds it hard to express her feelings and hates being pushed to speak out if she doesn't want to. And she is much more conventional than Aquarius, and often taken aback by his eccentric behaviour. Capricorn wants him to be an upstanding and respected citizen, one she can model herself on, and can be perplexed by his highly original and unusual ways.

Aquarius will teach Capricorn the valuable lesson that it's

okay to be herself and she doesn't have to check constantly that her behaviour is acceptable. He'll show her there's more to life than money and ambition, and that new ideas and new inventions can be fascinating. She may think he'll never put any of his grand ideas into practice, but she'll learn to dream and enjoy life.

The day will come when she'll start to think up ways of translating Dad's schemes into solid reality – and she's sure to make money out of them somewhere along the way!

Capricorn child with a Pisces mother

Kind and gentle Pisces Mum knows the way to her little Capricorn's heart. She's so in tune that she picks up just how her child is feeling, something that very few others can do. She gives warmth and love that help to break down Capricorn's wall of reserve, but she must watch that she is not too soft and indulgent. Capricorn likes firm guidance and sensible discipline to show her just where she stands. Mum needs to try to create a good balance.

Adaptable Pisces finds it easy to mould herself to fit in with Capricorn's character. She admires Capricorn's determination and the way she sticks at something until it's done. Mum lacks Capricorn's sense of purpose, and her life is likely to be far less structured than her child would like. Capricorn wants to feel firm support all around her, while Mum swims as the tide takes her and makes few definite plans.

Capricorn needs praise for her achievements at school and sensitive Pisces will be quick to reassure her that she's doing well. But Pisces is unlikely to share the driving ambition of her Capricorn child and must try not to show any doubts she may have about her child's abilities. Capricorn's confidence needs building up if she is to reach her potential. Pisces mustn't bend the truth, either. Capricorn will stop trusting her if she feels Mum is not being straightforward about things. Use tact and sensitivity instead.

Mum can blow her top under stress and should watch

that little Capricorn isn't taking her outbursts too much to heart. Capricorn doesn't show feelings on the surface but will hurt inside. Mum should also watch that she doesn't grow to rely on her child too much. Capricorn may be sensible and grown-up, but it's important that she is also encouraged to be a child sometimes.

Capricorn child with a Pisces father

Pisces Dad is delighted that Capricorn is so conventional and well behaved. He feels this is very important as, being a bit of an oddball himself, his greatest wish is for his children to fit in. Yet Dad is a worrier and can be too protective of his young Capricorn. She needs reassurance that he believes in her abilities in order to build her fragile self-confidence.

Dad is brilliant at bringing out Capricorn's artistic and musical talents. He's very creative and inspiring and teaches Capricorn to dream and enjoy herself. But he is very emotional and Capricorn can find it hard to deal with his mood swings and changes of mind. Capricorn likes everything to be predictable and reliable and hates the unexpected.

Yet she finds Pisces very kind and supportive in many ways. He indulges her with presents that make her the envy of her friends – wonderful for status-conscious Capricorn. His love and warmth certainly help to make Capricorn feel more secure, but his lack of a stable lifestyle can worry her a lot. Capricorn craves stability, normality and routine to an extent that other signs would find boring.

Pisces encourages Capricorn to talk and express her feelings as no-one else can. He understands children well and finds it easy to communicate on their level. But Capricorn can't understand how he can make decisions based on intuition and feelings. She's far more practical and believes you can do anything if you work hard enough at it.

Capricorn would like firmer discipline and structure in her family life. Yet she benefits from Pisces Dad's lessons in how to use her imagination and is less likely to live life in a rut because of his influence.

AQUARIUS
Stars for Life

STAR BABY

Aquarius is a real charmer – but so stubborn! He (or she*) is sociable, smiling and fast to grab at anything interesting dangled over his cot. But once he's had enough of sitting on Dad's knee, or thinks he's been anchored too long in his highchair, he'll be set on going walkabout. There's no holding independent Aquarius.

Mealtimes can be a trial with this fusspot, who develops strange and picky tastes. Don't be surprised if he turns down everything except prawn cocktail and lychees. No need to worry – tomorrow some new fad will have caught his fancy.

Crawling and walking come early and he's soon busily exploring his home. Better tie everything down, especially anything with lights on which fascinate him. He digs in his heels when you tell him to keep his paws out of the plantpots and away from the video. It's not easy to make determined Aquarius listen to sense!

Potty training can be a chore, as once again he refuses to be told what to do. But Aquarius will respond well to reason. Explain that everyone has to go through this stage and he'll mull it over, then train himself when you're not looking.

FIRST STEPS FOR AQUARIUS

Your sweet Aquarius will often turn into a cross and both-

*'He' is used to cover he and she for Aquarius child.

ered toddler, refusing to move and making a scene. Again, sensible explanation as to why he should or should not do something can help. Shouting matches will just make him even more determined to go his own way.

Aquarius will benefit from attending a nursery school. He needs pals of his own age and is happiest in a group. He loves lively games, especially running around with other children, although he'll still want to do things his own way and can be a naughty little terror at times.

His verbal abilities are evident early. He's a fine little talker, full of original phrases and quirky statements. But all too often he uses his gift of the gab to defy you. This little rebel needs firm but caring control to show him his limits. Don't let him get away with too much. He's determined that he knows best and hates any kind of authority, but he needs to learn that some rules are there for his own protection. It's great that he can think for himself – but this needs to be balanced with sense and consideration too, tell him.

Yet there's a surprisingly mature side to Aquarius, too, and he'll love talking around a subject with you, asking profound questions and expressing unusual insights. He's full of concern for those less fortunate than himself. If he sees a beggar, he'll demand to know all about homelessness – and will want to do something, however small, to help. Try to involve him if you are donating to charity, or just helping out a neighbour. His social conscience is evident from a very early age and needs nurturing.

Little Aquarius loves to help others, but he's shy about asking for help for himself. He needs to know you're ready to lend a hand. This little individual tends to go his own way too much and ends up believing he has to rely only on himself. He's not openly affectionate and can seem detached. Show him you love and accept him however he acts and that you're there with support when he needs it.

He loves being part of a group at nursery, but will make sure he still maintains his specialness in a crowd. He fits in easily and enjoys being surrounded by other children. He likes, too, the opportunity to learn new things, satisfying his immense curiosity.

Yet Aquarius keeps a part of himself secret, even from his parents. He finds it rather hard to get close to people, fearing he'll be rejected if he reveals his deepest thoughts. He prefers to invent a little world of his own where he can dream and no-one can hurt him. He can get lost in his thoughts, bumping into doors, forgetting what you've just told him. Aquarius is busy on another plane!

His quicksilver mind darts from one thing to another and he's always on the lookout for something new to occupy his busy brain. He's a young visionary, with science-fiction style ideas, dreaming of things that will one day become reality. Whatever you do, don't laugh at his big dreams. He wants to be listened to and treated with respect. Tell him he's full of hot air and you'll dampen his spark. His best pals are usually other little visionaries, and it's hard for more average children to make sense of him.

Aquarius likes to think of himself as very grown-up and may believe he's better at looking after himself than he is. Keep an eye on what he's getting up to and try to instill as much common sense into him as you can, without dragging him down. Tactfully help him through life's decisions, teaching him to discover his true desires, and he'll repay your care with touching loyalty. He depends on you a lot more than he shows.

SCHOOL RULES FOR AQUARIUS

At school he'll be as bright as a button, his head buzzing with all the new information he's taking in. He soon thinks he knows it all and can switch off if lessons are boring. He wants to look all round a subject, going off at tangents. While his creative thinking may prove useful in the future, he needs to be taught how to handle the job in hand and concentrate on one thing at a time.

He adores reading and his room at home will be packed with books on a wide range of subjects. He throws himself into those fields he loves, while ignoring those he dislikes. He'll argue back at the teachers if he thinks they've got their facts wrong.

Aquarius' ability to challenge and discriminate can make him an awkward pupil, who may not agree with the exam system and therefore won't try his best. He'll probably start to shine at his brightest in higher education, where his original perspective on life will be given more credit, and he can choose to specialise in what he's interested in.

TEENAGE TAKE-OFF FOR AQUARIUS

As a teenager, Aquarius will be unpredictable and troublesome at times. For a few years the manners you've tried so hard to teach him will be forgotten as he declares his freedom and acts how he wants, when he wants. He'll be out all the time with his weird and wonderful friends, experimenting, exploring, for he thrives on a busy social life during these years.

He'll always be disagreeing with you, acting unconventionally and asking tricky questions, then refusing to give straight answers. On the positive side, Aquarius teenager is full of fun, bursting with ideas and excitement. He's rarely selfish, would give away his last possession to someone in need and likes to help others as much as he can, probably through involvement with a charitable cause.

Because he likes to stay a little detached, he doesn't fling himself headlong into romance. Love may not hit him until he's rather older, but at least the worst of his teenage rebellion will be over then and he'll be in a better state to make choices that really suit him.

By then he'll be on his way to creating a lifestyle unique to him, having delighted you through his childhood with his sparkiness, inventiveness, intuition and his visionary outlook. You'll feel very proud of him indeed.

Aquarius child with an Aries mother

Mum loves the fact that her friendly little Aquarius is such a fast developer. She admires him for being a bit of a rebel, for being ahead of the times, a pioneering explorer. Both are honest, have lots of energy and hate routine. And both like to have their own way, so there could be some stubborn scenes between this determined pair.

Aries always leaps in and does something the moment it enters her head, while Aquarius takes time for logical planning. He's more of a thinker, although he changes his mind more often than Mum, who sets herself a goal and goes after it unfailingly.

Independent Aries is glad that Aquarius isn't a clingy child. He's happy in a crowd, leaving her free to talk, and he doesn't mind being left with people he knows so that she can go off and follow her own interests.

Aquarius loves to be part of a group, although he wants to stand out by being a bit different. He believes in fairness and equality and usually puts the needs of everyone before his own. Aries likes to be in charge of any group with which she's involved. She's a powerful leader who throws herself into things wholeheartedly, while Aquarius always keeps part of himself back. He's a private little creature who doesn't want people to get too close in case they hurt him in some way.

This child loves the way Mum treats him as a grown-up. She encourages him to be independent, yet she's firm when it comes to rules, a good combination for Aquarius. And she's not worried that he can be a little remote emotionally as she's not one for being demonstrative herself.

As long as she remembers that he needs more affection than he asks for, and seems more self-contained than he really is, then these two will enjoy a loving relationship.

Aquarius child with an Aries father

Dad admires his idealistic Aquarius child, especially the way he tries to put his big ideas into action. Aries is glad to see he's not just a dreamer. These two enjoy lively discussions about causes and issues that interest them both. They must both watch that they don't get too carried away with their enthusiasms.

Aries should be firm but not fierce with Aquarius, who needs logical discipline to help him behave. Aquarius loves to get his own way, but too much aggression in response could crush that idealistic spark Aries admires so much in his child.

This father is full of enthusiasm and drive, which inspires Aquarius to make the most of life and to have a wide range of interests. Dad has endless ideas for exciting things to do that keep Aquarius' lively mind buzzing.

Dad may take it personally if Aquarius does not excel at school in those early years. Aries can feel cross and let down, but Aquarius usually blossoms into an achiever as he grows up, so be patient. Aries should also watch that he doesn't impose his own ambitions on his child too much. Aquarius needs to feel free to find his own path through life.

Above all, Aries must accept that Aquarius is an individual who can act eccentrically sometimes. Dad should resist trying to force him to conform, for being unusual is all part of Aquarius' charm. And he should never forget that his Aquarius child is often ahead of his time.

Aquarius child with a Taurus mother

Warm Taurus Mum loves kind-hearted Aquarius, but she's puzzled by the way he sometimes struggles free of her cuddles. Mum is full of affection, and while Aquarius is friendly, he can also be rather detached and cool. Taurus should be reassured that he benefits from her warmth and needs affection like everyone else. It's just that he finds it hard to ask for and accept.

Aquarius can be a real little rebel, but stubborn Taurus Mum won't stand for any nonsense. Both want their own way, so there could be thunderous clashes from time to time. Mum can help to defuse her argumentative little Aquarius with logic and reason. He'll see sense in the end.

Traditional Taurus can't understand Aquarius' lack of respect for authority or his dislike of routine. She trusts what's tried and tested, while he seems to yearn for everything that's new. Mum must try not to overprotect Aquarius, who is a pioneering little explorer with a strong need for adventure.

Mum can also be very possessive, expecting Aquarius to do everything the way she thinks is best. She must learn to allow him to gradually find his own way in life. Her cosy style may not suit him at all, and Taurus must allow him to be himself.

Taurus will have to learn to keep up with her energetic Aquarius child. She plods steadily along, while he has bursts of hectic activity followed by quiet times. Mum will also be kept busy with his endless questions and curiosity.

Aquarius is full of bright ideas, and practical Mum can help by showing him which are workable and which are plain hare-brained. One thing Mum must watch closely is her tendency to feed her child up with hearty home cooking. Aquarius is naturally slim and will be happiest if he stays that way.

Aquarius will feel happy and loved with his Taurus mum and enjoy a childhood filled with all the home comforts he could wish for.

Aquarius child with a Taurus father

Dad likes his slippers by the fire and his cosy armchair after a hard day's work. He likes things to stay the same and doesn't want anyone to rock the boat. So he'll have his work cut out with Aquarius, who's raring for change and excitement! He wants to explore, investigate, have adventures, toss around ideas and enjoy himself. Dear old Taurus Dad can seem a real stick-in-the-mud to perky little Aquarius.

Yet Aquarius will benefit greatly from the old-fashioned

common sense that Dad teaches. Dad helps Aquarius to concentrate more, instead of dashing after every idea that comes into his head.

Aquarius is quirky and different, a real little individual, while Taurus is conventional and respectable. He doesn't always approve of Aquarius' odd band of friends, and he thinks Aquarius is way out of line when he argues back. Yet Dad's firm approach can stop Aquarius demanding his own way all the time, for he teaches his child that there are limits.

Dad must avoid blowing up with anger. Reason and logic work better than stormy scenes with this youngster. This applies especially during the teenage years, which could see a head-on confrontation if Taurus doesn't handle things gently.

Dad enjoys his cosy, materially comfortable life while Aquarius wants to launch off into the world of ideas. Aquarius wishes Dad could join him there, while Taurus wishes Aquarius would show some desire to settle down. Yet they will learn to accept each other and Taurus has a gentle and sensitive side which understands the bright desires of his child. And in his heart, Aquarius knows just how much his dad really cares.

Aquarius child with a Gemini mother

This talkative pair are bursting with ideas that they love to share with each other. Both think at the speed of light and are bouncing with energy and enthusiasm for life. They are big mind-changers, too, deciding on one thing one moment, then hopping on to something else the next. At least they're as bad as each other! They are not emotional, tending instead to think in a logical, intellectual way. Both enjoy looking forward to the future, dreaming up ideas that are ahead of their time.

Mum and child hate routine, so they are able to fit in with each other's anarchic lifestyle quite well. But there will be arguments, for these two are an unpredictable duo, given to bursts of temper. Both like to have their own way and think that their method of doing things is best. Mum must watch she doesn't try to take over her child's life too much. Rebellious Aquarius will stamp his feet and demand space. He hates to feel his freedom is being cramped in any way.

Mum will be delighted that Aquarius is a quick developer who talks early and enjoys a chat. He's a friendly child too, which pleases her as she loves her social life and will be glad that he's happy to tag along. She doesn't mind either that there's a part of him that seems emotionally distant, for she's very much the same.

She's a little more streetwise than him, though, and will teach him not to be too trusting. Otherwise she treats him as a grown-up, which he loves, though Mum must remember that he needs more care and reassurance than he shows.

Gemini lacks Aquarius' idealism, preferring to put her own need for amusement above most other considerations. But she'll give him the freedom to be himself, balanced with just the right amount of discipline. She's amused by his unconventionality, and he thinks she's tremendous fun. This pair are a good match and will always get a lot out of their relationship.

Aquarius child with a Gemini father

Gemini loves his adventurous little explorer. This child is full of enthusiasm and curiosity, just like Dad, and Gemini is secretly proud that Aquarius is a little rebel. Dad believes you should stand up to people who try to boss you about unfairly and is glad to see his child is a chip off the old block.

These two love words and Aquarius is always quick with a clever reply, which amuses fast-thinking Gemini. This child is also very honest, while Gemini tends to play little tricks with words. Aquarius is humanitarian and idealistic, always chasing after good causes, and makes Dad look rather selfish in comparison.

Dad can teach Aquarius how to function in the real world and how to make his ideas a workable reality. He will also help him to judge people and to make money. Dad has far more common sense than his little dreamer.

Both are very friendly but they can be rather remote at the same time. Aquarius won't risk revealing his true self, in case he gets hurt, while Gemini hides any inner insecurity under a blur of clever words.

Gemini is a very busy man and can feel a little unsure of whether he's a good father or not. He must learn to make time to be with his child and not give in too fast to boredom. Abruptly ended play may not seem to affect independent Aquarius, but he does feel so encouraged when Dad takes a real interest in him and his activities.

Dad will never make Aquarius feel silly for being slightly eccentric. He sees through to his child's originality and creativity, and encourages him to think for himself and express himself well, which is just what Aquarius needs.

Gemini is brilliant at thinking up stories to stimulate Aquarius' imagination, and there will be plenty of lively days out. Dad and Aquarius have a lot in common and fun is guaranteed for this pair.

Aquarius child with a Cancer mother

Protective Cancer Mum offers love and warmth to her child, but Aquarius is less emotional and dependent than her and values freedom more than almost anything. Cancer must be careful not to make claustrophobic demands on him for affection. Aquarius is a self-contained and independent little soul who will break free if Mum is too possessive.

Cancer must allow this child to explore, seek adventure, invent and dream. Aquarius has a vivid imagination and if Mum tries to restrict him he'll lose something that's basic to him. So let him be a bit unconventional, Mum, and don't sigh in despair at his eccentric little ways. Accept him as the creative and inventive personality he is.

Mum is far more conventional than Aquarius and values home, family, comfort and cooking above all other things. Aquarius wants to escape, travel, discuss ideas, share enthusiasms. Mum mustn't coop him up at home. She should get him into a good nursery or a school where his imagination is stretched, and take him out to meet people. Aquarius needs to mix.

Ideas don't appeal to Cancer in the way they do to her child. But Mum should try to do all she can to widen his horizons and should talk with him as much as possible. She shouldn't worry too much that Aquarius seems a bit remote. Cancer wants closeness and may feel frustrated that Aquarius keeps his distance. It's simply his nature and he needs love as much as any other child, and depends on his parents more than he shows. Mum mustn't try to manipulate him emotionally, though, for he'll just become more remote.

Mum will appreciate the way Aquarius wants to help others. Her caring nature finds expression in relationships and kindness, while Aquarius is set on changing the planet for the better. Mum doesn't think on this big scale, but can't help being proud of her child's ambitions.

Aquarius child with a Cancer father

Kind Cancer Dad is always happy to help Aquarius follow his latest interest and to organise educational days out that help keep that busy Aquarius brain buzzing. But Dad will expect to be thanked at the end of it, and Aquarius may forget. He lives life in a daydream and is vague, rather than affectionate.

Cancer finds disciplining his child difficult. Aquarius can be argumentative, always determined he's right, wanting his own way and stamping his feet. If Cancer isn't in the mood for a fight and feels tired, he'll just let Aquarius get away with it.

But if Cancer's swirling emotions get the better of him, he'll let fly with a tirade of anger. Aquarius never knows quite what to expect from Dad. Cancer has a lot of emotional ups and downs, which Aquarius deals with by making himself scarce and acting detached, ignoring Dad's loud protestations. He can also decide to argue back with unstoppable logic, which will make Cancer crosser than ever.

Aquarius does his best to evade helping in the home so that he can concentrate on dreaming up his latest scheme. Dad can't understand fast-developer Aquarius' big ideas and wishes he would come down from the clouds and help with the chores more often. He wants Aquarius to act more like a child instead of trying to engage adults in meaningful debate all the time.

These two are very different. Dad thinks with his emotions, while Aquarius is logical and intellectual. Aquarius takes risks, while Dad errs on the side of caution. Aquarius enjoys change, something Cancer dreads. And Cancer worries about everything while Aquarius is carefree in comparison. Dad needs rest and retreat to soothe his furrowed brow, and Aquarius only needs a rest after he's worn himself out with hectic activity. Aquarius is generous, where Cancer can be stingy. And Dad is very old-fashioned compared with his forward-looking child.

The key to these two getting on is for Dad not to be too controlling. If Aquarius has space to be himself, he'll appreciate Dad for all the good things he has to offer – kindness, encouragement, a comfortable home and complete family loyalty.

Aquarius child with a Leo mother

Aquarius may act cool and detached, but he can't help but glow in the warmth his Leo mum radiates. Generous, enthusiastic Leo brings out Aquarius' sunny side and makes him feel loved and wanted.

Mum must make a special effort to find out what makes Aquarius tick, what he's interested in and responds to. Leo can be far too imposing and forceful, insisting he does what she thinks is best. Stubborn Aquarius will argue back loudly, determined to make his own choices in life.

Proud Leo wants her child to do well, purely because of the glory it will bring her. Aquarius is very bright, yet he can be a late developer at school because he's so easily distracted. He'll suddenly shoot ahead in his teens and do really well, so Mum must be patient in the early years, gently helping him to concentrate without complaining to him.

Leo and Aquarius share a love of foreign holidays. This little explorer relishes adventure, but while Mum likes all her home comforts, Aquarius yearns to head off into the wide blue yonder with just his backpack once he's older. While he's young, though, he'll be happy with his holidays and days out and Mum will be rewarded each time she sees his eyes light up as he spots something new.

Both are great mixers. Aquarius is good at seeing everyone is kept happy, while Mum likes to be the centre of attention, radiating a warmth that brightens any event. These two are certainly a charming pair – when they're not arguing! Both are a bit eccentric, Aquarius in a quietly quirky way and Leo flamboyantly so. But they're also generous, friendly, optimistic and energetic. Independent Aquarius knows Mum has got a wise and serious side, too, and he'll come to her often for good advice as he grows up.

Aquarius child with a Leo father

All regal Leo Dad wants is for his child to respect, admire and look up to him adoringly. He certainly didn't bank on having a little rebel like Aquarius in the family! Aquarius doesn't give respect easily – people have to win it – and he won't obey authority unless there's a good reason to do so. As for adoration, Aquarius is far too detached to be so openly emotional.

Yet he'll get on well with his Leo father all the same. Both have nimble minds and enjoy discussing ideas. They love to laugh and are generous and kind-hearted. Aquarius isn't in the least embarrassed by Dad's dramatic way of carrying on either, or his different taste in clothes. Aquarius loves to stand out from the crowd, too, and is glad to have a father who understands why.

Aquarius won't be happy if Dad is heavy-handed with the

discipline. Aquarius needs boundaries as he can push his parents to the limit, but firm and logical explanation works best with him, not noisy shouting matches.

Dad wants his child to be perfect and may decide to be cruel to be kind. But harshness will only make Aquarius more detached and defiant. There are bound to be problems in the teenage years, when traditional Leo clashes with ahead-of-his-time Aquarius. Leo must stop being a tyrant and accept Aquarius for what he is.

Leo can offer wonderful guidance, helping Aquarius find practical ways to turn his ideas into reality. And Dad will be proud to have a child who is so bright and curious about life.

Aquarius child with a Virgo mother

Sensible Virgo likes a life of order and routine while Aquarius loves newness and excitement, games and ideas. Mum will just have to let the chores take care of themselves sometimes while she spends time chatting with her inventive little Aquarius. She'll find that there's a lot he wants to talk about!

Virgo would love to have a child who willingly helps around the house, but Aquarius will try to dodge anything he doesn't want to do. He needs bringing into line, something which Virgo will try to do firmly, refusing to let him have his own way all the time. But there can be arguments as Virgo has a critical tongue and Aquarius is quite prepared to argue back about anything he doesn't want to hear.

Mum must watch she doesn't hem Aquarius in with too many rules. He needs to have a sense of freedom and his bright, idealistic spark could be dimmed if he's made to obey orders all the time. He wants to explore, have adventures, get out and mix. Mum must let him be the creative, original and slightly quirky little person he is and not force him to conform.

Virgo isn't too bothered that Aquarius seems rather remote and detached. She's not emotional either and she understands his logical way of thinking. But she should still offer plenty of love and support to help him trust her enough to reveal his hopes and fears. Aquarius needs coaxing, for he's afraid of being hurt if he gives too much away.

Mum loves to do things to help others and is glad that Aquarius is kind and honest and wants to improve the lot of those worse off than himself. She may think that a lot of his idealistic dreams are just pie in the sky, but she'll be able to show him which will work, something that will help him greatly as he grows up.

Aquarius child with a Virgo father

Firm Virgo Dad makes sure Aquarius doesn't dodge his responsibilities. Unconventional Aquarius seems a real little rebel in his eyes, but this strict and sensible dad does his best to stop his child getting out of hand. Virgo wants his child to conform for his own benefit and so he insists on good behaviour and a regular routine.

Aquarius wants to have his own way too much and may ache to break free, but it will do him good to know his boundaries. Dad teaches him to organise his life, to take care of money, to apply himself more at school and to concentrate on one thing at a time instead of dashing after every bright idea that comes into his head.

Aquarius must be given space to explore, though, and encouragement for his bright ideas. He's a little visionary, often well ahead of his time, so he shouldn't be criticised or restricted too much. It could dim his lively personality.

Aquarius' habit of changing his mind disturbs Dad, who likes to think something through carefully before making a decision and sticking to it. Although Dad enjoys Aquarius' style of grown-up conversation, he still thinks of him as a wayward child while Aquarius wants his opinions to be taken seriously.

Virgo enjoys his child's lively-minded and curious questions. Quick-thinking Dad takes delight in giving detailed replies and explanations. This verbal pair have great fun talking together, although Dad isn't interested in all things new the way that Aquarius is. Deep down, Dad prefers what's tried and tested and reliable.

Dad may not approve of Aquarius' odd choice in friends and he certainly won't like his child's lack of respect for authority. He'll just have to accept that Aquarius sees life differently and has unusual interests. He can help his child best by constantly broadening his horizons, helping him to discover the world, and by not pouring cold water on Aquarius' bright and innocent ideas.

Aquarius child with a Libra mother

Sociable and friendly Libra Mum loves to mix and move and arranges all kinds of trips out that excite curious Aquarius. She's chatty and pleasant and gets along well with her talkative, inquisitive child. Mum's not too emotional and thinks in a logical way, so she can give Aquarius the space to be himself that he so needs. Aquarius will want to hang on to his individuality and there will always be an aura of mystery and detachment about him.

However, Mum will find his argumentative nature hard to cope with. She'll do anything to avoid a row, while Aquarius loves nothing better than a heated debate and will stand his ground to make his point and get his own way. Mum's a real softie who lets him get away with a lot, but there comes a point where she'll draw the line to stop him becoming a real little horror.

Neither is usually moody, although they both tend to hide their problems from others and even from themselves. Aquarius finds it hard to ask for reassurance and Libra ignores her troubles until they burst to the surface. She must make sure that she's honest with him about any difficulties so that he doesn't become confused and preoccupied in his secretive little world.

Both love anything new and like to be entertained. They'll have a great time talking about anything and everything, batting words back and forth. Aquarius is more likely than Libra to try to put his ideas into action, but she'll back him all the way with encouragement and practical tips.

Both believe in fairness and equality and Mum is happy to treat Aquarius as the little adult he wants to be. Aquarius is delighted that Mum gives him sensible guidance and leaves him free to choose his path ahead, and Libra is glad to have a clever and friendly child, so like herself.

Aquarius child with a Libra father

Logical Libra loves talking to his sunny little Aquarius. These two are bright and optimistic, friendly and sociable. Libra's a great listener and likes hearing all about Aquarius' latest big ideas. He'll throw in useful suggestions that help to keep the conversation flowing merrily along.

Libra understands his child well and appreciates his liveliness and intelligence. Dad is prepared to offer freedom and independence, still within sensible limits, which delights Aquarius who really hates to be hemmed in.

Here's a father who can open his child's eyes to the world of art, music and literature. Aquarius is very curious and loves to read and discover, and he'll lap up whatever Dad has to teach. These two find they've got a lot in common and Venus-ruled Libra will make a special effort to take an interest in the things that amuse his child. He finds it easy to see the world from his child's point of view.

Both need company. Libra is a lively mixer while Aquarius enjoys being part of a group in which he can express his individuality. Libra loves to find out what makes things tick, while Aquarius is always one step ahead, dreaming up ideas that will be a part of the future.

Dad listens to his child's views and respects them, but he won't be so pleased if quirky Aquarius lets him down in public. Libra needs to keep up appearances and his honest and slightly eccentric little Aquarius may sometimes blurt out the wrong thing. Yet his charm will make everyone laugh and Dad will quickly forget any embarrassment. He can't help but be bowled over by his bright and interesting little Aquarius.

Aquarius child with a Scorpio mother

Energetic Scorpio Mum loves her lively Aquarius child and has big dreams for his future. She encourages him to have lots of interests and is proud that he's so bright, curious and intelligent. However, Mum can make the mistake of wanting Aquarius to do all the things she never got a chance to do.

She must realise that this independent child needs to find his own way in life. Mum shouldn't expect him to succeed at the things she chooses for him. He needs to be closely involved in a subject to do well at it and he'll only do that if he's had some free choice in the matter.

Mum mustn't take over his hobbies, pry into his private life or restrict him too much. Aquarius needs controlling to some extent but he'll only thrive if he has a sense of freedom. The trouble is, Scorpio Mum fears everything will get out of hand if she offers freedom and independence. She should rest assured that this logical child has a sensible head on his shoulders and won't do anything silly.

Aquarius does need to be taught to behave and he can be argumentative and want his own way. But Mum should never be harsh with him. Firm talkings-to are all he needs. Aquarius won't be impressed if Mum tries to manipulate him, either. He's far more straightforward than she is and can't stand underhand dealings.

Neither of these two shows their feelings, for different reasons. Aquarius is the less emotional of the two and dreads being let down if he opens up too much. Scorpio thinks she will lose the upper hand if she reveals her true feelings. She likes to appear controlled, and keeps a tight grip on her strong emotions.

Scorpio must learn to allow Aquarius to be himself. He'll thank her forever if she can only give him the space he needs to grow.

Aquarius child with a Scorpio father

Aquarius admires his Scorpio dad for being effective, magnetic, powerful and clever. But Aquarius is quite prepared to stand his ground when Scorpio issues commands. Dad expects his word to be obeyed and won't stand for any nonsense. Aquarius will argue back and won't be told, even by big, bossy Dad.

Scorpio will have to become more flexible or it will be rows all the way between this pair. Aquarius hates to feel hemmed in and will wonder why Dad seems to think freedom spells trouble. There's a real danger that Aquarius' bright spontaneity and inventiveness will be crushed if Dad is too authoritarian.

This child needs the freedom to dream, to use his imagination and to create. Dad seems to think only of his own needs, plotting and planning to achieve his own ends, while Aquarius brightly schemes for the good of all mankind. Optimistic Aquarius wants to change the world and will feel thwarted if Dad tries to stop him.

Busy Dad can spend quite a lot of time working away from home, leading a complicated life full of dark intrigues that independent Aquarius must learn to steer clear of. But chances are that Scorpio will be a loving father whose only fault is inflexibility and an inability to see why his child might want to live life in a different way from him.

Aquarius is certainly more friendly than Scorpio, who can be open at times, although usually for his own ends. He's suspicious of Aquarius' grown-up ways and will try to keep him a child and under control. Scorpio doesn't like the child's adventurous spirit and the way he takes risks, yet he's proud of his fast mind and ability to adapt, and surprised at how easily his child gets on with people. Scorpio Dad may not fully understand his Aquarius child, but he certainly wants the very best for him.

Aquarius child with a Sagittarius mother

Both bright, lively, kind and friendly, this sunny pair get on very well. Mum understands the way her child thinks and can play with him and teach him in a way that he really enjoys. Aquarius delights in his funny and clever mum.

Both hate boring routine and love change and excitement. Mum is always full of bright ideas for things to do, and this pair enjoy games, travel, jokes, spending money and exploring. Life is certainly never dull for them!

But Mum can be a bit too relaxed when it comes to discipline. She can't be bothered to lay down tedious rules and, if she doesn't watch out, Aquarius can get wildly out of hand. She must make every effort to teach him what is acceptable behaviour and what isn't. Either way, these two will have lots of rows but they'll enjoy every minute of them! Aquarius loves standing up for his rights and Mum sneakily admires him for it.

Sagittarius will encourage her Aquarius child to think for himself, question authority and speak his mind. She believes in self-assertion and spontaneity and Aquarius is glad to have someone who understands and accepts his quirky little ways. Both like taking risks and neither likes to conform too much. Above all these two love to share ideas. They'll talk and dream about endless big schemes, never minding that few of them will ever become reality.

Aquarius is pleased that Mum treats him like a grown-up and he feels happy and encouraged in her lively company. He knows how to drive her mad with logic and her bluntness can annoy him more than he shows. But they both find life an exciting challenge and enjoy sharing it together.

Aquarius child with a Sagittarius father

Boyish Sagittarius Dad enjoys rough-and-tumble games, which aren't always to his Aquarius child's linking. Aquarius prefers to share Dad's intellectual bent, for these two are big thinkers, dreamers and debaters who love gathering and sharing information with anyone who'll listen.

They're sunny, bright, straightforward individuals, full of energy and fun. Dad is a good teacher for curious Aquarius, because he loves to talk about anything that interests him. They can both be a bit stubborn in an argument, but they are equally quick to forgive and forget. Dad will nudge

Aquarius out of any crossness with a beaming smile or a joke.

Dad will take Aquarius with him on his frequent travels, a real treat for this adventurous child. Sagittarius may well be a busy man, careerwise and socially, and will be glad that his little Aquarius is so independent and doesn't seem to mind his absences. But Aquarius will always need more affection and attention than he ever asks for or shows, so give him plenty of reassurance.

Sagittarius usually leaves emotional dealings to his partner and is pleased that this is not a particularly emotional child. He will take the time to explain what's right and wrong, though, and this does appeal to logical Aquarius. And Dad will encourage him to be creative and confident, too.

Sagittarius is less likely than his son to parcel up old clothes to help refugees, but is kind-hearted and admires his child's idealistic motives.

These two can be the best of friends because they see life in much the same inventive and straightforward way.

Aquarius child with a Capricorn mother

Capricorn can seem a little chilly, and working hard to make a good home and future for her child can leave her short of time for frivolous – yet still important – fun.

Aquarius likes to reach out to people and work with a group, while this mother creates her own world, and is the boss of it. Capricorn is naturally a fan of the traditional, while Aquarius looks forward and can seem rather odd to his mother.

This mother is working for herself and her family and pours energy into sorting out the practicalities of life, so she needs to be very careful that she doesn't steamroller Aquarius' natural idealism and imagination.

Because he seems to spend too much time in the mental world, it's tempting to take over control of Aquarius' life. But Capricorn should resist this and give her child freedom to find his own way through life, even though it may seem messy and she'd rather he settled down to something sensible.

But the relationship will thrive if she gives him plenty of praise for being clever and kind and interested in the future. Meanwhile, he will absorb a useful helping of practical common sense from his Capricorn mother.

Aquarius child with a Capricorn father

They admire each other's cool-set emotions and fairness, but Capricorn doesn't share Aquarius' belief that the world can be changed and wrongs righted. And at times his child's imagination can seem too crazy.

Dad is locked into hard, well-organised work and likes all the cash rewards and status he can get, so he may be baffled by his child's infatuation with ideas and failure to be impressed by money and possessions.

Yet, though Aquarius may seem independent, it's good to know Dad is solid and secure. And if Dad adds some patience to the relationship, it will grow closer, especially if they concentrate on what they can agree on, like books.

Disagreements can rock this twosome, though, as the discipline-loving, do-it-my-way dad clashes with the rule-hating Aquarius. Yet even as Aquarius seems to reject Dad's advice, a useful amount of it will sink in.

This is a mix of two very different people. Aquarius is generous – his Dad would say stupid – with money. Capricorn is very organised about money – his child might say mean. Capricorn may see his child as irresponsible, and full of crazy ideas. Yet, when he takes time to really listen, he'll see some of those ideas are world-beaters.

Aquarius child with an Aquarius mother

This pioneering pair think life is a big adventure to be enjoyed and together they'll try to make the most of every moment. But it can get too wild, sometimes, and short on common sense.

Yet they understand each other and can share ideas and dream up campaigning schemes to help others. They are an idealistic, brain-powered duo who love books and talk endlessly to each other about what they've been doing.

Both are rather detached and unemotional, except on subjects they feel passionate about. Then they will argue loudly, enjoying every noisy minute of it. Both believe in fairness and equality, honesty and freedom of thought.

Stubborn young Aquarius can be allowed too much rein by his Aquarius mother. He likes to get his own way, to be free to do what he pleases, and liberal-minded Mum will let him get away with a lot. She thinks it helps him to develop an independent mind, and believes he's simply learning to assert himself when he is argumentative. He needs to be shown that there are limits, otherwise he could become horribly rebellious.

With firm guidance, he'll be good-hearted, idealistic and sensitive to the needs of others. Mum can help him to express his creativity and expand his mind by answering all his questions and teaching him that his good actions can benefit society. Above all, she'll let him be himself, which is all he really wants.

Aquarius child with an Aquarius father

Aquarius Dad loves his rebellious little explorer and thinks he's a real chip off the old block. These two are bursting with ideas but unfortunately share a limited amount of common sense. So, while some of their schemes will prove to be excellent, they may be wise to get a second opinion before chasing off on some of their wilder projects and adventures.

Both love challenges and taking risks. They're full of energy and talk constantly to each other about anything and everything. They admire each other's honesty and integrity and are amused by the fact that they are both oddballs and often act in an unpredictable way.

Aquarius child could do with some outside influence to keep his feet somewhere near the ground. There's a danger that Dad will become too intellectual, caught up in books, social issues and good causes, and the child's emotional needs will be neglected. Aquarius must have someone he knows he can turn to on the rare occasions that he needs help.

Most of the time he's thrilled to be in his Dad's company. This father accepts his child for what he is and allows him to develop freely and naturally, without forcing him to follow any paths he doesn't feel entirely happy about. Dad will explain any rules, which suits his logical child, but he may be too idealistic in thinking that sensible explanations are all that's required to make Aquarius behave. Aquarius benefits from firm handling sometimes.

Dad will always listen to what his child has to say, help him with his homework, spend time talking and sharing thoughts with him. Both dislike routine and enjoy new things and both think ahead, spending their time looking to the future. Aquarius understands his child's unusual choice of friends, and treats him as a grown-up, which delights the child.

Aquarius child with a Pisces mother

Kind-hearted Pisces Mum loves her adventurous Aquarius child and spoils him like mad. This mother just wants to be loved and can't bear to be firm. She lets her little Aquarius get away with a lot, for she dreads the row that will follow if she puts her foot down. She should realise that Aquarius needs some discipline or he'll push Mum to breaking point if she lets him.

Pisces is puzzled that Aquarius seems so detached and unemotional. Mum is very emotional and wants to feel that she shares a strong bond of love with her children. Aquarius is almost remote and in a world of his own sometimes. Mum will just have to accept that that's the way he is. He's intellectual, logical and bookish, while she's sensitive and feels hurts deeply.

One thing Mum does admire in her little Aquarius is his budding sense of social justice. But she's not so keen to join him on banner-waving demonstrations aimed at changing the world. Caring Mum loves to help others, but on a more personal level. She's quick to offer a sympathetic shoulder to cry on, while Aquarius is busy penning letters to his local MP.

Aquarius is friendly, open and honest while Mum can sometimes bend the truth to avoid hurting others. Aquarius would much rather she was straightforward and less unpredictable. She's usually soft and easy-going, but she'll suddenly become angry and snappy if she feels under pressure.

She'll retreat from him, too, when life gets too much for her, so it's a good thing that Aquarius is so independent. At times like that, he'll take himself off to his own world and entertain himself. Aquarius can cope with Mum's lack of organisation and planning to a certain extent, too. He gets on with sorting out his own life, though he does like some sense of structure at home to help him feel more secure.

Pisces will find him an easy and pleasant child except when he's in an argumentative mood. He'll be especially glad of the way Mum encourages his artistic and creative streak. These two have huge imaginations and will spend many happy hours weaving colourful dreams together.

Aquarius child with a Pisces father

Pisces Dad allows Aquarius a fair amount of freedom, which is what this child wants most in the world. Dad thinks children should develop without too much interference, so he won't impose hefty restrictions that would dampen Aquarius' bright spirit.

Yet Pisces must provide some guidelines to stop wayward Aquarius taking advantage. This detached and intellectual child is determined he knows what's best for himself, but there are times when some grown-up wisdom is required to keep him from doing anything too crazy.

A little more routine and control at home wouldn't come amiss, either. Aquarius hates anything that threatens to hem him in, but he'll feel more secure if he knows what's expected of him and what his limits are.

Aquarius is bursting with energy, which Pisces can find hard to keep up with. Both are creative thinkers who conjure futuristic dreams together and have a lot of fun in the process. Aquarius is likely to be a lot more optimistic about what he can achieve than his doubting dad, though.

Aquarius is actually the deeper thinker of the two, delving into subjects, reading and gathering knowledge, while Dad relies more on his feelings when he's asked for an opinion on something.

Both are given to outbursts of temper when they're feeling wound up. Dad wants his child to be no problem at all, so he finds it hard when stubborn Aquarius stands his ground and argues logically – and loudly! Dad will feel like disappearing and leaving Mum to deal with the rumpus.

Artistic Pisces Dad opens up a world of colour and music to his equally creative child. He'll inspire him to use his imagination to widen his horizons and to make the most of life. Together they'll explore the future, and make the present a happy place to be.

PISCES
Stars for Life

STAR BABY

Baby Pisces looks the most angelic creature in the world, with her (or his*) translucent skin and little blinking eyes. She doesn't seem ready to take on the harsh realities of life – and indeed she isn't at first. She'll need calming cuddles and reassuring whispers – a soft and gentle introduction to life on earth.

Shield her from loud noises and make her cot as comfy and pretty as possible. She's sure to want to snuggle into your bed for comfort, though. And other times she'll drift away into a cotton wool land of her own where life is easy. Don't jolt her back to reality too fast.

But you shouldn't keep her molly-coddled forever. Pisces needs taking out into the big wide world in gentle stages if she is to toughen up in time for school. Pisces knows that using her charm will always get people on her side, yet she can become shy and cling to Mum when someone new comes along.

Don't worry or push her to be sociable before she's ready. She may seem reserved, but you'll soon find she has a lot of love and warmth to give. Let her be herself and she'll gradually grow in strength and confidence.

FIRST STEPS FOR PISCES

She's unlikely to be keen to walk early, so be prepared. She'll finally discover the joys of toddling once she's out in the fresh air, feeling the grass under her feet. She loves the

*'She' is used to cover she and he for Pisces child.

sea, so she will adore any trip to the beach. See her dipping her toes in the water and squealing with delight!

Pisces wants to please and will try hard to fit in with the family. But watch that she isn't trying too hard to be good. She needs to learn to express her own needs and feelings and must be reassured that she's loved and accepted just the way she is. Hugs and kisses will let her know she truly belongs.

If there is anything wrong at home, or someone is feeling down, she'll pick it up in a flash and try to do something to make things better. Help her see, though, that she can't put everything right that happens to the people around her. That would be too big a responsibility for one so small and sensitive.

Pisces hates having to live a regular lifestyle. She loves to do things when the mood takes her. And that includes eating. She's rarely hungry at lunchtime, then whines for a sandwich halfway through the afternoon. Toilet training can take time for the same reason.

Gently explain the point of it all, then leave her to go at her own pace. Don't forget to praise her when she does what's required, of course.

Pisces loves to draw, paint, dance to music, or leaf through books with bright pictures, pretending to read in a sing-song voice as she goes. She's got a creative imagination and entertains herself with daydreams, make-believe and fantasy. She rarely misbehaves, preferring to charm you into giving her what she wants.

But when life is boring or problematic, she'll slip off into her dream world. She can need teaching to stand up for herself instead of evading issues by always drifting into a daydream. But it's unlikely she'll ever have her two feet permanently on the ground. She's an ethereal creature who will take a long, long time to grow up – and maybe she never will.

She loves to tell you the weird and wonderful dream she had last night and wants you to interpret it for her. She pretends the fireside rug is a magic carpet and invites you to come fly with her. She takes teddy everywhere with her and the two have long and meaningful conversations. You'll think she's batty – but she's not, she's just got the most vivid imagination in the zodiac.

A Pisces child often finds reality too harsh to handle. Her fragile dreams can disappear when faced with the cold light of day, and she'll shrink tearfully from angry words. In turn, she hates to upset or hurt anyone so she may well tell a few half-truths to avoid a scene. Gently encourage her to tell the truth, no matter how difficult.

And when she shows an interest in art or music, encourage it. It will help her learn to express her true self. And you never know, her superb capacity for creative thinking could one day turn her into an artist, musician or writer. If that's the case, be prepared to accept that she may want to sacrifice security and material gain for art. Boring responsibilities are not her style.

SCHOOL RULES FOR PISCES

Pisces needs lots of encouragement to do her best at school. She has a strong drive to learn and understand, yet she may be reserved in class and will probably feel uncomfortable with the structure of lessons. She'd rather be free to study in a flexible way. Yet that is not always possible – and in truth, she does need discipline to really apply herself.

She finds it hard to make choices, in case she opts for the wrong thing or upsets someone by her decision. This can slow her down a lot. She won't fight back if a classmate says something that upsets her. She'd rather suffer in silence than risk offending her assailant with a sharp response. Pisces needs to know that it's okay to assert herself.

Pisces is a sweet and caring child who will have plenty of friends. But she'll worry a lot that her work isn't up to scratch, that people don't really like her and that something terrible will happen if she doesn't pass her next test. Pisces needs praise for the work that she does do well and realistic assessment of her progress. She's probably doing a lot better than she thinks. If she isn't reassured, though, she could just stop trying – so watch for this.

Bolster her up, help her learn to concentrate and apply herself, teach her how to stand up for herself and how to handle decision-making so that it doesn't overwhelm her. Show her how to plan her work, be thrilled at her successes and especially encourage any artistic talent. You'll have a much happier, more confident and fulfilled child on your hands.

TEENAGE TAKE-OFF FOR PISCES

Teenage Pisces continues to be sensitive to the feelings of others. She is a friendly and loving youngster who is happy to help anyone in need or listen to the woes of her friends. But it's unlikely she'll tell anyone her own troubles. She thinks no-one really wants to listen and can feel rather lonely, despite the fact that she's usually greatly valued by her family and friends.

She still drifts off into her land of dreams, where she seeks solace and rest from the harshness of life. It can help her to have charity or voluntary work into which she can channel her energies positively. She wants to make a contribution in life, but will need guidance to find a direction that really suits her.

Pisces still has a very active imagination and may get confused about what's expected of her in relationships with the opposite sex. She needs tactful advice to help her avoid getting involved too fast. She's emotional and vulnerable and she can be hurt all too easily.

What she's really searching for as she prepares to fly the nest is a soul mate who will cherish her. In return, she'll offer a warm heart, full of gentleness and tolerance, compassion and kindness – the qualities you have enjoyed so much in her since the day she was born.

Pisces child with an Aries mother

Energetic Aries Mum is full of drive and direction, leaping into action and making decisions almost without thinking. Meanwhile, Pisces ambles along waiting for inspiration to hit her. She won't make up her mind about anything till the last minute, and then she'll be worried about offending someone by making the wrong decision.

Mum is very much her own person, while Pisces seems to mould herself to whoever she is with, charming them with her easy-going ways. Aries often offends people with her bluntness and aggression, while Pisces pleases everyone with her sweet gentleness and kindness.

Aries lives life at a gallop, while Pisces prefers to stroll and enjoy the world around her. She's an artistic, creative dreamer, quite different from Mum who is a fierce go-getter, effective at whatever she tries. But Mum can learn a few things about appreciating her surroundings from her delightful Pisces child.

Praise is important to Pisces and Mum must be sure she gets plenty of it to build up her confidence. It's okay for Aries, brimming with self-esteem, but poor Pisces constantly doubts herself and relies on Mum to help her become more assertive and effective.

Mum can help her a lot, but she mustn't try to dominate young Pisces' life. This little fish needs help to find her own way to the sea, not a set of orders from abrasive Mum. Pisces thrives on kindness and praise. As long as Mum remembers that, Pisces will be happy.

Pisces child with an Aries father

Aries Dad must tread gently with his Pisces child, for she'll flood the place with tears if she's treated roughly. Dad's sudden outbursts might mean nothing to him, but Pisces will feel wounded to the heart, her confidence shattered, when he shouts.

Dad should give her lots of hugs and reassurance. Pisces needs to know that she belongs, that she's truly one of the family. Yet she needs kind but firm guidance, too. Dad should just watch that he's not too pushy or bullying.

Aries always looks merrily on the bright side, but Pisces daydreams, worries and broods. Busy Dad is always right on the ball, primed for action. He can't understand Pisces' reliance on feelings and emotions when she makes decisions. It's all far too vague and uncontrolled for him. He's baffled, too, by her little lies, even if she does only tell half-truths to avoid causing an upset. Straight-as-an-arrow Dad thinks everyone else should be completely truthful like him.

These two are very different. Dad has heaps of energy and stays up half the night, while Pisces flags early. She's not sporty like him and would prefer to spend her leisure time painting or learning a musical instrument.

Dad wants her to succeed and looks forward to basking in the reflected glory. But he'll have to accept that she may well have very different goals to his. Dad's ruthless ambition is simply not her style and this imaginative, intuitive child is far more likely to end up a struggling artist than a top executive. But at least she'll be happy, and doing her own thing.

This pair may be very different, but with affection and support Aries can help Pisces to become stronger, more decisive and able to stand up for herself. And Dad can take a lesson in kind-hearted caring from his good-natured Pisces child.

Pisces child with a Taurus mother

Warm-hearted Taurus Mum showers affection on her little Pisces, making this sensitive child feel loved, protected and wanted. Mum can see how much reassurance Pisces needs and knows just how to give it.

Pisces is more imaginative than practical-minded Taurus and needs adventures and outings to stimulate her. There's no point in Mum cooping her up at home. She should be out, exploring the world.

Taurus' calm and ordered ways will allow Pisces to find her feet at her own pace. Mum can help her by showing her how to concentrate, to see things through and make real achievements. Mum teaches her good manners, helping her to get on with others, but she shouldn't expect Pisces to fit into a strict routine or to become tidy all of a sudden.

This pair hate to row, yet both can explode under stress. And there can be upsets when Pisces evades most of Mum's rules. She'll tell fibs to cover her tracks and confuse Mum into believing her. Straightforward Mum will end up insisting Pisces always tells the truth.

Pisces and Taurus both love nature, and they share a hearty appetite, too. Mum must watch that Pisces doesn't grow plump on her home cooking. Both have a jolly sense of humour so there will be lots of laughs, although Mum also understands Pisces' emotional vulnerability and will do her best to soothe away any fears she has.

When it's time to fly the nest, Taurus will be puzzled that Pisces doesn't seem keen on making a home of her own and settling down. Her child is a dreamy wanderer who needs to explore and doesn't commit herself easily.

These two have a strong bond and will continue to enjoy a close relationship long after Pisces has gone her own way in life.

Pisces child with a Taurus father

Full of family loyalty, Taurus Dad offers love and care to his sensitive Pisces child. She feels very secure with him around and, although he can be a bit on the gruff side, she knows he's a big softie who understands her worries and wants her to be happy.

Patient Dad can lose his temper when pushed, though. He must watch his anger doesn't knock his Pisces youngster's confidence, although to his credit, Dad will be quick to reassure and to quell any tears. Pisces, too, is good at comforting him when he's down.

Taurus teaches Pisces to take a more commonsense

approach to life. He wants her to behave conventionally, and she wants to please. But Dad must watch she doesn't act like a good little girl just to make Dad happy, forgetting about her own needs and dreams. Pisces needs help to find her individual way forward. She should never be forced to act in a way that doesn't really suit her.

Pisces is more up to date than her staid dad, who likes what's tried and tested and distrusts anything new or fashionable. In adolescence there can be clashes as Pisces learns to strike out on her own. Taurus can seem like a real stick-in-the-mud to her then.

Dad must give Pisces credit for being more imaginative and intuitive than he is. It's helpful if he encourages her to find expression in art and music, and he shouldn't be shocked if she wants to become an artist, actor or musician. Dad would rather see her in a more secure line of work, but she'll never be that practical. As long as Dad accepts that, they'll get along fine.

Pisces child with a Gemini mother

Busy Gemini Mum is always bursting with ideas for things to do. But her main motive is to keep herself entertained, for she can't bear to be bored. Mum has to be out socialising every day and she'll take little Pisces along whether she wants to go or not. Mum should realise that Pisces is not a great mixer as a child and allow her to take things slowly.

Pisces will enjoy the sense of fun this bright and breezy mum creates. These two are both imaginative and will dream up great games together. They are real charmers, too, and know how to get what they want from other people – Gemini with clever words and Pisces with sweet smiles.

Gemini wants her child to develop quickly and will be frustrated when Pisces takes her time. Mum enjoys teaching her and will boost that lively Pisces imagination, although she certainly won't let her child drift off into daydreams for long.

Mum must watch her critical streak. Pisces takes harsh

words and teasing very badly and her confidence can crumple. Mum should be lavish with her praise and try to overlook any little failures. Pisces only thrives if reassured and encouraged. Mum should also watch that they don't tangle each other in white lies. Both signs are liable to tell fibs, but Mum should try to set Pisces a good example to discourage this tendency.

Gemini must avoid taking over her child's interests too much. Pisces wants to please and will let Mum march all over her rather than argue. In fact, this child has to be taught to make decisions for herself and encouraged to assert her needs more clearly. That way, these two will enjoy a rewarding and close relationship.

Pisces child with a Gemini father

Fast-thinking, fast-talking Gemini Dad travels at the speed of light compared with dreamy Pisces. She likes to live life in the slow lane, relying on her intuition, rather than on quick wit like her worldly dad.

Gemini plays tricks with words and Pisces will get her own back by telling little white lies to deceive him. She doesn't really mean any harm, but truth is very flexible to Pisces who shifts it to suit each new situation and person.

Neither is very straightforward, and neither wants a particularly settled life. Gemini likes moving house a lot, and adaptable Pisces is quite happy to follow. She fits in easily with Dad's plans but he must watch that she has a say in things sometimes. It's easy for Pisces to forget about her own needs and go along with everyone else's. Dad can help her by teaching her to be more assertive.

Dad must avoid teasing Pisces as she'll take it badly, sulking and brooding. And he should avoid insisting that his way is best. Pisces needs encouragement to find her own way of doing things, but she'll go along with Dad because she's afraid of upsetting him. She needs permission to disagree sometimes.

Don't be surprised if Pisces wants to dedicate herself to

art or music. She's not as materialistic as her father and will put enjoyment of her chosen career before financial security. Gemini will think she should do something that makes more money. Perhaps he can help her find sensible ways to increase her earnings.

With Dad's help, Pisces will grow up with a lively imagination. She'll have enjoyed his bouts of fun-filled play, but been hurt by his equally sudden attacks of boredom with her. Dad should be sure to hide his feelings when he gets tired of child's play, and take time out from his busy work and social life to see that Pisces is reassured and encouraged.

Gemini can teach Pisces to speak up for herself, handle tricky situations, concentrate and make decisions. All it takes is time. Gemini will love the gratitude he gets in return from his delightful child. Pisces will grow up less gullible and dreamy, more effective and forthright for having learned from her Gemini dad.

Pisces child with a Cancer mother

Kind Cancer Mum builds a cosy home where Pisces gets all the love and reassurance she so needs. Cancer understands her sensitive Pisces child and won't force her to socialise before she's ready, for she knows that Pisces will start life shy and take time to overcome it.

Mum must beware of a temptation to overprotect Pisces. There will come a time when she'll need to find her feet in company, and playgroups and family parties will give her a happy start.

These two are very close and will enjoy a strong bond. They're water signs, full of feelings, emotions, hurts and worries. Mum can sense when her child is down, and Pisces comforts Mum when life isn't going so well. Mum must avoid wrapping Pisces in cotton wool, though. She'll have to learn to stand up for herself one day.

It's important that Mum has a few interests of her own, otherwise she can end up trying to live through her child, which is no good for either of them. Pisces should have space and encouragement to develop as an individual, with needs of her own and the ability to express them.

Pisces feels happily at home with her Cancer mum. That strong emotional bond will even see them through teenage clash time, as long as Cancer doesn't cling too tight. In her heart Pisces knows she can always rely on her mum, and Cancer will be thankful to have a child who understands her so well.

Pisces child with a Cancer father

Caring Cancer Dad encourages Pisces to make the most of her talents. He'll take her swimming – they both love the water – help her paint and draw, and buy her a musical instrument when she asks for one. Dad will happily take her to all her activities, but he must watch she doesn't take advantage of his kind nature. Pisces likes being waited on, and she needs to learn some self-reliance.

This emotional water pair will clash at times. Both snap under pressure and Dad can suddenly become commanding and bossy in an attempt to assert his authority. Pisces will hate it when he shouts. Dad must remember to reassure her, otherwise she'll be upset and lose confidence.

Pisces needs lots of praise and encouragement to keep her self-esteem afloat. Dad must help her to make decisions and to ask for what she wants. It's a hard task for shy Cancer but he must do his best to teach Pisces to stand up for herself.

He should try to avoid endless rows over whether Pisces has tidied her room or not. She probably hasn't, but it's best to reason with her without raising voices.

Dad will be delighted to see what a caring charmer Pisces grows up to become, full of generosity and gentleness. He'll enjoy her company and stimulate that remarkable imagination of hers. Pisces will relish the security, direction and warmth that her Cancer dad offers her.

Pisces child with a Leo mother

Warm Leo Mum brightens Pisces' life with encouragement,

praise, love and affection. But power-house Mum must watch that she doesn't push Pisces too hard to achieve, for Pisces hasn't got Leo's energy and drive. She's a gentler soul, with artistic talents and a wonderful imagination.

Mum wants her child to do everything she never managed to. Pisces likes to have lots of interests but not to be overwhelmed. She needs help to find her own likes and dislikes, instead of being forced to do what Mum thinks will be good for her. Leo can easily dominate Pisces but must avoid the temptation because Pisces will simply give up if Mum takes over her life.

Pisces evades difficulties and hates tackling anything head on. She's soft-natured, generous and sweet and lacks Mum's decisive assertiveness, although she'll become more outgoing and friendly as she grows.

Vibrant Mum loves to meet people and be the centre of attention. She's bold and dramatic, while Pisces is quietly charming. Leo should introduce her gradually to her social whirl and remember not to hog all the limelight. Give Pisces her turn to shine too. Mum must also watch that fiery temper, for it can unsettle Pisces. But any angry words will be forgiven and forgotten in the warmth and love Leo gives her child. Pisces truly adores her charismatic mum.

Pisces child with a Leo father

Powerful Leo Dad has a warm heart but he does like to act tough. He can be imperious and commanding when little Pisces doesn't toe the line, thinking firm discipline is in her best interests. She will be unnerved by his behaviour and simply retreat into herself, upset and unhappy.

Leo wants his children to be perfect and thinks he can knock them into shape. But Pisces may not be destined to turn out the way he'd like. She has different goals from his and is gentle, dreamy and artistic where he's a fierce go-getter.

Pisces is indecisive while Dad makes up his mind in a flash. She doesn't value material security the way he does and may well end up as a penniless but very happy artist, while Dad would rather see her sensibly settled with a job in a bank.

Pisces can do very well in conventional terms if given more encouragement and praise and fewer harsh words. She needs appreciation, too, for being imaginative, creative, caring and idealistic, and less criticism for lacking push and direction. Pisces isn't keen on structuring her life, preferring to go where fate takes her.

If she does fail sometimes, shouting won't make her do any better. She usually wants to please, so there must be a genuine reason for things going wrong. Perhaps Pisces simply gave up trying because she felt there was too much pressure on her.

She hates upsetting Dad and will sometimes tell only half the truth to avoid a row. When Dad finds out, he'll be angry, but he should take into account that there's rarely any harm meant in her fibs. She just hates to say anything she thinks might anger people. Give her firm guidance by all means, though, for she needs to know what's right and what isn't.

Pisces can benefit greatly from Dad's influence if he teaches her to believe in herself as much as he believes in himself. She'll love his generosity and the soft heart she knows is hidden under that gruff exterior. Dad will love her for her adoring and sweet nature.

Pisces child with a Virgo mother

Virgo Mum enjoys being of service to others and Pisces has a kind and cheerful smile for anyone who's down, so these two have compatible natures. But Pisces lives in a dream world compared with practical Mum. She likes to drift off, imagine and create, while Virgo gets on with the basics of life, cleaning and sorting things out.

Mum is unlikely to get much help from Pisces when it comes to chores, for Pisces hates tidying up and is quite happy to live in a mess. Mum will heave a sigh, too, when it comes to Pisces' lack of money sense. This child is far too generous for thrifty Virgo, who would prefer her to save. Pisces may well want a pet, but she'll probably have to settle for a goldfish as Mum hates a mess.

Mum favours a traditional style of education and must try to ensure that it includes scope for Pisces' creative skills. She'll feel stifled by boring teaching methods. But Mum can teach her a useful lesson in how to be more effective in the real world, a doer instead of a dreamer.

Mum must take time from all her hard work to spare some affection for Pisces. This child needs reassurance that she's wanted. Shouting and reprimands can hurt her deeply and knock her confidence, as can Virgo's biting criticism. Mum must watch her sharp tongue with this child around.

Mum must be careful not to set unreachable standards for Pisces. This child sets high standards for herself anyway and can simply give up if she feels she's not up to scratch. Praise is what she needs.

Pisces will learn good manners from Mum and will value the secure home she creates. Mum will be amused and entranced by her imaginative little Pisces dreamer. She can't help but be charmed by her.

Pisces child with a Virgo father

Dad's aim is to keep his Pisces child in order, so he tells her exactly what's expected of her. He helps her develop interests, encourages and teaches her, and sees that she's heading in a positive direction. But he must watch that he doesn't insist she does everything his way. Pisces needs to gradually find her own feet in the world, and she won't if Dad runs her life for her.

And as for discipline, Dad can be quite strict in his bid to teach her manners, morals and good sense. He must watch that there aren't too many tellings-off, as Pisces takes them to heart so. She's a sensitive child who thrives on praise and hates criticism.

Dad does everything he can to see that Pisces has a secure future ahead of her. He'll be furious if she decides to live an unstructured life as a musician or painter. Dad is very practical and will want to know where the money is going to come from. He'd prefer to see her settled in a secure profession, but that wouldn't do for Pisces. She needs to be free and to see something of life. Her horizons are a lot broader than Dad's.

Yet Dad's down-to-earth approach will be of benefit to Pisces and she probably will act more sensibly in the end because of Virgo's good advice. There will be inevitable clashes in the teenage years between this emotional water child and her logical father, especially over the Pisces' habit of telling little white lies.

Pisces will one day thank her Virgo father for his sense, his reliability and support. He may not have Pisces' imagination, but his heart is in the right place and he's always there when Pisces needs him.

Pisces child with a Libra mother

Loving Libra Mum runs the risk of spoiling her Pisces child. She buys her plenty of presents and clothes, but can forget to be as generous with her encouragement and reassurance that Pisces is loved and very dear to the family. This will stand her in better stead than anything money can buy.

It's no good giving Pisces the impression that there's always going to be someone there to run around after her and do her bidding. It could make her grow up to be very demanding. It's better if Libra can slowly encourage her to be more independent. Pisces has to learn to stand on her own feet and do some things for herself.

Pisces needs help to make decisions, which can be a tricky area for indecisive Libra. She also needs help to find out what her real needs and wishes are. This pair both try to do what they think will please others. They want to be liked and, though they can rely on charm to get by in life, it's far better if Mum can teach Pisces to be firmer and to state clearly what she wants. She'll never become strong until she learns to speak up.

Libra loves to talk and play around with ideas and words, but Pisces prefers to daydream about how she can help the world. Mum is not nearly so idealistic. Like Mum, Pisces loves anything of beauty, but whereas Pisces is the creative one, working with art and music to make beautiful things, Mum is the perfect person to invite to admire them.

Mum loves to organise outings that stimulate Pisces' busy imagination and give her plenty to think about. Mum is more sociable than young Pisces, but this child will gradually learn to hold her own in a group, thanks to Mum's guidance as she learns to mix. Both charm everyone they meet, and they'll charm each other, too!

Pisces child with a Libra father

Optimistic Libra loves his Pisces child but wishes she wouldn't worry so much about whether she is as good as everyone else. Dad fits in with everyone he meets and gets by on friendly affability. Young Pisces will gradually learn the art from him but she starts life shy and in need of lots of reassurance.

Dad loves to see Pisces' vivid imagination at work, but he thinks in a cooler, more logical way than his emotional child. Sometimes he can be dominating and tough on her, which she won't like one little bit. Pisces prefers Dad to be warm and affectionate. Any harsh words will upset her and can badly shake her confidence. She needs rules and decisions to be gently explained to her.

Libra likes to treat his Pisces child as a miniature adult. He's not one to talk down to her, but he must watch he doesn't expect her to grow up too fast. Pisces appreciates being treated as a grown-up but she'll want to take her time over her development. In fact, many Pisces are still growing up late into middle age!

This father tends to hide any problems as he's very concerned with keeping up appearances. He may well bottle things up until they become too much and he finally explodes. Pisces intuitively picks up when something is wrong and may worry that it's her fault, if nothing is said. She'll need reassurance to keep her happy.

Pisces will thrive with Libra Dad because he lets her develop naturally and won't force her in any direction that doesn't suit her. And he helps her keep her feet on the ground too, instead of becoming too lost in dreams. He loves her caring and generous nature and is charmed by her sweetness. Libra wants the very best for his Pisces child, and she will enjoy a happy, caring childhood.

Pisces child with a Scorpio mother

Energetic Scorpio Mum will encourage Pisces to have all sorts of interests, which won't leave much time for daydreaming. Scorpio must watch that she doesn't push Pisces too hard in the wrong direction. Pisces will probably want to follow a creative, haphazard path through life, certainly not the go-getter's route to the top that Mum has mapped out.

Although this pair are both intuitive and emotional, Mum surrounds herself with a hard, protective shell and will be surprised at how unguarded her child is. Pisces is far more vulnerable and can't hide or control her feelings the way Scorpio can. Mum will want her Pisces child to toughen up.

Scorpio must realise that it's she who must protect Pisces while she's young, gradually teaching her to stand up for herself. Pisces is so sensitive and easily hurt by life, she needs Mum to gently teach her to be tougher.

Mum is a great one for extracting secrets from people, and Pisces is no exception. However, this private child needs space and time to herself and will even bend the truth to stop Mum finding out something that may upset her. Of course, Mum will be doubly cross when she finds out Pisces has lied to her, but she should avoid a big scene. Pisces takes outbursts very seriously and her confidence can easily dent.

Pisces tries to get her way with charm, while Mum is a master of manipulation. She'll think Pisces is useless with money, giving far too much away, and tell her that she should look after her own interests more. Yet her heart will soften at Pisces' sweet nature and Mum will learn a lesson in caring from her gentle water child.

Pisces child with a Scorpio father

Scorpio Dad enjoys frightening Pisces with scary stories, and must watch that he doesn't scare her in real life by being too bossy and commanding. Pisces needs love and encouragement to teach her to value her many good points. Bullying will knock her confidence for six.

Dad lives a complicated life that is way beyond the understanding of gentle Pisces. He gets involved in intrigues, revenges and plots, and makes enemies easily with his manipulative character. Pisces needs help to become independent enough to stay out of that side of his life or she could get hurt. She's simpler, more open and well intentioned. Dad can seem friendly and open, too, but there's always the risk he's just pretending. He's an expert at covering up his true feelings.

Pisces will find it hard to stand up to Scorpio Dad, who will always try to force his own point of view on her. He thinks his way of doing things is the only right way, yet it's probably far too narrow for Pisces, who is bound to have different goals. Pisces may forget her own needs in a bid to please Dad, which won't do her any good. Dad must make a big effort to help her find her true path in life. Imposing forceful views on her will only confuse her and stop her finding her way forward.

Dad is glad that Pisces is not a big risk-taker as it makes her easier to control. He must watch that he doesn't react too harshly if Pisces' exam results don't always come up to his high expectations. Tough criticism will only make her do worse. What she needs is love and affection, helpful teaching to be more assertive, praise and encouragement. As long as Scorpio gives her plenty of this, and rations the harder side of his character, he'll gain a lot of happiness from his relationship with Pisces.

Pisces child with a Sagittarius mother

Lively Sagittarius Mum helps Pisces feel sunnier about life with her optimistic outlook. She'll get her talking early, and encourage her to draw and make music. She'll also give her lots of encouragement and praise, which stops Pisces doubting herself.

Mum's free-and-easy ways mean that Pisces won't have to face harsh discipline, although Sagittarius must make sure the child is taught right from wrong. Somehow, though, she'll manage to pass on a wise attitude to life which will keep Pisces out of trouble.

Mum can be moody when she feels life is falling short of her idealistic expectations. At times like this, Pisces must be reassured that it's not her fault that Mum is down. Sagittarius must take time to help Pisces concentrate on her homework and finish things, as well as teach the child to stand up for herself and gradually develop a stronger sense of independence.

Sagittarius is very honest and simply can't hold things back, so it's hard for her to lie. Pisces will tell white lies to avoid an upset, which will annoy Mum. She will insist on the truth, and can't understand the reasons why people – and her child especially – need to be dishonest.

These two are both intuitive but Mum can sometimes lack sensitivity towards Pisces' emotional fragility. She can be too direct and Pisces takes any critical comments deeply to heart. Mum must learn to keep some of the more hurtful comments to herself, no matter how truthful they may be.

Mum should concentrate more on the sense of fun that she's so good at creating. That way, she'll enjoy a happy time with her Pisces child.

Pisces child with a Sagittarius father

Friendly Sagittarius Dad enjoys life with his Pisces child. Pisces may not be as sporty as Dad, but she'll benefit from his energetic ways. Dad also brings her down to earth and stops her daydreaming too much. He teaches her just how much fun there is to be had out of real life and real people.

Sagittarius encourages his child to sing, dance, draw and make music. He takes Pisces on the kind of holidays that stretch her imagination and teach her to be more daring. And if she ever looks down or worried, he'll shake her out of it by making her laugh.

Dad explains any do's and don'ts in a way that makes Pisces happily accept them. He encourages her to think for herself, stand up for herself, speak out and ask for what she wants.

He'll have to accept, though, that Pisces may be less competitive than he is, and that she won't always take up the opportunities he offers. She'll have different aims from him and may want to be a painter or a composer while he'd prefer that she did something more practical. There's no point in standing in her way, and anyway, in his heart of hearts, Dad's a dreamer too and will secretly admire her choice.

Some Sagittarius fathers find it hard to accept that their children develop into individuals. Yet it's so important that Pisces feels accepted, wanted and loved for the person she is. As long as Dad makes the effort to do that, he and Pisces will get along famously.

Pisces child with a Capricorn mother

Capricorn Mum may seem quiet but she knows what she wants. She's much more decisive, driven and definite than dreaming Pisces, who would love to float through life and has no fierce ambitions and expectations of wealth.

Mum is into status symbols, while Pisces is almost totally unmaterialistic. Mum likes to structure her life carefully, with everything in its place and under control, but Pisces likes a free-and-easy lifestyle that leaves her able to take up options as they come along. She hates to be tied down and Capricorn shouldn't expect Pisces to fit into a strict routine.

Mum will find Pisces totally unpractical, but there is a part of her that understands her child's dreamy creativeness.

Mum secretly loves music and art, too, and she'll encourage Pisces' interests in these fields. Of course, she'll give her plenty of warnings about the difficulties of making them a career, but she won't hold her back.

Once Pisces has chosen her path, there'll be strong pressure from Mum for her to succeed and be best. Mum can push too hard and there's a danger Pisces will simply give up and drift in response. Pisces is scared of failing and hates the thought of upsetting Mum. She dreads a scene and will dodge confrontations. Capricorn is not the warmest of signs, ruled by cool Saturn, so Mum may find it hard to show the affection that sensitive Pisces needs to reassure her and make her feel secure. Mum must show her love as best she can.

Her influence will help Pisces to find direction and to see sense. She'll teach her child to be tougher, too, so that life becomes less hard for her to cope with. Above all, Mum will organise Pisces, which is a big achievement in itself.

Pisces child with a Capricorn father

Capricorn Dad is the original upstanding citizen, respected by everyone. His only headache is that Pisces seems such an oddity. She hasn't got his logic and she's such a dreamer, following her feelings and demonstrating a vivid imagination.

She doesn't seem to value what he holds dear – a comfortable home, marriage, children, settling down in a stable lifestyle. Instead she grows up with plans to wander the world, living from day to day, searching for adventure, avoiding ties. Dad would prefer to see her surrounded by all the good things in life and admired for her status the way he is. He can't understand what she sees so wrong in that.

During the teenage years there are likely to be showdowns as stubborn and rigid Dad clashes head-on with emotional, wayward Pisces. He'll be surprised at her strong reactions and will remember fondly her infant days, when all she wanted was to please and fit in with his ordered lifestyle.

It could well be that Pisces was repressing her own needs at that time, to please him. Dad can reassure himself that his common-sense attitude will temper Pisces' free spirit and teach her to stay out of too much trouble.

Pisces may be less of a conformist than Dad, but he should understand that she also lacks his confidence. Capricorn can help her by offering encouragement, praise and approval. That's one way to keep her on the right track. Dad shouldn't put her down for being so free with money, either. She's just plain generous! She'll never see life in black and white the way Capricorn does. To her, it's in intuitive shades of the rainbow. Once Dad understands this, these two will have much to offer each other.

Pisces child with an Aquarius mother

Aquarius is delighted that her sensitive Pisces child shows signs of wanting to change the world and thinks everyone should be equal. She's a child after Mum's heart, for Aquarius always hoped for an offspring with a caring social conscience.

However, Pisces is not as fast as Mum to join the bandwagon and campaign for a shift in society. Pisces would prefer to change her own world first by being kind and caring to those around her.

Pisces understands why Mum thinks the way she does, and this helps them to get along well. Another thing they have in common is a rather detached and absent-minded dreamy aura. Mum is forever changing her mind, while Pisces spends all day making hers up as she's so afraid of upsetting someone by making the wrong decision.

Aquarius is an explorer, interested in new ideas and prepared to take risks. Pisces is more cautious when young, but her imagination will be boosted by Mum and her wide range of interests. Mum introduces her to books, politics and social issues, and teaches her to speak up and state her views.

Aquarius gives Pisces plenty of freedom, and enough advice

to see she doesn't get into trouble. She encourages Pisces to be an individual and not to simply try to please others. She enjoys watching her Pisces child's artistic and musical skills blossom. Mum will always encourage but won't ever push Pisces in a direction that's not right for her.

Intellectual Aquarius can seem too cool to emotional Pisces at times. Mum must remember that her child needs lots of affection. If she can learn to comfort Pisces when she's feeling at odds with the world, hug her and reassure her that she's loved, then these two will have a wonderful relationship.

Pisces child with an Aquarius father

Unpredictable Aquarius Dad is full of ideas. Pisces child thinks he's tremendous fun but gets a little confused sometimes at his hectic lifestyle. He's always in a rush!

Dad's great when it comes to helping Pisces with her homework, but he isn't so good at dealing with her emotional ups and downs. Pisces is sensitive and easily hurt by the world, while Aquarius brushes hurts off. He's more detached and feels embarrassed by other people's strong feelings.

Aquarius is likely to be caught up in politics and social issues, business or science. He sees life from an intellectual point of view, while Pisces is more interested in the intuitive and creative worlds of art and music. How she feels about something matters a lot more to her than what anyone else thinks about it. Dad must remember this when he's trying to raise her interest in a subject. If she really feels involved, she'll study harder.

Dad will encourage Pisces to be herself, although he must remember that she needs plenty of love and affection, along with reassurance to boost her confidence. He must find time in his busy schedule to spend with Pisces. She'll feel shut out if he is too tied up in his own world.

Pisces is thrilled to have a dad who is so fair, rarely raises his voice and carefully explains any rules. Pisces shrinks from commands, but because she wants to please, she'll go along with sensible discipline. She'll be glad that Dad is so understanding and obviously wants the best for her.

Pisces child with a Pisces mother

These two understand each other well. Usually Pisces feels she has to say what others want to hear, but with this caring mum, she'll reveal what she really thinks and feels. Mum is so openly kind and affectionate, Pisces will feel very reassured by her.

Pisces Mum listens to her child and picks up any fears and worries with her almost psychic intuition. Mum has a great empathy with Pisces and will feel every upset that her child feels.

Mum is imaginative and inspiring, always ready to join in games. Young Pisces will treasure her fun-filled upbringing. But there are a few pitfalls. This pair both tend to doubt their own abilities and Mum may find it hard to bolster her child's confidence. Pisces Mum must heap praise and encouragement on her child to help her believe in her many talents.

Pisces is not strong on discipline, either, and should watch that she doesn't become too indulgent. It could make young Pisces end up very demanding. Yet Pisces child is glad Mum isn't the bossy type, for this child hates being shouted at.

Mum encourages Pisces to be herself and there won't be any strict routines imposed on her. Young Pisces may miss out on practical matters and advice about life, but there will be lots of love and fun, which is what Pisces needs most.

Pisces child with a Pisces father

Young Pisces is delighted that Dad accepts her for the kind, caring, creative and gentle person she is. He doesn't push her too hard to achieve, and he'll be able to teach her how to get on with others. He insists on good manners and reasonable standards of behaviour, so that Pisces will fit in with society. He would hate his child to end up an oddball.

She can get confused at the way Dad wavers his way through life, though, often changing his mind and never making definite plans. Young Pisces may well turn out the same, but as a child she values some sense of stability and security. Dad has to admit he lives an unstructured life, and it would be good if he could settle down more for the sake of his child.

Dad has outbursts of temper from time to time. He tries to control the swirling emotions within himself, but when he's under stress he can explode. It's important that he reassures his child that it's not her fault when he loses his temper. She takes these things so seriously, blaming herself and brooding.

This pair are both guilty of embroidering the truth sometimes and must watch that they don't confuse each other. Both seem to change their behaviour according to the person they are with and it can be hard to pin either of them down.

Both are unmaterialistic, kind and creative. Dad will stretch his child's imagination, encourage her to follow her star, and listen when she's feeling at odds with the world. He's pleased to have a child so much on his own wavelength, and she'll be delighted to be so loved and so accepted.

PART FOUR

Venus: the key to your emotions

Look up your date of birth in the Venus tables to find the zodiac sign that helps you understand your own emotions in love and life

Where was planet Venus the day you were born?

You know your sun sign from the sign of the zodiac the sun was in on the day you were born. For example, if you were born on 27 May, you know you are a Gemini. But the planet Venus was also moving through the zodiac signs, too, and at its own speed. So, depending on the year you were born, that birthdate of 27 May can give you a Venus sign of Aries, Taurus, Gemini, Cancer or Leo. And whatever your sun sign, you could be one of five zodiac Venus signs (this can be the same as your sun sign, the two before, or the two after, as the sun and Venus are never very far apart).

It is important that you know which of your five choices it is, so please look up your year and day of birth in the Venus tables on the following pages.

Knowing your Venus sign helps you complete the star code to understanding your emotions, and how they affect the way you let love into your life and develop relationships. You'll know how to keep a better balance between good, caring relationships and being too dependent on other people. And between having the right amount of independence and keeping your own emotions locked away.

Although your sun sign is the senior partner in your personality, your Venus sign helps you understand the contradictions and changes that make you interesting to know, and sometimes difficult to understand. For example, if your sun sign is Aries, and yet you don't always have a full measure of love daring, then your Venus sign could be in the deeper, sympathetic, reassurance-needing Pisces.

But if your sun sign is Pisces, yet you sometimes shock even yourself with a bout of love daring, then a Venus sign in Aries will explain it.

Once you know both your sun sign and your Venus sign, you can draw on the strengths of both to get and give the best in your life and relationships.

Don't be disappointed if you are one of those people whose Venus and sun signs are the same, because this makes you a doubly interesting version of both. Though it can also make you love dynamite . . .

VENUS

The times and dates below indicate the point at which Venus entered each zodiac sign, for example, Venus entered Pisces on 20 January 1900 at 01:37, and stayed there till it entered Aries on 13 February 1900 at 14:08, so someone born at 02:00 on 20 January 1900 would have a Venus sign of Pisces.

All times are GMT and based on the 24-hour clock – don't forget to check the British Summer Time and World Time Zone tables for those not born in Britain if they apply to your time of birth (page 846–50).

VENUS

20 Jan 1900	01:37	Pisces
13 Feb 1900	14:08	Aries
10 Mar 1900	18:09	Taurus
6 Apr 1900	04:16	Gemini
5 May 1900	15:47	Cancer
8 Sep 1900	20:52	Leo
8 Oct 1900	13:31	Virgo
3 Nov 1900	21:28	Libra
28 Nov 1900	21:52	Scorpio
23 Dec 1900	07:47	Sagittarius
16 Jan 1901	11:28	Capricorn
9 Feb 1901	13:06	Aquarius
5 Mar 1901	14:51	Pisces
29 Mar 1901	18:02	Aries
22 Apr 1901	23:32	Taurus
17 May 1901	07:31	Gemini
10 Jun 1901	17:34	Cancer
5 Jul 1901	05:19	Leo
29 Jul 1901	19:11	Virgo
23 Aug 1901	12:31	Libra
17 Sep 1901	11:27	Scorpio
12 Oct 1901	19:13	Sagittarius
7 Nov 1901	19:25	Capricorn
5 Dec 1901	13:34	Aquarius
11 Jan 1902	17:47	Pisces
6 Feb 1902	23:00	Aquarius
4 Apr 1902	19:32	Pisces
7 May 1902	07:04	Aries
3 Jun 1902	23:57	Taurus
30 Jun 1902	06:25	Gemini
25 Jul 1902	18:56	Cancer
19 Aug 1902	18:26	Leo
13 Sep 1902	07:17	Virgo
7 Oct 1902	12:06	Libra
31 Oct 1902	11:50	Scorpio
24 Nov 1902	09:03	Sagittarius
18 Dec 1902	05:28	Capricorn
11 Jan 1903	02:13	Aquarius
4 Feb 1903	00:41	Pisces
28 Feb 1903	02:57	Aries
24 Mar 1903	11:49	Taurus
18 Apr 1903	06:39	Gemini
13 May 1903	16:23	Cancer
9 Jun 1903	03:09	Leo
7 Jul 1903	20:40	Virgo
17 Aug 1903	22:14	Libra
6 Sep 1903	01:32	Virgo
8 Nov 1903	14:44	Libra
9 Dec 1903	14:39	Scorpio

Date	Time	Sign
5 Jan 1904	03:38	Sagittarius
30 Jan 1904	09:23	Capricorn
24 Feb 1904	03:04	Aquarius
19 Mar 1904	15:58	Pisces
13 Apr 1904	03:24	Aries
7 May 1904	14:49	Taurus
1 Jun 1904	02:24	Gemini
25 Jun 1904	13:24	Cancer
19 Jul 1904	22:55	Leo
13 Aug 1904	06:46	Virgo
6 Sep 1904	13:43	Libra
30 Sep 1904	20:58	Scorpio
25 Oct 1904	05:33	Sagittarius
18 Nov 1904	16:37	Capricorn
13 Dec 1904	09:05	Aquarius
7 Jan 1905	14:36	Pisces
3 Feb 1905	04:47	Aries
6 Mar 1905	05:26	Taurus
9 May 1905	09:39	Aries
28 May 1905	11:44	Taurus
8 Jul 1905	11:57	Gemini
6 Aug 1905	08:13	Cancer
1 Sep 1905	20:11	Leo
27 Sep 1905	03:58	Virgo
21 Oct 1905	18:27	Libra
14 Nov 1905	22:35	Scorpio
8 Dec 1905	21:27	Sagittarius
1 Jan 1906	18:19	Capricorn
25 Jan 1906	15:08	Aquarius
18 Feb 1906	13:07	Pisces
14 Mar 1906	13:35	Aries
7 Apr 1906	17:52	Taurus
2 May 1906	03:06	Gemini
26 May 1906	18:10	Cancer
20 Jun 1906	16:30	Leo
16 Jul 1906	01:15	Virgo
11 Aug 1906	03:20	Libra
7 Sep 1906	15:34	Scorpio
9 Oct 1906	10:40	Sagittarius
15 Dec 1906	09:12	Scorpio
26 Dec 1906	01:04	Sagittarius
6 Feb 1907	16:26	Capricorn
6 Mar 1907	20:39	Aquarius
2 Apr 1907	01:21	Pisces
27 Apr 1907	12:22	Aries
22 May 1907	15:13	Taurus
16 Jun 1907	13:10	Gemini
11 Jul 1907	06:38	Cancer
4 Aug 1907	19:03	Leo
29 Aug 1907	02:24	Virgo
22 Sep 1907	05:44	Libra
16 Oct 1907	06:46	Scorpio
9 Nov 1907	06:58	Sagittarius
3 Dec 1907	07:16	Capricorn
27 Dec 1907	08:45	Aquarius
20 Jan 1908	13:45	Pisces
14 Feb 1908	02:52	Aries
10 Mar 1908	08:04	Taurus
5 Apr 1908	20:55	Gemini
5 May 1908	17:46	Cancer
8 Sep 1908	22:28	Leo
8 Oct 1908	06:06	Virgo
3 Nov 1908	11:22	Libra
28 Nov 1908	10:37	Scorpio
22 Dec 1908	19:56	Sagittarius
15 Jan 1909	23:15	Capricorn
9 Feb 1909	00:36	Aquarius
5 Mar 1909	02:07	Pisces
29 Mar 1909	05:08	Aries
22 Apr 1909	10:30	Taurus
16 May 1909	18:25	Gemini
10 Jun 1909	04:30	Cancer
4 Jul 1909	16:25	Leo
29 Jul 1909	06:36	Virgo
23 Aug 1909	00:29	Libra
17 Sep 1909	00:16	Scorpio
12 Oct 1909	09:24	Sagittarius
7 Nov 1909	12:10	Capricorn
5 Dec 1909	13:02	Aquarius

15 Jan 1910	21:29	Pisces	7 Jan 1913	05:26	Pisces
29 Jan 1910	07:55	Aquarius	2 Feb 1913	23:21	Aries
5 Apr 1910	09:56	Pisces	6 Mar 1913	17:06	Taurus
7 May 1910	02:24	Aries	2 May 1913	04:45	Aries
3 Jun 1910	14:53	Taurus	31 May 1913	09:59	Taurus
29 Jun 1910	19:27	Gemini	8 Jul 1913	09:15	Gemini
25 Jul 1910	06:57	Cancer	5 Aug 1913	23:30	Cancer
19 Aug 1910	05:52	Leo	1 Sep 1913	09:17	Leo
12 Sep 1910	18:26	Virgo	26 Sep 1913	16:02	Virgo
6 Oct 1910	23:07	Libra	21 Oct 1913	06:00	Libra
30 Oct 1910	22:49	Scorpio	14 Nov 1913	09:53	Scorpio
23 Nov 1910	20:03	Sagittarius	8 Dec 1913	08:36	Sagittarius
17 Dec 1910	16:31	Capricorn			
			1 Jan 1914	05:24	Capricorn
			25 Jan 1914	02:08	Aquarius
10 Jan 1911	13:20	Aquarius	18 Feb 1914	00:01	Pisces
3 Feb 1911	11:55	Pisces	14 Mar 1914	00:25	Aries
27 Feb 1911	14:21	Aries	7 Apr 1914	04:43	Taurus
23 Mar 1911	23:30	Taurus	1 May 1914	14:05	Gemini
17 Apr 1911	18:53	Gemini	26 May 1914	05:29	Cancer
13 May 1911	05:42	Cancer	20 Jun 1914	04:23	Leo
8 Jun 1911	18:50	Leo	15 Jul 1914	14:10	Virgo
7 Jul 1911	19:09	Virgo	10 Aug 1914	18:14	Libra
9 Nov 1911	00:53	Libra	7 Sep 1914	11:02	Scorpio
9 Dec 1911	09:17	Scorpio	10 Oct 1914	01:55	Sagittarius
			5 Dec 1914	22:50	Scorpio
			30 Dec 1914	23:17	Sagittarius
4 Jan 1912	18:32	Sagittarius			
29 Jan 1912	22:39	Capricorn	6 Feb 1915	15:53	Capricorn
23 Feb 1912	15:26	Aquarius	6 Mar 1915	13:09	Aquarius
19 Mar 1912	03:46	Pisces	1 Apr 1915	15:13	Pisces
12 Apr 1912	14:46	Aries	27 Apr 1915	00:52	Aries
7 May 1912	01:53	Taurus	22 May 1915	02:54	Taurus
31 May 1912	13:15	Gemini	16 Jun 1915	00:21	Gemini
25 Jun 1912	00:07	Cancer	10 Jul 1915	17:30	Cancer
19 Jul 1912	09:39	Leo	4 Aug 1915	05:46	Leo
12 Aug 1912	17:37	Virgo	28 Aug 1915	13:04	Virgo
6 Sep 1912	00:47	Libra	21 Sep 1915	16:28	Libra
30 Sep 1912	08:21	Scorpio	15 Oct 1915	17:38	Scorpio
24 Oct 1912	17:21	Sagittarius	8 Nov 1915	18:01	Sagittarius
18 Nov 1912	05:01	Capricorn	2 Dec 1915	18:34	Capricorn
12 Dec 1912	22:22	Aquarius	26 Dec 1915	20:18	Aquarius

20 Jan 1916	01:40	Pisces
13 Feb 1916	15:25	Aries
9 Mar 1916	21:51	Taurus
5 Apr 1916	13:32	Gemini
5 May 1916	20:38	Cancer
8 Sep 1916	22:22	Leo
7 Oct 1916	22:07	Virgo
3 Nov 1916	00:56	Libra
27 Nov 1916	23:05	Scorpio
22 Dec 1916	07:49	Sagittarius
15 Jan 1917	10:46	Capricorn
8 Feb 1917	11:52	Aquarius
4 Mar 1917	13:10	Pisces
28 Mar 1917	16:01	Aries
21 Apr 1917	21:16	Taurus
16 May 1917	05:06	Gemini
9 Jun 1917	15:13	Cancer
4 Jul 1917	03:17	Leo
28 Jul 1917	17:49	Virgo
22 Aug 1917	12:17	Libra
16 Sep 1917	12:58	Scorpio
11 Oct 1917	23:33	Sagittarius
7 Nov 1917	05:02	Capricorn
5 Dec 1917	13:17	Aquarius
5 Apr 1918	20:11	Pisces
6 May 1918	20:56	Aries
3 Jun 1918	05:24	Taurus
29 Jun 1918	08:09	Gemini
24 Jul 1918	18:41	Cancer
18 Aug 1918	17:05	Leo
12 Sep 1918	05:24	Virgo
6 Oct 1918	09:59	Libra
30 Oct 1918	09:42	Scorpio
23 Nov 1918	06:59	Sagittarius
17 Dec 1918	03:31	Capricorn
10 Jan 1919	00:24	Aquarius
2 Feb 1919	23:04	Pisces
27 Feb 1919	01:40	Aries
23 Mar 1919	11:06	Taurus
17 Apr 1919	07:03	Gemini
12 May 1919	19:01	Cancer
8 Jun 1919	10:39	Leo
7 Jul 1919	18:24	Virgo
9 Nov 1919	08:02	Libra
9 Dec 1919	03:25	Scorpio
4 Jan 1920	09:16	Sagittarius
29 Jan 1920	11:51	Capricorn
23 Feb 1920	03:45	Aquarius
18 Mar 1920	15:31	Pisces
12 Apr 1920	02:06	Aries
6 May 1920	12:54	Taurus
31 May 1920	00:04	Gemini
24 Jun 1920	10:51	Cancer
18 Jul 1920	20:23	Leo
12 Aug 1920	04:26	Virgo
5 Sep 1920	11:49	Libra
29 Sep 1920	19:41	Scorpio
24 Oct 1920	05:08	Sagittarius
17 Nov 1920	17:26	Capricorn
12 Dec 1920	11:44	Aquarius
6 Jan 1921	20:32	Pisces
2 Feb 1921	18:35	Aries
7 Mar 1921	09:16	Taurus
25 Apr 1921	23:26	Aries
2 Jun 1921	04:31	Taurus
8 Jul 1921	05:57	Gemini
5 Aug 1921	14:39	Cancer
31 Aug 1921	22:21	Leo
26 Sep 1921	04:05	Virgo
20 Oct 1921	17:32	Libra
13 Nov 1921	21:09	Scorpio
7 Dec 1921	19:45	Sagittarius
31 Dec 1921	16:30	Capricorn
24 Jan 1922	13:11	Aquarius
17 Feb 1922	11:02	Pisces
13 Mar 1922	11:25	Aries
6 Apr 1922	15:45	Taurus
1 May 1922	01:16	Gemini

25 May 1922	16:59	Cancer
19 Jun 1922	16:29	Leo
15 Jul 1922	03:22	Virgo
10 Aug 1922	09:32	Libra
7 Sep 1922	07:21	Scorpio
10 Oct 1922	22:49	Sagittarius
28 Nov 1922	21:12	Scorpio

2 Jan 1923	07:27	Sagittarius
6 Feb 1923	14:30	Capricorn
6 Mar 1923	05:33	Aquarius
1 Apr 1923	05:10	Pisces
26 Apr 1923	13:32	Aries
21 May 1923	14:47	Taurus
15 Jun 1923	11:44	Gemini
10 Jul 1923	04:34	Cancer
3 Aug 1923	16:40	Leo
27 Aug 1923	23:55	Virgo
21 Sep 1923	03:23	Libra
15 Oct 1923	04:41	Scorpio
8 Nov 1923	05:16	Sagittarius
2 Dec 1923	05:59	Capricorn
26 Dec 1923	07:58	Aquarius

19 Jan 1924	13:42	Pisces
13 Feb 1924	04:07	Aries
9 Mar 1924	11:53	Taurus
5 Apr 1924	06:45	Gemini
6 May 1924	01:49	Cancer
8 Sep 1924	21:42	Leo
7 Oct 1924	14:11	Virgo
2 Nov 1924	14:38	Libra
27 Nov 1924	11:43	Scorpio
21 Dec 1924	19:51	Sagittarius

14 Jan 1925	22:24	Capricorn
7 Feb 1925	23:12	Aquarius
4 Mar 1925	00:18	Pisces
28 Mar 1925	03:00	Aries
21 Apr 1925	08:09	Taurus
15 May 1925	15:57	Gemini
9 Jun 1925	02:08	Cancer
3 Jul 1925	14:24	Leo
28 Jul 1925	05:19	Virgo
22 Aug 1925	00:22	Libra
16 Sep 1925	02:00	Scorpio
11 Oct 1925	14:08	Sagittarius
6 Nov 1925	22:35	Capricorn
5 Dec 1925	15:16	Aquarius

6 Apr 1926	03:58	Pisces
6 May 1926	15:09	Aries
2 Jun 1926	19:54	Taurus
28 Jun 1926	20:58	Gemini
24 Jul 1926	06:36	Cancer
18 Aug 1926	04:30	Leo
11 Sep 1926	16:33	Virgo
5 Oct 1926	21:04	Libra
29 Oct 1926	20:46	Scorpio
22 Nov 1926	18:06	Sagittarius
16 Dec 1926	14:41	Capricorn

9 Jan 1927	11:40	Aquarius
2 Feb 1927	10:26	Pisces
26 Feb 1927	13:09	Aries
22 Mar 1927	22:51	Taurus
16 Apr 1927	19:23	Gemini
12 May 1927	08:32	Cancer
8 Jun 1927	02:52	Leo
7 Jul 1927	18:59	Virgo
9 Nov 1927	13:26	Libra
8 Dec 1927	21:21	Scorpio

3 Jan 1928	00:00	Sagittarius
29 Jan 1928	01:08	Capricorn
22 Feb 1928	16:11	Aquarius
18 Mar 1928	03:21	Pisces
11 Apr 1928	13:31	Aries
5 May 1928	23:59	Taurus
30 May 1928	10:55	Gemini
23 Jun 1928	21:36	Cancer
18 Jul 1928	07:08	Leo
11 Aug 1928	15:21	Virgo
4 Sep 1928	22:58	Libra

29 Sep 1928 07:11 Scorpio
23 Oct 1928 17:07 Sagittarius
17 Nov 1928 06:04 Capricorn
12 Dec 1928 01:21 Aquarius

6 Jan 1929 11:58 Pisces
2 Feb 1929 14:34 Aries
8 Mar 1929 07:38 Taurus
20 Apr 1929 01:05 Aries
3 Jun 1929 09:55 Taurus
8 Jul 1929 01:57 Gemini
5 Aug 1929 05:35 Cancer
31 Aug 1929 11:19 Leo
25 Sep 1929 16:08 Virgo
20 Oct 1929 05:07 Libra
13 Nov 1929 08:30 Scorpio
7 Dec 1929 07:00 Sagittarius
31 Dec 1929 03:40 Capricorn

24 Jan 1930 00:18 Aquarius
16 Feb 1930 22:06 Pisces
12 Mar 1930 22:27 Aries
6 Apr 1930 02:50 Taurus
30 Apr 1930 12:30 Gemini
25 May 1930 04:30 Cancer
19 Jun 1930 04:36 Leo
14 Jul 1930 16:34 Virgo
10 Aug 1930 00:56 Libra
7 Sep 1930 04:10 Scorpio
12 Oct 1930 03:02 Sagittarius
22 Nov 1930 06:47 Scorpio

3 Jan 1931 20:07 Sagittarius
6 Feb 1931 12:20 Capricorn
5 Mar 1931 21:40 Aquarius
31 Mar 1931 18:58 Pisces
26 Apr 1931 02:06 Aries
21 May 1931 02:36 Taurus
14 Jun 1931 23:02 Gemini
9 Jul 1931 15:32 Cancer
3 Aug 1931 03:26 Leo
27 Aug 1931 10:37 Virgo
20 Sep 1931 14:09 Libra
14 Oct 1931 15:37 Scorpio
7 Nov 1931 16:24 Sagittarius
1 Dec 1931 17:22 Capricorn
25 Dec 1931 19:39 Aquarius

19 Jan 1932 01:49 Pisces
12 Feb 1932 16:57 Aries
9 Mar 1932 02:06 Taurus
5 Apr 1932 00:18 Gemini
6 May 1932 09:04 Cancer
13 Jul 1932 09:46 Gemini
28 Jul 1932 13:07 Cancer
8 Sep 1932 19:40 Leo
7 Oct 1932 05:41 Virgo
2 Nov 1932 03:58 Libra
27 Nov 1932 00:04 Scorpio
21 Dec 1932 07:41 Sagittarius

14 Jan 1933 09:54 Capricorn
7 Feb 1933 10:29 Aquarius
3 Mar 1933 11:24 Pisces
27 Mar 1933 13:57 Aries
20 Apr 1933 18:58 Taurus
15 May 1933 02:44 Gemini
8 Jun 1933 12:57 Cancer
3 Jul 1933 01:25 Leo
27 Jul 1933 16:42 Virgo
21 Aug 1933 12:21 Libra
15 Sep 1933 14:53 Scorpio
11 Oct 1933 04:33 Sagittarius
6 Nov 1933 16:05 Capricorn
5 Dec 1933 18:04 Aquarius

6 Apr 1934 09:21 Pisces
6 May 1934 08:51 Aries
2 Jun 1934 10:08 Taurus
28 Jun 1934 09:35 Gemini
23 Jul 1934 18:20 Cancer
17 Aug 1934 15:45 Leo

11 Sep 1934	03:32	Virgo
5 Oct 1934	07:56	Libra
29 Oct 1934	07:36	Scorpio
22 Nov 1934	04:56	Sagittarius
16 Dec 1934	01:35	Capricorn
8 Jan 1935	22:39	Aquarius
1 Feb 1935	21:32	Pisces
26 Feb 1935	00:26	Aries
22 Mar 1935	10:28	Taurus
16 Apr 1935	07:38	Gemini
11 May 1935	22:03	Cancer
7 Jun 1935	19:13	Leo
7 Jul 1935	20:35	Virgo
9 Nov 1935	16:27	Libra
8 Dec 1935	14:29	Scorpio
3 Jan 1936	14:12	Sagittarius
28 Jan 1936	13:58	Capricorn
22 Feb 1936	04:14	Aquarius
17 Mar 1936	14:53	Pisces
11 Apr 1936	00:41	Aries
5 May 1936	10:53	Taurus
29 May 1936	21:39	Gemini
23 Jun 1936	08:15	Cancer
17 Jul 1936	17:49	Leo
11 Aug 1936	02:08	Virgo
4 Sep 1936	09:59	Libra
28 Sep 1936	18:34	Scorpio
23 Oct 1936	04:59	Sagittarius
16 Nov 1936	18:35	Capricorn
11 Dec 1936	14:52	Aquarius
6 Jan 1937	03:20	Pisces
2 Feb 1937	10:42	Aries
9 Mar 1937	13:11	Taurus
14 Apr 1937	04:28	Aries
4 Jun 1937	06:43	Taurus
7 Jul 1937	21:13	Gemini
4 Aug 1937	20:13	Cancer
31 Aug 1937	00:06	Leo
25 Sep 1937	04:02	Virgo
19 Oct 1937	16:33	Libra
12 Nov 1937	19:43	Scorpio
6 Dec 1937	18:07	Sagittarius
30 Dec 1937	14:43	Capricorn
23 Jan 1938	11:15	Aquarius
16 Feb 1938	08:59	Pisces
12 Mar 1938	09:18	Aries
5 Apr 1938	13:42	Taurus
29 Apr 1938	23:31	Gemini
24 May 1938	15:52	Cancer
18 Jun 1938	16:37	Leo
14 Jul 1938	05:47	Virgo
9 Aug 1938	16:30	Libra
7 Sep 1938	01:41	Scorpio
13 Oct 1938	18:59	Sagittarius
15 Nov 1938	15:46	Scorpio
4 Jan 1939	21:45	Sagittarius
6 Feb 1939	09:14	Capricorn
5 Mar 1939	13:23	Aquarius
31 Mar 1939	08:30	Pisces
25 Apr 1939	14:26	Aries
20 May 1939	14:12	Taurus
14 Jun 1939	10:10	Gemini
9 Jul 1939	02:24	Cancer
2 Aug 1939	14:10	Leo
26 Aug 1939	21:21	Virgo
20 Sep 1939	00:59	Libra
14 Oct 1939	02:36	Scorpio
7 Nov 1939	03:36	Sagittarius
1 Dec 1939	04:48	Capricorn
25 Dec 1939	07:22	Aquarius
18 Jan 1940	13:58	Pisces
12 Feb 1940	05:50	Aries
8 Mar 1940	16:26	Taurus
4 Apr 1940	18:12	Gemini
6 May 1940	18:49	Cancer
5 Jul 1940	15:51	Gemini
1 Aug 1940	02:40	Cancer
8 Sep 1940	16:58	Leo

6 Oct 1940	21:07	Virgo
1 Nov 1940	17:20	Libra
26 Nov 1940	12:29	Scorpio
20 Dec 1940	19:34	Sagittarius
13 Jan 1941	21:28	Capricorn
6 Feb 1941	21:48	Aquarius
2 Mar 1941	22:32	Pisces
27 Mar 1941	00:56	Aries
20 Apr 1941	05:50	Taurus
14 May 1941	13:32	Gemini
7 Jun 1941	23:48	Cancer
2 Jul 1941	12:28	Leo
27 Jul 1941	04:07	Virgo
21 Aug 1941	00:25	Libra
15 Sep 1941	03:59	Scorpio
10 Oct 1941	19:21	Sagittarius
6 Nov 1941	10:19	Capricorn
5 Dec 1941	23:11	Aquarius
6 Apr 1942	13:12	Pisces
6 May 1942	02:20	Aries
2 Jun 1942	00:19	Taurus
27 Jun 1942	22:12	Gemini
23 Jul 1942	06:06	Cancer
17 Aug 1942	03:01	Leo
10 Sep 1942	14:36	Virgo
4 Oct 1942	18:54	Libra
28 Oct 1942	18:36	Scorpio
21 Nov 1942	16:01	Sagittarius
15 Dec 1942	12:46	Capricorn
8 Jan 1943	09:56	Aquarius
1 Feb 1943	08:55	Pisces
25 Feb 1943	11:59	Aries
21 Mar 1943	22:21	Taurus
15 Apr 1943	20:10	Gemini
11 May 1943	11:56	Cancer
7 Jun 1943	12:10	Leo
8 Jul 1943	00:02	Virgo
9 Nov 1943	18:23	Libra
8 Dec 1943	07:39	Scorpio

3 Jan 1944	04:38	Sagittarius
28 Jan 1944	03:06	Capricorn
21 Feb 1944	16:36	Aquarius
17 Mar 1944	02:41	Pisces
10 Apr 1944	12:06	Aries
4 May 1944	22:00	Taurus
29 May 1944	08:35	Gemini
22 Jun 1944	19:06	Cancer
17 Jul 1944	04:40	Leo
10 Aug 1944	13:06	Virgo
3 Sep 1944	21:10	Libra
28 Sep 1944	06:06	Scorpio
22 Oct 1944	17:01	Sagittarius
16 Nov 1944	07:20	Capricorn
11 Dec 1944	04:43	Aquarius
5 Jan 1945	19:17	Pisces
2 Feb 1945	08:08	Aries
11 Mar 1945	11:31	Taurus
7 Apr 1945	18:18	Aries
4 Jun 1945	23:05	Taurus
7 Jul 1945	16:18	Gemini
4 Aug 1945	10:55	Cancer
30 Aug 1945	12:59	Leo
24 Sep 1945	16:00	Virgo
19 Oct 1945	04:04	Libra
12 Nov 1945	07:01	Scorpio
6 Dec 1945	05:18	Sagittarius
30 Dec 1945	01:51	Capricorn
22 Jan 1946	22:22	Aquarius
15 Feb 1946	20:04	Pisces
11 Mar 1946	20:24	Aries
5 Apr 1946	00:53	Taurus
29 Apr 1946	10:52	Gemini
24 May 1946	03:34	Cancer
18 Jun 1946	04:57	Leo
13 Jul 1946	19:22	Virgo
9 Aug 1946	08:37	Libra
7 Sep 1946	00:23	Scorpio
16 Oct 1946	11:36	Sagittarius
8 Nov 1946	07:28	Scorpio

5 Jan 1947	16:45	Sagittarius
6 Feb 1947	05:36	Capricorn
5 Mar 1947	05:03	Aquarius
30 Mar 1947	22:09	Pisces
25 Apr 1947	02:58	Aries
20 May 1947	02:02	Taurus
13 Jun 1947	21:32	Gemini
8 Jul 1947	13:27	Cancer
2 Aug 1947	01:03	Leo
26 Aug 1947	08:13	Virgo
19 Sep 1947	11:54	Libra
13 Oct 1947	13:41	Scorpio
6 Nov 1947	14:51	Sagittarius
30 Nov 1947	16:16	Capricorn
24 Dec 1947	19:08	Aquarius
18 Jan 1948	02:09	Pisces
11 Feb 1948	18:47	Aries
8 Mar 1948	06:57	Taurus
4 Apr 1948	12:39	Gemini
7 May 1948	08:29	Cancer
29 Jun 1948	07:09	Gemini
3 Aug 1948	02:37	Cancer
8 Sep 1948	13:40	Leo
6 Oct 1948	12:22	Virgo
1 Nov 1948	06:39	Libra
26 Nov 1948	00:51	Scorpio
20 Dec 1948	07:24	Sagittarius
13 Jan 1949	08:57	Capricorn
6 Feb 1949	09:03	Aquarius
2 Mar 1949	09:36	Pisces
26 Mar 1949	11:51	Aries
19 Apr 1949	16:39	Taurus
14 May 1949	00:20	Gemini
7 Jun 1949	10:42	Cancer
1 Jul 1949	23:35	Leo
26 Jul 1949	15:39	Virgo
20 Aug 1949	12:36	Libra
14 Sep 1949	17:11	Scorpio
10 Oct 1949	10:19	Sagittarius
6 Nov 1949	04:57	Capricorn
6 Dec 1949	06:15	Aquarius

6 Apr 1950	15:08	Pisces
5 May 1950	19:14	Aries
1 Jun 1950	14:14	Taurus
27 Jun 1950	10:41	Gemini
22 Jul 1950	17:47	Cancer
16 Aug 1950	14:16	Leo
10 Sep 1950	01:37	Virgo
4 Oct 1950	05:50	Libra
28 Oct 1950	05:31	Scorpio
21 Nov 1950	02:59	Sagittarius
14 Dec 1950	23:49	Capricorn
7 Jan 1951	21:05	Aquarius
31 Jan 1951	20:10	Pisces
24 Feb 1951	23:23	Aries
21 Mar 1951	10:04	Taurus
15 Apr 1951	08:33	Gemini
11 May 1951	01:41	Cancer
7 Jun 1951	05:10	Leo
8 Jul 1951	04:55	Virgo
9 Nov 1951	18:45	Libra
8 Dec 1951	00:15	Scorpio
2 Jan 1952	18:42	Sagittarius
27 Jan 1952	15:57	Capricorn
21 Feb 1952	04:41	Aquarius
16 Mar 1952	14:17	Pisces
9 Apr 1952	23:17	Aries
4 May 1952	08:54	Taurus
28 May 1952	19:18	Gemini
22 Jun 1952	05:43	Cancer
16 Jul 1952	15:19	Leo
9 Aug 1952	23:53	Virgo
3 Sep 1952	08:13	Libra
27 Sep 1952	17:33	Scorpio
22 Oct 1952	04:59	Sagittarius
15 Nov 1952	20:01	Capricorn
10 Dec 1952	18:31	Aquarius
5 Jan 1953	11:12	Pisces
2 Feb 1953	05:57	Aries
14 Mar 1953	18:55	Taurus

31 Mar 1953	04:50	Aries
5 Jun 1953	10:31	Taurus
7 Jul 1953	10:27	Gemini
4 Aug 1953	01:06	Cancer
30 Aug 1953	01:32	Leo
24 Sep 1953	03:46	Virgo
18 Oct 1953	15:26	Libra
11 Nov 1953	18:12	Scorpio
5 Dec 1953	16:24	Sagittarius
29 Dec 1953	12:53	Capricorn
22 Jan 1954	09:20	Aquarius
15 Feb 1954	07:00	Pisces
11 Mar 1954	07:18	Aries
4 Apr 1954	11:51	Taurus
28 Apr 1954	22:00	Gemini
23 May 1954	15:03	Cancer
17 Jun 1954	17:06	Leo
13 Jul 1954	08:45	Virgo
9 Aug 1954	00:37	Libra
6 Sep 1954	23:32	Scorpio
23 Oct 1954	22:07	Sagittarius
27 Oct 1954	10:52	Scorpio
6 Jan 1955	06:42	Sagittarius
6 Feb 1955	01:10	Capricorn
4 Mar 1955	20:17	Aquarius
30 Mar 1955	11:28	Pisces
24 Apr 1955	15:13	Aries
19 May 1955	13:36	Taurus
13 Jun 1955	08:38	Gemini
8 Jul 1955	00:15	Cancer
1 Aug 1955	11:42	Leo
25 Aug 1955	18:51	Virgo
18 Sep 1955	22:38	Libra
13 Oct 1955	00:34	Scorpio
6 Nov 1955	01:58	Sagittarius
30 Nov 1955	03:39	Capricorn
24 Dec 1955	06:51	Aquarius
17 Jan 1956	14:21	Pisces
11 Feb 1956	07:47	Aries

7 Mar 1956	21:34	Taurus
4 Apr 1956	07:25	Gemini
8 May 1956	02:16	Cancer
23 Jun 1956	12:00	Gemini
4 Aug 1956	09:46	Cancer
8 Sep 1956	09:23	Leo
6 Oct 1956	03:11	Virgo
31 Oct 1956	19:38	Libra
25 Nov 1956	13:00	Scorpio
19 Dec 1956	19:06	Sagittarius
12 Jan 1957	20:23	Capricorn
5 Feb 1957	20:17	Aquarius
1 Mar 1957	20:40	Pisces
25 Mar 1957	22:46	Aries
19 Apr 1957	03:27	Taurus
13 May 1957	11:06	Gemini
6 Jun 1957	21:32	Cancer
1 Jul 1957	10:39	Leo
26 Jul 1957	03:07	Virgo
20 Aug 1957	00:43	Libra
14 Sep 1957	06:21	Scorpio
10 Oct 1957	01:19	Sagittarius
5 Nov 1957	23:51	Capricorn
6 Dec 1957	15:33	Aquarius
6 Apr 1958	15:55	Pisces
5 May 1958	11:54	Aries
1 Jun 1958	04:03	Taurus
26 Jun 1958	23:06	Gemini
22 Jul 1958	05:25	Cancer
16 Aug 1958	01:29	Leo
9 Sep 1958	12:35	Virgo
3 Oct 1958	16:43	Libra
27 Oct 1958	16:24	Scorpio
20 Nov 1958	13:56	Sagittarius
14 Dec 1958	10:50	Capricorn
7 Jan 1959	08:11	Aquarius
31 Jan 1959	07:23	Pisces
24 Feb 1959	10:50	Aries
20 Mar 1959	21:54	Taurus

14 Apr 1959	21:07	Gemini	23 May 1962	02:41	Cancer
10 May 1959	15:45	Cancer	17 Jun 1962	05:28	Leo
6 Jun 1959	22:42	Leo	12 Jul 1962	22:31	Virgo
8 Jul 1959	12:09	Virgo	8 Aug 1962	17:14	Libra
20 Sep 1959	01:00	Leo	7 Sep 1962	00:15	Scorpio
25 Sep 1959	10:31	Virgo			
9 Nov 1959	18:07	Libra	6 Jan 1963	17:36	Sagittarius
7 Dec 1959	16:37	Scorpio	5 Feb 1963	20:30	Capricorn
			4 Mar 1963	11:34	Aquarius
2 Jan 1960	08:39	Sagittarius	30 Mar 1963	00:54	Pisces
27 Jan 1960	04:43	Capricorn	24 Apr 1963	03:35	Aries
20 Feb 1960	16:45	Aquarius	19 May 1963	01:17	Taurus
16 Mar 1960	01:51	Pisces	12 Jun 1963	19:53	Gemini
9 Apr 1960	10:30	Aries	7 Jul 1963	11:13	Cancer
3 May 1960	19:53	Taurus	31 Jul 1963	22:33	Leo
28 May 1960	06:08	Gemini	25 Aug 1963	05:42	Virgo
21 Jun 1960	16:30	Cancer	18 Sep 1963	09:35	Libra
16 Jul 1960	02:06	Leo	12 Oct 1963	11:42	Scorpio
9 Aug 1960	10:49	Virgo	5 Nov 1963	13:18	Sagittarius
2 Sep 1960	19:24	Libra	29 Nov 1963	15:14	Capricorn
27 Sep 1960	05:08	Scorpio	23 Dec 1963	18:47	Aquarius
21 Oct 1960	17:07	Sagittarius			
15 Nov 1960	08:54	Capricorn	17 Jan 1964	02:48	Pisces
10 Dec 1960	08:35	Aquarius	10 Feb 1964	21:06	Aries
			7 Mar 1964	12:37	Taurus
5 Jan 1961	03:35	Pisces	4 Apr 1964	03:06	Gemini
2 Feb 1961	04:53	Aries	9 May 1964	03:30	Cancer
5 Jun 1961	19:26	Taurus	17 Jun 1964	17:25	Gemini
7 Jul 1961	04:29	Gemini	5 Aug 1964	09:05	Cancer
3 Aug 1961	15:23	Cancer	8 Sep 1964	04:53	Leo
29 Aug 1961	14:13	Leo	5 Oct 1964	18:06	Virgo
23 Sep 1961	15:38	Virgo	31 Oct 1964	08:49	Libra
18 Oct 1961	02:55	Libra	25 Nov 1964	01:19	Scorpio
11 Nov 1961	05:31	Scorpio	19 Dec 1964	06:57	Sagittarius
5 Dec 1961	03:38	Sagittarius			
29 Dec 1961	00:03	Capricorn	12 Jan 1965	07:57	Capricorn
			5 Feb 1965	07:39	Aquarius
21 Jan 1962	20:26	Aquarius	1 Mar 1965	07:53	Pisces
14 Feb 1962	18:03	Pisces	25 Mar 1965	09:50	Aries
10 Mar 1962	18:22	Aries	18 Apr 1965	14:25	Taurus
3 Apr 1962	22:57	Taurus	12 May 1965	22:01	Gemini
28 Apr 1962	09:16	Gemini	6 Jun 1965	08:32	Cancer

30 Jun 1965	21:52	Leo
25 Jul 1965	14:45	Virgo
19 Aug 1965	13:02	Libra
13 Sep 1965	19:48	Scorpio
9 Oct 1965	16:47	Sagittarius
5 Nov 1965	19:39	Capricorn
7 Dec 1965	04:49	Aquarius
6 Feb 1966	11:37	Capricorn
25 Feb 1966	11:44	Aquarius
6 Apr 1966	15:50	Pisces
5 May 1966	04:27	Aries
31 May 1966	17:54	Taurus
26 Jun 1966	11:35	Gemini
21 Jul 1966	17:08	Cancer
15 Aug 1966	12:44	Leo
8 Sep 1966	23:37	Virgo
3 Oct 1966	03:40	Libra
27 Oct 1966	03:23	Scorpio
20 Nov 1966	01:00	Sagittarius
13 Dec 1966	22:01	Capricorn
6 Jan 1967	19:28	Aquarius
30 Jan 1967	18:47	Pisces
23 Feb 1967	22:25	Aries
20 Mar 1967	09:52	Taurus
14 Apr 1967	09:51	Gemini
10 May 1967	06:03	Cancer
6 Jun 1967	16:48	Leo
8 Jul 1967	22:18	Virgo
9 Sep 1967	11:00	Leo
1 Oct 1967	18:39	Virgo
9 Nov 1967	16:30	Libra
7 Dec 1967	08:45	Scorpio
1 Jan 1968	22:35	Sagittarius
26 Jan 1968	17:31	Capricorn
20 Feb 1968	04:52	Aquarius
15 Mar 1968	13:29	Pisces
8 Apr 1968	21:47	Aries
3 May 1968	06:55	Taurus
27 May 1968	17:00	Gemini

21 Jun 1968	03:16	Cancer
15 Jul 1968	12:54	Leo
8 Aug 1968	21:44	Virgo
2 Sep 1968	06:35	Libra
26 Sep 1968	16:41	Scorpio
21 Oct 1968	05:12	Sagittarius
14 Nov 1968	21:45	Capricorn
9 Dec 1968	22:40	Aquarius
4 Jan 1969	20:10	Pisces
2 Feb 1969	04:50	Aries
6 Jun 1969	01:49	Taurus
6 Jul 1969	22:01	Gemini
3 Aug 1969	05:26	Cancer
29 Aug 1969	02:43	Leo
23 Sep 1969	03:23	Virgo
17 Oct 1969	14:15	Libra
10 Nov 1969	16:39	Scorpio
4 Dec 1969	14:40	Sagittarius
28 Dec 1969	11:02	Capricorn
21 Jan 1970	07:24	Aquarius
14 Feb 1970	05:00	Pisces
10 Mar 1970	05:20	Aries
3 Apr 1970	10:01	Taurus
27 Apr 1970	20:30	Gemini
22 May 1970	14:18	Cancer
16 Jun 1970	17:49	Leo
12 Jul 1970	12:17	Virgo
8 Aug 1970	10:01	Libra
7 Sep 1970	01:57	Scorpio
7 Jan 1971	00:55	Sagittarius
5 Feb 1971	14:53	Capricorn
4 Mar 1971	02:22	Aquarius
29 Mar 1971	14:01	Pisces
23 Apr 1971	15:43	Aries
18 May 1971	12:47	Taurus
12 Jun 1971	06:57	Gemini
6 Jul 1971	22:02	Cancer
31 Jul 1971	09:14	Leo
24 Aug 1971	16:24	Virgo

Date	Time	Sign
17 Sep 1971	20:23	Libra
11 Oct 1971	22:39	Scorpio
5 Nov 1971	00:27	Sagittarius
29 Nov 1971	02:39	Capricorn
23 Dec 1971	06:31	Aquarius
16 Jan 1972	15:01	Pisces
10 Feb 1972	10:09	Aries
7 Mar 1972	03:28	Taurus
3 Apr 1972	22:51	Gemini
10 May 1972	13:46	Cancer
11 Jun 1972	20:11	Gemini
6 Aug 1972	01:32	Cancer
7 Sep 1972	23:29	Leo
5 Oct 1972	08:34	Virgo
30 Oct 1972	21:39	Libra
24 Nov 1972	13:22	Scorpio
18 Dec 1972	18:33	Sagittarius
11 Jan 1973	19:16	Capricorn
4 Feb 1973	18:45	Aquarius
28 Feb 1973	18:47	Pisces
24 Mar 1973	20:35	Aries
18 Apr 1973	01:04	Taurus
12 May 1973	08:41	Gemini
5 Jun 1973	19:18	Cancer
30 Jun 1973	08:54	Leo
25 Jul 1973	02:12	Virgo
19 Aug 1973	01:12	Libra
13 Sep 1973	09:08	Scorpio
9 Oct 1973	08:11	Sagittarius
5 Nov 1973	15:42	Capricorn
7 Dec 1973	21:43	Aquarius
29 Jan 1974	20:07	Capricorn
28 Feb 1974	14:13	Aquarius
6 Apr 1974	14:09	Pisces
4 May 1974	20:17	Aries
31 May 1974	07:16	Taurus
25 Jun 1974	23:43	Gemini
21 Jul 1974	04:35	Cancer
14 Aug 1974	23:48	Leo
8 Sep 1974	10:28	Virgo

Date	Time	Sign
8 Sep 1974	10:28	Virgo
2 Oct 1974	14:28	Libra
26 Oct 1974	14:12	Scorpio
19 Nov 1974	11:55	Sagittarius
13 Dec 1974	09:03	Capricorn
6 Jan 1975	06:37	Aquarius
30 Jan 1975	06:03	Pisces
23 Feb 1975	09:53	Aries
19 Mar 1975	21:43	Taurus
13 Apr 1975	22:27	Gemini
9 May 1975	20:13	Cancer
6 Jun 1975	10:56	Leo
9 Jul 1975	11:05	Virgo
2 Sep 1975	15:25	Leo
4 Oct 1975	05:32	Virgo
9 Nov 1975	13:52	Libra
7 Dec 1975	00:29	Scorpio
1 Jan 1976	12:15	Sagittarius
26 Jan 1976	06:09	Capricorn
19 Feb 1976	16:50	Aquarius
15 Mar 1976	00:59	Pisces
8 Apr 1976	08:57	Aries
2 May 1976	17:49	Taurus
27 May 1976	03:43	Gemini
20 Jun 1976	13:54	Cancer
14 Jul 1976	23:33	Leo
8 Aug 1976	08:32	Virgo
1 Sep 1976	17:41	Libra
26 Sep 1976	04:14	Scorpio
20 Oct 1976	17:20	Sagittarius
14 Nov 1976	10:42	Capricorn
9 Dec 1976	12:55	Aquarius
4 Jan 1977	13:04	Pisces
2 Feb 1977	05:58	Aries
6 Jun 1977	06:06	Taurus
6 Jul 1977	15:04	Gemini
2 Aug 1977	19:14	Cancer
28 Aug 1977	15:06	Leo
22 Sep 1977	15:04	Virgo

17 Oct 1977	01:37	Libra
10 Nov 1977	03:51	Scorpio
4 Dec 1977	01:48	Sagittarius
27 Dec 1977	22:07	Capricorn
20 Jan 1978	18:27	Aquarius
13 Feb 1978	16:03	Pisces
9 Mar 1978	16:24	Aries
2 Apr 1978	21:09	Taurus
27 Apr 1978	07:50	Gemini
22 May 1978	02:02	Cancer
16 Jun 1978	06:19	Leo
12 Jul 1978	02:16	Virgo
8 Aug 1978	03:11	Libra
7 Sep 1978	05:11	Scorpio
7 Jan 1979	06:37	Sagittarius
5 Feb 1979	09:12	Capricorn
3 Mar 1979	17:15	Aquarius
29 Mar 1979	03:15	Pisces
23 Apr 1979	04:00	Aries
18 May 1979	00:27	Taurus
11 Jun 1979	18:12	Gemini
6 Jul 1979	09:00	Cancer
30 Jul 1979	20:04	Leo
24 Aug 1979	03:12	Virgo
17 Sep 1979	07:15	Libra
11 Oct 1979	09:41	Scorpio
4 Nov 1979	11:43	Sagittarius
28 Nov 1979	14:14	Capricorn
22 Dec 1979	18:29	Aquarius
16 Jan 1980	03:33	Pisces
9 Feb 1980	23:38	Aries
6 Mar 1980	18:56	Taurus
3 Apr 1980	19:50	Gemini
12 May 1980	21:10	Cancer
5 Jun 1980	04:43	Gemini
6 Aug 1980	14:30	Cancer
7 Sep 1980	17:55	Leo
4 Oct 1980	23:02	Virgo
30 Oct 1980	10:33	Libra
24 Nov 1980	01:30	Scorpio
18 Dec 1980	06:18	Sagittarius
11 Jan 1981	06:46	Capricorn
4 Feb 1981	06:05	Aquarius
28 Feb 1981	05:59	Pisces
24 Mar 1981	07:40	Aries
17 Apr 1981	12:04	Taurus
11 May 1981	19:40	Gemini
5 Jun 1981	06:23	Cancer
29 Jun 1981	20:14	Leo
24 Jul 1981	14:00	Virgo
18 Aug 1981	13:43	Libra
12 Sep 1981	22:52	Scorpio
9 Oct 1981	00:07	Sagittarius
5 Nov 1981	12:43	Capricorn
8 Dec 1981	21:07	Aquarius
23 Jan 1982	02:20	Capricorn
2 Mar 1982	11:36	Aquarius
6 Apr 1982	12:15	Pisces
4 May 1982	12:21	Aries
30 May 1982	20:57	Taurus
25 Jun 1982	12:10	Gemini
20 Jul 1982	16:19	Cancer
14 Aug 1982	11:07	Leo
7 Sep 1982	21:35	Virgo
2 Oct 1982	01:29	Libra
26 Oct 1982	01:14	Scorpio
18 Nov 1982	23:00	Sagittarius
12 Dec 1982	20:12	Capricorn
5 Jan 1983	17:51	Aquarius
29 Jan 1983	17:25	Pisces
22 Feb 1983	21:29	Aries
19 Mar 1983	09:47	Taurus
13 Apr 1983	11:23	Gemini
9 May 1983	10:55	Cancer
6 Jun 1983	06:05	Leo
10 Jul 1983	05:32	Virgo
27 Aug 1983	10:40	Leo
5 Oct 1983	19:57	Virgo

9 Nov 1983 10:51 Libra
6 Dec 1983 16:11 Scorpio

1 Jan 1984 01:56 Sagittarius
25 Jan 1984 18:46 Capricorn
19 Feb 1984 04:48 Aquarius
14 Mar 1984 12:31 Pisces
7 Apr 1984 20:11 Aries
2 May 1984 04:51 Taurus
26 May 1984 14:36 Gemini
20 Jun 1984 00:44 Cancer
14 Jul 1984 10:26 Leo
7 Aug 1984 19:35 Virgo
1 Sep 1984 05:01 Libra
25 Sep 1984 16:00 Scorpio
20 Oct 1984 05:41 Sagittarius
13 Nov 1984 23:53 Capricorn
9 Dec 1984 03:28 Aquarius

4 Jan 1985 06:28 Pisces
2 Feb 1985 08:38 Aries
6 Jun 1985 08:51 Taurus
6 Jul 1985 07:57 Gemini
2 Aug 1985 09:05 Cancer
28 Aug 1985 03:34 Leo
22 Sep 1985 02:50 Virgo
16 Oct 1985 13:02 Libra
9 Nov 1985 15:07 Scorpio
3 Dec 1985 12:58 Sagittarius
27 Dec 1985 09:15 Capricorn

20 Jan 1986 05:32 Aquarius
13 Feb 1986 03:06 Pisces
9 Mar 1986 03:26 Aries
2 Apr 1986 08:13 Taurus
26 Apr 1986 19:05 Gemini
21 May 1986 13:43 Cancer
15 Jun 1986 18:50 Leo
11 Jul 1986 16:22 Virgo
7 Aug 1986 20:45 Libra
7 Sep 1986 10:18 Scorpio

7 Jan 1987 10:19 Sagittarius
5 Feb 1987 02:59 Capricorn
3 Mar 1987 07:52 Aquarius
28 Mar 1987 16:17 Pisces
22 Apr 1987 16:04 Aries
17 May 1987 11:53 Taurus
11 Jun 1987 05:13 Gemini
5 Jul 1987 19:48 Cancer
30 Jul 1987 06:47 Leo
23 Aug 1987 13:56 Virgo
16 Sep 1987 18:07 Libra
10 Oct 1987 20:43 Scorpio
3 Nov 1987 23:00 Sagittarius
28 Nov 1987 01:48 Capricorn
22 Dec 1987 06:26 Aquarius

15 Jan 1988 16:02 Pisces
9 Feb 1988 13:05 Aries
6 Mar 1988 10:25 Taurus
3 Apr 1988 17:16 Gemini
17 May 1988 17:06 Cancer
27 May 1988 06:22 Gemini
6 Aug 1988 23:27 Cancer
7 Sep 1988 11:38 Leo
4 Oct 1988 13:13 Virgo
29 Oct 1988 23:16 Libra
23 Nov 1988 13:31 Scorpio
17 Dec 1988 17:55 Sagittarius

10 Jan 1989 18:09 Capricorn
3 Feb 1989 17:16 Aquarius
27 Feb 1989 16:59 Pisces
23 Mar 1989 18:32 Aries
16 Apr 1989 22:51 Taurus
11 May 1989 06:26 Gemini
4 Jun 1989 17:14 Cancer
29 Jun 1989 07:18 Leo
24 Jul 1989 01:30 Virgo
18 Aug 1989 01:58 Libra
12 Sep 1989 12:24 Scorpio
8 Oct 1989 16:02 Sagittarius
5 Nov 1989 10:14 Capricorn
10 Dec 1989 05:02 Aquarius

16 Jan 1990	15:24	Capricorn
3 Mar 1990	17:52	Aquarius
6 Apr 1990	09:10	Pisces
4 May 1990	03:49	Aries
30 May 1990	10:12	Taurus
25 Jun 1990	00:14	Gemini
20 Jul 1990	03:42	Cancer
13 Aug 1990	22:06	Leo
7 Sep 1990	08:21	Virgo
1 Oct 1990	12:13	Libra
25 Oct 1990	12:02	Scorpio
18 Nov 1990	09:55	Sagittarius
12 Dec 1990	07:15	Capricorn
5 Jan 1991	05:01	Aquarius
29 Jan 1991	04:43	Pisces
22 Feb 1991	09:01	Aries
18 Mar 1991	21:44	Taurus
13 Apr 1991	00:11	Gemini
9 May 1991	01:31	Cancer
6 Jun 1991	01:20	Leo
11 Jul 1991	05:09	Virgo
21 Aug 1991	15:02	Leo
6 Oct 1991	21:21	Virgo
9 Nov 1991	06:38	Libra
6 Dec 1991	07:22	Scorpio
31 Dec 1991	15:19	Sagittarius
25 Jan 1992	07:13	Capricorn
18 Feb 1992	16:40	Aquarius
13 Mar 1992	23:58	Pisces
7 Apr 1992	07:18	Aries
1 May 1992	15:43	Taurus
26 May 1992	01:19	Gemini
19 Jun 1992	11:22	Cancer
13 Jul 1992	21:05	Leo
7 Aug 1992	06:24	Virgo
31 Aug 1992	16:07	Libra
25 Sep 1992	03:30	Scorpio
19 Oct 1992	17:46	Sagittarius
13 Nov 1992	12:50	Capricorn
8 Dec 1992	17:52	Aquarius

3 Jan 1993	23:57	Pisces
2 Feb 1993	12:40	Aries
6 Jun 1993	09:59	Taurus
6 Jul 1993	00:18	Gemini
1 Aug 1993	22:35	Cancer
27 Aug 1993	15:46	Leo
21 Sep 1993	14:22	Virgo
16 Oct 1993	00:14	Libra
9 Nov 1993	02:08	Scorpio
2 Dec 1993	23:54	Sagittarius
26 Dec 1993	20:09	Capricorn
19 Jan 1994	16:27	Aquarius
12 Feb 1994	14:02	Pisces
8 Mar 1994	14:25	Aries
1 Apr 1994	19:18	Taurus
26 Apr 1994	06:23	Gemini
21 May 1994	01:27	Cancer
15 Jun 1994	07:24	Leo
11 Jul 1994	06:34	Virgo
7 Aug 1994	14:38	Libra
7 Sep 1994	17:15	Scorpio
7 Jan 1995	12:06	Sagittarius
4 Feb 1995	20:11	Capricorn
2 Mar 1995	22:11	Aquarius
28 Mar 1995	05:10	Pisces
22 Apr 1995	04:07	Aries
16 May 1995	23:21	Taurus
10 Jun 1995	16:19	Gemini
5 Jul 1995	06:39	Cancer
29 Jul 1995	17:32	Leo
23 Aug 1995	00:41	Virgo
16 Sep 1995	04:58	Libra
10 Oct 1995	07:45	Scorpio
3 Nov 1995	10:15	Sagittarius
27 Nov 1995	13:21	Capricorn
21 Dec 1995	18:21	Aquarius
15 Jan 1996	04:31	Pisces
9 Feb 1996	02:33	Aries
6 Mar 1996	02:05	Taurus
3 Apr 1996	15:31	Gemini

7 Aug 1996	06:16	Cancer	24 Oct 1998	23:03	Scorpio
7 Sep 1996	05:06	Leo	17 Nov 1998	21:02	Sagittarius
4 Oct 1996	03:19	Virgo	11 Dec 1998	18:28	Capricorn
29 Oct 1996	11:59	Libra			
23 Nov 1996	01:32	Scorpio	4 Jan 1999	16:20	Aquarius
17 Dec 1996	05:33	Sagittarius	28 Jan 1999	16:12	Pisces
			21 Feb 1999	20:46	Aries
10 Jan 1997	05:32	Capricorn	18 Mar 1999	09:56	Taurus
3 Feb 1997	04:28	Aquarius	12 Apr 1999	13:16	Gemini
27 Feb 1997	04:01	Pisces	8 May 1999	16:30	Cancer
23 Mar 1997	05:24	Aries	5 Jun 1999	21:28	Leo
16 Apr 1997	09:40	Taurus	12 Jul 1999	15:26	Virgo
10 May 1997	17:16	Gemini	15 Aug 1999	13:25	Leo
4 Jun 1997	04:13	Cancer	7 Oct 1999	17:03	Virgo
28 Jun 1997	18:34	Leo	9 Nov 1999	02:19	Libra
23 Jul 1997	13:15	Virgo	5 Dec 1999	22:39	Scorpio
17 Aug 1997	14:31	Libra	31 Dec 1999	04:51	Sagittarius
12 Sep 1997	02:18	Scorpio			
8 Oct 1997	08:26	Sagittarius	24 Jan 2000	19:49	Capricorn
5 Nov 1997	08:52	Capricorn	18 Feb 2000	04:40	Aquarius
12 Dec 1997	05:04	Aquarius	13 Mar 2000	11:34	Pisces
			6 Apr 2000	18:35	Aries
9 Jan 1998	20:23	Capricorn	1 May 2000	02:46	Taurus
4 Mar 1998	16:15	Aquarius	25 May 2000	12:11	Gemini
6 Apr 1998	05:33	Pisces	18 Jun 2000	22:10	Cancer
3 May 1998	19:12	Aries	13 Jul 2000	07:56	Leo
29 May 1998	23:30	Taurus	6 Aug 2000	17:26	Virgo
24 Jun 1998	12:26	Gemini	31 Aug 2000	03:29	Libra
19 Jul 1998	15:16	Cancer	24 Sep 2000	15:20	Scorpio
13 Aug 1998	09:18	Leo	19 Oct 2000	06:15	Sagittarius
6 Sep 1998	19:22	Virgo	13 Nov 2000	02:14	Capricorn
30 Sep 1998	23:11	Libra	8 Dec 2000	08:50	Aquarius

Venus in Aries

HOW YOU LET LOVE IN

Hasty-hearted and outspoken, you always want to be the first to say, 'I love you'. You'll want love fast and direct, so it's not going to be good for your emotions if the object of your dreams spends long periods away or can't be as close to you as you would like. You haven't the patience for long-distance or star-crossed romance, either.

Aries Venus signs just can't help but be aggressive, so anyone who catches your fancy will soon be aware of the fact. Bold moves, linked with incorrigible flirting, are your tactics and what you lack in subtlety you more than make up with results.

You have no problems in sorting the sheep from the goats and speedily despatch the mismatches who wouldn't be interested in your tactile displays of affection. Those who do enjoy your kind of bold approach find you amusing and relish your powerful blend of physicality and hidden romanticism. Needless to say, any long-lasting love will probably have an ego at least as large as your own.

You thrive on emotional conquests and enjoy making your partner jealous. Whichever your sex, you have chauvinistic double standards and you are very competitive, forever striving to push your partner under your thumb but perversely threatening to leave them if they are weak enough to allow you to dictate to them.

New people and passions are vital to you and you are proud of visible signs of intense affection like scratches or small bruises. It boosts your ego and makes you feel – and look – loved and wanted.

Outgoing, enthusiastic and eager to take the initiative, you can make the mistake of concentrating too much on immediate, selfish pleasure. You can occasionally turn what should be a tender, passionate wooing into a relentless pursuit, and you have the ability to ruin a romantic moment with hasty, ill-chosen words.

You quite genuinely have trouble choosing between a deeply emotional relationship and instant attraction, often going for the showy and obvious when you have the chance of so much more. Your closest friends are often better judges of your suitors than you are and make far better guardians of your emotional wellbeing.

The clashes in your lovelife reflect the tension in this zodiac position. Love planet Venus is positively pulsating with ultra-female energy, while Aries is the pushy male leader of the 12 signs. But there is a softer, more romantic side to you and you must learn to listen to it and give in to it sometimes. No-one ever wins the kind of battle of the sexes you seem to take pleasure in.

YOUR LOVE PATH

Part of your attraction and charm lies in your childlike qualities. In those early, heady days of an affair, you give love innocently and trustingly. It's all so uncomplicated. But along with those childlike qualities there is also a childish streak, which isn't so appealing. You can't turn off the impulse for childish behaviour and, once slapped down, you retreat into a corner and sulk. You may be aching inside to be comforted, but behaving badly is not going to get the response you crave.

Most of the time, your partner will recognise and tolerate your emotional immaturity and want to smother you with understanding. But while this comforting pillow of love often makes you drowsy with contentment, there are times when you feel smothered by it. You'll fight off their clinging hands, avoid their caresses – and hurt their feelings badly in the process. Before things get this far, explain to your partner, kindly and calmly, that you need plenty of room to breathe and the freedom to be you.

Your self-confidence is high and others always find you attractive – too attractive for your own good, in fact, because it's very hard for you to be faithful. Teasing and pleasing are all too easy for you and you can never resist taking flirtation further. In your book, stopping short of the bedroom door is letting people down. One-night stands hold no guilt for you, even if you are living with your idea of a perfect lover.

Yet you're such a romantic idealist deep down and you'd be horrified if the tables were turned and your partner cheated on you. You're not really a hypocrite, it's simply those Aries–Venus double standards switching you between free-loving hedonism and a possessive urge to mate for life. When you feel tempted to stray, stop and think first how you'd react if it was your partner doing the cheating. Remind yourself that you are happy and that your emotional needs are being met. Is it worth risking all that for a brief encounter that will do no more than satisfy a fleeting physical need?

Luckily, no matter how long-standing your relationship, you're unlikely to get into a rut. Routine has no place in your bedroom! You're bewitched by a partner who keeps you amused and attentive in bed, and you positively devour sexy books and films in a bid to feed your fertile imagination and keep your partner interested. You're a thoughtful lover and would hate to think you've left your bedmate unfulfilled. Your own passion places are your face, head and hair – and you love being kissed in the space between your eyebrows!

The worst offence any lover can commit with you is to make a feeble, half-hearted advance. If someone wants to make love to you, you like being told in the sexiest way possible, leaving no room for doubt. You don't mince words yourself and you're so keen on caresses – and where they lead – that you can sometimes misinterpret physical signals. As far as you're concerned, a warm body close to yours can only mean one thing!

You are at your most romantic after loving and it's then – and often only then – that tender words and gestures pour straight from your heart, more than making up for your pre-sex bluntness. In fact, your partner then has the best of both worlds – wild, forceful, passionate lover, and caring, tender soul mate.

You won't find it too easy to express your feelings in words. But even when you have a blazing row with your partner, it will never be unduly drawn out or poisoned by wicked, well-chosen words. Short and sharp, it will be over in a flash. And while your sexual encounters may be equally blazing yet brief, you're quick to arouse again.

Aries sunshine and Venus happiness are bound to bless a partnership with plenty of laughter. You may be a bit of a rule-breaker, especially in love, and you can slip easily into the role of lovable eccentric, but you clown around for a purpose and no-one should ever mistake you for a fool. Your partner should realise it takes intelligence and a lot of rehearsing to put on your kind of show.

You're convinced that you always give of your best in a love match, and most of the time you do. Just occasionally you need to take a break to recharge your emotional batteries. Your partner may wonder what they've done to upset you, but they have no need to worry. Reassurance, kindness and warmth from them will always get a loving response from you.

You have great visions for the future and always include your partner in them. They can't help but be fascinated and flattered that they're always in your thoughts. What they don't realise is that, for you, sharing your world with your partner is second nature as you don't like anyone to feel left out, especially your nearest and dearest. In fact, your emotional generosity and trusting heart are an irresistible mix.

So why is it often hard for you to stay with someone? Usually, you're the quitter, and you mostly leave one lover for another. You do thrive on tension and can encourage emotional upset and jealousy just for the thrill of it. Learn to love the gentler, less exciting side of life instead of shouting so much. Work to maintain domestic harmony by giving in occasionally and letting your partner win, no matter who you think is right. Otherwise you'll spend your life swopping lovers and simply repeating the same emotional errors again and again.

Keep some of your wilder plans filed away until the time is ripe if you don't want to be labelled a bulldozer. Study a few gentle romantic gestures and practise them. Above all, stop hanging on to your partner's steering wheel so tightly and yanking it in your latest direction. Remember how much you hate being pushed yourself.

Most of all, make room for some romance and displays of gentle, caring emotion sometimes. You're a strong, passionate, whirlwind lover and even more desirable once you've tempered your wildness with tenderness.

Venus in Taurus

HOW YOU LET LOVE IN

Sensual, affectionate, considerate, Venus is truly at home in Taurus. This placing makes you love to touch and be touched and want to share your deepest heart-thoughts with your partner.

You are an avid collector of lovers – and of the material evidence of their affection. But you are easily satisfied, both physically and emotionally, and your approach to love and its many pleasures is essentially passive. This means that, once you have found a satisfying routine, you'll enjoy doing the same old thing, day in, day out. Your lovelife probably needs a good kick to get it out of a rut. Your romantic asset is great physical sensitivity. You love stroking and being stroked and make a delightful virtue out of indulging your senses – especially eating!

You need lots of affection and cuddles and take great trouble to make the moment right with the perfect setting, soft music and low lights. You find it hard to let go and release your feelings unless you feel completely safe, not only with your surroundings but also with your partner.

Above all, you like to feel that you've got the best, from the best home and objects money can buy to the best lover you can win for yourself. In this respect, you set yourself high targets and it's only when you have settled into a love relationship that you stop trying so hard. Beware overwhelming a new lover with sentimental gestures – you can overdo things sometimes.

Once you are committed, it takes a major upheaval to

make you leave a partner. You will usually put up with a lot rather than make the break. Secretly, you are pretty much in awe of love. It's a big, risky venture as far as you're concerned, worthy of nothing less than your total concentration. You tend to marry for security and are loath to rock the boat at any price. Price probably plays a part in your decision to stay put, too, because you are only too aware of how expensive a split can be.

There is a danger, especially in the early part of your life, of you becoming permanently tied to someone who appears exciting largely because of your lack of worldly experience. You may waste your emotions on someone who doesn't have your capacity for love and affection, which would be a great shame.

Your heart will get bruised, despite your best efforts to shield it, and you could nurse endless grudges and hit out roughly and without discrimination when you are hurt. If you feel threatened, you can be jealous and powerful, dominating less strong partners.

But on the whole, once you feel secure in a relationship, you are loving and tender, blending emotional warmth with consideration for your partner.

YOUR LOVE PATH

You usually sail through a lovelife that is steadfast, sexy and secure – even more so when your partner has the added bonus of earning a good living.

Adoring and adorable, you need few lessons in love, just guidance in bringing out the best in your relationships and making the most of your practical, faithful nature. Safety and stability are your emotional keys. They're what you yearn to feel, and strained atmospheres in relationships cause chaos for you. If everything feels right and wonderful, then your love flows.

You feel close to earth and nature and are tuned in to all your senses. But perhaps touch is the most highly developed of them. You have a real need to touch people, which is why you simply can't live without loving. This makes it hard sometimes to untangle love from lust. Try asking yourself if you are merely using someone to satisfy your burning craving for a close, physical relationship.

Your heart is brimming with love and you attract many lovers. But you know deep down that your ideal mate has to provide all the emotional and physical security you yearn for, so choose carefully. By all means enjoy the attraction of opposites and go for someone headstrong, flighty and spontaneous. Realise, though, that you are probably wasting your time – and love – because they'll never be able to give you that precious, safe, all-enveloping relationship you need.

You'll always opt for the traditional rather than the new and trendy. You love possessions and display them like trophies, tending to do the same with lovers. That's all very well if they like being shown off. Eventually, however, they may want to break free from such claustrophobic love, so try to curb your possessive streak with those you really care for.

You often demand rather than seek love, although it's always with a smile to cover your grim determination. And you'll stamp your foot in rage if it's not forthcoming. You're unlikely ever to pick a partner who can't give you a tender sexual relationship, though. You like the physical side of loving to be sensuous and romantic, and foreplay can be just as important to you as the actual act. Often the initial attraction will be your partner's status or earning power, although for reasons of security rather than greed.

You need familiar surroundings in which to make love and are most vulnerable to being seduced in your own cosy home, largely because you hate strange places. In fact, you can become so obsessed and worried trying to make every trivial detail just right that you often find you're simply too exhausted to make the most of your partner. Try not to take small criticisms to heart, either. Just because your partner tells you they don't like one aspect of sex play doesn't mean they don't like you.

Love relationships are investments as far as you're

concerned and you expect a return. You could pour all your energies and emotions into your private life than into your work, so your career may take second place. If you do decide to shine at work, it's usually in order to boost your standing in your lover's eyes.

Your loyalty to your partner is admirable and endures through thick and thin. You can stubbornly refuse to believe that they have any faults at all and will turn a blind eye to much that's wrong in a relationship – because you idealise partners so much.

You are horribly prone to jealousy and can't believe that the rest of the world doesn't fancy your partner as much as you do. You tend to misinterpret a situation and overreact to real or imagined infidelity, throwing your emotions into complete turmoil. Tone down your over-sensitive radar, for your own peace of mind, and try trusting partners instead of constantly double-checking whether every word of love sounds as if it comes straight from the heart.

Once you feel relaxed with someone, they can safely unburden themselves emotionally to you. You'll do everything in your power to solve a partner's problems – it's how you make yourself so indispensable. Your greatest weakness is your inability to recognise change and see when a relationship has moved on. You'd rather keep your blinkers on. Beware, too, of being greedy, both emotionally and sexually.

No-one is more impressed by money than you, but a cash-rich relationship can quickly become love-poor unless you learn to stop spoiling partners with gifts you can ill afford and they probably don't want. Money really can't buy the sort of secure and faithful love you need.

The value you put on love is huge, but be wary of making it so precious that when your partner fails you in some way, your whole world falls apart. You're basically a lover, not a warrior, but there are times when you'll have to fight. Don't be afraid to stand by your views and get your message across, even if it does cause the odd argument. Your great appetite for food will mean that keeping slim is going to be another battle for you, but if you want to stay feeling attractive, you'll have to get down to more of the exercise you dislike.

Most of all, please be easy on yourself. A lover will rarely leave you, because no-one knows how to please better than you. And even when you're far apart, your lover will still feel the warmth of your love. That's how powerful you are.

Venus in Gemini

HOW YOU LET LOVE IN

You are so popular, so sociable, that you can find it hard to settle down in a one-to-one relationship. And any relationship you do commit to, however exciting the lovemaking is, will also have a large element of brother–sister friendship about it. It's not that you don't like affection, but that you value good conversation even more. Like minds will always attract you and go on exerting their pull for years, while merely physical relationships will soon fizzle out.

One factor that hinders permanence in your lovelife is your sometimes shallow emotional ability to take other people's feelings seriously enough. You're not one for deep emotional involvement yourself, and you can't understand that not everyone is as delightfully casual about love as you are. You like lovers who retreat from you because it adds to the fun and keeps life interesting. You find it easy to love two or even three people simultaneously. Light, warm, extremely friendly and always eager to renew an acquaintance, you're hard to pin down.

Your major strength is your ability to bounce back from emotional disaster. Your heart mends speedily and you either find yourself a replacement from your vast network or you divert your sorrows by spending time with friends. You're good at soothing others' heartache, too, even though you're not as good a listener as you might be.

Your craving for variety in all things spills into your lovelife, making it very difficult for you to settle on one partner. Any lover has to be as adaptable as you and possess a personality as colourfully chameleon-like as your own to hold your interest. And once the flame of sexual desire has died in a relationship, it can never be rekindled for you. You will be turned off that person, physically, for life.

However, on an intellectual level, you can happily carry on communications with old flames indefinitely. You should try to be understanding if your present partner finds this disturbing, though, because they could be suffering unnecessary pangs of jealousy.

Mental stimulation is even more important to you than an active sex life. Put the two together and your lovelife looks set to last. But even if the physical side falls short of your ideal, you can make a go of it provided you have built up a natural, mutual understanding and still enjoy talking together.

New lovers will quickly spot that you enjoy talking about love and there's a danger that you'll be all words and no action. But verbal foreplay is as vital to you as the air you breathe, and strong, silent types or those who fail to match your intelligence won't last five minutes with you.

YOUR LOVE PATH

Sexually attractive and incredibly imaginative, you've got a lot going for you. But there's a big lesson you have to learn, and that's how to stay in love with just one person.

You've lots of personality and natural sparkle and easily set lovers alight. But although you excite them, you are also capable of shocking them with your behaviour and, worse still, not even realising the chaos you're causing. You can be cruel in your carelessness, refusing to let deep love develop. You're the classic lover and leaver, smart enough to be able to act the innocent and pretend to be bewildered by the jealous storms you whip up.

Your emotions tell you that if only you could find your true love match, you'd be faithful and caring. Well, you can look in the mirror to find your ideal partner, or go for the kind of soul mate who attracts you because they're every bit as bright, breezy and bold as you are. Then you can sit back and wait for the clash. This would be not so much a meeting of minds and a melting of bodies as a monstrous mistake. Constantly vying with one another in the popularity stakes, you'd talk each other to death and never be serious long enough to cement your relationship.

You need someone far more understanding, serious-minded and mature than you are. They have to tolerate being put on hold while you jettison a romantic evening with them in favour of a party full of strangers. You reckon there's plenty of time for intimacy with your special lover after you've had your fill of fun.

Whimsical and skittish, you can be so unreliable and irresponsible. Partners must get used to being let down, and be secure enough to realise that you still care for them. It's all or nothing with you, and every chance you get you'll unburden your most detailed thoughts at length on your partner. You also love a good gossip and your passion for intrigue and low boredom threshold mean you enjoy being a stirrer. It goes without saying that there's a childish side to your character, but this is precisely what keeps your relationships young and fresh.

If you relax long enough to look at your life, you'll realise that there's an empty space deep down in your flighty soul, aching to be filled. Bring more emotional satisfaction into your relationship by spending more time with your partner, showing them appreciation and thinking more about them than yourself. Terms of endearment don't come easily for you, and you need to listen to your head less and your heart more. Practise those tender phrases that will help make your partner feel more secure and loved, but don't overdo it.

The plus side to not pinning your heart to your sleeve is that you can be emotionally objective and sort out your love-life with the detachment of a professional counsellor, weighing up issues and characters wisely. Solutions to any problems will come to you with great clarity, and co-operating with others is second nature to you. You'll find yourself involved in all aspects of your lover's life, from their family to their job and, while you never find this a burden, you'll probably wonder if they are taking your advice seriously enough. That's because you can come over as gossipy and lightweight unless you are careful. It takes you time to tune yourself into serious matters and produce the right sort of response.

The way to seduce you is through your mind. You want to talk before, during and after sex and the more clever the conversation, the better the loving will be. Any lover will have to be prepared to talk frankly about sex with you and to be as honest about their past as you are prepared to be about yours.

You have a fascination with lips and, whenever you speak to someone, you tend to focus on their mouth rather than their eyes. You're naturally good at kissing, preferring to use your mouth on your lover's body rather than your hands. Any partner will have to avoid becoming too routine in approach. Repetition is the surest way of sending you in search of a more exciting bedmate.

You can be faithful and true, but you'll need an unusually cooperative partner. First, you'll have to establish with them that you must have complete freedom, no matter how wayward they fear you'll be. Let your partner know that, in return for keeping pace with your different moods and personality changes, there will be a stimulating and lively relationship. Never allow yourself to be influenced by others, and don't listen to idle gossip, especially if it involves your partner.

When you think you've found the love of your life, give them more of yourself than you would to others. The rewards will be worth it.

Venus in Cancer

HOW YOU LET LOVE IN

You let love into your life through a thousand different doors because you are such an instinctive lover and you live for love. At times, you are a positive slave to your heart and make, perhaps, too many sacrifices for those you care about.

You are a dreamer, vulnerable to be being fooled by anyone who fits your fantasies and, once you fall in love, you don't ever want to let go.

You are an emotional mood-swinger, sweet and tender one minute, irritable and demanding the next. Sometimes you want to lavish loved-ones with affection and fuss over them; at other times, you worry so much about being rejected that you can hardly bear to talk to anyone.

Any lover gets a complex package of deep emotions when they take up with you. But they also get a bedmate with the ability to communicate without words, one who can speedily discover a lover's sensitivities without being told.

Best of all, you like a partner who really needs you. And though you are normally rather shy, you'll soon zoom in on someone who looks as if they need a good, square meal and plenty of love and affection. Beware of charming con artists, for you're far from streetwise and often have problems sifting the good from the bad when choosing lovers. And you can be hurt, since you usually give far more emotionally than any partner in close relationships, believing it's better to give than to receive.

Given the green light, you can't wait to move in with your partner and, since you always create a happy home atmosphere, few lovers object. If you have a major emotional weakness, it's taking on hopeless lame ducks and trying to reform the impossible. Your friends will worry about you until they realise what fulfilment you find in some of these odd relationships.

Although you're as old-fashioned and romantic as it's possible to be, you don't want a love that is trouble-free. The meaner and moodier your mate, the more magnificent a lover they are in your eyes. It gives you more scope to lavish lots of tender loving care and attempt the kind of complete personality makeover you delight in.

You're great fun to live with and your changing moods keep monotony at bay. You'll be mother hen one day (whichever your sex), cool and distant the next, injecting all your roles with the maximum amount of high drama – especially if you can enjoy a good cry or sulk into the bargain.

YOUR LOVE PATH

The emotional bonds you form with people are very strong, whether it's friends and lovers or family and workmates. You are devoted to your closest relationships and they mean absolutely everything to you. Home is definitely where your heart resides and you blossom in familiar surroundings, alongside familiar faces.

You crave security more than most signs and long for the perfect love match. Your ideal partner will be so closely in tune with you that you will share an almost telepathic, highly intuitive relationship. Once you've entered an affair, you give your all – and expect everything in return. Your heart is huge and you're one of nature's carers, an eager listener and an enthusiastic problem-solver.

With Venus being the planet of attraction, you will always end up with a harmonious home, a secure way of life and a caring partner. You are unlikely to forge ahead in your career because you're too home- and family-centred to develop the kind of stay-late, workaholic lifestyle that will shoot you to the top. You feel that your real job of work is your partner and any children you may have. And even if all you come home to is a goldfish, you'll still rush back at the end of your working day to feed it and have a chat, with compliments.

Both sexes with this planet placing crave emotional commitment. The men are old-fashioned and like to choose the ring themselves and get down on one knee to propose. The women won't settle for living with someone when marriage is an option. Both sexes need to share an almost overwhelming intimacy with their chosen mate. You'll have your own private jokes that only the two of you understand, and you'll almost delight in seeing others feeling left out.

Yet you are also a loyal friend who'll never give away a secret, especially one confided by a lover. That's one of the reasons why you are so popular. When you make a promise, you always keep it. When you say you love someone, you mean it, and when you pledge to stay with them forever, they know they can believe it.

Because love makes your inner world revolve, do be prepared to experience every emotion in the book. You'll have to take the rough with the smooth and you won't be able to sidestep hurtful, damaging feelings. Probably the only sentiment you'll never experience is hatred. Your heart is too warm to ice over with such a steel-cold emotion.

You are very gentle with everyone you know, but watch out that you don't allow timidity to keep you quiet when you should be standing up for your rights. Don't ever let yourself become a doormat, even though the one thing you do hate is hurting people's feelings.

Nurturing is second nature to you and you'll take your emotional cue from your partner. If they've had a setback, you'll make sure they are treated with kid gloves. If they're on cloud nine, you'll expect everyone to be as happy as they are. You are even capable of telling your partner that you love them after your feelings have died, just because you don't want them to be hurt. It's rarely you who leaves a relationship, and you are protective to the very end.

Foolishly, you often doubt your attractiveness. That's all part of your shyness and faltering confidence. In fact, you have so many desirable qualities and put so much into your relationships that you deserve the very best in return. Don't feel guilty about demanding it.

You'll also go out of your way to avoid widening your world, especially if it means going somewhere unfamiliar and a little threatening and meeting new faces. Try to remember that each of your close friends was a stranger once, and push yourself to be more socially adventurous.

Try to be more relaxed about sharing your lover's company in public, too. You can feel so obsessively jealous about them that, shyness or no, you'll barge right in to push someone out if you fear they've got too close. Luckily, once your relationship is well established, you become more relaxed and less smothering.

When you have built up a relationship that gives you security, you lose your shyness during lovemaking. Cool shades of green and silver, as well as water, are powerful turn-ons for you, so seaside holidays and bathtimes offer potential chances to seal your mutual affection.

You don't mind discussing your most intimate feelings, but where sexual technique is concerned you'd rather let your actions do the talking. Above all, you hate innuendo and double meanings. Your loving doesn't lack warmth and passion, but it's an intensely private affair for you.

Smothering and mothering could be your only downfalls in relationships. You'll have to stop fighting your partner's battles for them, and realise how belittling your caring can be. And don't buy so many things for your shared home together without consulting your partner first, even if you don't trust their taste.

Sometimes, you can be so concerned about the quantity of loving you are getting that you overlook the quality. But please don't short-change yourself. Realise, too, that if you put every last ounce of energy and interest into your home and family, you could be left with an empty shell in years to come, with no real interests of your own. Strive for a healthier emotional balance and please find more room in your oversized heart for yourself.

Venus in Leo

HOW YOU LET LOVE IN

Bursting with passionate Leo emotion, you put an enormous amount of energy into pursuing love and, like everything else, you tend to overdo things once you do become romantically involved. You are searching for the ideal partner, someone you can look up to, even if you'll try to boss them about once you've put them on that pedestal. And if your idea of perfection happens to be already involved with someone else, you know that you'll have no trouble wooing them away. Not that you'd be so confident if the boot was on the other foot – then pride would be your overriding emotion and you'd probably convince yourself that they weren't worth the effort anyway.

You dream of a grand, old-fashioned, perfect love and it's not surprising that modern affairs can be a disappointment to you. You tend to blow up small signals of affection into grand passions and fan minor disagreements into major scenes. And if you can't call the shots and take complete control of an affair, then you don't want to play at all.

Yet you can be a huge-hearted and romantic lover, forever buying extravagant gifts and thinking up exciting ways to please your partner. It's just that when you're feeling thwarted, misunderstood or just plain unappreciated, you'll revert to the actions of a spoiled child, prepared to try anything, from sulking to outright emotional blackmail, to get your own way.

You just have to be boss in any relationship and your ideal match will be the person who always lets you think you're in charge – whether or not you are. You'll never spot the difference because, in certain emotional matters, you are delightfully naive.

When it comes to attention, you lap it up. But although you love being waited on, you get as much pleasure from lavishing loving attention on someone else. Even when you're comfortably settled in a relationship, you'll look for any excuse to treat your partner to a big night out. Not for you the quiet table tucked away in the corner, either. You want to be under the bright lights and, with this planetary placing, it's quite likely you are well known anyway.

YOUR LOVE PATH

Emotionally, you're very healthy and this is reflected in your successful relationships with others. Of all the Venus variations, yours is amongst the most likely to stay loyal and loving in a partnership.

People are drawn to your brand of proud strength and are eager to be your slave. But in some ways you are the slave to your own emotions and it's easy for someone to break down the barriers of your heart and get you hooked.

Nothing is ever too romantic or sentimental as far as you're concerned, and a lover who sends you soppy, old-fashioned cards and who sits sobbing alongside you through a tear-jerker film is definitely your soul mate.

In return, you make that person feel truly treasured, protected by the lion's share of your love and sheltered from life's nastier aspects. You have a superb instinct for giving comfort and support to a partner in times of trouble. It's no wonder you gather admirers with ease. Being held in such high esteem never worries you a bit, and with your supreme self-confidence you feel quite at home being admired.

Anyone who falls for you has much more to gain than love. Whatever is in your power to bestow – money, social position, a fine home or a new circle of friends – you'll want to give it to your lover.

You're good fun to be with, a great storyteller and an

entertaining raconteur of jokes. One of the main reasons why lovers find you uplifting and relaxing is because your innate sense of emotional self-preservation means you're never dragged down by a partner's low moods. 'Onwards and upwards' is your motto, and such positive energy and optimism rubs off.

The minus side is your desperate desire to always keep the upper hand in any relationship. Deep down, you are insecure and worry that you're not actually as caring and lovable as others think you are. You fear that your expansive image might be shattered if someone gets too close and discovers the truth.

The one thing that terrifies you is rejection, although you'll never admit it. If your lover goes away for a while, or appears preoccupied, you go to pieces emotionally. Any casual coolness on their part will create a wound in your heart which is difficult to heal. Lovers soon learn that it takes more than a kiss to make up with you.

You also expect a lover to have a never-ending supply of loving for you, even if your own supply has begun to dwindle. You can stay in a relationship when your love has ceased because you can't bear to be without someone. You'll also stay for appearances' sake, too, especially if you make a 'handsome couple'. You have a tendency to boast and exaggerate your standing in the love stakes – in your view, you were the love of every ex-lover's life and they're all pining away without you!

Most of the time, your lovelife is like a dramatic play with lots of action, passion and excitement, plenty of highs and lows. Your feelings are never neutral – you either love or hate. You'll carefully conceal any pain in the immediate aftermath of a break-up but, once hurt by someone you care for, you'll never, ever forgive them.

Your completely unforgiving nature has meant the end of many relationships in the past. But although you pride yourself on your own unflagging loyalty, you often stray in your imagination, although you don't think this counts. Your vanity – something else you won't admit to – actually helps your lovelife by ensuring you take as much care over your performance in bed as you do over your appearance in the mirror. You like to adapt yourself thoroughly to any partner's needs and wants, but you'd have to see true love shining in their eyes for the encounter to be perfect.

Those born with Venus in Leo are the undisputed lions of the love kingdom, and it's when you start to lord it over your lover that problems can begin. Naturally superior, you don't even notice when you're drowning your partner out. So if you want to keep your home life sweet, learn to let your partner have their say, share responsibilities and take a vote on joint decisions more often.

You hate the outside world to see you snarl and roar, but you'll do it in private. Usually the reason is a social gaffe on your partner's part. The worst crime they can commit is to show you up in front of other people, for you worry terribly about appearances. Try calming techniques like yoga or meditation to temper your rage. You should also try to curb your obsessions about your body. You worry particularly about your hair, constantly fussing and seeking new ways of styling it, which can be very boring for others. Be careful, too, not to undermine a partner's confidence when you turn your critical eye on their personal style.

It's hard to be a leader all the time, and you should try to step down now and again. Perhaps you are afraid to show your partner that you're as vulnerable as they are. If you did, they would love and respect you even more.

Venus in Virgo

HOW YOU LET LOVE IN

You need a happy lovelife for the sake of your emotional health. Without it, your feelings go into a decline and you become obsessed with tidiness and trivia. You're an exacting lover with very definite likes and dislikes. For a start, you want sex to be a squeaky-clean affair, with a lover who smells nice, bathes often and has a body that looks trim and fit. You can't stand dirt, mess and too much raw physicality. Yet no matter how neat your partner looks, you still have the urge to give them a complete makeover. It's all part of your critical nature.

You enjoy – and need – all the ritual and trappings of a traditional courtship and cannot bear to be rushed into making love if your heart is still undecided. Your deepest romantic emotions will only bloom in a setting of good taste and delicacy.

Your approach can keep love at arm's length, and in some ways that's just where you want it. You often fall for people who are primarily wedded to their work or who can't give their whole heart for some reason. This often suits you because you couldn't bear to have a partner under your feet all the time, getting in the way.

The world sees you as prim and a bit buttoned-up. Little do they know how much you fantasise about being overwhelmed by a passionate lover. Secretly, you half dread, half long for someone to muss up your hair and ruffle your strict business suit.

You fuss over lovers and love doing so, even if they would

rather be left alone. It's not surprising, then, that sometimes you can make new partners nervous and ill at ease. It's your odd combination of cosy cushion-plumping and calculating gaze that does it. While you try to make their immediate surroundings homely and comfortable, you're coolly weighing them up for possible flaws.

You often judge a would-be romance far too fast and the first five minutes of an encounter can be make or break time for you. Your memory for past affairs is elephantine and you pick over the bones of both past and present loves with great dedication. You are so picky that you go for long spells without any love interest and it can take you ages to find an ideal mate and marry.

You need a lover who is strong yet tolerant. Learn to curb your criticism and give potential lovers a chance. Somewhere out there is the perfect match for you.

YOUR LOVE PATH

Before you can really get the most out of your lovelife, you will probably have to overcome some inhibitions about sex and cultivate a more relaxed approach.

You may have to begin by lowering your standards. You've such a lofty view of love – your lover has to be immaculate and must never put a foot wrong – that even minor setbacks and disappointments are bound to knock you for six.

You tend to draw up a mental shopping list of qualities before you've even met someone. Top of the list is a moral and beautiful soul. You peer into the depths of prospective partners, picking up their good and bad character points. The trouble is, you are so put off by failings that your crusade for a life partner can take practically a lifetime.

Once someone has passed your first love test, you send out subtle signals. A gentle hand on their arm, a lingering gaze or a warm smile. Your courtships can go on and on, largely because you want to build an almost encyclopaedic knowledge of your potential partner well before you commit yourself.

Because you are so intelligent and level-headed yourself, it's rare that you'll form a relationship with someone who you think is not up to your intellectual standard. That's why you so often meet your mate at work, where you've had ample time to explore their background, assess their personality and judge their intelligence. There's no risk involved, either, as you can always pass off your interest as that of a friendly colleague. Your partner must have a firm sense of integrity and you'll often end up with someone who has a high standing in society, perhaps a lawyer or a doctor.

Honesty is vital in your relationship, as is fidelity. Yet if you do waver in a relationship and temporarily set aside your high morals, you can go off the rails in a really big way, lying and cheating on your partner. Although such a lapse will shock you both, it does at least make you seem more human and less saintly.

Shyness means that you often find it almost impossible to make the first move in forming a relationship, even when the other person has made it plain that they would welcome your advances. You may agonise and long for a particular person for ages and sometimes risk losing them through such hesitation.

When you do take a chance on someone, you usually find it quite hard to adapt to their ways. You want your domestic life to be uneventful and routine. If Friday night is when you usually go to an evening class, you won't thank your partner for deciding on a romantic, spur-of-the-moment dinner instead. You don't even like nice surprises from your lover. Your life direction is straight ahead, with few stops along the way. At least you are no fool about love and are rarely thrown when life has settled into a comfortable pattern.

Ritual is important to you, even in bed. You like to make elaborate preparations, often ensuring you look as well groomed undressed as you do dressed. You positively relish repetition, using the same tried-and-tested positions with your partner time and time again.

You are an unselfish lover, dedicated to giving pleasure,

although you are quite happy for your partner to take over sometimes. You tend to have a store of well-worked-out, elaborate fantasies that keep your spirits up during your lone periods of celibacy.

You do like to talk about making love before you actually start, but only with a trusted partner. The longer you know someone, the more easy you find it to shed your outer armour of inhibitions.

Long term, you have all the right qualities to stay the course in a love affair. With this planet placing, yours is a caring heart combined with a thoughtful nature. And once you've finally found a mate who's good enough for you, you have a fund of passion to fuel your physical relationship.

Your biggest problem remains your endless quest for perfection. Try to be less disappointed when you first discover your partner's inadequacies. No human being is devoid of them, after all.

Curb the carping if you don't want to lose every lover you have. There's no fun being left with just a long list of their faults to chew over with your friends. You have a natural tendency to nag and to worry at something like a terrier with a bone. You think this will get everything out in the open and force others to face up to the error of their ways, but even the most long-suffering partner will eventually respond badly to such tactics. Ask anyone who's ever loved – and left – a Venus in Virgo and they'll say they felt they could never measure up to their lover's high standards, or that the constant fault-finding drove them away.

Remember, too, that while you are conscientious about your job and believe in devoting time to your employer, it's not easy to maintain a loving relationship if you aren't around, especially if your partner takes their job less seriously. Be kinder on yourself when trying to juggle so many aspects of your life to perfection. No-one expects you to fulfil all your obligations all of the time.

You may take a long while to unearth a kindred spirit, but it will be worth the wait – for both of you.

Venus in Libra

HOW YOU LET LOVE IN

The influence of Venus is so strong in your case that you are often seduced by the mere idea of being in love. You have no problems falling head over heels for someone and letting the whole world know how you feel. The trouble is, you can end up with a partner who you are merely fond of, rather than madly in love with. You can like the idea of being in a partnership so much that you grab the first offer that comes along with scarcely a second thought.

When Venus in Libra is your emotions-ruler, you usually can't fulfil your potential in life unless you do have a partner. You would hate to go to see a film on your own, take a trip or eat a meal in a restaurant alone. Often, you snatch the most expedient option on offer and play at being in love, because even an unsatisfying relationship is better than none at all.

It's not as though you are stuck for choice. You are sociable and popular and spoil your lovers rotten. This is because you tend to see people as more attractive than they really are. No small favour is too tedious for you, no sorry saga too long for you to listen to sympathetically. You are usually your lover's best friend.

You need to pamper and cosset, groom and cultivate everyone. But, surprisingly, those who get close to you often end up thinking you are cold. It could be because you lavish exactly the same degree of affection on everyone, which makes it seem rather calculated. Or perhaps because they realise that you are really rather cerebral, and not as emotional as you first appear. You may live in your lover's pocket, eagerly sharing every second of their life, but you could probably behave exactly the same with any one of a number of others.

Your love dreams are heightened by a desire for luxury and expensive surroundings. Coupled with a natural streak of indolence, this can lead to a marriage of convenience and, despite your protestations, you are just as likely to end up with a poor partner as you are to stay single. Maybe less likely.

For you, love will soon fade unless your partner can offer or contribute to a good lifestyle. Even when you do realise that a relationship is emotionally barren and based more on politeness than passion, you rarely quit. You so hate confrontation that you'd rather grit your teeth and soldier on, gradually and diplomatically substituting hobbies for the physical side of your relationship.

You may want an easy life with your lover, but you could end up working very hard for it.

YOUR LOVE PATH

You have a highly idealised notion of what love is all about, and you aim at finding the perfect relationship as young as possible. You probably can't even remember a time when you weren't in love. Pretty soon you found you couldn't exist without the thrill of this heady emotion and you were hooked. But there was and always will be one pre-condition for you. Any potential partner must look pleasing, for you hate anything or anyone ugly.

You are certainly not a hunter, but you position yourself very carefully to ensure that you are caught. You've a strong eye for beauty and an impeccable sense of style, so this part of the courtship isn't hard for you. Wrappings are what count with you and, as long as your suitor has looks and charm, your affair usually gets off to a flying start. It's only later, when you begin to discover the real person behind the image, that problems can arise. This is often when you decide to bail out and begin all over again with someone new, just to experience those first heady moments yet again. You always attract admirers and it gives you a natural halo of self-confidence that boosts your appeal.

You can make each lover truly believe that they are the love of your life. And even if you know it won't last, it doesn't stop you keeping the charm flowing. You don't waste your time and effort on someone who obviously wouldn't be prepared to try and woo you back, though.

You don't nurse a grudge for years when things go wrong. Even if you part from someone with initial bitterness, you still enjoy an easy friendship with many former lovers.

You need to share all your feelings, including any doubts, with your lover. If they open their heart to you in the same way, you fall even more deeply in love with them.

You usually mould yourself smoothly to your partner, adopting their interests – anything to bring you even closer. One of your greatest assets is an excellent memory, and your ability to remember birthdays, anniversaries and other significant occasions creates a great impression. Keeping up with your tastes can be expensive and you yearn for long-term financial security. Unless you marry a millionaire, you'll never quite satisfy this desire, but take comfort from the fact that, although you may let money slip through your fingers, you will always have a rich lovelife and be able to charm the world well into old age.

You are scrupulously fair in your dealings with everyone. If anything, you are so fair and honest that you can be too harsh on yourself. You are also hopeless at hiding your feelings, much as you wish this wasn't the case. They are so near the surface that you are usually an open book, not only to your lover but to everyone else, too. However, on occasion, your charm can be a cover for your real feelings and you are brilliant at disguising the fact that you haven't taken to someone.

Rarely do you have a shouting match, for it would upset

the balance of your world too much. You far prefer a quiet chat that airs all aspects of an argument, followed by a compromise solution.

You are often labelled vain and you do feel unhappy when you know that you're not looking your best. On an 'off' day, you prefer to hide away, even from your lover.

Although you usually lend a sympathetic ear to their woes, partners can't always count on you when really serious problems arise. You protect your own emotions and hesitate to expose them to risk. You are also frequently unsettled, never quite satisfied with the way things are, although you are too lazy to make major changes in your life.

You will only find happiness with someone who is gentle, fair-minded and fun, but who has a bit more caution and far-sightedness than you. You may fling yourself into intense, physical relationships as soon as you reckon you're in love, but ultimately you want to settle down and, despite your chequered love past, you want a conventionally romantic marriage. Although you'll never stop flirting, you can be faithful.

The biggest obstacle to long-term bliss is your inability to face up to problems when they arise. You tend to slide everything under the carpet. You must confront conflicts between you and your partner if your love is to survive and grow. That's the only way to keep the balance you need in your life – to upset the apple cart once in a while and restack it afresh.

You do have an extraordinary talent for understanding people even if you can't always tolerate their weaknesses. You should also learn to accept that life will always throw the odd spanner your way and that, just because your love-life has been damaged temporarily, it has not necessarily been dealt a death blow.

Because you get and give love so easily, you can also abuse your lover's affections, testing their loyalty and teasing them with pretend affairs. If you want your luck to last, banish this tricky behaviour forever.

Venus in Scorpio

HOW YOU LET LOVE IN

Your emotions run at two very different speeds. One produces a slow semi-detachment from other people, but the second launches your feelings with a burst of passion that takes you right over the top. For you, love usually takes the form of obsession, although you can easily endure long spells between affairs by involving yourself intensely in your work and friendships. You can also satisfy your considerable sex drive through liaisons that are chiefly physical while you put your emotions on hold.

When you do fall in love, you need to take over your lover totally. As a first step, you try to find out all you can about them and you would happily hire a team of private detectives if you could afford it. The trouble with this over-zealous delving, especially into their past affairs, is that it often unleashes almost unbearable jealousy in you. You should try to satisfy your need to know with the facts your lover supplies voluntarily.

What you long to find, above all else, is depth in a person. Yet when you do discover what you want, you can find it hard to give unstinting devotion to your partner. You can be extremely moody – icy cold and dismissive one moment, boiling over with passion the next. You are afraid to lose control of your emotions because you know how very powerful they are, and you hate to feel that another has sway over your heart.

Your interest in secrets may also lead you down a path that diverts you from long-term happiness. Because you are loyal to the core and can keep a secret, you can easily become someone's secret lover, for whatever reason. It's a role you relish, at first. But it ultimately pushes you into the background and never allows you to make decisions or enjoy a full, open relationship.

Sometimes you are drawn to people with emotional problems or mental quirks. Certainly, you never judge by appearances alone, nor do you make your mind up about someone until you've seen them several times – and grilled them thoroughly. Sex is vital to any close relationship you experience and it should be intense and frequent.

You take romance very seriously and go all out when you want to woo a new lover. However, your pride can hinder your feelings. You're not much of a flirt, for instance, and can take a jokey approach quite the wrong way. If you're jilted, you won't rest until you've had your revenge. You can sever your tie with a straying lover with staggering abruptness, and you will erase their name from your heart, and engrave it onto your hate list.

YOUR LOVE PATH

Your loving is so powerful and potent that it can take a partner's breath away. Your affairs begin slowly and softly, like a piece of classical music, but they soon build to a crashing crescendo.

Since you do nothing by halves, you either loathe people or are completely crazy about them. When you fall madly in love, you like to take risks. You won't pick anyone safe – that's far too boring. You go for an extreme personality, either a total extrovert or a complete introvert. If a potential relationship looks set for a stormy course, then that's the one for you.

You are notoriously power-hungry and you express your passion for power through sex. You seek to dominate your partner through your physical relationship, although you won't be happy unless they retaliate. A perpetual power struggle keeps sparkle in a relationship, as long as you always retain a slight psychological edge over your partner. This edge gives you the ability to walk alone if necessary.

You've one of the strongest characters in the zodiac and you can handle most of what life throws at you with calm, clinical efficiency. Coupledom isn't the only way of life for you and you don't need to be half of a constant pair.

You have a reputation as a seducer and you rarely make a false move, accurately assessing those lovers who will be putty in your hands. You seem to have a sixth sense about which relationships will work, a skill that you can also use for your friends' romances. Few realise what emotional turmoil seethes inside your heart. And you'd have it no other way – it's so exciting.

When you do find a suitable match, you certainly don't want to settle down to a quiet life. You'll enjoy sparking off blazing rows over nothing, just for the emotional thrill of it. You enjoy pushing your partner to the limits, then passionately making up. Sometimes, they can't stand the emotion and upheaval and leave. That's when their problems really start because, with your own strong emotions, if they walk out on you, you feel as if you've lost a limb and the only cure for you is revenge. If you can't release the poison inside by slurring your ex-lover's reputation, phoning them at odd hours of the night and generally causing them distress, then you can sink into a deep depression. Yet, considering that you'll stoop to almost any depths to get even, you always retain your dignity, usually by keeping your outrageous behaviour a secret.

You can keep others' secrets as well as your own, and you expect the same from your partner. If they ever divulged details of your shared lovelife, it would probably damage your relationship fatally.

Venus in Scorpio makes you magnetic and attractive to others. But because you so value total intimacy and loyalty, you can resist the temptation to be unfaithful if you are completely committed to your partner.

This won't stop you suspiciously checking for signs of

disloyalty from them. You can tolerate their flirting with others, though, provided that you know it's an act. You can even put up with them being more popular than you or in a better job. What you can't take is ridicule and any lover who pokes fun at you in public will suffer for it.

Fighting and loving are closely connected for you. Your perfect night of passion usually starts with a blazing row. You like to generate an air of danger and uncertainty because, once it has been dispelled by apologies and then laughter, you know that your longing for each other will have been heightened.

Deeply sensual and seemingly tireless, you are at your most tender in the afterglow of sex. Partners can be quite surprised at this thoughtful, gentle side of you.

Ideally, you like to be the one doing the seducing and you feel uncomfortable when someone makes an obvious play for you because it upsets your notions of power balance. Partners find you such an intriguing, magnetic package that they rarely have the strength to leave you, no matter how much of a roller coaster ride you give their feelings. It's you who needs to come to terms with your habit of ending relationships abruptly and angrily on the spur of the moment.

Even when you regret having shown your lover the door rather hastily, your pride is too powerful for you to admit your mistake. You should let partners into the deepest recesses of your heart more often if you want to avoid the sudden deaths of relationships. Let your lover know what you yearn for, and together you may achieve your desires.

There is a line that you draw in all your relationships and once it's been crossed you seem to think there's no going back. But often you don't bother to show your partner where that line is, so they have no idea they've crossed a forbidden boundary. Try to be more forgiving and allow them one foot over sometimes.

There are other ways of keeping your lovelife exciting than engineering fiery arguments and steamy reconciliations. They merely try your lover's patience and become less and less effective as time goes by.

You need to channel your emotional energies away from such self-destructive behaviour, preferably into some physically exhausting sport. And don't be afraid to occasionally give just that bit more than your 50 per cent share to a relationship if you want to keep a perfect balance in the end.

Venus in Sagittarius

HOW YOU LET LOVE IN

Enthusiastic, bounding with energy and full of warm feelings, you don't have the slightest problem in communicating these to your lover. But anyone with this Venus placing is also very independent so you may not want to be too closely tied to just one person. You won't necessarily two-time your partner with another lover, but you'll always have one or more close friends who take up as much of your time as your partner does. Despite your own fear of being emotionally committed to one person, you still enjoy love and view it as one of the most exciting adventures that life has to offer.

Reckless and rather aggressive, you fling yourself into love with the same enthusiasm that you would a risky sport. In fact, you think having an affair is a great game and something to be enjoyed. You find it hard to take life too seriously so, even when your heart is being put through some tough paces, you can always see the bright side and no moment is too passionate to inspire a joke. But tenderness is never far from your clowning.

You relish surprises, like falling head over heels for the most unlikely person you know. You are attracted to bright, original people – real one-offs – and your flirty, outgoing personality ensures that you have no trouble attracting lovers.

Now and then you can sabotage a budding romance with your wounding honesty and your inability to pick the best time to speak out. Some of this tactlessness is not accidental. It's probably the only way you know of giving yourself a bit more elbow-room once you begin to feel you're emotionally hemmed in.

You often begin a love affair starry-eyed and over keen, with an impossibly idealised vision of how your lover should behave. Once you spot flaws, you cannot help but be frank, which may be fine when you're talking about your own feelings but can be very wounding when turned on a partner. Generally, you are an unsubtle soul who misses the finer shades of others' emotions.

You always seek a further dimension in your affairs. Sexual passion alone won't do and neither will merely having fun together. You want a lover who can teach you more about life. Although you come across as more of a good friend than a passionate partner, you are more easily hurt than your cheerful manner might suggest. Fair-minded to a fault, you suffer your greatest love setbacks when someone else behaves unfairly. You can't understand how anyone can be playing to a completely different set of rules, especially when you've put your trust in them.

If a romance founders, you are the noblest of leave-takers. You always allow the other party to keep face, and despite your easy-come, easy-go manner, you give far more than you ever take.

YOUR LOVE PATH

Fresh, fun and physical, an affair with you is fiercely unforgettable and you make sure you pack as much living as you can into everything you do. Your strong sense of fantasy and light-hearted nature ensure that your approach to love will never be very practical. You'd never do anything as safe and ordinary as falling for the boy or girl next door, for instance.

An attractive foreigner scores 10 in your love ratings, and if your lover isn't naturally exotic then chances are they will have travelled widely. Another must is a healthy, athletic body. You won't give a second glance to someone who looks as if they spend hours slumped in front of the television set or who has obviously never played any kind of sport, preferably one that's physically risky and exhilarating.

Whoever you fall for, they'll never manage to totally tie you down. You're too easy-going to show signs of itchy feet by engineering rows or sulking. You're more likely to do something obvious like book yourself a long holiday – alone.

Partners may accuse you of being selfish and only chasing your own dreams. You're perfectly happy to chase others, providing they look exciting enough. In some ways, you are a Peter Pan who's never fully matured, but this won't cause problems in relationships as long as you pick emotionally young-at-heart lovers.

You'll usually fall in love with a fun personality full of high spirits, and cheery extroverts will win over quiet, meaningful types every time. Your love path is bound to be long and extremely interesting, with some exciting detours. You'll make sure that you don't miss out on anything, so it's likely that you'll have many affairs.

Negative emotions don't surface often. Your solution to nastiness is simply to shrug your shoulders and walk away. You'll never stay and suffer in an unsatisfactory relationship, or make another's life miserable with your discontent. Trouble is, you find it hard to distinguish between a major problem and a minor one and you ought to be prepared to give lovers more second chances. You tend to shrug off responsibility whenever possible and when you do make promises to a partner you've usually got your fingers firmly crossed behind your back, just in case!

You're loyal and can be lastingly loving, but you also don't see why a broken promise or a casual fling should mean the end of your main relationship. You're also honest and will always admit to a transgression – if you're asked. Otherwise, you believe that what your partner doesn't know won't grieve them.

Beneath your flirty, flighty exterior, your thoughts run deep. Like your heart, your mind has a huge capacity, so a lover must provide mental stimulation to match their sexual prowess. You'll soon leave any lover who can't keep your busy brain entertained.

Lovers soon have to learn to share you. You collect friends from all walks of life, the way others collect ornaments. You'll always be the last to leave any get-together and your home is often full of visitors, too. Pity your partner when all they want to do is slam the door on the world and have you all to themselves!

Lovers may say that you're hard to please and certainly you have difficulties finding a flesh-and-blood partner who fits your idealised dreams of romance. You also expect unrealistically speedy emotional responses from others. Once your eye has settled on someone, you immediately want to know whether an affair with them is on the cards or not. It's no good wooing you with platitudes as you've a very keen nose – and a very cold shoulder – for anything that reeks of insincerity. And if someone doesn't fancy you, then you'd rather have the honest truth.

You are capable of making an emotional commitment, but you're likely to want to keep all your options open for as long as possible. And you sometimes view the addition of children to your relationship as more of a tie than a blessing!

You are proud of your good points and your achievements. Coupled with your sense of adventure, they rule out some of the not-so-noble reasons why many people settle down. You'd never need a lover to live through, to boost your ego or to act as emotional prop. Nor would you ever get caught for life in a relationship that you knew was purely physical.

It's a shame, though, that your sense of self-worth often strikes partners as big-headedness and that your carefree spirit can be seen as carelessness. You know that you can be tempted and succumb and still not alter your original loyalties, but few lovers are able to take infidelity as lightly as you.

Temptation will always be the biggest threat to your love

relationships. If you're serious about a cure, one solution is to take your partner with you whenever and wherever you can. Opportunity follows you around, probably because your wicked smile indicates that you're game for adventure. You'll either have to minimise your opportunities or settle for someone who never asks what you've been up to.

Make life easier for the person who's trying to share yours by setting yourself deadlines. Instead of shelving commitments indefinitely, tell your partner when you'll make a decision. You probably won't always fulfil all your promises, but at least they'll begin thinking of you as unpredictable rather than plain unreliable.

Take a more active interest in your partner's dreams, even if they're not as thrilling as your own. And instead of walking away from traumas, seek advice from those more experienced than you. It won't make you dull, merely help you to stay loved and lovable long term.

Venus in Capricorn

HOW YOU LET LOVE IN

Prudent, practical and pragmatic, you choose wisely in love. Not for you a romance that hurts or hinders, you're only interested in true love that can enrich your life. Unrequited passion, long-distance affairs and secret liaisons are not for you. And once you've given your heart, you're likely to stand firm as a rock for you truly believe in a 'till death us do part' relationship.

However, one major obstacle has to be surmounted before a loving relationship can be established. It is difficult for you to express your feelings and, until you overcome emotional inhibitions and are able to tell your lover exactly how much you feel for them, you won't get the best out of any relationship.

You may spend so much time studying or working to make your future as secure and financially rewarding as possible that dating takes a back seat. Then you suddenly realise that something is missing in your life and you logically and deliberately set about finding yourself a mate. Your sturdy emotions make you highly unlikely to be struck by the lightning bolt of love at first sight. You may choose a lover who is primarily a status symbol and, for that reason, not necessarily an ideal match. But you will rarely end up with an entirely unsuitable partner.

You see sex as rather naughty and you can be something of a connoisseur, with a range of fantasies to surprise your lover. You tend to divide your potential partners into the thrilling and outrageous who can never be introduced to family or friends, and the clean-cut, suitable type you want to be seen with. You feel emotionally secure with conventional people, preferably those with a sound bank balance and, in a really perfect world, an impeccable family tree.

You enjoy a formal courtship, especially if it involves writing letters. And for any affair to get off the ground, it is vital that you should first admire your lover from afar and feel a need to please and win them.

At first, you can appear chilly and tongue-tied, but the observant lover will realise that this is largely due to shyness. Once committed, few can match your loyalty and ability to stick with your partner through the kind of traumas, especially financial, that would mean the kiss of death to most relationships.

You respect those who like to be alone occasionally and can tolerate moodiness. But however much you love and respect someone, you won't want to feel solely responsible for them. You like a partner who can earn their own living, stand on their own feet in your absence, and perhaps even take over your business concerns if necessary. You value your lover as much for their usefulness as for their looks, and even there you go for healthiness rather than glamour. You always have one eye on the future, the other on your pension fund, and if some think you're unromantic, ask them again in 40 years' time. Yours is the kind of thoughtful, thought-out love that endures.

YOUR LOVE PATH

You may be very reserved and serious on the outside, but inside there's more passion, warmth and fun bubbling than people suspect. You are just waiting for the right person to release these feelings.

Cautious and careful even as a child, you will rarely plunge headlong into love without testing the water first. You realise better than most that you'll stand no chance of forming a loving, lasting relationship with anyone other than exactly your kind of person.

Your affairs can be slow at the start and you certainly don't rush from one stage to the next. You're the one person capable of keeping lust simmering.

You must have a mature relationship, a grown-up affair with a lover who's a real adult. You're attracted to those who have done well for themselves, brimming with confidence and successful in their field. And you won't hesitate to approach someone who appears, at first sight, to be above you in social standing or financial status. After all, you know that you're going places.

You are level-headed about love, but that doesn't mean that you can't still enjoy most of its excitements. First, though, you'll weigh up the good and bad points of a potential mate before deciding whether they're worth your commitment. And if they're not, you'll tell them straight, for you don't keep lovers dangling.

You aren't afraid of settling down, although you may not do so for some years. And when you feel that conditions are right, you can be as romantic as the next person, making the tenderest gestures and showing surprising generosity. You won't make a public fuss about it, though. Neither do you go in for a lover who's all show. Your emotions are strong and true and are kept safely locked away in your heart. Only you know the combination and that's a secret you'll share with only a privileged few throughout your life.

You're not particularly demonstrative and don't use body language to flirt, but you can't help liking people who are more physical than you. When a partner needs love words you may hesitate because, so often, words don't come out as you've intended. Usually, you'll only whisper words of love when you're in the mood. You should aim for a little-and-often approach if you want to keep lovers sweet.

Loyalty is your shining quality. Partners know that they can trust you and that you'll always safeguard their interests with a fierce, caring sense of responsibility.

Above all, you need stability. This can mean that you stay in a relationship that's gone cold and stale and it takes a near-earthquake for you to break out of a rut once you've set your course. Any emotional break takes its toll on your normally excellent health and is usually revealed only when your valued work begins to suffer through relationship problems.

You avoid money minefields and rarely get into financial difficulties. Wisely, you usually make it one of the conditions of your partnership with a lover that you hold the purse strings.

For the most part, your life and loves are played out according to well-defined rules. Just occasionally, however, you'll stray wildly off the straight and narrow and pick a deeply unconventional partner or take up an offbeat cause with all the aggression of pent-up desire. Such behaviour is infrequent, though, and makes no serious waves in the long term. But while you are basically sensible and down to earth, you realise that there must be some magic and romance to keep love alive. Coming from you, a shameless[illegible]y sentimental gesture will have maximum impact. Your timing is immaculate, too[illegible]

Anyon[illegible]ou soon discovers that ther[illegible]hat cool exterior. Your secretly [illegible]harply with your normally restraine[illegible] to surprise your partner. You rarely [illegible]e, though, and believe that sex is for do[illegible]ng about. However, you won't be seduced if you're not in the mood, no matter what tricks your partner may try. One plus for any lover is that you are seduced by someone's mind and personality, not their looks, so a perfect body is not a vital ingredient of romance for you. It can take time for you to relax with a new partner and you'll probably prefer someone who is more sexually experienced than yourself. The idea of being taught loving techniques really appeals to you.

Use yoga, massage and simple breathing exercises to help banish the emotional demons that won't let you relax fully. Your lovelife will be among the first areas of your life to benefit.

You don't always feel the need to show your lover how much you appreciate them, and they may think that you don't need many signs of devotion, either. It's a cause and effect that is entirely within your power to improve. Looking at love as a business proposition doesn't always bring the highest returns, either. Cultivate that sentimental corner of your heart.

Partners rarely have need to fear that you'll run off with someone else but they have every reason to feel jealous of your work. Put extra hours and effort into those togetherness areas of your life that sometimes don't show neglect until it's too late. That way, you'll really make the most of your loyal brand of loving.

Venus in Aquarius

HOW YOU LET LOVE IN

Your remarkable popularity is a mixed blessing. You exert a charismatic pull over a large crowd but, although you enjoy basking in the glow, you may find it difficult to settle down with just one person. Few come across as friendly as you, but your wide smile lights up with the readiness of a professional entertainer and there's nothing remotely personal about it. Part of you likes the idea of an intimate, one-to-one relationship, but the rest of you isn't sure that a partnership is worth the sacrifices.

Inside, you're far more fussy and cool than your manner suggests and you may have to work your way through a long list of potential admirers before you find the right one for you. The unsuccessful contenders will never know where they went wrong, because your manner will stay as friendly as ever with them.

You can love with great fidelity and a strong sense of idealism once you've found your perfect match. But you will always express your emotions rather coolly to your partner. They shouldn't be too disappointed if you say that you admire their mind, because there's no higher form of praise in your book.

Indeed, you love with your head and your heart may have little say but, because of your extreme sociability and friendly manner, few understand you. Your love burns hottest when the object of your desire is far away, and a lover who is close at hand and over-attentive can be thoroughly neglected. You'd never knowingly cause another pain, but you can be woefully inconsiderate. You want your lover to respond with passion when you're in a romantic mood, but you can't repay the compliment.

In many ways, you prefer casual affairs because full-blooded ones could tangle your emotional life too much. Marriage doesn't come easily to you and your most successful partnership will always be with a lover who carefully hides all signs of jealousy and gives you an extremely long lead.

Almost always, you'll finally settle with a former best friend who knows you inside out and shares all your interests. They never ask you where you're off to or what time you'll be back.

Any affair that survives the six-month mark will probably go on for years, for you like to test your lover rigorously to begin with, making sure you really can depend on them. If they can stand up to your fickle behaviour, then you admire them all the more and you'll be more prepared to settle down.

Clearly, it's no good you seeking lasting emotional fulfilment with a tender, subjective soul who mirrors your every mood. You will only be happy with a cool partner who remains strong and independent enough to provide a balance.

YOUR LOVE PATH

You dare to be different, so love with you is never less than sparky and full of fun. You want an equally unusual partner, someone who can surprise you every day.

In return, you give them a mixture of freedom and passion, letting them off the leash one moment and gathering them up with an overpowering warm embrace the next. You feed on excitement and find the chase especially thrilling. Falling for an ordinary, run-of-the-mill type is definitely out. What you want is a real character, an eccentric to match you.

You certainly appreciate head-turning looks in your

lover, but you're more smitten by what's on their mind. And no matter what you share with your partner behind the bedroom door, what truly counts in your life are those relaxed, good times together with friends. In fact, what you're looking for in a relationship is an enhanced friendship. You may be short on traditional romantic gestures but you're good at surprises. You stay friends with past loves, too. Old flames never completely go out – they just settle down to a cosy glow.

Jealousy has absolutely no place in your heart. You possess no-one and no-one possesses you. You may bind your lover to you emotionally with love and caring, but never with chains. In love, you may never provide a heavy, steamy, tortured passion, but you'll never give anyone the cold shoulder either. Your feelings won't seesaw and lovers will know exactly where they stand with you.

The only ingredient that could rock the boat is the complication of too many lovers. You are always open to temptation and you choose the sort of partner who gives you the chance to philander. You certainly like to play and may even end up having to choose between lovers.

You can, sometimes, successfully juggle a highly unorthodox lifestyle, but although it may be enjoyable, ultimately you would miss out on intimacy. Still, you would never act in a way that you'd find intolerable in a partner. Neither would you make a decision without consulting them. It's just that you don't much like the idea of settling down too soon in life.

When you do marry or form a permanent commitment, it probably won't be until later in life. Your family will have to fit in with your work and your hobbies, but you will always be welcoming, approachable and fun to be with.

One of your best points is your readiness to do battle on your partner's behalf. You get involved in their problems and are more than happy to fight for them. You will also be pleased if your partner wants to join one of your pet crusades, like saving the world! However, you can live equally well with a partner who has opposing views on all the major issues. A difference of opinion will never provoke a bitter argument.

You put great trust in a partner, right up to the moment they confess that your trust was misplaced. Even then, you may well be so impressed by their honesty that you decide to let them stay. Clinging lovers are not tolerated so easily, though. You'll quickly shake off anyone who tries to hang onto your arm while you circulate at a party, or who keeps checking up on you. Such tactics will bring you closest to blowing an emotional fuse.

Just as you enjoy maximum variety in your life, so sex should be equally as imaginative. You'll seek out the most unusual places in which to make love, or make a pass at your lover at the most unlikely moment. You want every encounter to be exciting and satisfying and, although you can't expect perfection every time, it's a good goal to aim for. Your appetite for a rich sex life is never dulled, not even by age.

You have limitless supplies of energy and you can go on and on with a relationship as long as there's a spark of life left in it. It may not be the same relationship as the one you began together, but you're readily adaptable. Your partner may get fed up sharing you, but they'll never leave you because they're bored!

Confrontations and complications will always litter your love path but you can change and make your life easier if you really want to. You will never accept being told how to mend your ways by a partner, even when you know that they are right. You can be incredibly stubborn. What you must do is weigh up your need for your partner and your need for a fling, and try to assess the risks more realistically. Remember, too, that your partner may not be able to live life at quite the breakneck speed you favour, and may not appreciate the way you are forever questioning them as if they were on a witness stand. It may amuse you but it can irritate them. You attract love easily – don't throw it away carelessly.

Venus in Pisces

HOW YOU LET LOVE IN

What with your urge to be swept off your feet and dominated, and your need to be constantly reassured that you are desired, anyone with Venus in Pisces looks set for emotional trouble. Yet yours is one of the very best love signs you could possibly have.

You have all the right ingredients for a happy lovelife. Few are more kind-hearted and sympathetic to others' feelings, few understand the frailties and fantasies of the human heart better than you. Emotionally intuitive, you are entirely dependent on the mood of the person you're with. If anyone has a love problem, they'll come to you first.

You are attractive, although you probably never believe this wholeheartedly enough to reap the self-confident benefits you merit. You are prepared to make a lot of sacrifices for love's sake, yet you so often run into emotional snags because you waste your tenderest affections on partners who don't deserve you. Ever receptive to a hard-luck story, you can be cruelly mismatched with those who despise your gifts and take advantage of your soft nature. It's partly your own fault, because you place lovers on pedestals of such dizzying height.

Deaf to the sensible opinions of friends, you exaggerate your partner's virtues and completely ignore their vices or, worse, embrace them yourself in a bid to understand more deeply what makes your lover tick. Once you've fallen in love – a frequent occurrence – any remaining crumbs of objectivity you might possess are shaken out of the window.

Do steer away from these energy-sapping lovers because you deserve far better. You can become totally emotionally dependent on a lover, so for the sake of your psychological health you need to be with a success, not a failure. You are not good at discriminating and your sense of emotional self-preservation isn't that wonderful either. You need to be needed, but you also have a shaky ego that requires plenty of warm reassurance in return. Bear in mind how reluctant you are to hurt another's feelings and the contorted lengths you go to in order to avoid it. Demand that your lover treats you with equal sensitivity.

Although you believe that you can handle unlimited emotional pain, both your own and other people's, you could be storing up unpleasant feelings that will spill out in the end. The longer you put up with someone battering your heart, the less able you will feel to stand up for your rights, so try to act quickly and decisively. Avoid taking the easy way out, too, when conflict threatens. You are an idealist, one of the noblest, nicest lovers in the zodiac. You deserve the best.

YOUR LOVE PATH

Sensitive, compassionate and caring, all you need is a soul mate to whisk you away. Together, you'll leave reality far behind and share a made-in-heaven love affair.

You reach out to everyone, touching them with your glowing, kind personality. You can make anyone feel special and it's no wonder that forming relationships has always come so easily to you. You're never short of admirers, but it's the perfect lover you're after, so you don't want to waste time with anyone who means fun rather than fairytale passion.

If the object of your desire looks as if they need saving, so much the better. You can't wait to wade in with sympathy and endless patience. Not surprisingly, you often end up with a partner who is flawed in some way and you enjoy being their prop, nursing them along and listening to their woes. And although you'd like to get them back on their feet, you have a secret worry that they might not need you quite so much then. You find good points in absolutely everybody, but one quality you do stipulate in your lover is that they must share your caring concern for all living creatures.

You don't care about worldly wealth or what your partner does for a living, although it would suit you if it was something creative. Once you have given your heart, you want to weave a protective spell around your lover, fearful that the wrong word or a careless gesture will undo the magic. You secretly fear that your partner will wake up one day and wonder what on earth they are doing with you. You dread them falling out of love with you and go to great lengths to forestall such a tragedy. Like a good cook, you know exactly the right portions of loving to serve at any given time. You'll never starve your partner of affection.

You are so sensitive to your surroundings that they can make or break a budding romance for you. You have near-psychic powers of observation, too, and can see friends' love problems clearly. Yet sometimes you fail to see the truth about your own relationships and your over-eager heart can be taken in by smooth talkers, only coming down to earth long after your friends have tried to warn you.

When your emotions are shattered, you tend to retreat from the world altogether. Life's uglier side is something you find impossible to deal with. You long to escape and be told, like a child, that everything is going to be all right. Unless you're wary, this ache to be comforted can lead you straight from one painful relationship to another, and drink and drugs are especially dangerous for you.

Meek and mild is how you come across when someone first meets you, but soon you reveal your hidden strengths. If anyone tries to muscle in on your relationship, for instance, you'll fight to the death and use every trick in the book if you have to see off a rival.

In other areas of your life, though, you often underestimate yourself and may never quite achieve your aims. You can be afraid of making demands on your partner, so you never ask anything of them. Far too easily influenced by others, you try too hard to be what your lover wants you to be, or what you think they want. Like softened wax, you allow yourself to be moulded this way and that, even giving up your friends and hobbies to meet with your lover's approval.

But no matter how much you sacrifice for love's sake, you never feel that life's driven too hard a bargain. You're not one for bitterness and recriminations, always believing that it's far better to give than to receive.

Whatever your lover does, they know that you'll forgive them. Even if they want to cool the relationship, you're so understanding that you'll comply. You have the patience to wait until they're ready to reseal your love – which they often do.

You never like to rush into bed with someone you've only just met. But your natural sensuousness more than makes up for lost time once an affair has become established. You take the trouble to make sure that your lovemaking never becomes stale or routine.

Your fragile self-confidence gets a potent boost whenever your lover gives you tangible proof of their feelings, especially if it's a proclamation of undying love or a long, passionate letter.

Sometimes you'd rather dream about the perfect lover than risk rebuff by going out there to find one. You must recognise this for what it is – laziness and a touch of emotional cowardice. Try to be more realistic and outgoing or you may get your emotions in a terrible muddle, falling in love but retaining a nagging feeling that something is missing. That will be one of the many occasions when you mistake compassion for love. You really do need to learn to differentiate between the two.

Short of growing another layer of skin, you cannot protect yourself from all the emotional knocks that come your way, and you find ridicule and criticism especially upsetting. You could definitely help yourself by telling your partner more clearly what wounds your sensitive feelings. Often the only clue they get that you've been hurt is silence.

Don't always volunteer first to make a sacrifice, either. Give your partner a chance to do something for you for a change, to help even the score. You have so much to give to a relationship, make sure you get plenty back in return.

PART FIVE

Mars:
what drives you on

Look up your date of birth in the Mars tables to find which of the 12 zodiac signs is the key to your sexuality, work and health

Where was planet Mars the day you were born?

The position of the sun on the day you were born gives you your sun sign. So, if you were born on 2 August, you know you are a Leo. Yet there is a part of you that could belong to any one of the 12 zodiac signs. Yes, the planet Mars, ruler of willpower, aggression and action, was also moving through the zodiac when you were born. And, because it moves in a different way, that same day, 2 August, could give you a Mars sign in Aries, or Virgo, or any of the other signs depending on the year of your birth.

Please look up your year and day of birth in the Mars tables on the following pages to find your Mars sign. Once you know it, you'll understand why, at times, you just don't act like your sun sign.

Although your sun sign is the senior partner, Mars is going to explain your sex drive at its most basic. If your sun sign makes you one of the gentler signs, like Cancer, but your sexual drive is, at times, much more impulsive, then your Mars sign could be Aries. But if you are a sun sign Aries, whose sex drive is, at times, seductively slow and marvellously imaginative, then your Mars sign could be in the zodiac sign of Cancer.

To get what you truly need from your working life, you should let your Mars sign have a share in the decisions. It can reveal that you are suppressing a need for real security, or a need for fame. You can be a sun sign Libra, full of charm and reason, yet, because Mars is in the harsher, power-seeking sign of Capricorn, in the workplace you need to be the boss, and will be a tough one.

In all kinds of relationships, you should look up both of your Mars signs, because the person with the strongest Mars sign could grab too much power in the relationship, unless both of you are aware of that danger.

In health, too, your Mars sign pinpoints your problems and suggests solutions, too. So when you get into stress situations, think about what Mars is really contributing. Then you'll find living with this part of your personality the exciting challenge it should be.

Don't be disappointed if you are one of those people whose Mars and sun signs are the same – though you'll never be easy to live with, it does make you a truly fascinating person.

MARS

The times and dates below indicate the point at which Mars entered each zodiac sign, for example Mars entered Aquarius on 21 January 1900 at 18:54, and stayed there until it entered Pisces on 28 February 1900 at 22:13, so someone born at 19:00 on 1 February 1900 would have a Mars sign of Aquarius.

All times are GMT – don't forget to check the British Summer Time and World Time Zone tables if they apply to your time of birth (pages 846–50).

MARS

Date	Time	Sign
21 Jan 1900	18:54	Aquarius
28 Feb 1900	22:13	Pisces
8 Apr 1900	03:51	Aries
17 May 1900	08:55	Taurus
27 Jun 1900	09:14	Gemini
10 Aug 1900	01:13	Cancer
26 Sep 1900	18:16	Leo
23 Nov 1900	09:11	Virgo
1 Mar 1901	17:50	Leo
11 May 1901	06:45	Virgo
13 Jul 1901	20:12	Libra
31 Aug 1901	18:26	Scorpio
14 Oct 1901	12:57	Sagittarius
24 Nov 1901	04:57	Capricorn
2 Jan 1902	00:08	Aquarius
9 Feb 1902	00:07	Pisces
19 Mar 1902	04:42	Aries
27 Apr 1902	10:54	Taurus
7 Jun 1902	11:21	Gemini
20 Jul 1902	17:42	Cancer
4 Sep 1902	14:49	Leo
23 Oct 1902	22:59	Virgo
20 Dec 1902	03:54	Libra
19 Apr 1903	18:49	Virgo
30 May 1903	18:39	Libra
6 Aug 1903	16:46	Scorpio
22 Sep 1903	13:55	Sagittarius
3 Nov 1903	05:31	Capricorn
12 Dec 1903	09:54	Aquarius
19 Jan 1904	15:48	Pisces
27 Feb 1904	03:14	Aries
6 Apr 1904	18:08	Taurus
18 May 1904	03:36	Gemini
30 Jun 1904	14:55	Cancer
15 Aug 1904	03:20	Leo
1 Oct 1904	13:47	Virgo
20 Nov 1904	06:19	Libra
13 Jan 1905	19:38	Scorpio
21 Aug 1905	20:28	Sagittarius
8 Oct 1905	00:41	Capricorn
18 Nov 1905	04:36	Aquarius
27 Dec 1905	13:58	Pisces
4 Feb 1906	23:45	Aries
17 Mar 1906	11:47	Taurus
28 Apr 1906	16:50	Gemini
11 Jun 1906	19:28	Cancer

27 Jul 1906	13:59	Leo
12 Sep 1906	12:36	Virgo
30 Oct 1906	04:03	Libra
17 Dec 1906	11:43	Scorpio
5 Feb 1907	09:01	Sagittarius
1 Apr 1907	18:03	Capricorn
13 Oct 1907	15:07	Aquarius
29 Nov 1907	05:06	Pisces
11 Jan 1908	05:11	Aries
23 Feb 1908	03:48	Taurus
7 Apr 1908	04:15	Gemini
22 May 1908	14:13	Cancer
8 Jul 1908	03:46	Leo
24 Aug 1908	06:30	Virgo
10 Oct 1908	05:44	Libra
25 Nov 1908	13:51	Scorpio
10 Jan 1909	03:18	Sagittarius
24 Feb 1909	01:28	Capricorn
9 Apr 1909	19:34	Aquarius
25 May 1909	21:45	Pisces
21 Jul 1909	06:24	Aries
27 Sep 1909	01:35	Pisces
20 Nov 1909	19:29	Aries
23 Jan 1910	01:54	Taurus
14 Mar 1910	07:21	Gemini
1 May 1910	20:54	Cancer
19 Jun 1910	03:31	Leo
6 Aug 1910	00:55	Virgo
22 Sep 1910	00:08	Libra
6 Nov 1910	13:30	Scorpio
20 Dec 1910	12:05	Sagittarius
31 Jan 1911	21:15	Capricorn
13 Mar 1911	23:41	Aquarius
23 Apr 1911	07:51	Pisces
2 Jun 1911	21:01	Aries
15 Jul 1911	15:02	Taurus
5 Sep 1911	13:44	Gemini
30 Nov 1911	07:24	Taurus
30 Jan 1912	19:53	Gemini
5 Apr 1912	11:18	Cancer
28 May 1912	08:11	Leo
17 Jul 1912	02:40	Virgo
2 Sep 1912	17:02	Libra
18 Oct 1912	02:36	Scorpio
30 Nov 1912	07:39	Sagittarius
10 Jan 1913	13:44	Capricorn
19 Feb 1913	08:01	Aquarius
30 Mar 1913	05:54	Pisces
8 May 1913	02:57	Aries
17 Jun 1913	00:26	Taurus
29 Jul 1913	10:12	Gemini
15 Sep 1913	16:42	Cancer
1 May 1914	20:18	Leo
26 Jun 1914	04:46	Virgo
14 Aug 1914	14:12	Libra
29 Sep 1914	10:39	Scorpio
11 Nov 1914	10:45	Sagittarius
22 Dec 1914	03:46	Capricorn
30 Jan 1915	06:09	Aquarius
9 Mar 1915	12:55	Pisces
16 Apr 1915	20:43	Aries
26 May 1915	03:11	Taurus
6 Jul 1915	06:29	Gemini
19 Aug 1915	09:13	Cancer
7 Oct 1915	20:51	Leo
28 May 1916	18:46	Virgo
23 Jul 1916	05:35	Libra
8 Sep 1916	18:01	Scorpio
22 Oct 1916	03:13	Sagittarius
1 Dec 1916	17:23	Capricorn
9 Jan 1917	13:04	Aquarius
16 Feb 1917	13:35	Pisces
26 Mar 1917	17:36	Aries

4 May 1917	22:07	Taurus
14 Jun 1917	20:52	Gemini
28 Jul 1917	03:57	Cancer
12 Sep 1917	10:51	Leo
2 Nov 1917	10:54	Virgo
11 Jan 1918	08:54	Libra
25 Feb 1918	19:31	Virgo
23 Jun 1918	19:18	Libra
17 Aug 1918	04:20	Scorpio
1 Oct 1918	07:52	Sagittarius
11 Nov 1918	10:32	Capricorn
20 Dec 1918	09:30	Aquarius
27 Jan 1919	11:45	Pisces
6 Mar 1919	19:10	Aries
15 Apr 1919	05:16	Taurus
26 May 1919	09:46	Gemini
8 Jul 1919	17:17	Cancer
23 Aug 1919	06:18	Leo
10 Oct 1919	03:51	Virgo
30 Nov 1919	12:10	Libra
31 Jan 1920	23:09	Scorpio
23 Apr 1920	21:22	Libra
10 Jul 1920	17:31	Scorpio
4 Sep 1920	20:08	Sagittarius
18 Oct 1920	13:11	Capricorn
27 Nov 1920	13:38	Aquarius
5 Jan 1921	07:46	Pisces
13 Feb 1921	05:36	Aries
25 Mar 1921	06:45	Taurus
6 May 1921	02:03	Gemini
18 Jun 1921	20:51	Cancer
3 Aug 1921	11:13	Leo
19 Sep 1921	11:46	Virgo
6 Nov 1921	16:18	Libra
26 Dec 1921	12:00	Scorpio
18 Feb 1922	16:32	Sagittarius
13 Sep 1922	12:45	Capricorn
30 Oct 1922	18:37	Aquarius
11 Dec 1922	12:54	Pisces
21 Jan 1923	09:58	Aries
4 Mar 1923	00:41	Taurus
16 Apr 1923	02:56	Gemini
30 May 1923	21:25	Cancer
16 Jul 1923	01:32	Leo
1 Sep 1923	01:01	Virgo
18 Oct 1923	04:17	Libra
4 Dec 1923	02:08	Scorpio
19 Jan 1924	19:01	Sagittarius
6 Mar 1924	19:05	Capricorn
24 Apr 1924	16:02	Aquarius
24 Jun 1924	16:35	Pisces
24 Aug 1924	16:52	Aquarius
19 Oct 1924	17:47	Pisces
19 Dec 1924	10:46	Aries
5 Feb 1925	10:00	Taurus
24 Mar 1925	00:25	Gemini
9 May 1925	22:34	Cancer
26 Jun 1925	09:03	Leo
12 Aug 1925	21:10	Virgo
28 Sep 1925	18:57	Libra
13 Nov 1925	13:55	Scorpio
28 Dec 1925	00:23	Sagittarius
9 Feb 1926	03:19	Capricorn
23 Mar 1926	04:19	Aquarius
3 May 1926	16:44	Pisces
15 Jun 1926	00:38	Aries
1 Aug 1926	09:01	Taurus
22 Feb 1927	00:23	Gemini
17 Apr 1927	01:15	Cancer
6 Jun 1927	11:23	Leo
25 Jul 1927	07:41	Virgo
10 Sep 1927	14:18	Libra
26 Oct 1927	00:21	Scorpio
8 Dec 1927	11:01	Sagittarius

19 Jan 1928	02:00	Capricorn
28 Feb 1928	06:20	Aquarius
7 Apr 1928	14:07	Pisces
16 May 1928	21:11	Aries
26 Jun 1928	08:37	Taurus
9 Aug 1928	03:45	Gemini
3 Oct 1928	03:04	Cancer
20 Dec 1928	06:49	Gemini
10 Mar 1929	22:30	Cancer
13 May 1929	02:10	Leo
4 Jul 1929	09:47	Virgo
21 Aug 1929	21:43	Libra
6 Oct 1929	12:24	Scorpio
18 Nov 1929	13:34	Sagittarius
29 Dec 1929	10:57	Capricorn
6 Feb 1930	18:37	Aquarius
17 Mar 1930	06:10	Pisces
24 Apr 1930	17:38	Aries
3 Jun 1930	03:19	Taurus
14 Jul 1930	12:47	Gemini
28 Aug 1930	11:15	Cancer
20 Oct 1930	14:26	Leo
16 Feb 1931	15:33	Cancer
30 Mar 1931	03:12	Leo
10 Jun 1931	14:40	Virgo
1 Aug 1931	16:22	Libra
17 Sep 1931	08:24	Scorpio
30 Oct 1931	12:31	Sagittarius
10 Dec 1931	03:00	Capricorn
18 Jan 1932	00:33	Aquarius
25 Feb 1932	02:43	Pisces
3 Apr 1932	07:16	Aries
12 May 1932	11:13	Taurus
22 Jun 1932	09:40	Gemini
4 Aug 1932	20:13	Cancer
20 Sep 1932	19:57	Leo
13 Nov 1932	21:36	Virgo

6 Jul 1933	22:15	Libra
26 Aug 1933	06:35	Scorpio
9 Oct 1933	11:28	Sagittarius
19 Nov 1933	07:05	Capricorn
28 Dec 1933	03:29	Aquarius
4 Feb 1934	04:01	Pisces
14 Mar 1934	09:02	Aries
22 Apr 1934	15:40	Taurus
2 Jun 1934	16:29	Gemini
15 Jul 1934	21:48	Cancer
30 Aug 1934	14:04	Leo
18 Oct 1934	05:22	Virgo
11 Dec 1934	10:09	Libra
29 Jul 1935	18:06	Scorpio
16 Sep 1935	13:24	Sagittarius
28 Oct 1935	18:36	Capricorn
7 Dec 1935	04:43	Aquarius
14 Jan 1936	14:01	Pisces
22 Feb 1936	04:05	Aries
1 Apr 1936	21:25	Taurus
13 May 1936	09:13	Gemini
25 Jun 1936	21:54	Cancer
10 Aug 1936	09:50	Leo
26 Sep 1936	15:04	Virgo
14 Nov 1936	15:11	Libra
5 Jan 1937	21:05	Scorpio
13 Mar 1937	04:54	Sagittarius
14 May 1937	20:12	Scorpio
8 Aug 1937	23:11	Sagittarius
30 Sep 1937	09:43	Capricorn
11 Nov 1937	19:03	Aquarius
21 Dec 1937	18:15	Pisces
30 Jan 1938	13:04	Aries
12 Mar 1938	08:02	Taurus
23 Apr 1938	18:45	Gemini
7 Jun 1938	01:30	Cancer

22 Jul 1938	22:27	Leo
7 Sep 1938	20:25	Virgo
25 Oct 1938	06:28	Libra
11 Dec 1938	23:35	Scorpio
29 Jan 1939	10:01	Sagittarius
21 Mar 1939	07:42	Capricorn
25 May 1939	00:51	Aquarius
21 Jul 1939	18:54	Capricorn
24 Sep 1939	01:09	Aquarius
19 Nov 1939	15:58	Pisces
4 Jan 1940	00:15	Aries
17 Feb 1940	02:08	Taurus
1 Apr 1940	18:51	Gemini
17 May 1940	14:50	Cancer
3 Jul 1940	10:29	Leo
19 Aug 1940	15:52	Virgo
5 Oct 1940	14:14	Libra
20 Nov 1940	17:11	Scorpio
4 Jan 1941	19:44	Sagittarius
17 Feb 1941	23:40	Capricorn
2 Apr 1941	11:58	Aquarius
16 May 1941	05:13	Pisces
2 Jul 1941	05:15	Aries
11 Jan 1942	21:35	Taurus
7 Mar 1942	07:42	Gemini
26 Apr 1942	06:03	Cancer
14 Jun 1942	03:40	Leo
1 Aug 1942	08:09	Virgo
17 Sep 1942	09:48	Libra
1 Nov 1942	22:11	Scorpio
15 Dec 1942	16:27	Sagittarius
26 Jan 1943	18:50	Capricorn
8 Mar 1943	12:31	Aquarius
17 Apr 1943	10:19	Pisces
27 May 1943	09:29	Aries
7 Jul 1943	23:17	Taurus
24 Aug 1943	00:13	Gemini

28 Mar 1944	09:31	Cancer
22 May 1944	13:56	Leo
12 Jul 1944	02:39	Virgo
29 Aug 1944	00:07	Libra
13 Oct 1944	11:47	Scorpio
25 Nov 1944	15:45	Sagittarius
5 Jan 1945	19:02	Capricorn
14 Feb 1945	09:28	Aquarius
25 Mar 1945	03:15	Pisces
2 May 1945	20:06	Aries
11 Jun 1945	11:40	Taurus
23 Jul 1945	08:51	Gemini
7 Sep 1945	20:59	Cancer
11 Nov 1945	21:24	Leo
26 Dec 1945	14:44	Cancer
22 Apr 1946	19:24	Leo
20 Jun 1946	08:26	Virgo
9 Aug 1946	13:13	Libra
24 Sep 1946	16:29	Scorpio
6 Nov 1946	18:15	Sagittarius
17 Dec 1946	10:45	Capricorn
25 Jan 1947	11:29	Aquarius
4 Mar 1947	16:26	Pisces
11 Apr 1947	22:39	Aries
21 May 1947	03:16	Taurus
1 Jul 1947	03:13	Gemini
13 Aug 1947	21:12	Cancer
1 Oct 1947	02:19	Leo
1 Dec 1947	11:34	Virgo
12 Feb 1948	10:25	Leo
18 May 1948	20:49	Virgo
17 Jul 1948	05:22	Libra
3 Sep 1948	13:54	Scorpio
17 Oct 1948	05:44	Sagittarius
26 Nov 1948	22:01	Capricorn
4 Jan 1949	17:54	Aquarius
11 Feb 1949	18:08	Pisces

21 Mar 1949	22:00	Aries
30 Apr 1949	02:26	Taurus
10 Jun 1949	00:46	Gemini
23 Jul 1949	05:42	Cancer
7 Sep 1949	04:39	Leo
27 Oct 1949	00:51	Virgo
26 Dec 1949	05:27	Libra
28 Mar 1950	10:34	Virgo
11 Jun 1950	20:40	Libra
10 Aug 1950	16:49	Scorpio
25 Sep 1950	19:47	Sagittarius
6 Nov 1950	06:34	Capricorn
15 Dec 1950	08:55	Aquarius
22 Jan 1951	13:06	Pisces
1 Mar 1951	22:06	Aries
10 Apr 1951	09:40	Taurus
21 May 1951	15:35	Gemini
3 Jul 1951	23:43	Cancer
18 Aug 1951	10:53	Leo
5 Oct 1951	00:20	Virgo
24 Nov 1951	06:17	Libra
20 Jan 1952	02:01	Scorpio
27 Aug 1952	19:37	Sagittarius
12 Oct 1952	05:12	Capricorn
21 Nov 1952	19:54	Aquarius
30 Dec 1952	21:42	Pisces
8 Feb 1953	01:06	Aries
20 Mar 1953	06:50	Taurus
1 May 1953	06:05	Gemini
14 Jun 1953	03:46	Cancer
29 Jul 1953	19:22	Leo
14 Sep 1953	17:53	Virgo
1 Nov 1953	14:11	Libra
20 Dec 1953	11:15	Scorpio
9 Feb 1954	19:23	Sagittarius
12 Apr 1954	17:19	Capricorn
3 Jul 1954	03:08	Sagittarius
24 Aug 1954	16:13	Capricorn
21 Oct 1954	13:05	Aquarius
4 Dec 1954	08:32	Pisces
15 Jan 1955	05:13	Aries
26 Feb 1955	10:49	Taurus
10 Apr 1955	23:25	Gemini
26 May 1955	00:57	Cancer
11 Jul 1955	09:25	Leo
27 Aug 1955	10:11	Virgo
13 Oct 1955	11:13	Libra
29 Nov 1955	01:18	Scorpio
14 Jan 1956	02:07	Sagittarius
28 Feb 1956	19:33	Capricorn
14 Apr 1956	23:06	Aquarius
3 Jun 1956	07:16	Pisces
6 Dec 1956	11:49	Aries
28 Jan 1957	14:44	Taurus
17 Mar 1957	22:00	Gemini
4 May 1957	15:40	Cancer
21 Jun 1957	12:32	Leo
8 Aug 1957	05:37	Virgo
24 Sep 1957	04:36	Libra
8 Nov 1957	21:04	Scorpio
23 Dec 1957	01:27	Sagittarius
3 Feb 1958	18:45	Capricorn
17 Mar 1958	06:51	Aquarius
27 Apr 1958	01:56	Pisces
7 Jun 1958	05:37	Aries
21 Jul 1958	06:16	Taurus
21 Sep 1958	03:12	Gemini
29 Oct 1958	02:59	Taurus
10 Feb 1959	13:38	Gemini
10 Apr 1959	09:49	Cancer
1 Jun 1959	02:33	Leo
20 Jul 1959	11:11	Virgo
5 Sep 1959	22:51	Libra
21 Oct 1959	09:44	Scorpio
3 Dec 1959	18:12	Sagittarius

14 Jan 1960	05:03	Capricorn
23 Feb 1960	04:15	Aquarius
2 Apr 1960	06:24	Pisces
11 May 1960	07:10	Aries
20 Jun 1960	08:52	Taurus
2 Aug 1960	04:09	Gemini
21 Sep 1960	03:36	Cancer
6 May 1961	01:04	Leo
28 Jun 1961	23:49	Virgo
17 Aug 1961	00:42	Libra
1 Oct 1961	20:00	Scorpio
13 Nov 1961	21:46	Sagittarius
24 Dec 1961	17:45	Capricorn
1 Feb 1962	23:03	Aquarius
12 Mar 1962	07:57	Pisces
19 Apr 1962	16:59	Aries
28 May 1962	23:50	Taurus
9 Jul 1962	03:50	Gemini
22 Aug 1962	11:32	Cancer
11 Oct 1962	23:40	Leo
3 Jun 1963	06:29	Virgo
27 Jul 1963	04:18	Libra
12 Sep 1963	09:17	Scorpio
25 Oct 1963	17:36	Sagittarius
5 Dec 1963	09:04	Capricorn
13 Jan 1964	06:09	Aquarius
20 Feb 1964	07:23	Pisces
29 Mar 1964	11:12	Aries
7 May 1964	14:27	Taurus
17 Jun 1964	11:32	Gemini
30 Jul 1964	18:15	Cancer
15 Sep 1964	05:13	Leo
6 Nov 1964	03:05	Virgo
29 Jun 1965	00:54	Libra
20 Aug 1965	12:17	Scorpio
4 Oct 1965	06:57	Sagittarius
14 Nov 1965	07:35	Capricorn

23 Dec 1965	05:53	Aquarius
30 Jan 1966	07:17	Pisces
9 Mar 1966	13:06	Aries
17 Apr 1966	20:38	Taurus
28 May 1966	22:04	Gemini
11 Jul 1966	03:06	Cancer
25 Aug 1966	15:42	Leo
12 Oct 1966	18:29	Virgo
4 Dec 1966	00:43	Libra
12 Feb 1967	11:26	Scorpio
31 Mar 1967	08:17	Libra
19 Jul 1967	22:22	Scorpio
10 Sep 1967	01:23	Sagittarius
23 Oct 1967	02:07	Capricorn
1 Dec 1967	20:13	Aquarius
9 Jan 1968	10:01	Pisces
17 Feb 1968	03:36	Aries
28 Mar 1968	00:01	Taurus
8 May 1968	14:31	Gemini
21 Jun 1968	05:15	Cancer
5 Aug 1968	17:14	Leo
21 Sep 1968	18:42	Virgo
9 Nov 1968	06:09	Libra
29 Dec 1968	22:11	Scorpio
25 Feb 1969	06:29	Sagittarius
21 Sep 1969	06:21	Capricorn
4 Nov 1969	18:34	Aquarius
15 Dec 1969	14:12	Pisces
24 Jan 1970	21:29	Aries
7 Mar 1970	01:33	Taurus
18 Apr 1970	19:10	Gemini
2 Jun 1970	07:03	Cancer
18 Jul 1970	06:56	Leo
3 Sep 1970	05:06	Virgo
20 Oct 1970	11:02	Libra
6 Dec 1970	16:38	Scorpio

23 Jan 1971	01:43	Sagittarius
12 Mar 1971	10:23	Capricorn
3 May 1971	21:23	Aquarius
6 Nov 1971	12:27	Pisces
26 Dec 1971	17:59	Aries
10 Feb 1972	13:58	Taurus
27 Mar 1972	04:30	Gemini
12 May 1972	13:16	Cancer
28 Jun 1972	16:16	Leo
15 Aug 1972	01:07	Virgo
30 Sep 1972	23:28	Libra
15 Nov 1972	22:17	Scorpio
30 Dec 1972	16:10	Sagittarius
12 Feb 1973	05:46	Capricorn
26 Mar 1973	20:57	Aquarius
8 May 1973	04:14	Pisces
20 Jun 1973	21:03	Aries
12 Aug 1973	15:11	Taurus
29 Oct 1973	22:49	Aries
24 Dec 1973	07:52	Taurus
27 Feb 1974	10:04	Gemini
20 Apr 1974	08:12	Cancer
9 Jun 1974	00:54	Leo
27 Jul 1974	14:08	Virgo
12 Sep 1974	19:14	Libra
28 Oct 1974	07:11	Scorpio
10 Dec 1974	22:10	Sagittarius
21 Jan 1975	18:49	Capricorn
3 Mar 1975	05:23	Aquarius
11 Apr 1975	19:02	Pisces
21 May 1975	07:55	Aries
1 Jul 1975	03:40	Taurus
14 Aug 1975	20:41	Gemini
17 Oct 1975	08:25	Cancer
25 Nov 1975	18:58	Gemini
18 Mar 1976	13:04	Cancer
16 May 1976	11:01	Leo

6 Jul 1976	23:20	Virgo
24 Aug 1976	05:52	Libra
8 Oct 1976	20:27	Scorpio
21 Nov 1976	00:03	Sagittarius
1 Jan 1977	00:56	Capricorn
9 Feb 1977	12:12	Aquarius
20 Mar 1977	02:33	Pisces
27 Apr 1977	15:51	Aries
6 Jun 1977	02:56	Taurus
17 Jul 1977	15:03	Gemini
1 Sep 1977	00:00	Cancer
26 Oct 1977	18:22	Leo
26 Jan 1978	03:03	Cancer
10 Apr 1978	18:03	Leo
14 Jun 1978	02:17	Virgo
4 Aug 1978	08:45	Libra
19 Sep 1978	20:36	Scorpio
2 Nov 1978	01:02	Sagittarius
12 Dec 1978	17:29	Capricorn
20 Jan 1979	17:06	Aquarius
27 Feb 1979	20:32	Pisces
7 Apr 1979	01:20	Aries
16 May 1979	04:39	Taurus
26 Jun 1979	02:10	Gemini
8 Aug 1979	13:36	Cancer
24 Sep 1979	21:23	Leo
19 Nov 1979	21:30	Virgo
11 Mar 1980	21:30	Leo
4 May 1980	01:57	Virgo
10 Jul 1980	17:41	Libra
29 Aug 1980	05:33	Scorpio
12 Oct 1980	06:02	Sagittarius
22 Nov 1980	01:16	Capricorn
30 Dec 1980	22:04	Aquarius
6 Feb 1981	22:27	Pisces
17 Mar 1981	02:25	Aries
25 Apr 1981	07:09	Taurus

5 Jun 1981	05:27	Gemini
18 Jul 1981	08:59	Cancer
2 Sep 1981	01:59	Leo
21 Oct 1981	02:02	Virgo
16 Dec 1981	00:19	Libra
3 Aug 1982	11:55	Scorpio
20 Sep 1982	01:19	Sagittarius
31 Oct 1982	22:59	Capricorn
10 Dec 1982	06:02	Aquarius
17 Jan 1983	12:50	Pisces
24 Feb 1983	23:58	Aries
5 Apr 1983	13:42	Taurus
16 May 1983	21:25	Gemini
29 Jun 1983	06:41	Cancer
13 Aug 1983	16:49	Leo
30 Sep 1983	00:11	Virgo
18 Nov 1983	10:24	Libra
11 Jan 1984	03:24	Scorpio
17 Aug 1984	20:10	Sagittarius
5 Oct 1984	06:22	Capricorn
15 Nov 1984	18:26	Aquarius
25 Dec 1984	06:48	Pisces
2 Feb 1985	17:24	Aries
15 Mar 1985	05:01	Taurus
26 Apr 1985	09:01	Gemini
9 Jun 1985	10:27	Cancer
25 Jul 1985	03:52	Leo
10 Sep 1985	01:24	Virgo
27 Oct 1985	15:10	Libra
14 Dec 1985	19:02	Scorpio
2 Feb 1986	06:30	Sagittarius
28 Mar 1986	03:43	Capricorn
9 Oct 1986	00:52	Aquarius
26 Nov 1986	02:38	Pisces
8 Jan 1987	12:32	Aries
20 Feb 1987	14:56	Taurus

5 Apr 1987	16:44	Gemini
21 May 1987	03:01	Cancer
6 Jul 1987	16:42	Leo
22 Aug 1987	19:46	Virgo
8 Oct 1987	19:22	Libra
24 Nov 1987	03:19	Scorpio
8 Jan 1988	15:28	Sagittarius
22 Feb 1988	10:23	Capricorn
6 Apr 1988	21:51	Aquarius
22 May 1988	07:46	Pisces
13 Jul 1988	19:50	Aries
24 Oct 1988	09:22	Pisces
1 Nov 1988	01:47	Aries
19 Jan 1989	07:48	Taurus
11 Mar 1989	08:36	Gemini
29 Apr 1989	04:30	Cancer
16 Jun 1989	14:05	Leo
3 Aug 1989	13:26	Virgo
19 Sep 1989	14:26	Libra
4 Nov 1989	05:17	Scorpio
18 Dec 1989	04:47	Sagittarius
29 Jan 1990	14:08	Capricorn
11 Mar 1990	15:57	Aquarius
20 Apr 1990	22:21	Pisces
31 May 1990	07:29	Aries
12 Jul 1990	15:05	Taurus
31 Aug 1990	12:12	Gemini
14 Dec 1990	07:02	Taurus
21 Jan 1991	01:36	Gemini
3 Apr 1991	00:52	Cancer
26 May 1991	12:22	Leo
15 Jul 1991	12:36	Virgo
1 Sep 1991	06:35	Libra
16 Oct 1991	18:56	Scorpio
29 Nov 1991	02:05	Sagittarius
9 Jan 1992	09:31	Capricorn
18 Feb 1992	04:21	Aquarius

28 Mar 1992	01:53	Pisces
5 May 1992	21:33	Aries
14 Jun 1992	16:02	Taurus
26 Jul 1992	19:19	Gemini
12 Sep 1992	06:34	Cancer
28 Apr 1993	00:03	Leo
23 Jun 1993	07:57	Virgo
12 Aug 1993	01:23	Libra
27 Sep 1993	02:25	Scorpio
9 Nov 1993	05:33	Sagittarius
20 Dec 1993	00:32	Capricorn
28 Jan 1994	03:58	Aquarius
7 Mar 1994	10:50	Pisces
14 Apr 1994	17:48	Aries
23 May 1994	22:23	Taurus
3 Jul 1994	22:25	Gemini
16 Aug 1994	19:17	Cancer
4 Oct 1994	16:06	Leo
2 Dec 1994	12:57	Virgo
22 Jan 1995	21:39	Leo
25 May 1995	16:31	Virgo
21 Jul 1995	09:33	Libra
7 Sep 1995	07:13	Scorpio
20 Oct 1995	21:14	Sagittarius
30 Nov 1995	14:10	Capricorn
8 Jan 1996	11:12	Aquarius
15 Feb 1996	11:56	Pisces
24 Mar 1996	15:13	Aries
2 May 1996	18:12	Taurus
12 Jun 1996	14:36	Gemini
25 Jul 1996	18:25	Cancer
9 Sep 1996	20:00	Leo
30 Oct 1996	07:13	Virgo
3 Jan 1997	08:40	Libra
8 Mar 1997	18:48	Virgo
19 Jun 1997	08:51	Libra
14 Aug 1997	08:51	Scorpio
28 Sep 1997	22:23	Sagittarius
9 Nov 1997	05:34	Capricorn
18 Dec 1997	06:40	Aquarius
25 Jan 1998	09:31	Pisces
4 Mar 1998	16:25	Aries
13 Apr 1998	01:09	Taurus
24 May 1998	03:43	Gemini
6 Jul 1998	08:57	Cancer
20 Aug 1998	19:13	Leo
7 Oct 1998	12:25	Virgo
27 Nov 1998	10:14	Libra
26 Jan 1999	12:24	Scorpio
5 May 1999	19:46	Libra
5 Jul 1999	05:11	Scorpio
2 Sep 1999	19:52	Sagittarius
17 Oct 1999	01:46	Capricorn
26 Nov 1999	06:59	Aquarius
4 Jan 2000	02:54	Pisces
12 Feb 2000	00:55	Aries
23 Mar 2000	01:16	Taurus
3 May 2000	19:08	Gemini
16 Jun 2000	12:20	Cancer
1 Aug 2000	01:09	Leo
17 Sep 2000	00:03	Virgo
4 Nov 2000	01:42	Libra
23 Dec 2000	14:24	Scorpio

Mars in Aries

SEX LIFE DRIVE

Aries is the natural home for aggressive, fiery planet Mars, driving you to want sex hot, exciting, and soon. So your sex life will be intense and busy. There are no cunning love detours with you. And, although this helps avoid misunderstandings with potential lovers, you can fall into the trap of being too impulsive. A too-hasty approach puts off shyer sex partners – not that you always rate these as much of a loss.

You like to explore untried territory with a partner who is as bold and unconventional as you. And you naturally bring out the passion in others, with the exception of the oversensitive who may never even get as far as the first kiss with you.

Once you spot someone you want, you are not easily deterred, although you hate the feeling of just following in someone else's love steps and can be frozen in your tracks if you happen to spot a photograph of your lover's previous partner lying carelessly around the house or, worse still, displayed like a trophy on the bedside table.

If all the signals are right, your response to sexual triggers is always eager, spontaneous and extra energetic. For this reason, you will sometimes leap into intimate relationships with people you don't actually like. Fortunately, this is where your Aries bluntness and courage over confrontation pays off. It means you can easily walk away from any sexual relationship that is no longer satisfactory for you. And anyone who tries to cheat on you can expect a blazing row. You are, however, supremely unobservant, so traces of a rival's presence might go undetected by you for quite some time before the explosion occurs.

Your assertiveness can be a great asset to your sex life, but it can also mean that you turn encounters into a battleground sooner or later. You rather enjoy loveplay that's rough (without being nasty) and think that the occasional quarrel in bed spices things up. But this can be very wearing on your partner, and become off-putting over a long period.

On the plus side, you don't go in for psychological game-playing or undue teasing. But against that, your lovemaking can be selfish and you pay scant attention to your mate's moods or wishes – or, for that matter, to any sweet nothings they may be murmuring.

Unsubtle you may be between the sheets, but at least your lovers won't get many shocks or unwelcome surprises. With you, what they see is what they get. And because you're never afraid to make the first move, your company can be a relief to those who find relationships more difficult.

Deep down, you are a true romantic, however, and you long to be swept off your feet. Allow this more vulnerable, tender side of yourself to show if you don't always want to do all the work yourself. Your sign tends to look sexy and you sparkle and glow noticeably when someone's caught your eye. Your overall attitude to sex is healthy if hasty!

With your great stamina, you are capable of long, satisfying lovemaking sessions, although you are usually too impatient to spin out the pleasure. Yours is one of the few signs that can get a lot out of even a very brief encounter – and it's so easy for you to find a willing partner. Yet, you always keep a segment of yourself apart and independent.

MARS AND YOUR WORK

When you choose a job, you go for cash and glory. You're a natural hard worker and love a challenge, but you may run into problems because you can't stand taking a submissive role. You need to control your career, and day-to-day work you do, as you can't tolerate having a boss looking over your shoulder all the time. If anyone tries to push you around, you are too easily tempted to quit.

Given your own patch to rule, you like a busy atmosphere, expect high standards from everyone else, and you work efficiently, and very fast. Occasionally, you can be slapdash, but few get more done by the end of the day than you.

Courageous and daring, you are at your best whenever others can handle routine and detail for you, and you don't mind switching jobs, or even careers, at short notice. You are ideal freelance material, and with this Mars sign your work energy flows in abundance.

Zappy and persuasive, you never have trouble enlisting help from others because workmates admire your enthusiasm, sparkle and confidence-inspiring honest personality.

Always game for new ideas, you're too enterprising ever to find yourself short of money. But your great mental energy and physical stamina is always geared to winning, no matter what, and you won't leave the ring until you've been laid out cold, whether it's a takeover battle or an office row over who gets the seat near the window.

You have the ingredients to be a bold entrepreneur, tough tycoon, professional sportsperson or gambler. You haven't the patience for brick-by-brick career moves. You want to be rich and successful overnight.

MARS AND YOUR HEALTH

Physical power and a great deal of nervous and mental energy are quite normal for you because of the way Mars affects your body. You are usually very healthy but, because you find life's an eternal conflict, you have a high level of inbuilt stress, too.

Your busy brain never stops ticking away and your fighting instinct will make you prone to headaches, indigestion, sleep problems and sinus troubles.

You're preprogrammed to pitch in, come what may, flinging yourself at life and never retreating from problems.

This results in many minor accidents and your body is rarely free of bumps and bruises.

Gut reactions count with you. You're never wary of acting out, or showing, your anger and such assertiveness is good news for your health. Your impatience means you enjoy more convenience foods than are good for you and you leap away from the table too fast or eat on the run, which is bad news for your digestion. You should take longer to eat and chew food more thoroughly.

Your excellent stamina means you're good at marathons and other long-distance endurance sports and should make more time for them. You can get very depressed, even though you usually get worries off your chest, and you'll find that vigorous exercise drives gloom out of your system.

You get the most out of any exercise if you're trying to beat the clock or an opponent (even if it's only a weights machine). Mars in Aries gives your system a high-octane energy buzz but it needs discipline if you are to make the most of your positive, self-assertive inner strengths.

LIVING WITH MARS IN ARIES

Life will be high-energy excitement for you, from loving to living. You'll enjoy a satisfying sex life and a challenging career, but you must temper your enthusiasms with a few sensible precautions if you want to avoid burnout. Practise some simple relaxation techniques, let the Mars energy help you to pace yourself and try to curb your impatience. That way, you'll enjoy your busy, buzzy life to the full.

Mars in Taurus

SEX LIFE DRIVE

You ooze earthy sexiness and, even when your motive's not blatantly sexual, you're the type who likes to put down whatever you're doing just to give someone a satisfying hug. This Mars position ensures that you're one of the most sensual types around and you enjoy your body to the full whether you're making love, eating or just luxuriating in a hot, foamy bath.

But although you love getting physical, you need to call the shots and to have the right atmosphere and setting for lovemaking. Everything has to be just right before you can express your desire. Your ideal night of passion would always be preceded by a wonderful meal – pity you were born too late to enjoy a Roman banqueting orgy. You like a masterplan, too, deciding what you want – and who you want to do it with – and moving ahead to the next love-making phase with pure persistence.

Your approach is welcomed by those who need others to push them into action and help them overcome their chronic tendency to dither. But, at your worst, you can come across as someone who won't take no for an answer and who pays little attention to a lover's wants and responses. You might skimp on foreplay because you honestly can't see the point of it, and you are one of the least mysterious bedmates. Your approach can veer towards the selfish and you usually make your move regardless of your partner's feelings. So, you'll make a late-night phone call to a lover who's already asleep in bed just because you're feeling in the mood.

You take a while to warm up to lovemaking (probably on account of the large meal you've just enjoyed) but your pace is steady, unfaltering and you've lots of stamina. You may allow plenty of time for lovemaking, but you could definitely benefit from a more varied approach.

Your sex drive needs a regular outlet, ideally with a permanent partner because you enjoy building up long-term relationships and need to feel comfortable with bedmates. In fact, finding a new partner is a task you dislike, for you find it hard to adjust to others' quirks and needs.

You have no trouble, though, in expressing your feelings physically and you enjoy giving love tokens – anything from teddies to tenderly prepared favourite foods – to your one-and-only.

Sexual frustration can make you feel physically ill and certainly makes itself glaringly obvious through your worsening temper. Sex for you is primarily a physical, not an intellectual, thrill and you can enjoy a satisfying liaison in which few words are spoken. All you require is that your lover is as earthy and warm as you are. Shared interests or even a shared language come much lower down your list of priorities.

You never lose interest in lovemaking, whether it's between new sheets, on a cool parquet floor or a thick fur rug – and no matter what your age. If spurned, you'll take your revenge, but the partner who stays on glowing terms with you will always be treated to Rolls Royce category love.

MARS AND YOUR WORK

The size of your bank balance is terribly important to you, so you'll be loath to take a low-paid job. This is because Mars channels your energies into earning power and you feel, quite strongly, that your financial status will make you more sexually attractive.

This is true, up to a point. But you can direct too much physical and mental energy into your job and starve your private life of the necessary time to enjoy the fruits of your labour. In other words, you can end up too busy burning the midnight oil to test how your affluence aids your attractiveness.

You're a conscientious hard worker by nature and a good shoulder-to-the-wheel, resilient type to have around in a financial crisis. You can be determined and aggressive, and a loyal and persistent employee. Your great endurance and steely willpower are among your chief assets and you'll persevere with any task until it's done.

Quality, not quantity, is what counts with you. You need to know that you're appreciated and you like to work within a framework of rules, everything clearly mapped out and everyone in their rightful place. You hate having your work routine disturbed and are probably best working alone, in your own room, within a large organisation.

You're extremely trustworthy and very patient and can be generously encouraging to those lower down the work ladder. But your temper is short and fearsome and you can be drawn to a job for reasons of social snobbery. Your skills combine the practical and the artistic and, although you move slowly and deliberately, you work very hard to achieve your goals.

MARS AND YOUR HEALTH

Good food plays a large part in your life and you expend a lot of energy on what goes down that throat of yours. You may have had a weight problem since childhood, and you'll certainly have to watch that you don't pile on the pounds once you're past early adulthood. That's when you tend to be working too hard and too long to take sufficient time off for exercise and sport.

But although Mars in this sign steers you in the dubious direction of physical over-indulgence, it also makes you very body conscious. You'll want to turn your body into something that can be admired. And, once you've seen the light about calories and indolence, you can become a work-out bore. Watch that you don't fall into the trap of being obsessive about exercise. And keep away from sunbeds – you have a tendency to fall asleep on them.

You're physically very strong and, if you can sidestep obesity, you tend to suffer only minor ailments. Your chief health problems affect your throat, voicebox and the glands around your neck. You must watch out, too, that overwork doesn't run down your system and lay you open to viral infections like glandular fever. Your temper is another problem area. Letting off steam is good for your mental health but physical injuries, sometimes the result of fights, can come your way. Learn a measure of self-control, and try yoga breathing techniques to stop the red mist of anger blinding you into a rage.

LIVING WITH MARS IN TAURUS

You can be too determined and persistent for your own good. Relax, loosen up and introduce a little spontaneity into all areas of your life, from bedroom to boardroom. Curb your craving for the good life, whether it's food or financial reward, and don't be sidetracked by over-indulgence. Live life to the full by all means, but not so full that it overflows!

Mars in Gemini

SEX LIFE DRIVE

Mars energy glides in, making you a sensitive, artful lover. Adaptable and versatile, you learn your love tricks early in life and few can rival your subtle, gentle touch in bed.

You're highly observant and forever storing away techniques and potent loving phrases that you've read, heard, or seen on film somewhere. You're always clever enough, however, to disguise such tricks as all your own work.

No partner could ever complain that you're dull in bed, but you can try to pack the whole *Kama Sutra* into one steamy, energetic night. Your major failing as a sex mate is probably impatience. And you rapidly become bored if you always go through the same lovemaking routines. You must have a partner who's willing to experiment and go along with your ideas. Failing that, you'll settle for more than one – you are, after all, one of the biggest flirts in the zodiac.

You enjoy lovemaking props and toys, although these need be no more mechanical than well-styled undies or flamboyant cushions, or perhaps some fun dressing-up sessions. Your attitude to sex is as jokey and light-hearted as the rest of your outlook on life.

Your chief weapon of seduction is your witty tongue and you can be pretty chatty in bed. Physically attractive, you exude an irresistible vitality that ensures you're never short of would-be partners. But your most potent sex organ is, in fact, your mind. You lack staying power and, to some extent, stamina, but you have finesse and originality on your side. Your erotic know-how and sweet talk alone can bring others to boiling point.

You can fall down when it comes to emotional depth, and many who find you the most satisfying of sexual partners can feel that you don't truly care about them deep down. Most of the time, you can stifle such doubts with your delicate, tender manner.

Sometimes, you can spend more time thinking about passionate encounters than simply getting on and living them. You tend to intellectualise sex, and people with Mars in Gemini often turn out to be excellent writers of sexual fantasies for others to enjoy, keeping their own physical fulfilment at arm's length.

You're happiest with a partner who enjoys your kind of sexy talking, without wanting to grab you straightaway. You enjoy all the preliminaries of lovemaking, and relish verbal foreplay and even a few arguments.

Anyone who's too overtly raunchy, or whose intellect lags far behind your own, won't end up anywhere near your sheets. More action, less stalling and far fewer words might inject a greater degree of satisfaction into your lovelife. And learn to bite your tongue when it comes to making jokes during lovemaking, which can so easily ruin your partner's confidence.

You've a reputation for sexual straying but, although you need variety, you can be happy with just one lover as long as that lover is versatile!

MARS AND YOUR WORK

You need work. Your brain needs to be kept busy, your hands never idle, or your energies will turn inwards and you'll fidget and fret yourself into ever-decreasing circles. Enforced idleness, whether it's a short delay while waiting for a phone call to be put through, or a long lay-off like compulsory redundancy, can drive you up the wall. So, with Mars in this sign, you must stick at it, even if you're doing a job for love, not money. If no-one will employ you, start up on your own. If that's impossible, treat a hobby as if it was a major career – it could even turn into one.

You're inquiring, restless, impatient, burning to know the answers and desperate to communicate what you know in the shortest possible time. You've a flair for writing and for energetic talking, and a great feel for language generally. Alert, always busy, you're not likely to let a break pass you by and you can be motivated by several goals at the same time. You can instigate activity for its own sake and you loathe seeing others idle.

Do guard against working erratically as your energies splutter and fizz in fits and starts. This is because you find it hard to sustain any project to the end unless you're deeply fascinated by it, and drop jobs at the first hint of boredom.

Travel, making personal contacts, and any self-employed, non-conformist work suits you. Spend less time talking and you'll get more done! You're best off channelling your energies into journalism and other kinds of communicating, including selling and fast-thinking jobs like politics.

MARS AND YOUR HEALTH

All your energies are directed towards intense, short-lived nervous activity. This is fine provided you're getting lots of sleep, eating whole, fresh foods and scheduling sufficient energy-boosting exercise into your life. But introduce one factor too many, like an unexpected deadline, sudden loss, or a change in your lifestyle such as moving home, or a rocky relationship, and the whole house of cards will fall about your ears as your stretched nerves finally rip.

That's the time your immune system will cave in and your body pick up an infection. But it's your mind that bears the brunt of strain, working in tandem with your body to produce a host of allergies or pushing you to the verge of mental breakdown.

You tend to spread yourself too thin, trying to do too much and be too many things to please too many people. Often chronically disorganised, you must have more self-discipline if confusion, or even panic, are not to set in.

Your best health tips are a light diet and plenty of restful sleep. You may appear to thrive on catnaps for weeks on end but you actually need a good seven hours at least. You'll benefit from shutting down your system during the day, too. Try short spells of meditation and deep relaxation for 15 minutes in the middle of your busiest, most stretched periods and you'll be amazed how refreshed you'll feel. Brisk walking, swimming and cycling have the same effect.

LIVING WITH MARS IN GEMINI

Beware going through life without some sort of strategy. You're bright and clever, a prized lover and a hard worker, but your lack of staying power could be your downfall, both emotionally and materially. Set yourself simple goals and try not to veer off-course too much. Your energies need concentrating, not scattering, if you are to achieve the fascinating life that can be yours.

Mars in Cancer

SEX LIFE DRIVE

It's no good – you simply can't make love unless the mood is right. And that goes for the setting, too. It must be tasteful, elegantly comfortable and extremely private. You like to lock the doors, dim the lights, take the phone off the hook and make well and truly sure that no-one and nothing is going to disturb you and your partner.

You can be rather shy about sex and may try to cover this up, dressing and acting more raunchily than you feel, hiding behind a teasing and suggestive vocabulary. But any lover who takes you at face value is in for a surprise, and a too-brusque or direct approach is destined to drive you far away.

You can be so psychologically tied to your parents that your sex life is positively emaciated and you never give yourself the chance to grow up and experiment in this vital area. You can be very touchy, even oversensitive, and find it hard to trust anyone sufficiently to want to make love with them.

Once you are satisfied that you're not going to be suddenly, brutally let down – or worse, rejected at your first tentative approach – you express your sex drive by being extremely protective of your lover. You're always keen to offer food, gifts, even a bed for the night – not necessarily with passion as part of the deal – because you view these as symbols of your love. Meanwhile, your partner could be craving other, but equally essential demonstrations of affection from you.

Your sexual energies flow in uneven rhythms, often overwhelming partners with their intensity if they have been blocked for lengthy periods. And although you have hot, loving moods, there are also times when you simply want sensual, tender gestures like cuddling and hand-holding instead of full lovemaking. You need a versatile, sensitive partner who can pick up on your strongly felt, but exceedingly changeable pattern of desires.

Your remarkable intuition helps you tune into a lover's unspoken needs, however, and you'd be an ideal partner for someone who's physically shyer or younger than you. Your lovemaking has all the delicacy and art idealised in Oriental erotic prints but you can tire quite easily and be difficult to arouse if you're feeling down.

You can become overprotective and sexually jealous, even interfering in your partner's social life because you worry that they are about to meet, and bed, someone who you think is more attractive than you. But once you have widened your sexual experience, your self-confidence tends to improve and this unattractive clinging declines.

Thoughtful and caring, you make your partner feel very secure and emotionally close to you and you go out of your way to be physically pleasing. Anyone with Mars in this position can usually keep a lover by their side for years.

MARS AND YOUR WORK

Work helps soothe your craving for security. Nothing makes you feel as safe as your nest-egg savings and you derive enormous satisfaction from opening up yet another account with lots of interest building up.

You are ambitious and tenacious so, when employers are looking to lighten their load, you are rarely among the first to be asked to look for another job. You won't job-hop by choice, either, much preferring to give long and faithful service to one organisation and collecting your gold retirement watch at the end. If you choose acting, your natural home may be a 10-year stint in a soap opera.

But although you're a diligent worker, you are also a bit of a split personality. No matter how tied up you are with your job, you're equally involved in what's going on at home, so you'll be on the phone to whoever's manning the domestic fort throughout your working day. And whenever you do have a break, you tend to whizz off on some vital errand like buying food for the freezer or DIY equipment.

Wherever you work, you'll turn your duty station into a home from home, sticking up pictures and arranging pot plants or filling your desk with useful items like sticking plasters, screwdrivers and needle and cotton.

Constructive, shrewd and with a phenomenal memory, you work best alone but within a framework. You always finish what you start, even if it means taking work home, and only an emotional upset can make you waver. One thing you must have to achieve goals is enthusiastic family support.

MARS AND YOUR HEALTH

You find it hard to say what you mean. And Mars in Cancer emotions run so deep and are subject to such changes, they can take a heavy toll on your health.

You have great difficulty expressing anger in a straightforward way. Instead, you turn it inwards and, as a result, suffer a range of problems with your digestive tract, from over-acidity to ulcers and irritable bowel syndrome. Your blood pressure can ultimately become raised if, after every argument, you spend hours wishing you'd said something bald and to the point, or you've been terribly nice to people who actually make you reach for the indigestion tablets.

You certainly need to be more self-assertive and should relax much more than you do. You also tend to worry yourself into knots whenever the subject of your family crops up, whether it involves an ageing parent, lover, problem teenager or preschool tearaway. Put a little more space between you and your nearest and dearest because your overprotectiveness doesn't do anyone any good in the long run. Learn when to let go.

You are, however, on good terms with your subconscious

mind and can learn a lot from your dreams. Psychologically, you can be too withdrawn and self-analytical at times and must beware obsessive traits. Physically, your Mars energies suggest long life and, though you dread illness, you heal and recuperate remarkably well.

LIVING WITH MARS IN CANCER

The keyword for success in all areas of your life is relaxation. You must learn to relax mentally and physically, not to take things so much to heart and to trust others – and most importantly yourself – far more than you do. Value yourself and the contribution you make in life. It will do wonders for your self-esteem and confidence, and the positive results will show in everything you do.

Mars in Leo

SEX LIFE DRIVE

You're just about the most open and warm sex mate in the zodiac. For you, making love is fun and natural and you view sex as a nice way of hotting up an excellent friendship. You also like to stay friends with your lovers, no matter how deep and steamy your relationship becomes.

You've a powerful and creative sex drive, and if it's not given an immediate outlet in bed, then you use it to fuel your tremendous capacity for work. Most partners would count themselves lucky to run into you, chiefly because you make them feel really relaxed.

True, if your partner wants plenty of preliminaries such as light-hearted chitchat and delicate dalliance before getting physical, then they've picked the wrong playmate in you. Once you get the green light, your forceful Mars placement fuels your physical interest immediately. The only foreplay you require is plumping up the soft furnishings and fiddling with the CD and lighting. As long as the setting's plush and luxurious enough, then you see no reason not to strike while love feelings run hot!

You sometimes do take great trouble, and expense, to impress a lover – often far more than is necessary – with your home, the amount of cash you earn and other purely materialistic things. You'd be better advised to consider your partner's wishes more instead. Some can even find your over-lavish preparations off-putting.

Once you find a lovemaking routine that works for you, you'll stick to it. You don't even realise that you're doing it, either. This doesn't bother some partners a bit, but why not ask them for some new directions now and then?

You're generous to a fault with partners. You enjoy showering them with love tokens, the more glittering and expensive the better. Your general zest for life is reflected in your lovemaking style, which is always playful. You find it puzzling that anyone can actually have a problem with sex, even if they're shy or repressed in any way. Occasionally, your failure to grasp that such difficulties can exist helps them overcome their hang-ups. You're either refreshing or shocking, depending on the other person's sexual stance. But you're certainly at your best when you've a partner who's as fun-loving and open as you are.

Sex is a joyful recreation in your life. You can do without it if you have to, but you're physically and mentally more balanced and feel far healthier once you've found a loving outlet for your sexual energy. Mars intensifies your enjoyment of the sheer physical part of loving, but you do need romantic involvement to make your pleasure perfect.

MARS AND YOUR WORK

Clear the decks, light the lights, you're the type who likes everyone to know you're working on a major project. In fact, you're probably in charge of it. Your Mars sign means you need to direct your work energy towards a showy outlet and that you like to act on impulse. Competitive, ambitious and enthusiastic, you enjoy hard work – but not in a lowly capacity. You aim to have your name on the door and can't stand being shoved into a back room and being told just to get on with it!

It's not that you can't take orders, just that you'd rather give them if you've any say at all in the matter. You're brilliant at organising and can inspire others considerably. You've also a talent for publicity and you're able to put big ideas into practice, largely because you rarely lose your nerve and are prepared to take a gamble.

Excellent at deputising, you give clear, effective instructions and never give less than your best. You don't ride on others' backs, no matter how much power you wield. Professional, responsible and a natural leader, you also champion good working conditions for everyone. You feel that you must create a good impression first time, but you can waste energy courting applause and popularity at work. Work brings you success, but you'll probably end up working too hard.

MARS AND YOUR HEALTH

Mars helps feed your already potent vitality. You never seem short of energy and, overall, your health tends to be excellent. If you are ever ill you make a terrible patient, full of self-pity and forever demanding small favours from your long-suffering carers. It's just as well this isn't a role you play very often.

You have scant sympathy with others who are sick. You don't understand what it's like being ill because you are so seldom sick yourself. But, once you do see that someone is feeling down in the mouth because of a health problem, you are generous with gifts to cheer them up.

With your powerful Mars sign you overcrowd your timetable and forget to allow yourself time to relax. You tend to take on far too much and are too stubborn and arrogant to accept offers of help. Soldiering on, you put strain on your most vulnerable body areas – your back, heart and blood circulatory system. Strokes and coronaries are your chief risks in later life, so change your punishing work routine and too-frantic social style now.

You really must schedule yourself time off to play more. Games, even gambling within limits, get rid of tensions, and as you find emotional release in taking risks, go ahead! Competitive sport and nerve-testing pastimes like rock climbing suit you, as does working out at a prestigious gym. Building your body suits your vanity perfectly.

LIVING WITH MARS IN LEO

Forceful and enthusiastic, your appetite for loving and living is larger than life. Yet a basic insecurity makes you crave material possessions and demands that you find favour with everyone you meet. Calm down, unwind and go with the flow of that Mars energy. Take the time to savour all that life has to offer and try not to care so much about what others think. Learn to be as strong inside as you appear to others by admitting you're not always fearless.

Mars in Virgo

SEX LIFE DRIVE

Sensitive, ultra-careful who you pick for a sex partner, you are a highly fastidious lover. Mars in this sign makes you concerned with all the little details of lovemaking. You put hours of thought into preparing the scene, which rather rules out a spontaneous romp.

Even if you did decide to make love in a hayfield, you'd check it out a few hours in advance, just to make sure that it was newly mown, free of thistles and not situated slap in the middle of a local ramblers' route!

You usually favour a cosy, indoor setting in a smart bedroom and you often have the forethought to take the phone off the hook before removing even a single item of clothing. When you do make love to someone, you concentrate on all sorts of delicate details. You've probably developed a great technique – but have you lost sight of passion and laughs on the way?

You take sex very seriously, so seriously that you may avoid it altogether because your overly health-conscious side worries that, these days, a new lover is too risky a business. There's no need to warn you to practise safe sex – you've rarely done anything else!

Physical cleanliness and peak health are of vital importance to you. You only want a partner who reaches your high standards and you're turned off in a big way by what you see as tacky. Nicotine-stained fingers, grubby undies, unwashed hair and unbrushed teeth are big passion-killers as far as you're concerned. And you're not particularly keen on body hair, either.

Your sex routine can be a ritual as silent and precise as the Japanese tea ceremony – a thing of beauty but emotionally formal and cool. You can liven up your lovemaking by unleashing those locked-away emotions more often. And don't let earthbound Virgo block out the loving needs of the moment. Try being more flexible and stray now and then from your planned path when you make love, letting your partner guide you.

Because you have learned many love skills, you may concentrate excessively on pleasing your partner. They're probably not complaining, yet, but your own desires are important, too, and need satisfying just as much. Fantasies can open up your sexual personality and liven up your attitudes, especially when you share them with a sympathetic partner.

Although you're faddy and play hard to get – not because you like those flirty, psychological games but because you genuinely find few who appeal to you sexually – plenty of people are attracted to you. Once you do find someone who suits, you can be one of the most thoughtful, sensitive lovers in the world. You try to fulfil their every physical whim – and you're unlikely to suddenly disappear, leaving them craving more!

MARS AND YOUR WORK

Any job you take must offer you security. That's the way you're made, and if you launch out on seemingly risky ventures, you have usually checked them out.

You're a deeply modest worker, and often quite happy to be behind the scenes. You don't relish dealing with the public, face to face, and much prefer your own office or working area with a closed door or partition between you and the rest of the world. Though you're an excellent nurse, too.

This can lead to loneliness, but you prefer to make the running where workmates are concerned and don't generally like stopping what you're doing for casual chats unless you've decided to award yourself a break. With this Mars slant, your energies are thrust towards personal achievement, making you active and dynamic, with a definite sense of direction. You need to get things done and can become easily irritated and impatient with others whose work pace doesn't match your own.

Dedicated, loyal and truly hard-working, you're perfect company material and you enjoy order, routine, facts and formulae, discipline and detail. You're a perfectionist who quickly becomes absorbed in your tasks and you willingly give your time and energy. In fact, you often drive yourself to the brink of fatigue.

Much of your work is centred on caring for others, though you won't allow anyone to take advantage, and will insist that they pull their weight. You think no-one can do a job as well as you can – and chances are, you're right.

MARS AND YOUR HEALTH

You can waste much of your vital energy fiddling over unnecessary detail and worrying about what outsiders might view as very minor problems. Consequently, you burn up calories and exhaust brain cells doing things that you shouldn't be bothering with at all.

You rarely relax and find it so hard to let go of tensions that you can teeter towards neurosis in no time at all. You are pernickety, overcritical and sometimes quirky, and you worry yourself inside out.

In fact, it's your insides that take the brunt. Your intestines and glandular system can rebel, causing ulcers and immune system problems. And when you do become ill, it can take you a long time to recuperate. Your health is directly affected by your diet and by weather conditions. You usually eat carefully, but there's little you can do about the weather. You suffer headaches and feelings of tightness and depression before thunderstorms and often become agitated in windy weather.

Helping others and having your special skills acknowledged act as a great pick-me-up. But you can feel very low-spirited when your abilities aren't acknowledged or appreciated. Your self-esteem is too easily bruised and you must guard against allowing others' opinions to dictate your wellbeing. You are your own best health monitor.

LIVING WITH MARS IN VIRGO

You can be far too uptight about the little details to see things on a grand scale. Let some of that Mars power open up your life and unlock your emotional door. You need to give in to the moment more and allow yourself to be selfish sometimes. It's all there for the taking, if you'll allow yourself to really reach out for it.

Mars in Libra

SEX LIFE DRIVE

You're a charming, highly popular lover. This Mars placing moves diplomatically behind the scenes to make sure that you're never stuck in a dreary, static affair and it's usually you who rings the changes when you feel that's the wisest option. But whether you're bidding a lover a fond farewell or trying to inject a few much-needed innovations into a relationship, you do it very smoothly. Your partner may not even wake up to the fact that you've got your own way until long after the event.

Usually, you're the one who takes the initiative in starting a new affair, and you'll probably hover delicately between two for a time, making sure the new one's up and running before snapping off the old, dead one at the roots. Though not many people will notice that you're hedging your bets.

You find it easy to attract sexual partners. You're not as flexible as you appear, but you do work at being pleasant and amusing. Your flirty laugh has as much pulling power as your rather good looks. But with Mars in Libra you can all too easily slide into an ultimately self-destructive pattern of sexual musical chairs, changing partners because you don't want to miss out on any exciting new encounters or deprive yourself of any fresh sensual experiences. You should take time to examine existing partners more closely before finally deciding to shrug them off.

Although secretly steely and wilful, you're prepared to play second fiddle from time to time – provided, that is, you can alternate roles in the power play of love games. Physically very affectionate, you're keen to please in bed and always make a point of learning what your lover enjoys best. You can provide a unique, special type of attention that proves irresistible once you've got someone physically hooked on you.

Your lovemaking is volatile and active and you really need a partner who's as responsive as you. Generally, you go for strenuous, intense affairs that demand a great deal of energy. You can run into rows over who's boss, but you actually relish emotionally charged situations that many other types would go to the ends of the earth to avoid. You find it intensifies your pleasure – anger and passion make good bedfellows for you.

You may find, however, that such ructions rock your relationships into ruin, especially when they're engineered by you to hot up the pace. You're best with a regular partner who's around most of the time because you recharge your batteries by making love. You don't enjoy sleeping alone and, when there's no love on the horizon, you'll share your bed with pets, stuffed toys, anything that provides some warm, cuddly company.

Your sexual energies propel you towards early romance, so you may well have got married or moved in with someone while you were very young. But with Mars making your sexual attraction so strong, you'll have to add some self-discipline to make it last.

MARS AND YOUR WORK

Your work-directed Mars energy runs very smoothly and you can apply intense concentration and genuine hard work – but only when you are fully involved in a work project. And there's the problem. Once your attention begins to stray, you're disappearing off on a self-awarded break or reaching for the phone. You have to conquer so many distractions before you can get down to business, and one of the chief attention-seekers is your lovelife.

However, once you have chained yourself to your task,

the only vital ingredient you need is a congenial work atmosphere. You hardly function at all without it. You're a deeply sociable animal and must have contact with others, so it's likely that you'll be strongly drawn to work that's to do with people. You have a keen sense of social duty and make an excellent team leader, too.

Mars in Libra also makes you a natural workplace mediator, able to live in the middle of conflict. Generally patient with colleagues, courteous to bosses and tactfully helpful to those junior to you, you work best in a partnership. However, your caring and friendly demeanour can suddenly erupt into quarrelling and you cannot, will not, be hassled and hurried along.

When distracted by sexual attraction, either within or outside your workplace, you can be disappointingly slapdash. But when you're wearing your serious working blinkers, you are a perfectionist. You need a stable business partner who's able to compensate for your odd lapses – or better still, fend them off.

MARS AND YOUR HEALTH

You devote far too much stressful mental energy to other people's opinions. You can be both passive and aggressive at the same time, trying to make others react to you without coming out and stating directly what you want. You also want to be liked by everyone all of the time and, when something enrages you, you feel hampered and unable to show your anger. Instead, you divert it, perhaps flirting in order to get your own back on an annoying lover, or mentally rerunning the row you wished you'd had at work on the bus home.

Self-assertiveness training is what you need and if you can't afford the time or the cash to do a proper course, then take a deep breath each time your nerves are set on edge by someone's actions and tell them calmly, but bluntly, how you feel.

The price you'll pay for continuing to submerge your

anger is poor skin, bad circulation and kidney problems. You can be prone to urinary infections and troubles in the adrenal glands, probably because your fight–flight reaction is so often exchanged for a sit-tight-and-don't-rock-the-boat attitude. Eventually, you may even suffer increased blood pressure.

You lack self-discipline when it comes to what you eat and any weight control regime will have to be entered into with other people – and be socially pleasant – if it's going to work for you. But the good news for your general health is that, if you have friends to accompany you, you'll diligently follow any keep-fit plan or even take up a sport. You just need a prod.

LIVING WITH MARS IN LIBRA

There's no chance of you getting stuck in a rut with Mars at your heels. As long as you are in a relationship and a job that captures your imagination and interest, then your life will be harmony and balance. If not, you'll waste precious energy in all the wrong places. Look at your life and use that strong, direct Mars power to decide what you really want from life – and go for it!

Mars in Scorpio

SEX LIFE DRIVE

You are passionate and intense with a jealous sexual nature and highly secretive about your sexlife. However, a bit of detective work will reveal that it's all going on, bubbling away beneath the surface. You never like to let the right hand know what the left is doing, though, and you'll never give away the name of the person you're secretly sleeping with. You'll even keep everyone in the dark about any wedding plans, too.

You always make the first move, usually striking when it's least expected. Maximum surprise and impact is what you're after and you usually catch a potential love mate off guard so that they give in before they've realised what's hit them.

Sexual repression doesn't suit you at all, as it can lead to violent, explosive outbursts of temper. You must have regular sex to stop these forceful zodiac rhythms being blocked. Your smouldering sex drive thrives on bedroom fantasy – and secrecy, of course – and you often hunger for someone for a long time before letting it show. Then your intense desire can almost overwhelm your partner.

Physically, you are demanding, tireless and unorthodox. But the only aspect of your nature that usually causes real problems is your jealousy. There's no fairness in it, either, for while you'd like to clamp your lover in a chastity belt or lock them safely in a dungeon while you pop out for the paper, the same rules don't apply when it comes to your roving eye.

It's probably your own voracious appetite and hidden off-the-record lusts (not always fulfilled) that make you feel so suspicious. Bear in mind that being faithful comes a lot more easily to some people.

In any relationship, sexual or otherwise, it's likely that you'll be the dominant partner. You also need someone who'll match your energy and who's able to let themselves go completely. If they happen to fall in love with you, and you with them, so much the better, but you'll settle for purely physical passion, provided it's strong enough. However, an air of mystery must always be maintained, or the affair's doomed.

Sex brightens you up – it really does have an invigorating effect on you. However, it's not always possible to avoid periods without it, when your mental and physical energies are tied up and working against each other. When this happens, you need to sublimate these powers in work or sport, otherwise you'll be tied in emotional knots!

Of all the Mars signs, yours is the most able to release a lover's buried innermost desires. You're turned on by anyone who plays hard to get, and by circumstances that contrive to stand in your way. If they don't exist already, you might even invent some!

When you fall out with your bedmate, the cause is usually a physical, sexual incompatibility, though you'll pin it on some other reason. You'll continue with someone who makes you jealous even when you no longer feel anything for them nor find them attractive because you won't let someone else win them from you. Your sex drive may look cool as ashes on the surface. But it's white hot within and just waiting to burst into flame.

MARS AND YOUR WORK

You attack tasks with zeal and passion, working in short, intense bursts, and overcommitment to work can be a serious problem for you. You're never far from a row either, whether it's over pay, output or deadlines. It's usually instigated by your extreme demands on others. Aggressive and dynamic, you bring a highly determined approach to any job you tackle. You've an unwavering sense of purpose, do nothing by halves and will work flat out for success, not only for yourself but for the benefit of others, too.

You won't ease up until the project in hand has been completed, even if that means staying up all night or taking work home. Chances are you're in charge of others but you're not an easy boss because you expect everyone to jump to it and react immediately. Yours is a powerful kind of energy and you need to see that you're making rapid headway, which makes you a classic candidate for overwork.

Quick and persistent, accurately observant and deeply committed, you ask only that your job is highly absorbing and offers you ample scope for advancement. If a job looks dead-end and low-key, you'll quit without a qualm and rarely have trouble landing something new.

Employers would be mad not to hire you, but they'd be equally crazy to give you too large an empire. Power goes to your head and you can start imagining that you're surrounded by enemies who are after your job. You take risks, but not all of them are wise.

MARS AND YOUR HEALTH

You've been blessed with prodigious energy and lots of stamina and your constitution is strong. Yet you are your body's own worst enemy because you tend to undermine these natural assets with overwork, over-indulgence and misdirected emotion.

You sap your vitality by working round the clock – and then some! You like to play hard, too, and eat and drink richly and to excess, compounding the damage by skimping on sleep. Your over-active sex life burns up any vigour that's left, and then you torture yourself mentally, wasting yet more energy, with complicated mind-games and lingering jealousies.

You are slow to venom, but you've a killer rage. Massive

temper explosions probably do you more good than harm, but you can grow moody and bitter while you're working up to this release and that's far from a healthy frame of mind.

Your body would benefit from inner-cleansing treatments such as a high-fibre, low-fat diet, and your liver should be allowed more of a rest from heavy meat. Avoid toxins, everything from food additives to alcohol and so-called 'recreational' drugs, because your system can't handle them at all.

Force yourself to clear a space in your life when you don't even think about work. Don't cram it with socialising, either. Just shut down your system for a few hours, cancel all available stimulation and drift into a trance. Your mental health will benefit. Your strengths are an ability to cope with crisis and to stay in tune with your instincts. Your weakness is obsessiveness.

LIVING WITH MARS IN SCORPIO

You have a dark side to your nature that harbours negative characteristics with a passionate intensity. Please re-direct that hidden power to more positive and harmonious traits. You can be obsessive and volatile – use it to work for you, not against you. Simplify your life, sort out your priorities and make the most of your forceful energy and magnetic personality.

Mars in Sagittarius

SEX LIFE DRIVE

You approach sex with gusto and bags of energy, leaping into the centre of action without many preliminaries. Your Mars sign frees you to try your luck with all kinds of people, though you also have a knack for picking suitable types. Sometimes you can spot a partner who's potentially ideal for you even when friends have ruled them out, although you always do follow your own headstrong route.

You can be breathtakingly hasty in forming liaisons, sometimes hardly bothering to ask someone's name before flinging yourself into an affair! As for finding out details like their job or where they live, you're simply not interested in such minor points. You go by gut reactions and are rarely proved wrong.

But you can tend to rush others into bed without building up sufficient steaming mutual passion first. So spend a bit longer on the foreplay, it's probably your only weakness.

Open, positive and gleeful in your enjoyment of the pleasures of the flesh, you are usually able to take any lover to cloud nine. Your brand of lovemaking is irresistible and you make it all seem so easy. But behind your skills lies a dedicated athlete who has gone to great lengths to keep body fit and imagination unfettered. Your own physical cleverness ensures that you never tire your love partner – or put their back out! Provided that you don't short-change when it comes to tenderness, your sex life should be much more than satisfactory.

It's only when a sex partner begins to make tying-down

demands that they may be in for disappointment. You're at your best as a no-strings partner, or with a lover who lives some distance away. Anyone who plans to keep you around had better disguise their intentions pretty well to avoid bringing you out in a hot flush of panicky paranoia.

You probably feel happier in an 'unofficial' partnership than a legalised one. But although you are seldom without a bedmate, you can be unfulfilled emotionally. This is not just because you fear the commitment of a continuing affair, but because you don't allow yourself enough room for sexual fantasy. You need variety in your lovelife and the security to express yourself freely.

Luckily, you build bonds quickly and relatively easily with others. You're drawn to the idea of travel for your sexual thrills and you prefer foreign lovers. Holiday romances are an all-year-round business where you're concerned and you secretly long to be asked to linger in some exotic spot, although you'd hate to live abroad forever.

Your impulsiveness and desire for freedom at all costs can result in problems with a partner's family. And you have been known to laugh at the worst possible moment.

MARS AND YOUR WORK

You're definitely one of the lucky ones. Your work energy is linked directly to your considerable ambition, meaning that you target the job you want as efficiently as a bullet speeding down the barrel of a gun. That's once your trigger is squeezed, of course, and if a job doesn't catch your fancy and fire your imagination, forget it.

You have to be highly motivated or all that physical and mental energy, all that adventurous explorer's spirit, goes straight down the drain. At school, you were either top of the form or class dunce, depending on whether you were enthralled or bored.

Still, you love a challenge and, once you've connected, you are an indefatigable worker. You can be a difficult employee, though, demanding total freedom and forever questioning everything and everyone around you. You're cooperative, versatile and something of an intellectual even though you express everything in plain terms. You need plenty of scope and don't really want responsibility – and sometimes you hate the idea of having staff working for you.

If you're not careful, your freewheeling nature can scatter your work drive to the four winds. You can be all speed and no endurance and, without more self-discipline, your impetuous bursts of fiery energy may fizzle out into exhaustion.

Time and again, you get going on a project in a rush and flurry, only to run out of steam. You always have enough zip to start again, but why waste your assets? Slow down and learn to pace yourself instead.

MARS AND YOUR HEALTH

You are actually quite highly strung, although you hide it well with lots of clowning around. Nervous exhaustion may stalk you and it's fortunate that you have great powers of emotional endurance.

Physically, you're usually in prime condition and it's practically impossible to tire you out bodily. But mentally you can become taut and overstretched, a state made worse when you're boxed in by a job or relationship from which you'd rather break away.

Both psychologically and physically you benefit from vigorous exercise. It's what you enjoy and the more challenging and near-Olympic in standard, the better.

Parts of your body to take extra care of are your upper legs, hips and sciatic nerves. Walking, riding, swimming and dance-movement will offset any tendency to seize up. You may also experience problems with your liver and circulation, so stick to the plain wholefoods that you actually prefer, even when you're eating out or keen not to offend someone's home cooking. You can suffer bilious attacks or migraine set off by a too-rich diet.

Your mental health can survive severe and shocking turns

of events and your ability to cope in strange and difficult circumstances is one of your chief strengths. You are good at adopting entirely new patterns of behaviour for yourself, too. Never let your agile, expansive mind stay unchallenged. You have the ability to learn at any age.

LIVING WITH MARS IN SAGITTARIUS

Slow down – life doesn't have to be all or nothing. You'll get more out of everything you do if you take the time to savour it, decide on a course of action and follow it through. Let the Mars influence set a pace to your life and help you to see the way ahead.

Mars in Capricorn

SEX LIFE DRIVE

You hold very definite views about what you want – and don't want – to do in bed. You tend to make up your mind very early in life, too, and rarely vary your lovemaking routine to suit others' tastes. This is okay if you've been lucky enough to find a partner who suits your most intimate needs. But if circumstances dictate a change of lover – something you dislike and dread – then you can't easily adapt physically to the newcomer.

You're an astute lover when you and your bedmate are in tune with one another. But there are times when you insist on doing it all your way and that's when a gaping communications gap usually yawns! Sexually faithful as a rule, you'll skip extra thrills rather than tussle with learning new tricks, and you conserve your powers by developing and refining one relationship over a period of time.

You are fairly conservative and prefer your lovemaking to have certain boundaries, doing only what you feel is acceptable. In any affair, you need to know that you have the situation well under control, which can mean you eventually grow tired of always being the one to call the shots.

Above all, you want to keep your sex life private, yet, much to your dismay, others have always taken far too much interest in what you're up to. Your affairs have a powerful effect on your career, too, often working to your benefit. Not surprisingly, this can cause jealous ructions with colleagues.

You lend a whole new meaning to the term 'sleeping

partner', for it's quite likely that you're with someone for work and play, right round the clock. Fortunately, you are highly self-disciplined and are able to keep your lovelife in one compartment, your job in another. You won't let slip an out-of-place 'darling' at a business meeting or prod someone awake to take a note of your latest idea.

But beware the double backwash any breakup is bound to bring. You can quite easily handle having to carry on working with the person you're no longer carrying on with, but a partner may not cope so well. Often, though, you're such a workaholic that unless your sex mate shared your working day, they'd see little of you!

Come nightfall, you can be too zonked for sex. So get out your diaries and make a few lunchtime-loving appointments if you want to keep a healthy balance in your life. Even better, schedule some getaway breaks into that rigidly serious timetable to ginger up existing romance.

You don't lack sexual passion but you can set it aside when you think more important matters merit your attention. This can make you appear more cold-blooded than you actually are. You're never short of admirers and your important work role turns people on. And although no-one could ever find you an accommodating, self-sacrificing lover, you do please in other ways. You're straightforward, you don't mind a big age gap and you don't judge on looks alone. You always shoulder responsibility for things like birth control, and you're always prepared to put in the hard work that ensures that an affair lasts a lifetime.

MARS AND YOUR WORK

You don't waste a single drop of your work energy. You're driven towards achieving worldly success and it probably means more to you than personal satisfaction. Extremely ambitious, completely self-reliant and chock-full of initiative, you are a highly organised worker. You excel at making plans and are valued accordingly. But you also find it hard to blend into a large organisation because your desire for power and authority gives you too many hard, sharp corners for others' comfort.

Serious and determined, you will also work hard to improve yourself. You're the classic case of someone who's wrenched themselves up by their bootstraps from unpromising beginnings. You are also fairly unusual in that you enjoy routine and can tolerate some pretty monotonous tasks.

You stick to your decisions, never take short cuts and, once your intense concentration and amazing persistence are beamed onto the right target, you zoom to the top. Any job you take on must offer you recognition, power, security and good money, in that order.

Punctilious and demanding, you expect a lot of fellow workers, though you have their good at heart. You don't baulk at barrackings and sackings and you can dish out criticism calmly and constructively. This is a great Mars placing for big business, taking you from errand-runner to boss, and brings happiness provided you don't become a workaholic.

MARS AND YOUR HEALTH

Built to last, you've the kind of good bones that mean you'll look great well into your later years. Your vital energies are all geared towards endurance. Certainly, you have a rare ability to tolerate extremes of physical discomfort and your body has a wiry resistance that seems to thrive on insufficient sleep or sustenance.

Just about your only possible weaknesses are back, joint and knee problems, and occasional painful bouts of teeth trouble. But most of these worries are linked to the ageing process and are not out of the ordinary. Short of moving to a warmer, gentler, drier climate, there really isn't much you can do to improve your basically healthy physique.

Mentally, however, you could do with some help. Your tendency to weave your own private network of escalating worries will etch itself on your face and hamper digestion.

You waste far too much energy constructing an elaborate public image that you are afraid others will see through. You rarely, if ever, seek help or sympathy, preferring to fight your problems alone – a needless extension of your suffering. Gloomy moods last longer than they need because of your stubborn, go-it-alone attitude.

Learn to bother less about your reputation and take positive steps to unwind if you want to tackle depression once and for all. You probably take life too seriously and would benefit from any therapy that reminds you what fun life can be. Try to change your lifestyle and let more love in, too.

LIVING WITH MARS IN CAPRICORN

Use all that Mars energy to drive you onwards and upwards. The sky's the limit for you, as long as you keep an open mind and see opportunities for what they are. Don't expect too much of others – allow partners and friends to have some human failings. A little more kindness for others along the way will make your success all the sweeter.

Mars in Aquarius

SEX LIFE DRIVE

Variety spices your sex life and you like to play the field. Fulfilment comes in many shapes and guises and, being an unconventional, independent type, you want to make the most of each new opportunity. There's an overwhelming temptation in your case to become a complete playboy or playgirl and, because you are remarkably unaffected by sexual jealousy yourself, you see little harm in having more than one partner on the go at once.

However, your goals are both variety and intimacy in your sex life, a tough combination to fit together. Your best bet is probably one partner who's as experimentally minded as you. You are highly desirable and go out of your way to find out your lover's favourite fantasies and then try to re-enact them. Freedom's a vital part of any pairing you enter into, even if you don't always exercise your right to it.

You should be more aware of the devastating effect your casual attitude can have on others. Partners often find slipping into an affair with you as easy as falling off a log. But deep and dangerous emotions are often stirred up once your free-loving approach becomes obvious. Some people find it painful to stay in an intimate relationship with you. What's more, you're often blissfully unaware of seething rivalries and jealousies.

On the plus side, you rarely disapprove of anything your lover does and won't turn a hair at anything in their past. You invest lots of energy in your sex life and, despite your willingness to launch off into unexplored new territory, you like your love affairs to last a satisfyingly long time.

You always want the best and so when you pick a partner you tend to gravitate towards the most attractive and those with reputations for being good lovers.

Although you make every effort to ensure that anyone who shares sex with you is in for a beautiful, unforgettable experience, you can concentrate too much on technique. Secretly, non-physical intimacy worries you and so you're scared of falling in love. This explains why you occasionally leave partners at the most passionate moments and dash off to visit some of your many friends. You also frequently jeopardise established affairs by chasing after potential fun on the side, and tend to get involved with married lovers and other unsatisfactory bedmates who can't give you everything that you really need.

You can show a remarkable lack of caution in choosing those you sleep with but often you genuinely don't care what other people think. You also like to stay friends with past lovers once the flame of lust has died. You don't like lulls between partners but your sex life is usually at its most glowing once you stop looking for potential lovers.

MARS AND YOUR WORK

Friends play a part in helping you to achieve your working ambitions. But set against this unexpected advantage is your own tendency to pick jobs and work partners rather unwisely. As a boss, you're prone to hire people you've met at a party, promoting them beyond their abilities. As an employee, you sign contracts for the flimsiest of reasons.

You often neglect work for the sake of your social life, too. When you do get your head down, though, you're an original and independent asset. Provided you have a firm objective, you will certainly put in long hours. And your imagination makes you a brilliant inventor.

You find it hard to cope with any job where you're asked to handle other people's ideas, preferring to produce your own. You are a stranger to fatigue or burnout, and others admire and envy your willpower, quick reactions and determination. Highly observant and with a well-developed sense of duty, you're keen on work that's linked to any kind of reform, human rights, freedom, science and progress.

You can't bear behind-the-scenes wheeler-dealing or any underhand behaviour. You loathe political manoeuvring at work and rely instead on intuition, originality and a flair for hitting it off with people at all levels. You need a job with a good measure of built-in excitement and scope for getting on. If it doesn't contribute to the happiness of mankind, then you'll work for a good cause in your spare time. Any work problems can usually be traced to missed appointments and rebelliousness on your part. You should try to be more open to colleagues' suggestions.

MARS AND YOUR HEALTH

The way you relate to other people is both your chief psychological strength and your greatest weakness. You thrive in networks, filtering your own ideas effectively through them and multiplying your ability to get things done by enlisting wide support. But you're also far more influenced by people pressure than you realise. You waste time and energy worrying whether people will like you or not, despite your outward air of devil-may-care individuality and this can lead to psychological problems.

This applies in particular to your working life. You express your feelings with some difficulty and a degree of inconsistency. Once someone has become truly intimate with you – which is much harder than your friendly veneer would suggest – it's always one step forwards and two back. In fact, you can go for years without telling a partner or close friend how much they mean to you. You tend to be more emotionally open with total strangers and so respond to therapy.

However, all this is no surprise to you because you're pretty hot on self-knowledge, though you lack the discipline to make those changes you know are needed. Only you realise that sometimes you're not half as caring as you come across to others.

Physically, you have to watch your circulation system as you get older. You can offset any inherited artery troubles by cutting animal fats almost entirely from your diet and by walking instead of going everywhere by car. Allow more time, keep up a brisk pace, and do your body a favour. Your ankles, calves and Achilles' tendons are also weak spots, so if you join the kind of sports club that you love socially, never skimp on those vital warm-ups before you exercise.

LIVING WITH MARS IN AQUARIUS

Channel your feelings in a positive direction. Don't be scared by the force of your emotions. Refusing to accept them or simply backing away when the going gets tough – or hot – won't achieve anything. You'll get more out of lovers and colleagues if you understand the effect you have on those around you.

Mars in Pisces

SEX LIFE DRIVE

Intuitive and adaptable you may be, but you can be too subtle for some tastes. You live much of your sex life inside your mind, and few lovers can surpass you when it comes to highly imaginative lovemaking that mirrors fantasies. You help others fulfil their wildest dreams.

And yet you're not first and foremost a sexual being. Thoughts and feelings count more with you than physicality. But while you may lack the kind of raw aggression that bowls people over and into bed, you more than compensate in a love relationship with all the gestures of affection you make to your partner.

Capable of immense self-sacrifice and always preferring others to take the lead, you must guard against allowing yourself to slip into a suffering sexual role. You need the kind of relationship in which you share a deep, unspoken understanding. You hate all that's crude or over-explicit.

Yet you are also often driven and obsessed by secret sex fantasies. You are both drawn to and repelled by unexplored dreams, so starting an affair isn't always simple for you. And although you can create some uniquely powerful partnerships, you're also likely to run into a few kinky individuals on your way.

It's not easy finding someone to play mind-games with you. There are likely to be long periods of unfulfilment, and you may have to travel widely to find those special partners who'll inspire you. At such times, frustration can make you act rashly, falling into bed and asking questions the next day, especially once your weakness for drink and late nights has been given free rein.

Experience is your best teacher. You never heed advice from worldlywise friends anyway and eventually your none-too-hot judgment will improve of its own accord. Anyway, you'll always reckon the rewards of some of your odder or more difficult liaisons are well worth it. But don't overlook health risks just because you're more interested in emotional ones.

Drawn to secret love affairs, you often live in fearful anticipation that your sexual relationships are going to meet with disapproval, whether or not there's a logical reason for this. You can be so keyed up to expect the kind of perfect pairing only found in romantic fiction and films that you hesitate to plunge into a real flesh-and-blood romance.

You find other people's imperfections, both physical and emotional, hard to accept. But your helpless streak makes plenty of people want to take you under their wing. You use your intuition to pick out what turns a lover on, then hone your technique. You may be passive and shy at the start of lovemaking, but you'll soon grow bolder in the right bed.

MARS AND YOUR WORK

Versatile and with strong artistic inclinations, you have creative talents galore. You couple this with a deeply genuine concern for people in need, so you'd be happiest working in fields such as music or the theatre, or anywhere you can put others in touch with a world beyond day-to-day reality.

You may do quite a lot of work for nothing in order to satisfy this altruistic streak, or take a low salary for a job. Provided that your work absorbs you, heart and soul, that more than compensates for any lack of financial satisfaction, as long as you've enough to get by on. You aren't greedy or particularly materialistic.

But despite your love of others, you prefer to work alone and you react badly to obvious pressure because you need to take daydreaming breaks from time to time for inspiration. Your working energies are considerable but they ebb and flow. Mars in Pisces absorbs others' ideas like a sponge, and what you read and hear influences you totally.

It's almost as if you become the last person you talked to. It would suit you to start out as the invaluable assistant of a powerful figure, who would influence you completely. Eventually, you would take this person's ideas one stage further, moulding them and making them your own.

You can be hampered by impracticality and need a work partner who can balance your creative touch with management and money-handling skills. Without a focus, your career could dissolve into a mist of disjointed false starts.

MARS AND YOUR HEALTH

Lack of daring can create psychological problems for you in the long term. Remember that later regrets usually centre on all those things you didn't do when you had the chance. You are prone to emotional disturbances and stress because you are so ultra-sensitive to other people. Your only defence – and it's one you already use quite naturally – is to tune out altogether from time to time. You cope with overstimulation by not seeing anyone for a while and by sleeping a lot. This is a healthier solution than your other occasional escape routes from the rigours of reality – sex, TV, over-eating, drinking – and worse.

You are far too idealistic and tend to deny your anger. You get swamped by uncomfortable but potent feelings and then act irrationally, even with violence. But because you are so open to suggestion, you're easily hypnotised and any therapy which helps you acknowledge all your feelings will be of benefit.

Apart from a lifelong tendency to put on too much weight, your constitution is generally good. Self-destructive habits such as a bad diet and too much alcohol will undermine it, though, and highlight your weak points – your bodily fluids system, glands, and the route to your stomach.

Your feet, too, may play up, but this is probably linked to your escalating weight!

Meditation, water-tank rebirthing, swimming and dancing are relaxants that suit your temperament. Drugs trigger allergy problems for you, so talk to your doctor about trying natural remedies whenever possible.

LIVING WITH MARS IN PISCES

Anchor your intuitive sensitivity in day-to-day reality. You tend to view life through rosy-tinted binoculars and, close to, it will never live up to your expectations. But although life may never be totally perfect, it's within your power to make it as good as it can possibly be.

Sun Sign Tables

Our year has 365 days, but the sun takes an extra five hours and 50 minutes each year to move through all the signs of the zodiac. So the time of day, and the date, it enters each sign varies from year to year. When dates like 23 July to 23 August are given for Leo, for example, this can only mean that most years the sun was in Leo for most of 23 July. But some years it was already in Leo by the evening of the 22 July, sometimes it spends quite a lot of the 23 July still in Cancer, and just three times this century it didn't move into Leo until the early hours of the 24 July.

If you were born near the beginning or end of your sun sign, please turn to that sun sign in these tables and check your year, day and time of birth to get your true sun sign.

Times used in the tables are GMT.

SUN INTO ARIES

Day	Year	Time of Day
21 March	1900	01:38
21 March	1901	07:23
21 March	1902	13:16
21 March	1903	19:14
21 March	1904	00:58
21 March	1905	06:57
21 March	1906	12:52
21 March	1907	18:32
21 March	1908	00:27
21 March	1909	06:13
21 March	1910	12:02
21 March	1911	17:54
20 March	1912	23:28
21 March	1913	05:18
21 March	1914	11:10
21 March	1915	16:51
20 March	1916	22:47
21 March	1917	04:37
21 March	1918	10:25
21 March	1919	16:19
20 March	1920	21:59
21 March	1921	03:51
21 March	1922	09:48
21 March	1923	15:28
20 March	1924	21:21
21 March	1925	03:12
21 March	1926	09:01
21 March	1927	14:59
20 March	1928	20:44
21 March	1929	02:35
21 March	1930	08:30
21 March	1931	14:06
20 March	1932	19:54
21 March	1933	01:43
21 March	1934	07:28
21 March	1935	13:18
20 March	1936	18:57
21 March	1937	00:45
21 March	1938	06:43

Day	Year	Time of Day
21 March	1939	12:28
20 March	1940	18:24
21 March	1941	00:20
21 March	1942	06:10
21 March	1943	12:03
20 March	1944	17:48
20 March	1945	23:37
21 March	1946	05:32
21 March	1947	11:12
20 March	1948	16:57
20 March	1949	22:48
21 March	1950	04:35
21 March	1951	10:26
20 March	1952	16:14
20 March	1953	22:00
21 March	1954	03:53
21 March	1955	09:35
20 March	1956	15:21
20 March	1957	21:16
21 March	1958	03:06
21 March	1959	08:55
20 March	1960	14:43
20 March	1961	20:32
21 March	1962	02:30
21 March	1963	08:20
20 March	1964	14:10
20 March	1965	20:05
21 March	1966	01:53
21 March	1967	07:37
20 March	1968	13:22
20 March	1969	19:09
21 March	1970	00:57
21 March	1971	06:38
20 March	1972	12:21
20 March	1973	18:13
21 March	1974	00:07
21 March	1975	05:57
20 March	1976	11:50
20 March	1977	17:43

20 March	1978	23:34	20 March	1990	21:20
21 March	1979	05:22	21 March	1991	03:02
20 March	1980	11:10	20 March	1992	08:49
20 March	1981	17:03	20 March	1993	14:41
20 March	1982	22:56	20 March	1994	20:29
21 March	1983	04:39	21 March	1995	02:15
20 March	1984	10:25	20 March	1996	08:04
20 March	1985	16:14	20 March	1997	13:56
20 March	1986	22:03	20 March	1998	19:55
21 March	1987	03:52	21 March	1999	01:47
20 March	1988	09:40	20 March	2000	07:36
20 March	1989	15:29	20 March	2001	13:32

SUN INTO TAURUS

Day	*Year*	*Time of Day*	*Day*	*Year*	*Time of Day*
20 April	1900	13:27	20 April	1925	14:51
20 April	1901	19:13	20 April	1926	20:36
21 April	1902	01:04	21 April	1927	02:32
21 April	1903	06:58	20 April	1928	08:16
20 April	1904	12:41	20 April	1929	14:10
20 April	1905	18:43	20 April	1930	20:06
21 April	1906	00:39	21 April	1931	01:39
21 April	1907	06:17	20 April	1932	07:28
20 April	1908	12:11	20 April	1933	13:19
20 April	1909	17:58	20 April	1934	19:00
20 April	1910	23:45	21 April	1935	00:50
21 April	1911	05:36	20 April	1936	06:31
20 April	1912	11:11	20 April	1937	12:19
20 April	1913	17:02	20 April	1938	18:15
20 April	1914	22:53	20 April	1939	23:55
21 April	1915	04:28	20 April	1940	05:51
20 April	1916	10:24	20 April	1941	11:51
20 April	1917	16:17	20 April	1942	17:39
20 April	1918	22:05	20 April	1943	23:32
21 April	1919	03:59	20 April	1944	05:17
20 April	1920	09:39	20 April	1945	11:07
20 April	1921	15:32	20 April	1946	17:02
20 April	1922	21:28	20 April	1947	22:39
21 April	1923	03:05	20 April	1948	04:25
20 April	1924	08:59	20 April	1949	10:17

20 April	1950	15:59	19 April	1976	23:03
20 April	1951	21:48	20 April	1977	04:58
20 April	1952	03:36	20 April	1978	10:50
20 April	1953	09:25	20 April	1979	16:36
20 April	1954	15:19	19 April	1980	22:23
20 April	1955	20:57	20 April	1981	04:19
20 April	1956	02:44	20 April	1982	10:08
20 April	1957	08:41	20 April	1983	15:50
20 April	1958	14:27	19 April	1984	21:38
20 April	1959	20:17	20 April	1985	03:26
20 April	1960	02:06	20 April	1986	09:13
20 April	1961	07:55	20 April	1987	14:58
20 April	1962	13:51	19 April	1988	20:46
20 April	1963	19:36	20 April	1989	02:39
20 April	1964	01:27	20 April	1990	08:27
20 April	1965	07:26	20 April	1991	14:09
20 April	1966	13:12	19 April	1992	19:57
20 April	1967	18:56	20 April	1993	01:49
20 April	1968	00:42	20 April	1994	07:37
20 April	1969	06:27	20 April	1995	13:22
20 April	1970	12:16	19 April	1996	19:11
20 April	1971	17:54	20 April	1997	01:04
19 April	1972	23:38	20 April	1998	06:58
20 April	1973	05:31	20 April	1999	12:47
20 April	1974	11:19	19 April	2000	18:40
20 April	1975	17:08	20 April	2001	00:37

SUN INTO GEMINI

Day	*Year*	*Time of Day*	*Day*	*Year*	*Time of Day*
21 May	1900	13:17	22 May	1911	05:18
21 May	1901	19:04	21 May	1912	10:56
22 May	1902	00:53	21 May	1913	16:49
22 May	1903	06:45	21 May	1914	22:37
21 May	1904	12:28	22 May	1915	04:10
21 May	1905	18:31	21 May	1916	10:05
22 May	1906	00:24	21 May	1917	15:58
22 May	1907	06:03	21 May	1918	21:45
21 May	1908	11:58	22 May	1919	03:39
21 May	1909	17:45	21 May	1920	09:21
21 May	1910	23:30	21 May	1921	15:16

21 May	1922	21:10	21 May	1962	13:17
22 May	1923	02:45	21 May	1963	18:58
21 May	1924	08:40	21 May	1964	00:50
21 May	1925	14:33	21 May	1965	06:51
21 May	1926	20:15	21 May	1966	12:32
22 May	1927	02:08	21 May	1967	18:18
21 May	1928	07:52	21 May	1968	00:06
21 May	1929	13:47	21 May	1969	05:50
21 May	1930	19:42	21 May	1970	11:38
22 May	1931	01:15	21 May	1971	17:15
21 May	1932	07:07	20 May	1972	23:00
21 May	1933	12:57	21 May	1973	04:55
21 May	1934	18:35	21 May	1974	10:36
22 May	1935	00:25	21 May	1975	16:24
21 May	1936	06:07	20 May	1976	22:21
21 May	1937	11:57	21 May	1977	04:15
21 May	1938	17:50	21 May	1978	10:10
21 May	1939	23:26	21 May	1979	15:55
21 May	1940	05:23	20 May	1980	21:43
21 May	1941	11:23	21 May	1981	03:40
21 May	1942	17:09	21 May	1982	09:23
21 May	1943	23:03	21 May	1983	15:07
21 May	1944	04:50	20 May	1984	20:58
21 May	1945	10:41	21 May	1985	02:43
21 May	1946	16:34	21 May	1986	08:28
21 May	1947	22:09	21 May	1987	14:11
21 May	1948	03:57	20 May	1988	19:57
21 May	1949	09:51	21 May	1989	01:54
21 May	1950	15:27	21 May	1990	07:38
21 May	1951	21:15	21 May	1991	13:20
21 May	1952	03:04	20 May	1992	19:13
21 May	1953	08:53	21 May	1993	01:02
21 May	1954	14:48	21 May	1994	06:49
21 May	1955	20:24	21 May	1995	12:35
21 May	1956	02:13	20 May	1996	18:24
21 May	1957	08:10	21 May	1997	00:19
21 May	1958	13:51	21 May	1998	06:06
21 May	1959	19:42	21 May	1999	11:53
21 May	1960	01:34	20 May	2000	17:50
21 May	1961	07:22	20 May	2001	23:45

SUN INTO CANCER

Day	Year	Time of Day
21 June	1900	21:40
22 June	1901	03:27
22 June	1902	09:15
22 June	1903	15:04
21 June	1904	20:51
22 June	1905	02:51
22 June	1906	08:41
22 June	1907	14:23
21 June	1908	20:19
22 June	1909	02:06
22 June	1910	07:49
22 June	1911	13:35
21 June	1912	19:16
22 June	1913	01:09
22 June	1914	06:54
22 June	1915	12:29
21 June	1916	18:24
22 June	1917	00:14
22 June	1918	05:59
22 June	1919	11:53
21 June	1920	17:40
21 June	1921	23:35
22 June	1922	05:26
22 June	1923	11:02
21 June	1924	16:59
21 June	1925	22:50
22 June	1926	04:30
22 June	1927	10:22
21 June	1928	16:06
21 June	1929	22:00
22 June	1930	03:53
22 June	1931	09:28
21 June	1932	15:23
21 June	1933	21:12
22 June	1934	02:48
22 June	1935	08:38
21 June	1936	14:22
21 June	1937	20:12
22 June	1938	02:04

Day	Year	Time of Day
22 June	1939	07:39
21 June	1940	13:36
21 June	1941	19:33
22 June	1942	01:16
22 June	1943	07:13
21 June	1944	13:02
21 June	1945	18:52
22 June	1946	00:45
22 June	1947	06:19
21 June	1948	12:10
21 June	1949	18:02
21 June	1950	23:36
22 June	1951	05:25
21 June	1952	11:12
21 June	1953	17:00
21 June	1954	22:54
22 June	1955	04:32
21 June	1956	10:24
21 June	1957	16:20
21 June	1958	21:57
22 June	1959	03:49
21 June	1960	09:42
21 June	1961	15:30
21 June	1962	21:25
22 June	1963	03:04
21 June	1964	08:57
21 June	1965	14:56
21 June	1966	20:34
22 June	1967	02:23
21 June	1968	08:13
21 June	1969	13:56
21 June	1970	19:43
22 June	1971	01:20
21 June	1972	07:06
21 June	1973	13:01
21 June	1974	18:38
22 June	1975	00:27
21 June	1976	06:24
21 June	1977	12:15

21 June	1978	18:11	21 June	1990	15:33
21 June	1979	23:57	21 June	1991	21:19
21 June	1980	05:47	21 June	1992	03:15
21 June	1981	11:46	21 June	1993	09:00
21 June	1982	17:24	21 June	1994	14:48
21 June	1983	23:09	21 June	1995	20:35
21 June	1984	05:03	21 June	1996	02:24
21 June	1985	10:45	21 June	1997	08:21
21 June	1986	16:30	21 June	1998	14:03
21 June	1987	22:11	21 June	1999	19:50
21 June	1988	03:57	21 June	2000	01:48
21 June	1989	09:54	21 June	2001	07:38

SUN INTO LEO

Day	*Year*	*Time of Day*	*Day*	*Year*	*Time of Day*
23 July	1900	08:36	23 July	1925	09:44
23 July	1901	14:23	23 July	1926	15:24
23 July	1902	20:10	23 July	1927	21:16
24 July	1903	01:58	23 July	1928	03:02
23 July	1904	07:49	23 July	1929	08:53
23 July	1905	13:45	23 July	1930	14:42
23 July	1906	19:32	23 July	1931	20:21
24 July	1907	01:17	23 July	1932	02:18
23 July	1908	07:14	23 July	1933	08:05
23 July	1909	13:00	23 July	1934	13:42
23 July	1910	18:43	23 July	1935	19:33
24 July	1911	00:28	23 July	1936	01:18
23 July	1912	06:13	23 July	1937	07:07
23 July	1913	12:04	23 July	1938	12:57
23 July	1914	17:46	23 July	1939	18:36
23 July	1915	23:26	23 July	1940	00:34
23 July	1916	05:21	23 July	1941	06:26
23 July	1917	11:07	23 July	1942	12:07
23 July	1918	16:51	23 July	1943	18:04
23 July	1919	22:44	22 July	1944	23:56
23 July	1920	04:35	23 July	1945	05:46
23 July	1921	10:30	23 July	1946	11:37
23 July	1922	16:19	23 July	1947	17:14
23 July	1923	22:00	22 July	1948	23:07
23 July	1924	03:57	23 July	1949	04:57

23 July	1950	10:29	22 July	1976	17:19
23 July	1951	16:21	22 July	1977	23:04
22 July	1952	22:08	23 July	1978	05:01
23 July	1953	03:52	23 July	1979	10:49
23 July	1954	09:45	22 July	1980	16:42
23 July	1955	15:25	22 July	1981	22:40
22 July	1956	21:20	23 July	1982	04:16
23 July	1957	03:15	23 July	1983	10:05
23 July	1958	08:50	22 July	1984	15:59
23 July	1959	14:45	22 July	1985	21:37
22 July	1960	20:37	23 July	1986	03:25
23 July	1961	02:23	23 July	1987	09:07
23 July	1962	08:18	22 July	1988	14:51
23 July	1963	13:59	22 July	1989	20:46
22 July	1964	19:53	23 July	1990	02:22
23 July	1965	01:48	23 July	1991	08:11
23 July	1966	07:23	22 July	1992	14:09
23 July	1967	13:16	22 July	1993	19:51
22 July	1968	19:08	23 July	1994	01:42
23 July	1969	00:48	23 July	1995	07:30
23 July	1970	06:37	22 July	1996	13:19
23 July	1971	12:15	22 July	1997	19:16
22 July	1972	18:03	23 July	1998	00:56
22 July	1973	23:56	23 July	1999	06:45
23 July	1974	05:31	22 July	2000	12:43
23 July	1975	11:22	22 July	2001	18:27

SUN INTO VIRGO

Day	*Year*	*Time of Day*	*Day*	*Year*	*Time of Day*
23 August	1900	15:20	24 August	1910	01:27
23 August	1901	21:07	24 August	1911	07:13
24 August	1902	02:53	23 August	1912	13:01
24 August	1903	08:41	23 August	1913	18:48
23 August	1904	14:36	24 August	1914	00:29
23 August	1905	20:28	24 August	1915	06:15
24 August	1906	02:13	23 August	1916	12:08
24 August	1907	08:03	23 August	1917	17:53
23 August	1908	13:57	23 August	1918	23:36
23 August	1909	19:43	24 August	1919	05:28

23 August	1920	11:21
23 August	1921	17:15
23 August	1922	23:04
24 August	1923	04:51
23 August	1924	10:47
23 August	1925	16:33
23 August	1926	22:14
24 August	1927	04:05
23 August	1928	09:53
23 August	1929	15:41
23 August	1930	21:26
24 August	1931	03:10
23 August	1932	09:06
23 August	1933	14:51
23 August	1934	20:32
24 August	1935	02:24
23 August	1936	08:10
23 August	1937	13:58
23 August	1938	19:46
24 August	1939	01:31
23 August	1940	07:28
23 August	1941	13:17
23 August	1942	18:58
24 August	1943	00:55
23 August	1944	06:46
23 August	1945	12:35
23 August	1946	18:27
24 August	1947	00:09
23 August	1948	06:02
23 August	1949	11:48
23 August	1950	17:23
23 August	1951	23:16
23 August	1952	05:03
23 August	1953	10:45
23 August	1954	16:36
23 August	1955	22:19
23 August	1956	04:15
23 August	1957	10:08
23 August	1958	15:46
23 August	1959	21:43
23 August	1960	03:34
23 August	1961	09:18
23 August	1962	15:13
23 August	1963	20:57
23 August	1964	02:51
23 August	1965	08:42
23 August	1966	14:18
23 August	1967	20:12
23 August	1968	02:03
23 August	1969	07:43
23 August	1970	13:34
23 August	1971	19:15
23 August	1972	01:03
23 August	1973	06:54
23 August	1974	12:29
23 August	1975	18:24
23 August	1976	00:19
23 August	1977	06:01
23 August	1978	11:57
23 August	1979	17:47
22 August	1980	23:41
23 August	1981	05:39
23 August	1982	11:16
23 August	1983	17:08
22 August	1984	23:01
23 August	1985	04:36
23 August	1986	10:26
23 August	1987	16:10
22 August	1988	21:55
23 August	1989	03:47
23 August	1990	09:21
23 August	1991	15:13
22 August	1992	21:11
23 August	1993	02:51
23 August	1994	08:44
23 August	1995	14:35
22 August	1996	20:23
23 August	1997	02:19
23 August	1998	08:00
23 August	1999	13:52
22 August	2000	19:49
23 August	2001	01:28

SUN INTO LIBRA

Day	*Year*	*Time of Day*	*Day*	*Year*	*Time of Day*
23 September	1900	12:20	23 September	1939	22:49
23 September	1901	18:08	23 September	1940	04:45
23 September	1902	23:55	23 September	1941	10:32
24 September	1903	05:43	23 September	1942	16:16
23 September	1904	11:40	23 September	1943	22:11
23 September	1905	17:29	23 September	1944	04:01
23 September	1906	23:14	23 September	1945	09:49
24 September	1907	05:08	23 September	1946	15:41
23 September	1908	10:58	23 September	1947	21:29
23 September	1909	16:44	23 September	1948	03:21
23 September	1910	22:30	23 September	1949	09:06
24 September	1911	04:17	23 September	1950	14:43
23 September	1912	10:08	23 September	1951	20:37
23 September	1913	15:52	23 September	1952	02:23
23 September	1914	21:33	23 September	1953	08:06
24 September	1915	03:23	23 September	1954	13:55
23 September	1916	09:14	23 September	1955	19:41
23 September	1917	15:00	23 September	1956	01:35
23 September	1918	20:45	23 September	1957	07:26
24 September	1919	02:35	23 September	1958	13:09
23 September	1920	08:28	23 September	1959	19:08
23 September	1921	14:19	23 September	1960	00:58
23 September	1922	20:09	23 September	1961	06:42
24 September	1923	02:03	23 September	1962	12:36
23 September	1924	07:58	23 September	1963	18:23
23 September	1925	13:43	23 September	1964	00:17
23 September	1926	19:26	23 September	1965	06:06
24 September	1927	01:17	23 September	1966	11:43
23 September	1928	07:05	23 September	1967	17:38
23 September	1929	12:52	22 September	1968	23:26
23 September	1930	18:36	23 September	1969	05:06
24 September	1931	00:23	23 September	1970	10:59
23 September	1932	06:15	23 September	1971	16:45
23 September	1933	12:00	22 September	1972	22:33
23 September	1934	17:44	23 September	1973	04:21
23 September	1935	23:38	23 September	1974	09:59
23 September	1936	05:26	23 September	1975	15:55
23 September	1937	11:13	22 September	1976	21:48
23 September	1938	17:00	23 September	1977	03:30

23 September	1978	09:26	23 September	1990	06:56
23 September	1979	15:17	23 September	1991	12:49
22 September	1980	21:09	22 September	1992	18:43
23 September	1981	03:06	23 September	1993	00:23
23 September	1982	08:47	23 September	1994	06:20
23 September	1983	14:42	23 September	1995	12:13
22 September	1984	20:33	22 September	1996	18:00
23 September	1985	02:08	22 September	1997	23:56
23 September	1986	07:59	23 September	1998	05:38
23 September	1987	13:45	23 September	1999	11:32
22 September	1988	19:29	22 September	2000	17:28
23 September	1989	01:20	22 September	2001	23:05

SUN INTO SCORPIO

Day	*Year*	*Time of Day*	*Day*	*Year*	*Time of Day*
23 October	1900	20:54	23 October	1924	16:44
24 October	1901	02:45	23 October	1925	22:30
24 October	1902	08:35	24 October	1926	04:18
24 October	1903	14:22	24 October	1927	10:07
23 October	1904	20:18	23 October	1928	15:54
24 October	1905	02:07	23 October	1929	21:41
24 October	1906	07:54	24 October	1930	03:26
24 October	1907	13:50	24 October	1931	09:15
23 October	1908	19:36	23 October	1932	15:03
24 October	1909	01:22	23 October	1933	20:47
24 October	1910	07:11	24 October	1934	02:35
24 October	1911	12:58	24 October	1935	08:28
23 October	1912	18:50	23 October	1936	14:18
24 October	1913	00:34	23 October	1937	20:06
24 October	1914	06:17	24 October	1938	01:54
24 October	1915	12:09	24 October	1939	07:46
23 October	1916	17:56	23 October	1940	13:39
23 October	1917	23:43	23 October	1941	19:27
24 October	1918	05:32	24 October	1942	01:15
24 October	1919	11:21	24 October	1943	07:08
23 October	1920	17:12	23 October	1944	12:55
23 October	1921	23:02	23 October	1945	18:43
24 October	1922	04:52	24 October	1946	00:35
24 October	1923	10:50	24 October	1947	06:26

			Day	Year	Time of Day
23 October	1948	12:18	24 October	1975	01:06
23 October	1949	18:03	23 October	1976	06:58
23 October	1950	23:44	23 October	1977	12:41
24 October	1951	05:36	23 October	1978	18:37
23 October	1952	11:22	24 October	1979	00:28
23 October	1953	17:06	23 October	1980	06:17
23 October	1954	22:56	23 October	1981	12:13
24 October	1955	04:43	23 October	1982	17:58
23 October	1956	10:34	23 October	1983	23:55
23 October	1957	16:24	23 October	1984	05:46
23 October	1958	22:11	23 October	1985	11:22
24 October	1959	04:11	23 October	1986	17:14
23 October	1960	10:01	23 October	1987	23:01
23 October	1961	15:47	23 October	1988	04:44
23 October	1962	21:40	23 October	1989	10:36
24 October	1963	03:29	23 October	1990	16:15
23 October	1964	09:20	23 October	1991	22:06
23 October	1965	15:10	23 October	1992	03:58
23 October	1966	20:51	23 October	1993	09:38
24 October	1967	02:44	23 October	1994	15:37
23 October	1968	08:29	23 October	1995	21:32
23 October	1969	14:10	23 October	1996	03:19
23 October	1970	20:04	23 October	1997	09:15
24 October	1971	01:53	23 October	1998	14:59
23 October	1972	07:41	23 October	1999	20:53
23 October	1973	13:30	23 October	2000	02:48
23 October	1974	19:11	23 October	2001	08:26

SUN INTO SAGITTARIUS

Day	*Year*	*Time of Day*	*Day*	*Year*	*Time of Day*
22 November	1900	17:47	22 November	1909	22:20
22 November	1901	23:40	23 November	1910	04:11
23 November	1902	05:34	23 November	1911	09:55
23 November	1903	11:20	22 November	1912	15:48
22 November	1904	17:15	22 November	1913	21:35
22 November	1905	23:04	23 November	1914	03:20
23 November	1906	04:53	23 November	1915	09:13
23 November	1907	10:51	22 November	1916	14:57
22 November	1908	16:34	22 November	1917	20:44

23 November	1918	02:37
23 November	1919	08:25
22 November	1920	14:15
22 November	1921	20:05
23 November	1922	01:55
23 November	1923	07:53
22 November	1924	13:46
22 November	1925	19:35
23 November	1926	01:27
23 November	1927	07:14
22 November	1928	13:00
22 November	1929	18:48
23 November	1930	00:34
23 November	1931	06:24
22 November	1932	12:10
22 November	1933	17:53
22 November	1934	23:43
23 November	1935	05:34
22 November	1936	11:25
22 November	1937	17:16
22 November	1938	23:06
23 November	1939	04:58
22 November	1940	10:49
22 November	1941	16:37
22 November	1942	22:30
23 November	1943	04:21
22 November	1944	10:07
22 November	1945	15:55
22 November	1946	21:46
23 November	1947	03:37
22 November	1948	09:29
22 November	1949	15:16
22 November	1950	21:02
23 November	1951	02:51
22 November	1952	08:35
22 November	1953	14:22
22 November	1954	20:14
23 November	1955	02:01
22 November	1956	07:50
22 November	1957	13:39
22 November	1958	19:29
23 November	1959	01:27
22 November	1960	07:18
22 November	1961	13:07
22 November	1962	19:01
23 November	1963	00:49
22 November	1964	06:39
22 November	1965	12:29
22 November	1966	18:14
23 November	1967	00:05
22 November	1968	05:49
22 November	1969	11:31
22 November	1970	17:24
22 November	1971	23:13
22 November	1972	05:02
22 November	1973	10:54
22 November	1974	16:39
22 November	1975	22:31
22 November	1976	04:21
22 November	1977	10:07
22 November	1978	16:04
22 November	1979	21:54
22 November	1980	03:41
22 November	1981	09:36
22 November	1982	15:24
22 November	1983	21:19
22 November	1984	03:11
22 November	1985	08:51
22 November	1986	14:44
22 November	1987	20:30
22 November	1988	02:12
22 November	1989	08:05
22 November	1990	13:47
22 November	1991	19:36
22 November	1992	01:26
22 November	1993	07:07
22 November	1994	13:06
22 November	1995	19:02
22 November	1996	00:50
22 November	1997	06:48
22 November	1998	12:35
22 November	1999	18:25
22 November	2000	00:20
22 November	2001	06:01

SUN INTO CAPRICORN

Day	Year	Time of Day	Day	Year	Time of Day
22 December	1900	06:40	22 December	1939	18:05
22 December	1901	12:36	21 December	1940	23:54
22 December	1902	18:34	22 December	1941	05:44
23 December	1903	00:19	22 December	1942	11:39
22 December	1904	06:13	22 December	1943	17:28
22 December	1905	12:03	21 December	1944	23:14
22 December	1906	17:52	22 December	1945	05:03
22 December	1907	23:50	22 December	1946	10:53
22 December	1908	05:33	22 December	1947	16:42
22 December	1909	11:19	21 December	1948	22:33
22 December	1910	17:11	22 December	1949	04:23
22 December	1911	22:53	22 December	1950	10:13
22 December	1912	04:44	22 December	1951	16:00
22 December	1913	10:34	21 December	1952	21:43
22 December	1914	16:22	22 December	1953	03:31
22 December	1915	22:15	22 December	1954	09:24
22 December	1916	03:58	22 December	1955	15:11
22 December	1917	09:45	21 December	1956	21:00
22 December	1918	15:41	22 December	1957	02:49
22 December	1919	21:27	22 December	1958	08:40
22 December	1920	03:17	22 December	1959	14:34
22 December	1921	09:08	21 December	1960	20:26
22 December	1922	14:57	22 December	1961	02:19
22 December	1923	20:53	22 December	1962	08:15
22 December	1924	02:45	22 December	1963	14:02
22 December	1925	08:37	21 December	1964	19:50
22 December	1926	14:33	22 December	1965	01:41
22 December	1927	20:18	22 December	1966	07:28
22 December	1928	02:03	22 December	1967	13:16
22 December	1929	07:52	21 December	1968	19:00
22 December	1930	13:39	22 December	1969	00:44
22 December	1931	19:29	22 December	1970	06:35
22 December	1932	01:14	22 December	1971	12:23
22 December	1933	06:57	21 December	1972	18:13
22 December	1934	12:49	22 December	1973	00:08
22 December	1935	18:36	22 December	1974	05:56
22 December	1936	00:26	22 December	1975	11:46
22 December	1937	06:21	21 December	1976	17:35
22 December	1938	12:13	21 December	1977	23:23

22 December	1978	05:21	22 December	1990	03:07
22 December	1979	11:10	22 December	1991	08:54
21 December	1980	16:56	21 December	1992	14:44
21 December	1981	22:51	21 December	1993	20:27
22 December	1982	04:38	22 December	1994	02:23
22 December	1983	10:31	22 December	1995	08:18
21 December	1984	16:23	21 December	1996	14:07
21 December	1985	22:08	21 December	1997	20:08
22 December	1986	04:02	22 December	1998	01:57
22 December	1987	09:46	22 December	1999	07:44
21 December	1988	15:28	21 December	2000	13:38
21 December	1989	21:22	21 December	2001	19:22

SUN INTO AQUARIUS

Day	*Year*	*Time of Day*	*Day*	*Year*	*Time of Day*
20 January	1900	11:31	21 January	1924	07:29
20 January	1901	17:16	20 January	1925	13:20
20 January	1902	23:11	20 January	1926	19:13
21 January	1903	05:13	21 January	1927	01:12
21 January	1904	10:57	21 January	1928	06:56
20 January	1905	16:51	20 January	1929	12:42
20 January	1906	22:42	20 January	1930	18:33
21 January	1907	04:30	21 January	1931	00:17
21 January	1908	10:27	21 January	1932	06:07
20 January	1909	16:10	20 January	1933	11:52
20 January	1910	21:58	20 January	1934	17:37
21 January	1911	03:51	20 January	1935	23:28
21 January	1912	09:29	21 January	1936	05:11
20 January	1913	15:19	20 January	1937	11:01
20 January	1914	21:11	20 January	1938	16:58
21 January	1915	02:59	20 January	1939	22:50
21 January	1916	08:53	21 January	1940	04:43
20 January	1917	14:37	20 January	1941	10:33
20 January	1918	20:24	20 January	1942	16:23
21 January	1919	02:20	20 January	1943	22:19
21 January	1920	08:04	21 January	1944	04:06
20 January	1921	13:54	20 January	1945	09:53
20 January	1922	19:48	20 January	1946	15:44
21 January	1923	01:35	20 January	1947	21:31

21 January	1948	03:18
20 January	1949	09:09
20 January	1950	15:00
20 January	1951	20:52
21 January	1952	02:38
20 January	1953	08:21
20 January	1954	14:11
20 January	1955	20:01
21 January	1956	01:49
20 January	1957	07:39
20 January	1958	13:29
20 January	1959	19:19
21 January	1960	01:10
20 January	1961	07:01
20 January	1962	12:58
20 January	1963	18:54
21 January	1964	00:41
20 January	1965	06:29
20 January	1966	12:20
20 January	1967	18:08
20 January	1968	23:54
20 January	1969	05:39
20 January	1970	11:24
20 January	1971	17:13
20 January	1972	22:59
20 January	1973	04:49
20 January	1974	10:46
20 January	1975	16:36
20 January	1976	22:25
20 January	1977	04:15
20 January	1978	10:04
20 January	1979	16:00
20 January	1980	21:49
20 January	1981	03:36
20 January	1982	09:31
20 January	1983	15:17
20 January	1984	21:06
20 January	1985	02:58
20 January	1986	08:47
20 January	1987	14:40
20 January	1988	20:25
20 January	1989	02:07
20 January	1990	08:02
20 January	1991	13:47
20 January	1992	19:33
20 January	1993	01:24
20 January	1994	07:08
20 January	1995	13:01
20 January	1996	18:54
20 January	1997	00:44
20 January	1998	06:47
20 January	1999	12:38
20 January	2000	18:24
20 January	2001	00:17

SUN INTO PISCES

Day	*Year*	*Time of Day*
19 February	1900	02:01
19 February	1901	07:44
19 February	1902	13:39
19 February	1903	19:40
20 February	1904	01:24
19 February	1905	07:20
19 February	1906	13:14
19 February	1907	18:57
20 February	1908	00:53
19 February	1909	06:38
19 February	1910	12:27
19 February	1911	18:20
19 February	1912	23:55
19 February	1913	05:44
19 February	1914	11:37
19 February	1915	17:23
19 February	1916	23:18
19 February	1917	05:04

19 February	1918	10:52	19 February	1960	15:27
19 February	1919	16:47	18 February	1961	21:17
19 February	1920	22:29	19 February	1962	03:15
19 February	1921	04:20	19 February	1963	09:09
19 February	1922	10:16	19 February	1964	14:57
19 February	1923	15:59	18 February	1965	20:48
19 February	1924	21:52	19 February	1966	02:38
19 February	1925	03:43	19 February	1967	08:24
19 February	1926	09:35	19 February	1968	14:09
19 February	1927	15:34	18 February	1969	19:55
19 February	1928	21:19	19 February	1970	01:42
19 February	1929	03:07	19 February	1971	07:27
19 February	1930	09:00	19 February	1972	13:11
19 February	1931	14:40	18 February	1973	19:02
19 February	1932	20:29	19 February	1974	00:59
19 February	1933	02:16	19 February	1975	06:50
19 February	1934	08:01	19 February	1976	12:40
19 February	1935	13:52	18 February	1977	18:31
19 February	1936	19:32	19 February	1978	00:21
19 February	1937	01:20	19 February	1979	06:13
19 February	1938	07:19	19 February	1980	12:02
19 February	1939	13:09	18 February	1981	17:52
19 February	1940	19:03	18 February	1982	23:46
19 February	1941	00:56	19 February	1983	05:31
19 February	1942	06:46	19 February	1984	11:17
19 February	1943	12:40	18 February	1985	17:08
19 February	1944	18:27	18 February	1986	22:58
19 February	1945	00:14	19 February	1987	04:50
19 February	1946	06:08	19 February	1988	10:36
19 February	1947	11:52	18 February	1989	16:21
19 February	1948	17:37	18 February	1990	22:14
18 February	1949	23:27	19 February	1991	03:58
19 February	1950	05:18	19 February	1992	09:44
19 February	1951	11:10	18 February	1993	15:36
19 February	1952	16:56	18 February	1994	21:22
18 February	1953	22:41	19 February	1995	03:12
19 February	1954	04:32	19 February	1996	09:02
19 February	1955	10:18	18 February	1997	14:53
19 February	1956	16:05	18 February	1998	20:56
18 February	1957	21:58	19 February	1999	02:47
19 February	1958	03:49	19 February	2000	08:34
19 February	1959	09:38	18 February	2001	14:28

British Summer Time (Daylight Saving Time)

If you were born during the times when the clocks were put forward, you need to deduct one hour (or two where double summer time is marked) to get back to Greenwich Mean Time.

The changes happen at 02.00 (but double summer time at 03.00)

1900 to 1915	No time changes
1916	21 April to 1 October
1917	8 April to 17 September
1918	24 March to 30 September
1919	30 March to 29 September
1920	28 March to 25 October
1921	3 April to 3 October
1922	26 March to 8 October
1923	22 April to 8 October
1924	13 April to 21 September
1925	19 April to 4 October
1926	18 April to 3 October
1927	10 April to 2 October
1928	22 April to 7 October
1929	21 April to 6 October
1930	4 April to 5 October
1931	19 April to 4 October
1932	17 April to 2 October
1933	9 April to 8 October
1934	22 April to 7 October
1935	14 April to 6 October

1936	19 April to 4 October
1937	18 April to 3 October
1938	10 April to 2 October
1939	16 April to 19 November
1940	25 February to 31 December
1941	all year (deduct two hours from 4 May to 10 August)
1942	all year (deduct two hours from 5 April to 9 August)
1943	all year (deduct two hours from 4 April to 15 August)
1944	all year (deduct two hours from 2 April to 17 September)
1945	all year (deduct two hours from 2 April to 15 July)
1946	14 April to 6 October (no doubles this year)
1947	16 March to 2 November (deduct two hours from 13 April to 10 August)
1948	18 April to 31 October
1949	3 April to 30 October
1950	16 April to 22 October
1951	15 April to 21 October
1952	20 April to 26 October
1953	19 April to 4 October
1954	11 April to 3 October
1955	17 April to 2 October
1956	22 April to 7 October
1957	14 April to 6 October
1958	2 April to 5 October
1959	19 April to 4 October
1960	10 April to 2 October
1961	26 March to 29 October
1962	24 March to 28 October
1963	31 March to 27 October
1964	22 March to 25 October
1965	21 March to 24 October
1966	20 March to 23 October

1967	19 March to 23 October
1968	18 February, then all year
1969	all year
1970	all year
1971	all year, up to 31 October
1972	19 March to 29 October
1973	18 March to 28 October
1974	17 March to 27 October
1975	16 March to 26 October
1976	21 March to 24 October
1977	20 March to 23 October
1978	19 March to 22 October
1979	18 March to 28 October
1980	16 March to 26 October
1981	28 March to 25 October
1982	28 March to 24 October
1983	27 March to 23 October
1984	25 March to 28 October
1985	31 March to 27 October
1986	30 March to 26 October
1987	29 March to 25 October
1988	27 March to 23 October
1989	26 March to 29 October
1990	25 March to 28 October
1991	31 March to 27 October
1992	29 March to 25 October
1993	28 March to 24 October
1994	27 March to 23 October
1995	26 March to 29 October
1996*	31 March to 27 October
1997	30 March to 26 October
1998	29 March to 25 October
1999	28 March to 24 October
2000	26 March to 29 October

* From 1996, dates are estimates and could be changed by the government.

World Time Zones

Astrological timings are traditionally based on Greenwich Mean Time (GMT) which is the time used in the United Kingdom and Eire. If you were born outside this time zone you need to adjust your time of birth to use Venus, Mars and Sun Sign tables. Where there is a minus sign next to your country, you are behind GMT so you need to add the number of hours shown. If there is a plus sign next to your country, you are ahead of GMT so you need to deduct the number of hours shown. You should also allow for that country's own summer or winter daylight saving time.

Time differences

Hours and minutes plus or minus GMT

Accra	00.00	Chicago	−06.00
Adelaide	+09.30	Christchurch NZ	+12.00
Alexandria	+02.00	Colombo	+05.30
Amsterdam	+01.00	Copenhagen	+01.00
Athens	+02.00	Delhi	+05.30
Baghdad	+03.00	Durban	+02.00
Bangkok	+07.00	Gibraltar	+01.00
Bombay	+05.30	Helsinki	+02.00
Brussels	+01.00	Hong Kong	+08.00
Buenos Aires	−03.00	Honolulu	−10.00
Cairo	+02.00	Houston	−06.00
Calcutta	+05.30	Istanbul	+02.00
Calgary	−07.00	Jakarta	+07.00
Cape Town	+02.00	Karachi	+05.00

Lagos	+01.00	Rangoon	+06.30
Lima	−05.00	Rio de Janeiro	−03.00
Lisbon	00.00	Rome	+01.00
London	00.00	St Petersburg	+02.00
Los Angeles	−08.00	San Francisco	−08.00
Madrid	+01.00	Santiago	−04.00
Malta	+01.00	Sierra Leone	00.00
Mauritius	+04.00	Singapore	+08.00
Melbourne	+10.00	Stockholm	+01.00
Montevideo	−03.00	Sydney NSW	+10.00
Montreal	−05.00	Tehran	+03.30
Moscow	+03.00	Tokyo	+09.00
Nairobi	+03.00	Toronto	−05.00
New York	−05.00	Vancouver	−08.00
Oslo	+01.00	Wellington NZ	+12.00
Paris	+01.00	Winnipeg	−06.00
Peking	+08.00	Yokohama	+09.00
Perth WA	+08.00